THE NORTON BOOK OF
CLASSICAL LITERATURE

THE NORTON BOOK OF
CLASSICAL LITERATURE

 Edited by BERNARD KNOX

W·W·NORTON & COMPANY·NEW YORK·LONDON

Printed in the United States of America.

The text of this book is composed in Avanta (Electra),
with the display set in Bernhard Modern.
Composition and Manufacturing by
The Haddon Craftsman, Inc.
Book design by Antonina Krass.

First Edition

Library of Congress Cataloging-in-Publication Data

The Norton book of classical literature / edited by Bernard Knox.
p.   cm.
Includes index.
1. Classical literature—Translations into English.   I. Knox,
Bernard MacGregor Walker.
PA3621.N6   1993
880'.09—dc20   92–10378

ISBN 0-393-03426-7

W.W. Norton & Company, Inc., 500 Fifth Avenue, New York, NY 10110
W.W. Norton & Company Ltd., 10 Coptic Street, London WC1A1PU

1 2 3 4 5 6 7 8 9 0

FOR BIANCA, ONCE AGAIN

CONTENTS

The Archaic Lyric and Iambus

ROME · 593

PREFACE

The literature of the classical world that has survived is a pitiful remnant of what once existed; we have, for example, only seven of the seventy-nine plays of Aeschylus that were available in the great library of Alexandria in the third century B.C. But this remnant is large enough to confront the anthologist with painful choices and some readers with unpleasant surprises as they search the pages of this book in vain for some long-remembered passage. It seems appropriate here to set forth briefly some of the principles that governed the editor's selections.

First of all, translatability; some texts are more translatable than others. Classical Greek literature, for example, the literature from Homer to Plato, is so new, so direct and forceful, that no matter how poor, stilted, or affected the translation, much of the original fire still burns—even in the utterly dreary Victorian version of Sophocles in the Loeb Classical Library a few sparks are still visible. Alexandrian Greek poetry, however, is another matter. These poets are men of letters, scholars and librarians, writing for an audience that will catch allusions, will appreciate imitations, parodies, or implicit repudiations of the classical models. In translation this intertextual depth is inevitably lost; even the overt allusions are often to exotic texts or obscure myths that demand a footnote. And even Theocritus, whose pastoral swains have never been near a library, can on occasion puzzle modern commentators with an arcane version of a familiar myth.

But this density of literary texture is prevalent in Latin literature from the very beginning; Latin literature was in every one of its many genres, except satire, an imitation of Greek models. Horace's claim to have "pioneered / a way to fit Greek rhythm to our tongue" (tr. James Michie) is not the whole of it; more than meter is involved. His ode celebrating the suicide of Cleopatra (p. 621), for example, begins with the words *Nunc est bibendum*—"Today is the day to drink"—that exactly reproduce, in meter, word lengths, and meaning, the opening words,

Nun chre methusthen, of Alcaeus' poem that celebrates the death of Myrsilus. Horace does not explain why today is the day to drink until line 7 of the poem, where the word *regina* makes it clear. But the educated reader knew as soon as he read or heard that first line that the poem was going to celebrate the death of an enemy and a tyrant. Translation cannot cope with this. Nor can it cope with the multiple allusiveness of Virgil, whose lines describing the death of Priam, for example (p. 651), would have brought to the mind of his Roman reader the headless corpse of Pompey on the Egyptian shore, a man who, like Priam, "in other days / Had ruled in pride so many lands and peoples / The power of Asia." For these reasons—its greater originality and translatability— Greek literature predominates in this book, in the proportion of three to one.

The initial choice was not the only problem facing the editor; the length of the item selected was another. The only long text printed in full is the *Antigone* of Sophocles. It seemed only right that there should be one complete play, and *Antigone* is not only one of the supreme masterpieces of the Attic stage, it has also, as George Steiner demonstrated in his brilliant book *Antigones,* exercised a commanding influence over modern Western thought and feeling. In general, however, other units, whether complete or excerpts, are short; the editor's hope was to give some idea of the extraordinary variety of the literature. One can get a fair idea of the nature of extant Sophoclean drama from reading the *Antigone* alone, but Euripides has such a wide dramatic range— the "most tragic of the poets" was also the precursor of the next century's New Comedy—that excerpts from a larger number of plays seemed more appropriate.

The book is no more than a sampler. The texts have been chosen with one idea in mind: to whet the reader's appetite for more. The permissions acknowledgments at the back of the book indicate the source of each translation, and For Further Reading suggests several excellent general introductions to the subject.

INTRODUCTION

The word "literature" has many meanings. When scholars, for example, speak of the literature of a subject, what they are referring to is the vast bibliography of criticism, interpretation, and polemic that has attached itself over the years to every field of study, humanistic and scientific. Such material rarely has any claim to literary distinction; some of it, in fact, especially of recent years, is barely intelligible. Campaign "literature," distributed by political parties, though intelligible, has even less claim to literary merit. When, however, we use such phrases as "American literature" or "French literature," we have something quite different in mind: a written tradition, available to a large literate public, preserving a canon of great works that define the identity of a civilization, proclaim its ideals but also brood over its problems and defects, and set a standard against which later writers measure their own achievement as they strive to adapt, reject, or surpass them. The first such literature in the history of the West is that of Greece.

This is not to claim that other ancient civilizations had no written literary works. Ancient Egyptian papyri contain stories and love poems in addition to a large corpus of religious texts, but ancient Egyptian culture, to quote an Egyptologist, "was not expressed in epic or drama, nor did it produce authors to rival Homer or Virgil, Aeschylus, Sophocles and Euripides, thinkers to match Plato and Aristotle or lyric poets on a level with Sappho or Catullus."[1] The clay tablets of the civilizations of the Tigris-Euphrates River basin have preserved for us religious poems of great interest—a Creation myth, for example—as well as a genuine epic poem, the tale of the hero Gilgamesh. And of course the sacred books of the Hebrews, the Biblical Old Testament, contain masterly narratives of a mythical religious nature, historical accounts of the triumphs and de-

---

[1]William Kelly Simpson, ed., *The Literature of Ancient Egypt* (New Haven: Yale University Press, 1972), p. 2.

feats of the Israelites and of the greatness and the wickedness of their
kings, as well as love poetry and, in the Book of Job, a powerful explora-
tion of the problem of undeserved human suffering, framed, after a
narrative prologue, entirely in dialogue—a sort of embryonic drama.

But all these written traditions lacked one element essential to the
definition proposed above: a large literate public that could read them.
The scripts in which they were recorded could be employed and read
only by professional scribes, whose competence came from many years
of training. The Egyptian hieroglyphs were an extremely complicated
medium of communication, consisting of logograms, which pictured the
object denoted; phonograms, which represented sounds; and determina-
tives, which helped the reader decide on the precise meaning intended.
The cuneiform scripts of the Middle East were simpler—there were no
logograms—but they were syllabaries: different combinations of wedge-
shaped incisions in the wet clay stood for syllables—consonant plus
vowel—each one represented by a different character. Obviously such a
system placed on the user the onus of learning many different signs, but
this was not the only thing that made reading and writing difficult. Here,
for example, is what an expert offers as a simplified explanation for the
lay person of the way the Sumerian script works.

> In Sumerian the word for barley is *š* (pronounced "she" as in shepherd), so
> the sign for barley also became the sign for the syllable *se.* The Sumerian
> for ox is *gu;* but the word for thread is also *gu,* so already you have two
> possible ways of writing the sound *gu.* There are, in fact, some fourteen
> ways of writing *gu,* so for convenience we (but not the Sumerians) mark
> thread as *gu* and ox as *gu*₄. The word for arrow is *ti,* but so is the word for
> life, so to write "life" you need only write the sign for arrow. The word for
> mouth is *ka* (represented as a head with the teeth clearly marked), but the
> sign *ka* is also used for the idea of shouting, which is again *gu* (*gu*₃ or *gù*);
> so the sign *KA* already has two values, *ka* and *gu*₃ (and in fact it can also be
> used for *zú* "tooth," *du,* "speak" and *inim* "word"). . . . The principle of
> using several signs to represent the same sound *(gu)* is called homophony,
> and giving one sign several values (like *KA*) is called polyphony. Both
> principles are fundamental features of cuneiform writing throughout its
> 3,000 year history.[2]

The Greeks too, in the second millennium B.C., had a syllabic script
that resembled those of the civilizations of the Tigris-Euphrates River
Valley, though it was much simpler. It appears on clay tablets discovered

[2]C. B. F. Walker, *Reading the Past. Cuneiform* (Berkeley: University of California Press,
1987), p. 12.

on Greek Bronze Age sites—Pylos and Mycenae on the mainland and Cnossus on Crete. It was evidently adapted by Greek speakers from a system designed to represent an unknown language, for it is far from satisfactory as a medium for the sounds of Greek. To cite one example only, it has no signs for syllables beginning with the sound we represent by the letter *l* and uses for them signs for syllables beginning with the sound we represent as *r*. So the name of the goddess Lato appears as *ra-to,* and the important word for "slave," *doulos,* as *doero.* The script is unable to indicate a consonantal closing to a syllable and it cannot deal with aspirated consonants. Consequently the Greek word for "sword," *phasganon,* appears as *pa-ga-no.* Small wonder that many of the tablets (which are for the most part lists of equipment or supplies on hand) show, in addition to their written content, an explanatory pictographic sign—a chariot wheel, a sword, a tripod. But inadequate representation of the sounds of the Greek language is not the only defect of this sylla-bary; it also, with its eighty-seven characters, makes formidable demands on the memory of its user. In any case, all memory of this writing system perished during the destruction of the Mycenean palaces in the last years of the second millennium; the clay tablets, baked to brick hardness by the fire, remained below ground awaiting the spades of the excavators in the late nineteenth and early twentieth centuries.

Of all these early scripts, the North Semitic, a group that included Hebrew and Phoenician, was the simplest. These writing systems were a radical departure from the pictographic style of Egyptian hieroglyphic, as well as from the syllabaries of the cuneiform tablets which had im-posed such heavy burdens on the memory of the scribes and, with their polyphony and homophony, demanded such prodigies of interpretation from their readers. The North Semitic scripts used characters that repre-sented the consonantal sounds of their languages; this reduced the num-ber of signs to be learned to somewhere in the neighborhood of twenty.

This was a giant step toward clarity and easy readability. "Write the vision," says the Lord to the Hebrew prophet Habakkuk, "and make it plain upon tables, that he may run who readeth it." (The "tables" of the King James Version means "tablets," as in Hamlet's "My tables—meet it is I set it down . . . "). The script was certainly clearer than anything developed so far, but the absence of notation for the vowels was a possi-ble source of confusion; many consonantal groups could be differently pronounced and the correct reading determined only by context or prec-edent—a situation rich in potential for disagreement. In one spectacular case, the vowels are no longer known; the memory of them was lost some time after the return of the Jews from exile in Babylonia. The sacred name of God, which was never pronounced, consists of four consonantal signs (hence its designation as the Tetragrammaton); they are *Y.H.W.H.* The usual scholarly consensus is for *Jahweh* (or, if you happen to be a German scholar, *Jahveh*), but the learned English and Scottish bishops who translated the Bible for King James the First of Great Britain—the Authorized Version—took over from Tyndale's earlier English version a different reading of the consonants. It was the name that resounded outside Fort Ticonderoga in 1775 when Ethan Allen summoned the British commander to surrender. Asked in whose name, he replied (according to his own account): "In the name of the Great Jehovah and the Continental Congress."

In Israel, the distance between the sacred books and the lay reader widened considerably after the Israelites returned from exile in Babylonia, where they had been deported by the Babylonian king Nebuchadrezzar II in 597 B.C. They were released by order of Cyrus, the Persian conqueror of Babylon in 537, but few of the returning exiles still spoke Hebrew. Their language was now Aramaic, the predominant Semitic language of the Middle East. The sacred texts had to be translated into Aramaic for use in the synagogues, and first-hand contact with the great literature of the past became the pride and privilege of scholars.

GREECE

It was a decisive innovation on the part of the Greeks that produced what we know as the alphabet. From their Phoenician trading partners they adopted a consonantal system. It proclaims its origin not only by the letter shapes but also by their Greek names—*alpha, beta, gamma,* and *delta* mean nothing in Greek, but Phoenician *aleph* means "ox," *beth* means "house," *gimel* (probably) means "camel," and *delta* is probably related to Hebrew *daleth,* "door." But the Greeks used some of the Phoenician signs that stood for consonants or consonantal combinations nonexistent in Greek to represent vowels. The resultant alphabet of twenty-four letters could represent, without ambiguity, all the sounds of the Greek language; it made writing and reading, for the first time in history, something available, without enormous effort, to everyone in the culture.

The earliest Greek alphabetic writing that has come down to us is scribbled on broken pieces of pottery; these shards come from archeological sites all over the Mediterranean and can be dated, by archeological criteria, to the second half of the eighth century B.C. Pottery, of course, is almost indestructible, but since other writing materials—leather, for example, or Egyptian papyrus—are not so longlasting, it has been argued that the Greeks may have been writing on such materials long before 750 B.C. Support for this hypothesis has been found in the shapes of the earliest Greek letters, which resemble those of Phoenician documents of the ninth and tenth centuries. It seems strange, however, that if that were indeed the case, no one thought of writing on whole pots or broken pieces until the middle of the eighth century.

Whatever the date of its appearance may have been, the Greek alphabet was destined to have a long history. Much later the Romans adopted it, with some slight modifications, from the Greek colonists of southern Italy and Sicily, or perhaps from the Etruscans of central Italy—a people engaged in voluminous trade with the Greeks from the sixth century on. The Roman version of the Greek alphabet is the one we still use whenever we write or print capital letters.

When this innovative, fully alphabetic script came into use all over the Greek world, no memory of the Mycenean syllabary remained. But a dim vision of the Mycenean age, of its gold, its bronze armor, and its wars, had been preserved by poetry—the songs of illiterate bards who sang of the deeds of heroic figures of the past, participants, most of them, in a great all-Greek expedition that sacked and burned the rich city of Troy in Asia Minor. This poetic oral tradition was the raw material from which a great poet, whom the Greeks called Homer, created the two epics that became the classic texts of Greek literature: the *Iliad*, the tale of the wrath of Achilles;[3] and the *Odyssey*, the long and dangerous return home from Troy of the hero Odysseus.

Internal evidence—historical, archeological, and linguistic—suggests that the two long poems were given their present form around the end of the eighth century, just at the time when the new alphabetic script was coming into use in the Greek world. Homer certainly knew of its existence, for in a passage in the sixth book of the *Iliad* he describes a written message; the word he uses for the act of writing, *graphein*, and the word used for the waxed tablets on which the message was written,

[3]In the selection from Richmond Lattimore's translation of the *Iliad* (p. 64), this name appears with the spelling Achilleus, and the name Hector as Hektor. Robert Fagles, however, prints Achilles and Hector. All through the Greek portion of this book the reader will find similar discrepancies—Nausikaa, Nausicaa; Alkinoos, Alcinous; Aias, Ajax; and so on. Achilles and Hector are the Latin forms of the names. Before the sixteenth century, it was through Latin poetry that Western readers made their acquaintance with Greek myth, so these forms became naturalized in English and have been used by English writers from Shakespeare to Tennyson and beyond. In recent years, however, some translators have felt that a closer approximation to the ancient Greek spelling—*k* for *c*, *-os* for *-us*—would give their lines a more authentic sound. In the introductory remarks, I have adhered to the Latin forms of the names—B.K.

deltoi, are those in common use in later, more literate, centuries. Scholars are still debating the question whether writing was used at this time or a little later to record the great epic poems that had been orally composed, or whether it was the ability to write that made possible the creation of poems of such length and structural intricacy.

Before the the Homeric texts were fixed in writing, the exploits of the heroes at Troy and the adventures of their returns home were the theme of improvised songs, chanted to the accompaniment of a stringed instrument, by oral poets who relied for their presentation of the old stories on a repertoire of formulaic phrases and set scenes. As the Homeric versions of the wrath of Achilles and the return of Odysseus came to be accepted as canonical, they were recited, no longer sung, by professional performers called "rhapsodes," who, like actors, had memorized the text. Even though written texts existed and circulated, Homer for many centuries to come would be more heard than read, and this is true of almost all Greek literature until the late years of the fourth century B.C. But the new alphabet meant not only that the text could be fixed but also that the writer could identify himself and claim it as his own, could speak in his own person.

Homer does not. Though he may well have used writing to construct and fix his monumental poems, he is the last and greatest of a long line of oral poets who thought of themselves as the anonymous voices of the Muses—the daughters of the goddess Mnemosyne, whose name means "Memory." Homer does not claim authorship of his great poems. "Sing to me, Muse, of the man . . . " is how the *Odyssey* begins, and the *Iliad* opens with: "Sing, goddess, the rage of Peleus' son, Achilles . . . " The first poet who does identify himself is another product of the oral tradition, composing in the same strict meter and the same highly formulaic language as Homer. His name was Hesiod, and he tells us that he came from what he himself describes as the miserable village of Ascra in Boeotia, an area of central Greece northwest of Athens. It was there that his father retired after failing to make a fortune as a merchant on the high seas. He tells us, too, how the Muses called him from his occupation as a shepherd on Mount Helicon and told him to sing of the everlasting race of the gods, as he does in his long poem the *Theogony.*

But Hesiod does not, like Homer, ask the Muse to sing. The voice and the power to "sing the story of things, the future and the past," have been given to him by the Muses, and he begins his epic recital of the pedigree of the Olympians with the words: "Come you, let us begin from the Muses . . . " The "you" he is addressing is himself. He still, of course, sang his songs for a audience; in fact he tells us that he won the prize in a poetic contest that was part of the funeral honors for Amphidamas, king of Chalcis. But, unlike Homer, he left behind him poems stamped with his own personality. In the *Works and Days*—a long poem that departs radically from the traditional matter of epic bards to celebrate work on the land—he addresses his lazy brother Perses, whom he accuses of taking more than his fair share of the land inherited from their father.

Homer was not the only poet who drew on the vast repertoire of the oral tradition to create long poems of his own. We hear from late sources of "the story of Oedipus by Cinaethon in six thousand, six hundred lines"; of the *Cypria*, which covered the events leading up to the Trojan War "in eleven books"; the *Aethiopis*, "in five books," which carried the story on from the end of the *Iliad* to cover the death of Achilles and the quarrel between Ajax and Odysseus over his arms; the *Little Iliad*, which continued the tale to the point where the Trojans take the horse into the city, "in four books"; *The Sack of Troy* in two books, followed by *The Returns*, the voyage home of the Achaean chieftains and the various receptions they met. Of all this "Epic Cycle," as the ancient critics called it, nothing remains but a few scattered verbatim quotations and some uninspired prose summaries.

But the Epic Cycle is not all that we have lost. After the *Odyssey* and *Iliad* of Homer, and the *Theogony* and *Works and Days* of Hesiod, the next complete works of literature of any considerable size that we possess are both from the fifth century B.C.: Pindar's tenth Pythian Ode for Hippocleas of Thessaly, victor in the boys' race in 498 B.C.; and Aeschylus' tragedy *The Persians*, staged in the Theater of Dionysus at Athens in 472. This does not mean that no literature was produced in the long span of years between. There was a huge, varied literature, most of it poetic; its authors were men and women from every corner of the Greek world. But almost all of it is lost.

The magnitude of this loss can, in some cases, be measured exactly. We have less than 300 verses of the Athenian legislator and poet Solon, but a writer of the third century A.D. tells us that he wrote 5,000. We have, at a rough count, some 300 intelligible lines of the sixth-century poet Sappho of Lesbos, but the Alexandrian scholars of the third century arranged her poems in nine books (that is, probably, in nine papyrus rolls). The first of these contained 333 Sapphic stanzas; that is to say, almost 1,000 lines. The library at Alexandria had the Spartan poet Alcman in six books, Mimnermus in two, Tyrtaeus in seven, Alcaeus of Lesbos in ten, Ibycus of Rhegium in seven, the same number for Anacreon of Teos, and no less than twenty-six books for the Sicilian Greek poet Stesichorus of Himera, of whose work we have now only scraps. The poetry of an immensely creative period was almost entirely

lost at some stage of the long, capricious process by which what we have
of Greek literature was preserved through the centuries between the end
of the pagan world and the fall of Constantinople to the Turks in 1453.
We do not know exactly when, but it seems likely that the last remaining
copies of Sappho's work were destroyed not by Christian bishops, as one
widespread story has it, nor by the infidel Turks, but by the rabble of
Norman, German, and Venetian mercenaries who sacked and burned
the Christian city of Constantinople in the piratical raid known as the
Fourth Crusade.

We can take some measure of consolation for the loss of the Epic
Cycle from Aristotle's assertion of Homer's "marvelous superiority to
the others," but in the case of the loss of most of the poetry of the next
two centuries, the seventh and sixth, no such comfort is available. It is
clear from what little has survived that this was a richly creative period,
an age of great poets whose fragments give us unforgettable glimpses
into a brilliant archaic world, a Greek civilization expanding mentally as
well as economically, but threatened by the huge kingdoms of the East,
and in danger too from its own fatal tendency to internecine strife. This
was the world of the city-state—the *polis,* to give it its Greek name—an
institution which, almost absent from the heroic world of Homer and
the rural world of Hesiod, had become, by the seventh century, the
characteristic form of Greek communal life. What had been scattered
farms and villages united to form a larger community, centered on a
defensible hill or rock—the acropolis—where the temples of the city's
patron gods were built. Citizenship was a closely guarded privilege; government was usually the task and prerogative of a caste of hereditary
large landowners. The *polis* was by modern standards a very small unit.
Aristotle, writing in the fourth century B.C., imagined his ideal *polis* as
one in which every citizen would be able to hear the voice of the town
crier. But because the *polis* was usually at odds and often at war with its
neighbors over disputed borders or grazing rights, it was a tightly cohesive unit. In the infantry battle line, every man's safety depended in part
on the shield of the man to his right, just as his own shield offered partial
protection to the man on his left. The fragments of the Spartan poet
Tyrtaeus hymn the discipline that holds the line firm, and warn of the
terrors unleashed by breaking from the line—"the spirit of the whole
army falls apart."

But this solidarity in the face of the enemy was often sadly wanting in
time of peace; the *polis* in the archaic period was all too often a place of
civil strife. A growing population put pressure on an almost exclusively
agricultural economy dominated by the aristocratic lords of large estates.
In some communities a wealthy class of merchants, excluded from politi-

cal power, added a new unstable element. The pressure was temporarily relieved in many cases by the departure of dissatisfied groups, who sailed off in search of a place to found a *polis* of their own. They looked for an arable plain near the sea, with a hill or rock formation for their acropolis—at first a fortress in which to defend themselves against the natives who would try to expel them, later (if the colony prospered), the site of the temples of the new city's patron gods. The climate of the Mediterranean coasts is uniform; the settlers found the hinterland of their new cities suitable for the cultivation of the staples of the Greek diet: cereals, the olive, and the vine. It was not long before new Greek cities appeared as far west as the south coast of France (Marseilles, Antibes, and Nice began life as Massilia, Antipolis, and Nikaia), and as far south as Cyrene on the coast of what is now Libya. Southern Italy and Sicily were so studded with Greek cities that the Romans referred to the area as *Magna Graecia:* Naples, Taranto, Messina, Reggio Calabria, Gela, and Syracuse all have Greek foundations.

The Greek cities of the Asia Minor coast, Miletus prominent among them, established colonies all round the Black Sea; Olbia on the Bug River and several Greek cities on the Crimean peninsula grew rich from the export of grain to the Greeks of the homeland. More than one of the new cities, in fact, soon became richer and more powerful than its mother city, and though family, dialect, and religion were powerful bonds, relations were not always friendly. One of the incidents that brought on the Peloponnesian War was Athenian intervention in a dispute between Corinth and its colony Corcyra (modern Corfu).

Colonial ventures reduced the tensions in the home cities, but the relief was only temporary; the old economic and political pressure soon built up toward the explosion point once more. The rich, fertile island of Lesbos, home of the poets Sappho and Alcaeus, was the scene in the late seventh century of factional disputes that escalated to civil war. Alcaeus was a violent partisan, who fought on what turned out to be the losing side; he ended his days in exile. Even Sappho, probably because of political activity on the part of her family, spent some time, most likely in her youth, in exile in Sicily. Theognis of Megara, in mainland Greece, spent his later years, like Alcaeus, in exile; his poems are the voice of a bitter, defeated aristocrat who can neither forget nor forgive.

In many cities, the outcome of civil dissension was the appearance of a figure the Greeks called a *tyrannos.* It is our word "tyrant," but the Greek word did not originally carry all the bad connotations it eventually acquired. A *tyrannos* was a man who mobilized the classes excluded from power against the aristocratic regime and made himself absolute ruler. The typical *tyrannos* encouraged trade and manufacture, engaged in large-scale public works, pursued a vigorous foreign policy of expansion, and also maintained a splendid court, which attracted poets and artists whose role was to celebrate the triumphs of the regime. Polycrates of Samos, for example, built a formidable navy; completed, if he did not initiate, the great Temple of Hera and the 1,200-yard tunneled aqueduct that brought water to the city under a hill 1,000 feet high; and maintained at his court the poet Anacreon and the artist Theodorus. Even more splendid were the tyrannies of the two great Sicilian cities, Syracuse and Gela. Hiero of Syracuse commissioned odes for his victories in the chariot race at Olympia from Pindar and Bacchylides; Simonides spent his last years at Hiero's court; and Aeschylus wrote and produced at Syracuse a play that celebrated Hiero's foundation of a new city on the slopes of Mount Etna.

In Athens, which sent out no colonial expeditions, the early years of the sixth century were, as elsewhere, a time of crisis; but instead of a *tyrannos*, there emerged the figure of the lawgiver Solon, entrusted by his fellow citizens with the task of writing new laws that would restore civil peace and establish some measure of social justice. Solon was his own poet, and we have significant fragments of his defense of the steps he took to avert civil war. His laws, however, were not a permanent solution to Athens' social and political problems, and Athens too eventually had its tyrant, Pisistratus, who after several unsuccessful attempts became master of the city in 546 B.C. He began construction of the huge Temple of Olympian Zeus—some of its immense columns still stand in Athens—and it was during his regime that the Festival of Dionysus first included a competition between tragic poets in which one Thespis won the first prize.

A *tyrannos* had to be a brilliant politician to maintain the power he had seized. Such talent is rarely inherited, and the tyrant's son often failed to combine the threat of force with the winning of popular favor as skillfully as his father had done. The fall of the tyranny usually resulted in the establishment of an oligarchic regime—a city ruled by an alliance of the old landed aristocrats and the new merchant class that had profited from the tyrant's expansionist policies. But in Athens something different happened, something new. When Pisistratus' son Hippias was driven out in 509 B.C., dissension among the aristocrats who had engineered his fall ended with the victory of Clisthenes, of the powerful Alcmeonid family. Although his rivals had the backing of Sparta, which had helped and encouraged the rebellion, Clisthenes won power by appealing to the people. He proposed a series of reforms which, when finally adopted, made Athens a democracy, a *polis* in which the assembly of male citizens was invested with full sovereignty.

This date marks the end of the archaic age, what has often been called the lyric age of Greece. Although Pindar, Bacchylides, and Simonides continued to celebrate the aristocratic virtues and to connect their well-born or princely clients with the great mythic heroes in the odes they composed to celebrate victories in the great games, Athenian democracy, as its power and influence grew with the years, came to dominate the literary world—not least through the work of the three great dramatists who year by year throughout the century produced their tragedies in the Theater of Dionysus.

The new democracy had hardly begun to test its institutions when it had to face a mortal danger. In 490 B.C. the deposed tyrant Hippias, backed by a formidable Persian expeditionary force, landed on the shore of the bay of Marathon, northeast of Athens. The Athenians called for help from their fellow Greeks against the common enemy (the Persians had already annexed the Greek cities of Asia Minor and many of the islands of the Aegean), but no help came except from the small city of Plataea, north of Athens. Nevertheless, the Athenians marched out to Marathon and there, to the astonishment of both sides, decisively defeated the army of Darius the Great King. Ten years later his successor Xerxes came in person, with a huge fleet and army; he captured and sacked Athens but was defeated at sea by the combined Greek naval forces, in which the largest contingent was Athenian, at Salamis. Xerxes went home, leaving the land army behind him. It was defeated in its turn in the next year, at Plataea.

The Athenians followed the Persian retreat across the Aegean, liberating the islands and cities that had been under Persian rule and carrying on the war against Persia by land and sea. They formed a league of cities for defense against Persia, providing it with the main naval force and also with aggressive leadership. The league soon became not an association of equals but an empire of subject cities under Athenian domination, paying tribute for the maintenance of a war fleet that was now no longer the fleet of the league, but the Athenian fleet. Athens was launched on its great imperial century, which saw the new democracy assume pride of place in the Greek world; its new magnificence was symbolized by the building, on the Acropolis, of the Parthenon, the Erechtheum, and the Propylaea to replace the temples destroyed by the Persians. All through the fifth century the Theater of Dionysus at the foot of the Acropolis saw the production of masterpieces by the three great tragic poets. In 479, with the burnt-out ruins of the city above and around them, the Athenians watched Aeschylus' play *The Persians*, which presented the defeat of Xerxes not as a triumph of Greek arms but as the divine punishment visited on a man who had tried to transgress the limits set by the gods to human greatness. This was not Aeschylus' first production; he had been at work in the theater as dramatist, director, and actor since near the beginning of the century—his first victory in the contest was in 484, six years after he had fought in the infantry battle line at Marathon.

The origins of Athenian tragedy, and so of Western theater, are veiled in mystery. The only coherent account we have, that of Aristotle in the *Poetics*, is full of problems; it conflicts, at several points, with evidence from other sources. All we can be sure of is that Athenian drama developed from some kind of choral dance and that it was from the first associated with the worship of the god Dionysus, whose image was brought into the theater to watch the performance and whose priest sat in a reserved seat in the front row. The crucial innovation that turned choral performance into drama was attributed to Thespis, who confronted a singing (and dancing) chorus as a masked actor. His spoken verses, framed in the iambic meter which, as Aristotle points out, most closely resembles normal speech, changed what had been choral monologue into dialogue. Aeschylus, like Thespis, acted in his own plays, but he added a second masked actor. Audience attention could now be directed to action and reaction, question and answer, conflict or cooperation between the actors rather than between actor and chorus. Sophocles added a third actor. This made possible not only three-cornered dramatic scenes but also, since the masks allowed an actor to play more than one part, plays with a large cast of characters, such as Euripides' *Phoenician Women*, which has no less than eleven speaking roles.

Aeschylus' *Persians* was an unusual departure for Athenian tragedy, which normally shunned recent history and drew its plots from the rich tradition of heroic myth. Also unusual was the fact that it was not part of a trilogy, Aeschylus' favorite medium, in which the three plays offered by the poet were devoted to the development of the same mythic core, with characters reappearing from play to play as the plot spans the generations of a tragic family. This is the form of Aeschylus' surviving masterpiece, the *Oresteia*, which traces the fatal sequence of retribution, blood for blood, through the generations of the house of Atreus to the solution of the dilemma, which is the foundation in Athens of the *Areopagus*, the first court of law.

Sophocles, like Aeschylus, produced his own plays; the inscriptions recording his victories in the dramatic contest use the formula *Sophokles edidasken*, literally, "Sophocles was the teacher," that is, he taught the chorus and the actors their lines. But though he is reported to have made a hit as Nausicaa in a play he based on the sixth book of the *Odyssey*, he gave up acting because, we are told, he had too small a voice. He was in any case a very busy man. In addition to producing over 120 plays, he served as ambassador, as general (an elected office in Athens), and in 411 B.C. as one of the emergency committee set up by the assembly to deal with the catastrophic situation Athens faced after the loss of its army and fleet in Sicily. He was proof of the truth of Pericles' proud claim for Athenian democracy, that its citizens were "capable . . . of the utmost dexterity and grace in the widest range of activities."

Unlike Aeschylus, Sophocles avoids trilogic form; his plays are self-contained. Instead of showing action and reaction over generations, he concentrates on a critical moment in a heroic life: Antigone's symbolic burial of her brother in defiance of the ruler's edict; Oedipus' relentless search for the truth about the death of Laius, which ends by revealing his own polluted identity; Ajax's decision to commit suicide. The tension is heightened by his masterly use of dramatic irony, which seems to emphasize the helplessness of heroes enmeshed in nets spread for them by the gods. Yet his emphasis is always on the greatness of the heroes; they may be as stubborn and uncompromising as Antigone, as unapproachable and murderous as Ajax, as embittered and full of hate as Philoctetes, but we never lose our admiration for their heroic consistency. And though the will of the gods remains a mystery, Sophocles somehow suggests that far from being malevolent, it is, in some strange way that is beyond explanation, just. This suggestion is conveyed, more often than not, in the choral lyric songs, which are among the greatest masterpieces of Greek poetry.

Euripides, who was Sophocles' rival and contemporary (they both died in 406 B.C.), was called by Aristotle "the most tragic of the poets." He seems to have meant that Euripides was the most successful at arousing pity and fear in the audience. It is true that many of his tragedies—*Trojan Women, Medea,* and *Hippolytus,* for example—end on an even grimmer note than those of Sophocles; there appears to be no consolation for suffering. On the other hand, Euripides can also serve up a happy ending, as in *Helen* or *Iphigenia in Tauris;* and in some of these plays, particularly in the *Ion,* he is a precursor of the fourth-century New Comedy of Menander and Philemon, with its intricate plotting of unknown or mistaken identity ending in recognition and restoration of lost or abandoned children to their proper station.

From midcentury on, the Theater of Dionysus was also the home of comedy, the uninhibited Old Comedy of Aristophanes and his rivals Eupolis and Cratinus. It was the most extraordinary exercise in all history of a freedom the Athenians prized as the epitome of the blessings of democracy—what they called *parrhesia,* freedom of speech. In Old Comedy, no theme was taboo. Leading statesmen, present in the audience, were caricatured and treated to scurrilous abuse: Cleon, for example, successor of Pericles as leader of the democracy, appears in *The Knights* of Aristophanes (424 B.C.) as a Paphlagonian slave in the house of a foolish old man called Demos, whom he lulls to sleep with servile flattery while robbing him blind. When Aristophanes produced *The Acharnians* in 425, the Athenians had been at war for six years, cooped up in the city, decimated by plague, powerless to intervene as they watched the Spartan armies outside the walls ravage the Attic countryside. Yet the hero of the play makes a separate peace with the Spartans for himself and family, imports all the luxuries the Athenians have been denied for years, announcing that the Athenians are just as much to blame for the war as the Spartans, and at the end of the play comes in drunk from a feast supported by two ladies of the night as an actor playing Lamachus, a general present in the audience, is carried on, wounded from the battle, lamenting his sad fate in mock-tragic style.

Even the gods were fair game. In *The Frogs,* Dionysus, the patron god of the theater, appears. He is bound for the lower world to bring Euripides back from the dead—since Sophocles and Euripides died, tragedy has been a disaster area. He has assumed the costume and attributes of Heracles, who had once gone down there to kidnap the dog Cerberus, but is unable to live up to the reputation of his heroic model. At one point, frightened by a phantom of some kind, he runs clear across the stage area to implore the priest of Dionysus, seated in the front row, to protect him. Later, confronted by Aeacus, one of the judges of the dead, who, taking him for Heracles, threatens him with all the furies and torments Hell can muster, he loses control of his bowels. The level of humor is not elevated by the dramatist's frequent resort to explicit sexual and scatological language, not to mention the fact that most of the actors sported, as part of their costume, a long leather *phallos* hanging from their lower belly. But these low jokes are balanced by the verbal wit of the dialogue and the high fantasy of the plots, as well as by the poetic genius of Aristophanes, who in many a choral ode shows himself to be a lyric poet of consummate artistry. Old Comedy is the feast of unreason, of "the world turned upside down"—that social safety valve that at Rome took the form of the Saturnalia, the day on which slaves were allowed to do as they liked, and that in medieval England became the season of the Lord of Misrule, when for a day authority was mocked.

Fifth-century Athens was not only an imperial capital, a center of wealth and power; it was also, because of its primacy in literature and the arts, a magnet for talent from all over the Greek world. It became, in fact, in the famous phrase of its leader Pericles, "the education of Greece." Herodotus of Halicarnassus, a city on the coast of Asia Minor, came to Athens to give readings from his fascinating history of the Great

Persian War and of all the nations and cities engaged in it; he became a friend of Sophocles and went off to live and die at Thurii in southern Italy, a Panhellenic colony organized by Pericles. Athens was the goal of the so-called "Sophists," the teachers of rhetoric and philosophy whose unsettling ideas and arguments are echoed in the speeches of Euripides' characters, developed in the paired speeches of Thucydides' history of the Peloponnesian War, and subjected to relentless, hostile analysis by Plato in those brilliant dialogues that recreate for us not only the figure of Socrates but also the intense atmosphere of Athenian intellectual life in the last years of Athens' great age as an imperial power.

That age ended in 404 B.C. as the twenty-seven-year war against Sparta and its allies ended in the unconditional surrender of Athens, the loss of the empire, and the replacement of democracy by a dictatorial committee of thirty, which, backed by a Spartan garrison, ruled by terror. The historian of that war, Thucydides, was an Athenian; in fact, he was in command of an Athenian fleet in the northern Aegean when, in 424 B.C., he failed to prevent the Spartan seizure of the strategic Athenian colony of Amphipolis and was exiled as a result. His history, which starts exactly where Herodotus left off, is incomplete. We know from his own comments that he lived to see the end of the war, but his narrative stops short in a passage describing the events of the summer of 411 B.C. Yet his book is a masterpiece that has served as a model for historians ever since, not only because of its dedication to accuracy and the power of its narrative but also because of the clarity and profundity of its analysis of power politics. Thucydides, wrote Thomas Hobbes, who published his translation of the *History* in 1634, "is accounted the most politic historiographer that ever writ."

The rule of the Thirty Tyrants, as they came to be known, lasted no more than eighteen months; their savagery alienated even those who had deplored the excesses and the mistakes of the imperial democratic regime. The democracy was restored and remained stable until the main Greek city-states, weakened by sixty years of internecine warfare, were decisively defeated in 338 B.C. by the army of Philip of Macedon at Chaeronea. Athens was never a fully independent city again. The forms of democracy remained, yet the city was, in reality, governed from now on by an oligarchy subservient to a succession of Hellenistic kings and finally to the Senate and People of Rome.

All through the fourth century B.C. the tragic and comic contests at the Festival of Dionysus continued, but of the plays of those years we have only titles and fragments. Significantly, the plays of the three great tragedians of the previous century could be, and often were, produced in competition with the offerings of contemporary poets. The canonical

stature of the three was officially recognized when the Athenian statesman Lycurgus, some time in the thirties of the century, set up statues of
them in the rebuilt Theater of Dionysus. Comedy too stayed alive: two
of the extant plays of Aristophanes, *The Women in Congress* and
Plutus, were produced in the first two decades of the century. They lack
the wild freedom and personal satire of the earlier plays; comedy has
been tamed, and by the last decades of the century, in the comedies of
Menander, it has been domesticated. Political and personal satire has
disappeared altogether, and so has fantasy: no Peisthetaerus organizes
the birds to cut off the smoke of sacrifice from Zeus and the Olympians,
no Trygaeus mounts to heaven on a dungbeetle to implore Zeus to stop
the Peloponnesian War. Instead, young sons of irascible, prosperous
Athenian fathers fall in love with slave girls who, through the intrigues of
clever slaves, are finally revealed as the long-lost daughters of rich neighbors by recognition of a ring or similar token that had been left with the
child when it was abandoned. This whole bag of tricks—the staple of the
New Comedy—is summarized by a third-century Alexandrian critic,
Satyrus, in a headless sentence from a papyrus fragment of his biography
of Euripides: " . . . toward wife, and father toward son and servants
toward master and also the whole business of vicissitudes, raping of
young women, substitution of children, recognition by means of rings
and necklaces."

Shopworn now, these stage conventions seemed brand new then
(though Euripides, as Satyrus pointed out, had used some of them in
tragedy). In the Menander who has come back to life from the sands of
Egypt (papyrus discoveries since 1900 have given us one complete play
and the better part of two others), we can see the deftness of characterization, the elegance of language, and the brilliant manipulation of intricate plot that made Menander one of the most admired literary figures
of the ancient world.

Menander, like his predecessors and contemporaries in the theater,
wrote in verse, but the fourth century is predominantly the age of
prose—of the orators Lysias, Isocrates, Aeschines, and above all Demosthenes, and of Plato, and his successors Aristotle and Theophrastus.
From a literary point of view, the greatest of these writers is of course
Plato. As a philosopher he rated the spoken word, the oral pursuit of
definition in question and answer, far above any written text; in a famous
passage of the *Phaedrus* he makes Socrates compare written words with
paintings—they "seem to talk to you as though they were intelligent but
if you ask them anything about what they are saying . . . they go on
telling you just the same thing for ever." Yet Plato was one of the
greatest writers who ever lived, and we can well believe that to achieve

the perfection of his dramatic style, he must himself have often suffered the agonies of the writer he describes elsewhere in the *Phaedrus*, who spends hours on his phrases, "twisting them this way and that, pasting them together and pulling them apart." There is a story that among his papers was found a draft of several different versions of the first words of *The Republic*. Nothing could be more effective than the one he finally chose: four Greek words that mean simply: "I went down yesterday to Piraeus."

Plato belongs of course to the history of philosophy as well as that of literature. He founded, and directed, in the grove of the hero Academus, a school for philosophical training and discussion that is the ancestor of the modern university. One of his students was Aristotle, who later founded a rival school of his own, the Lyceum, where he was succeeded as director by Theophrastus. Though Aristotle, like Plato, wrote philosophical dialogues that were praised for their elegant style by no less an authority than Cicero, none of them has survived. What we have is an impressive collection of philosophical and scientific treatises that were obviously not intended for general circulation; they sound more like the notes and outlines of a lecturer than finished treatises. One of them, however, *The Poetics*, is perhaps the most influential work of literary criticism ever written. Theophrastus, too, left us what are for the most part scientific texts (a huge work on plants, for example), but he also wrote a collection of sketches known as *Characters* that presents a remarkable series of portraits of Athenian types, most of them far from admirable.

Aristotle spent some time away from Athens in Macedon as tutor to Alexander, the son of Philip II, who had put an end to the independence of the Greek cities. Soon after he came to the throne in 336 B.C., Alexander set out on an expedition that changed the world. When he died, probably of malaria, in Babylon in 323 B.C., he was master of an empire that stretched from Greece to Afghanistan and from the Black Sea to the upper Nile. His generals divided up the conquered territory, the lands of the old Persian Empire, appointed themselves kings of their acquisitions, and proceeded to fight each other for supremacy. Meanwhile into the new kingdoms flowed a tide of Greeks from the homeland; they came, however, not as poor immigrants but as conquerors, to form the governing classes—soldiers, entrepreneurs, and bureaucrats— of the cities. Many of these cities had a long history behind them. They now acquired a Greek ruling class and the outward and visible signs of Greek culture: a theater, a gymnasium, an assembly area for the town meeting, and covered colonnades, what the Greeks called *stoas*, for strolling and conversation in the shade. Some of the cities were new foundations; the most famous of these was Alexandria in Egypt, its city plan laid out by Alexander himself.

Though the Far Eastern provinces of Alexander's conquests soon regained their independence, the area we know as the Middle East—modern Turkey, Iraq, Syria, Jordan, Palestine, and Egypt—was from that time until the Arab conquests of the eighth century A.D. dominated by a Greek-speaking upper class. Greek language and culture retained their primacy even when the whole area, from the second century B.C. on, was absorbed by the Roman Empire. When the Apostles wrote their accounts of the life and teachings of Jesus, whose native language was Aramaic, they wrote them in the language that would carry their message to the educated classes of the whole huge area—Greek.

In this new, so-called "Hellenistic" age, the city-states of the Greek homeland were no longer powers to be reckoned with. Athens remained an important cultural center because of its magnificent buildings and the fame of its philosophical schools, but the Greek cities of the East were now the centers of literary activity, often under royal patronage, as the Hellenistic monarchs, following the example of the archaic tyrants, welcomed poets and artists to their courts. The most important cultural center was Alexandria, where Ptolemy I, one of Alexander's generals who had seized Egypt as his share of the booty, established a library and a "Museum," which was not a showplace for exhibits but a shrine of the Muses, a residential center for scholars, scientists, and men of letters. The two institutions were separate, but the resident savants used the library and some of them worked there; the poet Callimachus, for example, made the catalogue. Ptolemy's agents bought books from all over the Greek world and the Alexandrian Library soon became the world's largest collection of Greek literature. It was here that the riches of the literary tradition from Homer to Plato were edited. The resident scholars and poets undertook the formidable task of producing sound editions of texts that came to them marred by all the vices of a handwritten tradition: errors corrected to produce still worse aberrations, interpolations, lacunae, and misattributions. They even had to deal with literary forgery, for in the absence of biographical data for even such recent figures as Sophocles and Euripides, hack writers had proceeded to satisfy public curiosity with collections of letters. We still have letters attributed to Euripides, Demosthenes, Heraclitus, Hippocrates, and Aristotle, many of them patent forgeries, and twelve letters supposed to be by Plato, two of which may be genuine or at least by a contemporary.

The great literary scholars of Alexandria—prominent among them Aristophanes of Byzantium and his successor as chief librarian Aristarchus of Samothrace—established the texts of the main authors, wrote

commentaries on them, and also established the literary canons that governed the educational system as long as Greek literature was read and studied in the ancient and medieval worlds. They singled out Homer and Hesiod among the epic poets, added to the already established Athenian tragic canon of Aeschylus, Sophocles, and Euripides a comic one (Aristophanes, Eupolis, and Cratinus), selected as preeminent ten lyric poets (Sappho, Alcaeus, Pindar, Anacreon, and Alcman among them), and ten orators (Demosthenes, Lysias, and Isocrates leading the list).

This selection was a crucial factor in the ultimate survival of what we still have of some of these writers. As ancient civilization, in the late third century A.D., began to disintegrate under the impact of external pressure, civil war, and economic collapse, libraries fell into disrepair, were damaged and destroyed; the district of Alexandria that housed the library was reduced to ruins in A.D. 273 when the Roman emperor Aurelian suppressed a rebellion there. Books were no longer produced in quantity. Papyrus does not have a long life except in extremely dry conditions, and so only those texts would survive that were transferred to the more durable, but more expensive, medium of parchment. As the situation grew more desperate, the canon contracted, and by late antiquity, though Homer and Hesiod were still preserved intact, the choice of tragedies for Aeschylus and Sophocles had narrowed to seven each—the ones we still have. The library at Alexandria had seventy-eight plays of Sophocles and at least seventy-nine of Aeschylus.

The great scholar-editors who established the texts and canons of Greek literature worked in the second century B.C. In the early days of the Museum and library, however, during the reign of Ptolemy II (285–246 B.C.), the Museum was the home of a circle of important poets whose work was to prove highly influential. Among them were Callimachus of Cyrene, Apollonius of Rhodes, and Theocritus of Syracuse. Another poet, Herodes, whose work has become known to us only in modern times through papyrus finds, had as far as we know no connection with the Museum, but he lived on the island of Cos, which was under Ptolemaic rule.

There is one great difference between these poets and their predecessors in archaic and classical Greece. From Homer to Menander, poets appealed to a wide audience that shared a common cultural, mythic, and religious tradition to which the poets could confidently refer. And the conditions of performance—the Homeric recitation, the archaic symposium, the victory song performed for the athletic patron, the competition in the huge Theater of Dionysus—all demanded from the poet a level of immediate intelligibility. He could be weighty and profound, even mysterious, as in some of the great Aeschylean choral odes; what he could not be was learned, deliberately obscure and riddling, or completely dependent on recognition of arcane literary allusions for his effect. Many of the Alexandrian poets were all of these things. One of them, Lycophron, has left us a poem of 1,474 lines which is a dramatic speech in iambic verse put into the mouth of Cassandra, the prophet daughter of Priam of Troy. It is from start to finish so darkly obscure that hardly a line in it can be understood without reference to explanatory footnotes. Here is a specimen: "I see the winged firebrand running to seize the bitch of Pephnos, the dove brought to birth by the vulture that moves on the water . . . " Only a highly literate reader would realize that Lycophron is talking about Paris and his abduction of Helen. Hecuba dreamed that she gave birth to a firebrand (Paris, whose action led to the burning of Troy), and Helen was one of the products of the union of Leda and Zeus who had assumed the form of a swan. This is of course an extreme case, a grotesque display of arcane allusion, but the literary reference and the taste for mythic exotica are characteristic also of the poetry of Callimachus and Apollonius.

Callimachus is the high priest of elegance and concision. "Big book, big evil," is one of his most famous remarks. He favors the low key: "Don't expect from me high sounding song . . . Thunder is not my business—that's for Zeus." He preaches novelty, avoidance of hackneyed themes: "Tread the path no carriages follow . . . ," choose "untrodden ways, even if they are narrower." In his poems there is a constant effort to "make it new," and one aspect of this is his treatment of the Olympian gods. They are no longer the awesome and often fearsome figures of Homer and the tragic stage; in Callimachus and Alexandrian poetry generally they have been scaled down to near human stature, their intrigues, foibles, and weakness the stuff of Baroque light opera rather than of epic grandeur or tragic *terribilità*. This is apparent in Callimachus' treatment of the myth of Tiresias' blinding in the poem called *The Bath of Pallas*, and in Apollonius' account of the way Athena and Hera enlist the support of Aphrodite in order to have Medea fall in love with Jason.

Apollonius defied the Callimachean injunction against big books and turned to epic. His *Argonautica* recounts, in Homeric hexameters and in a diction based on Homer's but full of learned novelties, the story of the good ship *Argo* and of its crew of heroes, its captain Jason and his successful quest for the Golden Fleece, successful only because the king's daughter Medea fell in love with him and gave him indispensable help and counsel. The poem is especially remarkable for its sympathetic and convincing handling of a theme rare in Greek literature—the emotions of a young woman passionately in love.

Theocritus, who wrote in a literary version of the Doric dialect of his native Sicily, seems to have been the inventor of a new genre: pastoral poetry. Seven of his short poems present us with shepherds and goatherds who tend their flocks in pastures far from the city and its adjacent plowland, whiling away the long days by competing in song, hymning the praises of their mistresses (Amaryllis, Galatea), or mourning the death of a fellow shepherd (Daphnis). These are of course elegant fictions; Mediterranean shepherds were (and still are) inhabitants of the mountains, poor vagrants, often outcasts from society. But it was a fiction that was to have a long literary history. Not all of the Theocritean idylls (as these short poems came to be called) deal with shepherds, however. Theocritus can handle other themes as well—the woman who casts a love spell to bring her lost lover back to her arms, the charming picture of two Alexandrian ladies in conversation, a scene of everyday life in upper-class Alexandria. Everyday life, but this time low life, is the material preferred by Herodes, whose dramatic mimes, written in an archaizing Ionic dialect, regale us with, among others of the same ilk, a procuress trying to fix up with a lover a wife whose husband is away in the army, and a pander pleading his case in court.

The Alexandrian poetic achievement of the third century B.C. was not by any means the end of pagan Greek literature. For another six or seven centuries poets, philosophers, historians, satirists, orators, and novelists went on producing voluminous works, which have survived in much greater bulk than the products of the archaic and classical ages. But from a strictly literary viewpoint, it is, compared with what preceded it, inferior. Plutarch's famous *Lives* are a bright exception, some of the satirical dialogues of Lucian of Samosata are still enjoyable reading, and there are many gems to be found in the huge collection known as *The Greek Anthology.* Yet on the whole one is inclined to agree with Louis MacNeice's disenchanted estimate:

> *And free speech shivered on the pikes of Macedonia*
> *And later on the swords of Rome*
> *And Athens became a mere university city*
> *And the goddess born of the foam*
> *Became the kept hetaera, heroine of Menander,*
> *And the philosopher narrowed his focus, confined*
> *His efforts to putting his own soul in order*
> *And keeping a quiet mind.*
> *And for a thousand years they went on talking,*
> *Making such apt remarks,*
> *A race no longer of heroes but of professors*

And crooked business men and secretaries and clerks
Who turned out dapper little elegiac verses
On the ironies of fate, the transience of all
Affections, carefully shunning an over-statement
But working the dying fall.[4]

ROME

In 273 B.C. King Ptolemy II of Egypt made a treaty with Rome, a city in central Italy. It did not commit either party to anything but was a mere exchange of diplomatic courtesies. The Romans had just defeated a Macedonian army led by one of the great Hellenistic generals of the age, Pyrrhus of Epirus, who had invaded the south of Italy in support of the Greek cities against Rome. The treaty was a recognition on the part of one of the most powerful Hellenistic kingdoms that Rome was a force to be reckoned with. But it seems unlikely that anyone in Alexandria could have foreseen at the time that by 146 B.C., Macedonia, Alexander's homeland, would be a Roman province, mainland Greece another—that over the next hundred years the Greek kingdoms of the Middle East would follow suit, and that in 30 B.C., with the suicide of the last Ptolemy, Cleopatra II, Egypt itself would come under Roman rule.

The Romans were a people very different from the Greeks. For all their brilliance in the spheres of literature, art, philosophy, and science, the Greeks had never learned the one thing essential to their survival as an independent nation—how to unite. Even in the great Persian War of 480 B.C. some Greek cities, including the powerful city of Thebes, fought, and fought well, on the Persian side. And the attempts of one city-state to unite all Greece under its leadership came, each in their turn, to nothing. Athens, Sparta, and Thebes had tried it and failed, before, united at last but too late, they were crushed by Philip of Macedon at Chaeronea. But the Romans, starting some time in the eighth century as a city upriver from the sea on the Tiber, with a fine defensible site, the Seven Hills, and a fertile plain, had gradually brought into a federation under their leadership city after city in central Italy. They cleverly devised for each new acquisition a different form of relationship to what became the imperial city. *Divide et impera*—"Divide and rule,"

[4]From "Autumn Journal," *The Collected Poems of Louis MacNeice* (Oxford: Oxford University Press, 1967), p. 118.

was their maxim. They conquered and absorbed the great Etruscan civilization to the north and the Greek cities to the south. They fought and won three separate wars against the republic of Carthage, a Phoenician power with a base in what is now Tunisia and an empire in western Sicily and Spain.

Involvement in the problems of the Hellenistic kingdoms led to acquisition of the whole of the Greek-speaking Middle East; Julius Caesar in the first century B.C. added what is now France and Belgium to the empire, and in A.D. 43 Britain became its most northerly province. In his epic poem the *Aeneid*, which tells the story of the Trojan hero Aeneas, whose descendants would, in the fullness of time, found the city of Rome, Virgil puts in the mouth of the hero's father Anchises a speech that points up the differences between Greeks and Romans. "Others," he says (see p. 698), obviously referring to the Greeks,

> *Others will cast more tenderly in bronze*
> *Their breathing figures, I can well believe,*
> *And bring more lifelike portraits out of marble;*
> *Argue more eloquently, use the pointer*
> *To trace the paths of heaven accurately*
> *And accurately foretell the rising stars.*
> *Roman, remember by your strength to rule*
> *Earth's peoples—for your arts are to be these:*
> *To pacify, to impose the rule of law,*
> *To spare the conquered, battle down the proud.*

And that is what they did.

Unlike the brilliant, inventive Greeks, they had national characteristics suitable for a race of conquerors and organizers. They admired what they called *gravitas*, a high seriousness, especially in matters concerning politics, morals, and religion. They had a horror of disorder and a deep respect for established institutions; political experiments such as democracy were not likely to attract them. They deferred to *auctoritas*, the power and respect won by experience and successful leadership. Above all, they had a keen sense of the necessity for discipline, a quality that made the Roman legions the most formidable fighting force the world had ever seen.

Every Roman soldier carried with him, in addition to his weapon and his rations, a spade; every evening at the end of the day's march, he took his part in digging a deep ditch around a square. The earth from the ditch was thrown up inside the square to form a rampart, the *vallum*, now protected by the *fossa*, the ditch; on the rampart each soldier fixed one of the heavy pointed wooden stakes that were also part of his load. Four gates in the *vallum* allowed access to the roads, crossing at right angles, that divided the tents. This was a fortified camp—*castra* is the Roman word—and all over Europe as the empire was built up, camps that had been located at strategic points became permanent garrison posts and later cities. In England their names remain, though changed in form from *castra* to *-caster* or *-chester:* Chester, Manchester, Lancaster, Winchester. As the new territories were pacified, the legions built roads connecting the forts and cities, roads so solidly constructed that some of them, in the Middle East, are still in use and others are the foundations of modern roads on which the heavy traffic of Europe rolls. They also built stone bridges: at Alacantara a Roman bridge still joins Spain and Portugal across the Tagus River; its roadbed is 156 feet above the water. They built, everywhere they settled, public baths. They also built stone amphitheaters, which still exist in Paris, Lyon, Orange, Verona, and Amman in Jordan; some of them, the ones at Verona and Orange, for example, are still used for performances of opera and spectacles of various kinds.

Of course the Roman record of consolidation and construction was not uninterrupted. As the empire grew to embrace the whole of the Mediterranean area, the institutions of the small city-state of Rome proved unsuited for the administration of such a huge and varied conglomeration of nations and territories. The Roman constitution, with its two supreme magistrates changing every year, could not guarantee consistency of policy; and the corruption of provincial governors (whose supreme power over prosperous cities gave tempting opportunities for enrichment) led to oppression and rebellion and, at home, faction which ended more than once in civil war. After a century or more of political chaos and violence, the republic was superseded. Following his decisive victory over Antony and Cleopatra at Actium in 31 B.C., Octavius, who was soon to assume the name Augustus, concentrated power in his own hands as *princeps*, first citizen, and *imperator*, victorious general, while maintaining the republican forms—Senate, consuls, tribunes, and popular assemblies. When he died in A.D. 14, the republic was dead for ever; his successors were emperors. And though there were bad times to come under such rulers as Caligula and Nero, the principal sufferers under their regimes were the Roman aristocrats of the capital; the provinces continued to enjoy the efficient and for the most part honest government that the republic had been unable to provide. By the second century A.D., under the rule of the so-called "good emperors"—Nerva, Trajan, Hadrian, Antoninus Pius, and Marcus Aurelius—the system was functioning brilliantly. It is of this period—A.D. 98 to 180—that Edward Gibbon wrote, in his *Decline and Fall of the Roman Empire:*

> In the second century of the Christian Aera, the empire of Rome comprehended the fairest part of the earth, and the most civilized portion of mankind. The frontiers of that extensive monarchy were guarded by ancient renown and disciplined valour. The gentle, but powerful influence of laws and manners had gradually cemented the union of the provinces. Their peaceful inhabitants enjoyed and abused the advantages of wealth and luxury. The image of a free constitution was preserved with decent reverence. The Roman senate appeared to possess the sovereign authority, and devolved on the emperors all the executive powers of government. During a happy period of more than fourscore years, the public administration was conducted by the virtue and abilities of Nerva, Trajan, Hadrian, and the two Antonines. . . .
> If a man were called to fix the period in the history of the world during which the condition of the human race was most happy and prosperous, he would, without hesitation, name that which elapsed from the death of Domitian [A.D. 98] to the accession of Commodus [180].

That may be thought an exaggeration—the empire was a slave society, and there were during this period persecutions of Christians—but it is nonetheless true that since the death of Marcus Aurelius, Europe has never seen a period even half as long as eighty years, in which from Scotland to the upper Nile, from Lisbon to Damascus, from Vienna to Tripoli, there were no frontiers, no customs barriers, no separate governments and police forces, and, above all, no war.

When the Romans conquered Greece and the kingdoms of the East, they came up against something that took them by surprise. They had absorbed a population that did not consist of barbarian tribes, as in Spain, nor one raised in an advanced but utterly alien culture, like that of Carthage, but a civilization of such sophistication, of such high artistic and literary achievement, that they were transformed by the contact. "Greece, conquered, took her rough conqueror captive," wrote the Roman poet Horace much later, "and brought her arts into rustic Latium." Before the Romans acquired the Greek cities of Sicily and later Athens and Pergamum (which had a library second only to that of Alexandria), they had not realized that a great nation should have a national literature. Once they did, they set out to create one. Of course there must have been Roman poetry before this, but we can only speculate about its nature and quality. Latin literature as we know it began with the performance of a tragedy, adapted from a Greek original, in 240 B.C.

Its author was Livius Andronicus, who came to Rome, probably as a prisoner of war, from the Greek city of Tarentum. He also made a Latin translation of the *Odyssey*, for which he used a native Italian meter, the Saturnian. The same meter was employed by Naevius, a native Italian who became a Roman citizen, for his epic poem on the First Punic War, in which he had served; it contained, among other things, the story of the departure of Aeneas from Troy and the eventual founding of Rome. His successor in the line of epic poets, Quintus Ennius, born in 239 B.C., composed *The Annals*, which presented the whole history of Rome from Aeneas' escape from the flames of Troy to the poet's own times (he died in 169). But Ennius abandoned the Saturnian meter and created a Latin adaptation of Homer's hexameter; he began the poem by telling of a dream in which Homer appeared to him and announced the transmigration of his own soul into the body of Ennius. This initiative was the beginning of full-scale adoption of Greek epic, iambic, and even lyric meters by Roman poets.

In the drama, however, adaptation from the Greek models had been going on for some time. Of the works of the Roman tragic poets of the republic we have only fragments, but we have some of the work of the comic poet Plautus (born c. 240 B.C.), and all of the six comedies of Terence (born 193 B.C.). Both of them adapted and sometimes combined plays by Menander and other Greek comic dramatists of the fourth century, keeping the Greek names and setting. Terence, writing for an aristocratic circle of which he was a protégé, preserved the discreet wit and decorum of the originals, but Plautus, probably drawing on native Italian comic routines, added elements of robust humor verging at times on the farcical. These made his plays popular favorites, as indeed they have remained through the centuries, in such adaptations as Shakespeare's *Comedy of Errors*, Molière's *Amphitryon*, and, more recently, *The Boys from Syracuse* and *A Funny Thing Happened on the Way to the Forum*.

The Latin hexameter line that Ennius created for his epic was later employed for a different purpose. In the first century B.C. Titus Lucretius Carus used it for his long poem *On the Nature of Things*, an introduction, for Roman readers, to the atomic theories of the fifth-century Greek philosophers Democritus and Leucippus, as they appear, often much modified, in the treatises of the later philosopher Epicurus. It is a remarkable achievement. Long, detailed passages of scientific exposition attempt to prove the thesis that the universe and all the creatures in it are the product of endless combinations and regroupings of material atoms, and that the soul dies with the body. Consequently it is as absurd to fear punishment in a future life as it is to worry about interference in human affairs on the part of gods. Lucretius knows that his subject matter is dark *(obscura)*, but his song, he claims, is clear *(lucida)*, for he "touches everything with the charm of the Muses." This is perhaps too much to grant him, for there are many passages that require deep concentration and sympathetic cooperation on the part of the reader, but it is true that for most of the way the poet is in control. The great set pieces, like the opening invocation to Venus or the exhortation not to fear death that concludes Book III, are justly famous, but even in the most tangled areas of his philosophical argument he can often clothe abstract thought or scientific doctrine in brilliant images drawn from nature or human experience. He compares the process to the physician's ruse to get children to taste wormwood—smearing the edge of the cup with honey.

Lucretius' great poem is dedicated to one Memmius; this may be the Caius Memmius who set out for the province of Bithynia, of which he had been appointed governor, in 57 B.C. On his staff was a young man called Caius Valerius Catullus. He was one of a group of young poets at Rome whom Cicero called the "new poets." What was new about them was, for one thing, the Greek models they followed: not the classic tragedians of the fifth century, not Homer and Hesiod, but the Alexandrians and, in particular, Callimachus. Catullus is the only one of them whose work has come down to us, and it too almost perished; our text comes from a single manuscript that surfaced in the fourteenth century at Verona, Catullus' home town, and then disappeared forever.

Callimachean influence can be seen in the brevity of the poems, which range from two-line epigrams to the 340 lines of a poem on the marriage of Peleus and Thetis, a poem clearly modeled on Callimachean and Theocritean short mythical scenes. This poem also shows the Alexandrian emphasis on literary allusion; but elsewhere, in the shorter poems that deal with contemporary themes, we are in a distinctly Roman world. Many of them are addressed, in friendship or in enmity, to contemporaries, and one series, which chronicles the poet's love affair with a woman he calls Lesbia, portrays the exaltation of love requited and the bitter agony of love betrayed with a directness and passion that has no parallel in ancient literature except some of the fragments of Sappho.

Catullus lived his short life in the last years of the republic—Julius Caesar and Cicero were among the contemporaries to whom he addressed poems—but Virgil and Horace lived to see, and benefit from, the establishment of the principate under Augustus. Both of them enjoyed imperial favor; Augustus, like the Greek tyrants and the Hellenistic monarchs, sought to legitimize and glorify his regime through the patronage of poets. For this he relied on the advice of his close friend and counselor Caius Maecenas, who cultivated the acquaintance of a circle of young poets that included Virgil and Horace. Both of them sang the praises of Augustus and his achievements, though they both politely declined a commission to write an epic in celebration of the new regime. Virgil, however, foreshadows, in the opening verses of the third book of his *Georgics*, the national epic of Rome's origins, the *Aeneid*, which was to be his crowning work. It is not specifically a celebration of Augustus, but its epic vision of the Roman mission was welcome at court; in 23 B.C. Virgil was invited to read Books II, IV, and VI to the imperial family.

Virgil's models are Greek: the *Odyssey* for the first half (the wanderings of Aeneas), the *Iliad* for the second (the wars in Italy). And the moving portrayal of Medea in love in the *Argonautica* of Apollonius of Rhodes made its contribution to Virgil's treatment of Dido in Books I and IV. But the final product is unmistakably Roman. Aeneas is a wanderer on the Mediterranean waters like Odysseus and, like him, goes to the lower world, the world of the dead. Once there, Odysseus sees his mother and his comrades who were killed at Troy or, like Agamemnon, on his return home, and he sees also the great heroic men and women of the distant past. Aeneas, however, sees his father, who shows him a pageant of great figures, not of the past but of the future: they are the warriors, statesmen, and legislators who will build the Roman Empire. Odysseus, at the end of his wanderings, returns home to his family, but Aeneas settles in a foreign land to fight and conquer a base for the empire to come and to die in battle before his time. The poem is not a heroic but a national epic. Aeneas is not just an individual hero; he is the personification of the sense of discipline and duty that brought Rome to the mastery of the world. What saves the poem from sounding like a patriotic manifesto is Virgil's brooding sense of the sadness of the Roman destiny, the sacrifice it entails. When he wrote the famous lines about the difference between the Greek and the Roman destinies, he was expressing his pride in the Roman achievement, but he was also listing, with infinite regret, the things a Roman had to renounce to be a Roman.

Horace—the English version of the name Quintus Horatius Flaccus—was, like Virgil, a protégé of Maecenas and one of the poets who helped to create the literary Augustan age. The admiration both poets expressed for Augustus was not mere adulation, nor was it the product of fear; like most of the inhabitants of the Roman world, they were thankful for the peace the empire had enjoyed ever since Augustus put an end to the civil war that had lasted for generations. Horace in fact showed a remarkable independence, treating Augustus almost as an equal. Invited to serve as Augustus' private secretary, he politely declined, preferring a quiet life on the Sabine farm near Rome that Maecenas had given him to the immense power the appointment would have put within his grasp. His refusal was all the more remarkable since, unlike Virgil, who seems to have come from a well-to-do family, he was the son of a *libertus*—that is to say, his father had started life as a slave.

Horace first made a reputation as a writer of poems known as Satires, a genre that owed little, for once, to Greek models—the Roman critic Quintilian later claimed: "Satire indeed is entirely our own." Horace's *Satires* use the same hexameter meter Virgil employed for his epic, but with metrical licenses that indicate the conversational style of the discourse; in fact, Horace usually refers to the poems as *Sermones*, Conversations. There is indeed a great deal of satire of men and manners in these apparently casual poems, but there is also much good humor. Above all, these poems give us a vivid picture of life in Augustan Rome as Horace surveys, with unfailing wit and astonishing literary skill, the follies and aberrations of Roman society.

But his main achievement was in another genre. He adapted for Latin verse the most complex meters of the Greek lyric poets. Catullus had written poems in the meter of Sappho; Horace uses this meter in abundance and adapts also the four-line stanza of Alcaeus as well as other Greek lyric meters in a variety of combinations. The result is an astonishing tour de force: these foreign verse forms, some of them extremely complicated arrangements of short and long syllables, move in Horace's *Odes* with an ease and point that seems to make them native to the language. It is significant that just as he had no real predecessor in these experiments, he had few followers; his success is unique. The *Odes*, exquisitely arranged for contrast and variety in four books, have a wide variety of tone: the somber seriousness of the so-called "Roman odes" (the first six of Book III); the mature sadness of poems that accept the shortness of human life and the transience of human happiness; the lightheartedness and wit of the love songs; the high spirits of the drinking songs—and everywhere a felicity of diction that has made him the admiration of readers ever since.

Sextus Propertius was the youngest member of the circle of Maecenas. All of his poetry is written in what is known as elegiac meter: couplets that consist of a hexameter line followed by a shorter one, a pentameter. The word "elegiac" is a possible source of confusion for the modern reader; there is no strict connotation of sadness or lament in the ancient, and especially the Latin, use of the term. Although the couplets could be, and often were, employed for funeral inscriptions (real or

imagined), they occur, in Greek poetry, as the medium for the martial
harangues of Tyrtaeus, the moral reflections of Solon, the bitter tirades
of Theognis, for Xenophanes' dismissal of the claim of victorious athletes to official honors, and also for Mimnermus' praise of the joys of
golden Aphrodite. The elegiac couplet was a favorite format of Callimachus, who used it for his long mythological poem *Aitia,* and even for
odes celebrating victories in athletic games. Almost half the poems in
Catullus' book are composed in this meter, and here too the subjects
range widely—personal invective, scurrilous epigram, a translation of
Callimachus' famous poem on the lock of Berenice's hair that became a
constellation—but many of them deal with his love for, and his later
alienation from, Lesbia. This subject, love, was to become the main
theme of Latin elegiac verse. The love elegy is in fact a Roman creation:
a series of poems in which the poet, in his own person, rings the changes
on his relations with a beloved mistress—Tibullus with Delia, Propertius
with Cynthia, Ovid with Corinna. These are fictitious names and may in
some cases be fictitious persons, though later critics have proposed real
identities for them.

Propertius is in some ways the most Alexandrian of these poets; sometimes the density of his mythological and literary allusions demands
lengthy explanation. Yet he can be witty and even humorous and he is
also, at his best, the most direct and passionate of the love elegists. The
Delia of Tibullus and Ovid's Corinna seem like paper dolls when compared to his Cynthia, their throes of passion contrived while his seem all
too real. And in his macabre vision of Cynthia dead, reproaching him for
his neglect, he combines desire, disgust, and regret in lines that evoke
Poe and Baudelaire. Robert Lowell's brilliant imitation (p. 725) gives
some idea of the power of the original.

Ovid was too young to be a member of the Maecenas salon. He
listened to Horace, he tells us, but "Virgil I only saw." He was also too
young to have known the realities of the long civil war, to have fought in
the republican ranks at Philippi, like Horace, or suffered the confiscation
of his family estates, like Virgil. His attitude toward Augustus could
hardly be as sincerely thankful as theirs, and in fact he managed to
offend the emperor so deeply that in A.D. 8 he was sent into exile at
Tomi, a bleak frontier post on the Black Sea, where he died nine years
later.

The specific offense that earned him the sentence of exile remains a
mystery to this day, but it is clear that Ovid, ever since the publication of
his first book of poems, the *Amores,* had been playing a risky game.
Augustus, who proposed around 20 B.C. an ambitious program of legislation aimed at restoration of the old Roman moral virtues celebrated in

Horace's Roman odes, must have been scandalized by the book—a witty, audacious chronicle of the author's love life with a married woman called Corinna (not to mention his dalliance with her maid). Ovid followed this up with the *Ars Amatoria*, a handbook of seduction, part one addressed to men, part two to women. The closing lines of the second part give explicit advice to the fair sex on the positions for sexual intercourse best suited for their figures and complexions, and the context makes it perfectly clear that the last person for whose delectation these positions are to be assumed is the lady's husband. Whatever it was that triggered the imperial decree of exile, there can be no doubt that Ovid had been in the emperor's bad books for a long time.

These poems are all in elegiac couplets, the traditional meter of love poetry, but his major work, completed just before he took ship for Tomi, is in hexameters, the Homeric and Virgilian epic line. The *Metamorphoses* is an epic of mythological transformations ". . . things that change, new being / Out of old . . . the shifting story of the world / From its beginning to the present hour." It starts with the creation of the universe—chaos transformed to order—and ends with the near contemporary murder of Julius Caesar in 44 B.C. and the transformation of his soul into a comet that blazed for seven nights while his adopted son Octavian, later to be Augustus, presided over funeral games in his memory. With a charm and wit that have rarely been surpassed, Ovid created what for most readers since has become the standard version of many a Greek story: Apollo and Daphne, Phaethon, Echo and Narcissus, Pyramus and Thisbe; Arachne the spinner changed into a spider, Niobe into a weeping cliff face, Philomela, Procne, and Tereus into birds. English poets from Shakespeare to Eliot have helped themselves liberally to stories and even phrases from this huge literary treasury.

When Ovid was banished to Tomi, the fiction that the republic had somehow been preserved, so carefully maintained by Augustus in the early years of his principate, had lost much of its power to deceive. Under the rule of his successors—Tiberius, Caligula, and Nero—the principate was clearly revealed as a despotism and, for the members of the old Roman aristocracy, a bloodily repressive one. Tiberius died in his bed, but both Caligula and Nero were assassinated by conspirators who, with good reason, feared for their own lives.

Nero (emperor A.D. 54–68) considered himself a poet ("What an artist perishes in me," he said as he died) and surrounded himself with poets and men of letters—Seneca, for example, the philosopher and tragic poet, and Lucan the epic poet, both of whom were eventually suspected of disloyalty and given the privilege of taking their own lives rather than facing the executioner. A similar fate was decreed for a man

who had been Nero's most admired courtier, one whose wit and taste
Nero so trusted that he was known as the *arbiter elegantiarum;* like
young Hamlet, he was "the glass of fashion and the mould of form."
Tacitus gives us an unforgettable description of his spectacular suicide
(p. 793). It seems likely that this man was the author of one of the most
extraordinary works in Latin literature, a sort of picaresque novel called
Satyricon, which is attributed in the manuscripts to Petronius Arbiter. It
is the story of two young Greco-Roman dropouts and their disreputable
adventures on the road in southern Italy and elsewhere. We have only
fragments of what was evidently a very long work, but one of them, a
description of a dinner at the house of a vulgar millionaire called Trimalchio, is a satiric and comic masterpiece.

Petronius did have models, of course, one of them the so-called
"Menippean satires." This was a genre invented by the third-century
Hellenistic poet Menippus of Gadara, a mixture of prose and verse that
combined homespun moral philosophy with broad humor. It had its
Latin imitators and Petronius undoubtedly owed something to them.
But the *Satyricon* has no parallel in either Greek or Latin literature for
its realistic creation of low-life characters—not just Trimalchio and his
trollop of a wife Fortunata, but also Echion the rag merchant, Phileros
the lawyer who once made his living as a peddler, and a whole crew of
upstart wealthy immigrants whose Latin, as served up by Petronius,
would, to use Milton's phrase, "have made Quintilian stare and gasp." It
is one of the few texts in Latin literature that reminds one, with a jolt,
that ordinary citizens of the empire did not, when they opened their
mouths, sound anything like Cicero.

The year that followed Nero's death in A.D. 68 is known as the year of
the four emperors: four claimants to the imperial power plunged the
empire into civil war for the first time since 30 B.C. The victor, Vespasian, and his son and successor Titus, gave the empire eleven years of
good government; but Titus' successor Domitian was another Nero. His
murder in A.D. 96 saw the elevation to the purple of Nerva, the first of
the "good emperors," the last of whom, Marcus Aurelius, died in 180.

It should be remembered that all through this period, even in the
most violent phases of the tyrannies of Caligula, Nero, and Domitian,
the provinces of the empire enjoyed better government than they had
under the rapacious regime of the aristocrats of the republic. The principal victims of the tyrannical regimes were the members of the upper
classes in Rome, who were (sometimes with reason) suspected of hostility to the regime and conspiracy against it. Unfortunately for the reputation of the early emperors, the greatest historian of the events of the first
century A.D., Cornelius Tacitus, though not himself from one of the

grcat Roman families, was a nostalgic admirer of the great days of Roman liberty and a severe critic of the imperial dynasty. He was also a writer of immense talent.

Tacitus spent the early years of his official career under the savagely repressive rule of Domitian (A.D. 81–96). "The reign of terror," he wrote, "was particularly ruthless at Rome. Rank, wealth and office, whether surrendered or retained, provided grounds for accusation, and the reward for virtue was inevitable death. . . . The profits made by the prosecutors were no less odious than their crimes. . . . Slaves were suborned to speak against their masters, freedmen against patrons, while those who had not an enemy in the world were ruined by their friends." His summing up of the effects of those fifteen years strikes a modern note in a world that has seen so many years of Fascist and Communist tyranny:

> There is no doubt that we have given the world a signal example of passivity. Former ages saw liberty carried to extremes of excess; we have experienced the extremes of slavery, for informers deprived us even of the freedom to converse with each other. We would have lost our memory as well as our voice, if it had been as much in our power to forget as to keep silent. . . . Fifteen years—no small portion of our life on earth—have seen many of us cut off by time and chance, the most active by the ferocity of the emperor, while we few survivors have outlived not only the others but, in a sense, ourselves. Since from our prime of life so many years have been cut out, years in which those of us who were young became old, those who were old reached the extreme limits of old age—and all without saying a word.

Tacitus had a distinguished career in the imperial administration—senator during the reign of Domitian, and later, under Nerva and Trajan, consul in Rome and governor of a large province, the eastern half of what is now Turkey. But he found time to write *The Annals*, a history of the empire from the death of Agustus in A.D. 14 to the murder of Nero in 96. Only about a third of the work has survived. We have most of the reign of Tiberius; none, unfortunately, of the lurid years of Caligula; about half of the reign of Claudius; and most of that of Nero. We have also, from *The Histories* (an earlier work that spanned the years from the death of Nero to that of Domitian), a riveting account of A.D. 69, the year of the four emperors, the civil war that followed the death of Nero and ended in the victory of Vespasian.

A contemporary of Tacitus (though there is no reason to think that they knew each other) was the satirist Juvenal, about whose life we have little reliable information. It seems likely that his official career, one on a much lower level than that of Tacitus, was interrupted by a sentence of exile under Domitian, and it appears from his writings that he knew all too well the humiliations of the search for support and patronage that occupied so much of the time of the middle-class Roman citizen. He uses for his *Satires* the same rather lax hexameter line that Horace used for his, but there is no trace of Horace's tolerant humor in Juvenal's vitriolic tirades. *Facit indignatio versum,* he says; it is indignation that drives him to write verses. His target is the corrupt society of a Rome that had become cosmopolitan, even polyglot, a world capital in which moral standards had long since been discarded. One entire satire is devoted to the horrors of life in the big city, and one of these is the omnipresence of Greeks. Horace had hailed the literary conquest of Rome by Greece as a blessing, but Juvenal is talking about something else—the Hellenistic Greek-speaking immigrants, many of them from cities with outlandish Eastern names, who had worked their way into every level of Roman society. Trimalchio's coarse guests at his dinner party all have recognizably Greek names; they were provincial millionaires, but some Greeks had climbed much higher. Under Claudius, Greek freedmen, such as Pallas and Narcissus, served the emperor as close advisers and accumulated wealth and power. Juvenal's vicious caricature of a Rome taken over by fast-talking, intriguing Greeks is a xenophobic classic. It was Samuel Johnson's model for his *London,* published in 1738, where, however, the target has changed: "I cannot bear a French metropolis." But it is much more than that; it is an awesome catalogue of the tribulations and dangers of life in the big city, and, from traffic jams to nocturnal bandits, they are all too familiar to the inhabitants of Los Angeles and New York.

The rule of the last of the "good emperors," Marcus Aurelius (A.D. 161–180), was that ideal proposed by Plato, the philosopher-king. He learned from Greek tutors and above all from the conversation of his adoptive father, the emperor Antoninus Pius, the ethical tenets of Stoic philosophy. Its name recalls the Stoa, the roofed colonnade in Athens, where Zeno first taught; his school was founded around 300 B.C. The basic Stoic principle was "harmony with nature"—that is, acceptance of whatever happens as the working of divine wisdom, and a consequent indifference to misfortune. Stoicism was introduced to the Romans in the second century B.C. by Greek teachers such as Panaetius, who adapted it along lines that made it attractive to men of action like the warriors and statesmen of the great days of the republic. Panaetius emphasized not only individual fortitude and virtue but also duty to the community. Under the first emperors Stoicism became the philosophy of the senatorial opposition; in fact, its teachers were twice banned from

Italy. But in the so-called *Meditations* of Marcus Aurelius—notes, written in Greek, addressed to himself and composed, most of them, during his campaigns in the Balkans defending the now permanently menaced Roman frontier—Stoicism is the philosophy of an enlightened monarch whose delight was in philosophy and literature, but whose sense of duty kept him for many years on the rough frontier where in 180 he died.

The empire had now seen its best days. With Marcus' son, Commodus, who was assassinated in 192, begins what Gibbon has immortalized in his title, the decline and fall of the Roman Empire. Commodus was an emperor in the tradition of Caligula and Nero rather than that of Hadrian, Antoninus, and Marcus Aurelius. His murder in 192 was followed by a war between rival army commanders that ended in the victory of Severus, a provincial from Africa, who reorganized and enlarged the Roman army to cope with the growing threat of invasion not only in the Balkans but also in the East. But when he died in 211, his son Caracalla held power for only six years; his murder was followed by fifty years of chaos and civil war (218–268), in which there were more than fifty claimants to the imperial purple, one short-lived emperor after another was killed by his own troops, and new and more formidable foreign enemies, the Goths to the north and the Persians to the east, ravaged the Balkan and Near Eastern provinces almost at will. When Rome celebrated the one thousandth year of its existence in 248, it must have seemed to many who took part in the ceremonies that the end was near.

It was to be delayed for more than a century. Under a series of soldier emperors—Gallienus, Claudius Gothicus (the second name is an honorific, meaning "conqueror of the Goths"), and Aurelian—the frontiers were secured. But the cost was tremendous. The increased taxation imposed for the upkeep of the legions, and the inflation that was partly due to the imperial government's progressive debasement of the gold and silver currency, began to undermine the whole economic and social system. Under Diocletian (284–305) an unprecedented measure designed to combat inflation, a decree fixing the maximum price of all goods and services in the empire, had little effect (except to drive goods off the market), but a reorganization of the tax system along more equitable lines helped to stabilize the regime. These and other measures, which aimed at strict control of the citizen body, were part of a program designed to unify the vast population of the empire in support of the emperor and the armies in the fight against the unrelenting pressure on the frontiers. The emperor assumed the semi-divinity of an Oriental monarch, and elaborate court ceremonial emphasized his role as the protector of Rome and its people.

To this program of totalitarian regimentation there was one influential group that refused cooperation—the Christian Church. In spite of sporadic persecutions, provoked by the Christian refusal to make the ritual offering to the divinity of the emperor, the Church, by the end of the third century, had become a widespread, well-organized community, especially strong in the cities of the empire. The persecutions under Diocletian were particularly severe, but failed to break the Church's hold on the minds of its adherents. In the turbulent years that followed Diocletian's retirement in 305, it grew from strength to strength; under the rule and leadership of its bishops, it became a sort of state within the state. Constantine, who emerged from a civil war as sole ruler of the empire in 323, declared himself a Christian and, though he accepted baptism only on his deathbed, favored the growth of the Church's power and influence. Christianity was at this time by no means the predominant religion of the empire, though it was stronger in the East than in the West, but Constantine was probably impressed by its capacity for growth and counted on it to organize support for his imperial regime. Under imperial patronage the Church flourished as never before, and though one of Constantine's successors, Julian (361–363), tried to restore the old pagan cults (hence the name given him by Christian historians—Julian the Apostate), the tide could not be turned back. In 391, the emperor Theodosius suppressed all pagan worship and Christianity became the official religion of the Roman state.

Theodosius ruled the empire not from Rome but from the "New Rome" Constantine had made for himself by rebuilding and enlarging the ancient Greek city of Byzantium, a strategic site on the straits that connect the Black Sea with the Mediterranean. Constantinople was a new Rome in more senses than one. Not only was it a newly constructed city, which meant that unlike old Rome, it was not crowded with huge temples dedicated to pagan gods; it was also the new center of imperial power in the East. It had become clear already in the late second century that Rome was too far from the Balkan and Eastern frontiers for effective control of the worsening military situation, and Diocletian had divided the responsibility for the empire's defense between himself in the East and his partner Maximian in the West. By 395, when Theodosius died, his two sons, Honorius in the West and Arcadius in the East, ruled their halves of the empire as separate and on occasion unfriendly powers. The two halves, separate in language, culture, and now under separate rule, grew steadily farther apart. The Eastern empire, ruled from Constantinople, was now launched on a thousand-year career as a Christian empire until the city was captured by the Turks in 1453. But in the West, the frontier defenses collapsed. Into France, Spain, and Italy came invading armies of Franks, Burgundians, Alans, Vandals, and Visigoths, to plunder and later to settle. Rome itself fell to the Visigoth Alaric in 410.

Although Rome was no longer a place of strategic importance, the fall of the city was a shock felt round the world. Saint Jerome, who while living in Rome in the years 382–385 had produced a new and improved Latin translation of the Bible, heard the news in Jerusalem. "When the brightest light of the whole earth was extinguished," he wrote, "when the Roman empire was deprived of its head . . . when the whole world perished in one city . . . my sorrow was stirred." The Roman Empire in the West had passed away, but the Roman Church survived, to convert the invaders, and from Rome to rule over a spiritual kingdom that still exists.

One of its most prominent figures in these desperate years was Aurelius Augustinus, born in 354 in the city of Hippo, in what is now Algeria. In 395 he was consecrated bishop of his home town, and there he remained until his death in 430. As he died, the Vandals, who had fought their way from Germany through France and Spain to North Africa, were besieging the city. During his thirty-five years as bishop, he had written over ninety-three books, many of them polemical treatises against what he regarded as heresies (for example, the rejection of the idea of Original Sin by the British monk Pelagius). Among them was an influential work on Christian education, *De Doctrina Christiana,* that recommended a program combining Roman literary culture with the study of the Bible. There was also an immense and formidably learned work, *The City of God,* which was, among many other things, a refutation of the idea—widely held by the still large pagan community—that Rome had fallen because it had abandoned its tutelary gods.

His most famous work, the *Confessions,* is an address to God, an account of his life before his late conversion and baptism at the age of thirty-three. *Sero te amavi,* he writes: "Late I came to love you, Beauty so ancient and so new." He presents a picture of his life seen as a slow and contested return journey to final recognition of the truth of the Christian vision in which his mother Monica had brought him up. Like Odysseus, he took years to come home, his voyage interrupted by many sirens and sorceresses: the call of worldly ambition in the pagan world as a brilliant professor of rhetoric (a lucrative and influential position in a society dominated by the spoken word); the charms of pagan philosophy (that of the skeptical Academics, who proved to their own satisfaction that true knowledge was unattainable); the exotic cult of the Manichees, who saw the world as a battleground between the forces of good and of evil and whose Elect lived a life of abstinence; but strongest of all these, the call of the flesh. To be accepted as a priest he would have to renounce the sexual love of women, and this he found hardest of all. As a young man he had prayed: "Grant me chastity and continence, but not yet." And later, even when his mind was made up, his "old loves" held him back. "They tugged at the garment of my flesh and whispered: 'Are you getting rid of us?' " As he wrestled with his conflicting desires in a garden near Milan, he heard a child's voice inside the house saying over and over again: *Tolle, lege*—"Pick up and read." He opened the book he had been reading and found himself looking at verses 12 and 13 of Saint Paul's Epistle to the Romans; they end with the words: " . . . put ye on the Lord Jesus Christ, and make no provision for the flesh, to fulfil the lusts thereof." The fall of Rome to the Visigoths in 410 is often cited as the end of ancient civilization and the beginning of a new age. But just as important, perhaps more important, for the future of Europe was this moment in the garden when Augustine took the decision that was to make him the dominant intellectual influence on the Western Church for many centuries to come.

GREECE

HOMER
Late 8th Century B.C.?

About Homer, who was believed to be the creator of two great epic poems, the Iliad *and the* Odyssey, *we know nothing certain. The ancient tradition that he was blind is probably based on the description of the blind bard Demodocus, who sings at the court of the Phaeacian king in the* Odyssey, *and the fact that seven cities claimed the honor of his birth suggests strongly that no real biographical data had been preserved. Some thought of him as living at the time of the Trojan War, the background of both epic poems (this would have placed him in the eleventh century B.C.); Herodotus, writing in the middle years of the fifth century B.C., believed that he lived "four hundred years before my time"; and modern scholars, appealing to linguistic, historical, and archeological criteria, date the poems to the last years of the eighth century B.C. Whether or not Homer was the author of both poems, it is generally agreed that the* Odyssey, *which deals with events that followed the fall of Troy, was composed later than the* Iliad.

THE ILIAD

The Iliad *opens with a violent quarrel between Agamemnon, king of Argos, whom the other Achaean chieftains acknowledge as commander of the expedition against Troy, and Achilles, son of Peleus, from Phthia in Thessaly, the bravest and most aggressive fighter in the Achaean host. Achilles is also the commander of the Myrmidons, the most formidable contingent of the army, who are loyal to him personally. The dispute occurs when Agamemnon is forced by public opinion to give up his share of the booty taken in a recent raid. His share was a woman, Chyseis, whose father, a priest of Apollo, has, by his prayer to the god, brought* down a lethal plague on the Achaeans. Agamemnon demands compensation from the army for his loss. Achilles tells him to wait until next time, but the king, infuriated, says he will take Achilles' own share of the booty, a woman called Briseis, to whom Achilles is much attached. Achilles' initial reaction is to reach for his sword, but he is restrained by the goddess Athena, who, together with Zeus' wife Hera and his brother Poseidon, is a bitter enemy of Troy and insists on its destruction. Achilles obeys the goddess but withdraws, with his troops, from the fighting. He also persuades his goddess mother Thetis to go to Zeus and ask him to give the Trojans the upper hand in the battle, so that the Achaeans will regret depriving him of that honor among warriors that he prizes above life itself. Zeus complies, and soon the Achaeans are hard pressed.

From BOOK VI

HECTOR AND ANDROMACHE

Meanwhile Hector, son of Priam, king of Troy, the main champion on the Trojan side, goes back into the city to tell his mother to organize a religious ceremony, an appeal to Athena for help. That done, he goes off to visit, for the last time as it turns out, his wife Andromache and his infant son Astyanax.

Richmond Lattimore, the translator of our first selection (and also of the third), tries to reproduce some of the peculiarities of the Homeric poetic language, Homer's legacy from generations of oral illiterate bards. They relied for their speed and agility in improvised recitation on standard phrases—"formulas"—that fit easily into place in the metrical pattern of their long line. In the following excerpt, for example, the repeated phrases "Hector of the shining helm" and "glorious Hector" represent Greek expressions that fit different lengths at the end of the line, just as "lovely-haired women of Troy" and "Hector slayer of men" correspond to formulas that are suitable for the beginning of the line. Lattimore has tried to find English equivalents for most of these expressions; he has also devised a line that, though it substitutes the native English patterns of stress for the variations of length of syllable of the Greek, does suggest, by its length and by the variations of the stress patterns from line to line, the sound of Homer's verse.

So speaking Hektor of the shining helm departed
and in speed made his way to his own well-established dwelling,
but failed to find in the house Andromache of the white arms;

for she, with the child, and followed by one fair-robed attendant,
had taken her place on the tower in lamentation, and tearful.
When he saw no sign of his perfect wife within the house, Hektor
stopped in his way on the threshold and spoke among the
    handmaidens:
"Come then, tell me truthfully as you may, handmaidens:
where has Andromache of the white arms gone? Is she
with any of the sisters of her lord or the wives of his brothers?
Or has she gone to the house of Athene, where all the other
lovely-haired women of Troy propitiate the grim goddess?"
    Then in turn the hard-working housekeeper gave him an answer:
"Hektor, since you have urged me to tell you the truth, she is not
with any of the sisters of her lord or the wives of his brothers,
nor has she gone to the house of Athene, where all the other
lovely-haired women of Troy propitiate the grim goddess,
but she has gone to the great bastion of Ilion, because she heard
    that
the Trojans were losing, and great grew the strength of the
    Achaians.
Therefore she has gone in speed to the wall, like a woman
gone mad, and a nurse attending her carries the baby."
    So the housekeeper spoke, and Hektor hastened from his home
backward by the way he had come through the well-laid streets. So
as he had come to the gates on his way through the great city,
the Skaian gates, whereby he would issue into the plain, there
at last his own generous wife came running to meet him,
Andromache, the daughter of high-hearted Eëtion;
Eëtion, who had dwelt underneath wooded Plakos,
in Thebe below Plakos, lord over the Kilikian people.
It was his daughter who was given to Hektor of the bronze helm.
She came to him there, and beside her went an attendant carrying
the boy in the fold of her bosom, a little child, only a baby,
Hektor's son, the admired, beautiful as a star shining,
whom Hektor called Skamandrios, but all of the others
Astyanax—lord of the city; since Hektor alone saved Ilion.
Hektor smiled in silence as he looked on his son, but she,
Andromache, stood close beside him, letting her tears fall,
and clung to his hand and called him by name and spoke to him:
    "Dearest,
your own great strength will be your death, and you have no pity
on your little son, nor on me, ill-starred, who soon must be your
    widow;
for presently the Achaians, gathering together,

will set upon you and kill you; and for me it would be far better
to sink into the earth when I have lost you, for there is no other
consolation for me after you have gone to your destiny—
only grief; since I have no father, no honoured mother.
It was brilliant Achilleus who slew my father, Eëtion,
when he stormed the strong-founded citadel of the Kilikians,
Thebe of the towering gates. He killed Eëtion
but did not strip his armour, for his heart respected the dead man,
but burned the body in all its elaborate war-gear
and piled a grave mound over it, and the nymphs of the mountains,
daughters of Zeus of the aegis, planted elm trees about it.
And they who were my seven brothers in the great house all went
upon a single day down into the house of the death god,
for swift-footed brilliant Achilleus slaughtered all of them
as they were tending their white sheep and their lumbering oxen;
and when he had led my mother, who was queen under wooded
    Plakos,
here, along with all his other possessions, Achilleus
released her again, accepting ransom beyond count, but Artemis
of the showering arrows struck her down in the halls of her father.
Hektor, thus you are father to me, and my honoured mother,
you are my brother, and you it is who are my young husband.
Please take pity upon me then, stay here on the rampart,
that you may not leave your child an orphan, your wife a widow,
but draw your people up by the fig tree, there where the city
is openest to attack, and where the wall may be mounted.
Three times their bravest came that way, and fought there to storm it
about the two Aiantes and renowned Idomeneus,
about the two Atreidai and the fighting son of Tydeus.
Either some man well skilled in prophetic arts had spoken,
or the very spirit within themselves had stirred them to the
    onslaught."
　　Then tall Hektor of the shining helm answered her: "All these
things are in my mind also, lady; yet I would feel deep shame
before the Trojans, and the Trojan women with trailing garments,
if like a coward I were to shrink aside from the fighting;
and the spirit will not let me, since I have learned to be valiant
and to fight always among the foremost ranks of the Trojans,
winning for my own self great glory, and for my father.
For I know this thing well in my heart, and my mind knows it:
there will come a day when sacred Ilion shall perish,
and Priam, and the people of Priam of the strong ash spear.

But it is not so much the pain to come of the Trojans
that troubles me, not even of Priam the king nor Hekabe,
not the thought of my brothers who in their numbers and valour
shall drop in the dust under the hands of men who hate them,
as troubles me the thought of you, when some bronze-armoured
Achaian leads you off, taking away your day of liberty,
in tears; and in Argos you must work at the loom of another,
and carry water from the spring Messeis or Hypereia,
all unwilling, but strong will be the necessity upon you;
and some day seeing you shedding tears a man will say of you:
'This is the wife of Hektor, who was ever the bravest fighter
of the Trojans, breakers of horses, in the days when they fought
     about Ilion.'
So will one speak of you; and for you it will be yet a fresh grief,
to be widowed of such a man who could fight off the day of your
     slavery.
But may I be dead and the piled earth hide me under before I
hear you crying and know by this that they drag you captive."
     So speaking glorious Hektor held out his arms to his baby,
who shrank back to his fair-girdled nurse's bosom
screaming, and frightened at the aspect of his own father,
terrified as he saw the bronze and the crest with its horse-hair,
nodding dreadfully, as he thought, from the peak of the helmet.
Then his beloved father laughed out, and his honoured mother,
and at once glorious Hektor lifted from his head the helmet
and laid it in all its shining upon the ground. Then taking
up his dear son he tossed him about in his arms, and kissed him,
and lifted his voice in prayer to Zeus and the other immortals:
"Zeus, and you other immortals, grant that this boy, who is my son,
may be as I am, pre-eminent among the Trojans,
great in strength, as am I, and rule strongly over Ilion;
and some day let them say of him: 'He is better by far than his
     father,'
as he comes in from the fighting; and let him kill his enemy
and bring home the blooded spoils, and delight the heart of his
     mother."
     So speaking he set his child again in the arms of his beloved
wife, who took him back again to her fragrant bosom
smiling in her tears; and her husband saw, and took pity upon her,
and stroked her with his hand, and called her by name and spoke to
     her:
"Poor Andromache! Why does your heart sorrow so much for me?

No man is going to hurl me to Hades, unless it is fated,
but as for fate, I think that no man yet has escaped it
once it has taken its first form, neither brave man nor coward.
Go therefore back to our house, and take up your own work,
the loom and the distaff, and see to it that your handmaidens
ply their work also; but the men must see to the fighting,
all men who are the people of Ilion, but I beyond others."
    So glorious Hektor spoke and again took up the helmet
with its crest of horse-hair, while his beloved wife went homeward,
turning to look back on the way, letting the live tears fall.
And as she came in speed into the well-settled household
of Hektor the slayer of men, she found numbers of handmaidens
within, and her coming stirred all of them into lamentation.
So they mourned in his house over Hektor while he was living
still, for they thought he would never again come back from the
        fighting
alive, escaping the Achaian hands and their violence.

Translated by Richmond Lattimore

From BOOK IX

THE EMBASSY TO ACHILLES

*The fighting goes so badly for the Achaeans that Agamemnon calls
together a council of the chieftains to decide what is to be done. Nestor,
the oldest and wisest of them, urges Agamemenon to send an embassy to
Achilles, begging him to return to the battle. Agamemnon agrees and
appoints three ambassadors: Odysseus, the most crafty and politic of the
Achaeans; Ajax, the bravest warrior next to Achilles; and Phoenix, whose
presence at the council is somewhat surprising, since he is commander of
one of the Myrmidon contingents and a much loved older friend and
retainer of Achilles. Agamemnon instructs them to recite to Achilles the
long and impressive list of gifts he offers in propitiation, and also his
promise to return Briseis, the woman he had taken away from Achilles,
and to swear that he had never touched her. But he does not offer
anything like an apology for his insults.*

*   Robert Fagles, the translator of this (and of our fourth) excerpt, has
chosen a line length more familiar to readers of English narrative verse—
the blank verse line of Milton, Tennyson, and for that matter of Shakespeare and the Elizabethan dramatists; he has profited from the work of
many modernist poets whose experiments have given the line increased*

flexibility. He has also chosen not to offer the same version of a Homeric formula every time it occurs, but instead to convey some aspects of its content and emotional effect in a variety of ways.

So Ajax and Odysseus made their way at once
where the battle lines of breakers crash and drag,
praying hard to the god who moves and shakes the earth
that they might bring the proud heart of Achilles
round with speed and ease.
Reaching the Myrmidon shelters and their ships,
they found him there, delighting his heart now,
plucking strong and clear on the fine lyre—
beautifully carved, its silver bridge set firm—
he won from the spoils when he razed Eetion's city.
Achilles was lifting his spirits with it now,
singing the famous deeds of fighting heroes . . .
Across from him Patroclus sat alone, in silence,
waiting for Aeacus' son to finish with his song.
And on they came, with good Odysseus in the lead,
and the envoys stood before him. Achilles, startled,
sprang to his feet, the lyre still in his hands,
leaving the seat where he had sat in peace.
And seeing the men, Patroclus rose up too
as the famous runner called and waved them on:
"Welcome! Look, dear friends have come our way—
I must be sorely needed now—my dearest friends
in all the Achaean armies, even in my anger."

So Prince Achilles hailed and led them in,
sat them down on settles with purple carpets
and quickly told Patroclus standing by, "Come,
a bigger winebowl, son of Menoetius, set it here.
Mix stronger wine. A cup for the hands of each guest—
here beneath my roof are the men I love the most."

He paused. Patroclus obeyed his great friend,
who put down a heavy chopping block in the firelight
and across it laid a sheep's chine, a fat goat's
and the long back cut of a full-grown pig,
marbled with lard. Automedon held the meats
while lordly Achilles carved them into quarters,

cut them well into pieces, pierced them with spits
and Patroclus raked the hearth, a man like a god
making the fire blaze. Once it had burned down
and the flames died away, he scattered the coals
and stretching the spitted meats across the embers,
raised them onto supports and sprinkled clean pure salt.
As soon as the roasts were done and spread on platters,
Patroclus brought the bread, set it out on the board
in ample wicker baskets. Achilles served the meat.
Then face-to-face with his noble guest Odysseus
he took his seat along the farther wall,
he told his friend to sacrifice to the gods
and Patroclus threw the first cuts in the fire.
They reached out for the good things that lay at hand
and when they had put aside desire for food and drink,
Ajax nodded to Phoenix. Odysseus caught the signal,
filled his cup and lifted it toward Achilles,
opening with this toast: "Your health, Achilles!
We have no lack of a handsome feast, I see that,
either in Agamemnon's tents, the son of Atreus,
or here and now, in yours. We can all banquet here
to our heart's content.
                              But it's not the flowing feast
that is on our minds now—no, a stark disaster,
too much to bear, Achilles bred by the gods,
that is what we are staring in the face
and we are afraid. All hangs in the balance now:
whether we save our beached ships or they're destroyed,
unless, of course, you put your fighting power in harness.
They have pitched camp right at our ships and rampart,
those brazen Trojans, they and their far-famed allies,
thousands of fires blaze throughout their armies . . .
Nothing can stop them now—that's their boast—
they'll hurl themselves against our blackened hulls.
And the son of Cronus sends them signs on the right,
Zeus' firebolts flashing. And headlong Hector,
delirious with his strength, rages uncontrollably,
trusting to Zeus—no fear of man or god, nothing—
a powerful rabid frenzy has him in its grip!
Hector prays for the sacred Dawn to break at once,
he threatens to lop the high horns of our sterns
and gut our ships with fire, and all our comrades

pinncd against thc hulls, panicked by thick smoke,
he'll rout and kill in blood!
A nightmare—I fear it, with all my heart—
I fear the gods will carry out his threats
and then it will be our fate to die in Troy,
far from the stallion-land of Argos . . .
                                        Up with you—
now, late as it is, if you *want* to pull our Argives,
our hard-hit armies, clear of the Trojan onslaught.
Fail us now? What a grief it will be to you
through all the years to come. No remedy,
no way to cure the damage once it's done.
Come, while there's still time, think hard:
how can you fight off the Argives' fatal day?
Oh old friend, surely your father Peleus urged you,
that day he sent you out of Phthia to Agamemnon,
'My son, victory is what Athena and Hera will give,
if they so choose. But you, you hold in check
that proud, fiery spirit of yours inside your chest!
Friendship is much better. Vicious quarrels are deadly—
put an end to them, at once. Your Achaean comrades,
young and old, will exalt you all the more.'
That was your aged father's parting advice.
It must have slipped your mind.
                                But now at last,
stop, Achilles—let your heart-devouring anger go!
The king will hand you gifts to match his insults
if only you'll relent and end your anger . . .
So come then, listen, as I count out the gifts,
the troves in his tents that Agamemnon vows to give you.
Seven tripods never touched by fire, ten bars of gold,
twenty burnished cauldrons, a dozen massive stallions,
racers who earned him trophies with their speed.
He is no poor man who owns what they have won,
not strapped for goods with all that lovely gold—
what trophies those high-strung horses carried off for him!
Seven women he'll give you, flawless, skilled in crafts,
women of Lesbos—the ones he chose, his privilege,
that day you captured the Lesbos citadel yourself:
they outclassed the tribes of women in their beauty.
These he will give, and along with them will go
the one he took away at first, Briseus' daughter,

and he will swear a solemn, binding oath in the bargain:
he never mounted her bed, never once made love with her . . .
the natural thing, my lord, men and women joined.
Now all these gifts will be handed you at once.
But if, later, the gods allow us to plunder
the great city of Priam, you shall enter in
when we share the spoils, load the holds of your ship
with gold and bronze—as much as your heart desires—
and choose for your pleasure twenty Trojan women
second only to Argive Helen in their glory.
And then, if we can journey home to Achaean Argos,
pride of the breasting earth, you'll be his son-by-marriage . . .
He will even honor you on a par with his Orestes,
full-grown by now, reared in the lap of luxury.
Three daughters are his in his well-built halls,
Chrysothemis and Laodice and Iphianassa—
and you may lead away whichever one you like,
with no bride-price asked, home to Peleus' house.
And he will add a dowry, yes, a magnificent treasure
the likes of which no man has ever offered with his daughter . . .
Seven citadels he will give you, filled with people,
Cardamyle, Enope, and the grassy slopes of Hire,
Pherae the sacrosanct, Anthea deep in meadows,
rolling Aepea and Pedasus green with vineyards.
All face the sea at the far edge of sandy Pylos
and the men who live within them, rich in sheep-flocks,
rich in shambling cattle, will honor you like a god
with hoards of gifts and beneath your scepter's sway
live out your laws in sleek and shining peace.
                                                   All this . . .
he would extend to you if you will end your anger.
But if you hate the son of Atreus all the more,
him and his troves of gifts, at least take pity
on all our united forces mauled in battle here—
they will honor you, honor you like a god.
Think of the glory you will gather in their eyes!
Now you can kill Hector—seized with murderous frenzy,
certain there's not a single fighter his equal,
no Achaean brought to Troy in the ships—
now, for once, you can meet the man head-on!"

   The famous runner Achilles rose to his challenge:
"Royal son of Laertes, Odysseus, great tactician . . .

I must say what I have to say straight out,
must tell you how I feel and how all this will end—
so you won't crowd around me, one after another,
coaxing like a murmuring clutch of doves.
I hate that man like the very Gates of Death
who says one thing but hides another in his heart.
I will say it outright. That seems best to me.
Will Agamemnon win me over? Not for all the world,
I swear it—nor will the rest of the Achaeans.
No, what lasting thanks in the long run
for warring with our enemies, on and on, no end?
One and the same lot for the man who hangs back
and the man who battles hard. The same honor waits
for the coward and the brave. They both go down to Death,
the fighter who shirks, the one who works to exhaustion.
And what's laid up for me, what pittance? Nothing—
and after suffering hardships, year in, year out,
staking my life on the mortal risks of war.

　　Like a mother bird hurrying morsels back
to her wingless young ones—whatever she can catch—
but it's all starvation wages for herself.
　　　　　　　　　So for me.
Many a sleepless night I've bivouacked in harness,
day after bloody day I've hacked my passage through,
fighting other soldiers to win their wives as prizes.
Twelve cities of men I've stormed and sacked from shipboard,
eleven I claim by land, on the fertile earth of Troy.
And from all I dragged off piles of splendid plunder,
hauled it away and always gave the lot to Agamemnon,
that son of Atreus—always skulking behind the lines,
safe in his fast ships—and he would take it all,
he'd parcel out some scraps but keep the lion's share.
Some he'd hand to the lords and kings—prizes of honor—
and they, they hold them still. From me alone, Achilles
of all Achaeans, he seizes, he keeps the wife I love . . .
Well *let* him bed her now—
enjoy her to the hilt!
　　　　　　　　Why must we battle Trojans,
men of Argos? Why did he muster an army, lead us here,
that son of Atreus? Why, why in the world if not
for Helen with her loose and lustrous hair?
Are *they* the only men alive who love their wives,

those sons of Atreus? Never! Any decent man,
a man with sense, loves his own, cares for his own
as deeply as I, I loved that woman with all my heart,
though I won her like a trophy with my spear . . .
But now that he's torn my honor from my hands,
robbed me, lied to me—don't let him try me now.
I know *him* too well—he'll never win me over!

                        No, Odysseus,
let him rack his brains with you and the other captains
how to fight the raging fire off the ships. Look—
what a mighty piece of work he's done without *me!*
Why, he's erected a rampart, driven a trench around it,
broad, enormous, and planted stakes to guard it. No use!
He still can't block the power of man-killing Hector!
No, though as long as *I* fought on Achaea's lines
Hector had little lust to charge beyond his walls,
never ventured beyond the Scaean Gates and oak tree.
There he stood up to me alone one day—
and barely escaped my onslaught.

                      Ah but now,
since I have no desire to battle glorious Hector,
tomorrow at daybreak, once I have sacrificed
to Zeus and all the gods and loaded up my holds
and launched out on the breakers—watch, my friend,
if you'll take the time and care to see me off,
and you will see my squadrons sail at dawn,
fanning out on the Hellespont that swarms with fish,
my crews manning the oarlocks, rowing out with a will,
and if the famed god of the earthquake grants us safe passage,
the third day out we raise the dark rich soil of Phthia.
There lies my wealth, hoards of it, all I left behind
when I sailed to Troy on this, this insane voyage—
and still more hoards from here: gold, ruddy bronze,
women sashed and lovely, and gleaming gray iron,
and I will haul it home, all I won as plunder.
All but my prize of honor . . .
he who gave that prize has snatched it back again—
what outrage! That high and mighty King Agamemnon,
that son of Atreus!

                    Go back and tell him all,
all I say—out in the open too—so other Achaeans
can wheel on him in anger if he still hopes—

who knows?—to deceive some other comrade.
                                    Shameless,
inveterate—armored in shamelessness! Dog that he is,
he'd never dare to look me straight in the eyes again.
No, I'll never set heads together with that man—
no planning in common, no taking common action.
He cheated me, did me damage, wrong! But never again,
he'll never rob me blind with his twisting words again!
Once is enough for him. Die and be damned for all I care!
Zeus who rules the world has ripped his wits away.
His gifts, I loathe his gifts . . .
I wouldn't give you a splinter for that man!
Not if he gave me ten times as much, twenty times over, all
he possesses now, and all that could pour in from the world's end—
not all the wealth that's freighted into Orchomenos, even into Thebes,
Egyptian Thebes where the houses overflow with the greatest troves of
        treasure,
Thebes with the hundred gates and through each gate battalions,
two hundred fighters surge to war with teams and chariots—
no, not if his gifts outnumbered all the grains of sand
and dust in the earth—no, not even then could Agamemnon
bring my fighting spirit round until he pays me back,
pays full measure for all his heartbreaking outrage!

    His daughter . . . I will marry no daughter of Agamemnon.
Not if she rivaled Aphrodite in all her golden glory,
not if she matched the crafts of clear-eyed Athena,
not even then would I make *her* my wife! No,
let her father pitch on some other Argive—
one who can please *him*, a greater king than I.
If the gods pull me through and I reach home alive,
Peleus needs no help to fetch a bride for me himself.
Plenty of Argive women wait in Hellas and in Phthia,
daughters of lords who rule their citadels in power.
Whomever I want I'll make my cherished wife—at home.
Time and again my fiery spirit drove me to win a wife,
a fine partner to please my heart, to enjoy with her
the treasures my old father Peleus piled high.
I say no wealth is worth my life! Not all they claim
was stored in the depths of Troy, that city built on riches,
in the old days of peace before the sons of Achaea came—
not all the gold held fast in the Archer's rocky vaults,

in Phoebus Apollo's house on Pytho's sheer cliffs!
Cattle and fat sheep can all be had for the raiding,
tripods all for the trading, and tawny-headed stallions.
But a man's life breath cannot come back again—
no raiders in force, no trading brings it back,
once it slips through a man's clenched teeth.
                                        Mother tells me,
the immortal goddess Thetis with her glistening feet,
that two fates bear me on to the day of death.
If I hold out here and I lay siege to Troy,
my journey home is gone, but my glory never dies.
If I voyage back to the fatherland I love,
my pride, my glory dies . . .
true, but the life that's left me will be long,
the stroke of death will not come on me quickly.

    One thing more. To the rest I'd pass on this advice:
sail home now! You will never set your eyes
on the day of doom that topples looming Troy.
Thundering Zeus has spread his hands above her—
her armies have taken heart!
                                        So you go back
to the great men of Achaea. You report my message—
since this is the privilege of senior chiefs—
let *them* work out a better plan of action,
use their imaginations now to save the ships
and Achaea's armies pressed to their hollow hulls.
This maneuver will never work for them, this scheme
they hatched for the moment as I raged on and on.
But Phoenix can stay and rest the night with us,
so he can voyage home, home in the ships with me
to the fatherland we love. Tomorrow at dawn.
But only if Phoenix wishes.
I will never force the man to go."
                                        He stopped.
A stunned silence seized them all, struck dumb—
Achilles' ringing denials overwhelmed them so.
At last Phoenix the old charioteer spoke out,
he burst into tears, terrified for Achaea's fleet:
"Sail home? Is *that* what you're turning over in your mind,
my glorious one, Achilles? Have you no heart at all
to fight the gutting fire from the fast trim ships?

The spirit inside you overpowered by anger!
How could I be severed from you, dear boy,
left behind on the beachhead here—alone?
The old horseman Peleus had me escort you,
that day he sent you out of Phthia to Agamemnon,
a youngster still untrained for the great leveler, war,
still green at debate where men can make their mark.
So he dispatched me, to teach you all these things,
to make you a man of words and a man of action too.
Cut off from you with a charge like that, dear boy?
I have no heart to be left behind, not even
if Zeus himself would swear to scrape away
the scurf of age and make me young again . . .
As fresh as I was that time I first set out
from Hellas where the women are a wonder,
fleeing a blood feud with my father, Amyntor,
Ormenus' son. How furious father was with me,
over his mistress with her dark, glistening hair.
How he would dote on her and spurn his wedded wife,
my own mother! And time and again she begged me,
hugging my knees, to bed my father's mistress down
and kill the young girl's taste for an old man.
Mother—I did your bidding, did my work . . .
But father, suspecting at once, cursed me roundly,
he screamed out to the cruel Furies—'Never,
never let me bounce on my knees a son of his,
sprung of his loins!'—and the gods drove home that curse,
mighty Zeus of the Underworld and grim Persephone.
So I, I took it into my head to lay him low
with sharp bronze! But a god checked my anger,
he warned me of what the whole realm would say,
the loose talk of the people, rough slurs of men—
they must not call me a father-killer, our Achaeans!
Then nothing could keep me there, my blood so fired up.
No more strolling about the halls with father raging.
But there was a crowd of kin and cousins round me,
holding me in the house, begging me to stay . . .
they butchered plenty of fat sheep, banquet fare,
and shambling crook-horned cattle, droves of pigs,
succulent, rich with fat—they singed the bristles,
splaying the porkers out across Hephaestus' fire,
then wine from the old man's jars, all we could drink.

Nine nights they passed the hours, hovering over me,
keeping the watch by rounds. The fires never died,
one ablaze in the colonnade of the walled court,
one in the porch outside my bedroom doors.
                                                    But then,
when the tenth night came on me, black as pitch,
I burst the doors of the chamber bolted tight
and out I rushed, I leapt the walls at a bound,
giving the slip to guards and women servants.
And alway I fled through the whole expanse of Hellas
and gaining the good dark soil of Phthia, mother of flocks,
I reached the king, and Peleus gave me a royal welcome.
Peleus loved me as a father loves a son, I tell you,
his only child, the heir to his boundless wealth,
he made me a rich man, he gave me throngs of subjects,
I ruled the Dolopes, settling down on Phthia's west frontier.
And I made you what you are—strong as the gods, Achilles—
I loved you from the heart. You'd never go with another
to banquet on the town or feast in your own halls.
Never, until I'd sat you down on my knees
and cut you the first bits of meat, remember?
You'd eat your fill, I'd hold the cup to your lips
and all too often you soaked the shirt on my chest,
spitting up some wine, a baby's way . . . a misery.
Oh I had my share of troubles for you, Achilles,
did my share of labor. Brooding, never forgetting
the gods would bring no son of mine to birth,
not from my own loins.
                                    So you, Achilles—
great godlike Achilles—I made you my son, I tried,
so someday *you* might fight disaster off my back.
But now, Achilles, beat down your mounting fury!
It's wrong to have such an iron, ruthless heart.
Even the gods themselves can bend and change,
and theirs is the greater power, honor, strength.
Even the gods, I say, with incense, soothing vows,
with full cups poured and the deep smoky savor
men can bring them round, begging for pardon
when one oversteps the mark, does something wrong.
We do have Prayers, you know, Prayers for forgiveness,
daughters of mighty Zeus . . . and they limp and halt,
they're all wrinkled, drawn, they squint to the side,

can't look you in the eyes, and always bent on duty,
trudging after Ruin, maddening, blinding Ruin.
But Ruin is strong and swift—
She outstrips them all by far, stealing a march,
leaping over the whole wide earth to bring mankind to grief.
And the Prayers trail after, trying to heal the wounds.
And then, if a man reveres these daughters of Zeus
as they draw near him, they will help him greatly
and listen to his appeals. But if one denies them,
turns them away, stiff-necked and harsh—off they go
to the son of Cronus, Zeus, and pray that Ruin
will strike the man down, crazed and blinded
until he's paid the price.
                  Relent, Achilles—you too!
See that honor attend these good daughters of Zeus,
honor that sways the minds of others, even heroes.
If Agamemnon were not holding out such gifts,
with talk of more to come, that son of Atreus,
if the warlord kept on blustering in his anger, why,
I'd be the last to tell you, 'Cast your rage to the winds!
Defend your friends!'—despite their desperate straits.
But now, look, he gives you a trove of treasures
right away, and vows there are more to follow.
He sends the bravest captains to implore you,
leaders picked from the whole Achaean army,
comrades-in-arms that you love most yourself.
Don't dismiss their appeal, their expedition here—
though no one could blame your anger, not before.
So it was in the old days too. So we've heard
in the famous deeds of fighting men, of heroes,
when seething anger would overcome the great ones.
Still you could bring them round with gifts and winning words.
There's an old tale I remember, an ancient exploit,
nothing recent, but this is how it went . . .
We are all friends here—let me tell it now.

   The Curetes were fighting the combat-hard Aetolians,
armies ringing Calydon, slaughtering each other,
Aetolians defending their city's handsome walls
and Curetes primed to lay them waste in battle.
It all began when Artemis throned in gold
loosed a disaster on them, incensed that Oeneus

offered her no first fruits, his orchard's crowning glory.
The rest of the gods had feasted full on oxen, true,
but the Huntress alone, almighty Zeus' daughter—
Oeneus gave her nothing. It slipped his mind
or he failed to care, but what a fatal error!
How she fumed, Zeus' child who showers arrows,
she loosed a bristling wild boar, his tusks gleaming,
crashing his savage, monstrous way through Oeneus' orchard,
ripping up whole trunks from the earth to pitch them headlong,
rows of them, roots and all, appleblossoms and all!
But the son of Oeneus, Meleager, cut him down—
mustering hunters out of a dozen cities,
packs of hounds as well. No slim band of men
could ever finish him off, that rippling killer,
he stacked so many men atop the tear-soaked pyre.
But over his body the goddess raised a terrific din,
a war for the prize, the huge beast's head and shaggy hide—
Curetes locked to the death with brave Aetolians.
                                                        Now,
so long as the battle-hungry Meleager fought,
it was deadly going for the Curetes. No hope
of holding their ground outside their *own* city walls,
despite superior numbers. But then, when the wrath
came sweeping over the man, the same anger that swells
the chests of others, for all their care and self-control—
then, heart enraged at his own dear mother Althaea,
Meleager kept to his bed beside his wedded wife,
Cleopatra . . . that great beauty. Remember her?
The daughter of trim-heeled Marpessa, Euenus' child,
and her husband Idas, strongest man of the men
who once walked the earth—he even braved Apollo,
he drew his bow at the Archer, all for Marpessa
the girl with lovely ankles. There in the halls
her father and mother always called Cleopatra Halcyon,
after the seabird's name . . . grieving once for her own fate
her mother had raised the halcyon's thin, painful cry,
wailing that lord Apollo the distant deadly Archer
had whisked her far from Idas.
                                        Meleager's Cleopatra—
she was the one he lay beside those days,
brooding over his heartbreaking anger.
He was enraged by the curses of his mother,

volleys of curses she called down from the gods.
So racked with grief for her brother he had killed
she kept pounding fists on the earth that feeds us all,
kept crying out to the god of death and grim Persephone,
flung herself on the ground, tears streaking her robes
and she screamed out, 'Kill Meleager, kill my son!'
And out of the world of darkness a Fury heard her cries,
stalking the night with a Fury's brutal heart, and suddenly—
thunder breaking around the gates, the roar of enemies,
towers battered under assault. And Aetolia's elders
begged Meleager, sent high priests of the gods,
pleading, 'Come out now! defend your people now!'—
and they vowed a princely gift.
Wherever the richest land of green Calydon lay,
there they urged him to choose a grand estate,
full fifty acres, half of it turned to vineyards,
half to open plowland, and carve it from the plain.
And over and over the old horseman Oeneus begged him,
he took a stand at the vaulted chamber's threshold,
shaking the bolted doors, begging his own son!
Over and over his brothers and noble mother
implored him—he refused them all the more—
and troops of comrades, devoted, dearest friends.
Not even they could bring his fighting spirit round
until, at last, rocks were raining down on the chamber,
Curetes about to mount the towers and torch the great city!
And then, finally, Meleager's bride, beautiful Cleopatra
begged him, streaming tears, recounting all the griefs
that fall to people whose city's seized and plundered—
the men slaughtered, citadel burned to rubble, enemies
dragging the children, raping the sashed and lovely women.
How his spirit leapt when he heard those horrors—
and buckling his gleaming armor round his body,
out he rushed to war. And so he saved them all
from the fatal day, he gave way to his own feelings,
but too late. No longer would they make good the gifts,
those troves of gifts to warm his heart, and even so
he beat off that disaster . . . empty-handed.

    But you, you wipe such thoughts from your mind.
Don't let your spirit turn you down that path, dear boy.
Harder to save the warships once they're up in flames.

Now—while the gifts still wait—go out and fight!
Go—the Achaeans all will honor you like a god!
But enter this man-killing war without the gifts—
your fame will flag, no longer the same honor,
even though you hurl the Trojans home!"

    But the swift runner Achilles answered firmly,
"Phoenix, old father, bred and loved by the gods,
what do I need with honor such as that?
I say my honor lies in the great decree of Zeus.
That gift will hold me here by the beaked ships
as long as the life breath remains inside my chest
and my springing knees will lift me. Another thing—
take it to heart, I urge you. Stop confusing
my fixed resolve with this, this weeping and wailing
just to serve his pleasure, Atreus' mighty son.
It degrades you to curry favor with that man,
and I will hate you for it, I who love you.
It does you proud to stand by me, my friend,
to attack the man who attacks me—
be king on a par with me, take half my honors!
These men will carry their message back, but you,
you stay here and spend the night in a soft bed.
Then, tomorrow at first light, we will decide
whether we sail home or hold out here."
                                                    With that,
he gave Patroclus a sharp glance, a quiet nod
to pile the bedding deep for Phoenix now,
a sign to the rest to think of leaving quickly.
Giant Ajax rose to his feet, the son of Telamon,
tall as a god, turned and broke his silence:
"Ready, Odysseus? Royal son of Laertes,
great tactician—come, home we go now.
There's no achieving our mission here, I see,
not with this approach. Best to return at once,
give the Achaeans a full report, defeating as it is.
They must be sitting there, waiting for us now.
                                                    Achilles—
he's made his own proud spirit so wild in his chest,
so savage, not a thought for his comrades' love—
we honored him past all others by the ships.

Hard, ruthless man . . .
Why, any man will accept the blood-price paid
for a brother murdered, a child done to death.
And the murderer lives on in his own country—
the man has paid enough, and the injured kinsman
curbs his pride, his smoldering, vengeful spirit,
once he takes the price.
                    You—the gods have planted
a cruel, relentless fury in your chest! All for a girl,
just one, and here we offer you seven—outstanding beauties—
that, and a treasure trove besides. Achilles,
put some human kindness in your heart.
Show respect for your own house. Here we are,
under your roof, sent from the whole Achaean force!
Past all other men, all other Achaean comrades,
we long to be your closest, dearest friends."

    And the swift runner Achilles answered warmly,
"Ajax, royal son of Telamon, captain of armies,
all well said, after my own heart, or mostly so.
But my heart still heaves with rage
whenever I call to mind that arrogance of his—
how he mortified me, right in front of the Argives—
that son of Atreus treating me like some vagabond,
like some outcast stripped of all my rights!
You go back to him and declare my message:
I will not think of arming for bloody war again,
not till the son of wise King Priam, dazzling Hector
batters all the way to the Myrmidon ships and shelters,
slaughtering Argives, gutting the hulls with fire.
But round my own black ship and camp this Hector
will be stopped, I trust, blazing for battle
as he goes—stopped dead in his tracks!"
                    So he finished.
Then each man, lifting his own two-handled cup,
poured it out to the gods, and back they went
along the ships, Odysseus in the lead.

                              Translated by Robert Fagles

From BOOK XXI

ACHILLES AND LYCAON

The battle resumes and now the Trojan onslaught, led by Hector, threatens the Achaean ships drawn up on the beach. Agamemnon, his brother Menelaus, Diomedes, and Odysseus are wounded one after another. Achilles' closest friend, Patroclus, sent by Achilles to find out how things stand in the Achaean camp, brings back the news and also pleads with Achilles to relent. He does so, but only partly: he agrees to let Patroclus take the Myrmidons into battle, wearing the distinctive shield and armor of Achilles. This is enough to turn the tide of battle; the Trojans in their turn are thrown back. But Patroclus is killed by the god Apollo, the protector of Troy, and by Hector, who strips Achilles' armor off the corpse and puts it on.

Achilles' rage is now directed against Hector, the killer of his dearest friend. He is reconciled with Agamemnon, and after his mother brings him a splendid new suit of armor made by the smith god Hephaestus, he leads the attack. He kills many Trojans as he fights his way toward Hector, among them Lycaon, a son of Priam. The lines that describe this encounter are remarkable not only for their ferocity but also for Achilles' use of the word "friend" to address the man he is about to kill. He can use it because war locks them both, killer and victim, in the same deadly trap; his own turn, as he says, will come all too soon. Wilfred Owen, the English poet who was killed in the last days of World War I, may have had this passage in mind when he wrote, in his great poem "Strange Meeting," "I am the enemy you killed, my friend . . ."

And there he came upon a son of Dardanian Priam
as he escaped from the river, Lykaon, one whom he himself
had taken before and led him unwilling from his father's gardens
on a night foray. He with the sharp bronze was cutting young
     branches
from a fig tree, so that they could make him rails for a chariot,
when an unlooked-for evil thing came upon him, the brilliant
Achilleus, who that time sold him as slave in strong-founded Lemnos
carrying him there by ship, and the son of Jason paid for him;
from there a guest and friend who paid a great price redeemed him,
Eëtion of Imbros, and sent him to shining Arisbe;
and from there he fled away and came to the house of his father.
For eleven days he pleasured his heart with friends and family

after he got back from Lemnos, but on the twelfth day once again
the god cast him into the hands of Achilleus, who this time
was to send him down unwilling on his way to the death god.
Now as brilliant swift-footed Achilleus saw him and knew him
naked and without helm or shield, and he had no spear left
but had thrown all these things on the ground, being weary and
    sweating
with the escape from the river, and his knees were beaten with
    weariness,
disturbed, Achilleus spoke to his own great-hearted spirit:
"Can this be? Here is a strange thing that my eyes look on.
Now the great-hearted Trojans, even those I have killed already,
will stand and rise up again out of the gloom and the darkness
as this man has come back and escaped the day without pity
though he was sold into sacred Lemnos; but the main of the grey
    sea
could not hold him, though it holds back many who are unwilling.
But come now, he must be given a taste of our spearhead
so that I may know inside my heart and make certain
whether he will come back even from there, or the prospering
earth will hold him, she who holds back even the strong man."
    So he pondered, waiting, and the other in terror came near him
in an agony to catch at his knees, and the wish in his heart was
to get away from the evil death and the dark fate. By this
brilliant Achilleus held the long spear uplifted above him
straining to stab, but he under-ran the stroke and caught him
by the knees, bending, and the spear went over his back and stood
    fast
in the ground, for all its desire to tear a man's flesh. Lykaon
with one hand had taken him by the knees in supplication
and with the other held and would not let go of the edged spear
and spoke aloud to him and addressed him in winged words:
    "Achilleus,
I am at your knees. Respect my position, have mercy upon me.
I am in the place, illustrious, of a suppliant who must be honoured,
for you were the first beside whom I tasted the yield of Demeter
on that day you captured me in the strong-laid garden
and took me away from my father and those near me, and sold me
away into sacred Lemnos, and a hundred oxen I fetched you.
My release was ransom three times as great; and this is
the twelfth dawn since I came back to Ilion, after
much suffering. Now again cursed destiny has put me

in your hands; and I think I must be hated by Zeus the father
who has given me once more to you, and my mother bore me
to a short life, Laothoë, daughter of aged Altes,
Altes, lord of the Leleges, whose delight is in battle,
and holds headlong Pedasos on the river Satnioeis.
His daughter was given to Priam, who had many wives beside her.
We are two who were born to her. You will have cut the throats
of both, since one you beat down in the forefront of the
     foot-fighters,
Polydoros the godlike, with a cast of the sharp spear. This time
the evil shall be mine in this place, since I do not think
I shall escape your hands, since divinity drove me against them.
Still, put away in your heart this other thing I say to you.
Do not kill me. I am not from the same womb as Hektor,
he who killed your powerful and kindly companion."
     So the glorious son of Priam addressed him, speaking
in supplication, but heard in turn the voice without pity:
"Poor fool, no longer speak to me of ransom, nor argue it.
In the time before Patroklos came to the day of his destiny
then it was the way of my heart's choice to be sparing
of the Trojans, and many I took alive and disposed of them.
Now there is not one who can escape death, if the gods send
him against my hands in front of Ilion, not one
of all the Trojans and beyond others the children of Priam.
So, friend, you die also. Why all this clamour about it?
Patroklos also is dead, who was better by far than you are.
Do you not see what a man I am, how huge, how splendid
and born of a great father, and the mother who bore me immortal?
Yet even I have also my death and my strong destiny,
and there shall be a dawn or an afternoon or a noontime
when some man in the fighting will take the life from me also
either with a spearcast or an arrow flown from the bowstring."
     So he spoke, and in the other the knees and the inward
heart went slack. He let go of the spear and sat back, spreading
wide both hands; but Achilleus drawing his sharp sword struck him
beside the neck at the collar-bone, and the double-edged sword
plunged full length inside. He dropped to the ground, face
     downward,
and lay at length, and the black blood flowed, and the ground was
     soaked with it.
Achilleus caught him by the foot and slung him into the river
to drift, and spoke winged words of vaunting derision over him:

"Lie there now among the fish, who will lick the blood away
from your wound, and care nothing for you, nor will your mother
lay you on the death-bed and mourn over you, but Skamandros
will carry you spinning down to the wide bend of the salt water.
And a fish will break a ripple shuddering dark on the water
as he rises to feed upon the shining fat of Lykaon.
Die on, all; till we come to the city of sacred Ilion,
you in flight and I killing you from behind; and there will not
be any rescue for you from your silvery-whirled strong-running
river, for all the numbers of bulls you dedicate to it
and drown single-foot horses alive in its eddies. And yet
even so, die all an evil death, till all of you
pay for the death of Patroklos and the slaughter of the Achaians
whom you killed beside the running ships, when I was not with
        them."

                         Translated by Richmond Lattimore

BOOK XXIV

ACHILLES AND PRIAM

Achilles finally meets and kills Hector. He lashes the corpse to his char-
iot and drags it to his tent, intending to throw it to the dogs and birds of
prey. For Patroclus he holds a magnificent funeral, complete with
human sacrifice and athletic and martial contests.

At the beginning of the last book of the Iliad, *Achilles is still locked in*
that rage which has been his dominant passion since the opening line
announced it as the subject of the poem—rage, first against Agamem-
non, and later, more deadly, against Hector. This unrelenting hate,
which drives him to go on maltreating Hector's corpse long after the life
has left it, is something inhuman. It resembles, in fact, the rage of gods
and goddesses—of Hera, Athena ("the girl with the blazing eyes"), and
Poseidon against Troy, for example. "Only if you could breach their
gates and their long walls," says Zeus to Hera in Book IV, "and devour
Priam and Priam's sons and the Trojan armies raw—then you might just
cure your rage at last." In fact, when in Book XXIV the gods debate the
question of bringing Achilles' desecration of the corpse of Hector to
an end, Hera defends Achilles along these lines, protesting that the
two men are not equal: "Hector is mortal . . . Achilles sprang from a god-
dess . . ." To Apollo the defender of Troy, Achilles is more like a wild
animal: ". . . like some lion, going his own barbaric way, giving in to his
power, his brute force and his pride . . ."

*God and animal—these are, in Greek feeling, the two extremes be-
tween which human nature should strike a mean. "The man," Aristotle
was to say much later, in the* Politics, *"who cannot be part of a community, or does not need to do so because he is self-sufficient, is not part of
the city, like a wild animal or a god." In the final book of the poem,
Achilles at last breaks out of the prison of his rage as he comes to feel
sympathy and admiration for another man—old Priam, Hector's father,
who has come alone, by night, to the tent of Troy's mortal enemy, to
ransom the corpse of his son.*

The games were over now. The gathered armies scattered,
each man to his fast ship, and fighters turned their minds
to thoughts of food and the sweet warm grip of sleep.
But Achilles kept on grieving for his friend,
the memory burning on . . .
and all-subduing sleep could not take him,
not now, he turned and twisted, side to side,
he longed for Patroclus' manhood, his gallant heart—
What rough campaigns they'd fought to an end together,
what hardships they had suffered, cleaving their way
through wars of men and pounding waves at sea.
The memories flooded over him, live tears flowing,
and now he'd lie on his side, now flat on his back,
now facedown again. At last he'd leap to his feet,
wander in anguish, aimless along the surf, and dawn on dawn
flaming over the sea and shore would find him pacing.
Then he'd yoke his racing team to the chariot-harness,
lash the corpse of Hector behind the car for dragging
and haul him three times round the dead Patroclus' tomb,
and then he'd rest again in his tents and leave the body
sprawled facedown in the dust. But Apollo pitied Hector—
dead man though he was—and warded all corruption off
from Hector's corpse and round him, head to foot,
the great god wrapped the golden shield of storm
so his skin would never rip as Achilles dragged him on.

And so he kept on raging, shaming noble Hector,
but the gods in bliss looked down and pitied Priam's son.
They kept on urging the sharp-eyed giant-killer Hermes
to go and steal the body, a plan that pleased them all,
but not Hera, Poseidon or the girl with blazing eyes.

They clung to their deathless hate of sacred Troy,
Priam and Priam's people, just as they had at first
when Paris in all his madness launched the war.
He offended Athena and Hera—both goddesses.
When they came to his shepherd's fold he favored Love
who dangled before his eyes the lust that loosed disaster.
But now, at the twelfth dawn since Hector's death,
lord Apollo rose and addressed the immortal powers:
"Hard-hearted you are, you gods, you live for cruelty!
Did Hector never burn in your honor thighs of oxen
and flawless, full-grown goats? Now you cannot
bring yourselves to save him—even his corpse—
so his wife can see him, his mother and his child,
his father Priam and Priam's people: how they'd rush
to burn his body on the pyre and give him royal rites!
But murderous Achilles—you gods, you *choose* to help Achilles.
That man without a shred of decency in his heart . . .
his temper can never bend and change—like some lion
going his own barbaric way, giving in to his power,
his brute force and wild pride, as down he swoops
on the flocks of men to seize his savage feast.
Achilles has lost all pity! No shame in the man,
shame that does great harm or drives men on to good.
No doubt some mortal has suffered a dearer loss than this,
a brother born in the same womb, or even a son . . .
he grieves, he weeps, but then his tears are through.
The Fates have given mortals hearts that can endure.
But this Achilles—first he slaughters Hector,
he rips away the noble prince's life
then lashes him to his chariot, drags him round
his beloved comrade's tomb. But why, I ask you?
What good will it do him? What honor will he gain?
Let that man beware, or great and glorious as he is,
we mighty gods will wheel on him in anger—look,
he outrages the senseless clay in all his fury!"

    But white-armed Hera flared at him in anger:
"Yes, there'd be some merit even in what *you* say,
lord of the silver bow—if all you gods, in fact,
would set Achilles and Hector high in equal honor.
But Hector is mortal. He sucked a woman's breast.
Achilles sprang from a goddess—one I reared myself:

I brought her up and gave her in marriage to a man,
to Peleus, dearest to all your hearts, you gods.
All you gods, you shared in the wedding rites,
and so did you, Apollo—there you sat at the feast
and struck your lyre. What company you keep now,
these wretched Trojans. You—forever faithless!"

   But Zeus who marshals the storm clouds warned his queen,
"Now, Hera, don't fly into such a rage at fellow gods.
These two can never attain the same degree of honor.
Still, the immortals loved Prince Hector dearly,
best of all the mortals born in Troy . . .
so *I* loved him, at least:
he never stinted with gifts to please my heart.
Never once did my altar lack its share of victims,
winecups tipped and the deep smoky savor. These,
these are the gifts we claim—they are our rights.
But as for stealing courageous Hector's body,
we must abandon the idea—not a chance in the world
behind Achilles' back. For Thetis is always there,
his mother always hovering near him night and day.
Now would one of you gods call Thetis to my presence?—
so I can declare to her my solemn, sound decree:
Achilles must receive a ransom from King Priam,
Achilles must give Hector's body back."
                                      So he decreed
and Iris, racing a gale-wind down with Zeus' message,
mid-sea between Samos and Imbros' rugged cliffs
dove in a black swell as groaning breakers roared.
Down she plunged to the bottom fast as a lead weight
sheathed in a glinting lure of wild bull's horn,
bearing hooked death to the ravenous fish.
And deep in a hollow cave she came on Thetis.
Gathered round her sat the other immortal sea-nymphs
while Thetis amidst them mourned her brave son's fate,
doomed to die, she knew, on the fertile soil of Troy,
far from his native land. Quick as the wind now
Iris rushed to the goddess, urging, "Rise, Thetis—
Zeus with his everlasting counsels calls you now!"
Shifting on her glistening feet, the goddess answered,
"Why . . . what does the great god want with me?
I cringe from mingling with the immortals now—

Oh the torment—never-ending heartbreak!
But go I shall. A high decree of the Father
must not come to nothing—whatever he commands."

   The radiant queen of sea-nymphs seized a veil,
blue-black, no robe darker in all the Ocean's depths,
and launched up and away with wind-swift Iris leading—
the ground swell round them cleaved and opened wide.
And striding out on shore they soared to the high sky
and found farseeing Zeus, and around him all the gods
who live in bliss forever sat in a grand assembly.
And Thetis took a seat beside the Father,
a throne Athena yielded. Hera placed in her hand
a burnished golden cup and said some words of comfort,
and taking a few quick sips, Thetis gave it back . . .
The father of men and gods began to address them:
"You have come to Olympus now, immortal Thetis,
for all your grief—what unforgettable sorrow
seizes on your heart. I know it well myself.
Even so, I must tell you why I called you here.
For nine whole days the immortals have been feuding
over Hector's corpse and Achilles scourge of cities.
They keep urging the sharp-eyed giant-killer Hermes
to go and steal the body. But that is not my way.
I will grant Achilles glory and so safeguard
your awe and love of me for all the years to come.
Go at once to the camp, give your son this order:
tell him the gods are angry with him now
and I am rising over them all in deathless wrath
that he in heartsick fury still holds Hector's body,
there by his beaked ships, and will not give him back—
perhaps in fear of me he'll give him back at once.
Then, at the same time, I am winging Iris down
to greathearted Priam, commanding the king
to ransom his dear son, to go to Achaea's ships,
bearing gifts to Achilles, gifts to melt his rage."
                                    So he decreed
and Thetis with her glistening feet did not resist a moment.
Down the goddess flashed from the peaks of Mount Olympus,
made her way to her son's camp, and there he was,
she found him groaning hard, choked with sobs.
Around him trusted comrades swung to the work,

preparing breakfast, steadying in their midst
a large fleecy sheep just slaughtered in the shelter.
But his noble mother, settling down at his side,
stroked Achilles gently, whispering his name: "My child—
how long will you eat your heart out here in tears and torment?
All wiped from your mind, all thought of food and bed?
It's a welcome thing to make love with a woman . . .
You don't have long to live now, well I know:
already I see them looming up beside you—death
and the strong force of fate. Listen to me,
quickly! I bring you a message sent by Zeus:
he says the gods are angry with you now
and he is rising over them all in deathless wrath
that you in heartsick fury still hold Hector's body,
here by your beaked ships, and will not give him back.
O give him back at once—take ransom for the dead!"

     The swift runner replied in haste, "So be it.
The man who brings the ransom can take away the body,
if Olympian Zeus himself insists in all earnest."

     While mother and son agreed among the clustered ships,
trading between each other many winged words,
Father Zeus sped Iris down to sacred Troy:
"Quick on your way now, Iris, shear the wind!
Leave our Olympian stronghold—
take a message to greathearted Priam down in Troy:
he must go to Achaea's ships and ransom his dear son,
bearing gifts to Achilles, gifts to melt his rage.
But let him go alone, no other Trojan attend him,
only a herald with him, a seasoned, older one
who can drive the mules and smooth-running wagon
and bring the hero's body back to sacred Troy,
the man that brilliant Achilles killed in battle.
Let him have no fear of death, no dread in his heart,
such a powerful escort we will send him—the giant-killer
Hermes will guide him all the way to Achilles' presence.
And once the god has led him within the fighter's shelter,
Achilles will not kill him—he'll hold back all the rest:
Achilles is no madman, no reckless fool, not the one
to defy the gods' commands. Whoever begs his mercy

he will spare with all the kindness in his heart."
                              So he decreed
and Iris ran his message, racing with gale force
to Priam's halls where cries and mourning met her.
Sons huddled round their father deep in the courtyard,
robes drenched with tears, and the old man amidst them,
buried, beaten down in the cloak that wrapped his body . . .
Smeared on the old man's head and neck the dung lay thick
that he scraped up in his own hands, groveling in the filth.
Throughout the house his daughters and sons' wives wailed,
remembering all the fine brave men who lay dead now,
their lives destroyed at the fighting Argives' hands.
And Iris, Zeus' crier, standing alongside Priam,
spoke in a soft voice, but his limbs shook at once—
"Courage, Dardan Priam, take heart! Nothing to fear.
No herald of doom, I come on a friendly mission—
I come with all good will.
I bring you a message sent by Zeus, a world away
but he has you in his heart, he pities you now . . .
Olympian Zeus commands you to ransom royal Hector,
to bear gifts to Achilles, gifts to melt his rage.
But you must go alone, no other Trojan attend you,
only a herald with you, a seasoned, older one
who can drive the mules and smooth-running wagon
and bring the hero's body back to sacred Troy,
the man that brilliant Achilles killed in battle.
But have no fear of death, no dread in your heart,
such a powerful escort will conduct you—the giant-killer
Hermes will guide you all the way to Achilles' presence.
And once the god has led you within the fighter's shelter,
Achilles will not kill you—he'll hold back all the rest:
Achilles is no madman, no reckless fool, not the one
to defy the gods' commands. Whoever begs his mercy
he will spare with all the kindness in his heart!"

    And Iris racing the wind went veering off
and Priam ordered his sons to get a wagon ready,
a good smooth-running one, to hitch the mules
and strap a big wicker cradle across its frame.
Then down he went himself to his treasure-chamber,
high-ceilinged, paneled, fragrant with cedarwood

and a wealth of precious objects filled its chests.
He called out to his wife, Hecuba, "Dear woman!
An Olympian messenger came to me from Zeus—
I must go to Achaea's ships and ransom our dear son,
bearing gifts to Achilles, gifts to melt his rage.
Tell me, what should I do? What do *you* think?
Myself—a terrible longing drives me, heart and soul,
down to the ships, into the vast Achaean camp."

But his wife cried out in answer, "No, no—
where have your senses gone?—that made you famous once,
both among outland men and those you rule in Troy!
How can you think of going down to the ships, alone,
and face the glance of the man who killed your sons,
so many fine brave boys? You have a heart of iron!
If he gets you in his clutches, sets his eyes on you—
that savage, treacherous man—he'll show no mercy,
no respect for your rights!
                                    Come, all we can do now
is sit in the halls, far from our son, and wail for Hector . . .
So this, this is the doom that strong Fate spun out,
our son's life line drawn with his first breath—
the moment I gave him birth—
to glut the wild dogs, cut off from his parents,
crushed by the stronger man. Oh would to god
that I could sink my teeth in his liver, eat him raw!
That would avenge what he has done to Hector—
no coward the man Achilles killed—my son stood
and fought for the men of Troy and their deep-breasted wives
with never a thought of flight or run for cover!"

But the old and noble Priam answered firmly,
"I will go. My mind's made up. Don't hold me back.
And don't go flying off on your own across the halls,
a bird of evil omen—you can't dissuade me now.
If someone else had commanded me, some mortal man,
some prophet staring into the smoke, some priest,
I'd call it a lie and turn my back upon it.
Not now. I heard her voice with my own ears,
I looked straight at the goddess, face-to-face.
So I am going—her message must not come to nothing.
And if it is my fate to die by the beaked ships

of Achaeans armed in bronze, then die I shall.
Let Achilles cut me down straightway—
once I've caught my son in my arms and wept my fill!"

He raised back the carved lids of the chests
and lifted out twelve robes, handsome, rich brocades,
twelve cloaks, unlined and light, as many blankets,
as many big white capes and shirts to go with them.
He weighed and carried out ten full bars of gold
and took two burnished tripods, four fine cauldrons
and last a magnificent cup the Thracians gave him once—
he'd gone on an embassy and won that priceless treasure—
but not even *that* did the old man spare in his halls,
not now, consumed with desire to ransom back his son.
Crowds of Trojans were mobbing his colonnades—
he gave them a tongue-lashing, sent them packing:
"Get out—you good-for-nothings, public disgraces!
Haven't you got enough to wail about at home
without coming here to add to all my griefs?
You think it nothing, the pain that Zeus has sent me?—
he's destroyed my best son! You'll learn too, in tears—
easier game you'll be for Argive troops to slaughter,
now my Hector's dead. But before I have to see
my city annihilated, laid waste before my eyes—
oh let me go down to the House of Death!"

He herded them off with his staff—they fled outside
before the old man's fury. So he lashed out at his sons,
cursing the sight of Helenus, Paris, noble Agathon,
Pammon, Antiphonus, Polites loud with the war cry,
Deiphobus and Hippothous, even lordly Dius—
the old man shouted at all nine, rough commands:
"Get to your work! My vicious sons—my humiliations!
If only you'd all been killed at the fast ships
instead of my dear Hector . . .
But I—dear god, my life so cursed by fate!—
I fathered hero sons in the wide realm of Troy
and now, now not a single one is left, I tell you.
Mestor the indestructible, Troilus, passionate horseman
and Hector, a god among men—no son of a mortal man,
he seemed a deathless god's. But Ares killed them all
and all he left me are these, these disgraces—liars,

dancers, heroes only at beating the dancing-rings,
you plunder your own people for lambs and kids!
Why don't you get my wagon ready—now, at once?
Pack all these things aboard! We must be on our way!"

   Terrified by their father's rough commands
the sons trundled a mule-wagon out at once,
a good smooth-running one,
newly finished, balanced and bolted tight,
and strapped a big wicker cradle across its frame.
They lifted off its hook a boxwood yoke for the mules,
its bulging pommel fitted with rings for guide-reins,
brought out with the yoke its yoke-strap nine arms long
and wedged the yoke down firm on the sanded, tapered pole,
on the front peg, and slipped the yoke-ring onto its pin,
strapped the pommel with three good twists, both sides,
then lashed the assembly round and down the shaft
and under the clamp they made the lashing fast.
Then the priceless ransom for Hector's body:
hauling it up from the vaults they piled it high
on the wagon's well-made cradle, then they yoked the mules—
stamping their sharp hoofs, trained for heavy loads—
that the Mysians once gave Priam, princely gifts.
And last they yoked his team to the king's chariot,
stallions he bred himself in his own polished stalls.

   No sooner were both men harnessed up beneath the roofs,
Priam and herald, minds set on the coming journey,
than Hecuba rushed up to them, gaunt with grief,
holding a gold cup of mellow wine in her right hand
so the men might pour libations before they left.
She stood in front of the horses, crying up at Priam,
"Here, quickly—pour a libation out to Father Zeus!
Pray for a safe return from all our mortal enemies,
seeing you're dead set on going down to the ships—
though you go against my will. But if go you must,
pray, at least, to the great god of the dark storm cloud,
up there on Ida, gazing down on the whole expanse of Troy!
Pray for a bird of omen, Zeus's wind-swift messenger,
the dearest bird in the world to his prophetic heart,
the strongest thing on wings—clear on the right
so you can see that sign with your own eyes

and trust your life to *it* as you venture down
to Achaea's ships and the fast chariot-teams.
But if farseeing Zeus does *not* send you that sign—
his own messenger—then I urge you, beg you,
don't go down to the ships—
not for all the passion in your heart!"

    The old majestic Priam gave his answer:
"Dear woman, surely I won't resist your urging now.
It's well to lift our hands and ask great Zeus for mercy."

    And the old king motioned a steward standing by
to pour some clear pure water over his hands,
and she came forward, bearing a jug and basin.
He rinsed his hands, took the cup from his wife
and taking a stand amidst the forecourt, prayed,
pouring the wine to earth and scanning the high skies,
Priam prayed in his rich resounding voice: "Father Zeus!
Ruling over us all from Ida, god of greatness, god of glory!
Grant that Achilles will receive me with kindness, mercy.
Send me a bird of omen, your own wind-swift messenger,
the dearest bird in the world to your prophetic heart,
the strongest thing on wings—clear on the right
so I can see that sign with my own eyes
and trust my life to *it* as I venture down
to Achaea's ships and the fast chariot-teams!"

    And Zeus in all his wisdom heard that prayer
and straightaway the Father launched an eagle—
truest of Zeus's signs that fly the skies—
the dark marauder that mankind calls the Black-wing.
Broad as the door of a rich man's vaulted treasure-chamber,
well-fitted with sturdy bars, so broad each wing of the bird
spread out on either side as it swept in through the city
flashing clear on the right before the king and queen.
All looked up, overjoyed—the people's spirits lifted.

    And the old man, rushing to climb aboard his chariot,
drove out through the gates and echoing colonnades.
The mules in the lead hauled out the four-wheeled wagon,
driven on by seasoned Idaeus. The horses came behind
as the old man cracked the lash and urged them fast

throughout the city with all his kinsmen trailing . . .
weeping their hearts out, as if he went to his death.
But once the two passed down through crowded streets
and out into open country, Priam's kin turned back,
his sons and in-laws straggling home to Troy.
But Zeus who beholds the world could hardly fail
to see the two men striking out across the plain.
As he watched the old man he filled with pity
and quickly summoned Hermes, his own dear son:
"Hermes—escorting men is your greatest joy,
you above all the gods,
and you listen to the wish of those you favor.
So down you go. Down and conduct King Priam there
through Achaea's beaked ships, so none will see him,
none of the Argive fighters recognize him now,
not till he reaches Peleus' royal son."

                        So he decreed
and Hermes the giant-killing guide obeyed at once.
Under his feet he strapped the supple sandals,
never-dying gold, that wing him over the waves
and boundless earth with the speed of gusting winds.
He seized the wand that enchants the eyes of men
whenever Hermes wants, or wakes them up from sleep.
That wand in his grip he flew, the mighty giant-killer
touching down on Troy and the Hellespont in no time
and from there he went on foot, for all the world
like a young prince, sporting his first beard,
just in the prime and fresh warm pride of youth.

                                And now,
as soon as the two drove past the great tomb of Ilus
they drew rein at the ford to water mules and team.
A sudden darkness had swept across the earth
and Hermes was all but on them when the herald
looked up, saw him, shouted at once to Priam,
"Danger, my king—think fast! I see a man—
I'm afraid we'll both be butchered on the spot—
into the chariot, hurry! Run for our lives
or fling ourselves at his knees and beg for mercy!"

    The old man was stunned, in a swirl of terror,
the hairs stood bristling all over his gnarled body—
he stood there, staring dumbly. Not waiting for welcome

the running god of luck went straight up to Priam,
clasped the old king's hands and asked him warmly,
"Father—where do you drive these mules and team
through the godsent night while other mortals sleep?
Have you no fear of the Argives breathing hate and fury?
Here are your deadly enemies, camping close at hand.
Now what if one of them saw you, rolling blithely on
through the rushing night with so much tempting treasure—
how would you feel then? You're not so young yourself,
and the man who attends you here is far too old
to drive off an attacker spoiling for a fight.
But I would never hurt you—and what's more,
I'd beat off any man who'd do you harm:
you remind me of my dear father, to the life."

   And the old and noble Priam said at once,
"Our straits are hard, dear child, as you say.
But a god still holds his hands above me, even me.
Sending such a traveler here to meet me—
what a lucky omen! Look at your build . . .
your handsome face—a wonder. And such good sense—
your parents must be blissful as the gods!"

   The guide and giant-killer answered quickly,
"You're right, old man, all straight to the mark.
But come, tell me the truth now, point by point:
this treasure—a king's ransom—do you send it off
to distant, outland men, to keep it safe for you?
Or now do you all abandon sacred Troy,
all in panic—such was the man who died,
your finest, bravest man . . . your own son
who never failed in a fight against the Argives?"

   But the old majestic Priam countered quickly,
"Who are *you*, my fine friend?—who are your parents?
How can you speak so well of my doomed son's fate?"

   And the guide and giant-killer answered staunchly,
"You're testing me, old man—asking of noble Hector.
Ah, how often I watched him battling on the lines
where men win glory, saw the man with my own eyes!
And saw him drive Achaeans against the ships that day

he kept on killing, cutting them down with slashing bronze
while we stood by and marveled—Achilles reined us in:
no fighting for us while he raged on at Agamemnon.
I am Achilles' aide, you see,
one and the same good warship brought us here.
I am a Myrmidon, and my father is Polyctor,
and a wealthy man he is, about as old as you . . .
He has six sons—I'm the seventh—we all shook lots
and it fell to me to join the armies here at Troy.
I've just come up from the ships to scout the plain—
at dawn the fiery-eyed Achaeans fight around the city.
They chafe, sitting in camp, so bent on battle now
the kings of Achaea cannot hold them back."

   And the old and noble Priam asked at once,
"If you really are the royal Achilles' aide,
please, tell *me* the whole truth, point by point.
My son—does he still lie by the beached ships,
or by now has the great Achilles hacked him
limb from limb and served him to his dogs?"

   The guide and giant-killer reassured him:
"So far, old man, no birds or dogs have eaten him.
No, there he lies—still there at Achilles' ship,
still intact in his shelters.
This is the twelfth day he's lain there, too,
but his body has not decayed, not in the least,
nor have the worms begun to gnaw his corpse,
the swarms that devour men who fall in battle.
True, dawn on fiery dawn he drags him round
his beloved comrade's tomb, drags him ruthlessly
but he cannot mutilate his body. It's marvelous—
go see for yourself how he lies there fresh as dew,
the blood washed away, and no sign of corruption.
All his wounds sealed shut, wherever they struck . . .
and many drove their bronze blades through his body.
Such pains the blissful gods are lavishing on your son,
dead man though he is—the gods love him dearly!"

   And the old man rejoiced at that, bursting out,
"O my child, how good it is to give the immortals
fit and proper gifts! Now take my son—

or was he all a dream? Never once in his halls
did he forget the gods who hold Olympus, never,
so now they remember *him* . . . if only after death.
Come, this handsome cup: accept it from me, I beg you!
Protect me, escort me now—if the gods will it so—
all the way till I reach Achilles' shelter."

      The guide and giant-killer refused him firmly,
"You test me again, old man, since I am young,
but you will not persuade me,
tempting me with a gift behind Achilles' back.
I fear the man, I'd die of shame to rob him—
just think of the trouble I might suffer later.
But I'd escort you with all the kindness in my heart,
all the way till I reached the shining hills of Argos
bound in a scudding ship or pacing you on foot—
and no marauder on earth, scorning your escort,
would dare attack you then."
                              And the god of luck,
leaping onto the chariot right behind the team,
quickly grasped the whip and reins in his hands
and breathed fresh spirit into the mules and horses.
As they reached the trench and rampart round the fleet,
the sentries had just begun to set out supper there
but the giant-killer plunged them all in sleep . . .
he spread the gates at once, slid back the bars
and ushered Priam in with his wagon-load of treasure.
Now, at last, they approached royal Achilles' shelter,
the tall, imposing lodge the Myrmidons built their king,
hewing planks of pine, and roofed it high with thatch,
gathering thick shaggy reeds from the meadow banks,
and round it built their king a spacious courtyard
fenced with close-set stakes. A single pine beam
held the gates, and it took three men to ram it home,
three to shoot the immense bolt back and spread the doors—
three average men. Achilles alone could ram it home himself.
But the god of luck now spread the gates for the old man,
drove in the glinting gifts for Peleus' swift son,
climbed down from behind the team and said to Priam,
"Old man, look, I am a god come down to you,
I am immortal Hermes—
my Father sent me here to be your escort.

But now I will hasten back. I will not venture
into Achilles' presence: it would offend us all
for a mortal man to host an immortal face-to-face.
But you go in yourself and clasp Achilles' knees,
implore him by his father, his mother with lovely hair,
by his own son—so you can stir his heart!"
                                        With that urging
Hermes went his way to the steep heights of Olympus.
But Priam swung down to earth from the battle-car
and leaving Idaeus there to rein in mules and team,
the old king went straight up to the lodge
where Achilles dear to Zeus would always sit.
Priam found the warrior there inside . . .
many captains sitting some way off, but two,
veteran Automedon and the fine fighter Alcimus
were busy serving him. He had just finished dinner,
eating, drinking, and the table still stood near.
The majestic king of Troy slipped past the rest
and kneeling down beside Achilles, clasped his knees
and kissed his hands, those terrible, man-killing hands
that had slaughtered Priam's many sons in battle.
Awesome—as when the grip of madness seizes one
who murders a man in his own fatherland and flees
abroad to foreign shores, to a wealthy, noble host,
and a sense of marvel runs through all who see him—
so Achilles marveled, beholding majestic Priam.
His men marveled too, trading startled glances.
But Priam prayed his heart out to Achilles:
"Remember your own father, great godlike Achilles—
as old as *I* am, past the threshold of deadly old age!
No doubt the countrymen round about him plague him now,
with no one there to defend him, beat away disaster.
No one—but at least he hears you're still alive
and his old heart rejoices, hopes rising, day by day,
to see his beloved son come sailing home from Troy.
But I—dear god, my life so cursed by fate . . .
I fathered hero sons in the wide realm of Troy
and now not a single one is left, I tell you.
Fifty sons I had when the sons of Achaea came,
nineteen born to me from a single mother's womb
and the rest by other women in the palace. Many,
most of them violent Ares cut the knees from under.

But one, one was left me, to guard my walls, my people—
the one you killed the other day, defending his fatherland,
my Hector! It's all for him I've come to the ships now,
to win him back from you—I bring a priceless ransom.
Revere the gods, Achilles! Pity me in my own right,
remember your own father! I deserve more pity . . .
I have endured what no one on earth has ever done before—
I put to my lips the hands of the man who killed my son."

   Those words stirred within Achilles a deep desire
to grieve for his own father. Taking the old man's hand
he gently moved him back. And overpowered by memory
both men gave way to grief. Priam wept freely
for man-killing Hector, throbbing, crouching
before Achilles' feet as Achilles wept himself,
now for his father, now for Patroclus once again,
and their sobbing rose and fell throughout the house.
Then, when brilliant Achilles had had his fill of tears
and the longing for it had left his mind and body,
he rose from his seat, raised the old man by the hand
and filled with pity now for his gray head and gray beard,
he spoke out winging words, flying straight to the heart:
"Poor man, how much you've borne—pain to break the spirit!
What daring brought you down to the ships, all alone,
to face the glance of the man who killed your sons,
so many fine brave boys? You have a heart of iron.
Come, please, sit down on this chair here . . .
Let us put our griefs to rest in our own hearts,
rake them up no more, raw as we are with mourning.
What good's to be won from tears that chill the spirit?
So the immortals spun our lives that we, we wretched men
live on to bear such torments—the gods live free of sorrows.
There are two great jars that stand on the floor of Zeus' halls
and hold his gifts, our miseries one, the other blessings.
When Zeus who loves the lightning mixes gifts for a man,
now he meets with misfortune, now good times in turn.
When Zeus dispenses gifts from the jar of sorrows only,
he makes a man an outcast—brutal, ravenous hunger
drives him down the face of the shining earth,
stalking far and wide, cursed by gods and men.
So with my father, Peleus. What glittering gifts
the gods rained down from the day that he was born!

He excelled all men in wealth and pride of place,
he lorded the Myrmidons, and mortal that he was,
they gave the man an immortal goddess for a wife.
Yes, but even on him the Father piled hardships,
no powerful race of princes born in his royal halls,
only a single son he fathered, doomed at birth,
cut off in the spring of life—
and I, I give the man no care as he grows old
since here I sit in Troy, far from my fatherland,
a grief to you, a grief to all your children . . .
And you too, old man, we hear you prospered once:
as far as Lesbos, Macar's kingdom, bounds to seaward,
Phrygia east and upland, the Hellespont vast and north—
that entire realm, they say, you lorded over once,
you excelled all men, old king, in sons and wealth.
But then the gods of heaven brought this agony on you—
ceaseless battles round your walls, your armies slaughtered.
You must bear up now. Enough of endless tears,
the pain that breaks the spirit.
Grief for your son will do no good at all.
You will never bring him back to life—
sooner you must suffer something worse."

    But the old and noble Priam protested strongly:
"Don't make me sit on a chair, Achilles, Prince,
not while Hector lies uncared-for in your camp!
Give him back to me, now, no more delay—
I must see my son with my own eyes.
Accept the ransom I bring you, a king's ransom!
Enjoy it, all of it—return to your own native land,
safe and sound . . . since now you've spared my life."

    A dark glance—and the headstrong runner answered,
"No more, old man, don't tempt my wrath, not now!
My own mind's made up to give you back your son.
A messenger brought me word from Zeus—my mother,
Thetis who bore me, the Old Man of the Sea's daughter.
And what's more, I can see through you, Priam—
no hiding the fact from me: one of the gods
has led you down to Achaea's fast ships.
No man alive, not even a rugged young fighter,
would dare to venture into our camp. Never—

how could he slip past the sentries unchallenged?
Or shoot back the bolt of my gates with so much ease?
So don't anger me now. Don't stir my raging heart still more.
Or under my own roof I may not spare your life, old man—
suppliant that you are—may break the laws of Zeus!"

The old man was terrified. He obeyed the order.
But Achilles bounded out of doors like a lion—
not alone but flanked by his two aides-in-arms,
veteran Automedon and Alcimus, steady comrades,
Achilles' favorites next to the dead Patroclus.
They loosed from harness the horses and the mules,
they led the herald in, the old king's crier,
and sat him down on a bench. From the polished wagon
they lifted the priceless ransom brought for Hector's corpse
but they left behind two capes and a finely-woven shirt
to shroud the body well when Priam bore him home.
Then Achilles called the serving-women out:
"Bathe and anoint the body—
bear it aside first. Priam must not see his son."
He feared that, overwhelmed by the sight of Hector,
wild with grief, Priam might let his anger flare
and Achilles might fly into fresh rage himself,
cut the old man down and break the laws of Zeus.
So when the maids had bathed and anointed the body
sleek with olive oil and wrapped it round and round
in a braided battle-shirt and handsome battle-cape,
then Achilles lifted Hector up in his own arms
and laid him down on a bier, and comrades helped him
raise the bier and body onto the sturdy wagon . . .
Then with a groan he called his dear friend by name:
"Feel no anger at me, Patroclus, if you learn—
even there in the House of Death—I let his father
have Prince Hector back. He gave me worthy ransom
and you shall have your share from me, as always,
your fitting, lordly share."
                              So he vowed
and brilliant Achilles strode back to his shelter,
sat down on the well-carved chair that he had left,
at the far wall of the room, leaned toward Priam
and firmly spoke the words the king had come to hear:
"Your son is now set free, old man, as you requested.

Hector lies in state. With the first light of day
you will see for yourself as you convey him home.
Now, at last, let us turn our thoughts to supper.
Even Niobe with her lustrous hair remembered food,
though she saw a dozen children killed in her own halls,
six daughters and six sons in the pride and prime of youth.
True, lord Apollo killed the sons with his silver bow
and Artemis showering arrows killed the daughters.
Both gods were enraged at Niobe. Time and again
she placed herself on a par with their own mother,
Leto in her immortal beauty—how she insulted Leto:
'All you have borne is two, but I have borne so many!'
So, two as they were, they slaughtered all her children.
Nine days they lay in their blood, no one to bury them—
Cronus' son had turned the people into stone . . .
then on the tenth the gods of heaven interred them.
And Niobe, gaunt, worn to the bone with weeping,
turned her thoughts to food. And now, somewhere,
lost on the crags, on the lonely mountain slopes,
on Sipylus where, they say, the nymphs who live forever,
dancing along the Achelous River run to beds of rest—
there, struck into stone, Niobe still broods
on the spate of griefs the gods poured out to her.

So come—we too, old king, must think of food.
Later you can mourn your beloved son once more,
when you bear him home to Troy, and you'll weep many tears."

Never pausing, the swift runner sprang to his feet
and slaughtered a white sheep as comrades moved in
to skin the carcass quickly, dress the quarters well.
Expertly they cut the meat in pieces, pierced them with spits,
roasted them to a turn and pulled them off the fire.
Automedon brought the bread, set it out on the board
in ample wicker baskets. Achilles served the meat.
They reached out for the good things that lay at hand
and when they had put aside desire for food and drink,
Priam the son of Dardanus gazed at Achilles, marveling
now at the man's beauty, his magnificent build—
face-to-face he seemed a deathless god . . .
and Achilles gazed and marveled at Dardan Priam,

beholding his noble looks, listening to his words.
But once they'd had their fill of gazing at each other,
the old majestic Priam broke the silence first:
"Put me to bed quickly, Achilles, Prince.
Time to rest, to enjoy the sweet relief of sleep.
Not once have my eyes closed shut beneath my lids
from the day my son went down beneath your hands . . .
day and night I groan, brooding over the countless griefs,
groveling in the dung that fills my walled-in court.
But now, at long last, I have tasted food again
and let some glistening wine go down my throat.
Before this hour I had tasted nothing."
                              He shook his head
as Achilles briskly told his men and serving-women
to make beds in the porch's shelter, to lay down
some heavy purple throws for the beds themselves
and over them spread blankets and thick woolly robes,
a warm covering laid on top. Torches held in hand,
they went from the hall and fell to work at once
and in no time two good beds were spread and made.
Then Achilles nodded to Priam, leading the king on
with brusque advice: "Sleep outside, old friend,
in case some Achaean captain comes to visit.
They keep on coming now, huddling beside me,
making plans for battle—it's their duty.
But if one saw you here in the rushing dark night
he'd tell Agamemnon straightaway, our good commander.
Then you'd have real delay in ransoming the body.
One more point. Tell me, be precise about it—
how many days do you need to bury Prince Hector?
I will hold back myself
and keep the Argive armies back that long."

    And the old and noble Priam answered slowly,
"If you truly want me to give Prince Hector burial,
full, royal honors, you'd show me a great kindness,
Achilles, if you would do exactly as I say.
You know how crammed we are inside our city,
how far it is to the hills to haul in timber,
and our Trojans are afraid to make the journey.
Well, nine days we should mourn him in our halls,

on the tenth we'd bury Hector, hold the public feast,
on the eleventh build the barrow high above his body—
on the twelfth we'd fight again . . . if fight we must."

   The swift runner Achilles reassured him quickly:
"All will be done, old Priam, as you command.
I will hold our attack as long as you require."

   With that he clasped the old king by the wrist,
by the right hand, to free his heart from fear.
Then Priam and herald, minds set on the journey home,
bedded down for the night within the porch's shelter.
And deep in his sturdy well-built lodge Achilles slept
with Briseis in all her beauty sleeping by his side.

   Now the great array of gods and chariot-driving men
slept all night long, overcome by gentle sleep.
But sleep could never hold the running Escort—
Hermes kept on turning it over in his mind . . .
how could he convoy Priam clear of the ships,
unseen by devoted guards who held the gates?
Hovering at his head the Escort rose and spoke:
"Not a care in the world, old man? Look at you,
how you sleep in the midst of men who'd kill you—
and just because Achilles spared your life. Now, yes,
you've ransomed your dear son—for a king's ransom.
But wouldn't the sons you left behind be forced
to pay three times as much for *you* alive?
What if Atrides Agamemnon learns you're here—
what if the whole Achaean army learns you're here?"

   The old king woke in terror, roused the herald.
Hermes harnessed the mules and team for both men,
drove them fast through the camp and no one saw them.

   Once they reached the ford where the river runs clear,
the strong, whirling Xanthus sprung of immortal Zeus,
Hermes went his way to the steep heights of Olympus
as Dawn flung out her golden robe across the earth,
and the two men, weeping, groaning, drove the team
toward Troy and the mules brought on the body.
No one saw them at first, neither man nor woman,

none before Cassandra, golden as goddess Aphrodite.
She had climbed to Pergamus heights and from that point
she saw her beloved father swaying tall in the chariot,
flanked by the herald, whose cry could rouse the city.
And Cassandra saw *him* too . . .
drawn by the mules and stretched out on his bier.
She screamed and her scream rang out through all Troy:
"Come, look down, you men of Troy, you Trojan women!
Behold Hector now—if you ever once rejoiced
to see him striding home, home alive from battle!
He was the greatest joy of Troy and all our people!"

Her cries plunged Troy into uncontrollable grief
and not a man or woman was left inside the walls.
They streamed out at the gates to meet Priam
bringing in the body of the dead. Hector—
his loving wife and noble mother were first
to fling themselves on the wagon rolling on,
the first to tear their hair, embrace his head
and a wailing throng of people milled around them.
And now, all day long till the setting sun went down
they would have wept for Hector there before the gates
if the old man, steering the car, had not commanded,
"Let me through with the mules! Soon, in a moment,
you can have your fill of tears—once I've brought him home."

So he called and the crowds fell back on either side,
making way for the wagon. Once they had borne him
into the famous halls, they laid his body down
on his large carved bed and set beside him singers
to lead off the laments, and their voices rose in grief—
they lifted the dirge high as the women wailed in answer.
And white-armed Andromache led their songs of sorrow,
cradling the head of Hector, man-killing Hector
gently in her arms: "O my husband . . .
cut off from life so young! You leave me a widow,
lost in the royal halls—and the boy only a baby,
the son we bore together, you and I so doomed.
I cannot think he will ever come to manhood.
Long before *that* the city will be sacked,
plundered top to bottom! Because you are dead,
her great guardian, you who always defended Troy,

who kept her loyal wives and helpless children safe,
all who will soon be carried off in the hollow ships
and I with them—
                        And you, my child, will follow me
to labor, somewhere, at harsh, degrading work,
slaving under some heartless master's eye—that,
or some Achaean marauder will seize you by the arm
and hurl you headlong down from the ramparts—horrible death—
enraged at you because Hector once cut down his brother,
his father or his son, yes, hundreds of armed Achaeans
gnawed the dust of the world, crushed by Hector's hands!
Your father, remember, was no man of mercy . . .
not in the horror of battle, and that is why
the whole city of Troy mourns you now, my Hector—
you've brought your parents accursed tears and grief
but to me most of all you've left the horror, the heartbreak!
For you never died in bed and stretched your arms to me
or said some last word from the heart I can remember,
always, weeping for you through all my nights and days!"

    Her voice rang out in tears and the women wailed in answer
and Hecuba led them now in a throbbing chant of sorrow:
"Hector, dearest to me by far of all my sons . . .
and dear to the gods while we still shared this life—
and they cared about you still, I see, even after death.
Many the sons I had whom the swift runner Achilles
caught and shipped on the barren salt sea as slaves
to Samos, to Imbros, to Lemnos shrouded deep in mist!
But you, once he slashed away your life with his brazen spear
he dragged you time and again around his comrade's tomb,
Patroclus whom you killed—not that he brought Patroclus
back to life by that. But I have you with me now . . .
fresh as the morning dew you lie in the royal halls
like one whom Apollo, lord of the silver bow,
has approached and shot to death with gentle shafts."

    Her voice rang out in tears and an endless wail rose up
and Helen, the third in turn, led their songs of sorrow:
"Hector! Dearest to me of all my husband's brothers—
my husband, Paris, magnificent as a god . . .
he was the one who brought me here to Troy—
Oh how I wish I'd died before that day!
But this, now, is the twentieth year for me

since I sailed here and forsook my own native land,
yet never once did I hear from *you* a taunt, an insult.
But if someone else in the royal halls would curse me,
one of your brothers or sisters or brothers' wives
trailing their long robes, even your own mother—
not your father, always kind as my own father—
why, you'd restrain them with words, Hector,
you'd win them to my side . . .
you with your gentle temper, all your gentle words.
And so in the same breath I mourn for you and me,
my doom-struck, harrowed heart! Now there is no one left
in the wide realm of Troy, no friend to treat me kindly—
all the countrymen cringe from me in loathing!"

Her voice rang out in tears and vast throngs wailed
and old King Priam rose and gave his people orders:
"Now, you men of Troy, haul timber into the city!
Have no fear of an Argive ambush packed with danger—
Achilles vowed, when he sent me home from the black ships,
not to do us harm till the twelfth dawn arrives."

At his command they harnessed oxen and mules to wagons,
they assembled before the city walls with all good speed
and for nine days hauled in a boundless store of timber.
But when the tenth Dawn brought light to the mortal world
they carried gallant Hector forth, streaming tears,
and they placed his corpse aloft the pyre's crest,
flung a torch and set it all aflame.
                At last,
when young Dawn with her rose-red fingers shone once more,
the people massed around illustrious Hector's pyre . . .
And once they'd gathered, crowding the meeting grounds,
they first put out the fires with glistening wine,
wherever the flames still burned in all their fury.
Then they collected the white bones of Hector—
all his brothers, his friends-in-arms, mourning,
and warm tears came streaming down their cheeks.
They placed the bones they found in a golden chest,
shrouding them round and round in soft purple cloths.
They quickly lowered the chest in a deep, hollow grave
and over it piled a cope of huge stones closely set,
then hastily heaped a barrow, posted lookouts all around
for fear the Achaean combat troops would launch their attack

before the time agreed. And once they'd heaped the mound
they turned back home to Troy, and gathering once again
they shared a splendid funeral feast in Hector's honor,
held in the house of Priam, king by will of Zeus.

And so the Trojans buried Hector breaker of horses.

Translated by Robert Fagles

THE ODYSSEY

From BOOK I

PROEM

Sing in me, Muse, and through me tell the story
of that man skilled in all ways of contending,
the wanderer, harried for years on end,
after he plundered the stronghold
on the proud height of Troy.
                              He saw the townlands
and learned the minds of many distant men,
and weathered many bitter nights and days
in his deep heart at sea, while he fought only
to save his life, to bring his shipmates home.
But not by will nor valor could he save them,
for their own recklessness destroyed them all—
children and fools, they killed and feasted on
the cattle of Lord Hêlios, the Sun,
and he who moves all day through heaven
took from their eyes the dawn of their return.

Of these adventures, Muse, daughter of Zeus,
tell us in our time, lift the great song again.
Begin when all the rest who left behind them
headlong death in battle or at sea
had long ago returned, while he alone still hungered
for home and wife. Her ladyship Kalypso
clung to him in her sea-hollowed caves—
a nymph, immortal and most beautiful,
who craved him for her own.

Translated by Robert Fitzgerald

From BOOK V

ODYSSEUS AND CALYPSO

The opening of the Odyssey *locates its hero on Calypso's island; the time is ten years after the fall of Troy. Before Homer tells us about Odysseus and Calypso, however, he devotes four whole books, one sixth of the poem, to the situation on the island of Ithaca, Odysseus' home. The hero's son Telemachus has come of age to face a difficult situation. A huge crowd of suitors for the hand of his mother Penelope, certain after twenty years of absence that Odysseus must be dead, have occupied the house, refusing to leave until she chooses one of them as her new husband. Meanwhile they feast and carouse, at her, and Telemachus', expense.*

The goddess Athena, who has persuaded the Olympian gods to allow Odysseus to return home at last, goes to Ithaca, and, assuming the identity of Mentes, an overseas friend of Odysseus, encourages Telemachus to start on a voyage to Pylos and Sparta, where he asks first Nestor, then Menelaus, for news of his father. Meanwhile Hermes, the herald and messenger of the Olympian gods, arrives at Calypso's island with a message from Zeus: "Send him back in haste."

Especially remarkable in the following excerpt is the fact (twice mentioned) that Calypso is so passionately intent on keeping Odysseus as her consort that she has offered him the exclusive prerogative of the gods: immortality. Of course this was not a gift to be accepted lightly. The dawn goddess, Eos, fell in love with a Trojan prince called Tithonus, and asked Zeus to make him immortal. Her wish was granted, but she had forgotten to ask also for the gift of eternal youth. Tithonus lived for ever but grew immensely old; when the goddess arose to light up the morning sky, he remained in bed. He grew feeble, and so small that he was kept in a basket; eventually he changed into a cicada. But Calypso offers to make Odysseus ageless as well as immortal. "I . . . sang that he should not die / nor grow old, ever . . ." (Robert Fitzgerald's translation here weakens the force of the original, for the word he renders "sang" is much more emphatic—"I promised, I undertook that . . .")

Calypso offers this gift again in their final interview, as she points out that the alternative is for Odysseus to set out once again on the sea where he has already suffered so much. "If you could see it all . . . all the adversity you face at sea— you would stay here." But he refuses. He refuses an everlasting life of youth and tranquility, with a goddess as his bride, choosing instead whatever the sea still holds in store for him after

the loss of all his ships and all his men, whatever waits for him at home,
and, finally, his death.

Calypso's name is a Greek word that means "I shall conceal." But
Odysseus, like Achilles, lives for fame; his fame, he says later, when he
reveals his identity to the Phaeacians, "has gone abroad to the sky's rim."
His refusal is one of many gestures on the part of the Homeric heroes
that emphasize the one great difference between immortal gods and
mortal men: heroism is something to which the gods can never aspire,
for in its defiance and acceptance of death, it is exclusively human.

Once again we rely on two translators. Lattimore uses the same long
line as in his Iliad, *a line that enables him to organize the words in*
approximately the same space as in the original, thus preserving some
significant enjambments; he also retains much of the formularity of the
epic language. Robert Fitzgerald chooses a shorter, flexible line, one
closer to the norm of English narrative verse, and in general avoids
Homeric formulas, though he sometimes retains formulaic epithets.

That goddess most divinely made
shuddered before him, and her warm voice rose:
"Oh you vile gods, in jealousy supernal!
You hate it when we choose to lie with men—
immortal flesh by some dear mortal side.
So radiant Dawn once took to bed Orion
until you easeful gods grew peevish at it,
and holy Artemis, Artemis throned in gold,
hunted him down in Delos with her arrows.
Then Dêmêtêr of the tasseled tresses yielded
to Iasion, mingling and making love
in a furrow three times plowed; but Zeus found out
and killed him with a white-hot thunderbolt.
So now you grudge me, too, my mortal friend.
But it was I who saved him—saw him straddle
his own keel board, the one man left afloat
when Zeus rent wide his ship with chain lightning
and overturned him in the winedark sea.
Then all his troops were lost, his good companions,
but wind and current washed him here to me.
I fed him, loved him, sang that he should not die
nor grow old, ever, in all the days to come.
But now there's no eluding Zeus' will.
If this thing be ordained by him, I say

so be it, let the man strike out alone
on the vast water. Surely I cannot 'send' him.
I have no long-oared ships, no company
to pull him on the broad back of the sea.
My counsel he shall have, and nothing hidden,
to help him homeward without harm."

To this the Wayfinder made answer briefly:

"Thus you shall send him, then. And show more grace
in your obedience, or be chastised by Zeus."

The strong god glittering left her as he spoke,
and now her ladyship, having given heed
to Zeus' mandate, went to find Odysseus
in his stone seat to seaward—tear on tear
brimming his eyes. The sweet days of his life time
were running out in anguish over his exile,
for long ago the nymph had ceased to please.
Though he fought shy of her and her desire,
he lay with her each night, for she compelled him.
But when day came he sat on the rocky shore
and broke his own heart groaning, with eyes wet
scanning the bare horizon of the sea.
Now she stood near him in her beauty, saying:

"O forlorn man, be still.
Here you need grieve no more; you need not feel
your life consumed here; I have pondered it,
and I shall help you go.
Come and cut down high timber for a raft
or flatboat; make her broad-beamed, and decked over,
so you can ride her on the misty sea.
Stores I shall put aboard for you—bread, water,
and ruby-colored wine, to stay your hunger—
give you a seacloak and a following wind
to help you homeward without harm—provided
the gods who rule wide heaven wish it so.
Stronger than I they are, in mind and power."

For all he had endured, Odysseus shuddered.
But when he spoke, his words went to the mark:

"After these years, a helping hand? O goddess,
what guile is hidden here?
A raft, you say, to cross the Western Ocean,
rough water, and unknown? Seaworthy ships
that glory in god's wind will never cross it.
I take no raft you grudge me out to sea.
Or yield me first a great oath, if I do,
to work no more enchantment to my harm."

At this the beautiful nymph Kalypso smiled
and answered sweetly, laying her hand upon him:

"What a dog you are! And not for nothing learned,
having the wit to ask this thing of me!
My witness then be earth and sky
and dripping Styx that I swear by—
the gay gods cannot swear more seriously—
I have no further spells to work against you.
But what I shall devise, and what I tell you,
will be the same as if your need were mine.
Fairness is all I think of. There are hearts
made of cold iron—but my heart is kind."

Swiftly she turned and led him to her cave,
and they went in, the mortal and immortal.
He took the chair left empty now by Hermês,
where the divine Kalypso placed before him
victuals and drink of men; then she sat down
facing Odysseus, while her serving maids
brought nectar and ambrosia to her side.
Then each one's hands went out on each one's feast
until they had had their pleasure; and she said:

"Son of Laërtês, versatile Odysseus,
after these years with me, you still desire
your old home? Even so, I wish you well.
If you could see it all, before you go—
all the adversity you face at sea—
you would stay here, and guard this house, and be
immortal—though you wanted her forever,
that bride for whom you pine each day.
Can I be less desirable than she is?

Less interesting? Less beautiful? Can mortals
compare with goddesses in grace and form?"

To this the strategist Odysseus answered:

"My lady goddess, here is no cause for anger.
My quiet Penélopê—how well I know—
would seem a shade before your majesty,
death and old age being unknown to you,
while she must die. Yet, it is true, each day
I long for home, long for the sight of home.
If any god has marked me out again
for shipwreck, my tough heart can undergo it.
What hardship have I not long since endured
at sea, in battle! Let the trial come."

Now as he spoke the sun set, dusk drew on,
and they retired, this pair, to the inner cave
to revel and rest softly, side by side.

Translated by Robert Fitzgerald

BOOK VI

ODYSSEUS AND NAUSICAA

It was only because Poseidon, Zeus' brother, was absent from the Olym-
pian council that the decision to set Odysseus free was unanimous.
Poseidon, whose son Polyphemus the Cyclops had been blinded by
Odysseus, was determined to delay the hero's return home as long as
possible. He returns from his visit to the far-off Ethiopians just in time to
catch Odysseus at sea on the raft he has built on Calypso's island. His
domain is the sea; he sends down a storm that shatters the raft and leaves
Odysseus in rough waves off a rocky coast. Finally, battered and ex-
hausted, Odysseus struggles ashore at a rivermouth; he has landed on
Scheria, the home of the Phaeacians, a people famous for their magically
swift ships. He goes to sleep on a bed of leaves in a thicket near the shore.
The figure of the young princess Nausicaa is one of Greek literature's
most charming creations. She is a young girl, but very much a princess.
She is able to deal with an unusual social situation—an almost naked
strange man emerging suddenly from a bush—in royal style, and she has
no trouble making her deepest wishes clear in ways that do not commit

*her fully and openly. In the speech in which she instructs Odysseus to
fall behind when they reach the town, for example, her description of
the kind of talk she is anxious to avoid giving rise to is a discreet suggestion that she would be prepared to consider favorably a proposal of
marriage.*

Far gone in weariness, in oblivion,
the noble and enduring man slept on;
but Athena in the night went down the land
of the Phaiákians, entering their city.
In days gone by, these men held Hypereia,
a country of wide dancing grounds, but near them
were overbearing Kyklopês, whose power
could not be turned from pillage. So the Phaiákians
migrated thence under Nausíthoös
to settle a New World across the sea,
Skhería Island. That first captain walled
their promontory, built their homes and shrines,
and parcelled out the black land for the plow.
But he had gone down long ago to Death.
Alkínoös ruled, and Heaven gave him wisdom,
so on this night the goddess, grey-eyed Athena,
entered the palace of Alkínoös
to make sure of Odysseus' voyage home.
She took her way to a painted bedchamber
where a young girl lay fast asleep—so fine
in mould and feature that she seemed a goddess—
the daughter of Alkínoös, Nausikaa.
On either side, as Graces might have slept,
her maids were sleeping. The bright doors were shut,
but like a sudden stir of wind, Athena
moved to the bedside of the girl, and grew
visible as the shipman Dymas' daughter,
a girl the princess' age, and her dear friend.
In this form grey-eyed Athena said to her:

"How so remiss, and yet thy mother's daughter?
leaving thy clothes uncared for, Nausikaa,
when soon thou must have store of marriage linen,
and put they minstrelsy in wedding dress!

Beauty, in these, will make the folk admire,
and bring thy father and gentle mother joy.
Let us go washing in the shine of morning!
Beside thee will I drub, so wedding chests
will brim by evening. Maidenhood must end!
Have not the noblest born Phaiákians
paid court to thee, whose birth none can excel?
Go beg thy sovereign father, even at dawn,
to have the mule cart and the mules brought round
to take thy body-linen, gowns and mantles.
Thou shouldst ride, for it becomes thee more,
the washing pools are found so far from home."

On this word she departed, grey-eyed Athena,
to where the gods have their eternal dwelling—
as men say—in the fastness of Olympos.
Never a tremor of wind, or a splash of rain,
no errant snowflake comes to stain that heaven,
so calm, so vaporless, the world of light.
Here, where the gay gods live their days of pleasure,
the grey-eyed one withdrew, leaving the princess.

And now Dawn took her own fair throne, awaking
the girl in the sweet gown, still charmed by dream.
Down through the rooms she went to tell her parents,
whom she found still at home: her mother seated
near the great hearth among her maids—and twirling
out of her distaff yarn dyed like the sea—;
her father at the door, bound for a council
of princes on petition of the gentry.
She went up close to him and softly said:
"My dear Papà, could you not send the mule cart
around for me—the gig with pretty wheels?
I must take all our things and get them washed
at the river pools; our linen is all soiled.
And you should wear fresh clothing, going to council
with counselors and first men of the realm.
Remember your five sons at home: though two
are married, we have still three bachelor sprigs;
they will have none but laundered clothes each time
they go to the dancing. See what I must think of!"

She had no word to say of her own wedding,
though her keen father saw her blush. Said he:

"No mules would I deny you, child, nor anything.
Go along, now; the grooms will bring your gig
with pretty wheels and the cargo box upon it."

He spoke to the stableman, who soon brought round
the cart, low-wheeled and nimble;
harnessed the mules, and backed them in the traces.
Meanwhile the girl fetched all her soiled apparel
to bundle in the polished wagon box.
Her mother, for their luncheon, packed a hamper
with picnic fare, and filled a skin of wine,
and, when the princess had been handed up,
gave her a golden bottle of olive oil
for softening girls' bodies, after bathing.
Nausikaa took the reins and raised her whip,
lashing the mules. What jingling! What a clatter!
But off they went in a ground-covering trot,
with princess, maids, and laundry drawn behind.
By the lower river where the wagon came
were washing pools, with water all year flowing
in limpid spillways that no grime withstood.
The girls unhitched the mules, and sent them down
along the eddying stream to crop sweet grass.
Then sliding out the cart's tail board, they took
armloads of clothing to the dusky water,
and trod them in the pits, making a race of it.
All being drubbed, all blemish rinsed away,
they spread them, piece by piece, along the beach
whose pebbles had been laundered by the sea;
then took a dip themselves, and, all anointed
with golden oil, ate lunch beside the river
while the bright burning sun dried out their linen.
Princess and maids delighted in that feast;
then, putting off their veils,
they ran and passed a ball to a rhythmic beat,
Nausikaa flashing first with her white arms.

So Artemis goes flying after her arrows flown
down some tremendous valley-side—

                       Taÿgetos, Erymanthos—
chasing the mountain goats or ghosting deer,
with nymphs of the wild places flanking her;
and Lêto's heart delights to see them running,
for, taller by a head than nymphs can be,
the goddess shows more stately, all being beautiful.
So one could tell the princess from the maids.

Soon it was time, she knew, for riding homeward—
mules to be harnessed, linen folded smooth—
but the grey-eyed goddess Athena made her tarry,
so that Odysseus might behold her beauty
and win her guidance to the town.

                       It happened
when the king's daughter threw her ball off line
and missed, and put it in the whirling stream,—
at which they all gave such a shout, Odysseus
awoke and sat up, saying to himself:

"Now, by my life, mankind again! But who?
Savages, are they, strangers to courtesy?
Or gentle folk, who know and fear the gods?
That was a lusty cry of tall young girls—
most like the cry of nymphs, who haunt the peaks,
and springs of brooks, and inland grassy places.
Or am I amid people of human speech?
Up again, man; and let me see for myself."
He pushed aside the bushes, breaking off
with his great hand a single branch of olive,
whose leaves might shield him in his nakedness;
so came out rustling, like a mountain lion,
rain-drenched, wind-buffeted, but in his might at ease,
with burning eyes—who prowls among the herds
or flocks, or after game, his hungry belly
taking him near stout homesteads for his prey.
Odysseus had this look, in his rough skin
advancing on the girls with pretty braids;
and he was driven on by hunger, too.
Streaked with brine, and swollen, he terrified them,
so that they fled, this way and that. Only

Alkínoös' daughter stood her ground, being given
a bold heart by Athena, and steady knees.

She faced him, waiting. And Odysseus came,
debating inwardly what he should do:
embrace this beauty's knees in supplication?
or stand apart, and, using honeyed speech,
inquire the way to town, and beg some clothing?
In his swift reckoning, he thought it best
to trust in words to please her—and keep away;
he might anger the girl, touching her knees.
So he began, and let the soft words fall:

"Mistress: please: are you divine, or mortal?
If one of those who dwell in the wide heaven,
you are most near to Artemis, I should say—
great Zeus' daughter—in your grace and presence.
If you are one of earth's inhabitants,
how blest your father, and your gentle mother,
blest all your kin. I know what happiness
must send the warm tears to their eyes, each time
they see their wondrous child go to the dancing!
But one man's destiny is more than blest—
he who prevails, and takes you as his bride.
Never have I laid eyes on equal beauty
in man or woman. I am hushed indeed.
So fair, one time, I thought a young palm tree
at Delos near the altar of Apollo—
I had troops under me when I was there
on the sea route that later brought me grief—
but that slim palm tree filled my heart with wonder:
never came shoot from earth so beautiful.
So now, my lady, I stand in awe so great
I cannot take your knees. And yet my case is desperate:
twenty days, yesterday, in the winedark sea,
on the ever-lunging swell, under gale winds,
getting away from the Island of Ogýgia.
And now the terror of Storm has left me stranded
upon this shore—with more blows yet to suffer,
I must believe, before the gods relent.
Mistress, do me a kindness!
After much weary toil, I come to you,

and you are the first soul I have seen—I know
no others here. Direct me to the town,
give me a rag that I can throw around me,
some cloth or wrapping that you brought along.
And may the gods accomplish your desire:
a home, a husband, and harmonious
converse with him—the best thing in the world
being a strong house held in serenity
where man and wife agree. Woe to their enemies,
joy to their friends! But all this they know best."

Then she of the white arms, Nausikaa, replied:

"Stranger, there is no quirk or evil in you
that I can see. You know Zeus metes out fortune
to good and bad men as it pleases him.
Hardship he sent to you, and you must bear it.
But now that you have taken refuge here
you shall not lack for clothing, or any other
comfort due to a poor man in distress.
The town lies this way, and the men are called
Phaiákians, who own the land and city.
I am daughter to the Prince Alkínoös,
by whom the power of our people stands."

Turning, she called out to her maids-in-waiting:

"Stay with me! Does the sight of a man scare you?
Or do you take this one for an enemy?
Why, there's no fool so brash, and never will be,
as to bring war or pillage to this coast,
for we are dear to the immortal gods,
living here, in the sea that rolls forever,
distant from other lands and other men.
No: this man is a castaway, poor fellow;
we must take care of him. Strangers and beggars
come from Zeus: a small gift, then, is friendly.
Give our new guest some food and drink, and take him
into the river, out of the wind, to bathe."

They stood up now, and called to one another
to go on back. Quite soon they led Odysseus

under the river bank, as they were bidden;
and there laid out a tunic, and a cloak,
and gave him olive oil in the golden flask.
"Here," they said, "go bathe in the flowing water."
But heard now from that kingly man, Odysseus:

"Maids," he said, "keep away a little; let me
wash the brine from my own back, and rub on
plenty of oil. It is long since my anointing.
I take no bath, however, where you can see me—
naked before young girls with pretty braids."

They left him, then, and went to tell the princess.
And now Odysseus, dousing in the river,
scrubbed the coat of brine from back and shoulders
and rinsed the clot of sea-spume from his hair;
got himself all rubbed down, from head to foot,
then he put on the clothes the princess gave him.
Athena lent a hand, making him seem
taller, and massive too, with crisping hair
in curls like petals of wild hyacinth,
but all red-golden. Think of gold infused
on silver by a craftsman, whose fine art
Hephaistos taught him, or Athena: one
whose work moves to delight: just so she lavished
beauty over Odysseus' head and shoulders.
Then he went down to sit on the sea beach
in his new splendor. There the girl regarded him,
and after a time she said to the maids beside her:

"My gentlewomen, I have a thing to tell you.
The Olympian gods cannot be all averse
to this man's coming here among our islanders.
Uncouth he seemed, I thought so, too, before;
but now he looks like one of heaven's people.
I wish my husband could be fine as he
and glad to stay forever on Skhería!

But have you given refreshment to our guest?"

At this the maids, all gravely listening, hastened
to set out bread and wine before Odysseus,

and ah! how ravenously that patient man
took food and drink, his long fast at an end.

The princess Nausikaa now turned aside
to fold her linens; in the pretty cart
she stowed them, put the mule team under harness,
mounted the driver's seat, and then looked down
to say with cheerful prompting to Odysseus:

"Up with you now, friend; back to town we go;
and I shall send you in before my father
who is wondrous wise; there in our house with him
you'll meet the noblest of the Phaiákians.
You have good sense, I think; here's how to do it:
while we go through the countryside and farmland
stay with my maids, behind the wagon, walking
briskly enough to follow where I lead.
But near the town—well, there's a wall with towers
around the Isle, and beautiful ship basins
right and left of the causeway of approach;
seagoing craft are beached beside the road
each on its launching ways. The agora,
with fieldstone benches bedded in the earth,
lies either side Poseidon's shrine—for there
men are at work on pitch-black hulls and rigging,
cables and sails, and tapering of oars.
The archer's craft is not for the Phaiákians,
but ship designing, modes of oaring cutters
in which they love to cross the foaming sea.
From these fellows I will have no salty talk,
no gossip later. Plenty are insolent.
And some seadog might say, after we passed:
'Who is this handsome stranger trailing Nausikaa?
Where did she find him? Will he be her husband?
Or is she being hospitable to some rover
come off his ship from lands across the sea—
there being no lands nearer. A god, maybe?
a god from heaven, the answer to her prayer,
descending now—to make her his forever?
Better, if she's roamed and found a husband
somewhere else: none of our own will suit her,
though many come to court her, and those the best.'

This is the way they might make light of me.
And I myself should hold it shame
for any girl to flout her own dear parents,
taking up with a man, before her marriage.

Note well, now, what I say, friend, and your chances
are excellent for safe conduct from my father.
You'll find black poplars in a roadside park
around a meadow and fountain—all Athena's—
but Father has a garden in the place—
this within earshot of the city wall.
Go in there and sit down, giving us time
to pass through town and reach my father's house.
And when you can imagine we're at home,
then take the road into the city, asking
directions to the palace of Alkínoös.
You'll find it easily: any small boy
can take you there; no family has a mansion
half so grand as he does, being king.
As soon as you are safe inside, cross over
and go straight through into the mégaron
to find my mother. She'll be there in firelight
before a column, with her maids in shadow,
spinning a wool dyed richly as the sea.
My father's great chair faces the fire, too;
there like a god he sits and takes his wine.
Go past him; cast yourself before my mother,
embrace her knees—and you may wake up soon
at home rejoicing, though your home be far.
On Mother's feeling much depends; if she
looks on you kindly, you shall see your friends
under your own roof in your father's country."

At this she raised her glistening whip, lashing
the team into a run; they left the river
cantering beautifully, then trotted smartly.
But then she reined them in, and spared the whip,
so that her maids could follow with Odysseus.
The sun was going down when they went by
Athena's grove. Here, then, Odysseus rested,
and lifted up his prayer to Zeus's daughter:

"Hear me, unwearied child of royal Zeus!
O listen to me now—thou so aloof
while the Earthshaker wrecked and battered me.
May I find love and mercy among these people."

He prayed for that, and Pallas Athena heard him—
although in deference to her father's brother
she would not show her true form to Odysseus,
at whom Poseidon smoldered on
until the kingly man came home to his own shore.

Translated by Robert Fitzgerald

BOOK IX

ODYSSEUS AND THE CYCLOPS

*Odysseus takes Nausicaa's advice, and once in the palace, throws himself
at the feet of her mother, Queen Arete—"On mother's feeling much
depends," she had told him. He is accepted as a guest and promised a
passage home in one of the Phaeacian swift ships. His identity is still a
mystery, but when the court bard Demodocus sings the song of the
Wooden Horse, the capture of Troy, and the role Odysseus played in all
these events, the hero cannot conceal his emotions and the Phaeacian
king, Alcinous, courteously asks him to reveal his name and country.
Odysseus in reply rells the long tale of his wanderings, all the way from
Troy to the island of the Phaeacians.*

Now this was the reply Odysseus made:

"Alkínoös, king and admiration of men,
how beautiful this is, to hear a minstrel
gifted as yours: a god he might be, singing!
There is no boon in life more sweet, I say,
than when a summer joy holds all the realm,
and banqueters sit listening to a harper
in a great hall, by rows of tables heaped
with bread and roast meat, while a steward goes
to dip up wine and brim your cups again.
Here is the flower of life, it seems to me!
But now you wish to know my cause for sorrow—

and thereby give me cause for more.
                                    What shall I
say first? What shall I keep until the end?
The gods have tried me in a thousand ways.
But first my name: let that be known to you,
and if I pull away from pitiless death,
friendship will bind us, though my land lies far.

I am Laërtês' son, Odysseus.
                              Men hold me
formidable for guile in peace and war:
this fame has gone abroad to the sky's rim.
My home is on the peaked sea-mark of Ithaka
under Mount Neion's wind-blown robe of leaves,
in sight of other islands—Doulíkhion,
Samê, wooded Zakynthos—Ithaka
being most lofty in that coastal sea,
and northwest, while the rest lie east and south.
A rocky isle, but good for a boy's training;
I shall not see on earth a place more dear,
though I have been detained long by Kalypso,
loveliest among goddesses, who held me
in her smooth caves, to be her heart's delight,
as Kirkê of Aiaia, the enchantress,
desired me, and detained me in her hall.
But in my heart I never gave consent.
Where shall a man find sweetness to surpass
his own home and his parents? In far lands
he shall not, though he find a house of gold.

What of my sailing, then, from Troy?
                                       What of those years
of rough adventure, weathered under Zeus?
The wind that carried west from Ilion
brought me to Ismaros; on the far shore,
a strongpoint on the coast of the Kikonês.
I stormed that place and killed the men who fought.
Plunder we took, and we enslaved the women,
to make division, equal shares to all—
but on the spot I told them: 'Back, and quickly!
Out to sea again!' My men were mutinous,
fools, on stores of wine. Sheep after sheep

they butchered by the surf, and shambling cattle,
feasting,—while fugitives went inland, running
to call to arms the main force of Kikonês.
This was an army, trained to fight on horseback
or, where the ground required, on foot. They came
with dawn over that terrain like the leaves
and blades of spring. So doom appeared to us,
dark word of Zeus for us, our evil days.
My men stood up and made a fight of it—
backed on the ships, with lances kept in play,
from bright morning through the blaze of noon
holding our beach, although so far outnumbered;
but when the sun passed toward unyoking time,
then the Akhaians, one by one, gave way.
Six benches were left empty in every ship
that evening when we pulled away from death.
And this new grief we bore with us to sea:
our precious lives we had, but not our friends.
No ship made sail next day until some shipmate
had raised a cry, three times, for each poor ghost
unfleshed by the Kikonês on that field.

Now Zeus the lord of cloud roused in the north
a storm against the ships, and driving veils
of squall moved down like night on land and sea.
The bows went plunging at the gust; sails
cracked and lashed out strips in the big wind.
We saw death in that fury, dropped the yards,
unshipped the oars, and pulled for the nearest lee:
then two long days and nights we lay offshore
worn out and sick at heart, tasting our grief,
until a third Dawn came with ringlets shining.
Then we put up our masts, hauled sail, and rested,
letting the steersmen and the breeze take over.

I might have made it safely home, that time,
but as I came round Malea the current
took me out to sea, and from the north
a fresh gale drove me on, past Kythera.
Nine days I drifted on the teeming sea
before dangerous high winds. Upon the tenth
we came to the coastline of the Lotos Eaters,

who live upon that flower. We landed there
to take on water. All ships' companies
mustered alongside for the mid-day meal.
Then I sent out two picked men and a runner
to learn what race of men that land sustained.
They fell in, soon enough, with Lotos Eaters,
who showed no will to do us harm, only
offering the sweet Lotos to our friends—
but those who ate this honeyed plant, the Lotos,
never cared to report, nor to return:
they longed to stay forever, browsing on
that native bloom, forgetful of their homeland.
I drove them, all three wailing, to the ships,
tied them down under their rowing benches,
and called the rest: 'All hands aboard;
come, clear the beach and no one taste
the Lotos, or you lose your hope of home.'
Filing in to their places by the rowlocks
my oarsmen dipped their long oars in the surf,
and we moved out again on our sea faring.

In the next land we found were Kyklopês,
giants, louts, without a law to bless them.
In ignorance leaving the fruitage of the earth in mystery
to the immortal gods, they neither plow
nor sow by hand, nor till the ground, though grain—
wild wheat and barley—grows untended, and
wine-grapes, in clusters, ripen in heaven's rain.
Kyklopês have no muster and no meeting,
no consultation or old tribal ways,
but each one dwells in his own mountain cave
dealing out rough justice to wife and child,
indifferent to what the others do.
                                    Well, then:
across the wide bay from the mainland
there lies a desert island, not far out,
but still not close inshore. Wild goats in hundreds
breed there; and no human being comes
upon the isle to startle them—no hunter
of all who ever tracked with hounds through forests
or had rough going over mountain trails.
The isle, unplanted and untilled, a wilderness,

pastures goats alone. And this is why:
good ships like ours with cheekpaint at the bows
are far beyond the Kyklopês. No shipwright
toils among them, shaping and building up
symmetrical trim hulls to cross the sea
and visit all the seaboard towns, as men do
who go and come in commerce over water.
This isle—seagoing folk would have annexed it
and built their homesteads on it: all good land,
fertile for every crop in season: lush
well-watered meads along the shore, vines in profusion,
prairie, clear for the plow, where grain would grow
chin high by harvest time, and rich sub-soil.
The island cove is landlocked, so you need
no hawsers out astern, bow-stones or mooring:
run in and ride there till the day your crews
chafe to be under sail, and a fair wind blows.
You'll find good water flowing from a cavern
through dusky poplars into the upper bay.
Here we made harbor. Some god guided us
that night, for we could barely see our bows
in the dense fog around us, and no moonlight
filtered through the overcast. No look-out,
nobody saw the island dead ahead,
nor even the great landward rolling billow
that took us in: we found ourselves in shallows,
keels grazing shore: so furled our sails
and disembarked where the low ripples broke.
There on the beach we lay, and slept till morning.

When Dawn spread out her finger tips of rose
we turned out marvelling, to tour the isle,
while Zeus' shy nymph daughters flushed wild goats
down from the heights—a breakfast for my men.
We ran to fetch our hunting bows and long-shanked
lances from the ships, and in three companies
we took our shots. Heaven gave us game a-plenty:
for every one of twelve ships in my squadron
nine goats fell to be shared; my lot was ten.
So there all day, until the sun went down,
we made our feast on meat galore, and wine—
wine from the ship, for our supply held out,

so many jars were filled at Ismaros
from stores of the Kikonês that we plundered.
We gazed, too, at Kyklopês Land, so near,
we saw their smoke, heard bleating from their flocks.
But after sundown, in the gathering dusk,
we slept again above the wash of ripples.

When the young Dawn with finger tips of rose
came in the east, I called my men together
and made a speech to them:

                              'Old shipmates, friends,
the rest of you stand by; I'll make the crossing
in my own ship, with my own company,
and find out what the mainland natives are—
for they may be wild savages, and lawless,
or hospitable and god fearing men.'

At this I went aboard, and gave the word
to cast off by the stern. My oarsmen followed,
filing in to their benches by the rowlocks,
and all in line dipped oars in the grey sea.

As we rowed on, and nearer to the mainland,
at one end of the bay, we saw a cavern
yawning above the water, screened with laurel,
and many rams and goats about the place
inside a sheepfold—made from slabs of stone
earthfast between tall trunks of pine and rugged
towering oak trees.
                         A prodigious man
slept in this cave alone, and took his flocks
to graze afield—remote from all companions,
knowing none but savage ways, a brute
so huge, he seemed no man at all of those
who eat good wheaten bread; but he seemed rather
a shaggy mountain reared in solitude.
We beached there, and I told the crew
to stand by and keep watch over the ship;
as for myself I took my twelve best fighters
and went ahead. I had a goatskin full
of that sweet liquor that Euanthês' son,

Maron, had given me. He kept Apollo's
holy grove at Ismaros; for kindness
we showed him there, and showed his wife and child,
he gave me seven shining golden talents
perfectly formed, a solid silver winebowl,
and then this liquor—twelve two-handled jars
of brandy, pure and fiery. Not a slave
in Maron's household knew this drink; only
he, his wife and the storeroom mistress knew;
and they would put one cupful—ruby-colored,
honey-smooth—in twenty more of water,
but still the sweet scent hovered like a fume
over the winebowl. No man turned away
when cups of this came round.
                                    A wineskin full
I brought along, and victuals in a bag,
for in my bones I knew some towering brute
would be upon us soon—all outward power,
a wild man, ignorant of civility.

We climbed, then, briskly to the cave. But Kyklops
had gone afield, to pasture his fat sheep,
so we looked round at everything inside:
a drying rack that sagged with cheeses, pens
crowded with lambs and kids, each in its class:
firstlings apart from middlings, and the 'dewdrops,'
or newborn lambkins, penned apart from both.
And vessels full of whey were brimming there—
bowls of earthenware and pails for milking.
My men came pressing round me, pleading:

                                    'Why not
take these cheeses, get them stowed, come back,
throw open all the pens, and make a run for it?
We'll drive the kids and lambs aboard. We say
put out again on good salt water!'

                    Ah,
how sound that was! Yet I refused. I wished
to see the caveman, what he had to offer—
no pretty sight, it turned out, for my friends.
We lit a fire, burnt an offering,

and took some cheese to eat; then sat in silence
around the embers, waiting. When he came
he had a load of dry boughs on his shoulder
to stoke his fire at suppertime. He dumped it
with a great crash into that hollow cave,
and we all scattered fast to the far wall.
Then over the broad cavern floor he ushered
the ewes he meant to milk. He left his rams
and he-goats in the yard outside, and swung
high overhead a slab of solid rock
to close the cave. Two dozen four-wheeled wagons,
with heaving wagon teams, could not have stirred
the tonnage of that rock from where he wedged it
over the doorsill. Next he took his seat
and milked his bleating ewes. A practiced job
he made of it, giving each ewe her suckling;
thickened his milk, then, into curds and whey,
sieved out the curds to drip in withy baskets,
and poured the whey to stand in bowls
cooling until he drank it for his supper.
When all these chores were done, he poked the fire,
heaping on brushwood. In the glare he saw us.

'Strangers,' he said, 'who are you? And where from?
What brings you here by sea ways—a fair traffic?
Or are you wandering rogues, who cast your lives
like dice, and ravage other folk by sea?'

We felt a pressure on our hearts, in dread
of that deep rumble and that mighty man.
But all the same I spoke up in reply:

'We are from Troy, Akhaians, blown off course
by shifting gales on the Great South Sea;
homeward bound, but taking routes and ways
uncommon; so the will of Zeus would have it.
We served under Agamémnon, son of Atreus—
the whole world knows what city
he laid waste, what armies he destroyed.
It was our luck to come here; here we stand,
beholden for your help, or any gifts
you give—as custom is to honor strangers.

We would entreat you, great Sir, have a care
for the gods' courtesy; Zeus will avenge
the unoffending guest.'

                    He answered this
from his brute chest, unmoved:

                         'You are a ninny,
or else you come from the other end of nowhere,
telling me, mind the gods! We Kyklopês
care not a whistle for your thundering Zeus
or all the gods in bliss; we have more force by far.
I would not let you go for fear of Zeus—
you or your friends—unless I had a whim to.
Tell me, where was it, now, you left your ship—
around the point, or down the shore, I wonder?'

He thought he'd find out, but I saw through this,
and answered with a ready lie:

                         'My ship?
Poseidon Lord, who sets the earth a-tremble,
broke it up on the rocks at your land's end.
A wind from seaward served him, drove us there.
We are survivors, these good men and I.'

Neither reply nor pity came from him,
but in one stride he clutched at my companions
and caught two in his hands like squirming puppies
to beat their brains out, spattering the floor.
Then he dismembered them and made his meal,
gaping and crunching like a mountain lion—
everything: innards, flesh, and marrow bones.
We cried aloud, lifting our hands to Zeus,
powerless, looking on at this, appalled;
but Kyklops went on filling up his belly
with manflesh and great gulps of whey,
then lay down like a mast among his sheep.
My heart beat high now at the chance of action,
and drawing the sharp sword from my hip I went
along his flank to stab him where the midriff
holds the liver. I had touched the spot

when sudden fear stayed me: if I killed him
we perished there as well, for we could never
move his ponderous doorway slab aside.
So we were left to groan and wait for morning.

When the young Dawn with finger tips of rose
lit up the world, the Kyklops built a fire
and milked his handsome ewes, all in due order,
putting the sucklings to the mothers. Then,
his chores being all dispatched, he caught
another brace of men to make his breakfast,
and whisked away his great door slab
to let his sheep go through—but he, behind,
reset the stone as one would cap a quiver.
There was a din of whistling as the Kyklops
rounded his flock to higher ground, then stillness.
And now I pondered how to hurt him worst,
if but Athena granted what I prayed for.
Here are the means I thought would serve my turn:

a club, or staff, lay there along the fold—
an olive tree, felled green and left to season
for Kyklops' hand. And it was like a mast
a lugger of twenty oars, broad in the beam—
a deep-sea-going craft—might carry:
so long, so big around, it seemed. Now I
chopped out a six foot section of this pole
and set it down before my men, who scraped it;
and when they had it smooth, I hewed again
to make a stake with pointed end. I held this
in the fire's heart and turned it, toughening it,
then hid it, well back in the cavern, under
one of the dung piles in profusion there.
Now came the time to toss for it: who ventured
along with me? whose hand could bear to thrust
and grind that spike in Kyklops' eye, when mild
sleep had mastered him? As luck would have it,
the men I would have chosen won the toss—
four strong men, and I made five as captain.

At evening came the shepherd with his flock,
his woolly flock. The rams as well, this time,

entered the cave: by some sheep-herding whim—
or a god's bidding—none were left outside.
He hefted his great boulder into place
and sat him down to milk the bleating ewes
in proper order, put the lambs to suck,
and swiftly ran through all his evening chores.
Then he caught two more men and feasted on them.
My moment was at hand, and I went forward
holding an ivy bowl of my dark drink,
looking up, saying:

         'Kyklops, try some wine.
Here's liquor to wash down your scraps of men.
Taste it, and see the kind of drink we carried
under our planks. I meant it for an offering
if you would help us home. But you are mad,
unbearable, a bloody monster! After this,
will any other traveller come to see you?'

He seized and drained the bowl, and it went down
so fiery and smooth he called for more:

'Give me another, thank you kindly. Tell me,
how are you called? I'll make a gift will please you.
Even Kyklopês know the wine-grapes grow
out of grassland and loam in heaven's rain,
but here's a bit of nectar and ambrosia!'

Three bowls I brought him, and he poured them down.
I saw the fuddle and flush come over him,
then I sang out in cordial tones:

         'Kyklops,
you ask my honorable name? Remember
the gift you promised me, and I shall tell you.
My name is Nohbdy: mother, father, and friends,
everyone calls me Nohbdy.'

         And he said:
'Nohbdy's my meat, then, after I eat his friends.
Others come first. There's a noble gift, now.'

Even as he spoke, he reeled and tumbled backward,
his great head lolling to one side; and sleep
took him like any creature. Drunk, hiccuping,
he dribbled streams of liquor and bits of men.

Now, by the gods, I drove my big hand spike
deep in the embers, charring it again,
and cheered my men along with battle talk
to keep their courage up: no quitting now.
The pike of olive, green though it had been,
reddened and glowed as if about to catch.
I drew it from the coals and my four fellows
gave me a hand, lugging it near the Kyklops
as more than natural force nerved them; straight
forward they sprinted, lifted it, and rammed it
deep in his crater eye, and I leaned on it
turning it as a shipwright turns a drill
in planking, having men below to swing
the two-handled strap that spins it in the groove.
So with our brand we bored that great eye socket
while blood ran out around the red hot bar.
Eyelid and lash were seared; the pierced ball
hissed broiling, and the roots popped.

                                        In a smithy
one sees a white-hot axehead or an adze
plunged and wrung in a cold tub, screeching steam—
the way they make soft iron hale and hard—:
just so that eyeball hissed around the spike.
The Kyklops bellowed and the rock roared round him,
and we fell back in fear. Clawing his face
he tugged the bloody spike out of his eye,
threw it away, and his wild hands went groping;
then he set up a howl for Kyklopês
who lived in caves on windy peaks nearby.
Some heard him; and they came by divers ways
to clump around outside and call:

                                        'What ails you,
Polyphêmos? Why do you cry so sore
in the starry night? You will not let us sleep.
Sure no man's driving off your flock? No man
has tricked you, ruined you?'

Out of the cave
the mammoth Polyphêmos roared in answer:

'Nohbdy, Nohbdy's tricked me, Nohbdy's ruined me!'

To this rough shout they made a sage reply:

'Ah well, if nobody has played you foul
there in your lonely bed, we are no use in pain
given by great Zeus. Let it be your father,
Poseidon Lord, to whom you pray.'

So saying
they trailed away. And I was filled with laughter
to see how like a charm the name deceived them.
Now Kyklops, wheezing as the pain came on him,
fumbled to wrench away the great doorstone
and squatted in the breach with arms thrown wide
for any silly beast or man who bolted—
hoping somehow I might be such a fool.
But I kept thinking how to win the game:
death sat there huge; how could we slip away?
I drew on all my wits, and ran through tactics,
reasoning as a man will for dear life,
until a trick came—and it pleased me well.
The Kyklops' rams were handsome, fat, with heavy
fleeces, a dark violet.

Three abreast
I tied them silently together, twining
cords of willow from the ogre's bed;
then slung a man under each middle one
to ride there safely, shielded left and right.
So three sheep could convey each man. I took
the woolliest ram, the choicest of the flock,
and hung myself under his kinky belly,
pulled up tight, with fingers twisted deep
in sheepskin ringlets for an iron grip.
So, breathing hard, we waited until morning.

When Dawn spread out her finger tips of rose
the rams began to stir, moving for pasture,
and peals of bleating echoed round the pens

where dams with udders full called for a milking.
Blinded, and sick with pain from his head wound,
the master stroked each ram, then let it pass,
but my men riding on the pectoral fleece
the giant's blind hands blundering never found.
Last of them all my ram, the leader, came,
weighted by wool and me with my meditations.
The Kyklops patted him, and then he said:

'Sweet cousin ram, why lag behind the rest
in the night cave? You never linger so,
but graze before them all, and go afar
to crop sweet grass, and take your stately way
leading along the streams, until at evening
you run to be the first one in the fold.
Why, now, so far behind? Can you be grieving
over your Master's eye? That carrion rogue
and his accurst companions burnt it out
when he had conquered all my wits with wine.
Nohbdy will not get out alive, I swear.
Oh, had you brain and voice to tell
where he may be now, dodging all my fury!
Bashed by this hand and bashed on this rock wall
his brains would strew the floor, and I should have
rest from the outrage Nohbdy worked upon me.'

He sent us into the open, then. Close by,
I dropped and rolled clear of the ram's belly,
going this way and that to untie the men.
With many glances back, we rounded up
his fat, stiff-legged sheep to take aboard,
and drove them down to where the good ship lay.
We saw, as we came near, our fellows' faces
shining; then we saw them turn to grief
tallying those who had not fled from death.
I hushed them, jerking head and eyebrows up,
and in a low voice told them: 'Load this herd;
move fast, and put the ship's head toward the breakers.'
They all pitched in at loading, then embarked
and struck their oars into the sea. Far out,
as far off shore as shouted words would carry,
I sent a few back to the adversary:

'O Kyklops! Would you feast on my companions?
Puny, am I in a Caveman's hands?
How do you like the beating that we gave you,
you damned cannibal? Eater of guests
under your roof! Zeus and the gods have paid you!'

The blind thing in his doubled fury broke
a hilltop in his hands and heaved it after us.
Ahead of our black prow it struck and sank
whelmed in a spuming geyser, a giant wave
that washed the ship stern foremost back to shore.
I got the longest boathook out and stood
fending us off, with furious nods to all
to put their backs into a racing stroke—
row, row, or perish. So the long oars bent
kicking the foam sternward, making head
until we drew away, and twice as far.
Now when I cupped my hands I heard the crew
in low voices protesting:

                    'Godsake, Captain!
Why bait the beast again? Let him alone!'

'That tidal wave he made on the first throw
all but beached us.'

                    'All but stove us in!'
'Give him our bearing with your trumpeting,
he'll get the range and lob a boulder.'

                    'Aye
He'll smash our timbers and our heads together!'

I would not heed them in my glorying spirit,
but let my anger flare and yelled:

                    'Kyklops,
if ever mortal man inquire
how you were put to shame and blinded tell him
Odysseus, raider of cities, took your eye:
Laërtês' son, whose home's on Ithaka!'

At this he gave a mighty sob and rumbled:

'Now comes the weird upon me, spoken of old.
A wizard, grand and wondrous, lived here—Télemos,
a son of Eurymos; great length of days
he had in wizardry among the Kyklopês,
and these things he foretold for time to come:
my great eye lost, and at Odysseus' hands.
Always I had in mind some giant, armed
in giant force, would come against me here.
But this, but you—small, pitiful and twiggy—
you put me down with wine, you blinded me.
Come back, Odysseus, and I'll treat you well,
praying the god of earthquake to befriend you—
his son I am, for he by his avowal
fathered me, and, if he will, he may
heal me of this black wound—he and no other
of all the happy gods or mortal men.'

Few words I shouted in reply to him:

'If I could take your life I would and take
your time away, and hurl you down to hell!
The god of earthquake could not heal you there!'

At this he stretched his hands out in his darkness
toward the sky of stars, and prayed Poseidon:

'O hear me, lord, blue girdler of the islands,
if I am thine indeed, and thou art father:
grant that Odysseus, raider of cities, never
see his home: Laërtês' son, I mean,
who kept his hall on Ithaka. Should destiny
intend that he shall see his roof again
among his family in his father land,
far be that day, and dark the years between.
Let him lose all companions, and return
under strange sail to bitter days at home.'

In these words he prayed, and the god heard him.
Now he laid hands upon a bigger stone
and wheeled around, titanic for the cast,
to let it fly in the black-prowed vessel's track.

But it fell short, just aft the steering oar,
and whelming seas rose giant above the stone
to bear us onward toward the island.
                                          There
as we ran in we saw the squadron waiting,
the trim ships drawn up side by side, and all
our troubled friends who waited, looking seaward.
We beached her, grinding keel in the soft sand,
and waded in, ourselves, on the sandy beach.
Then we unloaded all the Kyklops' flock
to make division, share and share alike,
only my fighters voted that my ram,
the prize of all, should go to me. I slew him
by the sea side and burnt his long thighbones
to Zeus beyond the stormcloud, Kronos' son,
who rules the world. But Zeus disdained my offering;
destruction for my ships he had in store
and death for those who sailed them, my companions."

Translated by Robert Fitzgerald

From BOOK X

ODYSSEUS AND CIRCE

*After his adventure in the land of the Cyclops, Odysseus arrives at the
island of Aeolus, lord of the winds, who is so delighted when he hears the
tale of Troy that he arranges for a West Wind to waft Odysseus home.
All the other winds he confines in a leather bag and gives to Odysseus to
take onboard ship. Odysseus gets near enough to Ithaca to see the onshore smoke of fires, but then, exhausted, falls asleep. His crew, convinced that the bag holds gold and silver of which they are to be denied a
share, open the bag. The ship is blown all the way back to the island of
Aeolus, who angrily tells Odysseus to find his own way home this time.
What he finds his way to next is the land of the Laestrygonians, giant
cannibals, who hurl rocks from the cliffs and sink every one of his squadron of twelve ships except his own. With that one ship and crew, he
arrives at another island; it turns out to be the home of Circe.*

"There we brought our ship in to the shore, in silence,
at a harbor fit for ships to lie, and some god guided us
in. There we disembarked, and for two days and two nights
we lay there, for sorrow and weariness eating our hearts out.

But when the fair-haired Dawn in her rounds brought on the third
    day,
then at last I took up my spear again, my sharp sword,
and went up quickly from beside the ship to find a lookout
place, to look for some trace of people, listen for some sound.
I climbed to a rocky point of observation and stood there,
and got a sight of smoke which came from the halls of Circe
going up from wide-wayed earth through undergrowth and forest.
Then I pondered deeply in my heart and my spirit,
whether, since I had seen the fire and smoke, to investigate;
but in the division of my heart this way seemed the best to me,
to go back first to the fast ship and the beach of the sea, and give
my companions some dinner, and then go forward and investigate.
But on my way, as I was close to the oar-swept vessel,
some god, because I was all alone, took pity upon me,
and sent a great stag with towering antlers right in my very
path; he had come from his range in the forest down to the river
to drink, for the fierce strength of the sun was upon him. As he
stepped out, I hit him in the middle of the back, next to
the spine, so that the brazen spearhead smashed its way clean
    through.
He screamed and dropped in the dust and the life spirit fluttered
    from him.
I set my foot on him and drew the bronze spear out of
the wound it had made, and rested it on the ground, while I
pulled growing twigs and willow withes and, braiding them into
a rope, about six feet in length, and looping them over
the feet of this great monster on both sides, lashed them together,
and with him loaded over my neck went toward the black ship,
propping myself on my spear, for there was no way to carry him
on the shoulder holding him with one hand, he was such a very
big beast. I threw him down by the ship and roused my
    companions,
standing beside each man and speaking to him in kind words:
'Dear friends, sorry as we are, we shall not yet go down into
the house of Hades. Not until our day is appointed.
Come then, while there is something to eat and drink by the fast
    ship,
let us think of our food and not be worn out with hunger.'
"So I spoke, and they listened at once to me and obeyed me,
and unveiling their heads along the beach of the barren water
they admired the stag, and truly he was a very big beast.
But after they had looked at him and their eyes had enjoyed him,

they washed their hands and set to preparing a communal high
feast.
So for the whole length of the day until the sun's setting
we sat there feasting on unlimited meat and sweet wine.
But when the sun went down and the sacred darkness came over,
then we lay down to sleep along the break of the seashore;
but when the young Dawn showed again with her rosy fingers,
then I held an assembly and spoke forth to all of them:
'Hear my words, my companions, in spite of your hearts' sufferings.
Dear friends, for we do not know where the darkness is nor the
sunrise,
nor where the Sun who shines upon people rises, nor where
he sets, then let us hasten our minds and think, whether there is
any course left open to us. But I think there is none.
For I climbed to a rocky place of observation and looked at
the island, and the endless sea lies all in a circle
around it, but the island itself lies low, and my eyes saw
smoke rising in the middle through the undergrowth and the forest.'
    "So I spoke, and the inward heart in them was broken,
as they remembered Antiphates the Laistrygonian
and the violence of the great-hearted cannibal Cyclops,
and they wept loud and shrill, letting the big tears fall,
but there came no advantage to them for all their sorrowing.
    "I counted off all my strong-greaved companions into two
divisions, and appointed a leader for each, I myself
taking one, while godlike Eurylochos had the other.
Promptly then we shook the lots in a brazen helmet,
and the lot of great-hearted Eurylochos sprang out. He then
went on his way, and with him two-and-twenty companions,
weeping, and we whom they left behind were mourning also.
In the forest glen they came on the house of Circe. It was
in an open place, and put together from stones, well polished,
and all about it there were lions, and wolves of the mountains,
whom the goddess had given evil drugs and enchanted,
and these made no attack on the men, but came up thronging
about them, waving their long tails and fawning, in the way
that dogs go fawning about their master, when he comes home
from dining out, for he always brings back something to please
them;
so these wolves with great strong claws and lions came fawning
on my men, but they were afraid when they saw the terrible big
beasts.
They stood there in the forecourt of the goddess with the glorious

hair, and heard Circe inside singing in a sweet voice
as she went up and down a great design on a loom, immortal
such as goddesses have, delicate and lovely and glorious
their work. Now Polites leader of men, who was
the best and dearest to me of my friends, began the discussion:
'Friends, someone inside going up and down a great piece
of weaving is singing sweetly, and the whole place murmurs to the
    echo
of it, whether she is woman or goddess. Come, let us call her.'
    "So he spoke to them, and the rest gave voice, and called her,
and at once she opened the shining doors, and came out, and
    invited
them in, and all in their innocence entered; only
Eurylochos waited outside, for he suspected treachery.
She brought them inside and seated them on chairs and benches,
and mixed them a potion, with barley and cheese and pale honey
added to Pramneian wine, but put into the mixture
malignant drugs, to make them forgetful of their own country.
When she had given them this and they had drunk it down, next
    thing
she struck them with her wand and drove them into her pig pens,
and they took on the look of pigs, with the heads and voices
and bristles of pigs, but the minds within them stayed as they had
    been
before. So crying they went in, and before them Circe
threw down acorns for them to eat, and ilex and cornel
buds, such food as pigs who sleep on the ground always feed on.
    "Eurylochos came back again to the fast black ship,
to tell the story of our companions and of their dismal
fate, but he could not get a word out, though he was trying
to speak, but his heart was stunned by the great sorrow, and both
    eyes
filled with tears, he could think of nothing but lamentation.
But after we had wondered at him and asked him questions,
at last he told us about the loss of his other companions:
'We went, O glorious Odysseus, through the growth as you
told us, and found a fine house in the glen. It was
in an open place, and put together from stones, well polished.
Someone, goddess or woman, was singing inside in a clear voice
as she went up and down her loom, and they called her, and spoke
    to her,
and at once she opened the shining doors, and came out and invited

them in, and all in their innocence entered, only
I waited for them outside, for I suspected treachery.
Then the whole lot of them vanished away together, nor did one
single one come out, though I sat and watched for a long time.'
    "So he spoke, and I slung my great bronze sword with the silver
nails across my shoulders, and hung my bow on also,
and told him to guide me back by the same way he had gone;
but he, clasping my knees in both hands, entreated me,
and in loud lamentation spoke to me and addressed me:
'Illustrious, do not take me against my will there. Leave me
here, for I know you will never come back yourself, nor bring back
any of your companions. Let us rather make haste, and with these
who are left, escape, for we still may avoid the day of evil.'
    "So he spoke, and I answered again in turn and said to him:
'Eurylochos, you may stay here eating and drinking, even
where you are and beside the hollow black ship; only
I shall go. For there is strong compulsion upon me.'
    "So I spoke, and started up from the ship and the seashore.
But as I went up through the lonely glens, and was coming
near to the great house of Circe, skilled in medicines,
there as I came up to the house, Hermes, of the golden
staff, met me on my way, in the likeness of a young man
with beard new grown, which is the most graceful time of young
        manhood.
He took me by the hand and spoke to me and named me, saying:
'Where are you going, unhappy man, all alone, through the hilltops,
ignorant of the land-lay, and your friends are here in Circe's
place, in the shape of pigs and holed up in the close pig pens.
Do you come here meaning to set them free? I do not think
you will get back yourself, but must stay here with the others.
But see, I will find you a way out of your troubles, and save you.
Here, this is a good medicine, take it, and go into Circe's
house; it will give you power against the day of trouble.
And I will tell you all the malevolent guiles of Circe.
She will make you a potion, and put drugs in the food, but she will
        not
even so be able to enchant you, for this good medicine
which I give you now will prevent her. I will tell you the details
of what to do. As soon as Circe with her long wand strikes you,
then drawing from beside your thigh your sharp sword, rush
forward against Circe, as if you were raging to kill her,
and she will be afraid, and invite you to go to bed with her.

Do not then resist and refuse the bed of the goddess,
for so she will set free your companions, and care for you also;
but bid her swear the great oath of the blessed gods, that she
has no other evil hurt that she is devising against you,
so she will not make you weak and unmanned, once you are naked.'
  "So spoke Argeïphontes, and he gave me the medicine,
which he picked out of the ground, and he explained the nature
of it to me. It was black at the root, but with a milky
flower. The gods call it moly. It is hard for mortal
men to dig up, but the gods have power to do all things.
  "Then Hermes went away, passing over the wooded island,
toward tall Olympos, and I meanwhile made my way to the house
of Circe, but my heart was a storm in me as I went. Now
I stood outside at the doors of the goddess with the glorious
hair, and standing I shouted aloud; and the goddess heard me,
and at once she opened the shining doors and came out and invited
me in; and I, deeply troubled in my heart, went in with her.
She made me sit down in a chair that was wrought elaborately
and splendid with silver nails, and under my feet was a footstool.
She made a potion for me to drink and gave it in a golden
cup, and with evil thoughts in her heart added the drug to it.
Then when she had given it and I drank it off, without being
enchanted, she struck me with her wand and spoke and named me:
'Go to your sty now and lie down with your other friends there.'
  "So she spoke, but I, drawing from beside my thigh the sharp
      sword,
rushed forward against Circe as if I were raging to kill her,
but she screamed aloud and ran under my guard, and clasping both
      knees
in loud lamentation spoke to me and addressed me in winged words:
'What man are you and whence? Where are your city and parents?
The wonder is on me that you drank my drugs and have not been
enchanted, for no other man beside could have stood up
under my drugs, once he drank and they passed the barrier
of his teeth. There is a mind in you no magic will work on.
You are then resourceful Odysseus. Argeïphontes
of the golden staff was forever telling me you would come
to me, on your way back from Troy with your fast black ship.
Come then, put away your sword in its sheath, and let us
two go up into my bed so that, lying together
in the bed of love, we may then have faith and trust in each other.'
  "So she spoke, and I answered her again and said to her:

'Circe, how can you ask me to be gentle with you, when it
is you who turned my companions into pigs in your palace?
And now you have me here myself, you treacherously
ask me to go into your chamber, and go to bed with you,
so that when I am naked you can make me a weakling, unmanned.
I would not be willing to go to bed with you unless
you can bring yourself, O goddess, to swear me a great oath
that there is no other evil hurt you devise against me.'
    "So I spoke, and she at once swore me the oath, as I asked her,
But after she had sworn me the oath, and made an end of it,
I mounted the surpassingly beautiful bed of Circe.
    "Meanwhile, the four maidservants, who wait on Circe
in her house, were busy at their work, all through the palace.
These are daughters born of the springs and from the coppices
and the sacred rivers which flow down to the sea. Of these
one laid the coverlets, splendid and stained in purple, over
the backs of the chairs, and spread on the seats the cloths to sit on.
The second drew up the silver tables and placed them in front of
the chairs, and laid out the golden serving baskets upon them.
The third mixed wine, kindly sweet and fragrant, in the silver
mixing bowl, and set out the golden goblets. The fourth one
brought in water, then set about building up an abundant
fire, underneath the great caldron, and the water heated.
But when the water had come to a boil in the shining bronze, then
she sat me down in the bathtub and washed me from the great
        caldron,
mixing hot and cold just as I wanted, and pouring it
over shoulders and head, to take the heart-wasting weariness
from my limbs. When she had bathed me and anointed me with
        olive oil,
she put a splendid mantle and a tunic upon me,
and made me sit down in a chair that was wrought elaborately
and splendid with silver nails, and under my feet was a footstool.
A maidservant brought water for us and poured it from a splendid
and golden pitcher, holding it above a silver basin,
for us to wash, and she pulled a polished table before us.
A grave housekeeper brought in the bread and served it to us,
adding many good things to it, generous with her provisions,
and told us to eat, but nothing pleased my mind, and I sat there
thinking of something else, mind full of evil imaginings.
    "When Circe noticed how I sat there without ever putting
my hands out to the food, and with the strong sorrow upon me,

she came close, and stood beside me and addressed me in winged
    words:
'Why, Odysseus, do you sit so, like a man who has lost his
voice, eating your heart out, but touch neither food nor drink. Is it
that you suspect me of more treachery? But you have nothing
to fear, since I have already sworn my strong oath to you.'
    "So she spoke, but I answered her again and said to her:
'Oh, Circe, how could any man right in his mind ever
endure to taste of the food and drink that are set before him,
until with his eyes he saw his companions set free? So then,
if you are sincerely telling me to eat and drink, set them
free, so my eyes can again behold my eager companions.'
    "So I spoke, and Circe walked on out through the palace,
holding her wand in her hand, and opened the doors of the pigsty,
and drove them out. They looked like nine-year-old porkers. They
    stood
ranged and facing her, and she, making her way through their
ranks, anointed each of them with some other medicine,
and the bristles, grown upon them by the evil medicine Circe
had bestowed upon them before, now fell away from them,
and they turned back once more into men, younger than they had
    been
and taller for the eye to behold and handsomer by far.
They recognized me, and each of them clung to my hand. The
    lovely
longing for lamentation came over us, and the house echoed
terribly to the sound, and even the goddess took pity,
and she, shining among goddesses, came close and said to me:
'Son of Laertes and seed of Zeus, resourceful Odysseus,
go back down now to your fast ship and the sand of the seashore,
and first of all, drag your ship up on the land, stowing
your possessions and all the ship's running gear away in the sea
    caves,
and then come back, and bring with you your eager companions.'
    "So she spoke, and the proud heart in me was persuaded,
and I went back down to my fast ship and the sand of the seashore,
and there I found beside the fast ship my eager companions
pitiful in their lamentation and weeping big tears.
And as, in the country, the calves, around the cows returning
from pasture back to the dung of the farmyard, well filled with
    grazing,
come gamboling together to meet them, and the pens no longer

can hold them in, but lowing incessantly they come running
around their mothers, so these men, once their eyes saw me,
came streaming around me, in tears, and the spirit in them made
    them
feel as if they were back in their own country, the very
city of rugged Ithaka, where they were born and raised up.
So they came in tears about me, and cried in winged words:
'O great Odysseus, we are as happy to see you returning
as if we had come back to our own Ithakan country.
But come, tell us about the death of our other companions.'
    "So they spoke, but I answered in soft words and told them:
'First of all, let us drag our ship up on the land, stowing
our possessions and all the ship's running gear away in the sea caves,
and then make haste, all of you, to come along with me,
so that you can see your companions, in the sacred dwelling
of Circe, eating and drinking, for they have all in abundance.'
    "So I spoke, and at once they did as I told them. Only
Eurylochos was trying to hold back all my other
companions, and he spoke to them and addressed them in winged
    words
'Ah, poor wretches. Where are we going? Why do you long for
the evils of going down into Circe's palace, for she will
transform the lot of us into pigs or wolves or lions,
and so we shall guard her great house for her, under compulsion.
So too it happened with the Cyclops, when our companions
went into his yard, and the bold Odysseus was of their company;
for it was by this man's recklessness that these too perished.'
    "So he spoke, and I considered in my mind whether
to draw out the long-edged sword from beside my big thigh,
and cut off his head and throw it on the ground, even though
he was nearly related to me by marriage; but my companions
checked me, first one then another speaking, trying to soothe me:
'Zeus-sprung Odysseus, if you ask us to, we will leave
this man here to stay where he is and keep watch over
the ship. You show us the way to the sacred dwelling of Circe.'
    "So they spoke, and started up from the ship and the seashore;
nor would Eurylochos be left alone by the hollow
ship, but followed along in fear of my fierce reproaches.
    "Meanwhile, inside the house, Circe with loving care bathed
the rest of my companions, and anointed them well with olive oil,
and put about them mantles of fleece and tunics. We found them
all together, feasting well in the halls. When my men

looked each other in the face and knew one another,
they burst into an outcry of tears, and the whole house echoed,
But she, shining among goddesses, came close and said to us:
'Son of Laertes and seed of Zeus, resourceful Odysseus,
no longer raise the swell of your lamentation. I too
know all the pains you have suffered on the sea where the fish
    swarm,
and all the damage done you on the dry land by hostile
men. But come now, eat your food and drink your wine, until
you gather back again into your chests that kind of spirit
you had in you when first you left the land of your fathers
on rugged Ithaka. Now you are all dried out, dispirited
from the constant thought of your hard wandering, nor is there any
spirit in your festivity, because of so much suffering.'
    "So she spoke, and the proud heart in us was persuaded.
There for all our days until a year was completed
we sat there feasting on unlimited meat and sweet wine."

Translated by Richmond Lattimore

From BOOK XI

THE LAND OF THE DEAD

*One has the distinct impression that Odysseus would have stayed with
Circe much longer, but his crewmen urge him to resume the voyage
home. Circe tells him he must first go to the land of the dead, to consult
the shade of the Theban prophet Tiresias, who will show him how to get
home. Odysseus orders his men aboard ship.*

    "Yet I did not lead away my companions without some
loss. There was one, Elpenor, the youngest man, not terribly
powerful in fighting nor sound in his thoughts. This man,
apart from the rest of his friends, in search of cool air, had lain
down drunkenly to sleep on the roof of Circe's palace,
and when his companions stirred to go he, hearing their tumult
and noise of talking, started suddenly up, and never thought,
when he went down, to go by way of the long ladder,
but blundered straight off the edge of the roof, so that his neck
    bone
was broken out of its sockets, and his soul went down to Hades.
    "Now as my men were on their way I said a word to them:

'You think you are on your way back now to your own beloved
country, but Circe has indicated another journey
for us, to the house of Hades and of revered Persephone
there to consult with the soul of Teiresias the Theban.'
    "So I spoke, and the inward heart in them was broken.
They sat down on the ground and lamented and tore their hair out,
but there came no advantage to them for all their sorrowing.
    "When we came down to our fast ship and the sand of the
        seashore,
we sat down, sorrowful, and weeping big tears. Circe
meanwhile had gone down herself to the side of the black ship,
and tethered aboard it a ram and one black female, easily
passing by us unseen. Whose eyes can follow the movement
of a god passing from place to place, unless the god wishes?"
    "Now when we had gone down again to the sea and our vessel,
first of all we dragged the ship down into the bright water,
and in the black hull set the mast in place, and set sails,
and took the sheep and walked them aboard, and ourselves also
embarked, but sorrowful, and weeping big tears. Circe
of the lovely hair, the dread goddess who talks with mortals,
sent us an excellent companion, a following wind, filling
the sails, to carry from astern the ship with the dark prow.
We ourselves, over all the ship making fast the running gear,
sat still, and let the wind and the steersman hold her steady.
All day long her sails were filled as she went through the water,
and the sun set, and all the journeying-ways were darkened.
    "She made the limit, which is of the deep-running Ocean.
There lie the community and city of Kimmerian people,
hidden in fog and cloud, nor does Helios, the radiant
sun, ever break through the dark, to illuminate them with his
        shining,
neither when he climbs up into the starry heaven,
nor when he wheels to return again from heaven to earth,
but always a glum night is spread over wretched mortals.
Making this point, we ran the ship ashore, and took out
the sheep, and ourselves walked along by the stream of the Ocean
until we came to that place of which Circe had spoken.
    "There Perimedes and Eurylochos held the victims
fast, and I, drawing from beside my thigh my sharp sword,
dug a pit, of about a cubit in each direction,
and poured it full of drink offerings for all the dead, first
honey mixed with milk, and the second pouring was sweet wine,

and the third, water, and over it all I sprinkled white barley.
I promised many times to the strengthless heads of the perished
dead that, returning to Ithaka, I would slaughter a barren
cow, my best, in my palace, and pile the pyre with treasures,
and to Teiresias apart would dedicate an all-black
ram, the one conspicuous in all our sheep flocks.
Now when, with sacrifices and prayers, I had so entreated
the hordes of the dead, I took the sheep and cut their throats
over the pit, and the dark-clouding blood ran in, and the souls
of the perished dead gathered to the place, up out of Erebos,
brides, and young unmarried men, and long-suffering elders,
virgins, tender and with the sorrows of young hearts upon them,
and many fighting men killed in battle, stabbed with brazen
spears, still carrying their bloody armor upon them.
These came swarming around my pit from every direction
with inhuman clamor, and green fear took hold of me.
Then I encouraged my companions and told them, taking
the sheep that were lying by, slaughtered with the pitiless
bronze, to skin these, and burn them, and pray to the divinities,
to Hades the powerful, and to revered Persephone,
while I myself, drawing from beside my thigh my sharp sword,
crouched there, and would not let the strengthless heads of the
      perished
dead draw nearer to the blood, until I had questioned Teiresias.
   "But first there came the soul of my companion, Elpenor,
for he had not yet been buried under earth of the wide ways,
since we had left his body behind in Circe's palace,
unburied and unwept, with this other errand before us.
I broke into tears at the sight of him, and my heart pitied him,
and so I spoke aloud to him and addressed him in winged words:
'Elpenor, how did you come here beneath the fog and the darkness?
You have come faster on foot than I could in my black ship.'
   "So I spoke, and he groaned aloud and spoke and answered:
'Son of Laertes and seed of Zeus, resourceful Odysseus,
the evil will of the spirit and the wild wine bewildered me.
I lay down on the roof of Circe's palace, and never thought,
when I went down, to go by way of the long ladder,
but blundered straight off the edge of the roof, so that my neck
      bone
was broken out of its sockets, and my soul went down to Hades.
But now I pray you, by those you have yet to see, who are not here,
by your wife, and by your father, who reared you when you were
      little,

and by Telemachos whom you left alone in your palace;
for I know that after you leave this place and the house of Hades
you will put back with your well-made ship to the island, Aiaia;
there at that time, my lord, I ask that you remember me,
and do not go and leave me behind unwept, unburied,
when you leave, for fear I might become the gods' curse upon you;
but burn me there with all my armor that belongs to me,
and heap up a grave mound beside the beach of the gray sea,
for an unhappy man, so that those to come will know of me.
Do this for me, and on top of the grave mound plant the oar
with which I rowed when I was alive and among my companions.'
  "So he spoke, and I in turn spoke to him in answer:
'All this, my unhappy friend, I will do for you as you ask me.'
  "So we two stayed there exchanging our sad words, I on
one side holding my sword over the blood, while opposite
me the phantom of my companion talked long with me.
  "Next there came to me the soul of my dead mother,
Antikleia, daughter of great-hearted Autolykos,
whom I had left alive when I went to sacred Ilion.
I broke into tears at the sight of her and my heart pitied her,
but even so, for all my thronging sorrow, I would not
let her draw near the blood until I had questioned Teiresias.
  "Now came the soul of Teiresias the Theban, holding
a staff of gold, and he knew who I was, and spoke to me:
'Son of Laertes and seed of Zeus, resourceful Odysseus,
how is it then, unhappy man, you have left the sunlight
and come here, to look on dead men, and this place without
      pleasure?
Now draw back from the pit, and hold your sharp sword away from
      me,
so that I can drink of the blood and speak the truth to you.'
  "So he spoke, and I, holding away the sword with the silver
nails, pushed it back in the sheath, and the flawless prophet,
after he had drunk the blood, began speaking to me.
'Glorious Odysseus, what you are after is sweet homecoming,
but the god will make it hard for you. I think you will not
escape the Shaker of the Earth, who holds a grudge against you
in his heart, and because you blinded his dear son, hates you.
But even so and still you might come back, after much suffering,
if you can contain your own desire, and contain your companions',
at that time when you first put in your well-made vessel
at the island Thrinakia, escaping the sea's blue water,
and there discover pasturing the cattle and fat sheep

of Helios, who sees all things, and listens to all things.
Then, if you keep your mind on homecoming, and leave these
      unharmed,
you might all make your way to Ithaka, after much suffering;
but if you do harm them, then I testify to the destruction
of your ship and your companions, but if you yourself get clear,
you will come home in bad case, with the loss of all your
      companions,
in someone else's ship, and find troubles in your household,
insolent men, who are eating away your livelihood
and courting your godlike wife and offering gifts to win her.
You may punish the violences of these men, when you come home.
But after you have killed these suitors in your own palace,
either by treachery, or openly with the sharp bronze,
then you must take up your well-shaped oar and go on a journey
until you come where there are men living who know nothing
of the sea, and who eat food that is not mixed with salt, who never
have known ships whose cheeks are painted purple, who never
have known well-shaped oars, which act for ships as wings do.
And I will tell you a very clear proof, and you cannot miss it.
When, as you walk, some other wayfarer happens to meet you,
and says you carry a winnow-fan on your bright shoulder,
then you must plant your well-shaped oar in the ground, and render
ceremonies sacrifice to the lord Poseidon,
one ram and one bull, and a mounter of sows, a boar pig,
and make your way home again and render holy hecatombs
to the immortal gods who hold the wide heaven, all
of them in order. Death will come to you from the sea, in
some altogether unwarlike way, and it will end you
in the ebbing time of a sleek old age. Your people
about you will be prosperous. All this is true that I tell you.'
    "So he spoke, but I in turn said to him in answer:
'All this, Teiresias, surely must be as the gods spun it.
But come now, tell me this and give me an accurate answer.
I see before me now the soul of my perished mother,
but she sits beside the blood in silence, and has not yet deigned
to look directly at her own son and speak a word to me.
Tell me, lord, what will make her know me, and know my
      presence?'
    "So I spoke, and he at once said to me in answer:
'Easily I will tell you and put it in your understanding.
Any one of the perished dead you allow to come up

to the blood will give you a true answer, but if you begrudge this
to any one, he will return to the place where he came from.'
    "So speaking, the soul of the lord Teiresias went back into
the house of Hades, once he had uttered his prophecies, while I
waited steadily where I was standing, until my mother
came and drank the dark-clouding blood, and at once she knew me,
and full of lamentation she spoke to me in winged words:
'My child, how did you come here beneath the fog and the darkness
and still alive? All this is hard for the living to look on,
for in between lie the great rivers and terrible waters
that flow, Ocean first of all, which there is no means of crossing
on foot, not unless one has a well-made ship. Are you
come now to this place from Troy, with your ship and your
        companions,
after wandering a long time, and have you not yet come
to Ithaka, and there seen your wife in your palace?'
    "So she spoke, and I in turn said to her in answer:
'Mother, a duty brought me here to the house of Hades.
I had to consult the soul of Teiresias the Theban.
For I have not yet been near Achaian country, nor ever
set foot on our land, but always suffering I have wandered
since the time I first went along with great Agamemnon
to Ilion, land of good horses, and the battle against the Trojans.
But come now, tell me this, and give me an accurate answer.
What doom of death that lays men low has been your undoing?
Was it a long sickness, or did Artemis of the arrows
come upon you with her painless shafts, and destroy you?
And tell me of my father and son whom I left behind. Is
my inheritance still with them, or does some other
man hold them now, and thinks I will come no more? Tell me
about the wife I married, what she wants, what she is thinking,
and whether she stays fast by my son, and guards everything,
or if she has married the best man among the Achaians.'
    "So I spoke, and my queenly mother answered me quickly:
'All too much with enduring heart she does wait for you
there in your own palace, and always with her the wretched
nights and the days also waste her away with weeping.
No one yet holds your fine inheritance, but in freedom
Telemachos administers your allotted lands, and apportions
the equal feasts, work that befits a man with authority
to judge, for all call him in. Your father remains, on the estate
where he is, and does not go to the city. There is no bed there

nor is there bed clothing nor blankets nor shining coverlets,
but in the winter time he sleeps in the house, where the thralls do,
in the dirt next to the fire, and with foul clothing upon him;
but when the summer comes and the blossoming time of harvest,
everywhere he has places to sleep on the ground, on fallen
leaves in piles along the rising ground of his orchard,
and there he lies, grieving, and the sorrow grows big within him
as he longs for your homecoming, and harsh old age is on him.
And so it was with me also and that was the reason I perished,
nor in my palace did the lady of arrows, well-aiming,
come upon me with her painless shafts, and destroy me,
nor was I visited by sickness, which beyond other
things takes the life out of the body with hateful weakness,
but, shining Odysseus, it was my longing for you, your cleverness
and your gentle ways, that took the sweet spirit of life from me.'
    "So she spoke, but I, pondering it in my heart, yet wished
to take the soul of my dead mother in my arms. Three times
I started toward her, and my heart was urgent to hold her,
and three times she fluttered out of my hands like a shadow
or a dream, and the sorrow sharpened at the heart within me,
and so I spoke to her and addressed her in winged words, saying:
'Mother, why will you not wait for me, when I am trying
to hold you, so that even in Hades with our arms embracing
we can both take the satisfaction of dismal mourning?
Or are you nothing but an image that proud Persephone
sent my way, to make me grieve all the more for sorrow?'
    "So I spoke, and my queenly mother answered me quickly:
'Oh my child, ill-fated beyond all other mortals,
this is not Persephone, daughter of Zeus, beguiling you,
but it is only what happens, when they die, to all mortals.
The sinews no longer hold the flesh and the bones together,
and once the spirit has left the white bones, all the rest
of the body is made subject to the fire's strong fury,
but the soul flitters out like a dream and flies away. Therefore
you must strive back toward the light again with all speed; but
        remember
these things for your wife, so you may tell her hereafter.' "

[*After his mother, Odysseus sees the shades of illustrious women of the
past, consorts of gods and mothers of heroes some of them, others great
victims or sinners—Phaedra, Ariadne, and Epicaste, wife of Oedipus*

*"whose great unwitting deed it was / to marry her own son." After this,
Odysseus breaks his long story off; the hour is late. But Alcinous demands more ("Here's a long night—an endless night before us . . .") and
Odysseus takes up the tale again. He now sees the shades of his companions at Troy: Agamemnon, killed by his wife on his return home;
Achilles, killed in battle by Paris and Apollo; and Ajax, who, enraged by
the award of the arms of Achilles to Odysseus instead of to himself, tried
to kill Odysseus and the royal judges, failed, and killed himself.]*

"There came the soul of Agamemnon, the son of Atreus,
grieving, and the souls of the other men, who died with him
and met their doom in the house of Aigisthos, were gathered around
    him.
He knew me at once, when he drank the dark blood, and fell to
lamentation loud and shrill, and the tears came springing,
and threw himself into my arms, meaning so to embrace me,
but there was no force there any longer, nor any juice left
now in his flexible limbs, as there had been in time past.
I broke into tears at the sight of him and my heart pitied him,
and so I spoke aloud to him and addressed him in winged words:
'Son of Atreus, most lordly and king of men, Agamemnon,
what doom of death that lays men low has been your undoing?
Was it with the ships, and did Poseidon, rousing a stormblast
of battering winds that none would wish for, prove your undoing?
Or was it on the dry land, did men embattled destroy you
as you tried to cut out cattle and fleecy sheep from their holdings,
or fighting against them for the sake of their city and women?'
"So I spoke, and he in turn said to me in answer:
'Son of Laertes and seed of Zeus, resourceful Odysseus,
not in the ships, nor did Poseidon, rousing a stormblast
of battering winds that none would wish for, prove my destruction,
nor on dry land did enemy men destroy me in battle;
Aigisthos, working out my death and destruction, invited
me to his house, and feasted me, and killed me there, with the help
of my sluttish wife, as one cuts down an ox at his manger.
So I died a most pitiful death, and my other companions
were killed around me without mercy, like pigs with shining
tusks, in the house of a man rich and very powerful,
for a wedding, or a festival, or a communal dinner.
You have been present in your time at the slaughter of many
men, killed singly, or in the strong encounters of battle;

but beyond all others you would have been sorry at heart
for this scene, how we lay sprawled by the mixing bowl and the
    loaded
tables, all over the palace, and the whole floor was steaming
with blood; and most pitiful was the voice I heard of Priam's
daughter Kassandra, killed by treacherous Klytaimestra
over me; but I lifted my hands and with them beat on
the ground as I died upon the sword, but the sluttish woman
turned away from me and was so hard that her hands would not
press shut my eyes and mouth though I was going to Hades.
So there is nothing more deadly or more vile than a woman
who stores her mind with acts that are of such sort, as this one
did when she thought of this act of dishonor, and plotted
the murder of her lawful husband. See, I had been thinking
that I would be welcome to my children and thralls of my
    household
when I came home, but she with thoughts surpassingly grisly
splashed the shame on herself and the rest of her sex, on women
still to come, even on the one whose acts are virtuous.'
    "So he spoke, and I again said to him in answer:
'Shame it is, how most terribly Zeus of the wide brows
from the beginning has been hateful to the seed of Atreus
through the schemes of women. Many of us died for the sake of
    Helen
and when you were far, Klytaimestra plotted treason against you.'
    "So I spoke, and he in turn said to me in answer:
'So by this, do not be too easy even with your wife,
nor give her an entire account of all you are sure of.
Tell her part of it, but let the rest be hidden in silence.
And yet you, Odysseus, will never be murdered by your wife.
The daughter of Ikarios, circumspect Penelope,
is all too virtuous and her mind is stored with good thoughts.
Ah well. She was only a young wife when we left her
and went off to the fighting, and she had an infant child then
at her breast. That child now must sit with the men and be
    counted.
Happy he! For his dear father will come back, and see him,
and he will fold his father in his arms, as is right. My wife
never even let me feed my eyes with the sight of
my own son, but before that I myself was killed by her.
And put away in your heart this other thing that I tell you.
When you bring your ship in to your own dear country, do it

secretly, not in the open. There is no trusting in women
But come now, tell me this and give me an accurate answer;
tell me if you happened to hear that my son was still living,
whether perhaps in Orchomenos, or in sandy Pylos,
or perhaps with Menelaos in wide Sparta; for nowhere
upon the earth has there been any death of noble Orestes.'
   "So he spoke, and I again said to him in answer:
'Son of Atreus, why do you ask me that? I do not know
if he is alive or dead. It is bad to babble emptily.'
   "So we two stood there exchanging our sad words, grieving
both together and shedding the big tears. After this,
there came to us the soul of Peleus' son, Achilleus,
and the soul of Patroklos and the soul of stately Antilochos,
and the soul of Aias, who for beauty and stature was greatest
of all the Danaans, next to the stately son of Peleus.
The soul of swift-footed Achilleus, scion of Aiakos, knew me,
and full of lamentation he spoke to me in winged words:
'Son of Laertes and seed of Zeus, resourceful Odysseus,
hard man, what made you think of this bigger endeavor, how could
     you
endure to come down here to Hades' place, where the senseless
dead men dwell, mere imitations of perished mortals?'
   "So he spoke, and I again said to him in answer:
'Son of Peleus, far the greatest of the Achaians, Achilleus,
I came for the need to consult Teiresias, if he might tell me
some plan by which I might come back to rocky Ithaka;
for I have not yet been near Achaian country, nor ever
set foot on my land, but always I have troubles. Achilleus,
no man before has been more blessed than you, nor ever
will be. Before, when you were alive, we Argives honored you
as we did the gods, and now in this place you have great authority
over the dead. Do not grieve, even in death, Achilleus.'
   "So I spoke, and he in turn said to me in answer:
'O shining Odysseus, never try to console me for dying.
I would rather follow the plow as thrall to another
man, one with no land allotted him and not much to live on,
than be a king over all the perished dead. But come now,
tell me anything you have heard of my proud son, whether
or not he went along to war to fight as a champion;
and tell me anything you have heard about stately Peleus,
whether he still keeps his position among the Myrmidon
hordes, or whether in Hellas and Phthia they have diminished

his state, because old age constrains his hands and feet, and I
am no longer there under the light of the sun to help him,
not the man I used to be once, when in the wide Troad
I killed the best of their people, fighting for the Argives. If only
for a little while I could come like that to the house of my father,
my force and my invincible hands would terrify such men
as use force on him and keep him away from his rightful honors.'
    "So he spoke, and I again said to him in answer:
'I have no report to give you of stately Peleus,
but as for your beloved son Neoptolemos, I will
tell you, since you ask me to do it, all the true story;
for I myself, in the hollow hull of a balanced ship, brought him
over from Skyros, to join the strong-greaved Achaians. Whenever
we, around the city of Troy, talked over our counsels,
he would always speak first, and never blunder. In speaking
only godlike Nestor and I were better than he was.
And when we Achaians fought in the Trojan plain, he never
would hang back where there were plenty of other men, nor stay
        with
the masses, but run far out in front, giving way to no man
for fury, and many were those he killed in the terrible fighting.
I could not tell over the number of all nor name all
the people he killed as he fought for the Argives, but what a great
        man
was one, the son of Telephos he slew with the brazen
spear, the hero Eurypylos, and many Keteian
companions were killed about him, by reason of womanish presents.
Next to great Memnon, this was the finest man I ever
saw. Again, when we who were best of the Argives entered
the horse that Epeios made, and all the command was given
to me, to keep close hidden inside, or sally out from it,
the other leaders of the Danaans and men of counsel
were wiping their tears away and the limbs were shaking under
each man of them; but never at any time did I see him
losing his handsome color and going pale, or wiping
the tears off his face, but rather he implored me to let him
sally out of the horse; he kept feeling for his sword hilt
and spear weighted with bronze, full of evil thoughts for the
        Trojans.
But after we had sacked the sheer citadel of Priam,
with his fair share and a princely prize of his own, he boarded
his ship, unscathed; he had not been hit by thrown and piercing
bronze, nor stabbed in close-up combat, as often happens

in fighting. The War God rages at all, and favors no man.'

"So I spoke, and the soul of the swift-footed scion of Aiakos
stalked away in long strides across the meadow of asphodel,
happy for what I had said of his son, and how he was famous.

"Now the rest of the souls of the perished dead stood near me
grieving, and each one spoke to me and told of his sorrows.
Only the soul of Telamonian Aias stood off
at a distance from me, angry still over that decision
I won against him, when beside the ships we disputed
our cases for the arms of Achilleus. His queenly mother
set them as prize, and the sons of the Trojans, with Pallas Athene,
judged; and I wish I had never won in a contest like this,
so high a head has gone under the ground for the sake of that
    armor,
Aias, who for beauty and for achievement surpassed
all the Danaans next to the stately son of Peleus.
So I spoke to him now in words of conciliation:
'Aias, son of stately Telamon, could you then never
even in death forget your anger against me, because of
that cursed armor? The gods made it to pain the Achaians,
so great a bulwark were you, who were lost to them. We Achaians
grieved for your death as incessantly as for Achilleus
the son of Peleus at his death, and there is no other
to blame, but Zeus; he, in his terrible hate for the army
of Danaan spearmen, visited this destruction upon you.
Come nearer, my lord, so you can hear what I say and listen
to my story; suppress your anger and lordly spirit.'

"So I spoke. He gave no answer, but went off after
the other souls of the perished dead men, into the darkness."

Translated by Richmond Lattimore

From BOOK XII

SIRENS; SCYLLA AND CHARYBDIS

*Odysseus returns to Circe's island, where she tells him what comes next:
first the Sirens; then Scylla and Charybdis; and finally Trinacria, the
island of the cattle of the Sun, which he is to avoid at all costs.*

"She, shining among goddesses, went away, up the island.
Then, going back on board my ship, I told my companions
also to go aboard, and to cast off the stern cables,

and quickly they went aboard the ship and sat to the oarlocks,
and sitting well in order dashed the oars in the gray sea;
but fair-haired Circe, the dread goddess who talks with mortals,
sent us an excellent companion, a following wind, filling
the sails, to carry from astern the ship with the dark prow.
We ourselves, over all the ship making fast the running gear,
sat there, and let the wind and the steersman hold her steady.
Then, sorrowful as I was, I spoke and told my companions:
'Friends, since it is not right for one or two of us only
to know the divinations that Circe, bright among goddesses,
gave me, so I will tell you, and knowing all we may either
die, or turn aside from death and escape destruction.
First of all she tells us to keep away from the magical
Sirens and their singing and their flowery meadow, but only
I, she said, was to listen to them, but you must tie me
hard in hurtful bonds, to hold me fast in position
upright against the mast, with the ropes' ends fastened around it;
but if I supplicate you and implore you to set me
free, then you must tie me fast with even more lashings.'
    "So as I was telling all the details to my companions,
meanwhile the well-made ship was coming rapidly closer
to the Sirens' isle, for the harmless wind was driving her onward;
but immediately then the breeze dropped, and a windless
calm fell there, and some divinity stilled the tossing
waters. My companions stood up, and took the sails down,
and stowed them away in the hollow hull, and took their places
for rowing, and with their planed oarblades whitened the water.
Then I, taking a great wheel of wax, with the sharp bronze
cut a little piece off, and rubbed it together in my heavy
hands, and soon the wax grew softer, under the powerful
stress of the sun, and the heat and light of Hyperion's lordling.
One after another, I stopped the ears of all my companions,
and they then bound me hand and foot in the fast ship, standing
upright against the mast with the ropes' ends lashed around it,
and sitting then to row they dashed their oars in the gray sea.
But when we were as far from the land as a voice shouting
carries, lightly plying, the swift ship as it drew nearer
was seen by the Sirens, and they directed their sweet song toward us:
'Come this way, honored Odysseus, great glory of the Achaians,
and stay your ship, so that you can listen here to our singing;
for no one else has ever sailed past this place in his black ship
until he has listened to the honey-sweet voice that issues

from our lips; then goes on, well pleased, knowing more than ever
he did; for we know everything that the Argives and Trojans
did and suffered in wide Troy through the gods' despite.
Over all the generous earth we know everything that happens."
    "So they sang, in sweet utterance, and the heart within me
desired to listen, and I signaled my companions to set me
free, nodding with my brows, but they leaned on and rowed hard,
and Perimedes and Eurylochos, rising up, straightway
fastened me with even more lashings and squeezed me tighter.
But when they had rowed on past the Sirens, and we could no
        longer
hear their voices and lost the sound of their singing, presently
my eager companions took away from their ears the beeswax
with which I had stopped them. Then they set me free from my
        lashings.
    "But after we had left the island behind, the next thing
we saw was smoke, and a heavy surf, and we heard it thundering.
The men were terrified, and they let the oars fall out of
their hands, and these banged all about in the wash. The ship
        stopped
still, with the men no longer rowing to keep way on her.
Then I going up and down the ship urged on my companions,
standing beside each man and speaking to him in kind words:
'Dear friends, surely we are not unlearned in evils.
This is no greater evil now than it was when the Cyclops
had us cooped in his hollow cave by force and violence,
but even there, by my courage and counsel and my intelligence,
we escaped away. I think that all this will be remembered
some day too. Then do as I say, let us all be won over.
Sit well, all of you, to your oarlocks, and dash your oars deep
into the breaking surf of the water, so in that way Zeus
might grant that we get clear of this danger and flee away from it.
For you, steersman, I have this order; so store it deeply
in your mind, as you control the steering oar of this hollow
ship; you must keep her clear from where the smoke and the
        breakers
are, and make hard for the sea rock lest, without your knowing,
she might drift that way, and you bring all of us into disaster.'
    "So I spoke, and they quickly obeyed my words. I had not
spoken yet of Skylla, a plague that could not be dealt with,
for fear my companions might be terrified and give over
their rowing, and take cover inside the ship. For my part,

I let go from my mind the difficult instruction that Circe
had given me, for she told me not to be armed for combat;
but I put on my glorious armor and, taking up two long
spears in my hands, I stood bestriding the vessel's foredeck
at the prow, for I expected Skylla of the rocks to appear first
from that direction, she who brought pain to my companions.
I could not make her out anywhere, and my eyes grew weary
from looking everywhere on the misty face of the sea rock.
    "So we sailed up the narrow strait lamenting. On one side
was Skylla, and on the other side was shining Charybdis,
who made her terrible ebb and flow of the sea's water.
When she vomited it up, like a caldron over a strong fire,
the whole sea would boil up in turbulence, and the foam flying
spattered the pinnacles of the rocks in either direction;
but when in turn again she sucked down the sea's salt water,
the turbulence showed all the inner sea, and the rock around it
groaned terribly, and the ground showed at the sea's bottom,
black with sand; and green fear seized upon my companions.
We in fear of destruction kept our eyes on Charybdis,
but meanwhile Skylla out of the hollow vessel snatched six
of my companions, the best of them for strength and hands' work,
and when I turned to look at the ship, with my other companions,
I saw their feet and hands from below, already lifted
high above me, and they cried out to me and called me
by name, the last time they ever did it, in heart's sorrow.
And as a fisherman with a very long rod, on a jutting
rock, will cast his treacherous bait for the little fishes,
and sinks the horn of a field-ranging ox into the water,
then hauls them up and throws them on the dry land, gasping
and struggling, so they gasped and struggled as they were hoisted
up the cliff. Right in her doorway she ate them up. They were
        screaming
and reaching out their hands to me in this horrid encounter.
That was the most pitiful scene that these eyes have looked on
in my sufferings as I explored the routes over the water.
    "Now when we had fled away from the rocks and dreaded
        Charybdis
and Skylla, next we made our way to the excellent island
of the god, where ranged the handsome wide-browed oxen, and
        many
fat flocks of sheep, belonging to the Sun God, Hyperion.
While I was on the black ship, still out on the open water,
I heard the lowing of the cattle as they were driven

home, and the bleating of sheep, and my mind was struck by the
     saying
of the blind prophet, Teiresias the Theban, and also
Aiaian Circe. Both had told me many times over
to avoid the island of Helios who brings joy to mortals.
Then sorrowful as I was I spoke and told my companions:
'Listen to what I say, my companions, though you are suffering
evils, while I tell you the prophecies of Teiresias
and Aiaian Circe. Both have told me many times over
to avoid the island of Helios who brings joy to mortals,
for there they spoke of the most dreadful disaster that waited
for us. So drive the black ship onward, and pass the island.'
     "So I spoke, and the inward heart in them was broken.
At once Eurylochos answered me with a bitter saying:
'You are a hard man, Odysseus. Your force is greater,
your limbs never wear out. You must be made all of iron,
when you will not let your companions, worn with hard work and
     wanting
sleep, set foot on this land, where if we did, on the seagirt
island we could once more make ready a greedy dinner;
but you force us to blunder along just as we are through the running
night, driven from the island over the misty face of the water.
In the nights the hard stormwinds arise, and they bring damage
to ships. How could any of us escape sheer destruction,
if suddenly there rises the blast of a storm from the bitter
blowing of the South Wind or the West Wind, who beyond others
hammer a ship apart, in despite of the gods, our masters?
But now let us give way to black night's persuasion; let us
make ready our evening meal, remaining close by our fast ship,
and at dawn we will go aboard and put forth onto the wide sea.'
     "So spoke Eurylochos, and my other companions assented.
I saw then what evil the divinity had in mind for us. . . ."

                              Translated by Richmond Lattimore

From BOOK XXIII

ODYSSEUS AND PENELOPE

*Odysseus' foreboding soon proves justified. Once ashore, they are kept
on the island for a month by onshore gales. Supplies run out, and finally,
when Odysseus is absent from their camp, the crew kill the cattle of the
Sun and roast the flesh. The wind changes, they put to sea, and Zeus, at
the request of the Sun god, sends a storm that wrecks the ship. Odysseus*

is the only survivor; holding onto a piece of the mast, he is carried back
to the strait between Scylla and Charybdis. This time it is Charybdis, the
gigantic whirlpool, that he has to pass. He does so, and finally reaches
Calypso's island—and the end of the long tale he has told his Phaeacian
hosts. They load him with precious gifts and promise him passage home
at once.

They do what they promised: they land Odysseus on Ithaca, pile up
beside him the treasure Alcinous and the Phaeacian lords gave him, and
depart, leaving him fast asleep on the beach. Athena, who has helped
him, behind the scene and in disguise, ever since he reached the Phaeacian island, now decides to reveal herself and prepare him for the dangers and trials that await him at home. The long dialogue between hero
and goddess that follows is, like Odysseus' refusal of Calypso's offer of
immortality, unparalleled in Greek literature. The relationship between
them resembles a love affair, as if they were equals. Odysseus in fact
reproaches her for not coming to his aid before he reached Phaeacia, and
Athena explains why she was unable to do so. Equally remarkable is the
intriguing fact that the account he gives of himself, a tale set firmly in
the real world of battle by land and commerce by sea, is—like the similar
tales he will spin later for the swineherd Eumaeus; for Antinous, the
leader of the suitors; and for Penelope—a lie from beginning to end,
whereas the stories told at the Phaeacian court—stories of goddesses,
sorceresses, one-eyed giants, cannibals, and man-eating sea monsters—
were true.

Meanwhile, on his island,
his father's shore, that kingly man, Odysseus,
awoke, but could not tell what land it was
after so many years away; moreover,
Pallas Athena, Zeus' daughter, poured
a grey mist all around him, hiding him
from common sight—for she had things to tell him
and wished no one to know him, wife or townsmen,
before the suitors paid up for their crimes.

The landscape then looked strange, unearthly strange
to the Lord Odysseus: paths by hill and shore,
glimpses of harbors, cliffs, and summer trees.
He stood up, rubbed his eyes, gazed at his homeland,
and swore, slapping his thighs with both his palms,
then cried aloud:

"What am I in for now?
Whose country have I come to this time? Rough
savages and outlaws, are they, or
godfearing people, friendly to castaways?
Where shall I take these things? Where take myself,
with no guide, no directions? These should be
still in Phaiákian hands, and I uncumbered,
free to find some other openhearted
prince who might be kind and give me passage.
I have no notion where to store this treasure;
first-comer's trove it is, if I leave it here.

My lords and captains of Phaiákia
were not those decent men they seemed, not honorable,
landing me in this unknown country—no,
by god, they swore to take me home to Ithaka
and did not! Zeus attend to their reward,
Zeus, patron of petitioners, who holds
all other mortals under his eye; he takes
payment from betrayers!
                                        I'll be busy.
I can look through my gear. I shouldn't wonder
if they pulled out with part of it on board."

He made a tally of his shining pile—
tripods, cauldrons, cloaks, and gold—and found
he lacked nothing at all.
                                        And then he wept,
despairing, for his own land, trudging down
beside the endless wash of the wide, wide sea,
weary and desolate as the sea. But soon
Athena came to him from the nearby air,
putting a young man's figure on—a shepherd,
like a king's son, all delicately made.
She wore a cloak, in two folds off her shoulders,
and sandals bound upon her shining feet.
A hunting lance lay in her hands.

                                        At sight of her
Odysseus took heart, and he went forward
to greet the lad, speaking out fair and clear:

"Friend, you are the first man I've laid eyes on
here in this cove. Greetings. Do not feel
alarmed or hostile, coming across me; only
receive me into safety with my stores.
Touching your knees I ask it, as I might
ask grace of a god.
                              O sir, advise me,
what is this land and realm, who are the people?
Is it an island all distinct, or part
of the fertile mainland, sloping to the sea?"

To this grey-eyed Athena answered:

                              "Stranger,
you must come from the other end of nowhere,
else you are a great booby, having to ask
what place this is. It is no nameless country.
Why, everyone has heard of it, the nations
over on the dawn side, toward the sun,
and westerners in cloudy lands of evening.
No one would use this ground for training horses,
it is too broken, has no breadth of meadow;
but there is nothing meager about the soil,
the yield of grain is wondrous, and wine, too,
with drenching rains and dewfall.
                              There's good pasture
for oxen and for goats, all kinds of timber,
and water all year long in the cattle ponds.
For these blessings, friend, the name of Ithaka
has made its way even as far as Troy—
and they say Troy lies far beyond Akhaia."

Now Lord Odysseus, the long-enduring,
laughed in his heart, hearing his land described
by Pallas Athena, daughter of Zeus who rules
the veering stormwind; and he answered her
with ready speech—not that he told the truth,
but, just as she did, held back what he knew,
weighing within himself at every step
what he made up to serve his turn.

                              Said he:
"Far away in Krete I learned of Ithaka—

in that broad island over the great ocean.
And here I am now, come myself to Ithaka!
Here is my fortune with me. I left my sons
an equal part, when I shipped out. I killed
Orsílokhos, the courier, son of Idómeneus.
This man could beat the best cross country runners
in Krete, but he desired to take away
my Trojan plunder, all I had fought and bled for,
cutting through ranks in war and the cruel sea.
Confiscation is what he planned; he knew
I had not cared to win his father's favor
as a staff officer in the field at Troy,
but led my own command.
                              I acted: I
hit him with a spearcast from a roadside
as he came down from the open country. Murky
night shrouded all heaven and the stars.
I made that ambush with one man at arms.
We were unseen. I took his life in secret,
finished him off with my sharp sword. That night
I found asylum on a ship off shore
skippered by gentlemen of Phoinikia; I gave
all they could wish, out of my store of plunder,
for passage, and for landing me at Pylos
or Elis Town, where the Epeioi are in power.

Contrary winds carried them willy-nilly
past that coast; they had no wish to cheat me,
but we were blown off course.
                              Here, then, by night
we came, and made this haven by hard rowing.
All famished, but too tired to think of food,
each man dropped in his tracks after the landing,
and I slept hard, being wearied out. Before
I woke today, they put my things ashore
on the sand here beside me where I lay,
then reimbarked for Sidon, that great city.
Now they are far at sea, while I am left
forsaken here."

                    At this the grey-eyed goddess
Athena smiled, and gave him a caress,
her looks being changed now, so she seemed a woman,

tall and beautiful and no doubt skilled
at weaving splendid things. She answered briskly:

"Whoever gets around you must be sharp
and guileful as a snake; even a god
might bow to you in ways of dissimulation.
You! You chameleon!
Bottomless bag of tricks! Here in your own country
would you not give your stratagems a rest
or stop spellbinding for an instant?

You play a part as if it were your own tough skin.

No more of this, though. Two of a kind, we are,
contrivers, both. Of all men now alive
you are the best in plots and story telling.
My own fame is for wisdom among the gods—
deceptions, too.
                    Would even you have guessed
that I am Pallas Athena, daughter of Zeus,
I that am always with you in times of trial,
a shield to you in battle, I who made
the Phaiákians befriend you, to a man?

Now I am here again to counsel with you—
but first to put away those gifts the Phaiákians
gave you at departure—I planned it so.
Then I can tell you of the gall and wormwood
it is your lot to drink in your own hall.
Patience, iron patience, you must show;
so give it out to neither man nor woman
that you are back from wandering. Be silent
under all injuries, even blows from men."

His mind ranging far, Odysseus answered:

"Can mortal man be sure of you on sight,
even a sage, O mistress of disguises?
Once you were fond of me—I am sure of that—
years ago, when we Akhaians made
war, in our generation, upon Troy.
But after we had sacked the shrines of Priam

and put to sea, God scattered the Akhaians;
I never saw you after that never
knew you aboard with me, to act as shield
in grievous times—not till you gave me comfort
in the rich hinterland of the Phaiákians
and were yourself my guide into that city.

Hear me now in your father's name, for I
cannot believe that I have come to Ithaka.
It is some other land. You made that speech
only to mock me, and to take me in.
Have I come back in truth to my home island?"

To this the grey-eyed goddess Athena answered:

"Always the same detachment! That is why
I cannot fail you, in your evil fortune,
coolheaded, quick, well-spoken as you are!
Would not another wandering man, in joy,
make haste home to his wife and children? Not
you, not yet. Before you hear their story
you will have proof about your wife.

                          I tell you,
she still sits where you left her, and her days
and nights go by forlorn, in lonely weeping.
For my part, never had I despaired; I felt
sure of your coming home, though all your men
should perish; but I never cared to fight
Poseidon, Father's brother, in his baleful
rage with you for taking his son's eye.

Now I shall make you see the shape of Ithaka.
Here is the cove the sea lord Phorkys owns,
there is the olive spreading out her leaves
over the inner bay, and there the cavern
dusky and lovely, hallowed by the feet
of those immortal girls, the Naiadês—
the same wide cave under whose vault you came
to honor them with hekatombs—and there
Mount Neion, with his forest on his back!"

She had dispelled the mist, so all the island
stood out clearly. Then indeed Odysseus'
heart stirred with joy. He kissed the earth,
and lifting up his hands prayed to the nymphs:

"O slim shy Naiadês, young maids of Zeus,
I had not thought to see you ever again!
                     O listen smiling
to my gentle prayers, and we'll make offering
plentiful as in the old time, granted I
live, granted my son grows tall, by favor
of great Athena, Zeus' daughter,
who gives the winning fighter his reward!"

The grey-eyed goddess said directly:

                     "Courage;
and let the future trouble you no more.
We go to make a cache now, in the cave,
to keep your treasure hid. Then we'll consider
how best the present action may unfold."

The goddess turned and entered the dim cave,
exploring it for crannies, while Odysseus
carried up all the gold, the fire-hard bronze,
and well-made clothing the Phaiákians gave him.
Pallas Athena, daughter of Zeus the storm king,
placed them, and shut the cave mouth with a stone,
and under the old grey olive tree those two
sat down to work the suitors death and woe.
Grey-eyed Athena was the first to speak, saying:

"Son of Laërtês and the gods of old,
Odysseus, master of land ways and sea ways,
put your mind on a way to reach and strike
a crowd of brazen upstarts.
                   Three long years
they have played master in your house: three years
trying to win your lovely lady, making
gifts as though betrothed. And she? Forever
grieving for you, missing your return,
she has allowed them all to hope, and sent

messengers with promises to each—
though her true thoughts are fixed elsewhere."

                                              At this
the man of ranging mind, Odysseus, cried:

"So hard beset! An end like Agamémnon's
might very likely have been mine, a bad end,
bleeding to death in my own hall. You forestalled it,
goddess, by telling me how the land lies.
Weave me a way to pay them back! And you, too,
take your place with me, breathe valor in me
the way you did that night when we Akhaians
unbound the bright veil from the brow of Troy!
O grey-eyed one, fire my heart and brace me!
I'll take on fighting men three hundred strong
if you fight at my back, immortal lady!"

The grey-eyed goddess Athena answered him:

"No fear but I shall be there; you'll go forward
under my arm when the crux comes at last.
And I foresee your vast floor stained with blood,
spattered with brains of this or that tall suitor
who fed upon your cattle.
                              Now, for a while,
I shall transform you; not a soul will know you,
the clear skin of your arms and legs shriveled,
your chestnut hair all gone, your body dressed
in sacking that a man would gag to see,
and the two eyes, that were so brilliant, dirtied—
contemptible, you shall seem to your enemies,
as to the wife and son you left behind.

But join the swineherd first—the overseer
of all your swine, a good soul now as ever,
devoted to Penélopê and your son.
He will be found near Raven's Rock and the well
of Arethousa, where the swine are pastured,
rooting for acorns to their hearts' content,
drinking the dark still water. Boarflesh grows
pink and fat on that fresh diet. There

stay with him, and question him, while I
am off to the great beauty's land of Sparta,
to call your son Telémakhos home again—
for you should know, he went to the wide land
of Lakedaimon, Meneláos' country,
to learn if there were news of you abroad."

Odysseus answered:

                "Why not tell him, knowing
my whole history, as you do? Must he
traverse the barren sea, he too, and live
in pain, while others feed on what is his?"

At this the grey-eyed goddess Athena said:

"No need for anguish on that lad's account.
I sent him off myself, to make his name
in foreign parts—no hardship in the bargain,
taking his ease in Meneláos' mansion,
lapped in gold.
             The young bucks here, I know,
lie in wait for him in a cutter, bent
on murdering him before he reaches home.
I rather doubt they will. Cold earth instead
will take in her embrace a man or two
of those who fed so long on what is his."

Speaking no more, she touched him with her wand,
shriveled the clear skin of his arms and legs,
made all his hair fall out, cast over him
the wrinkled hide of an old man, and bleared
both his eyes, that were so bright. Then she
clapped an old tunic, a foul cloak, upon him,
tattered, filthy, stained by greasy smoke,
and over that a mangy big buck skin.
A staff she gave him, and a leaky knapsack
with no strap but a loop of string.

                  Now then,
their colloquy at an end, they went their ways—
Athena toward illustrious Lakedaimon
far over sea, to join Odysseus' son.

[*Odysseus goes, as planned, to the quarters of Eumaeus the swincherd, where he finds a man loyal to the memory of his lord. Meanwhile Athena goes to Sparta and tells Telemachus to go home. Following her advice, he avoids the trap set for him by the suitors, landing not at the port of Ithaca but on a distant beach. He goes to Eumaeus' hut, where Odysseus, momentarily transformed back to his real shape by Athena, reveals his identity to his son and tells him the plan for the defeat and killing of the suitors. Transformed once again into a filthy old beggar by the goddess, he makes his way to the palace guided by Eumaeus, who still does not know who he is. He finds the suitors feasting, and, passing among them begging for food, endures their taunts and insults, even blows, as both Antinous, their leader, and Eurymachus, his rival, hurl footstools at him. At night Penelope comes to question him, hoping for news of Odysseus; his false tale of seeing Odysseus on Crete on his way to Troy brings tears to her eyes. But when Eurycleia, his old nurse, ordered to wash his feet, recognizes him by the the scar on his thigh, he silences her; it is not yet time to reveal his identity. He finds another loyal man in Philoetius, the herdsman, and warns both him and Eumaeus that Odysseus will soon appear, enlisting them on his side.*

At this point Penelope, inspired by Athena, declares that any suitor who can bend and string the bow of Odysseus and then shoot an arrow through a line of ax-heads, will win her hand in marriage. The principal suitors try, one after another, to string the bow, but fail. Odysseus claims the right to try, strings it at once, and revealing his identity, shoots Antinous and Eurymachus. Then, aided by Telemachus, Eumaeus, and Philoetius, not to mention Athena, who turns aside the spears the suitors throw, he slaughters the whole lot of them. He directs a clean-up of the great hall, and sends Eurycleia to bring Penelope down from her room.]

The old nurse went upstairs exulting,
with knees toiling, and patter of slapping feet,
to tell the mistress of her lord's return,
and cried out by the lady's pillow:

                    "Wake,
wake up, dear child! Penélopê, come down,
see with your own eyes what all these years you longed for!
Odysseus is here! Oh, in the end, he came!
And he has killed your suitors, killed them all
who made his house a bordel and ate his cattle
and raised their hands against his son!"

                                        Penélopê said:
"Dear nurse . . . the gods have touched you.
They can put chaos into the clearest head
or bring a lunatic down to earth. Good sense
you always had. They've touched you. What is this
mockery you wake me up to tell me,
breaking in on my sweet spell of sleep?
I had not dozed away so tranquilly
since my lord went to war, on that ill wind
to Ilion.
              Oh, leave me! Back down stairs!
If any other of my women came in babbling
things like these to startle me, I'd see her
flogged out of the house! Your old age spares you that."

Eurýkleia said:

"Would I play such a trick on you, dear child?
It is true, true, as I tell you, he has come!
That stranger they were baiting was Odysseus.
Telémakhos knew it days ago—
cool head, never to give his father away,
till he paid off those swollen dogs!"

The lady in her heart's joy now sprang up
with sudden dazzling tears, and hugged the old one,
crying out:

               "But try to make it clear!
If he came home in secret, as you say,
could he engage them singlehanded? How?
They were all down there, still in the same crowd."

To this Eurýkleia said:

                            "I did not see it,
I knew nothing; only I heard the groans
of men dying. We sat still in the inner rooms
holding our breath, and marvelling, shut in,
until Telémakhos came to the door and called me—
your own dear son, sent this time by his father!
So I went out, and found Odysseus

erect, with dead men littering the floor
this way and that. If you had only seen him!
It would have made your heart glow hot!—a lion
splashed with mire and blood.
                              But now the cold
corpses are all gathered at the gate,
and he has cleansed his hall with fire and brimstone,
a great blaze. Then he sent me here to you.
Come with me: you may both embark this time
for happiness together, after pain,
after long years. Here is your prayer, your passion,
granted: your own lord lives, he is at home,
he found you safe, he found his son. The suitors
abused his house, but he has brought them down."

The attentive lady said:

                         "Do not lose yourself
in this rejoicing: wait: you know
how splendid that return would be for us,
how dear to me, dear to his son and mine;
but no, it is not possible, your notion
must be wrong.
                Some god has killed the suitors,
a god, sick of their arrogance and brutal
malice—for they honored no one living,
good or bad, who ever came their way.
Blind young fools, they've tasted death for it.
But the true person of Odysseus?
He lost his home, he died far from Akhaia."

The old nurse sighed:

                     "How queer, the way you talk!
Here he is, large as life, by his own fire,
and you deny he ever will get home!
Child, you always were mistrustful!
But there is one sure mark that I can tell you:
that scar left by the boar's tusk long ago.
I recognized it when I bathed his feet
and would have told you, but he stopped my mouth,
forbade me, in his craftiness.

                              Come down,
I stake my life on it, he's here!
Let me die in agony if I lie!"

                              Penélopê said:
"Nurse dear, though you have your wits about you,
still it is hard not to be taken in
by the immortals. Let us join my son, though,
and see the dead and that strange one who killed them."
She turned then to descend the stair, her heart
in tumult. Had she better keep her distance
and question him, her husband? Should she run
up to him, take his hands, kiss him now?
Crossing the door sill she sat down at once
in firelight, against the nearest wall,
across the room from the lord Odysseus.
                              There
leaning against a pillar, sat the man
and never lifted up his eyes, but only waited
for what his wife would say when she had seen him.
And she, for a long time, sat deathly still
in wonderment—for sometimes as she gazed
she found him—yes, clearly—like her husband,
but sometimes blood and rags were all she saw.
Telémakhos' voice came to her ears:

                              "Mother,
cruel mother, do you feel nothing,
drawing yourself apart this way from Father?
Will you not sit with him and talk and question him?
What other woman could remain so cold?
Who shuns her lord, and he come back to her
from wars and wandering, after twenty years?
Your heart is hard as flint and never changes!"

Penélopê answered:

                              "I am stunned, child.
I cannot speak to him. I cannot question him.
I cannot keep my eyes upon his face.
If really he is Odysseus, truly home,
beyond all doubt we two shall know each other

better than you or anyone. There are
secret signs we know, we two."

A smile
came now to the lips of the patient hero, Odysseus,
who turned to Telémakhos and said:

"Peace: let your mother test me at her leisure.
Before long she will see and know me best.
These tatters, dirt—all that I'm caked with now—
make her look hard at me and doubt me still.
As to this massacre, we must see the end.
Whoever kills one citizen, you know,
and has no force of armed men at his back,
had better take himself abroad by night
and leave his kin. Well, we cut down the flower of Ithaka,
the mainstay of the town. Consider that."

Telémakhos replied respectfully:

"Dear Father,
enough that you yourself study the danger,
foresighted in combat as you are,
they say you have no rival.
We three stand
ready to follow you and fight. I say
for what our strength avails, we have the courage."

And the great tactician, Odysseus, answered:

"Good.
Here is our best maneuver, as I see it:
bathe, you three, and put fresh clothing on,
order the women to adorn themselves,
and let our admirable harper choose a tune
for dancing, some lighthearted air, and strum it.
Anyone going by, or any neighbor,
will think it is a wedding feast he hears.
These deaths must not be cried about the town
till we can slip away to our own woods. We'll see
what weapon, then, Zeus puts into our hands."

They listened attentively, and did his bidding,
bathed and dressed afresh; and all the maids
adorned themselves. Then Phêmios the harper
took his polished shell and plucked the strings,
moving the company to desire
for singing, for the sway and beat of dancing,
until they made the manor hall resound
with gaiety of men and grace of women.
Anyone passing on the road would say:

"Married at last, I see—the queen so many courted.
Sly, cattish wife! She would not keep—not she!—
the lord's estate until he came."

                              So travellers'
thoughts might run—but no one guessed the truth.
Greathearted Odysseus, home at last,
was being bathed now by Eurýnomê
and rubbed with golden oil, and clothed again
in a fresh tunic and a cloak. Athena
lent him beauty, head to foot. She made him
taller, and massive, too, with crisping hair
in curls like petals of wild hyacinth
but all red-golden. Think of gold infused
on silver by a craftsman, whose fine art
Hephaistos taught him, or Athena: one
whose work moves to delight: just so she lavished
beauty over Odysseus' head and shoulders.
He sat then in the same chair by the pillar,
facing his silent wife, and said:

                              "Strange woman,
the immortals of Olympos made you hard,
harder than any. Who else in the world
would keep aloof as you do from her husband
if he returned to her from years of trouble,
cast on his own land in the twentieth year?

Nurse, make up a bed for me to sleep on.
Her heart is iron in her breast."

                         Penélopê
spoke to Odysseus now. She said:

                              "Strange man,
if man you are . . . This is no pride on my part
nor scorn for you—not even wonder, merely.
I know so well how you—how he—appeared
boarding the ship for Troy. But all the same . . .

Make up his bed for him, Eurýkleia.
Place it outside the bedchamber my lord
built with his own hands. Pile the big bed
with fleeces, rugs, and sheets of purest linen."

With this she tried him to the breaking point,
and he turned on her in a flash raging:

"Woman, by heaven you've stung me now!
Who dared to move my bed?
No builder had the skill for that—unless
a god came down to turn the trick. No mortal
in his best days could budge it with a crowbar.
There is our pact and pledge, our secret sign,
built into that bed—my handiwork
and no one else's!

                      And old trunk of olive
grew like a pillar on the building plot,
and I laid out our bedroom round that tree,
lined up the stone walls, built the walls and roof,
gave it a doorway and smooth-fitting doors.
Then I lopped off the silvery leaves and branches,
hewed and shaped that stump from the roots up
into a bedpost, drilled it, let it serve
as model for the rest. I planed them all,
inlaid them all with silver, gold and ivory,
and stretched a bed between—a pliant web
of oxhide thongs dyed crimson.
                              There's our sign!
I know no more. Could someone's else's hand
have sawn that trunk and dragged the frame away?"

Their secret! as she heard it told, her knees
grew tremulous and weak, her heart failed her.
With eyes brimming tears she ran to him,
throwing her arms around his neck, and kissed him,
murmuring:

              "Do not rage at me, Odysseus!
No one ever matched your caution! Think
what difficulty the gods gave: they denied us
life together in our prime and flowering years,
kept us from crossing into age together.
Forgive me, don't be angry. I could not
welcome you with love on sight! I armed myself
long ago against the frauds of men,
impostors who might come—and all those many
whose underhanded ways bring evil on!
Helen of Argos, daughter of Zeus and Leda,
would she have joined the stranger, lain with him,
if she had known her destiny? known the Akhaians
in arms would bring her back to her own country?
Surely a goddess moved her to adultery,
her blood unchilled by war and evil coming,
the years, the desolation; ours, too.
But here and now, what sign could be so clear
as this of our own bed?
No other man has ever laid eyes on it—
only my own slave, Aktoris, that my father
sent with me as a gift—she kept our door.
You make my stiff heart know that I am yours."

Now from his breast into his eyes the ache
of longing mounted, and he wept at last,
his dear wife, clear and faithful, in his arms,
longed for
              as the sunwarmed earth is longed for by a swimmer
spent in rough water where his ship went down
under Poseidon's blows, gale winds and tons of sea.
Few men can keep alive through a big surf
to crawl, clotted with brine, on kindly beaches
in joy, in joy, knowing the abyss behind:
and so she too rejoiced, her gaze upon her husband,
her white arms round him pressed as though forever.

The rose Dawn might have found them weeping still
had not grey-eyed Athena slowed the night
when night was most profound, and held the Dawn
under the Ocean of the East. That glossy team,
Firebright and Daybright, the Dawn's horses
that draw her heavenward for men—Athena
stayed their harnessing.

                    Then said Odysseus:
"My dear, we have not won through to the end.
One trial—I do not know how long—is left for me
to see fulfilled. Teirêsias' ghost forearned me
the night I stood upon the shore of Death, asking
about my friends' homecoming and my own.

But now the hour grows late, it is bed time,
rest will be sweet for us; let us lie down."

To this Penélopê replied:

                    "That bed,
that rest is yours whenever desire moves you,
now the kind powers have brought you home at last.
But as your thought has dwelt upon it, tell me:
what is the trial you face? I must know soon;
what does it matter if I learn tonight?"

The teller of many stories said:

                    "My strange one,
must you again, and even now,
urge me to talk? Here is a plodding tale;
no charm in it, no relish in the telling.
Teirêsias told me I must take an oar
and trudge the mainland, going from town to town,
until I discover men who have never known
the salt blue sea, nor flavor of salt meat—
strangers to painted prows, to watercraft
and oars like wings, dipping across the water.
The moment of revelation he foretold
was this, for you may share the prophecy:
some traveller falling in with me will say:

'A winnowing fan, that on your shoulder, sir?'
There I must plant my oar, on the very spot,
with burnt offerings to Poseidon of the Waters:
a ram, a bull, a great buck boar. Thereafter
when I come home again, I am to slay
full hekatombs to the gods who own broad heaven,
one by one.
            Then death will drift upon me
from seaward, mild as air, mild as your hand,
in my well-tended weariness of age,
contented folk around me on our island.
He said all this must come."

                    Penélopê said:
"If by the gods' grace age at least is kind,
we have that promise—trials will end in peace."

So he confided in her, and she answered.
Meanwhile Eurýnomê and the nurse together
laid soft coverlets on the master's bed,
working in haste by torchlight. Eurýkleia
retired to her quarters for the night,
and then Eurýnomê, as maid-in-waiting,
lighted her lord and lady to their chamber
with bright brands.

            She vanished.
                    So they came
into that bed so steadfast, loved of old,
opening glad arms to one another.

                    Translated by Robert Fitzgerald

[*The two great Alexandrian editors and critics of Homer, Aristophanes
of Byzantium and Aristarchus of Samothrace, seem to have stated that
this last line—"opening glad arms to one another"—verse 296 of Book
XXIII, was the "boundary" or "end" of the* Odyssey. *Modern scholars
are still debating the question, some finding a falling off in quality in the
rest of the poem. Yet, as Odysseus himself points out, there is more
trouble to come; they have "cut down the flower of Ithaca," 108 young
aristocrats, and their relatives are still to be reckoned with. And Odysseus has not yet met his father Laertes, who is still alive. It is to the house*

in the country to which old Laertes has retired that Odysseus and his three allies make their way, and it is there that a mob of angry Ithacans arrives in arms. Telemachus kills their leader, but Athena puts a stop to the fighting and reconciles the two sides.]

HESIOD
7th Century B.C.?

From *THE WORKS AND DAYS*

Hesiod's date is as uncertain as Homer's, but he is usually thought of as active around 700 B.C. Though he uses the same hexameter line as Homer, his poems are not epic in theme. The Theogony *begins with a description of the emergence of the universe from chaos and goes on the describe the genealogy of the gods. The* Works and Days, *on the other hand, deals with work—work on the land—and then, in a very brief section, with "the days that come from Zeus, all in the right order," special days of the month that have religious significance or are propitious for different occasions or enterprises. The poem is concerned, as no other extant Greek work of literature is, with the work that, until the coming of the Industrial Revolution in the West, has been the hard lot of the majority of humankind—the year-long, backbreaking incessant work of plowing, sowing, and reaping, of threshing, winnowing, and grinding. Such things are hardly mentioned elsewhere, except sometimes in a simile in Homer, where, used as a comparison with some phenomenon of battle or seafaring, they give us an occasional glimpse of the labor that supported the life style of the princes and warriors of the heroic tale.*

Our two translators, Richmond Lattimore and Apostolos Athanassakis, both use a long line modeled on Hesiod's hexameter, the meter of Homer; Lattimore breaks it up into two shorter units.

The opening section of the Works *tries to deal with the question: Why do we have to work so hard? It might have been different. It is the*

same question asked, and answered, by the story of Adam and Eve in the
Hebrew Genesis. There was no work in Eden, but because of the sin of
Eve and Adam, the Lord says to them: "Cursed is the ground for thy
sake; in sorrow shalt thou eat of it all thy life. . . . In the sweat of thy face
shalt thou eat bread. . . ." In Hesiod's explanation, humanity is not
directly responsible for its plight. The demigod Prometheus defied Zeus
and gave us the forbidden gift of fire, the basis of civilized arts and crafts.
Zeus, enraged, punished not only Prometheus but also the human race.
The instrument of punishment was a woman, Pandora, who let loose on
the world all the evils that still plague us—work, sickness, old age. In
both accounts it is a woman—Eve or Pandora—who is the cause of all
our troubles. Perhaps this emphasis is typical of peasant societies, in
which the birth of a daughter, who cannot push the plow and who must
have a dowry if she is to be married, is often viewed with misgiving
rather than joy.

PANDORA

For the gods have hidden and keep hidden
what could be men's livelihood.
It could have been that easily
in one day you could work out
enough to keep you for a year,
with no more working.
Soon you could have hung up your steering oar
in the smoke of the fireplace,
and the work the oxen and patient mules do
would be abolished,
but Zeus in the anger of his heart hid it away
because the devious-minded Prometheus had cheated him;
and therefore Zeus thought up dismal sorrows
for mankind.
He hid fire; but Prometheus, the powerful son
of Iapetos,
stole it again from Zeus of the counsels,
to give to mortals.
He hid it out of the sight of Zeus
who delights in thunder
in the hollow fennel stalk. In anger
the cloud-gatherer spoke to him:
"Son of Iapetos, deviser of crafts beyond all others,

you are happy that you stole thc firc,
  and outwitted my thinking;
but it will be a great sorrow to you,
  and to men who come after.
As the price of fire I will give them an evil,
  and all men shall fondle
this, their evil, close to their hearts,
  and take delight in it."
  So spoke the father of gods and mortals;
  and laughed out loud.
He told glorious Hephaistos to make haste, and plaster
earth with water, and to infuse it with a human voice
and vigor, and make the face
  like the immortal goddesses,
the bewitching features of a young girl;
  meanwhile Athene
was to teach her her skills, and how
  to do the intricate weaving,
while Aphrodite was to mist her head
  in golden endearment
and the cruelty of desire and longings
  that wear out the body,
but to Hermes, the guide, the slayer of Argos,
  he gave instructions
to put in her the mind of a hussy,
  and a treacherous nature.
  So Zeus spoke. And all obeyed Lord Zeus,
  the son of Kronos.
The renowned strong smith modeled her figure of earth,
  in the likeness
of a decorous young girl, as the son of Kronos
  had wished it.
The goddess gray-eyed Athene dressed and arrayed her;
  the Graces,
who are goddesses, and hallowed Persuasion
  put necklaces
of gold upon her body, while the Seasons,
  with glorious tresses,
put upon her head a coronal of spring flowers,
[and Pallas Athene put all decor upon her body].
But into her heart Hermes, the guide,
  the slayer of Argos,

put lies, and wheedling words
  of falsehood, and a treacherous nature,
made her as Zeus of the deep thunder wished,
  and he, the gods' herald,
put a voice inside her, and gave her
  the name of woman,
Pandora, because all the gods
  who have their homes on Olympos
had given her each a gift, to be a sorrow to men
who eat bread. Now when he had done
  with this sheer, impossible
deception, the Father sent the gods' fleet messenger,
  Hermes,
to Epimetheus, bringing her, a gift,
  nor did Epimetheus
remember to think how Prometheus had told him never
to accept a gift from Olympian Zeus,
  but always to send it
back, for fear it might prove
  to be an evil for mankind.
He took the evil, and only perceived it
  when he possessed her.
    Since before this time the races of men
  had been living on earth
free from all evils, free from laborious work,
  and free from
all wearing sicknesses that bring
  their fates down on men
[for men grow old suddenly
  in the midst of misfortune];
but the woman, with her hands lifting away the lid
  from the great jar,
scattered its contents, and her design
  was sad troubles for mankind.
Hope was the only spirit that stayed there
  in the unbreakable
closure of the jar, under its rim,
  and could not fly forth
abroad, for the lid of the great jar
  closed down first and contained her;
this was by the will of cloud-gathering Zeus
  of the aegis;

but there are other troubles by thousands
    that hover about men,
for the earth is full of evil things,
    and the sea is full of them;
there are sicknesses that come to men by day,
    while in the night
moving of themselves they haunt us,
    bringing sorrow to mortals,
and silently, for Zeus of the counsels
    took the voice out of them.

So there is no way to avoid what Zeus has intended.

                              Translated by Richmond Lattimore

THE FIVE AGES

*Hesiod proceeds to expound another myth that deals with the present
miserable state of humanity, the story of the five ages. It could have been
otherwise, he said at the beginning of the tale of Prometheus and Pandora; in the golden age, it was—the earth yielded its crops without men
having to do a hand's turn. But the golden age was succeeded by the
silver, the bronze, and the iron ages, each worse than the one before.
Our age, the iron, is the worst of all, and will get worse still. This myth of
human regress, expressed in terms of metallic ages, has many parallels in
the lore of the Middle East. The same four metals turn up in a Persian
myth; and in the Book of Daniel, Nebuchadnezzar, the Babylonian conqueror of Jerusalem, dreams of an image with a head of gold, breast and
arms of silver, belly and thighs of brass, and feet part iron and part clay.
The prophet Daniel interprets it as a succession of kingdoms, each inferior to its predecessor.*

*Hesiod's version, however, interrupts the process of steady degenera-
tion by inserting a non-metallic age just before the arrival of the iron age
in which we now live. It is the age of the "divine race of heroes" who
fought at seven-gated Thebes and at Troy; and although some died in
battle, others were settled by Zeus in the islands of the blessed, where
crops ripen three times a year. Hesiod interrupts the downhill sequence
with this glamorous vision because the Greeks all believed that there was
a great heroic age (a memory, perhaps, of Mycenean civilization) immediately preceding the miserable age they now lived in, and so it had to be
inserted, even though it is not associated with a metal and does not fit
the pattern of the story. What it does, though, is to intensify the wretch-*

edness of humanity's present state, a relapse into degeneration after a
glorious break with the relentless decline from the golden age.

At first the immortals who dwell on Olympos
created a golden race of mortal men.
That was when Kronos was king of the sky,
and they lived like gods, carefree in their hearts,
shielded from pain and misery. Helpless old age
did not exist, and with limbs of unsagging vigor
they enjoyed the delights of feasts, out of evil's reach.
A sleeplike death subdued them, and every good thing was theirs;
the barley-giving earth asked for no toil to bring forth
a rich and plentiful harvest. They knew no constraint
and lived in peace and abundance as lords of their lands,
rich in flocks and dear to the blessed gods.
But the earth covered this race,
and they became holy spirits that haunt it,
benign protectors of mortals that drive harm away
and keep a watchful eye over lawsuits and wicked deeds,
swathed in misty veils as they wander over the earth.
They are givers of wealth by kingly prerogative.
The gods of Olympos made a second race
—a much worse one—this time of silver,
unlike the golden one in thought or looks.
For a hundred years they were nurtured by their prudent mothers
as playful children—each a big baby in his house—
but when they grew up and reached adolescence
they lived only for a short while, plagued by the pains
of foolishness. They could not refrain from reckless violence
against one another and did not want to worship the gods
and on holy altars perform sacrifices for them,
as custom differing from place to place dictates.
In time Zeus, son of Kronos, was angered and buried them
because they denied the blessed Olympians their due honors.
The earth covered this race, too;
they dwell under the ground and are called blessed mortals—
they are second but, still, greatly honored.
Zeus the father made a third race of mortals,
this time of bronze, not at all like the silver one.
Fashioned from ash trees, they were dreadful and mighty
and bent on the harsh deeds of war and violence;

they ate no bread and their hearts were strong as steel.
No one could come near them, for their strength was great
and mighty arms grew from the shoulders of their sturdy bodies.
Bronze were their weapons, bronze their homes
and bronze was what they worked—there was no black iron then.
With their hands they worked one another's destruction
and they reached the dank home of cold Hades
nameless. Black death claimed them for all their fierceness,
and they left the bright sunlight behind them.
But when the earth covered this race, too,
Zeus, son of Kronos, made upon the nourishing land
yet another race—the fourth one—better and more just.
They were the divine race of heroes, who are called
demigods; they preceded us on this boundless earth.
Evil war and dreadful battle wiped them all out,
some fighting over the flocks of Oidipous
at seven-gated Thebes, in the land of Kadmos,
others over the great gulf of the sea in ships
that had sailed to Troy for the sake of lovely-haired Helen;
there death threw his dark mantle over them.
Yet others of them father Zeus, son of Kronos, settled at earth's
    ends,
apart from men, and gave them shelter and food.
They lived there with hearts unburdened by cares
in the islands of the blessed, near stormy Okeanos,
these blissful heroes for whom three times a year
the barley-giving land brings forth full grain sweet as honey.
I wish I were not counted among the fifth race of men,
but rather had died before, or been born after it.
This is the race of iron. Neither day nor night
will give them rest as they waste away with toil
and pain. Growing cares will be given them by the gods,
and their lot will be a blend of good and bad.
Zeus will destroy this race of mortals
when children are born gray at the temples.
Children will not resemble their fathers,
and there will be no affection between guest and host
and no love between friends or brothers as in the past.
Sons and daughters will be quick to offend their aging parents
and rebuke them and speak to them with rudeness
and cruelty, not knowing about divine retribution;
they will not even repay their parents for their keep—

these law-breakers—and they will sack one another's cities,
The man who keeps his oath, or is just and good,
will not be favored, but the evil-doers and scoundrels
will be honored, for might will make right and shame will vanish.
Base men will harm their betters with words
that are crooked and then swear they are fair.
And all toiling humanity will be blighted by envy,
grim and strident envy that takes its joy in the ruin of others.
Then Shame and Retribution will cover their fair bodies
with white cloaks and, leaving men behind,
will go to Olympos from the broad-pathed earth
to be among the race of the immortals, while grief and pain
will linger among men, whom harm will find defenseless.

Translated by Apostolos Athanassakis

WHEN TO PLOW

At the time when you hear the cry of the crane
   going over, that annual
voice from high in the clouds, you should take notice
   and make plans.
She brings the signal for the beginning of planting,
   the winter
season of rains, but she bites the heart
   of the man without oxen.
At this time, keep your horn-curved oxen indoors,
   and feed them.
It is easy to make a speech: "Please give me two oxen
   and a wagon."
But it's also easy to answer: "I have plenty of work
   for my oxen."
And a man, rich in his dreams, sees his wagon
   as built already,
the idiot, forgetting that the wagon has
   a hundred timbers,
and it takes some work to have these laid up at home,
   beforehand.
   At the first moment when the plowing season
   appears for mankind,
set hard to work, your servants, yourself,
   everybody together

plowing through wet weather and dry
  in the plowing season;
rise early and drive the work along, so your fields
  will be full.
Plow fallow in spring. Fallow land turned in summer
  will not disappoint you.
Fallow land should be sown while the soil
  is still light and dry.
Fallow land is kind to children, and keeps off
  the hexes.
  Make your prayers to Zeus of the ground
  and holy Demeter
that the sacred yield of Demeter may grow complete,
  and be heavy.
Do this when you begin your first planting, when,
  gripping the handle
in one hand, you come down hard with the goad
  on the backs of your oxen
as they lean into the pin of the straps.
  Have a small boy helping you
by following and making hard work for the birds
  with a mattock
covering the seed over. It is best to do things
  systematically,
since we are only human, and disorder
  is our worst enemy.
Do as I tell you, and the ears will
  sweep the ground in their ripeness,
if the Olympian himself grants that all
  shall end well;
and you can knock the spider-webs from your bins,
  and, as I hope,
be happy as you draw on all that substance
  that's stored up.
You will have plenty to make it till the next
  gray spring; you need not
gaze longingly at others. It's the other man
  who will need you.
  But if you have waited for the winter solstice
  to plow the divine earth,
you will have to squat down to reap, gathering it
  in thin handfuls,

down in the dust, cross-binding for the looks of it,
  not very happy;
you will bring it home in a basket,
  and there will be few to admire you.

Translated by Richmond Lattimore

SUMMER

When the thistle blooms and the chirping cicada
sits on trees and pours down shrill song
from frenziedly quivering wings in the toilsome summer,
then goats are fatter than ever and wine is at its best;
women's lust knows no bounds and men are all dried up,
because the dog star parches their heads and knees
and the heat sears their skin. Then, ah then,
I wish you a shady ledge and your choice wine,
bread baked in the dusk and mid-August's goat milk
and meat from a free-roving heifer that has never calved—
and from firstling kids. Drink sparkling wine,
sitting in the shade with your appetite sated,
and face Zephyr's breeze as it blows from mountain peaks.
Pour three measures of water fetched from a clear spring,
one that flows unchecked, and a fourth one of wine.

Translated by Apostolos Atharassakis

WINTER

*This description of the rigors of winter may come as a surprise to those
who know Greece only from visits in the summer months. Hesiod's
"month of Lenaion" is December–January. The smithy, with its furnace, is the only warm place in the village and so the natural center for
the men to congregate and gossip. "Mr. Boneless" is an example of
"kenning"; it is a riddling name for the octopus. The ancient Greeks
believed that the octopus nibbled at its tentacles when short of food.
Aristotle denied this, but modern zoologists have established that it does
sometimes happen, not from hunger but under stress.*

Walk past the smithy and its crowded lounge
in winter when cold keeps men away from work
—even then an industrious man can increase his fortune—

so that in the grip of an evil winter's needy impasse
you are not forced to rub your swollen feet with a scrawny hand.
The lazy man trusts in empty hope and is left
without means; so his mind is turned to wrongdoing.
It is the wrong kind of hope that courts the poor,
who do not have enough and yet gossip in idleness.
Before midsummer has passed tell your slaves:
"Build barns! It will not be summer forever."
In the month of Lenaion the days are bad;
they skin oxen alive. Beware of this month and its frosts
that grip the earth when the gusty north wind
stirs the broad sea and blows through Thrace
—that nurturer of horses—as land and forest bellow.
Up in the mountain woodlands it blows against many high-crested
    oaks and sturdy firs
and fells them to the rich earth as the vast forest groans.
Wild beasts shiver then and curl their tails under their bellies—
chilly wind pierces the shag that coats the breasts
even of animals whose skin is covered with deep fur;
it will go through the hide of an ox
and through a goat's long hair, but fleecy sheep
are safe from the blast of the north wind.
It sends an old man scurrying for protection,
but does not blow through to a maiden's tender skin,
for she stays indoors with her dear mother,
still unaware of golden Aphrodite's deeds;
she bathes her soft skin well and rubs it down
to sleekness with oil and then lies down, hidden away in her
    bedroom.
So it is in the winter when Mr. Boneless chews his foot
in the gloomy haunts, where his fireless house lies;
for the sun does not show him the way to the feeding grounds
but circles over those who dwell in the lands
of black men and is slow to shine on all the Greeks.
Then horned and hornless lodgers of the forest,
teeth chattering wretchedly, flee throughout the woodlands
and there is only one thought in their hearts:
they long to find shelter in windproof lairs
inside some hollow rock. Then mortals have three legs;
their backs are bent and their heads sweep the ground—
they are walking tripods fleeing the white snow.
Then you must clothe your body well
with a fringed tunic and a soft cloak over it.

Weave cloth in which there is much weft for little warp
and wear it, so that your hair does not stand on end
and bristle all over your body.
From the skin of a slaughtered ox make sandals
lined with felt and bind them snugly about your feet.
When the cold season comes stitch together skins
of firstling kids with an ox sinew and wrap your back
with them to keep the rain off; and on your head
wear a tight-fitting cap to keep your ears dry.
Mornings are cold when the north wind blows
and damp fog descends from the starry sky
and hovers like a chilly veil over men's wheat patches.
This is a mist drawn up from ever-flowing rivers
and then raised by stormy winds high above the earth;
sometimes it comes as evening rain and often as wind
when Thracian gusts whip thick clouds to frenzy.
Run faster than this wind; finish work and head for home,
wary of a dark cloud that swoops from the sky to envelope you
and soak your body and clothes until you are dripping wet.
Take precautions. This is a wintry and stormy month,
cruel for men and cruel for sheep.
Give oxen half rations and men more than their usual share
because the kindly nights are now too long.
Heed this advice until the end of the year,
when nights and days are no longer unequal
and until the earth, mother of all, gives her many fruits.

Translated by Apostolos Athanassakis

SAILING SEASONS

*Hesiod's admission that he is "not one who has much knowledge of ships
and sea voyages" is more than borne out by the length of the one sea
voyage he claims to have made. The distance from Aulis to the coast of
Euboea is about sixty-five meters.*

. . . Wait for the time to come when a voyage
is in season.
Then drag your swift ship down to the sea,
and put in a cargo
that will be suitable for it, so you can bring home
a profit,

as did my father, and yours too, O Perses,
  you great fool,
who used to sail in ships, for he wanted to live
  like a noble,
and once on a time, leaving Kyme of Aiolis,
  he came here
in his black ship, having crossed over
  a vast amount of water;
and it was not comfort he was fleeing, nor wealth,
  nor prosperity,
but that evil poverty that Zeus gives men
  for a present;
and settled here near Helikon in a hole of a village,
Askra, bad in winter, tiresome in summer,
  and good at no season.
  As for you, Perses, remember the timely seasons
  for all work
done, but remember it particularly about seafaring.
Admire a little ship, but put your cargo in a big one.
The bigger the cargo, the bigger will be
  the profit added
to profit—if only the winds hold off
  their harsh gales from it.
  But for when, turning your easily blown thoughts
  toward a merchant's
life, you wish to escape your debts,
  and unhappy hunger,
I will show you the measures
  of the much-thundering sea, I
who am not one who has much knowledge of ships
  and sea voyages;
for I never did sail in a ship across the wide water
except across to Euboia from Aulis, where once
  the Achaians
stayed out the storm and gathered together
  a great many people
from sacred Hellas to go to Troy,
  the land of fair women.
There I crossed over to Chalkis
  for the games held in honor
of gallant Amphidamas, for the sons
  of this great-hearted

man had set out many chosen prizes. There,
    I can claim,
I won the contest with a song
    and took off an eared tripod;
and this I set up as an offering
    to the Muses of Helikon,
where they first had made me a master
    of melodious singing.
This is all my experience with intricately bolted
ships, but still I can tell you the thought,
    which is of aegis-bearing
Zeus, for the Muses have taught me to sing
    immortal poetry.
    For fifty days, after the turn
    of the summer solstice,
when the wearisome season of the hot weather
    goes to its conclusion
then is the timely season for men to voyage.
    You will not
break up your ship, nor will the sea drown
    its people, unless
Poseidon, the shaker of the earth,
    of his own volition,
or Zeus, the king of the immortals, wishes
    to destroy it,
for with these rests authority for all outcomes,
    good or evil.
At that time the breezes can be judged,
    and the sea is untroubled.
At that time, trusting your swift ship to the winds,
    you can draw her
down to the sea at will, and load all your cargo
    inside her;
but make haste still, for the sake of
    an earlier homecoming,
and do not wait for the season of new wine,
    and the autumn
rain, and the winter coming on,
    and the hard-blowing southwind
who comes up behind the heavy rains that Zeus sends
    in autumn

and upheaves the sea and makes the open water
difficult.
There is one other sailing season for men,
in spring time.
At that point, when you first make out
on the topmost branches
of the fig tree, a leaf as big as the print
that a crow makes
when he walks; at that time also the sea is navigable
and this is called the spring sailing season.
I for my part
do not like it. There is nothing about it
that I find pleasant.
It's snatched. You will find it hard
to escape coming to grief. Yet still
and even so, men in their short-sightedness
do undertake it;
for acquisition means life to miserable mortals;
but it is an awful thing to die among the waves.
No, rather
I tell you to follow with all your attention,
as I instruct you.
Do not adventure your entire livelihood
in hollow ships.
Leave the greater part ashore and make
the lesser part cargo.
For it is awful to run on disaster in the waves
of the open
water, and awful to put an overwhelming load
on your wagon
and break the axle, and have all the freight
go to nothing.
Observe measures. Timeliness is best in all matters.

Translated by Richmond Lattimore

THE ARCHAIC LYRIC
AND IAMBUS

The poets who followed Hesiod wrote in a diversity of meters that ranges from the elegiac couplet—a combination of the regular epic hexameter with a shorter line, the pentameter (which has five metrical units instead of six)—to the complicated lyric lines of the Pindaric odes, which seem at first glance a sort of free verse but are in fact under rigid control, since the metrical pattern of what is often a long stanza is exactly repeated in the words of the stanza following (strophe, *to use the Greek terms, corresponding to* antistrophe). *Iambic rhythms are also frequent, often in poems that attack or blame an individual, though they can also appear as a medium for dignified discussion, as in the poems Solon wrote explaining and defending his famous legal reforms in Athens. Archilochus, the earliest of the lyric poets whose work has come down to us, uses a rich variety of iambic and lyric meters, as well as the elegiac couplet.*

ARCHILOCHUS
7th Century B.C.

We know that Archilochus of Paros was alive and writing in 648 B.C.; that is the date of the total eclipse of the sun visible in the Aegean that he refers to in our poem 15. But almost everything else about him that we know (or think we know) comes from his own poems. This was the case too for the Greeks of the fifth century B.C. Critias, himself a poet (and also the uncle of Plato and leader of the Thirty Tyrants) wrote about *Archilochus: "If he had not published to all the Greeks such an opinion about himself, we would never have found out that his mother Enipo was a slave . . . nor that he was an adulterer, that he was licentious and violent, and, most disgraceful of all, that he threw away his shield."* Unfortunately, a poet's lines are rarely reliable evidence for the facts of his life; in many cases we do not know (and Critias may not have known either) who the speaker is supposed to be. One fragment, our no. *18,* might well have been used by modern critics, hungry for biographical detail, as evidence for Archilochus' contempt for wealth and tyranny, if we did not know from our sources that the speaker is one Charon the carpenter.

Modern critics have made much of the poem cited by Critias as the most disgraceful of all; it has been seen as a repudiation of aristocratic and Homeric values by an individualist, a mercenary soldier. That Archilochus was a mercenary seems doubtful; he was fighting on Thasos, where his home city was attempting to form a colony, and in the only mention of mercenaries in our fragments he dismisses them as unreliable. As for the loss of his shield, Critias' strong condemnation is understandable: in fifth-century Sparta, mothers told their sons to come back with their shields or on them, and at Athens somebody called Cleonymus is mercilessly pilloried in one Aristophanic comedy after another because he threw away his shield. But this is the voice of the fifth-century polis, of the day of the solid hoplite phalanx, in which each man's life depended partly on the shield of his neighbor. There is no symbolic value attached to the shield in Homer, and the kind of fighting Archilochus was engaged in against the natives of Thasos was almost certainly quite unlike the collision of heavily armored, compact lines that Critias was thinking of. It is remarkable that the aristocratic poet Alcaeus, a fierce fighter in the civil wars of Lesbos, also (as we know from a tiny fragment) speaks of losing his shield. So too, a century later, does the love poet and playboy of the tyrants' courts at Samos and Athens, Anacreon of Teos—not to mention the Roman poet Horace, who claims to have left his shield disgracefully—relicta non bene parmula—at Philippi. Horace was of course fighting on the wrong side—against his present patron, the emperor Augustus.

1

And I know how to lead off
The sprightly dance
Of the Lord Dionysos,
    the dithyramb.

I do it thunderstruck
With wine.

2

My ash spear is my barley bread,
My ash spear is my Ismarian wine.
I lean on my spear and drink.

3

Kindly pass the cup down the deck
And keep it coming from the barrel,
Good red wine, and don't stir up the dregs,
And don't think why we shouldn't be,
More than any other, drunk on guard duty.

4

O that I might but touch
Neobulé's hand.

5

Attribute all to the gods.
They pick a man up,
Stretched on the black loam,
And set him on his two feet,
Firm, and then again
Shake solid men until
They fall backward
Into the worst of luck,
Wandering hungry,
Wild of mind.

6

Let us hide the sea-king's gifts,
The wrecked dead Poseidon brings.

7

One sizable thing I do know:
How to get back my own
With a man doing me wrong.

Translated by Guy Davenport

8

I am two things: a fighter who follows the Master of Battles,
and one who understands the gift of the Muses' love.

9

I don't like the towering captain with the spraddly length of leg,
one who swaggers in his lovelocks and cleanshaves beneath the chin.
Give me a man short and squarely set upon his legs, a man
full of heart, not to be shaken from the place he plants his feet.

10

Some barbarian is waving my shield, since I was obliged to
    leave that perfectly good piece of equipment behind
under a bush. But I got away, so what does it matter?
Let the shield go; I can buy another one equally good.

11

Here the island stands
stiff with wild timber like a donkey's bristling back.
This is no place of beauty, not desirable
nor lovely like the plains where the River Siris runs.

12

Heart, my heart, so battered with misfortune far beyond your
    strength,
up, and face the men who hate us. Bare your chest to the assault
of the enemy, and fight them off. Stand fast among the beamlike
    spears.
Give no ground; and if you beat them, do not brag in open show,
nor, if they beat you, run home and lie down on your bed and cry.

Keep some measure in the joy you take in luck, and the degree
you give way to sorrow. All our life is up-and-down like this.

13

. . . slammed by the surf on the beach
naked at Salmydéssos, where the screw-haired men
of Thrace, taking him in
will entertain him (he will have much to undergo,
chewing on slavery's bread)
stiffened with cold, and loops of seaweed from the slime
tangling his body about,
teeth chattering as he lies in abject helplessness
flat on his face like a dog
beside the beach-break where the waves come shattering in.
And let me be there to watch;
for he did me wrong and set his heel on our good faith,
he who had once been my friend.

14

The fox knows many tricks, the hedgehog only one.
One good one.

Translated by Richmond Lattimore

15

Nothing in the world can surprise me now. Nothing
is impossible or too wonderful, for Zeus, father
of the Olympians, has turned midday into black night
by shielding light from the blossoming sun,
and now dark terror hangs over mankind.
   Anything
may happen, so do not be amazed if beasts
on dry land seek pasture with dolphins in
the ocean, and those beasts who loved sunny hills
love crashing seawaves more than the warm mainland.

16

Say goodbye to the island Paros,
farewell to its figs and the seafaring life.

17

All, O all the calamities of all the Hellenes
are set loose on this battleground in Thasos.

18

The gold booty of Gyges means nothing to me.
I don't envy that Lydian king, nor am I jealous
of what gods can do, nor of the tyrants' great
powers. All these are realms beyond my vision.

19

When dead no man finds respect or glory from men
of his town. Rather, we hope while alive for some
favor from the living. The dead are always scorned.

Translated by Willis Barnstone

". . . BUT IF YOU'RE IN A HURRY AND CAN'T WAIT FOR ME"

*According to our ancient sources, Archilochus was promised the hand of
Neobule, daughter of Lycambes, but at some point the father broke off
the engagement. Archilochus took his revenge by composing songs
about Lycambes, Neobule, and her younger sister so scurrilous that all
three of his victims hanged themselves. The names Lycambes and Neobule do turn up in the fragments (Neobule in our no. 4, for example), but
on the whole this seems an unlikely story, especially its ending. In 1974,
however, a papyrus fragment was published that appears to bear directly
on the matter. It starts in the middle of a speech by Neobule's younger
sister. She is trying to persuade an importunate lover to wait until her
mourning period for her mother is over, or to transfer his attentions to
her elder sister.*

". . . but if you're in a hurry and can't wait for me
there's another girl in our house who's quite ready
to marry, a pretty girl, just right for you."
That was what she said, but I can talk too.
"Daughter of dear Amphimedo," I said,
"(a fine woman she was—pity she's dead)
there are plenty of kinds of pretty play

young men and girls can know and not go all the way
—something like that will do. As for marrying,
we'll talk about that again when your mourning
is folded away, god willing. But now
I'll be good, I promise—I do know how.
Don't be hard, darling. Truly I'll stay
out on the garden-grass, not force the doorway
—just try. But as for that sister of yours,
someone else can have her. The bloom's gone—she's coarse
—the charm too (she had it)—now she's on heat
the whole time, can't keep away from it—
damn her, don't let anyone saddle me with that.
With a wife like she is I shouldn't half
give the nice neighbours a belly-laugh.
You're all right, darling. You're simple and straight
—she takes her meat off anyone's plate.
I'd be afraid if I married her
my children would be like the bitch's litter
—born blind, and several months too early."
But I'd talked enough. I laid the girl
down among the flowers. A soft cloak spread,
my arm round her neck, I comforted
her fear. The fawn soon ceased to flee.
Over her breasts my hands moved gently,
the new-formed girlhood she bared for me;
over all her body, the young skin bare,
I spilt my white force, just touching her yellow hair.

Translated by Martin Robertson

If Neobule, her father Lycambes, and her younger sister were real people
and contemporaries of Archilochus living in the same city on Paros—
and if he circulated many more poems like this one—it is indeed possible
that they hanged themselves. For of course this is not a matter of
publication of poems in little magazines that nobody reads. An epode,
as its name implies, is a song, and a song such as this, performed at the
male symposia where the men of Greek society gathered to drink and
amuse themselves, would soon be the property of the whole community.
The destructive power of such poetry is in fact an argument for thinking
that the whole situation is fictional; that no real persons are involved.
Greek society being what it was, and for that matter still is, Archilochus'
life would have been in mortal danger from the male relatives of the

girls, who would not have rested until they saw the color of his blood. Fictional or not, it shows Archilochus in an unpleasant light, not entirely mitigated by the incredible skill of versification and characterization displayed in such short compass.

This poem helps us understand why Critias, and Pindar too, thought him a scoundrel. But he was also a great poet, and though perhaps he was the first, he was certainly not the last great poet to be a scoundrel as well.

TYRTAEUS
7th Century B.C.

Sparta was, for the fifth-century Greeks as it is for us, the classic exemplar of the military ethic. The courage, tenacity, and cohesion of the doomed band that held the pass at Thermopylae, fighting to the last man, were qualities expected of Spartan troops in any battle they entered, and expectations were rarely disappointed. The lifelong training that produced this military temper had been imposed on all Spartan male citizens as part of a radical social reform attributed to one Lycurgus, whose date cannot be fixed and whose very existence has been doubted. But it is generally agreed that the reforms were a result of the pressures of the war the Spartans waged to gain control of the plains of Messenia, on the other side of Taygetus, the mountain range that towers over Sparta. To win the war—and later to maintain their status as elite conquerors supported by the labor of enslaved field hands—they had to become an army in permanent readiness. The reforms were in one sense radical, amounting almost to the abolition of the private family in favor of a communal existence, for the males, in a lifelong military formation; but it seems clear that they were also in part a return to an older form of tribal organization native to other Doric communities, notably those in Crete.

The Spartan poet Tyrtaeus was the official voice of this warrior ethic. The remains of his poetry (the Alexandrians had five books) are all concerned with the crisis, the Messenian war and its aftermath, which had brought about the reorganization of Spartan life. One fragment mentions

> . . . *Our king Theopompus, loved by the gods*
> *with whom we took the wide plains of Messene,*
> *Messene, good to plough and good to plant.*
> *For it they fought for ten and nine more years*
> *without a break, their hearts highly resolved,*
> *those spearmen, fathers of our fathers.*
> *In the twentieth the foe left the rich fields*
> *in flight from the uplands of Ithome.*

As a result, the Messenians were enslaved; they became serfs on the estates that supported the Spartan citizen soldiers—Helots, a word form from the Greek root hel- ("capture"). Tyrtaeus describes their life:

> . . . *like donkeys weighed down with heavy loads*
> *bringing their masters under grim constraint*
> *half of whatever the ploughed land bears . . .*

And when a Spartan died, his Helots were obliged to mourn at his funeral:

> . . . *lamenting their master's death, man and wife alike,*
> *whenever the deadly fate came to take him.*

To the Spartans, Tyrtaeus repeated again and again the same messages: A man must stand firm in the battle line; better death than the dishonor that comes with cowardice. An Athenian orator of the fifth century tells us that still, in his day, Spartan troops called up for field duty went to the king's tent to listen to the poems of Tyrtaeus.

Tyrtaeus' language is not, as one might have expected, the Doric dialect that was the common speech of the Spartans; his language is in fact Ionic—it is almost relentlessly Homeric. The source and the inspiration for his martial heroics is the Iliad. His characteristic meter, however, is only partly Homeric; it is what, for want of a better word, we call elegiac verse—a sequence of couplets in which a regular Homeric hexameter is followed by a pentameter, a shorter line consisting of two dactylic half-lines. In these couplets the hexameter seems to rise to a high point; the pentameter, in two attempts to rise, falls ebbing back. It can be imitated in English with stressed syllables corresponding to the long syllables of the original, but this has not been a meter that has found favor with English poets. The Germans, Schiller and Goethe especially, used it to good effect; this is the meter for example of Goethe's Roman Elegies. Schiller wrote a couplet that exactly reproduces the rhythm while it conveys the effect, and Coleridge translated it into English:

In the hexameter rises the fountain's silvery column
In the pentameter aye falling in melody back.

Translators of Greek and Roman elegiac verse have in general not attempted to follow this lead and have preferred an alternation of long and
slightly shorter lines.

    In Greek and Latin poetry the elegiac couplet was destined to have a
long history. It was to serve not only for the martial harangues of Tyrtaeus but also for Xenophanes' criticism of the extravagant rewards given
to successful athletes; for Theognis' love poems to Cyrnus and his laments for the end of aristocratic rule in his city of Megara; for funeral
epigrams like those composed by Simonides for the Spartans who fell at
Thermopylae as well as for anonymous verse epitaphs for the graves of
obscure citizens; for the literary epigrams of the Alexandrians and their
many followers over the centuries; and, most notably, in Latin dress, for
the love elegies of Tibullus, Propertius, and Ovid.

THE SPARTAN CREED

I would not say anything for a man nor take account of him
    for any speed of his feet or wrestling skill he might have,
not if he had the size of a Cyclops and strength to go with it,
    not if he could outrun Bóreas, the North Wind of Thrace,
not if he were more handsome and gracefully formed than Tithónos,
    or had more riches than Midas had, or Kínyras too,
not if he were more of a king than Tantalid Pelops,
    or had the power of speech and persuasion Adrastos had,
not if he had all splendors except for a fighting spirit.
    For no man ever proves himself a good man in war
unless he can endure to face the blood and the slaughter,
    go close against the enemy and fight with his hands.
Here is courage, mankind's finest possession, here is
    the noblest prize that a young man can endeavor to win,
and it is a good thing his city and all the people share with him
    when a man plants his feet and stands in the foremost spears
relentlessly, all thought of foul flight completely forgotten,
    and has well trained his heart to be steadfast and to endure,
and with words encourages the man who is stationed beside him.
    Here is a man who proves himself to be valiant in war.
With a sudden rush he turns to flight the rugged battalions
    of the enemy, and sustains the beating waves of assault.
And he who so falls among the champions and loses his sweet life,
    so blessing with honor his city, his father, and all his people,

with wounds in his chest, where the spear that he was facing has
transfixed
that massive guard of his shield, and gone through his breastplate as
well,
why, such a man is lamented alike by the young and the elders,
and all his city goes into mourning and grieves for his loss.

His tomb is pointed to with pride, and so are his children,
and his children's children, and afterward all the race that is his.
His shining glory is never forgotten, his name is remembered,
and he becomes an immortal, though he lies under the ground,
when one who was a brave man has been killed by the furious War
God
standing his ground and fighting hard for his children and land.
But if he escapes the doom of death, the destroyer of bodies,
and wins his battle, and bright renown for the work of his spear,
all men give place to him alike, the youth and the elders,
and much joy comes his way before he goes down to the dead.
Aging, he has reputation among his citizens. No one
tries to interfere with his honors or all he deserves;
all men withdraw before his presence, and yield their seats to him,
the youth, and the men his age, and even those older than he.
Thus a man should endeavor to reach this high place of courage
with all his heart, and, so trying, never be backward in war.

Translated by Richmond Lattimore.

ALCMAN
Late 7th Century B.C.

*One extraordinary effect of the Lycurgan reorganization of male Spartan
life as a military initiation followed by many years in barracks was the
comparative emancipation of Spartan women. They were essential for
the breeding of perfect male physical specimens; newborn babies with
physical defects were exposed on the high slopes of Mount Taygetus.*

But the Spartan insistence on healthy offspring meant that girls were not allowed to marry at the very early age customary elsewhere in Greece, and the same deliberate policy was recognizable in the emphasis on women's athletics. The Spartan women were in fact notorious all over Greece for their free outdoor life, and their athletic dress earned them among other Greeks, who kept their women as covered and shut up as possible, the epithet phainomerides *("show-thighs").*

This side of Spartan life is reflected in the poor remnants of the work of a remarkable lyric poet, Alcman, whose poetry, as far as we can tell, steered completely clear of the martial themes of Tyrtaeus. It is possible that a small fragment—*"Weighed against steel a skilled hand on the lyre / Tips the scale . . ."*—is Alcman's claim to his own poetic territory and his assertion of its value.

Of the six books into which the Alexandrian editors divided Alcman's work, we know that at least two consisted of partheneia *(maiden songs).* In many of the tiny papyrus fragments of Alcman that have surfaced in recent years, too small to give us more than a single word, if that, of any line, we find time and again feminine terminations of adjectives and participles; the speakers seem to be, as in the only substantial fragment of a partheneion *that we have, female. It is written in the Doric dialect;* the powerful hold that Homeric dialect, meter, and formula exerted on the elegiacs of Tyrtaeus is absent here. Alcman sets the pattern for choral lyric from now on. Doric, real or literary, remains the standard dialect for this type of song—*in Pindar and Bacchylides, for example—* and even the Athenian tragic poets, in those songs they wrote for the choral dances in their tragedies, affected a sprinkling of Doric forms. Alcman's meters are complicated lyric units. They are strophic: an initial long passage written in an elaborate pattern of long and short syllables is followed by a stanza of exactly the same length arranged in exactly the same pattern of longs and shorts—strophe followed by antistrophe. This correspondence is the ground plan of the choreography, the dance notation, so to speak.

The long fragment of the partheneion *printed here (no. 2) is full of* unsolved puzzles. There is obviously some kind of competition going on. Is it a race? Or a metaphor for a competition in dance and song? Are Hagesichora and Agido rivals? Or perhaps partners? Who is the *"I"* of the poem? Are the Pleiades a rival girl chorus or the constellation? These are questions that will not be solved until we know much more than we do now about Spartan maiden festivals and early Spartan religious festivals, which seem to be involved. But one thing the poem does do for us is to create an atmosphere unlike anything we shall find elsewhere in the remains of Greek literature—a radiant vision of the grace and high spirits of young girlhood. Perhaps it was only in Sparta, where the regimentation of the men seems to have set women free, or at any rate freer than they were in other Greek cities, that such vigor and high spirits could be found among girls and given an official voice in the work of a male poet. Alcman seems to have been devoted to this kind of composition and the performance which was its fulfillment. The first poem in our selection sounds in fact like a farewell to the days when he could rehearse the girls in their dance—he is getting old.

There were, of course, four other books of his poems in the Alexandrian Library, but we have little idea of what they contained. Some of his songs may have been designed for banquets; the fragments treat wine and food in remarkably concrete fashion. Perhaps our fragment no. 3 comes from one of these. It names four seasons (Homer and Hesiod named only three), and reminds us that for communities utterly dependent on agriculture and close to the poverty level, the fearful and dangerous season is that darling of the Romantic poets, spring, when nothing has matured and the winter supplies are running low. Our fragment no. 4, an evocation of night, is one of the most beautiful passages in all Greek poetry. It is typical of the way survival of the Greek poets has been determined that we owe these marvelous lines to a lexicographer of the second century A.D. called Apollonius the Sophist, who quoted them to illustrate the words Alcman used to distinguish between reptiles, animals, and fish.

1

No longer, maiden voices sweet-calling, sounds of allurement,
can my limbs bear me up; oh I wish, I wish I could be a seabird
who with halcyons skims the surf-flowers of the sea water
with careless heart, a sea-blue-colored and sacred waterfowl.

Translated by Richmond Lattimore

2

And there is the vengeance of the gods.
He is a happy man who can weave his days,
No trouble upon the loom.
And I, I sing of Agido,
Of her light. She is like the sun
To which she makes our prayers,
The witness of its radiance.

Yet I can neither praise her nor blame her
Till I have sung of another,
Sung of our choirmaster,
Who stands among us as in a pasture
One splendid stallion
Paws the meadow, a champion racer,
A horse that runs in dreams.

Imagine her if you can. Her hair,
As gold as a Venetian mane,
Flowers around her silver eyes.
What can I say to make you see?
She is Hagesikhora and
Agido, almost, almost as beautiful,
Is a Kolaxaian filly running behind her
In the races at Ibeno.
A Pleiades of doves they are
Contending at dawn before the altar of Artemis
For the honor of offering the sacred plow
Which we have brought to the goddess.
They are the white star Sirius rising
In the honey and spice of a summer night.
Neither abundance of purple
Can defend us with its glory,
Nor golden snakes engraved with eyes and scales,
Nor bonnets from Lydia and brooches,
Nor our sweet violet eyes.
Nor can Nanno's hair, Areta's goddess face,
Thylakis nor Kleësithera,
Nor Ainesimbrota to whom we cry
Let Astaphis be ours,
Let Philylla look our way sometimes,
Damareta and the lovely Wianthemis,
Keep back defeat unless
Hagesikhora alone, our love,
Be our victory's shield.

And she is, she is our own,
The splendid-ankled Hagesikhora!
With Agido, by whose side she lingers,
She honors the rites with her beauty.
Accept her prayers O gods,

For she is your handiwork,
Perfect of her kind.
And I, I, O Choirmaster,
Am but an ordinary girl.
I hoot like an owl in the roof.
I long to worship the goddess of the dawn
Whose gift is peace. For Hagesikhora
We sing, for her we virgin girls
Make our lovely harmonies.

Translated by Guy Davenport

3

And he established three seasons,
summer, winter and autumn third
and a fourth, spring,
when everything blooms
but there is not enough to eat.

4

All asleep—the mountain peaks and gorges,
the forelands and ravines,
all the creeping things bred by the black earth,
the mountain beasts, the nations of the bees,
and the monsters in the deeps of the dark sea.
Asleep too the tribes of long-winged birds.

Translated by Bernard Knox

HIPPONAX

Middle 6th Century B.C.

Hipponax of Ephesus (a prosperous Greek city of the Aegean shore of Asia Minor) was famous, like Archilochus, for his scathing personal abuse, the characteristic vein of iambic poetry. (The name of the maid-

servant whose crude jokes cheered up the goddess Demeter when she was mourning the loss of her daughter Persephone was Iambe.) Like Archilochus, Hipponax was credited with some victims: the sculptors Bupalus and Athenis, targets because they had caricatured the poet's features in stone, were driven to suicide by his attacks. We know nothing about Lycambes and his daughters except what Archilochus tells us, but Bupalus and Athenis were real people, active in the Aegean area in the second half of the sixth century B.C. And the elder Pliny, in his excursus on the history of art, dismisses the story of their suicides as a fabrication. Athenis is rarely mentioned in our fragments, but Bupalus turns up often (no. 2), and usually as the object of scurrilous accusations or denigrating remarks, as in one fragment in which he is said to have slept with his mother, and in another where someone is asked the question: "Why did you go to bed with that scoundrel Bupalus?"

Hipponax adopted (or perhaps invented) an iambic line that is called choliambic *("lame iambic"); the last three syllables are long, which brings the line to a slow halt. (Nos. 1 and 4 attempt to reproduce the effect in English.) We have about 150 fragments, most of them mere phrases, single words, or tattered papyrus scraps. The tone is far from edifying; food, drink, copulation, and excretion seem to be the principal concerns of the sordid cast of characters, of whom Hipponax himself is not the least disreputable. But we would give much to have more; these bits and pieces give us every now and then precious glimpses of life in the Ionian cities, which produced not only poets such as Xenophanes and Mimnermus but also the first philosophers, Thales, Anaximander, and Anaximenes of Miletus. One such fragment reminds us that the hinterland of the coastal cities was where the Greek slavers went for their human merchandise:*

> . . . and if they catch any barbarians, they put them up for sale;
> the Phrygians to work the grain mills in Miletus . . .

Our no. 5 is the complaint of a man whose sons have eaten up his fortune, and no. 3 lists the tombs of the Lydian kings, including Gyges, who is the hero (if that is the right word) of one of Herodotus' most fascinating stories (p. 267).

1

Hermes, dear Hermes, Maia's son from Kylléne,
I pray to you, I'm suffering from extreme shivers,
so give an overcoat to Hippónax, give him
a cape, and sandals, and felt overshoes, sixty
pieces of gold to bury in his strong chamber.

2

Hold my jacket, somebody, while I hit Boúpalos in the eye.
I can hit with both hands, and I never miss punches.

3

Keep traveling, you swine, the whole way toward Smyrna.
Go through the Lydian land, past the tomb of Alyáttes,
the grave of Gyges and the pillar of Megástrys.
the monument of Atys, son of Alyáttes,
big chief, and point your paunch against the sun's setting.

Translated by Richmond Lattimore

4

It never happened to me. The god of wealth's stone blind.
He never came into my house and said to me: "Hipponax,
Here's money for you, thirty minae of pure silver
And a lot more besides." No, he's too hard-hearted.

5

For one of them spent whole days at ease at table
Swilling down tunafish and cheese in a steady stream
for all the world like a eunuch from Lampsacus
and so ate up the family fortune. I have to dig
rocks on the mountainside, munch medium-sized figs
and barley-wheat loaves—slave fodder.

Translated by Bernard Knox

ALCAEUS
Late 7th Century–Middle 6th Century B.C.

*Tyrtaeus' calls to arms date from the middle of the seventh century B.C.,
the time of the second Messenian war, a mass revolt of the Helots.
Alcman, judging by the little evidence we have (much of it conflicting),*

seems to have been of the same generation. Alcaeus and Sappho come later—born in the late seventh century and active in the sixth on the island of Lesbos in the Aegean.

In their poems we are in a different world from that of Archilochus— the sea voyages, the long-drawn-out fighting with the natives on Thasos—different too from the city-in-arms that was Sparta. Lesbos is a large and fertile island. Paros may have been famous for its figs and its marble, but Lesbos had rich farmland, olive groves, wide pastures, or- chards, vineyards, and gardens. Alcaeus and Sappho both belonged to the aristocracy of the island and lived in its principal city, Mitylene. The poems suggest an atmosphere of wealth and leisure. Not, however, in the case of Alcaeus, a tranquil atmosphere, for many of the poems are parti- san songs of civil strife. Yet the background is still that of a privileged upper class, confident of its right to a dominant position, though aware that it is threatened.

The two poets knew each other; they both composed their songs (and sang them to the accompaniment of a lyre) in the soft Lesbian dialect, which the scribes somehow preserved for us through all the vicissitudes of hand copying over so many centuries in which the sounds of that dialect were no longer heard. Though they both composed in a wide variety of lyric meters, Sappho was especially fond of one, which bears her name—Sapphic—and Alcaeus too had his characteristic stanza, the Alcaic. But their poetic concerns were very different. And so were the worlds—one a man's, the other a woman's—in which they lived.

Alcaeus' background is the fierce power struggle which raged in Mity- lene in the sixth century, as it did in so many of the cities of the Greek world. He was fully engaged in the political and military strife that plagued the city for years until Pittacus established a stable, peaceful government. Aristotle, citing our fragment no. 4 in the Politics, *discusses this regime as a case of what he calls "elected tyranny." Pittacus was voted sole ruler by the people of Mitylene for the purpose of repelling the exiles who planned to return; their leaders were Alcaeus the poet and his brother Antimenides. Alcaeus' poems, of which we have many fasci- nating but tantalizing papyrus scraps, give vivid glimpses of the life of a party chieftain, often in combat and just as often in exile. The descrip- tion of the armory (no. 5) has a loving, gloating tone, the authentic voice of civil war; these weapons, we can be sure, are for use, not for show. The poem about the ship in trouble (no. 6) is, we are told by ancient scho- lars, an allegory of "the evils caused by tyrants." Other fragments give us glimpses of one of Alcaeus' favorite themes—abuse of Pittacus, for whom he has a truly formidable collection of epithets (though Pit- tacus was obviously admired by Aristotle, and became in legend one of the Seven Sages, along with Solon and Thales). And we have a frag-*

ment of a poem that Alcaeus wrote far from Mitylene, in exile in the country:

> ... I am wretched; my life is that of a rough country man. I long to hear the assembly summoned to meeting . . . and the council. I am driven away from the estates my father and his father held all their lives, among these self-destructive citizens, an exile in the hinterland . . .

The social context of these songs was clearly a man's world; they were almost certainly composed for those male symposia in which the scurrilous songs of Archilochus were also at home. The symposium was one of those institutions which, like the gymnasium, were central to the culture of the archaic and classical Greeks. It was a drinking party, the celebrants male (the only females present were flute-girls and other ladies of the night); such gatherings were often, as Plato's literary Symposium suggests, the breeding ground for those homosexual attachments that seem to have been a phase, at least, in the life of most aristocratic Greeks in archaic and classical times. We have no trace of this element in the papyrus fragments so far, but it is one of the memorable characteristics of the poetry of Alcaeus listed by the Roman poet Horace, his admirer and imitator. Horace speaks of Alcaeus' themes as the hardships of sea voyages, exile, and war, but sees him as one who also sang of "Bacchus, the Muses, Venus and the boy who clings to her always, and of Lycus, glorious in the beauty of his dark eyes and jet-black hair."

The meter Alcaeus favors, the one named after him, is a brilliant rhythmic pattern, a four-line stanza in which the first two lines have an identical rocking rhythm, the third is shorter and ends with spondaic solemnity, while the last line races in dactyls to a close. Lattimore adapts it for English in our nos. 6 and 7. It so happens that one of the most technically accomplished of English poets tried his hand at this form, and his effort gives a better idea of the variety and solemnity the Alcaic stanza could achieve. Here is the first stanza of Tennyson's "Ode to John Milton":

> O mighty-mouthed inventor of harmonies,
> O skilled to sing of Time or Eternity,
>   God-gifted organ-voice of England,
>   Milton, a name to resound for ages.

1

Wash your gullet with wine for the Dog-Star returns with the heat of summer searing a thirsting earth.

Cicadas cry softly under high leaves, and pour down
shrill song incessantly from under their wings.
The artichoke blooms, and women are warm and wanton—
but men turn lean and limp for the burning Dog-
            Star parches their brains and knees.

2

Come with me now and leave the land of
Pelops, mighty sons of Zeus and Leda,
and in kindness spread your light on us,
            Kastor and Polydeukes.

You who wander above the long earth
and over all the seas on swift horses,
easily delivering mariners
            from pitiful death,

fly to the masthead of our swift ship,
and gazing over foremast and forestays,
light a clear path through the midnight gloom
            for our black vessel.

3

You have come home from the ends of the earth,
Antimenidas, my dear brother; come
with a gold and ivory handle to your sword.
You fought alongside the Babylonians
and your prowess saved them from annihilation
when you battled and cut down a warrior giant
who was almost eight feet tall.

4

                One and all,
you have proclaimed Pittakos, the lowborn,
to be tyrant of your lifeless and doomed
land. Moreover, you deafen him with praise.

Translated by Willis Barnstone

5

The great hall is aglare with bronze armament and the whole inside
    made fit for war
with helms glittering and hung high, crested over with white
    horse-manes that nod and wave
and make splendid the heads of men who wear them. Here are
    shining greaves made out of bronze,
hung on hooks, and they cover all the house's side. They are strong
    to stop arrows and spears.
Here are war-jackets quilted close of new linen, with hollow shields
    stacked on the floor,
with broad swords of the Chalkis make, many tunics and many belts
    heaped close beside.
These shall not lie neglected, now we have stood to our task and
    have this work to do.

6

I cannot understand how the winds are set
against each other. Now from this side and now
    from that the waves roll. We between them
    run with the wind in our black ship driven,

hard pressed and laboring under the giant storm.
All round the mast-step washes the sea we shipped.
    You can see through the sail already
    where there are opening rents within it.

The forestays slacken. . . .

7

Zeus rains upon us, and from the sky comes down
enormous winter. Rivers have turned to ice. . . .

Dash down the winter. Throw a log on the fire
and mix the flattering wine (do not water it
    too much) and bind on round our foreheads
    soft ceremonial wreaths of spun fleece.

We must not let our spirits give way to grief.
By being sorry we get no further on,
my Bukchis. Best of all defenses
is to mix plenty of wine, and drink it.

Translated by Richmond Lattimore

SAPPHO
A Contemporary of Alcaeus

Sappho (in her own dialect the name is Psappho) came from the same aristocratic caste as Alcaeus; she was married to a rich man from the island of Andros. Though she seems to have spent some time as an exile in Sicily (probably because of the political activities of her husband or her brothers), there is not a trace in her poems of the political concerns which Alcaeus could rarely forget. Her world is one of girlhood, marriage, and love; her themes the love of young women for each other, and the poignancy of their separation as they leave to assume wifely responsibilities. The context and audience for Alcaeus's songs was the male symposium; for Sappho's we do not know what it was. Some of the songs were probably designed for a women's festival, like that beauty contest Alcaeus watched in exile in the country, where "all around there rings the wondrous sound of the loud, holy cry of the women." Some of them were epithalamia, *songs for wedding celebrations. But the poems that deal with love and parting must have been composed and performed for some intimate circle of women friends. It may have been an association with a religious purpose, centered on the worship of a female deity— Artemis, Hera, or Aphrodite. The great German scholar and critic Wilamowitz, who was worried about Sappho's reputation, suggested a milieu for these songs that would perhaps explain and also make more respectable the emotions expressed in them; he imagined Sappho as the teacher in a sort of finishing school in which girls were prepared for marriage. This proposal did not arouse much enthusiasm, but a papyrus published in 1974 (Wilamowitz wrote his book in 1913) suggests that he may have been on the right track. It is a prose text that says: "But she, in peace and quiet, educating the best women not only of the local families but from all over Ionia . . . and she was held in such favorable respect by the citizens that Callias of Mitylene said in . . ." Sappho is not named, but Callias, in about 200 B.C., wrote a commentary on Sappho and Alacaeus. And perhaps the contemptuous poem addressed to another woman (no. 10) makes sense in such a context; the late anthologist who preserved it for us tells that it was aimed at "an uneducated woman." But we cannot be certain of the milieu in which these poems were composed; all we can say is that it was clearly and exclusively female. Its subject is a woman's life, from girlhood to marriage, evoked with a passion, tenderness, and immediacy that have seldom if ever been equaled.*

Just as Alcaeus had his favorite meter, so did Sappho. It is, as usually printed, a four-line stanza (three lines of exactly the same pattern, followed by a short dactylic clausula); it is perhaps better to think of it as two equal lines followed by a longer third. Lattimore, using stress for quantity, reproduces it in nos. 6, 7, and 8. It is not a meter easily adaptable for English verse. Swinburne tried his hand at it, and though the content, as so often in Swinburne, is—to put it mildly—inane, he does manage to reproduce in English the gliding smoothness of the Greek.

> Saw the white, implacable Aphrodite
> Saw the hair unbound and the feet unsandalled
> Shine as fire of sunset on Western waters
> Saw the reluctant
> Feet, the straining plumes of the doves that draw her,
> Looking always, looking with necks reverted
> Back to Lesbos, back to the hills where under
> Stood Mitylene.

It is in Sapphic stanzas that Sappho wrote her address to Aphrodite (no. 8), probably the opening poem of what the Alexandrian scholars arranged as her first book. The address starts as a conventional religious cletic hymn, that is, a hymn calling on the god to come to the suppliant's aid. It employs the usual formulas—you came once before, come to me now again—but then departs from the pattern; instead of dealing with the present, it gives an account of the previous visit of the goddess. The poem is quoted by an ancient literary critic as an example of "smooth and exuberant" style and also of cohesive construction. It is all of that, but it is also a brilliant example of refined, self-deprecating wit. The whole religious apparatus of the cletic hymn, including the epiphany of

the goddess, is put in motion so that Sappho can win the love of some
recalcitrant girl; furthermore it turns out that this is not the first time she
has brought Aphrodite down from Olympus to deal with her affairs. The
other poem that calls on Aphrodite (no. 5) is incomplete (what we have
was inscribed on a potsherd of the third century B.C.), but its tone seems
to be entirely different—an almost solemn reverence. In other poems
the goddess is not called on, but she is present in the passion that
breathes in the words. Sappho is the poet who has given the most concentrated, vivid expression to sexual passion in all Greek—perhaps in all
world—literature. The famous poem (no. 7) in which she describes her
sensations as she looks at the girl who is intent on the man sitting
opposite her presents the other side of the coin, which showed Aphrodite promising Sappho she would be pursued—here she is rejected, for
a man, whose good fortune makes him seem to her the equal of the
gods. There is not only passionate desire here but also jealousy, a fearsome combination that has seldom been so forcefully and physically por-
trayed.

Sometimes love is a tender emotion, though this aspect of it surfaces
always in reminiscence, never in presence. So in the beautiful poem (no.
6) that begins and ends with the Lydian horsemen ". . . remembering
Anaktoria / who has gone from me . . .", and so also in no. 1 (". . . she
recalls / gentle Atthis with desire . . ."), and no. 2 (". . . I loved you,
Atthis, / yes, long ago . . ."). Sometimes even memory fails and there is
only the loneliness, as in no. 11, a poem which many authoritative critics
refuse to accept as Sappho's work, but for which it is hard to imagine any
other author. Sometimes the memory of past happiness is blended with
the sadness of imminent separation, as in the fragmentary no. 4, where
the exquisite variations of dactylic and cretic line endings seem to project the yearning and regret to infinity. Sappho's attempt to comfort her
departing friend carries her away in increasingly passionate memories of
what they are both about to lose.

The final words of the fragment, with their clear allusion to sexual
contact, seem to touch on the question of whether Sappho—besides
being an inhabitant of Lesbos—was also a lesbian in the modern sense of
the word. It seems clear that the passion, spiritual and physical, of the
speaker of these poems is exclusively directed toward the young women
whose names turn up so often in the papyrus fragments: Atthis, Anac-
toria, Gorgo, Gongyla, Andromeda, Irana, Mnasidica, Gyrinno. On the
other hand, Sappho was married and had a daughter (no. 3), whom she
loved. In her time no word of reproach was uttered against her; Alcaeus
in fact called her hagna—pure, holy. Clearly her way of life was not

considered in any way abnormal in her place and time. She lived in a society in which evidently young women, at least young women of the upper classes, had an intense communal life of their own, a life of female occasions, festivals, and functions, in which their passionate natures were fully engaged with each other. This was presumably, for most of them, a stage preliminary to their later career as wives and mothers. The masculine tradition of later ages distorted the picture and made Lesbos and Sappho the target of crude obscenities, but they could not explain on this basis the honesty and the purity (Alcaeus was right to use the word hagna*) of the emotions caught for us in Sappho's unforgettable lines. The ancient readers had them all; we have only tattered fragments, and yet each new scrap of papyrus reveals the same inimitable mastery of rhythm, of verbal melody, and of crisp freshness of expression. No wonder that the later Greeks recognized her as the greatest of the lyric poets and added her name to those of the Nine Muses to make a tenth.*

1

[. . . Atthis,]
although she is in Sardis,
her thoughts often stray here, to us . . .

[. . . for you know that she honoured] you
as if you were a goddess
and, most of all, delighted in your song.

But now she surpasses all the women
of Lydia, like the moon,
rose-fingered, after the sun has set,

shining brighter than all the stars; its light
stretches out over the salt-
filled sea and the fields brimming with flowers:

the beautiful dew falls and the roses
and the delicate chervil
and many-flowered honey-clover bloom.

But wandering here and there, she recalls
gentle Atthis with desire
and her tender heart is heavy with grief . . .

2

Once upon a time, I loved you, Atthis,
                                    yes, long ago . . .
even when I thought of you as a small
                        and graceless girl . . .

3

I have a beautiful daughter, golden
like a flower, my beloved Cleis,
for her, in her place, I would not accept
the whole of Lydia, nor lovely . . .

Translated by Josephine Balmer

4

"Honest, I want to die," she said to me.
She was in tears when she went away,

Said to me not once but many times:
"Sappho, why must we suffer so?
It's not by choice; I don't want to leave you here."

And I, this is what I said to answer her:
"Farewell. Go in peace. But remember me.
Don't ever forget how well I took care of you.

If you do, let me recall to you
. . . .
All the good days we had together,

The wreathes you wore, of roses and violets
As we lay side by side, the necklaces
Woven from flowers to drape your soft shoulders,

The perfume, precious, fit for royalty
. . . .
How much you used, to anoint yourself!

The soft bed (where) you would satisfy . . . desire . . .

Translated by Bernard Knox

5

Leave Krete and come to this holy temple
where the graceful grove of apple trees
circles an altar smoking with frank-
        incense.

Here roses leave shadow on the ground
and cold springs babble through apple branches
where shuddering leaves pour down pro-
        found sleep.

In our meadow where horses graze
and wild flowers of spring blossom,
anise shoots fill the air with a-
        roma.

And here, Queen Aphrodite, pour
heavenly nectar into gold cups
and fill them gracefully with sud-
        den joy.

Translated by Willis Barnstone

6

Some there are who say that the fairest thing seen
on the black earth is an array of horsemen;
some, men marching; some would say ships; but I say
        she whom one loves best

is the loveliest. Light were the work to make this
plain to all, since she, who surpassed in beauty
all mortality, Helen, once forsaking
        her lordly husband,

fled away to Troy-land across the water.
Not the thought of child nor beloved parents
was remembered, after the Queen of Cyprus
        won her at first sight.

Since young brides have hearts that can be persuaded
easily, light things, palpitant to passion

as am I, remembering Anaktória
who has gone from me

and whose lovely walk and the shining pallor
of her face I would rather see before my
eyes than Lydia's chariots in all their glory
armored for battle.

7

Like the very gods in my sight is he who
sits where he can look in your eyes, who listens
close to you, to hear the soft voice, its sweetness
murmur in love and

laughter, all for him. But it breaks my spirit;
underneath my breast all the heart is shaken.
Let me only glance where you are, the voice dies,
I can say nothing,

but my lips are stricken to silence, underneath my skin the tenuous flame suffuses;
nothing shows in front of my eyes, my ears are
muted in thunder.

And the sweat breaks running upon me, fever
shakes my body, paler I turn than grass is;
I can feel that I have been changed, I feel that
death has come near me.

8

Throned in splendor, deathless, O Aphrodite,
child of Zeus, charm-fashioner, I entreat you
not with griefs and bitternesses to break my
spirit, O goddess;

standing by me rather, if once before now
far away you heard, when I called upon you,
left your father's dwelling place and descended,
yoking the golden

chariot to sparrows, who fairly drew you
down in speed aslant the black world, the bright air
trembling at the heart to the pulse of countless
        fluttering wingbeats.

Swiftly then they came, and you, blessed lady,
smiling on me out of immortal beauty,
asked me what affliction was on me, why I
        called thus upon you,

what beyond all else I would have befall my
tortured heart: "Whom then would you have Persuasion
force to serve desire in your heart? Who is it,
        Sappho, that hurt you?

Though she now escape you, she soon will follow;
though she take not gifts from you, she will give them:
though she love not, yet she will surely love you
        even unwilling."

In such guise come even again and set me
free from doubt and sorrow; accomplish all those
things my heart desires to be done; appear and
        stand at my shoulder.

9

Like the sweet apple turning red on the branch top, on the
top of the topmost branch, and the gatherers did not notice it,
rather, they did notice, but could not reach up to take it.

Like the hyacinth in the hills which the shepherd people
step on, trampling into the ground the flower in its purple.

10

You will die and be still, never shall be memory left of you
after this, nor regret when you are gone. You have not touched the
        flowers
of the Muses, and thus, shadowy still in the domain of Death,
you must drift with a ghost's fluttering wings, one of the darkened
        dead.

Translated by Richmond Lattimore

11

The moon has set,
And the Pleiades. It is
Midnight. Time passes.
I sleep alone.

Translated by Kenneth Rexroth

12

Percussion, salt and honey,
A quivering in the thighs;
He shakes me all over again,
Eros who cannot be thrown,
Who stalks on all fours
Like a beast.

13

Eros makes me shiver again
Strengthless in the knees,
Eros gall and honey,
Snake-sly, invincible.

Translated by Guy Davenport

XENOPHANES
570–Early 5th Century B.C.

Xenophanes left his native city, Colophon, on the coast of Asia Minor, in 545 B.C., when he was twenty-five years old (no. 2). The city was about to fall to the armies of the Persian Empire, which had defeated the Lydian king Croesus, with whom the Greek cities had lived in peace. Xenophanes recalls the days of peace when he and his fellow citizens enjoyed a luxurious standard of living (no. 6); for the rest of his long life, he was a wanderer in the free Greek world, and he died, far from home, probably at Elea on the west coast of southern Italy.

Xenophanes' protest against the Greek reverence for successful athletes (no. 1) is, as far as the archaic world was concerned, a voice crying in the wilderness; not until the fifth and fourth centuries were Euripides and Isocrates to express similar sentiments. Other fragments show that this was not the only unorthodox opinion put forward in his poems. In fact, the rejection of the idea of anthropomorphic gods implicit in nos. 3 and 4—as well as the approach to a monotheistic view in no. 5—find no echoes in Greek thought until very much later.

1

Now, supposing a man were to win the prize for the foot race
    at Olýmpia, there where the precinct of Zeus stands beside
the river, at Pisa: or if he wins the five-contests, or the wrestling,
    or if he endures the pain of boxing and wins, or that new
and terrible game they call the pankrátion, contest of all holds:
    why, such a man will obtain honor, in the citizens' sight,
and be given a front seat and be on display at all civic occasions,
    and he would be given his meals all at the public expense,
and be given a gift from the city to take and store for safekeeping.
    If he won with the chariot, too, all this would be granted to him,
and yet he would not deserve it, as I do. Better than brute strength
    of men, or horses either, is the wisdom that is mine.
But custom is careless in all these matters, and there is no justice
    in putting strength on a level above wisdom which is sound.
For if among the people there is one who is a good boxer,
    or one who excels in wrestling or in the five-contests,
or else for speed of his feet, and this is prized beyond other
    feats of strength that men display in athletic games,
the city will not, on account of this man, have better government.
    Small is the pleasure the city derives from one of its men
if he happens to come first in the games by the banks of Pisa.
    This does not make rich the treasure house of the state.

2

Now the Years are seven and sixty that have been tossing
    my restless intelligence up and down the land of the Greeks,
and to these there are five and twenty more still to be added
    before I began: at least if my addition is right.

Translated by Richmond Lattimore

3

If a horse or lion or a slow ox
had agile hands for paint and sculpture,
the horse would make his god a horse,
the ox would sculpt an ox.

4

Our gods have flat noses and black skins
say the Ethiopians. The Thracians say
our gods have red hair and hazel eyes.

5

There is one God—supreme among gods and men—
who is like mortals in neither body nor mind.

6

They acquired useless luxuries out of Lydia
while still free from her odious tyranny;
paraded to the market place in seapurple robes,
often in bright swarms of a thousand.
They were proud and pleased in their elaborate hairdo's
and hid body odor with rare perfumes.

7

The gods did not enrich man
with a knowledge of all things
from the beginning of life.
Yet man seeks, and in time
invents what may be better.

Translated by Willis Barnstone

MIMNERMUS
2nd Half of 7th Century B.C.

Mimnermus was born, like Xenophanes, in Colophon, but we have very little information about his life. He was active in the late seventh century. Probably because of the famous opening lines of no. 1, he was, and is, often thought of as a poet who sang of the joys of love; but in fact many of our fragments are, like the closing lines of no. 1, laments for the miseries of old age. One couplet is a wish for sixty years free of disease and oppressive troubles, and then death. Solon of Athens, who had presumably at the time passed his sixtieth birthday, addressed Mimnermus in a poem, telling him to wish to live until he was eighty.

1

What, then, is life if love the golden is gone? What is pleasure?
    Better to die when the thought of these is lost from my heart:
the flattery of surrender, the secret embrace in the darkness.
    These alone are such charming flowers of youth as befall
women and men. But once old age with its sorrows advances
    upon us, it makes a man feeble and ugly alike,
heart worn thin with the hovering expectation of evil,
    lost all joy that comes out of the sight of the sun.
Hateful to boys a man goes then, unfavored of women.
    Such is the thing of sorrow God has made of old age.

Translated by Richmond Lattimore

2

The sun works every day and there's no rest
    for him or for his horses once
the rose-fingered dawn leaves the ocean waters
    and begins to scale the firmament.
For with night the sun is swept across the waves
    in a hollow cup of gleaming gold,

a wondrous bed with wings, forged by Hephaistos;
it speeds him sleeping over salt foam
from the Hesperides to the Ethiopian desert.
There his fleet chariot and horses wait
till Dawn comes, early child of morning.

Translated by Willis Barnstone

THEOGNIS
6th Century B.C.

There was no such thing as copyright in the ancient world, not even the idea of literary property. Once a song had been sung or its text circulated among friends in handwritten copies, the author had no control over its fate. It could suffer interpolation or deletion; it could even, all or part of it, be incorporated in the body of an entirely different work, perhaps under another name. The first author we know of who was concerned about this matter and tried to do something about it was Theognis of Megara, a city that was later to fight and lose a war with Athens over the possession of the island of Salamis that lay between them.

In some lines addressed to a young man called Cyrnus, with whom he is in love, Theognis writes: "Cyrnus, as I compose my songs for you, let a seal be placed on the verses; if stolen they will never pass undetected nor will anyone exchange their present good content for worse—but everyone will say: 'They are the lines of Theognis of Megara, a name known to all mankind.'" The word "seal" is a metaphor from everyday business practice: he is thinking of the personal seal ring with which its owner could make an unmistakable impression on the wax that sealed the letter. But exactly what Theognis meant by this metaphor we cannot tell. This is the only passage that mentions his name, and even the frequent recurrence of the name of Cyrnus was obviously no effective bar to the literary forger. Whatever it was, it did not work. The book that has come down to us, consisting of some 700 elegiac couplets, contains lines that are elsewhere attributed to Solon, Mimnermus, and Tyrtaeus (and there may be more such material that we cannot at present identify); it contains a brilliant sequence that clearly refers to the danger faced by

Megara in the Persian invasion of 480 B.C. (the wrong century for Theognis); and it is full of needless repetitions and outright contradictions. What we have inherited looks rather like someone's private anthology of elegiac verse, of which Theognis' work formed the core.

The sequences addressed to Cyrnus, with the addition of lines attributed to Theognis by such authors of the fourth century B.C. as Aristotle and Plato, give us a total of some 300 lines. But they are enough to stamp on our memory the impression of a strong personality: an embittered aristocrat, warning Cyrnus against the violence and vulgarity of the lower classes (no. 3); a disappointed lover (no. 1); and finally an exile brooding on his wrongs (no. 7), reduced to poverty (no. 5) and despair (no. 4).

1

See, I have given you wings on which to hover uplifted
   high above earth entire and the great waste of the sea
without strain. Wherever men meet in festivals, as men
   gather, you will be there, your name will be spoken again
as the young singers, with the flutes clear piping beside them,
   make you into a part of the winsome verses, and sing
of you. And even after you pass to the gloom and the secret
   chambers of sorrow, Death's house hidden under the ground,
even in death your memory shall not pass, and it shall not
   die, but always, a name and a song in the minds of men,
Kyrnos, you shall outrange the land of Greece and the islands,
   cross the upheaving sea where the fish swarm, carried not
astride the back of a horse, but the shining gifts of the
     dark-wreathed
Muses shall be the force that carries you on your way.
For all wherever song is you shall be there for the singers.
   So long as earth endures and sun endures, you shall be.
I did this. But you give me not the smallest attention.
   You put me off with deceits as if I were a little child.

2

May wide and towering heaven collapse upon me in all its
   bronze and terror, catastrophe to the peoples of earth,
on that day when I no longer stand by my companions,
   on that day when I cease to harry my enemies.

3

Kyrnos, this city is still the same city, but its people are different.
Those who before knew nothing of lawsuits, nothing of laws,
who went about in goatskins flapping over their shoulders,
who lived on the ranges, far out from the town, like wild deer,
these are now the Great Men, son of Pólypas. Our former nobles
are Rabble now. Who could endure it when things are so?
They swindle each other, they mock at one another, and meanwhile
understand nothing at all of what good and bad men think.
Never make one of these citizens your friend, son of Pólypas,
however much you may need to use them: not from the heart:
pretend to all that you are their friend: talk as if you were one:
but never communicate to any one of these men
anything important. You must know that their purposes are
unpleasant,
and there is no trusting them in any matter at all,
but treachery, and deception, and catch-as-catch-can is their nature.
Such are the desperate men who have no future assured.

Translated by Richmond Lattimore

4

Best of all things—is never to be born,
never to know the light of sharp sun.
But being born, then best
to pass quickly as one can through the gates of Hell,
and there lie under the massive shield of earth.

5

Nothing destroys a good man quicker than poverty:
not malarial fever, Kyrnos, nor old age.
Better to hurl oneself into the abysmal sea
or over a blunt cliff—than be a victim
of poverty. The poor man can do or say nothing
worthwhile. Even his mouth is gagged.

6

In breeding donkeys, rams or horses, we seek out
the thoroughbred to get a good strain,

my Kyrnos. Yet now the noblest man will marry
    the lowest daughter of a base family,
if only she brings in money. And a lady
    will share her bed with a foul rich man,
preferring gold to pedigree. Money is all.
    Good breed with bad and race is lost
to riches. Don't wonder our city's blood is polluted
    when noble men will couple with upstarts.

7

I heard the sharp cry of the bird, O son of Polypas,
    who came to men with the message to plow
in good season; and it wounded my heart black
    that others own my flowering lands,
and not for me are mules dragging the curved plow,
    now, in my exile, on the wretched sea.

Translated by Willis Barnstone

SOLON

c. 640–After 561 B.C.

*All through the seventh century B.C., poets flourished in the Greek cities
of South Italy and Sicily, of the Aegean islands and of the coast of Asia
Minor, but Athens remained mute. When it was finally heard from, its
spokesman was not only a fine poet; he was also a great statesman. His
name was Solon, and he was a member of one of Athens' oldest aristocratic families. Already famous for his part in bringing about the victorious end of the war the Athenians waged against Megara for possession of
the island of Salamis, he was appointed, in 590 B.C., supreme magistrate
for a year with a commission to revise the laws in an attempt to prevent
the civil war that seemed inevitable as economic crisis gave a keener edge
to the hostility between rich and poor. He was successful in this; although Athens later came under the rule of a tyrant, civil war was
avoided.*

In some of the fragments of his poems (300 lines or so survive out of 5,000), we have his own account of his legislation and a defense of his actions. He wrote, in elegiac couplets (no. 2), a grim warning to his fellow citizens on the horrors of civil war: it *"invades the house of each citizen / and the courtyard doors no longer have strength to keep it away / but it overleaps the lofty wall . . ."* Once loosed, as in Beirut or Yugoslavia, it resists all attempts to contain it. In other fragments we find him writing iambic verse, but not for the same purpose as Archilochus or Hipponax. In no. 1 he discusses some of the measures he took to redress economic imbalance and restore social order, the remission of debts prominent among them; he also proudly refers to the way he prevented the reprisals both sides were ready to proceed with. Neither party, he says, was fully satisfied (no. 3), but both were held in check.

In these iambic poems, Solon developed a new style of discourse. The matter is elegantly organized, yet the sentences move with natural ease; the sequences are logical but the tone dramatic. It has been suggested that the early Attic tragic poets later found in these poems a model for the speech of the heroes of their plays. In one fragment (in iambic tetrameter) Solon even shows a gift for comedy. He puts a speech into the mouth of a critic, who blames and despises him for resigning at the end of his year in power, instead of becoming a tyrant:

> Solon was no deep thinker but a man devoid of sense, for the gods offered him blessings and he refused them. He had the catch inside his big net but in his amazement failed to pull it shut—as short of spirit as of brains. As for me, just to hold power, get wealth without limit and be despot of Athens for just one day, I'd be willing to be flayed alive to make a wine skin and have my whole line wiped out.

1

Where did I fail? When did I give up goals
for which I gathered my torn people together?
When the judgment of time descends on me,
call on my prime witness, Black Earth, supreme
excellent mother of the Olympian gods,
whose expanse was once pocked with mortgage stones,
which I dug out to free a soil in bondage.

Into our home, Athens, founded by the gods,
I brought back many sold unlawfully as slaves,
and throngs of debtors harried into exile,

drifting about so long in foreign lands
they could no longer use our Attic tongue;
here at home men who wore the shameful brand
of slavery and suffered the hideous moods
of brutal masters—all these I freed. Fusing
justice and power into an iron weapon,
I forced through every measure I had pledged.
I wrote the laws for good and bad alike,
and gave an upright posture to our courts.
Had someone else controlled the whip of power,
a bungler, a man of greed, he would not
have held the people in. Had I agreed
to do what satisfied opponents, or else
what their enemies planned in turn for them,
our dear city would be widowed of her men.
But I put myself on guard at every side,
spinning like a wolf among a pack of dogs.

Translated by Willis Barnstone

2

This city of ours will never be destroyed by the planning
   of Zeus, nor according to the wish of the immortal gods;
such is she who, great hearted, mightily fathered, protects us,
   Pallas Athene, whose hands are stretched out over our heads.
But the citizens themselves in their wildness are bent on destruction
   of their great city, and money is the compulsive cause.
The leaders of the people are evil-minded. The next stage
   will be great suffering, recompense for their violent acts,
for they do not know enough to restrain their greed and apportion
   orderly shares for all as if at a decorous feast.
· ·
   they are tempted into unrighteous acts and grow rich.
· ·
   sparing the property neither of the public nor of the gods,
they go on stealing, by force or deception, each from the other,
   nor do the solemn commitments of Justice keep them in check;
but she knows well, though silent, what happens and what has been
      happening,
   and in her time she returns to extract a full revenge;

for it comes upon the entire city as a wound beyond healing,
    and quickly it happens that foul slavery is the result,
and slavery wakens internal strife, and sleeping warfare,
    and this again destroys many in the pride of their youth,
for from enemies' devising our much-adored city is afflicted
    before long by conspiracies so dear to wicked men.
Such evils are churning in the home country, but, of the
    impoverished,
    many have made their way abroad on to alien soil,
sold away, and shamefully going in chains of slavery . . .

. . . .

Thus the public Ruin invades the house of each citizen,
    and the courtyard doors no longer have strength to keep it
    away,
but it overleaps the lofty wall, and though a man runs in
    and tries to hide in chamber or closet, it ferrets him out.
So my spirit dictates to me: I must tell the Athenians
    how many evils a city suffers from Bad Government,
and how Good Government displays all neatness and order,
    and many times she must put shackles on the breakers of laws.
She levels rough places, stops Glut and Greed, takes the force from
    Violence;
    she dries up the growing flowers of Despair as they grow;
she straightens out crooked judgments given, gentles the swollen
    ambitions, and puts an end to acts of divisional strife;
she stills the gall of wearisome Hate, and under her influence
    all life among mankind is harmonious and does well.

3

I gave the people as much privilege as they have a right to:
    I neither degraded them from rank nor gave them free hand;
and for those who already held the power and were envied for
    money,
    I worked it out that they also should have no cause for complaint.
I stood there holding my sturdy shield over both the parties;
    I would not let either side win a victory that was wrong.

. . . .

Thus would the people be best off, with the leaders they follow:
    neither given excessive freedom nor put to restraint;

for Glut gives birth to Greed, when great prosperity suddenly
befalls those people who do not have an orderly mind.

. . . .

Acting where issues are great, it is hard to please all.

Translated by Richmond Lattimore

ANACREON
c. 570–? B.C.

*When Polycrates, tyrant of Samos, fell into the hands of the Persians
and came to a ghastly end, Hipparchus, the last tyrant of Athens, sent a
fifty-oared ship to Samos to rescue and bring to his court the poet
Anacreon of Teos. Anacreon is the poet* par excellence *of the drinking
song and the frivolous love song; his erotic, symposiac poetry was admira-
bly suitable for the atmosphere of the tyrant's court at Athens, as it had
been on Samos, and there is no reason why he should have changed his
tune between one soft berth and another. He became extraordinarily
popular with the Athenians, as we could have guessed not only from the
statue of him set up later on the Acropolis but also from his frequent
appearance on Attic red-figure vases, which show him playing the lyre as
young men dance around him with abandon.*

*Critias, poet and tyrant of a different age and temper from Hippar-
chus and his father Pisistratus, paid tribute to this aspect of Anacreon's
muse: "Anacreon, you who once wove the strains of women's melodies,
who were the life of the male drinking party and the seducer of women
. . . affection for you shall never grow old as long as the boy carries round
the water mixed with wine." His name did in fact become proverbial as
the poet of wine, women (not to mention boys), and song. Though few
of us are conscious of the fact, we still pay tribute to Anacreon's memory
every time we sing the national anthem. When Francis Scott Key
watched the British bombardment of Fort McHenry and later wrote his
famous lines, he matched them to a melody that was running in his
head. It was the tune of a British drinking song that began: "To
Anacreon in Heaven / Our glasses we raise . . ."*

What little of his poetry has come down to us shows extraordinary artistry and an exquisite wit, playful rather than malicious. The short poem about the girl who turns away from him (no. 1) is typical in this respect, and the few drinking songs that survive show the same flair. He could be cutting when he wished: no. 2 shows him as master of the abusive iambic. Like Sappho and Alcaeus, he has a favored meter that was named after him, the Anacreontic. Lattimore reproduces it in English in no. 3.

1

The love god with his golden curls
puts a bright ball into my hand,
shows a girl in her fancy shoes,
and suggests that I take her.

Not that girl—she's the other kind,
one from Lesbos. Disdainfully,
nose turned up at my silver hair,
she makes eyes at the ladies.

2

Once he went out huddled about in dirty clothes with his hair
    skimped up,
buttons of wood hung in his ears for rings, and the hide of a
    threadbare ox
scrubbed from a cast-off shield to wrap
his bones to keep him warm. For friends all he could get was pastry
    cooks
or girls who walked the streets for fun. He was the lousy Ártemon.
He lived the life of a useless bum.
He got his neck framed in the pillory, he got whipped till his back
    was raw,
he had hairs pulled out of his head.
Look at him now, Kýke's boy; he rides in a coach and four, and
    wears
gold on his arms, gold on his neck, shaded by ivory parasols,
like some dame in society.

3

I have gone gray at the temples,
yes, my head is white, there's nothing
of the grace of youth that's left me,
and my teeth are like an old man's.
Life is lovely. But the lifetime
that remains for me is little.
For this cause I mourn. The terrors
of the Dark Pit never leave me.
For the house of Death is deep down
underneath; the downward journey
to be feared, for once I go there
I know well there's no returning.

Translated by Richmond Lattimore

4

My Thracian foal, why do you glare with disdain
and then shun me absolutely as if I knew
        nothing of this art?

I tell you I could bridle you with tight straps,
seize the reins and gallop you around the posts
        of the pleasant course.

But you prefer to graze on the calm meadow,
or frisk and gambol gayly—having no manly
        rider to break you in.

5

O sweet boy like a girl,
I see you though you will not look my way.
You are unaware that you handle the reins
        of my soul.

Translated by Willis Barnstone

6

Here lies Timokritos: soldier: valiant in battle.
Arês spares not the brave man, but the coward.

Translated by Dudley Fitts

"IF YOU CAN COUNT THE NUMBER"

Anacreon's characteristic themes and his meter were much admired and imitated in later centuries, and from those centuries we have inherited a fairly large collection of anonymous poems known as the Anacreontea. They were in their turn admired and imitated in the Renaissance, particularly in France, after they were first printed in 1554 by the great scholar and printer Henri Estienne. Ronsard, who began to write in the style and an approximation to the meter of Anacreon (at the time these poems were believed to be genuine), proclaimed his debt in a poetic toast to the publisher:

> *Je vais boire à Henry Estienne,*
> *Qui des enfers nous a rendu*
> *Du vieil Anacreon perdu*
> *La douce lyre Teïenne.*

Here is a specimen of the Anacreontea. It is a frivolous love piece, which could perhaps be aptly titled with a phrase from Mozart's Don Giovanni—*"Madamina, il catalogo e questo . . ."*

If you can count the number
of the leaves on all the branches,
or if you can find the total
of the waves in all the oceans,
I'll appoint you sole recorder—
you can catalogue my love life.

Now for Athens, just to start with,
write down the number thirty
and fifteen more for completeness.
After that, for Corinth, check off
love affairs in runs, in series
(for that city's in Achaea
where the girls are always handsome).
Then take down the score for Lesbos,
moving on towards Ionia
via Caria and Rhodos—
and the total now: two thousand.

What's the matter? Feeling dizzy?
Wait until I get to Syria,

to the yearning sighs of Egypt,
not to speak of Crete—the island
that has everything, where Eros
runs amok in all the cities.
And I will not even mention
love affairs beyond Gibraltar
and across the Indian border
in my amorous grand total.

Translated by Bernard Knox

IBYCUS
6th Century B.C.

Ibycus, who came from Rhegium in southern Italy, was another of the poets who were attracted to the court of Polycrates of Samos. He was famous for his love songs addressed to and about boys, but he also composed long mythological poems, like his fellow southern Italian Stesichorus. Some papyrus fragments of one of them—which ends with praise of Polycrates—have come to light. The poem is disappointing; compared to the two short pieces on love in our selection, it seems rather pedestrian.

1

In spring time the Kydonian
quinces, watered by running streams,
there where the maiden nymphs have
their secret garden, and grapes that grow
round in shade of the tendriled vine,
ripen.
      Now in this season for me
there is no rest from love.
Out of the hard bright sky,
a Thracian north wind blowing

with searing rages and hurt—dark,
pitiless, sent by Aphrodite—Love
rocks and tosses my heart.

Translated by Richmond Lattimore

2

Even now Eros looks at me with tenderness
from under dark eyelids, and casts me spellbound
into Aphrodite's nets where I lie caught
inextricably,

for I swear his mere approach makes me tremble
like an old champion chariot horse, as he
draws a swift cart unwillingly to the race.

Translated by Willis Barnstone

SIMONIDES
556–468 B.C.

*One more poet who was a guest of the tyrant of Samos, then of Hipparchus, tyrant of Athens—and who, like Anacreon, stayed on after the
democracy was set up in 509 B.C.—was Simonides, who came from
Ceos, an island about 15 miles southeast of the Attic coast. The pseudo-
Platonic dialogue* Hipparchus *tells us that the tyrant kept Simonides
happy with gifts and payments; we hear elsewhere of Simonides' insistence on high fees. All this may be merely a reflection of the fact that he
seems to have been the first openly professional bard, ready to go anywhere on commission—Thessaly, Sicily, Athens—and superbly
equipped to produce poetry of high quality in an amazing variety of
genres: choral lyric, dithyramb, victory odes for successful athletes,
dirges for the dead, epitaphs, elegiac verse, paeans (a special kind of
hymn to Apollo). We are even told that he composed tragedies, but of
his vast production only scraps remain.*

That he had an exquisite lyric style is clear from the fragment (no. 1) that describes Danae comforting her baby son Perseus in the wooden chest floating on the waves. Her father Acrisius, king of Argos, had been told by an oracle that he would be killed by his grandson. So he determined not to have one; he shut his daughter up in a bronze chamber under guard. But Zeus himself came to her, in the form of a shower of gold that filtered in through a crack in the roof, and she bore his son Perseus, who was to become the slayer of the Gorgon and eventually, by accident, of his grandfather. Acrisius set mother and son adrift on the sea in a locked wooden chest. In the fragment, Danae, after her moving words to the sleeping child, appeals in a somewhat peremptory tone to Zeus: "Let some change appear / Zeus, father, from you." One should not speak to a god like that, as she well knows. "This bold word and beyond justice / I speak, I pray you forgive it me." She is summoning Zeus to accept responsibility for his action. Which of course he does, and mother and son are rescued.

Although we know that the metrical organization of the fragment is strophic, we have no idea what kind of poem it came from. Nor do we know the context of no. 7, the long discussion of the difficulty of being a good man. We do know that the poem as a whole was addressed to Scopas, the ruler of the city of Crannon in Thessaly and one of Simonides' steady patrons. Simonides once wrote an ode celebrating a boxing champion, which had been commissioned by Scopas, and spent so much time celebrating the mythical prototypes of boxers, Castor and Polydeuces, that Scopas cut the fee in half. He told Simonides to ask Castor and Polydeuces for the rest of it. This is the only adverse comment preserved from antiquity on the mythical digression which had become a standard feature of the epinician ode.

The passage which deals with the difficulty of being good has been preserved because it is the subject of a dispute in Plato's dialogue Protagoras. *The Sophists Protagoras and Prodicus produce ethical interpretations of the passage, and Socrates outdoes them both with an interpretation that sounds like a parody of their methods, before Plato returns to more serious argument. The text itself is a remarkable specimen of sturdy, commonsense ethical thinking. Simonides is no philosopher, concerned, like Plato and Socrates, with defining goodness; and he is no Utopian, expecting more of human beings than they can give. He knew that circumstances can make all the difference—" it is not possible / for a man not to go bad / when he has more bad luck than he can handle . . . ," so he will not ask for too much, will not engage in the search for "the Utterly Blameless man . . ." And he can lighten this serious discourse with an ironic touch: "But if I find one, I will let you know." He is all too conscious of the instability of human life and fortune (no. 2).*

Simonides lived long enough to experience Greece's greatest moments, the Persian wars. The noble epitaph (no. 4) for the Spartan prophet who foresaw his death at Thermopylae but refused to withdraw, even though Leonidas would have sent him to the rear, is, as we know from Herodotus, his work; the seer Megistias was his friend. And it seems certain too that it was Simonides who composed the general epitaph for the three hundred Spartans who died there, the most famous two-line epitaph in all history (no. 3). But about the many other epitaphs attributed to him it is hard to be sure; his fame as a writer of epitaphs was such that in later times anything in this line that was worth remembering was attributed to him.

1

. . . when in the wrought chest
the wind blowing over
and the sea heaving
struck her with fear, her cheeks not dry,
she put her arm over Perseus and spoke: My child
such trouble I have.
And you sleep, your heart is placid;
you dream in the joyless wood;
in the night nailed in bronze,
in the blue dark you lie still and shine.
The salt water that towers above your head
as the wave goes by you
heed not, nor the wind's voice; you press
your bright face to the red blanket.
If this danger were danger to you,
your small ear would attend my words.
But I tell you: Sleep, my baby, and let the sea sleep, let
our trouble sleep; let some change appear

Zeus father, from you.
This bold word and beyond justice
I speak, I pray you, forgive it me.

2

Being no more than a man, you cannot tell what will happen
    tomorrow,
nor, when you see one walk in prosperity know for how much time
    it will be.
For overturn on the light-lifting wings of a dragonfly
is not more swift.

3

Traveler, take this word to the men of Lakedaímon:
    We who lie buried here did what they told us to do.

4

This is the grave of that Megístias, whom once the Persians
    and Medes killed when they crossed Spercheíos River; a seer
who saw clearly the spirits of death advancing upon him,
    yet could not bring himself to desert the Spartiate kings.

5

Friend, we once were alive in the harbor city of Korinth.
    Now the island city of Salamis is our grave.

Translated by Richmond Lattimore

6

Much have I eaten, much have I drunk and much have I slandered
Mankind. Now here I lie, Rhodian Timocrates.

Translated by Bernard Knox

7

To be a good man, without blame and without question,
foursquare founded hand and foot, mind also
faultless fashioned, is difficult.

Thus the word of Píttakos, but it does not
run right, though it was a wise man who said it:

that it is difficult to be excellent. Not difficult;
only a god could have this privilege; it is not *possible*
for a man not to go bad
when he has more bad luck than he can handle.
Any man is good while his luck is good,
bad when bad, and for the most part they are best
whom the gods love.

Therefore, I will not throw away my time and life
into unprofitable hope and emptiness, the search
for that object which cannot possibly be,
the Utterly Blameless Man among all of us who enjoy
man's food on the wide earth.
But if I find one, I will let you know.
No, I admire all, am a friend of any
who of his own will does nothing shameful. Against
necessity not even the gods can fight.

I do not like to find fault.
Enough for me if one is not
bad, not too unsteady, knows
what is right and good for his city,
a sound man. I will not
look out his faults. For the generation
of fools is endless. Take anything as good
which is not soiled with shame.

Translated by Richmond Lattimore

PINDAR

518–After 446 B.C.

Pindar, a native of Thebes, a mainland Greek city north of Athens, was a prolific lyric poet who composed in many different genres—hymns to the gods, dithyrambs to Dionysus, dirges for the dead, eulogies for the living, paeans *to Apollo—but the only complete works that have been preserved are four books of epinician odes dedicated to winners of athletic events at the principal athletic festivals celebrated in Greece. They are the games that were held at Nemea in the Peloponnese, at the Isthmus of Corinth, at Delphi, and at Olympia. The Olympian games, held every fourth year in the territory of Pisa near a hill named for Cronos, the father of Zeus, and the Alpheus River, were, as the opening lines of Pindar's First Olympian Ode proclaim, the most magnificent and famous. They were also the oldest, established in 776 B.C., a date that became the base of the most widely used Greek dating system.*

FIRST OLYMPIAN ODE (FOR HIERO OF SYRACUSE)

This ode celebrates an Olympic victory in the horse race, won by the horse Pherenikos ("Bringer of Victory") for Hiero of Syracuse in 476 B.C. Hiero did not of course ride the horse; that was the task of a jockey, whose name, for obvious reasons, is not mentioned. In the epinician ode it was customary, if not de rigueur, to associate the winner of the event with the mythic, heroic world of the past; woven into the complicated structures of praise for the victor and discreet self-advertisement for the poet was a mythical narrative that reflected glory on the patron and his city. Since the myths were usually familiar to the poet's audience— tyrant and court in this case, elsewhere the victor and his friends and family—the poet can be lightly allusive, touching only on those aspects of the story or stories that suit his present purpose. This can create difficulties for the modern reader. The First Olympian is particularly puzzling at first sight, since in addition to using only those details which fit his theme, Pindar makes radical changes in the well-known tale.

It is the story of Pelops, the foundation hero of the Olympic Games (and, incidentally, the man who gave his name to the main landmass of southern Greece), and his father Tantalus, king of Lydia. Tantalus was a friend of the gods, so dear a friend that they condescended to dine at his table. This gave him an overexalted idea of his stature; he felt himself to be their equal, and decided to put their powers and knowledge to a test. He killed his young son Pelops, carved and cooked the flesh, and served it to the gods. Only one of them, Demeter, goddess of the grain harvest, was deceived—she swallowed Pelops' shoulder. The gods reassembled Pelops and provided him with a prosthetic shoulder of ivory. Tantalus was condemned to everlasting punishment in the lower world. According to Homer, he was "tantalized" by food and water placed within reach, which retreated before him whenever he reached for it. Pindar follows the version that had him bound under a huge rock, always on the point of falling and crushing his head.

Pindar indignantly rejects the story of the cannibal feast. The sin of Tantalus was that he gave the divine nectar and ambrosia, food of the immortal gods, to mortal men. As for Pelops, he was taken up to Olympus by Poseidon to be his young lover, as Ganymede was by Zeus. When he could not be found, some malicious neighbor invented and spread the story of the cannibal feast. So far so good, but Pindar still has to deal with that ivory shoulder; it could not be excised since, for one thing, it was a sacred relic, on view at Olympia. So he has Pelops born with it: it was there when Clotho, one of the three Fates who presided over human births, drew him "out of the pure cauldron."

Because of the sin of Tantalus, the gods expelled Pelops from Olympus. When he came of age he asked Poseidon for help; he had decided to go to Greece and take up the challenge of Oenomaus, king of Pisa. The king had a daughter, Hippodamea (her name means "tamer of horses"), whom he did not wish to have married. He challenged her suitors to a chariot race: if a suitor won, he got the hand of the king's daughter; if he lost, he was killed. So far, thirteen had lost the race and their lives. Poseidon promised help, and Pelops went to Pisa, beat the king, who was killed in the race, married Hippodamea, and became king himself. Pindar does not mention it, but the usual story is that he bribed the king's groom, Myrtilus, to loosen the lynchpins of the royal chariot, so causing a wreck. The reason for the suppression of this detail is clear enough: Pindar is intent on investing Hiero's victory at Olympia with the mythic glory of Pelops' heroic decision and the divine blessing that gave him the victory. At the same time the story of Tantalus functions as a discreet warning to Hiero. An Olympic victory made a man feel almost equal to the gods; Hiero must, unlike Tantalus, "digest his great bliss." The ode concludes with a prayer that Hiero with "a god . . . as overseer [to] his ambitions" will one day, like Pelops, win a far greater prize—victory in the four-horse chariot race, the supreme event of the Olympic Games.

Our translator has preserved the original triadic metrical form of the original: strophe (Turn), antistrophe (Counterturn), and epode (Stand). In the parrheneion of Alcman these units were those of the dance. Whether these epinician odes were always delivered by a dancing chorus is a controversial question; for some of them, like our no. 2 (which is not an epinician ode at all but retains the form), performance by a chorus seems unlikely.

Turn 1
Water is preeminent and gold, like a fire
   burning in the night, outshines
all possessions that magnify men's pride.
   But if, my soul, you yearn
      to celebrate great games,
         look no further
         for another star
      shining through the deserted ether
   brighter than the sun, or for a contest
mightier than Olympia—
                              where the song
has taken its coronal
design of glory, plaited
in the minds of poets
   as they come, calling on Zeus' name,
   to the rich radiant hall of Hieron

Counterturn 1
who wields the scepter of justice in Sicily,
      reaping the prime of every distinction.
And he delights in the flare of music,
      the brightness of song circling
         his table from man to man.
         Then take the Dorian lyre
         down from its peg
      if the beauty of Pisa
   and of Pherenikos
somehow
         cast your mind
under a gracious spell,
when by the stream
of Alpheos, keeping his flanks
   ungrazed by the spur, he sped
      and put his lord in the embrace of power—

Stand 1
Syracusan knight and king, blazoned
      with glory in the land of Pelops:
Pelops, whom earth-cradling Poseidon loved,
since Klotho had taken him

out of the pure cauldron, his ivory shoulder
    gleaming in the hearth-light.
Yes! marvels are many, stories
starting from mortals somehow
    stretch truth to deception
woven cunningly on the loom of lies.

Turn 2
Grace, the very one who fashions every delight
    for mortal men, by lending her sheen
to what is unbelievable, often makes it believed.
        But the days to come
        are the wisest witness.
            It is proper for a man
        to speak well of the gods—
    the blame will be less.
Pelops, I will tell your story
differently from the men of old.
                    Your father Tantalos
had invited the gods to banquet
in his beloved Sipylos, providing
a stately feast in return
    for the feast they had given him.
    It was then Poseidon seized you,

Counterturn 2
overwhelmed in his mind with desire, and swept you
    on golden mares to Zeus' glorious palace
on Olympos, where, at another time, Ganymede came also
    for the same passion in Zeus.
        But after you had disappeared
        and searchers
        again and again
        returned to your mother
    without you, then one of the neighbors,
invidious, whispered
                that the gods had sliced you
limb by limb into the fury
of boiling water,
and then they passed
    morsels of your flesh
        around the table, and ate them.

Stand 2

No! I cannot call any of the blessed gods
    a savage: I stand apart.
Disaster has often claimed the slanderer.
If ever the watchlords of Olympos
honored a man, this was Tantalos.
    But he could not digest
his great bliss—in his fullness he earned the doom
that the father poised above him, the looming
        boulder which, in eternal
distraction, he strains to heave from his brow.

Turn 3

Such is the misery upon him, a fourth affliction
    among three others, because he robbed
the immortals—their nektar and ambrosia,
    which had made him deathless,
        he stole and gave
            to his drinking companions.
        But a man who hopes
        to hide his doings from the gods
    is deluded.
For this they hurled his son Pelops
                        back among the short-lived
generations of men.
But when he grew
toward the time of bloom
    and black down curled on his cheeks,
        he thought of a marriage there for his seeking—

Counterturn 3

to win from her Pisan father the girl Hippodameia.
    Going down by the dim sea,
alone in the dark, he called on the god
    of the trident, loud pounding
        Poseidon, who appeared
            and stood close by.
        "If in any way,"
        Pelops said to him,
    "the gifts of Aphrodite
count in my favor,
                    shackle the bronze spear of Oinomaos,

bring me on the swiftest chariot
to Elis, and put me
within the reach
   of power, for he has slain
      thirteen suitors now, and so he delays

Stand 3
his daughter's marriage. Great danger
   does not come upon
the spineless man, and yet, if we must die,
why squat in the shadows, coddling a bland
old age, with no nobility, for nothing?
   As for me, I will undertake this exploit.
And you—I beseech you: let me achieve it."
He spoke, and his words found fulfillment:
   the god made him glow with gifts—
a golden chariot and winged horses never weary.

Turn 4
He tore the strength from Oinomaos and took
   the maiden to his bed.
She bore him six sons, leaders of the people,
   intent on prowess.
      Now in the bright blood rituals
         Pelops has his share, reclining
      by the ford of Alpheos.
   Men gather at his tomb, near the crowded altar.
   The glory of the Olympiads
shoots its rays afar
               in his races, where speed
and strength are matched
in the bruise of toil.
But the victor,
   for the rest of his life,
      enjoys days of contentment,

Counterturn 4
as far as contests can assure them.
   A single day's blessing
is the highest good a mortal knows.
   I must crown him now
      to the horseman's tune,

in Aiolian rhythms,
for I believe
the shimmering folds of my song
shall never embrace
a host more lordly in power
or perception of beauty.
Hieron, a god is overseer
to your ambitions, keeping watch,
cherishing them as his own.
If he does not abandon you soon,
still sweeter the triumph I hope

Stand 4
will fall to your speeding chariot,
and may I be the one to praise it,
riding up the sunny Hill of Kronos!
The Muse is tempering her mightiest arrow for me.
Men are great in various ways, but in kingship
the ultimate crest is attained.
Peer no farther into the beyond.
For the time we have, may you continue to walk on high,
and may I for as long consort with victors,
conspicuous for my skill among Greeks everywhere.

Translated by Frank J. Nisetich

THIRD PYTHIAN ODE (FOR HIERO OF SYRACUSE)

This ode is not a celebration of an athletic victory won at the Pythian games at Delphi; in fact, it is not a victory ode in any sense of the word. It is a letter of comfort and consolation written by a friend to a man who is mortally ill. The man was Hiero of Syracuse, and the poem was composed probably about 472 B.C., not many years after the First Olympian Ode that sang of the victory of Hiero's horse Pherenikos.

The principal myth Pindar had recourse to here is the story of the birth (and the death) of Asclepius, the great healer—to whose sanctuaries all over the Greek world, and especially to the great complex of buildings at Epidaurus, men and women came seeking relief from disease. Asclepius was a son of Apollo, himself a healing god, though he could also dispense plague. His mother was a mortal woman, Koronis, daughter of Phlegyas, a Thessalian king who lived at Lakereia, near Lake

*Boibias. Pregnant by Apollo, Koronis took a mortal lover, Ischys, from
Arcadia. But Apollo knew at once, and sent his sister Artemis to kill
Koronis. As her corpse was placed on the pyre and the flames rose toward
it, Apollo rescued his son Asclepius and gave him to the centaur Chiron
to bring up. Chiron, half man and half horse, was, unlike the rest of the
centaurs, whose violence was notorious, a wise and gentle creature, a
great healer and a trainer of heroes, Achilles and Jason among them.
Under his tutelage Asclepius became the greatest healer of all, one to
whom men and women flocked to be cured. But he went too far; for
money, he restored a dead man to life, and Zeus blasted him out of
existence with a lightning bolt.*

*Pindar begins in the middle of the story, with a wish that Chiron were
still alive; if so, as he says many lines later, he could perhaps have
charmed him with song and "persuaded him even now / to give me a
healer against the burning sickness of great men . . ." But it is an impossible wish, like all the wishes of this poem. The leitmotif is "If only . . .";
the mood is the melancholy that phrase engenders. And the meaning of
the myth for Hiero is all too clear. He must not be like Koronis, who
"was in love with what was not there." Nor like Asclepius, who over-
stepped the boundaries prescribed for human action. Hiero is deathly
sick, and must often think angrily that his enormous wealth and supreme
power ought to exempt him from the common fate of humanity. Hiero
must "seek from the gods that which becomes us / knowing where we
belong . . ."*

*If only . . . If only Chiron were living yet. If only "I could have come
down from the sea / with a gift in either hand, golden health, and praise
. . ." But it cannot be. Hiero must accept his fate like a hero. "Men who
are as children cannot take this becomingly; / but the manly do, turning
the brightness outward." Heroes, too, even those who walked with gods,
knew affliction: Cadmus saw the sad fate of his daughters, and Peleus'
son Achilles fell at Troy. The one thing Hiero can think of now with
some comfort is his glory in time to come. That depends, like the fame
of Nestor and Sarpedon, on the words of the poets; and Hiero's glory,
Pindar is assuring him in the last lines, is in good hands.*

I could wish that Chiron, Philyra's son
(if such word of prayer from my lips could be published),
the departed, were living yet,
child wide-minded of Uranian Kronos, and ruled the Pelian glades,
    that beast of the hills

with the heart kindly to men, as of old when he reared
the gentle smith of pain's ease to heal bodies, Asklepios,
the hero who warded sickness of every kind.

Koronis, daughter of Phlegyas the great horseman,
before with the ministration of Eleithyia she brought her child to
    birth, was stricken
by the golden bow of Artemis
in a bedroom, and went down into the house of death
by design of Apollo. No slight thing
is the anger of the children of Zeus. She, making little of this
in her confused heart, accepted a second marriage, in secrecy
from her father,
she who had lain before with Phoibos of the loose hair

and carried the immaculate seed of the god.
She could not stay for the coming of the bride-feast,
not for hymen cry in many voices, such things
as the maiden companions of youth are accustomed to sing
at nightfall, using the old names of endearment. No.
She was in love with what was not there; it has happened to many.
There is a mortal breed most full of futility.
In contempt of what is at hand, they strain into the future,
hunting impossibilities on the wings of ineffectual hopes.

Willful elegantly-robed Koronis was taken
by even such an obsession. She went to bed with a stranger
who came from Arkadia, nor escaped
the Watcher. In his temple at Pytho, where the sheep are offered,
    King Loxias knew,
persuading his heart to the sheerest witness, his own
mind that knows all; he has no traffic with lies, nor god
nor man escapes him in purpose or deed of the hand.

Knowing the hospitality of bed given Ischys,
Eilatos' son, and the graceless treachery, he sent his sister inflamed
with anger that brooked no bar,
to Lakereia, for the girl lived by Boibias under the pendulous cliffs;
    her angel
shifted to evil and struck her down; and many a neighbor
shared, and was smitten together. Fire on a mountain leaping
from one seed will obliterate a great forest.

But when her kinsmen had laid the girl in the wall
of wood, and Hephaistos' greedy flame
ran high, then spoke Apollo: "No longer
will I endure in my heart the destruction of my own child
by a most pitiful death along with his mother's heavy suffering."
He spoke, and in the first stride was there and caught the boy
from the body, and the blaze of the pyre was divided before him.
Carrying him to the centaur in Magnesia, he gave him to be
      perfected
in the healing of sicknesses that bring many pains to men.

They came to him with ulcers the flesh had grown,
or their limbs mangled with the gray bronze, or bruised
with the stone flung from afar,
or the body stormed with summer fever, or chill; and he released
      each man and led him
from his individual grief. Some he treated with gentle incantations,
some with healing potions to drink; or he tended the limbs with
      salves
from near and far; and some by the knife he set on their feet again.

But even genius is tied to profit. Someone
turned even Asklepios with a lordly price, showing the gold in his
      hand,
to bring back from death a man
already gone. But Zeus Kronion, with a cast of his hand, tore life
      from the hearts of both men
instantly, and the shining thunder dashed them to death.
With our mortal minds we should seek from the gods that which
      becomes us,
knowing where we belong, and what lies before our feet.

Dear soul of mine, never urge a life beyond
mortality, but work the art that is yours to the end.
But if only temperate Chiron were living yet in his cave,
and the charm of these songs I make might have cast some spell
across his heart, I could have persuaded him even now
to give me a healer against the burning sickness of great men,
someone called son of Apollo or even of Zeus the father.
I could have come by ship, cutting the Ionian sea,
to the spring of Arethousa and my friend and host of Aitna.

He disposes in Syracuse as a king
mild to citizens, not envious of good men, to strangers a father
    admired.
If I could have come down from the sea
with a gift in either hand, golden health, and praise, glorious with
    garlands of the Pythian Games
Pherenikos won him once on a time, the best horse beside Kirrha,
I say that I would have crossed the deep sea bringing him light
to shine afar, more bright than a star in heaven.

But I am willing to pray to the Great Mother
to whom night after night before my doors, a stately goddess,
the maidens dance, and to Pan beside her.
But, Hieron, if you know how to take the straight issue of
words, you understand what the ancients said:
For every one good thing, the immortals bestow on men
two evils. Men who are as children cannot take this becomingly;
but the manly do, turning the brightness outward.

The portion of happiness has come your way.
Great destiny looks to you, if to any man, as a lord
and leader of people. But a life unshaken
befell neither Peleus called Aiakidas
nor godlike Kadmos, yet men say these two were given
blessedness beyond all mortals. They heard on the mountain
and at seven-gated Thebes the gold-chapleted Muses singing
when one married ox-eyed Harmonia, and the other
wise Nereus' legendary daughter, Thetis.

And the gods feasted beside them each in turn,
and they saw the kings, the sons of Kronos, in their golden chairs,
    and accepted
their gifts. And after troubles endured before
they won in requital the favor of Zeus, and their hearts were
    restored. But again in time
three daughters suffered and made Kadmos desolate
of gladness; though Zeus father came to the lovely embrace
of the fourth, white-armed Thyona.

And Peleus' son, the sole child
immortal Thetis bore him in Phthia, left life in battle, arrowstruck;
and his body, burned on the pyre,

stirred the Danaan grief. If any mortal keeps in mind the way of
  truth, he must take
with grace whatever the gods give. Various ways go the blasts
of the high-flown winds. Men's prosperity will not walk far
safe, when it fares under its own deep weight.

I will be small in small things, great among great.
I will work out the divinity that is busy within my mind
and tend the means that are mine.
If it were luxury and power God gave me
I hope I should find glory that would rise higher hereafter.
Nestor and Sarpedon of Lykia we know,
legends of men, from the sounding words that smiths of song in
  their wisdom
built to beauty. In the glory of poetry achievement of men
blossoms long; but to do this well is given to few.

Translated by Richmond Lattimore

BACCHYLIDES

6th–5th Centuries B.C.

*Bacchylides, a younger rival of Pindar, came—like his uncle Simo-
nides—from the island of Ceos. Until 1896 we had only fragments of his
work—citations by later authors—but in that year the British Museum
acquired portions of a papyrus roll that contained nineteen poems, some
of them complete. Thirteen of them are epinician odes, the rest dithyrambs.*

DITHYRAMB. THESEUS ON HIS WAY TO ATHENS

*One of Bacchylides' dithyrambs takes the form of a dramatic dialogue:
Aegeus, king of Athens, is questioned by a chorus of citizens about the
alarm signal that has been sounded on the trumpet and tells them what
little he knows. A "mighty man" on the Corinth road has performed a*

*series of epic feats, ridding the world of a crowd of monsters that preyed
on travelers. Sinis the giant tore his victims apart by tying them to the
tops of two pine trees he had bent down to ground level and then letting
the trees loose to swing back to their full height. An immense and savage
boar devoured men in the woods of Cremmyon. Sciron, sitting on a cliff
edge, forced travelers to wash his feet, and as they bent down to do so,
kicked them over the edge to be torn apart by a giant tortoise that was
waiting below. Cercyon challenged passers-by to a wrestling match,
which always ended in their deaths. And Procrustes (the Butcher), the
son of Polypemon, adjusted the size of his victims to his bed, cutting the
long ones short and flattening the short ones out with a hammer. The
young man on the road has killed them all—and he is on his way to
Athens.*

*Aegeus cannot tell the chorus who this redoubtable young man is, but
the audience knew that it was Theseus, a son born long ago to Aegeus
without his knowledge, whose mother has raised him and now sent him
on his way to claim his heritage. The audience knows also that the
apprehension clear in Aegeus' words is justified; many years later this boy
will, unintentionally, cause Aegeus' death.*

CHORUS OF ATHENIANS: King of our sacred Athens,
        Elegant Ionians' lord,
        Why this splitting warsong
        Blared from the brass horns?
        Does a marshal press
        His enemy raiders
        Around our borders?
        Or treacherous bandits
        Wrest the flocks
        From the shepherds
        And drive them off?
        Or worry tear your heart?
        Speak: you are the one,
        O Pandion's son and Creousa's,
        Backed by matchless young allies.
KING AEGEUS: Fresh from his heat
        On the Corinth road,
        A runner tells out
        Unbelievable acts
        Of a mighty man:
        He's brought down Sinis
        The Bender of Pines,

A son of Looser Poseidon
Who wracks the earth;
He's killed the boar
That devoured men
In the woods of Cremmyon,
Put an end
To the reckless Sciron,
Shut the wrestling ring
Of Cercyon, and snapped
Polypemon's club from the Butcher
Who met with a better man.
I dread where his works will end.
CHORUS OF ATHENIANS: What's his name?
His land? his equipment?
Does he head up an army
Massing along
In heavy gear?
Or trek alone
With his henchmen,
A wanderer out
For exotic lands?
Iron in heart
This invincible one
Who checks the strength
Of immense opponents;
A god is behind him,
Forging these laws
For a dragon-ridden land.
Outrage mounting on outrage
Always meets its retribution.
All ends in the drift of time.
KING AEGEUS: Only two keep his pace,
Over glistening shoulders
He slings a sword
With an ivory hilt,
Two sanded lances
Ride his grip,
A stitched Laconian
Skincap binds
His burnished locks,
Hugging his chest
A seablue tunic

And horseman's woolly cape;
From eyes like the Lemnos-fire
Leaps flaring flame,
And but a boy in the bud of youth,
Yet bent on the grim delights of war
And the din of bronze on bronze,
He strides on to illustrious Athens!

Translated by Robert Fagles

PRAXILLA
5th Century B.C.

Praxilla was a lyric poet who lived in Sicyon, a city near the southern shore of Gulf of Corinth. The beautiful fragment that follows comes from a poem called Adonis. *It is the reply Adonis makes to the question put to him by the shades of the Underworld when he arrives there after his death: "What was the most beautiful thing you left behind you?"*

The only reason we have this tantalizing fragment of Praxilla's work is that one Zenobius, who compiled a dictionary of proverbial phrases in the reign of the emperor Hadrian, quotes it to explain the proverb: "Sillier than Praxilla's Adonis." Anyone, he goes on, who would list cucumbers and so on together with the sun and the moon must be simple-minded.

Finest of all the things I have left is the light of the sun,
Next to that the brilliant stars and the face of the moon,
Cucumbers in their season, too, and apples and pears.

Translated by Bernard Knox

HERODOTUS
490–c. 425 B.C.

From THE HISTORY

Cicero called Herodotus the father of history; others have thought him the father of lies. There is truth in both verdicts. He is the first writer we know of to recreate, on an epic scale, the remote and immediate past of his contemporary world—not only of his native Greece but also of the great Eastern civilizations (Egypt, Babylon, and Persia), and of barbarian tribes in the Balkans and South Russia. On the other hand, for most of his narrative he is almost entirely dependent on oral sources, and in that area he is sometimes not as critical as modern historical standards would demand. "I consider it my duty," he remarks, "to report what people say, but I do not always feel obliged to believe it." Sometimes of course he has only one report to go on, and, true or not, he includes it. But since what so many of his informants passed on to him are fascinating stories, his readers are happy that his criteria were not too strict.

CANDAULES AND GYGES

Herodotus' purpose, he announces in the opening sentences of his History, is "to preserve the memory of the past by recording the amazing achievements of the Greeks and also of foreign peoples, and in addition, the reason they went to war with one another." As he works his way toward the climax of his story—the battles of Marathon (490 B.C.), Salamis (480), and Plataea (479)—he explores the history, customs, and religions of all the nations that were eventually involved in the great Persian War. In his enquiry into the causes, he starts with the man who, in modern times as opposed to the mythical time of the Trojan War, began the quarrel between East and West. It was Croesus, king of Lydia in Asia Minor, who annexed the Greek cities on the Ionian coastline.

But Herodotus begins several generations further back, with the founder of Croesus' royal dynasty, Gyges, and this enables him to offer his readers, very near the beginning of the long work, the extraordinary story of Candaules, the king who was too much in love with his own wife.

This Candaules fell in love with his own wife; and because he was so in love, he thought he had in her far the most beautiful of women. So he thought. Now, he had a bodyguard named Gyges, the son of Dascylus, who was his chief favorite among them. Candaules used to confide all his most serious concerns to this Gyges, and of course he was forever over-praising the beauty of his wife's body to him. Some time thereafter—for it was fated that Candaules should end ill—he spoke to Gyges thus: "Gyges, I do not think that you credit me when I tell you about the beauty of my wife; for indeed men's ears are duller agents of belief than their eyes. Contrive, then, that you see her naked." The other made outcry against him and said, "Master, what a sick word is this you have spoken, in bidding me look upon my mistress naked! With the laying-aside of her clothes, a woman lays aside the respect that is hers! Many are the fine things discovered by men of old, and among them this one, that each should look upon his own, only. Indeed I believe that your wife is the most beautiful of all women, and I beg of you not to demand of me what is unlawful."

With these words he would have fought him off, being in dread lest some evil should come to himself out of these things; but the other answered him and said: "Be of good heart, Gyges, and fear neither myself, lest I might suggest this as a trial of you, nor yet my wife, that some hurt might befall you from her. For my own part I will contrive it entirely that she will not know she has been seen by you. For I will place you in the room where we sleep, behind the open door. After my coming-in, my wife too will come to her bed. There is a chair that stands near the entrance. On this she will lay her clothes, one by one, as she takes them off and so will give you full leisure to view her. But when she goes from the chair to the bed and you are behind her, let you heed then that she does not see you as you go through the door."

Inasmuch, then, as Gyges was unable to avoid it, he was ready. Candaules, when he judged the hour to retire had come, led Gyges into his bedroom; and afterwards his wife, too, came in at once; and, as she came in and laid her clothes aside, Gyges viewed her. When she went to the bed and Gyges was behind her, he slipped out—but the woman saw him as he was going through the door. She understood then what had been done by her husband; and though she was so shamed, she raised no outcry nor let on to have understood, having in mind to take punishment on Candaules. For among the Lydians and indeed among the generality of the barbarians, for even a man to be seen naked is an occasion of great shame.

So for that time she showed nothing but held her peace. But when the day dawned, she made ready such of her household servants as she saw were most loyal to her and sent for Gyges. He gave never a thought to her knowing anything of what had happened and came on her summons, since he had been wont before this, also, to come in attendance whenever the queen should call him. As Gyges appeared, the woman said to him: "Gyges, there are two roads before you, and I give you your choice which you will travel. Either you kill Candaules and take me and the kingship of the Lydians, or you must yourself die straightway, as you are, that you may not, in days to come, obey Candaules in everything and look on what you ought not. For either he that contrived this must die or you, who have viewed me naked and done what is not lawful." For a while Gyges was in amazement at her words; but then he besought her not to bind him in the necessity of such a choice. But he did not persuade her—only saw that necessity truly lay before him: either to kill his master or himself be killed by others. So he chose his own survival. Then he spoke to her and asked her further: "Since you force me to kill my master, all unwilling, let me hear from you in what way we shall attack him." She answered and said: "The attack on him shall be made from the self-same place whence he showed me to you naked, and it is when he is sleeping that you shall attack him."

So they prepared their plot, and, as night came on—for there was no going back for Gyges, nor any riddance of the matter but that either himself or Candaules must die—he followed the woman into the bedroom. She gave him a dagger and hid him behind the very door. And after that, as Candaules was taking his rest, Gyges slipped out and killed him, and so it was that he, Gyges, had the wife and the kingship of Lydia. Archilochus of Paros, who lived at the same time, made mention of him in a poem of iambic trimeters.

Translated by David Grene

SOLON AND CROESUS

Since Croesus did not consolidate his hold on the throne of Lydia until 560 B.C., and Solon must have been a man of mature age when appointed supreme magistrate in 594 B.C., the meeting between them described in the following extract seems, on chronological grounds, un-

likely. It was in fact regarded as suspect in antiquity. Plutarch, in his Life
of Solon, *has some pertinent comments: "Some people think they can
expose this meeting as a fiction on chronological grounds. For my part,
this story is so famous, and so often quoted, and, what is more, so characteristic of Solon's magnanimity and wisdom, that I do not think it right
to reject it on such grounds. . . ."*

In the course of time Croesus subdued all the peoples west of the river
Halys, except the Cilicians and Lycians. The rest he kept in subjection—
Lydians, Phrygians, Mysians, Mariandynians, Chalybians, Paphlagoni-
ans, Thracians (both Thynian and Bithynian), Carians, Ionians, Dorians, Aeolians, and Pamphylians.

When all these nations had been added to the Lydian empire, and
Sardis was at the height of her wealth and prosperity, all the great Greek
teachers of that epoch, one after another, paid visits to the capital. Much
the most distinguished of them was Solon the Athenian, the man who at
the request of his countrymen had made a code of laws for Athens. He
was on his travels at the time, intending to be away ten years, in order to
avoid the necessity of repealing any of the laws he had made. That, at
any rate, was the real reason of his absence, though he gave it out that
what he wanted was just to see the world. The Athenians could not alter
any of Solon's laws without him, because they had solemnly sworn to
give them a ten years' trial.

For this reason, then—and also no doubt for the pleasure of foreign
travel—Solon left home and, after a visit to the court of Amasis in
Egypt, went to Sardis to see Croesus.

Croesus entertained him hospitably in the palace, and three or four
days after his arrival instructed some servants to take him on a tour of the
royal treasuries and point out the richness and magnificence of everything. When Solon had made as thorough an inspection as opportunity
allowed, Croesus said: "Well, my Athenian friend, I have heard a great
deal about your wisdom, and how widely you have travelled in the pursuit of knowledge. I cannot resist my desire to ask you a question: who is
the happiest man you have ever seen?"

The point of the question was that Croesus supposed himself to be the
happiest of men. Solon, however, refused to flatter, and answered in
strict accordance with his view of the truth. "An Athenian," he said,
"called Tellus."

Croesus was taken aback. "And what," he asked sharply, "is your
reason for this choice?"

"There are two good reasons," said Solon, "first, his city was prosperous, and he had fine sons, and lived to see children born to each of them, and all these children surviving; and, secondly, after a life which by our standards was a good one, he had a glorious death. In a battle with the neighbouring town of Eleusis, he fought for his countrymen, routed the enemy, and died like a soldier; and the Athenians paid him the high honour of a public funeral on the spot where he fell."

All these details about the happiness of Tellus, Solon doubtless intended as a moral lesson for the king; Croesus, however, thinking he would at least be awarded second prize, asked who was the next happiest person whom Solon had seen.

"Two young men of Argos," was the reply; "Cleobis and Biton. They had enough to live on comfortably; and their physical strength is proved not merely by their success in athletics, but much more by the following incident. The Argives were celebrating the festival of Hera, and it was most important that the mother of the two young men should drive to the temple in her ox-cart; but it so happened that the oxen were late in coming back from the fields. Her two sons therefore, as there was no time to lose, harnessed themselves to the cart and dragged it along, with their mother inside, for a distance of nearly six miles, until they reached the temple. After this exploit, which was witnessed by the assembled crowd, they had a most enviable death—a heaven-sent proof of how much better it is to be dead than alive. Men kept crowding round them and congratulating them on their strength, and women kept telling the mother how lucky she was to have such sons, when, in sheer pleasure at this public recognition of her sons' act, she prayed the goddess Hera, before whose shrine she stood, to grant Cleobis and Biton, who had brought her such honour, the greatest blessing that can fall to mortal man.

"After her prayer came the ceremonies of sacrifice and feasting; and the two lads, when all was over, fell asleep in the temple—and that was the end of them, for they never woke again.

"The Argives had statues made of them, which they sent to Delphi, as a mark of their particular respect."

Croesus was vexed with Solon for giving the second prize for happiness to the two young Argives, and snapped out: "That's all very well, my Athenian friend; but what of my own happiness? Is it so utterly contemptible that you won't even compare me with mere common folk like those you have mentioned?"

"My lord," replied Solon, "I know God is envious of human prosperity and likes to trouble us; and you question me about the lot of man. Listen then: as the years lengthen out, there is much both to see and to suffer which one would wish otherwise. Take seventy years as the span of a man's life: those seventy years contain 25,200 days, without counting intercalary months. Add a month every other year, to make the seasons come round with proper regularity, and you will have thirty-five additional months, which will make 1050 additional days. Thus the total of days for your seventy years is 26,250, and not a single one of them is like the next in what it brings. You can see from that, Croesus, what a chancy thing life is. You are very rich, and you rule a numerous people; but the question you asked me I will not answer, until I know that you have died happily. Great wealth can make a man no happier than moderate means, unless he has the luck to continue in prosperity to the end. Many very rich men have been unfortunate, and many with a modest competence have had good luck. The former are better off than the latter in two respects only, whereas the poor but lucky man has the advantage in many ways; for though the rich have the means to satisfy their appetites and to bear calamities, and the poor have not, the poor, if they are lucky, are more likely to keep clear of trouble, and will have besides the blessings of a sound body, health, freedom from trouble, fine children, and good looks.

"Now if a man thus favoured dies as he has lived, he will be just the one you are looking for: the only sort of person who deserves to be called happy. But mark this: until he is dead, keep the word 'happy' in reserve. Till then, he is not happy, but only lucky.

"Nobody of course can have all these advantages, any more than a country can produce everything it needs: whatever it has, it is bound to lack something. The best country is the one which has most. It is the same with people: no man is ever self-sufficient—there is sure to be something missing. But whoever has the greatest number of the good things I have mentioned, and keeps them to the end, and dies a peaceful death, that man, my lord Croesus, deserves in my opinion to be called happy.

"Look to the end, no matter what it is you are considering. Often enough God gives a man a glimpse of happiness, and then utterly ruins him."

These sentiments were not of the sort to give Croesus any pleasure; he let Solon go with cold indifference, firmly convinced that he was a fool. For what could be more stupid than to keep telling him to look at the "end" of everything, without any regard to present prosperity?

After Solon's departure Croesus was dreadfully punished, presumably because God was angry with him for supposing himself the happiest of men. It began with a dream he had about a disaster to one of his sons: a dream which came true. He had two sons: one with a physical disability, being deaf and dumb; the other, named Atys, as fine a young man as one can fancy. Croesus dreamt that Atys would be killed by a blow from an iron weapon. He woke from the dream in horror, and lost no time in getting his son a wife, and seeing to it that he no longer took the field with the Lydian soldiers, whom he used to command. He also removed all the weapons—javelins, spears and so on—from the men's rooms, and had them piled up in the women's quarters, because he was afraid that some blade hanging on the wall might fall on Atys' head.

The arrangements for the wedding were well in hand, when there came to Sardis an unfortunate stranger who had been guilty of manslaughter. He was a Phrygian, and related to the Phrygian royal house. This man presented himself at the palace and begged Croesus to cleanse him from blood-guilt according to the laws of the country (the ceremony is much the same in Lydia as in Greece): and Croesus did as he asked. When the formalities were over, Croesus, wishing to know who he was and where he came from, said: "What is your name, stranger, and what part of Phrygia have you come from, to take refuge with me? What man or woman did you kill?"

"Sire," the stranger replied, "I am the son of Gordias, and Midas was my grandfather. My name is Adrastus. I killed my brother by accident, and here I am, driven from home by my father and stripped of all I possessed."

"Your family and mine," said Croesus, "are friends. You have come to a friendly house. If you stay in my dominions, you shall have all you need. The best thing for you will be not to take your misfortune too much to heart." Adrastus, therefore, took up his residence in the palace.

Now it happened just at this time that Mount Olympus in Mysia was infested by a monstrous boar. This tremendous creature used to issue from his mountain lair and play havoc with the crops, and many times the Mysians had taken the field against him, but to no purpose. The unfortunate hunters received more damage than they were able to inflict. As a last resource the Mysians sent to Croesus.

"Sire," the messengers said, "a huge beast of a boar has appeared amongst us, and is doing fearful damage. We want to catch him, but we can't. Please, my lord, send us your son with a party of young men, and some dogs, so that we can get rid of the brute."

Croesus had not forgotten his dream, and in answer to this request forbade any further mention of his son.

"I could not send him," he said; "he is just married, and that keeps him busy. But I will certainly send picked men, with a complete hunting outfit, and I will urge them to do all they can to help rid you of the animal."

This answer satisfied the Mysians; but at that moment Atys, who had heard of their request, entered the room. The young man, finding that Croesus persisted in his refusal to let him join the hunting party, said to his father: "Once honour demanded that I should win fame as a huntsman and fighter; but now, father, though you cannot accuse me of cowardice or lack of spirit, you won't let me take part in either of these admirable pursuits. Think what a figure I must cut when I walk between here and the place of assembly! What will people take me for? What must my young wife think of me? That she hasn't married much of a husband, I fear! Now, father, either let me join this hunt, or give me an intelligible reason why what you're doing is good for me."

"My son," said Croesus, "of course you are not a coward or anything unpleasant of that kind. That is not the reason for what I'm doing. The fact is, I dreamt that you had not long to live—that you would be killed by an iron weapon. It was that dream that made me hasten your wedding; and the same thing makes me refuse to let you join in this enterprise. As long as I live, I am determined to protect you, and to rob death of his prize. You are my only son, for I do not count that wretched cripple, your brother."

"No one can blame you, father," Atys replied, "for taking care of me after a dream like that. Nevertheless there is something which you have failed to observe, and it is only right that I should point it out to you. You dreamt that I should be killed by an iron weapon. Very well: has a boar got hands? Can a boar hold this weapon you fear so much? Had you dreamt that I should be killed by a boar's tusk or anything of that sort, your precautions would be justified. But you didn't: it was a weapon which was to kill me. Let me go, then. It is only to hunt an animal, not to fight against men."

"My boy," said Croesus, "I own myself beaten. You interpret the dream better than I did. I cannot but change my mind, and allow you to join the expedition."

The king then sent for Adrastus the Phrygian, and said to him: "Through no fault of your own, Adrastus, you came to me in great distress and with an ugly stain on your character. I gave you ritual purification, welcomed you to my house, and have spared no expense to entertain you. Now I expect a fair return for my generosity: take charge of my son on this boar-hunt; protect him from footpads and cut-throats on the road. In any case it is your duty to go where you can distinguish yourself: your family honour demands it, and you are a stalwart fellow besides."

"Sire," Adrastus answered, "under ordinary circumstances I should have taken no part in this adventure. A man under a cloud has no business to associate with those who are luckier than himself. Indeed I have no heart for it, and there are many reasons to prevent my going. But your wishes make all the difference. It is my duty to gratify you in return for your kindness; so I am ready to do as you ask. So far as it lies in my power to protect your son, you may count on his returning safe and sound."

When Adrastus had given his answer, the party set out, men, dogs, and all. They made their way to Olympus and kept their eyes open for the boar. As soon as they spotted him, they surrounded him and let fly with spears—and then it was that the stranger—Adrastus, the very man whom Croesus had cleansed from the stain of blood—aimed at the boar, missed him, and struck the king's son. Croesus' dream had come true.

A messenger hurried off to Sardis, and Croesus was told of the encounter with the boar and the death of his son. The shock of the news was dreadful; and the horror of it was increased by the fact that the weapon had been thrown by the very man whom the king had cleansed from the guilt of blood. In the violence of his grief Croesus prayed to Zeus, calling on him as God of Purification to witness what he had suffered at the hands of his guest; he invoked him again under his title of Protector of the Hearth, because he had unwittingly entertained his son's murderer in his own house; and yet again as God of Friendship, because the man he had sent to guard his son had turned out to be his bitterest enemy.

Before long the Lydians arrived with the body, followed by the unlucky killer. He took his stand in front of the corpse, and stretching out his hands in an attitude of submission begged the king to cut his throat there and then upon the dead body of his son.

"My former trouble," he said, "was bad enough. But now that I have ruined the man who absolved me of my guilt, I cannot bear to live."

In spite of his grief Croesus was moved to pity by these words. "Friend," he said, "as you condemn yourself to death, there is nothing more I can require of you. Justice is satisfied. This calamity is not your fault; you never meant to strike the blow, though strike it you did. Some God is to blame—some God who long ago warned me of what was to happen."

Croesus buried his son with all proper ceremony; and as soon as everything was quiet after the funeral, Adrastus—the son of Gordias, the grandson of Midas: the man who had killed his brother and ruined the host who gave him purification—convinced that he was the unluckiest of all the men he had ever known, stabbed himself and fell dead upon the tomb.

Sardis was captured by the Persians and Croesus taken prisoner, after a reign of fourteen years and a siege of fourteen days. The oracle was fulfilled; Croesus had destroyed a mighty empire—his own.

The Persians brought their prisoner into the presence of the king, and Cyrus chained Croesus and placed him with fourteen Lydian boys on a great pyre that he had built; perhaps he intended them as a choice offering to some god of his, or perhaps he had made a vow and wished to fulfil it; or it may be that he had heard that Croesus was a godfearing man, and set him on the pyre to see if any divine power would save him from being burnt alive. But whatever the reason, that was what he did; and Croesus, for all his misery, as he stood on the pyre, remembered how Solon had declared that no man could be called happy until he was dead. It was as true as if God had spoken it. Till then Croesus had not uttered a sound; but when he remembered, he sighed bitterly and three times, in anguish of spirit, pronounced Solon's name.

Cyrus heard the name and told his interpreters to ask who Solon was; but for a while Croesus refused to answer the question and kept silent; at last, however, he was forced to speak. "He was a man," he said, "who ought to have talked with every king in the world. I would give a fortune to have had it so." Not understanding what he meant, they renewed their questions and pressed him so urgently to explain, that he could no longer refuse. He then related how Solon the Athenian once came to Sardis, and made light of the splendour which he saw there, and how everything he said—though it applied to all men and especially to those who imagine themselves fortunate—had in his own case proved all too true.

While Croesus was speaking, the fire had been lit and was already burning round the edges. The interpreters told Cyrus what Croesus had said, and the story touched him. He himself was a mortal man, and was burning alive another who had once been as prosperous as he. The thought of that, and the fear of retribution, and the realization of the instability of human things, made him change his mind and give orders that the flames should at once be put out, and Croesus and the boys brought down from the pyre. But the fire had got a hold, and the attempt to extinguish it failed. The Lydians say that when Croesus understood that Cyrus had changed his mind, and saw everyone vainly trying to master the fire, he called loudly upon Apollo with tears to come and save him from his misery, if any of his gifts had been pleasant to him. It was a clear and windless day; but suddenly in answer to Croesus' prayer clouds gathered and a storm broke with such violent rain that the flames were put out.

This was proof enough for Cyrus that Croesus was a good man whom the gods loved, so he brought him down from the pyre and said, "Tell me, Croesus; who was it who persuaded you to march against my country and be my enemy rather than my friend?"

"My lord," Croesus replied, "the luck was yours when I did it, and the loss was mine. The god of the Greeks encouraged me to fight you: the blame is his. No one is fool enough to choose war instead of peace—in peace sons bury fathers, but in war fathers bury sons. It must have been heaven's will that this should happen."

Cyrus had his chains taken off and invited him to sit by his side. He made much of him and looked at him with a sort of wonder, as did everyone else who was near enough to see.

Translated by Aubrey de Sélincourt

RHAMPSINITUS AND THE THIEF

The whole of Herodotus' second long second book (180 chapters) is devoted to the history, customs, and religion of Egypt, which he had visited. He mentions among his sources the Egyptian priests. They evidently gave him a great deal of reliable information; his account is one of the bases of the modern reconstruction of ancient Egypt's long history. They also told him some very good stories, like the following specimen, which would not be out of place in the tales Scheherezade told her sister one hour before daybreak for a thousand and one nights.

The king who succeeded Proteus was Rhampsinitus, said the priests. He is the king who left as his memorial the western propylaea of the temple of Hephaestus, and facing the propylaea he set up two statues, being in greatness thirty-eight feet high; the Egyptians call the one to the north Summer, the one to the south Winter. Summer they do obeisance to and treat well, but that which is called Winter they treat in the contrary fashion. This king had great wealth of silver; none of those who came after him exceeded him in this or came near him. As the king wished to store his treasure in safety, he built himself a stone chamber whereof one of the walls abutted upon the outer wall of his house. His workman laid a plot and contrived as follows: he took heed that one of the stones should be such as to be easily removed by two men or even one. When the chamber was completed, the king stored his treasures in it. Now, as time went on, the builder was at his life's end and called his sons to him—he had two of them—and explained to them his fore-thought on their behalf: that they might want for nothing, he had made his contrivance while building the king's treasure house. He showed them clearly all about the withdrawal of the stone and gave them the measurements of it. "Keep but these," he said, "and you shall be the stewards of the king's money." So he ended his life, and the boys were not long about it before they approached the royal palace by night, and, easily finding the stone in the chamber, shifted it and took out a great deal of the treasure. When the king chanced to open the chamber, he was amazed to see certain of the vessels short of their money, and no one could be found to blame for it, since all the seals were unbroken and the chamber shut tight. Twice and thrice more he opened the chamber, and each time the treasure always seemed to him to be less—for of course the thieves did not cease their raids. So this is what he did. He gave orders to have traps made and set them up around the vessels where the money was stored. The thieves came as they had done before; one of the two of them entered the chamber and, as he approached the treasure vessel, he was straightway caught in the trap. As soon as he realized in what case he stood, he called his brother and told him what had happened him. He bade him come in quickly and cut off his head so that he might not be seen and recognized and so destroy his brother as well. The brother thought he was right and was persuaded to do as he said; and having done so, he replaced the stone and went home, carrying his brother's head with him. At dawn the king came to the chamber, entered it, and was bewildered to see a headless thief caught in the trap but the chamber undisturbed, with no sign of entrance or exit. In his perplexity he did this: he hung the thief's body on the outer wall, set sentries over it, and gave them charge that whomever they saw mourning the dead or showing pity on him they should arrest and bring to the king.

So the corpse hung there; but his mother took it terribly to heart, and she had much to say to the surviving son and bade him, in whatever way he could, contrive to take down the hanging body of his brother and bring it home. If he neglected what she said, she threatened, she would herself go to the king and give information that her son had the money. So terribly did the mother rate the surviving son—and all he had to say to her went for nothing—that the boy made another contrivance. He got donkeys and filled some skins with wine and laded them on the donkeys and proceeded to drive them along. When they came to the spot where the corpse was hanging and where the sentinels were, he pulled down two or three of the corners of the wineskins, where the fastenings were, so as to loosen them. As the wine ran out, the young man started to beat his head and cry aloud, as though he did not know which of the donkeys to run to first. The guards, as soon as they saw the wine running freely, collected down to the road with buckets and began to scoop up the spilled wine, thinking themselves lucky fellows. The boy abused them all, pretending to be furious. The guards soothed him down, and at last he feigned to be pacified and to give over his anger, and at last he drove the donkeys off the road and tried to settle the loads on them. So they talked some more, and one of the soldiers mocked the boy with a joke and made him laugh (so the boy pretended), and so the boy ended by giving them one of the wineskins. The guards sat down, just where they were, and decided to drink. They took the boy in and told him to stay and drink with them. So of course he was convinced—and stayed. As they grew fond of him in the charitableness of their drinking, he gave them another of the wineskins. The guards had now had a great deal to drink and became totally drunk. The wine won out completely, and they went to sleep just where they had had their party. But the boy, as soon as the night was far advanced, took down the body of his brother and, by way of derision of the guards, shaved the right cheek of each of them, loaded the corpse on the donkeys, and went off home. He had done what his mother ordered.

The king, as soon as he heard that the body of the thief had been stolen, was in a fury. He wanted more than anything in the world to find out who it was that had played the trick, and so he did something— though I myself do not believe it. He set his daughter in a room and ordered her to consort with all the men that came to her, alike. But before they enjoyed her, she must compel each to tell her what was the cleverest and wickedest thing he had ever done in his life. Whoever told her the story of the thief, she was to lay hold of and not let get away. His child did what her father ordered her, and the thief, knowing why all this was being done, wanted to surpass the king in resourcefulness, and so *he* did something. He cut off the arm of a freshly dead man at the shoulder, and he took this with him under his cloak when he went to the chamber. So he went in to the king's daughter and was asked what all the rest were asked, and he said, "The wickedest thing I did was to cut off the head of my brother who was caught in a trap in the king's treasury; the cleverest is when I made the guards drunk and took down the body of my brother, which was hanging there." When she heard that, she grabbed at him. But the thief, in the dark room, stretched out to her the hand of the corpse. She took hold of it and held it, thinking she was grasping the hand of the man himself. Then the thief left it to her and made his escape through the doors.

When this news, too, was brought to the king, he was astounded at the wit and daring of the man, and finally he sent round to all the cities making proclamation of immunity and promising a great reward if the thief would come into his sight. The thief trusted him and came.

Rhampsinitus admired him greatly and gave him his daughter to wife, as being the man who understood more than anyone else in the world. "The Egyptians excel all others," he said, "and this man the rest of the Egyptians."

Translated by David Grene

AMASIS AND POLYCRATES

The Egyptian Pharoah Ahmose, whom Herodotus calls by his Greek name Amasis, was friendly to the Greeks. He married a Greek woman from Cyrene, a prosperous Greek city on the coast of what is now Libya; and he offered the Greeks trading concessions and contributed generously to the expenses of rebuilding the Temple of Apollo at Delphi, which had been ruined by a fire in 548 B.C. When Polycrates of Samos made his island into an important seapower, Amasis made an alliance with him. Herodotus tells us why that alliance was broken off.

Amasis was fully aware of the remarkable luck which Polycrates enjoyed, and it caused him some uneasiness; accordingly, when he heard of his ever-mounting tale of successes, he wrote him the following letter, and sent it to Samos: "Amasis to Polycrates:—It is a pleasure to hear of a friend and ally doing well, but, as I know that the gods are jealous of success, I cannot rejoice at your excessive prosperity. My own wish, both for myself and for those I care for, would be to do well in some things and badly in others, passing through life with alternate success and failure; for I have never yet heard of a man who after an unbroken run of luck was not finally brought to complete ruin. Now I suggest that you deal with the danger of your continual successes in the following way: think of whatever it is you value most—whatever you would most regret the loss of—and throw it away: throw it right away, so that nobody can ever see it again. If, after that, you do not find that success alternates with failure, then go on using the remedy I have advised."

Polycrates read the letter and approved of the advice which it contained; so he began to look around amongst his treasures for what he felt he would be most grieved to lose, and finally hit upon a ring. This was a signet-ring he used to wear, an emerald set in gold, the work of a Samian named Theodorus, the son of Telecles. Having decided that this was the thing to get rid of, he manned a galley, went aboard, and gave orders to put to sea. When the vessel was a long way off-shore, he took the ring from his finger, in full view of everyone on board, and threw it into the water. Then he rowed back to the island, returned to his house, and lamented his lost treasure.

Five or six days later it happened that a fisherman caught a fine big fish and thought it would make a worthy present for Polycrates. He took it to the door and asked for an audience; this being granted, he offered the fish, and said: "Master, I did not think it right to take this fish I caught to market, poor working man though I am; it is such a fine one that I thought it good enough for you and your greatness. So I have brought it here to give you."

Polycrates, much pleased with what the fisherman said, replied: "You have done very well, and I thank you twice over—once for your words, and again for your present. I invite you to take supper with me."

The fisherman then went home, very proud of the honour done him. Meanwhile Polycrates' servants cut up the fish, and found the signet-ring in its belly. The moment they saw it, they picked it up, and taking it to Polycrates in triumph, told him how it had been found. Seeing in this the hand of providence, Polycrates wrote a letter to Amasis in Egypt, and related to him everything he had done and what the result had been. Amasis read the letter, and at once realized how impossible it is for one man to save another from his destiny, and how certain it was that Polycrates, whose luck held even to the point of finding again what he deliberately threw away, would one day die a miserable death. He forthwith sent a messenger to Samos to say that the pact between Polycrates and himself was at an end. This he did in order that when the destined calamity fell upon Polycrates, he might avoid the distress he would have felt, had Polycrates still been his friend.

Translated by Aubrey de Sélincourt

[*The "destined calamity" was not far off. The Persian satrap (governor) of Sardis, on the nearby mainland, lured Polycrates to his court with a false promise of alliance, killed him in what must have been an especially barbaric manner—since Herodotus says it is not fit to be described—and exposed his crucified corpse to the elements.*]

HIPPOCLIDES DOESN'T CARE

The chief opponents of the tyranny of Pisistratus and his sons at Athens were the members of a powerful family, the Alcmeonidae, the descendants of Alcmeon, whose immense wealth, as Herodotus explains in the next extract, was acquired in a rather ludicrous fashion. His son, Mega-

cles, was one of many rich and distinguished suitors for the hand of Agarista, daughter of Clisthenes, the tyrant of Sicyon, a prosperous city on the Corinthian Gulf. The story Herodotus tells of the great banquet at which Clisthenes was to announce the name of his future son-in-law—and the way Hippoclides of Athens, the favorite so far, "danced away his wife," losing her to Megacles—is one of the most delightful in his book. Solo male dancing is of course still a feature of Greek festivities, and no one who has spent the late hours of the night in bouzouki joints in Piraeus will be surprised that Hippoclides calls for a table to dance on, and ends up doing a handstand on it, dancing with his feet in the air. At least he didn't try one of the high points of the modern dance known as the zeibekiko, in which the reveler clamps his teeth on the edge of a small table loaded with plates and glasses, straightens up, and dances a few complicated steps before setting it down, glasses and plates intact.

When Hipparchus was driven out of Athens, the Alcmeonidae, who had played an important role in his expulsion, returned to Athens. One of them, Megacles' son Clisthenes, was the founder of the new Athenian democracy.

Even in very early days the Alcmaeonidae were a distinguished family in Athens, and from the time of Alcmaeon, and afterwards of Megacles, they became very distinguished indeed. Alcmaeon, the son of Megacles, gave all the assistance in his power to the Lydians who came from Croesus at Sardis to consult the oracle at Delphi; and Croesus, when the Lydians told him of the good service he had rendered, invited him to Sardis and offered him, as a reward, as much gold as he could carry on his person at one time. Alcmaeon thought of a fine way of taking advantage of this unusual offer: he put on a large tunic, very loose and baggy in front, and a pair of the widest top-boots that he could find, and, thus clad, entered the treasury to which the king's servants conducted him. Here he attacked a heap of gold dust; he crammed into his boots, all up his legs, as much as they would hold, filled the baggy front of his tunic full, sprinkled the dust all over his hair, stuffed some more into his mouth, and then staggered out, scarcely able to drag one foot after another and looking, with his bulging cheeks and swollen figure, like anything rather than a man. When Croesus saw him he burst out laughing, and gave him all the gold he was carrying, and as much again in addition. In this way Alcmaeon's family suddenly found itself rich, and Alcmaeon was able to keep race-horses, with which he won the chariot race at Olympia.

In the next generation the family became much more famous than before through the distinction conferred upon it by Cleisthenes the master of Sicyon. Cleisthenes, the son of Aristonymus, grandson of Myron, and great-grandson of Andreas, had a daughter, Agarista, whom he wished to marry to the best man in all Greece. So during the Olympic games, in which he had himself won the chariot race, he had a public announcement made, to the effect that any Greek who thought himself good enough to become Cleisthenes' son-in-law should present himself in Sicyon within sixty days—or sooner if he wished—because he intended, within the year following the sixtieth day, to betroth his daughter to her future husband. Cleisthenes had had a race-track and a wrestling-ring specially made for his purpose, and presently the suitors began to arrive—every man of Greek nationality who had something to be proud of either in his country or in himself. From Sybaris in Italy (Sybaris was then at the height of its prosperity) came Smindyrides the son of Hippocrates, a man noted above all others for delicate and luxurious living, and from Siris, also in Italy, came Damascus the son of Amyris who was nicknamed the Philosopher. Then there was Amphimnestus, the son of Epistrophus, from Epidamnus on the Ionian Gulf, and Males from Aetolia—Males, the brother of Titormus who was the strongest man in Greece and went to live in the remotest part of Aetolia to avoid intercourse with his kind. Several came from the Peloponnese: first there was Leocedes the son of Pheidon, who was ruler of Argos and the man who brought in the system of weights and measures for the Peloponnese—and also turned out the Eleians whose duty it was to manage the Olympic games and proceeded to manage them himself—the wickedest and most arrogant thing ever done by a Greek. Next there was Amiantus, the son of Lycargus, from Trapezus in Arcadia, and Laphanes, an Azenian from Paeus, whose father Euphorion, the story goes, received Castor and Pollux under his own roof and afterwards kept open house for all comers; and, the last to come from the Peloponnese, there was Onomastus, the son of Agaeus. From Athens there were two: Megacles, whose father Alcmaeon visited the court of Croesus, and Tisander's son Hippocleides, the wealthiest and best-looking man in Athens. Euboea provided but a single suitor, Lysanias from Eretria, which at that time was at the height of its prosperity; then there was a Thessalian, Diactorides, one of the Scopadae, from Crannon, and, lastly, Alcon from Molossia. All these distinguished men came to Sicyon by the appointed day to try their luck for the bride.

Cleisthenes began by asking each in turn to name his country and parentage; then he kept them in his house for a year, to get to know them well, entering into conversation with them sometimes singly, sometimes all together, and testing each of them for his temper, accomplishments, manners, and all the virtues which a man should possess. Those who were not too old he would take to the gymnasia—but the most important test of all was their behaviour at the dinner-table. All this went on throughout their stay in Sicyon, and never, during the whole time, was their entertainment anything but most lavish.

For one reason or another it was the two Athenians who impressed Cleisthenes most favourably, and of the two Tisander's son Hippocleides came to be preferred, not only for his manly virtues but also because he was related some generations back to the noble Corinthian family of Cypselus.

At last the day came which had been fixed for the betrothal, and Cleisthenes had to declare his choice. He marked the day by the sacrifice of a hundred oxen, and then gave a great banquet, to which not only the suitors but everyone of note in Sicyon was invited. When dinner was over, the suitors began to compete with each other in music and in talking on a set theme to the assembled company. In both these accomplishments it was Hippocleides who proved by far the doughtiest champion, until at last, as more and more wine was drunk, he asked the flute-player to play him a tune and began to dance to it. Now it may well be that he danced to his own satisfaction; Cleisthenes, however, who was watching the performance, began to have serious doubts about the whole business. Presently, after a brief pause, Hippocleides sent for a table; the table was brought, and Hippocleides, climbing on to it, danced first some Laconian dances, next some Attic ones, and ended by standing on his head and beating time with his legs in the air. The Laconian and Attic dances were bad enough; but Cleisthenes, though he already loathed the thought of having a son-in-law who could behave so disgracefully in public, nevertheless restrained himself and managed to avoid an outburst; but when he saw Hippocleides beating time with his legs, he could bear it no longer. "Son of Tisander," he cried, "you have danced away your wife." "I could hardly care less," was the cheerful reply. Hence the common saying, "It's all one to Hippocleides."

Cleisthenes now called for silence and addressed the company. "Gentlemen," he said, "you are here as suitors for my daughter's hand. I have the highest opinion of you all; to distinguish one and reject the rest is not an agreeable task, and I would gladly, were it possible, show my favour to every one of you. Unfortunately, it is not possible; I have only one girl to dispose of, so how can I please you all? To each man, therefore, who has failed to win the bride I propose to give a talent of silver, to mark my appreciation of the honour he has done me by wishing to marry into my family, and to compensate him for his long absence from home; and my daughter Agarista I betroth, according to the Athenian law, to Megacles the son of Alcmaeon." Megacles declared that he accepted her, and the formalities of the betrothal were completed.

Such is the story of the Trial of the Suitors, and this was the way in which the Alcmaeonidae came to be talked of throughout Greece. The issue of the marriage was that Cleisthenes (named after his grandfather, Cleisthenes of Sicyon) who reorganized the Athenians into tribes and instituted the system of popular government in Athens. A second son of Megacles was Hippocrates, who became the father of another Megacles and another Agarista—the namesake of Cleisthenes' daughter—who married Xanthippus the son of Ariphron. This second Agarista dreamt during her pregnancy that she gave birth to a lion, and a few days later became the mother of Pericles.

Translated by Aubrey de Sélincourt

XERXES AND DEMARATUS

In 480 B.C. Xerxes, the Great King of the Persian Empire, marshaled a huge fleet and army for the invasion of Greece. According to Herodotus, his forces, excluding army servants, camp followers, crews of provision boats, and so on, numbered no less than 2,641,610 fighting men. He seems to have reached this impossible total by including in the expeditionary force the entire military resources of the Persian Empire. Herodotus' description of the many national contingents, including such exotic units as the Indians, the Arabians, the Libyans, and the Ethiopians, suggests that he may have had access to the Persian equivalent of the Army List. Nevertheless, though ancient logistic constraints alone rule out Herodotus' figure, there can be no doubt that the Persians came into Greece with overwhelming numerical superiority against a Greece that was, as usual, divided against itself; some of the Greek cities, including Thebes, one of the most powerful, fought on the Persian side.

Xerxes had brought with him on the march westward a former king of Sparta, Demaratus, who, exiled from his homeland through internal strife over the succession to the throne, had traveled to Susa and had there been treated as an honored guest. After crossing the Hellespont, Xerxes reviewed his army and navy; he then turned to Demaratus and asked him how the Greeks could possibly think of resisting his advance.

Having sailed from one end to the other of the line of anchored ships, Xerxes went ashore again and sent for Demaratus, the son of Ariston, who was accompanying him in the march to Greece. "Demaratus," he said, "it would give me pleasure at this point to put to you a few questions. You are a Greek, and a native, moreover, of by no means the meanest or weakest city in that country—as I learn not only from yourself but from the other Greeks I have spoken with. Tell me, then—will the Greeks dare to lift a hand against me? My own belief is that all the Greeks and all the other western peoples gathered together would be insufficient to withstand the attack of my army—and still more so if they are not united. But it is your opinion upon this subject that I should like to hear."

"My lord," Demaratus replied, "is it a true answer you would like, or merely an agreeable one?"

"Tell me the truth," said the king; "and I promise that you will not suffer by it." Encouraged by this Demaratus continued: "My lord, you bid me speak nothing but the truth, to say nothing which might later be proved a lie. Very well then; this is my answer: poverty is my country's inheritance from of old, but valour she won for herself by wisdom and the strength of law. By her valour Greece now keeps both poverty and bondage at bay.

"I think highly of all Greeks of Dorian descent, but what I am about to say will apply not to all Dorians, but to the Spartans only. First then, they will not under any circumstances accept terms from you which would mean slavery for Greece; secondly, they will fight you even if the rest of Greece submits. Moreover, there is no use in asking if their numbers are adequate to enable them to do this; suppose a thousand of them take the field—then that thousand will fight you; and so will any number, greater than this or less."

Xerxes laughed. "My dear Demaratus," he exclaimed, "what an extraordinary thing to say! Do you really suppose a thousand men would fight an army like mine? Now tell me, would *you*, who were once, as you say, king of these people, be willing at this moment to fight ten men single-handed? I hardly think so; yet, if things in Sparta are really as you have described them, then, according to your laws, you as king ought to take on a double share—so that if every Spartan is a match for ten men of mine, I should expect you to be a match for twenty. Only in that way can you prove the truth of your claim. But if you Greeks, who think so much of yourselves, are all of the size and quality of those I have spoken with when they have visited my court—and of yourself, Demaratus— there is some danger of your words being nothing but an empty boast. But let me put my point as reasonably as I can—how is it possible that a thousand men, or ten thousand, or fifty thousand, should stand up to an army as big as mine, especially if they were not under a single master, but all perfectly free to do as they pleased? Suppose them to have five thousand men: in that case we should be more than a thousand to one! If, like ours, their troops were subject to the control of a single man, then possibly for fear of him, in spite of the disparity in numbers, they might show some sort of factitious courage, or let themselves be whipped into battle; but, as every man is free to follow his fancy, it is not conceivable that they should do either. Indeed, my own opinion is that even on equal terms the Greeks could hardly face the Persians alone. We, too, have this thing that you were speaking of—I do not say it is common, but it does exist; for instance, amongst the Persians in my bodyguard there are men who would willingly fight with three Greeks together. But you know nothing of such things, or you could not talk such nonsense."

"My lord," Demaratus answered, "I knew before I began that if I spoke the truth you would not like it. But, as you demanded the plain truth and nothing less, I told you how things are with the Spartans. Yet you are well aware that I now feel but little affection for my countrymen, who robbed me of my hereditary power and privileges and made me a fugitive without a home—whereas your father welcomed me at his court and gave me the means of livelihood and somewhere to live. Surely it is unreasonable to reject kindness; any sensible man will cherish it. Personally I do not claim to be able to fight ten men—or two; indeed I should prefer not even to fight with one. But should it be necessary—should there be some great cause to urge me on—then nothing would give me more pleasure than to stand up to one of those men of yours who claim to be a match for three Greeks. So it is with the Spartans; fighting singly, they are as good as any, but fighting together they are the best soldiers in the world. They are free—yes—but not entirely free; for they have a master, and that master is Law, which they fear much more than your subjects fear you. Whatever this master commands, they do; and his command never varies: it is never to retreat in battle, however great the odds, but always to stand firm, and to conquer or die. If, my lord, you think that what I have said is nonsense—very well; I am willing henceforward to hold my tongue. This time I spoke because you forced me to speak. In any case, I pray that all may turn out as you desire."

Xerxes was not at all angry with Demaratus' answer. He turned it off with a laugh and good-humouredly let him go.

Translated by Aubrey de Sélincourt

THERMOPYLAE

Xerxes' way south lay along the coast, accompanied by his fleet. As he left the plains of Thessaly, he had to go through the pass at Thermopylae; at its narrowest point there were only fifty feet between the cliffs and the sea. (The coastline has changed, and the distance is now

several miles.) The united Greek council had decided to hold the pass,
but their action was late; when Xerxes arrived in the area, the pass was
held by a small advance party of some five thousand men, under the
command of one of the two Spartan kings, Leonidas, a descendant of
Heracles. His troops included three hundred full Spartan citizens, as well
as men from other parts of the Peloponnese; there were also local levies
from nearby Phocis and Locris. When, at the first news of the Persian
arrival in the area, a proposal was made to retreat, they opposed it, since
it would have left their home territory unprotected. There was also a
Theban detachment, who were there very much against their will;
Thebes had not yet openly declared for Xerxes, but the Greeks suspected
Theban intentions and these men were, in effect, hostages.

The Persian army was now close to the pass, and the Greeks, suddenly
doubting their power to resist, held a conference to consider the advisa-
bility of retreat. It was proposed by the Peloponnesians generally that
the army should fall back upon the Peloponnese and hold the Isthmus;
but when the Phocians and Locrians expressed their indignation at this
suggestion, Leonidas gave his voice for staying where they were and
sending, at the same time, an appeal for reinforcements to the various
states of the confederacy, as their numbers were inadequate to cope with
the Persians.

During the conference Xerxes sent a man on horseback to ascertain
the strength of the Greek force and to observe what the troops were
doing. He had heard before he left Thessaly that a small force was
concentrated here, led by the Lacedaemonians under Leonidas of the
house of Heracles. The Persian rider approached the camp and took a
thorough survey of all he could see—which was not, however, the whole
Greek army; for the men on the further side of the wall which, after its
reconstruction, was now guarded, were out of sight. He did, nonetheless,
carefully observe the troops who were stationed on the outside of the
wall. At that moment these happened to be the Spartans, and some of
them were stripped for exercise, while others were combing their hair.
The Persian spy watched them in astonishment; nevertheless he made
sure of their numbers, and of everything else he needed to know, as
accurately as he could, and then rode quietly off. No one attempted to
catch him, or took the least notice of him.

Back in his own camp he told Xerxes what he had seen. Xerxes was
bewildered; the truth, namely that the Spartans were preparing themselves to kill and to be killed according to their strength, was beyond his
comprehension, and what they were doing seemed to him merely ab-

surd. Accordingly he sent for Demaratus, the son of Ariston, who had come with the army, and questioned him about the spy's report, in the hope of finding out what the unaccountable behaviour of the Spartans might mean. "Once before," Demaratus said, "when we began our march against Greece, you heard me speak of these men. I told you then how I saw this enterprise would turn out, and you laughed at me. I strive for nothing, my lord, more earnestly than to observe the truth in your presence; so hear me once more. These men have come to fight us for possession of the pass, and for that struggle they are preparing. It is the common practice of the Spartans to pay careful attention to their hair when they are about to risk their lives. But I assure you that if you can defeat these men and the rest of the Spartans who are still at home, there is no other people in the world who will dare to stand firm or lift a hand against you. You have now to deal with the finest kingdom in Greece, and with the bravest men."

Xerxes, unable to believe what Demaratus said, asked further how it was possible that so small a force could fight with his army. "My lord," Demaratus replied, "treat me as a liar, if what I have foretold does not take place." But still Xerxes was unconvinced.

For four days Xerxes waited, in constant expectation that the Greeks would make good their escape; then, on the fifth, when still they had made no move and their continued presence seemed mere impudent and reckless folly, he was seized with rage and sent forward the Medes and Cissians with orders to take them alive and bring them into his presence. The Medes charged, and in the struggle which ensued many fell; but others took their places, and in spite of terrible losses refused to be beaten off. They made it plain enough to anyone, and not least to the king himself, that he had in his army many men, indeed, but few soldiers. All day the battle continued; the Medes, after their rough handling, were at length withdrawn and their place was taken by Hydarnes and his picked Persian troops—the King's Immortals—who advanced to the attack in full confidence of bringing the business to a quick and easy end. But, once engaged, they were no more successful than the Medes had been; all went as before, the two armies fighting in a confined space, the Persians using shorter spears than the Greeks and having no advantage from their numbers.

On the Spartan side it was a memorable fight; they were men who understood war pitted against an inexperienced enemy, and amongst the feints they employed was to turn their backs in a body and pretend to be retreating in confusion, whereupon the enemy would come on with a great clatter and roar, supposing the battle won; but the Spartans, just as the Persians were on them, would wheel and face them and inflict in the new struggle innumerable casualties. The Spartans had their losses too, but not many. At last the Persians, finding that their assaults upon the pass, whether by divisions or by any other way they could think of, were all useless, broke off the engagement and withdrew. Xerxes was watching the battle from where he sat; and it is said that in the course of the attacks three times, in terror for his army, he leapt to his feet.

Next day the fighting began again, but with no better success for the Persians, who renewed their onslaught in the hope that the Greeks, being so few in number, might be badly enough disabled by wounds to prevent further resistance. But the Greeks never slackened; their troops were ordered in divisions corresponding to the states from which they came, and each division took its turn in the line except the Phocian, which had been posted to guard the track over the mountains. So when the Persians found that things were no better for them than on the previous day, they once more withdrew.

How to deal with the situation Xerxes had no idea; but while he was still wondering what his next move should be, a man from Malis got himself admitted to his presence. This was Ephialtes, the son of Eurydemus, and he had come, in hope of a rich reward, to tell the king about the track which led over the hills to Thermopylae—and the information he gave was to prove the death of the Greeks who held the pass.

Later on, Ephialtes, in fear of the Spartans, fled to Thessaly, and during his exile there a price was put upon his head at an assembly of the Amphictyons at Pylae. Some time afterwards he returned to Anticyra, where he was killed by Athenades of Trachis. In point of fact, Athenades killed him not for his treachery but for another reason, which I will explain further on; but the Spartans honoured him nonetheless on that account. According to another story, which I do not at all believe, it was Onetes, the son of Phanagoras, a native of Carystus, and Corydallus of Anticyra who spoke to Xerxes and showed the Persians the way round by the mountain track; but one may judge which account is the true one, first by the fact that the Amphictyons, who must surely have known everything about it, set a price not upon Onetes and Corydallus but upon Ephialtes of Trachis, and, secondly, by the fact that there is no doubt that the accusation of treachery was the reason for Ephialtes' flight. Certainly Onetes, even though he was not a native of Malis, might have known about the track, if he had spent much time in the neighbourhood—but it was Ephialtes, and no one else, who showed the Persians the way, and I leave his name on record as the guilty one.

Xerxes found Ephialtes' offer most satisfactory. He was delighted with it, and promptly gave orders to Hydarnes to carry out the movement with the troops under his command. They left camp about the time the lamps are lit.

The track was originally discovered by the Malians of the neighbour-hood; they afterwards used it to help the Thessalians, taking them over it to attack Phocis at the time when the Phocians were protected from invasion by the wall which they had built across the pass. That was a long time ago, and no good ever came of it since. The track begins at the Asopus, the stream which flows through the narrow gorge, and, running along the ridge of the mountain—which, like the track itself, is called Anopaea—ends at Alpenus, the first Locrian settlement as one comes from Malis, near the rock known as Black-Buttocks' Stone and the seats of the Cercopes. Just here is the narrowest part of the pass.

This, then, was the mountain track which the Persians took, after crossing the Asopus. They marched throughout the night, with the mountains of Oeta on their right hand and those of Trachis on their left. By early dawn they were at the summit of the ridge, near the spot where the Phocians, as I mentioned before, stood on guard with a thousand men, to watch the track and protect their country. The Phocians were ready enough to undertake this service, and had, indeed, volunteered for it to Leonidas, knowing that the pass at Thermopylae was held as I have already described.

The ascent of the Persians had been concealed by the oak-woods which cover this part of the mountain range, and it was only when they reached the top that the Phocians became aware of their approach; for there was not a breath of wind, and the marching feet made a loud swishing and rustling in the fallen leaves. Leaping to their feet, the Phocians were in the act of arming themselves when the enemy was upon them. The Persians were surprised at the sight of troops preparing to resist; they had not expected any opposition—yet here was a body of men barring their way. Hydarnes asked Ephialtes who they were, for his first uncomfortable thought was that they might be Spartans; but on learning the truth he prepared to engage them. The Persian arrows flew thick and fast, and the Phocians, supposing themselves to be the main object of the attack, hurriedly withdrew to the highest point of the mountain, where they made ready to face destruction. The Persians, however, with Ephialtes and Hydarnes paid no further attention to them, but passed on along the descending track with all possible speed.

The Greeks at Thermopylae had their first warning of the death that was coming with the dawn from the seer Megistias, who read their doom in the victims of sacrifice; deserters, too, had begun to come in during the night with news of the Persian movement to take them in the rear, and, just as day was breaking, the look-out men had come running from the hills. At once a conference was held, and opinions were divided, some urging that they must on no account abandon their post, others taking the opposite view. The result was that the army split: some dispersed, the men returning to their various homes, and others made ready to stand by Leonidas.

There is another account which says that Leonidas himself dismissed a part of his force, to spare their lives, but thought it unbecoming for the Spartans under his command to desert the post which they had originally come to guard. I myself am inclined to think that he dismissed them when he realized that they had no heart for the fight and were unwilling to take their share of the danger; at the same time honour forbade that he himself should go. And indeed by remaining at his post he left a great name behind him, and Sparta did not lose her prosperity, as might otherwise have happened; for right at the outset of the war the Spartans had been told by the oracle, when they asked for advice, that either their city must be laid waste by the foreigner or one of their kings be killed. The prophecy was in hexameter verse and ran as follows:

> Hear your fate, O dwellers in Sparta of the wide spaces;
> Either your famed, great town must be sacked by Perseus' sons,
> Or, if that be not, the whole land of Lacedaemon
> Shall mourn the death of a king of the house of Heracles,
> For not the strength of lions or of bulls shall hold him,
> Strength against strength; for he has the power of Zeus,
> And will not be checked till one of these two he has consumed.

I believe it was the thought of this oracle, combined with his wish to lay up for the Spartans a treasure of fame in which no other city should share, that made Leonidas dismiss those troops; I do not think that they deserted, or went off without orders, because of a difference of opinion. Moreover, I am strongly supported in this view by the case of Megistias, the seer from Acarnania who foretold the coming doom by his inspection of the sacrificial victims: this man—he was said to be descended from Melampus—was with the army, and quite plainly received orders from Leonidas to quit Thermopylae, to save him from sharing the army's fate. But he refused to go, sending away instead an only son of his, who was serving with the forces.

Thus it was that the confederate troops, by Leonidas' orders, abandoned their posts and left the pass, all except the Thespians and the Thebans who remained with the Spartans. The Thebans were detained by Leonidas as hostages very much against their will—unlike the loyal

Thespians, who refused to desert Leonidas and his men, but stayed, and died with them. They were under the command of Demophilus the son of Diadromes.

In the morning Xerxes poured a libation to the rising sun, and then waited till about the time of the filling of the market-place, when he began to move forward. This was according to Ephialtes' instructions, for the way down from the ridge is much shorter and more direct than the long and circuitous ascent. As the Persian army advanced to the assault, the Greeks under Leonidas, knowing that the fight would be their last, pressed forward into the wider part of the pass much further than they had done before; in the previous days' fighting they had been holding the wall and making sorties from behind it into the narrow neck, but now they left the confined space and battle was joined on more open ground. Many of the invaders fell; behind them the company commanders plied their whips, driving the men remorselessly on. Many fell into the sea and were drowned, and still more were trampled to death by their friends. No one could count the number of the dead. The Greeks, who knew that the enemy were on their way round by the mountain track and that death was inevitable, fought with reckless desperation, exerting every ounce of strength that was in them against the invader. By this time most of their spears were broken, and they were killing Persians with their swords.

In the course of that fight Leonidas fell, having fought like a man indeed. Many distinguished Spartans were killed at his side—their names, like the names of all the three hundred, I have made myself acquainted with, because they deserve to be remembered. Amongst the Persian dead, too, were many men of high distinction—for instance, two brothers of Xerxes, Habrocomes and Hyperanthes, both of them sons of Darius by Artanes' daughter Phratagune.

There was a bitter struggle over the body of Leonidas; four times the Greeks drove the enemy off, and at last by their valour succeeded in dragging it away. So it went on, until the fresh troops with Ephialtes were close at hand; and then, when the Greeks knew that they had come, the character of the fighting changed. They withdrew again into the narrow neck of the pass, behind the walls, and took up a position in a single compact body—all except the Thebans—on the little hill at the entrance to the pass, where the stone lion in memory of Leonidas stands to-day. Here they resisted to the last, with their swords, if they had them, and, if not, with their hands and teeth, until the Persians, coming on from the front over the ruins of the wall and closing in from behind, finally overwhelmed them.

Of all the Spartans and Thespians who fought so valiantly on that day, the most signal proof of courage was given by the Spartan Dieneces. It is said that before the battle he was told by a native of Trachis that, when the Persians shot their arrows, there were so many of them that they hid the sun. Dieneces, however, quite unmoved by the thought of the terrible strength of the Persian army, merely remarked: "This is pleasant news that the stranger from Trachis brings us: for if the Persians hide the sun, we shall have our battle in the shade." He is said to have left on record other sayings, too, of a similar kind, by which he will be remembered. After Dieneces the greatest distinction was won by the two Spartan brothers, Alpheus and Maron, the sons of Orsiphantus; and of the Thespians the man to gain the highest glory was a certain Dithyrambus, the son of Harmatides.

The dead were buried where they fell, and with them the men who had been killed before those dismissed by Leonidas left the pass. Over them is this inscription, in honour of the whole force:

> Four thousand here from Pelops' land
> Against three million once did stand.

The Spartans have a special epitaph; it runs:

> Go tell the Spartans, you who read:
> We took their orders, and are dead.

For the seer Megistias there is the following:

> I was Megistias once, who died
> When the Mede passed Spercheius' tide.
> I knew death near, yet would not save
> Myself, but share the Spartans' grave.

The columns with the epitaphs inscribed on them were erected in honour of the dead by the Amphictyons—though the epitaph upon the seer Megistias was the work of Simonides, the son of Leoprepes, who put it there for friendship's sake.

Two of the three hundred Spartans, Eurytus and Aristodemus, are said to have been suffering from acute inflammation of the eyes, on account of which they were dismissed by Leonidas before the battle and went to Alpeni to recuperate. These two men might have agreed together to return in safety to Sparta; or, if they did not wish to do so, they might have shared the fate of their friends. But, unable to agree which course to take, they quarrelled, and Eurytus had no sooner heard that the

Persians had made their way round by the mountain track than he called for his armour, put it on, and ordered his servant to lead him to the scene of the battle. The servant obeyed, and then took to his heels, and Eurytus, plunging into the thick of things, was killed. Aristodemus, on the other hand, finding that his heart failed him, stayed behind at Alpeni. Now if only Aristodemus had been involved—if he alone had returned sick to Sparta—or if they had both gone back together, I do not think that the Spartans would have been angry; but as one was killed and the other took advantage of the excuse, which was open to both of them, to save his skin, they could hardly help being very angry indeed with Aristodemus.

There is another explanation of how Aristodemus got back alive to Sparta: according to this, he was sent from camp with a message, and though he might have returned in time to take part in the fighting, he deliberately loitered on the way and so saved himself, while the man who accompanied him on the errand joined in the battle and was killed. In any case, he was met upon his return with reproach and disgrace; no Spartan would give him a light to kindle his fire, or speak to him, and he was nicknamed the Trembler. However, he afterwards made amends for everything at the battle of Plataea.

There is also a story that one more of the three hundred—Pantites—survived. He had been sent with a message into Thessaly, and on his return to Sparta found himself in such disgrace that he hanged himself.

The Thebans under Leontiades remained for a time with the army and were compelled to make some show of resistance to the enemy; but as soon as they saw that things were going in favour of Persia, they took the opportunity of Leonidas' hurried retreat to the little hill, where his last stand was made, to detach themselves from his force; they then approached the enemy with outstretched hands, crying out that in their zeal for the Persian interest they had been amongst the first to give earth and water to the king, and had no share in the responsibility for the injury done him, because they had come to Thermopylae against their will. It was all too true—and, when it was backed up by the evidence of the Thessalians, it saved their lives. Nevertheless, their luck did not hold in every respect; for a few were killed by the Persians on their first approach, and all the rest were branded by Xerxes' orders with the royal mark, beginning with Leontiades their commander. Leontiades' son Eurymachus was afterwards killed by the Plataeans when he was leading a force of four hundred Theban troops at the capture of Plataea.

Such, then, is the story of the Greeks' struggle at Thermopylae.

Translated by Aubrey de Sélincourt

THEMISTOCLES AND ATHENS

Once through the pass at Thermopylae, Xerxes' army pressed on to Athens, where only a small remnant of the population remained, defending the Acropolis to the last. Athens was sacked and burned, the temples on the Acropolis were ruined, the statues mutilated.

The evacuation of Athens had been organized by Themistocles, the leader of the democracy. Women and children were sent by boat to the nearby island of Salamis, or to Troezen on the Peloponnesian mainland; the men boarded the 180 warships of the Athenian fleet and joined the rest of the Greek ships off Salamis. It was by far the largest contingent in the fleet, which numbered 378 ships. It was Themistocles who persuaded Eurybiades, the Spartan commander of the united fleet, to fight at Salamis rather than withdraw to the Isthmus, as the Corinthians and other Peloponnesian units were proposing. The result was a stunning victory for the Greeks. Xerxes went home to Susa, leaving only a land force behind him; it was decisively defeated in the following year, at Plataea.

Herodotus, writing much later, at a time when Athens had long since converted an original league of free island and coastal Aegean cities into an empire ruled by force, delivers his opinion of the importance of the Athenian contribution to the Persian defeat—an opinion, as he realizes and states, that will not be welcome in all quarters.

The purpose of Xerxes' expedition, which was directed nominally against Athens, was in fact the conquest of the whole of Greece. The various Greek communities had long been aware of this, but they viewed the coming danger with very different eyes. Some had already made their submission, and were consequently in good spirits, because they were sure of getting off lightly at the invaders' hands; others, who had refused to submit, were thrown into panic partly because there were not enough ships in Greece to meet the Persians with any chance of success, and partly because most of the Greeks were unwilling to fight and all too ready to accept Persian dominion. At this point I find myself compelled to express an opinion which I know most people will object to; nevertheless, as I believe it to be true, I will not suppress it. If the Athenians, through fear of the approaching danger, had abandoned their country, or if they had stayed there and submitted to Xerxes, there would have been no attempt to resist the Persians by sea; and, in the absence of a Greek fleet, it is easy to see what would have been the course of events on land. However many lines of fortification the Spartans had built across the Isthmus, they would have been deserted by their confederates; not that their allies would have wished to desert them, but they could not have helped doing so, because one by one they would have fallen victims to the Persian naval power. Thus the Spartans would have been left alone—to perform prodigies of valour and to die nobly. Or, on the other hand, it is possible that before things came to the ultimate test, the sight of the rest of Greece submitting to Persia might have driven them to make terms with Xerxes. In either case the Persian conquest of Greece would have been assured; for I cannot myself see what possible use there could have been in fortifying the Isthmus, if the Persians had command of the sea. In view of this, therefore, one is surely right in saying that Greece was saved by the Athenians. It was the Athenians who held the balance: whichever side they joined was sure to prevail. It was the Athenians, too, who, having chosen that Greece should live and preserve her freedom, roused to battle the other Greek states which had not yet submitted. It was the Athenians who—after God—drove back the Persian king. Not even the terrifying warnings of the oracle at Delphi could persuade them to abandon Greece; they stood firm and had the courage to meet the invader.

Prepared as they were to listen to the oracle's advice, the Athenians had sent their envoys to Delphi, and as soon as the customary rites were performed and they had entered the shrine and taken their seats, the Priestess Aristonice uttered the following prophecy:

> *Why sit you, doomed ones? Fly to the world's end, leaving*
> *Home and the heights your city circles like a wheel.*
> *The head shall not remain in its place, nor the body,*
> *Nor the feet beneath, nor the hands, nor the parts between;*
> *But all is ruined, for fire and the headlong God of War*
> *Speeding in a Syrian chariot shall bring you low.*
> *Many a tower shall he destroy, not yours alone,*
> *And give to pitiless fire many shrines of gods,*
> *Which even now stand sweating, with fear quivering,*
> *While over the roof-tops black blood runs streaming*
> *In prophecy of woe that needs must come. But rise,*
> *Haste from the sanctuary and bow your hearts to grief.*

The Athenian envoys were greatly perturbed by this prophetic utterance; indeed they were about to abandon themselves to despair at the dreadful fate which the oracle declared was coming upon them, when Timon, the son of Androbulus and one of the most distinguished men in

Delphi, suggested that they should re-enter the shrine with branches of olive in their hands and, in the guise of suppliants begging for a better fate, put their question a second time. The Athenians acted upon this suggestion and returned to the temple. "Lord Apollo," they said, "can you not, in consideration of these olive-boughs which we have brought you, give us some kindlier prophecy about our country? We will never go away until you do; indeed no: we'll stay here till we die."

Thereupon the Prophetess uttered her second prophecy, which ran as follows:

> *Not wholly can Pallas win the heart of Olympian Zeus,*
> *Though she prays him with many prayers and all her subtlety;*
> *Yet will I speak to you this other word, as firm as adamant:*
> *Though all else shall be taken within the bound of Cecrops*
> *And the gold of the holy mountain of Cithaeron,*
> *Yet Zeus the all-seeing grants to Athene's prayer*
> *That the wooden wall only shall not fall, but help you and your children.*
> *But await not the host of horse and foot coming from Asia,*
> *Nor be still, but turn your back and withdraw from the foe.*
> *Truly a day will come when you will meet him face to face.*
> *Divine Salamis, you will bring death to women's sons*
> *When the corn is scattered, or the harvest gathered in.*

This second answer seemed to be, as indeed it was, less menacing than the first; so the envoys wrote it down and returned to Athens. When it was made public upon their arrival in the city, and the attempt to explain it began, amongst the various opinions which were expressed there were two mutually exclusive interpretations. Some of the older men supposed that the prophecy meant that the Acropolis would escape destruction, on the grounds that the Acropolis was fenced in the old days with a thorn-hedge—the "wooden wall" of the oracle; but others thought that by this expression the oracle meant ships, and they urged in consequence that everything should be abandoned in favour of the immediate preparation of a fleet. There was, however, for those who believed "wooden wall" to mean ships, one disturbing thing—namely, the last two lines of the Priestess' prophecy:

> *Divine Salamis, you will bring death to women's sons*
> *When the corn is scattered, or the harvest gathered in.*

This was a very awkward statement and caused profound disturbance amongst all who took the wooden wall to signify ships; for the professional interpreters understood the lines to mean that if they prepared to fight at sea, they would be beaten at Salamis. There was, however, a man in Athens who had recently made a name for himself—Themistocles, more generally known as Neocles' son; and he it was who now came forward and declared that there was an important point in which the professional interpreters were mistaken. If, he maintained, the disputed passage really referred to the Athenians, it would not have been expressed in such mild language. "Hateful Salamis" would surely have been a more likely phrase than "divine Salamis," if the inhabitants of the island were really doomed to destruction. On the contrary, the true interpretation was that the oracle referred not to the Athenians but to their enemies. The "wooden wall" did, indeed, mean ships; so he advised his countrymen to prepare at once to meet the invader at sea.

The Athenians found Themistocles' explanation of the oracle preferable to that of the professional interpreters, who had not only tried to dissuade them from preparing to fight at sea but had been against offering opposition of any sort. The only thing to do was, according to them, to abandon Attica altogether and seek a home elsewhere.

Once on a previous occasion Themistocles had succeeded in getting his views accepted, to the great benefit of his country. The Athenians from the produce of the mines at Laurium had amassed a large sum of money, which they proposed to share out amongst themselves at the rate of ten drachmas a man; Themistocles, however, persuaded them to give up this idea and, instead of distributing the money, to spend it on the construction of two hundred warships for use in the war with Aegina. The outbreak of this war at that moment saved Greece by forcing Athens to become a maritime power. In point of fact the two hundred ships were not employed for the purpose for which they were built, and were consequently at the disposal of Greece in her hour of need. The Athenians also found it necessary to expand this existing fleet by laying down new ships, and they determined at a council, which was held after the discussion on the oracle, to take the god's advice and meet the invader at sea with all the force they possessed, and with any other Greeks who were willing to join them.

Translated by Aubrey de Sélincourt

AESCHYLUS
525–456 B.C.

Aeschylus was the first of the three great Athenian tragic poets. His initial victory at the Dionysiac festival was in 484 B.C.; it came between his participation in the Battle of Marathon in 490 and the decisive Battle of Salamis in 480 B.C.

From SEVEN AGAINST THEBES

THE FALL OF THE CITY

Seven Against Thebes, *produced in the theater of Dionysus in 467 B.C., was the third and final play of a trilogy that dealt with the story of the family of Oedipus; the titles of the preceding plays, now lost, were* Laius *and* Oedipus. *In the last play we are shown the fulfillment of the curse old Oedipus pronounced against his two sons: that they would kill each other. One of them, Polynices, exiled from Thebes, has brought a foreign army, led by seven champions, against his own city; his brother, Eteocles, defends it.*

In the following excerpt, a choral ode from the final play, the women of Thebes, hearing the sounds of an attack launched against the walls, imagine the horrors of the fall of the city to an invading army. Thebes, however, is spared. Eteocles repels the attack, but in the process kills and is killed by his brother.

The fall of a city was, for the Greeks, the ultimate horror—the slaughter of the male population, the enslavement of the women and children, the destruction of age-old hallowed shrines and divine images. It was only thirteen years since the Athenians had abandoned their city as the Persian invaders drew near; if they had stayed, the terrible fate envisioned by the chorus in this ode would have been theirs.

Pitiful and terrible it would be
to deliver so august, so famous a city
    to the Dark House of Death;
brought down in flaking ashes, like a felled beast,
    rent without pity
    or honor by the enslaving rod,
    the wooden-shafted spear
hurled by a fellow Hellene, backed by a god;
    and terrible, a pity
for all these women assembled here today,
the withered and white-headed, the young and fair,
to be led off, like horses, by the hair,
    their clothing ripped, their breasts
    exposed to the conqueror's view.
Eviscerated, the stunned city screams.
    Ulooloo, Ulooloo
The booty hauled away. Shouts. Brutal jokes.
I quake. I dream the most terrible of dreams.

O terrible, before a woman is ripe,
without accustomed procession, accustomed song,
to go the awful road from her own home
under the sword's compulsion. I say the man
who dies in battle is better off than this.
For when a city is doomed to armored rape,
blades flash in the firelight; murderers throng
the streets. Gigantic Ares, in his bliss,
dazed and insane with the towering flame and fume,
befouls the pieties, harvests his dead wealth,
and breathes from our black smoke his terrible health.

The city echoes with loud, bellowing howls;
it is a death-trap, fatally self-ensnared.
A thin blood-cry of infants, a shrill reed
    of nursling terror wails,
and lumbering spearmen pierce each other's bowels.
    Pillagers loot each other
in plundering brotherhood; greed joins with greed;
    the empty-handed hails
with rallying cry his empty-handed brother;
no one content with a lesser or equal share.

Who shall account for this portioning, by what law
comes this allotment of pain, grief, and despair?

It is a bitter sight for the housewife
to see, spilled piecemeal from her cherished store,
the foison and wealth of earth, the harvest riches,
grain, oil, and wine, dashed from their polished jars,
    sluicing the filthy ditches.
    And by the rule of strife,
the pale, unfamilied girl became the whore
and trophy of her captor, forced to spread
for the sweating soldier, triumphant, hate-inflamed.
Perhaps a dark deliverance may occur
    in that foul bridal, the untamed
violence of that battle-grounded bed.
    And there may come to her
    a species of relief,
an end of tidal groans, weeping, and grief.

Translated by Anthony Hecht and Helen H. Bacon

FROM PROMETHEUS BOUND

PROMETHEUS' GIFTS TO HUMANITY

We do not know the date of the first production of Prometheus Bound
in the theater of Dionysus. We know that there was a sequel, the Prometheus Unbound *(of which we have significant fragments), but about the
third play of the triology, and even the question whether there was in
fact a trilogy, we are in the dark. There is even doubt among modern
scholars about the attribution of the* Prometheus Bound *to Aeschylus.
Some have found the presentation of Zeus as tyrant, a persecutor of the
benefactor of mankind, irreconcilable with lofty idea of Zeus and his
justice prominent in all of his other extant plays, especially in the*
Oresteia. *A recent study has established that the choral songs of the play,
which are in any case much shorter and simpler than the Aeschylean
norm, are organized in metrical units and patterns that have no parallel
in the other plays. The ancient authorities, however, express no doubt on
the subject, and they had much more evidence than we have—the other
two Prometheus plays and the whole of Aeschylus' tragic corpus, of
which we possess only a pitiful remnant.*

The argument based on the picture of Zeus drawn in the play under-values the fact that in the second play, Prometheus is set free—and set free by a son of Zeus, Heracles. This sounds like a possible preliminary to the reconciliation of the two mighty opposites. The metrical inconcinnity, on the other hand, is hard to explain away; it is as if a composer suddenly produced a work that contained no trace of his habitual style, as if, to suggest an admittedly exaggerated example, a quartet assigned to Beethoven sounded more like the work of Boccherini or Rossini. But it should also be said that our ear for Aeschylean metrical technique is based solely on the lyric sections of the other six extant plays, all that remain of the seventy-nine available to the Alexandrian editors.

In any case, Aeschylean or not (or not entirely—perhaps Aeschylus left it unfinished at his death, and his son, a successful tragic poet in his own right, added the choral sections), Prometheus is one of the archetypal mythic figures of the Western tradition, the defiant demigod, humanity's champion and benefactor—chained, tortured, and threatened by the servants of the supreme power.

PROMETHEUS: Think not my silence is enforced by pride
Or obstinacy—by bitterness of heart
To see myself so savagely outraged.
    And yet for these new deities who else
Prescribed their powers and privileges but I?
Of that no more, for the tale that I could tell
Is known to you; but hearken to the plight
Of man, in whom, born witless as a babe,
I planted mind and the gift of understanding.
I speak of men with no intent to blame
But to expound my gracious services:
Who first, with eyes to see, did see in vain,
With ears to hear, did hear not, but as shapes
Figured in dreams throughout their mortal span
Confounded all things, knew not how to raise
Brick-woven walls sun-warmed, nor build in wood,
But had their dwelling, like the restless ant,
In sunless nooks of subterranean caves.
No token sure they had of winter's cold,
No herald of the flowery spring or season
Of ripening fruit, but laboured without wit
In all their works, till I revealed the obscure
Risings and settings of the stars of heaven.

Yea, and the art of number, arch-device,
I founded, and the craft of written words,
The world's recorder, mother of the Muse.
I first subdued the wild beasts of the field
To slave in pack and harness and relieve
The mortal labourer of his heaviest toil,
And yoked in chariots, quick to serve the rein,
The horse, prosperity's proud ornament;
And none but I devised the mariner's car
On hempen wing roaming the trackless ocean.
    Such the resources I have found for man,
Yet for myself, alas, have none to bring
From this my present plight deliverance.
CHORUS: Thy plight is cruel indeed: bereft of wit
And like a bad physician falling sick,
Thou dost despair and for thine own disease
Canst find no physic nor medicament.
PROMETHEUS: Nay, hear the rest and thou wilt marvel more,
What cunning arts and artifices I planned.
    Of all the greatest, if a man fell sick,
There was no remedy, nor shredded herb
Nor draught to drink nor ointment, and in default
Of physic their flesh withered, until I
Revealed the blends of gentle medicines
Wherewith they arm themselves against disease.
And many ways of prophecy I ordered,
And first interpreted what must come of dreams
In waking hours, and the obscure import
Of wayside signs and voices I defined,
And taught them to discern the various flight
Of taloned birds, which of them favourable
And which of ill foreboding, and the ways
Of life by each pursued, their mating-seasons,
Their hatreds and their loves one for another;
The entrails too, of what texture and hue
They must appear to please the sight of heaven;
The dappled figure of the gall and liver,
The thigh-bone wrapt in fat and the long chine
I burnt and led man to the riddling art
Of divination; and augury by fire,
For long in darkness hid, I brought to light.
Such help I gave, and more—beneath the earth,

The buried benefits of humanity,
Iron and bronze, silver and gold, who else
Can claim that he revealed to man but I?
None, I know well, unless an idle braggart.
    In these few words learn briefly my whole tale.
Prometheus founded all the arts of man.

Translated by George Thomson

THE ORESTEIA

From AGAMEMNON

THE WATCHMAN ON THE ROOF

*We are fortunate that the capricious gods who presided over the fate of
the Greek tragic texts saw fit to preserve for us one complete Aeschylean
trilogy, the* Oresteia. *As its name suggests, it is centered on Orestes'
killing of his mother Clytemnestra, an action which is the climactic
moment of the second play of the trilogy,* The Libation Bearers. *The
first play shows us Agamemenon's return from Troy and his death—
together with that of his captive mistress, the Trojan princess Cassandra—at the hands of his wife Clytemnestra. It opens with the speech of
a sentinel on the roof of Agamemnon's palace at Argos; he is on the
watch for a distant beacon fire, which will signal the fall of Troy.*

SCENE: *Argos, before the palace of King* AGAMEMNON. *The* WATCHMAN,
who speaks the opening lines, is posted on the roof of the palace.
CLYTAEMESTRA's *entrances are made from a door in the center of the
stage; all others, from the wings.*

[*The* WATCHMAN, *alone.*]
I ask the gods some respite from the weariness
of this watchtime measured by years I lie awake
elbowed upon the Atreidae's roof dogwise to mark
the grand processionals of all the stars of night
burdened with winter and again with heat for men,
dynasties in their shining blazoned on the air,
these stars, upon their wane and when the rest arise.

I wait; to read the meaning in that beacon light,
a blaze of fire to carry out of Troy the rumor
and outcry of its capture; to such end a lady's
male strength of heart in its high confidence ordains.
Now as this bed stricken with night and drenched with dew
I keep, nor ever with kind dreams for company:
since fear in sleep's place stands forever at my head
against strong closure of my eyes, or any rest:
I mince such medicine against sleep failed: I sing,
only to weep again the pity of this house
no longer, as once, administered in the grand way.
Now let there be again redemption from distress,
the flare burning from the blackness in good augury.
        [*A light shows in the distance.*]
Oh hail, blaze of the darkness, harbinger of day's
shining, and of processionals and dance and choirs
of multitudes in Argos for this day of grace.
Ahoy!
I cry the news aloud to Agamemnon's queen,
that she may rise up from her bed of state with speed
to raise the rumor of gladness welcoming this beacon,
and singing rise, if truly the citadel of Ilium
has fallen, as the shining of this flare proclaims.
I also, I, will make my choral prelude, since
my lord's dice cast aright are counted as my own,
and mine the tripled sixes of this torchlit throw.

May it only happen. May my king come home, and I
take up within this hand the hand I love. The rest
I leave to silence; for an ox stands huge upon
my tongue. The house itself, could it take voice, might speak
aloud and plain. I speak to those who understand,
but if they fail, I have forgotten everything.

                                Translated by Richmond Lattimore

                    THE SACRIFICE OF IPHIGENIA

*A chorus of old men comes on stage as the sentinel goes in through the
door of the palace with his news. Their song recalls the day, ten years
back, when the army departed for Troy and an omen appeared that the
prophet Calchas feared might have terrible consequences. A pair of*

eagles, royal birds, seized and devoured a pregnant hare; the kings, Calchas proclaimed, would destroy the city of Troy and its as yet unborn generations. But he foresaw the anger of the goddess Artemis, the protector of wild life, and feared she might send adverse winds to prevent the expedition from sailing. The winds came, as he feared, and kept the ships idle at Aulis.

So it was that day the king,
the steersman at the helm of Greece,
would never blame a word the prophet said—
swept away by the wrenching winds of fortune
he conspired! Weatherbound we could not sail,
our stores exhausted, fighting strength hard-pressed,
and the squadrons rode in the shallows off Chalkis
where the riptide crashes, drags,

and winds from the north pinned down our hulls at Aulis,
port of anguish . . . head winds starving,
sheets and the cables snapped
and the men's minds strayed,
the pride, the bloom of Greece
was raked as time ground on,
ground down, and then the cure for the storm
and it was harsher—Calchas cried,
"My captains, Artemis must have blood!"—
so harsh the sons of Atreus
dashed their sceptres on the rocks,
could not hold back the tears,

and I still can hear the older warlord saying,
"Obey, obey, or a heavy doom will crush me!—
Oh but doom *will* crush me
once I rend my child,
the glory of my house—
a father's hands are stained,
blood of a young girl streaks the altar.
Pain both ways and what is worse?
Desert the fleets, fail the alliance?
No, but stop the winds with a virgin's blood,
feed their lust, their fury?—feed their fury!—
Law is law!—
Let all go well."

And once he slipped his neck in the strap of Fate,
his spirit veering black, impure, unholy,
once he turned he stopped at nothing,
        seized with the frenzy
                blinding driving to outrage—
wretched frenzy, cause of all our grief!
Yes, he had the heart
        to sacrifice his daughter,
to bless the war that avenged a woman's loss,
        a bridal rite that sped the men-of-war.

"My father, father!"—she might pray to the winds;
no innocence moves her judges mad for war.
Her father called his henchmen on,
        on with a prayer,
                "Hoist her over the altar
like a yearling, give it all your strength!
She's fainting—lift her,
        sweep her robes around her,
but slip this strap in her gentle curving lips . . .
                here, gag her hard, a sound will curse the house"—

and the bridle chokes her voice . . . her saffron robes
pouring over the sand
                        her glance like arrows showering
wounding every murderer through with pity
        clear as a picture, live,
she strains to call their names . . .
I remember often the days with father's guests
when over the feast her voice unbroken,
        pure as the hymn her loving father
bearing third libations, sang to Saving Zeus—
transfixed with joy, Atreus' offspring
        throbbing out their love.

What comes next? I cannot see it, cannot say.
The strong techniques of Calchas do their work.
But Justice turns the balance scales,
        sees that we suffer
and we suffer and we learn.
And we will know the future when it comes.

Greet it too early, wccp too soon.
It all comes clear in the light of day.

Translated by Robert Fagles

HELEN AND TROY

Clytemnestra tells the chorus the great news announced by the beacon fire, and they proceed to sing a hymn of thanks to the gods for the victory, a Te Deum Laudamus. *They place the blame for the war and all the deaths it has caused squarely on the shoulders of Alexander (another name for Paris), and of Helen, who abandoned her husband to go with him to Troy. But as they vividly recall the keenness of Menelaus' sorrow at his loss, there comes over them the thought of all the other losses— the young men who have died so far from home, "and all for some strange woman." The victory hymn is turning into a lament for the dead and a covert condemnation of the war and the kings. It ends with a repudiation of what is happening in Troy: "let me not plunder cities . . ."*

CHORUS: O Zeus our lord and Night beloved,
bestower of power and beauty,
you slung above the bastions of Troy
the binding net, that none, neither great
nor young, might outleap
the gigantic toils
of enslavement and final disaster.
I gaze in awe on Zeus of the guests
who wrung from Alexander such payment.
He bent the bow with slow care, that neither
the shaft might hurdle the stars, nor fall
spent to the earth, short driven.

They have the stroke of Zeus to tell of.
This thing is clear and you may trace it.
He acted as he had decreed.
A man thought
the gods deigned not to punish mortals
who trampled down the delicacy of things
inviolable. That man was wicked.
The curse on great daring

shines clear; it wrings atonement
from those high hearts that drive to evil,
from houses blossoming to pride
and peril. Let there be
wealth without tears; enough for
the wise man who will ask no further.
There is not any armor
in gold against perdition
for him who spurns the high altar
of Justice down to the darkness.

Persuasion the persistent overwhelms him,
she, strong daughter of designing Ruin.
And every medicine is vain; the sin
smolders not, but burns to evil beauty.
As cheap bronze tortured
at the touchstone relapses
to blackness and grime, so this man
tested shows vain
as a child that strives to catch the bird flying
and wins shame that shall bring down his city.
No god will hear such a man's entreaty,
but whoso turns to these ways
they strike him down in his wickedness.
This was Paris: he came
to the house of the sons of Atreus,
stole the woman away, and shamed
the guest's right of the board shared.

She left among her people the stir and clamor
of shields and of spearheads,
the ships to sail and the armor.
She took to Ilium her dowry, death.
She stepped forth lightly between the gates
daring beyond all daring. And the prophets
about the great house wept aloud and spoke:
"Alas, alas for the house and for the champions,
alas for the bed signed with their love together.
Here now is silence, scorned, unreproachful.
The agony of his loss is clear before us.
Longing for her who lies beyond the sea
he shall see a phantom queen in his household.

Her images in their beauty
are bitterness to her lord now
where in the emptiness of eyes
all passion has faded."

Shining in dreams the sorrowful
memories pass; they bring him
vain delight only.
It is vain, to dream and to see splendors,
and the image slipping from the arms' embrace
escapes, not to return again,
on wings drifting down the ways of sleep.

Such have the sorrows been in the house by the hearthside;
such have there been, and yet there are worse than these.
In all Hellas, for those who swarmed to the host
the heartbreaking misery
shows in the house of each.
Many are they who are touched at the heart by these things.
Those they sent forth they knew;
now, in place of the young men
urns and ashes are carried home
to the houses of the fighters.

The god of war, money changer of dead bodies,
held the balance of his spear in the fighting,
and from the corpse-fires at Ilium
sent to their dearest the dust
heavy and bitter with tears shed
packing smooth the urns with
ashes that once were men.
They praise them through their tears, how this man
knew well the craft of battle, how another
went down splendid in the slaughter:
and all for some strange woman.
Thus they mutter in secrecy,
and the slow anger creeps below their grief
at Atreus' sons and their quarrels.
There by the walls of Ilium
the young men in their beauty keep
graves deep in the alien soil
they hated and they conquered.

The citizens speak: their voice is dull with hatred.
The curse of the people must be paid for.
There lurks for me in the hooded night
terror of what may be told me.
The gods fail not to mark
those who have killed many.
The black Furies stalking the man
fortunate beyond all right
wrench back again the set of his life
and drop him to darkness. There among
the ciphers there is no more comfort
in power. And the vaunt of high glory
is bitterness; for God's thunderbolts
crash on the towering mountains.
Let me attain no envied wealth,
let me not plunder cities,
neither be taken in turn, and face
life in the power of another.

Translated by Richmond Lattimore

CLYTEMNESTRA TRIUMPHANT

*Agamemnon comes on stage as the classic figure of the triumphant
conqueror returning home; he is in a chariot and by his side is the prize
awarded him by the army, the Trojan princess Cassandra. She was given,
as she tells us later after Agamemnon enters the palace, a priceless gift by
the god Apollo, the power of true prophecy; but when she refused him
the consummation of his love, he turned the gift into a curse by adding
the condition that no one would ever believe what she foretold. Clytemnestra, welcoming her husband in a speech loaded with fulsome compliments and rich in ironic undertones, lures him into the palace. She
comes back later for Cassandra, after a scene in which we see the poisoned gift of Apollo in action: Cassandra foretells not only the imminent
death of Agamemenon (and herself) but also, far in the future, the
return and revenge of Orestes. But the chorus does not understand.*

*After Cassandra leaves the stage, two cries of agony are heard off
stage—Agamemnon's last words. The chorus, in a panic, breaks up into
separate voices debating what should be done. The palace doors open.
Two corpses, those of Agamemnon and Cassandra, are laid out on the
steps. Over them stands Clytemnestra, who now, after so many veiled
words, speaks plain truth.*

CLYTAEMNESTRA: Words, endless words I've said to serve the
    moment—
now it makes me proud to tell the truth.
How else to prepare a death for deadly men
who seem to love you? How to rig the nets
of pain so high no man can overleap them?

I brooded on this trial, this ancient blood feud
year by year. At last my hour came.
Here I stand and here I struck
and here my work is done.
I did it all. I don't deny it, no.
He had no way to flee or fight his destiny—
    [Unwinding the robes from AGAMEMNON's body, spreading them
    before the altar where the old men cluster around them, unified as
    a CHORUS once again.]
our never-ending, all embracing net, I cast it
wide for the royal haul, I coil him round and round
in the wealth, the robes of doom, and then I strike him
once, twice, and at each stroke he cries in agony—
he buckles at the knees and crashes here!
And when he's down I add the third, last blow,
to the Zeus who saves the dead beneath the ground
I send that third blow home in homage like a prayer.

So he goes down, and the life is bursting out of him—
great sprays of blood, and the murderous shower
wounds me, dyes me black and I, I revel
like the Earth when the spring rains come down,
the blessed gifts of god, and the new green spear
splits the sheath and rips to birth in glory!

So it stands, elders of Argos gathered here.
Rejoice if you can rejoice—I glory.
And if I'd pour upon his body the libation
it deserves, what wine could match my words?
It is right and more than right. He flooded
the vessel of our proud house with misery,
with the vintage of the curse and now
he drains the dregs. My lord is home at last.
LEADER: You appal me, you, your brazen words—
    exulting over your fallen king.

CLYTAEMNESTRA: And you,
  you try me like some desperate woman.
  My heart is steel, well you know. Praise me,
  blame me as you choose. It's all one.
  Here is Agamemnon, my husband made a corpse
  by this right hand—a masterpiece of Justice.
  Done is done.
CHORUS: Woman!—what poison cropped from the soil
  or strained from the heaving sea, what nursed you,
  drove you insane? You brave the curse of Greece.
  You have cut away and flung away and now
  the people cast you off to exile,
  broken with our hate.
CLYTAEMNESTRA: And now you sentence me?—
  you banish *me* from the city, curses breathing
  down my neck? But *he*—
  name one charge you brought against him then.
  He thought no more of it than killing a beast,
  and his flocks were rich, teeming in their fleece,
  but he sacrificed his own child, our daughter,
  the agony I laboured into love
  to charm away the savage winds of Thrace.

  Didn't the law demand you banish him?—
  hunt him from the land for all his guilt?
  But now you witness what I've done
  and you are ruthless judges.
                         Threaten away!
  I'll meet you blow for blow. And if I fall
  the throne is yours. If god decrees the reverse,
  late as it is, old men, you'll learn your place.
CHORUS: Mad with ambition,
      shrilling pride!—some Fury
  crazed with the carnage rages through your brain—
    I can see the flecks of blood inflame your eyes!
  But vengeance comes—you'll lose your loved ones,
  stroke for painful stroke.
CLYTAEMNESTRA: Then learn this, too, the power of my oaths.
  By the child's Rights I brought to birth,
  by Ruin, by Fury—the three gods to whom
  I sacrificed this man—I swear my hopes
  will never walk the halls of fear so long

as Aegisthus lights the fire on my hearth.
Loyal to me as always, no small shield
to buttress my defiance.
                              Here he lies.
He brutalized me. The darling of all
the golden girls who spread the gates of Troy.
And here his spear-prize . . . what wonders she beheld!—
the seer of Apollo shared my husband's bed,
his faithful mate who knelt at the rowing-benches,
worked by every hand.
                              They have their rewards.
He as you know. And she, the swan of the gods
who lived to sing her latest, dying song—
his lover lies beside him.
She brings a fresh, voluptuous relish to my bed!

Translated by Robert Fagles

From THE LIBATION BEARERS

ORESTES' NURSE

Seven years after his father's murder, Orestes (grown to young manhood in exile) returns, in disguise, to Argos. The second play of the trilogy is named The Libation Bearers *after the chorus of women who come on stage in the opening scenes to pour liquid offerings on the grave of Agamemnon. Orestes and his friend Pylades watch from concealment as Electra, Orestes' elder sister, hesitates to perform the rite. She does not know how to address Agamemnon's spirit, since the offerings are sent by his killer Clytemnestra. The queen has been terrified by a dream in which she gave birth to a serpent, but when she gave suck, it drew blood. She fears it is a sign of Agamemnon's wrath and is trying to placate him. Orestes identifies himself, and together brother and sister make their own prayer to the dead king, a plea for help in their plan to avenge his murder. Orestes will gain admission to the palace by bringing a false report of his own death in exile; once inside he will do what must be done. Clytemnestra is the one who comes to the palace door to greet him, and it is she who invites him in and accompanies him and Pylades as they go inside. The audience now expects to hear a cry of agony offstage, but instead there is an unexpected entrance—that of an old slavewoman, one who had nursed Orestes when he was a child and is now grief-stricken at the report of his death. She has been sent to summon Aegisthus to the palace to hear the news.*

CHORUS: Queen of the Earth, rich mounded Earth,
  breasting over the lord of ships,
  the king's corpse at rest,
  hear us now, now help us,
    now the time is ripe—
  Down to the pit Persuasion goes
  with all her cunning. Hermes of Death,
  the great shade patrols the ring
  to guide the struggles, drive the tearing sword.
LEADER: And I think our new friend is at his mischief.
  Look, Orestes' nurse in tears.
    [*Enter* CILISSA.]
  Where now, old-timer, padding along the gates?
  With pain a volunteer to go your way.
NURSE: "Aegisthus,"
  your mistress calling, "hurry and meet your guests.
  There's news. It's clearer man to man, you'll see."

And she looks at the maids and pulls that long face
and down deep her eyes are laughing over the work
that's done. Well and good for her. For the house
it's the curse all over—the strangers make that plain.
But let *him* hear, he'll revel once he knows.
                      Oh god,
the life is hard. The old griefs, the memories
mixing, cups of pain, so much pain in the halls,
the house of Atreus . . . I suffered, the heart within me
always breaking, oh, but I never shouldered
misery like this. So many blows, good slave,
I took my blows.
             Now dear Orestes—
the sweetest, dearest plague of all our lives!

Red from your mother's womb I took you, reared you . . .
nights, the endless nights I paced, your wailing
kept me moving—led me a life of labour,

all for what?
              And such care I gave it . . .
baby can't think for itself, poor creature.
You have to nurse it, don't you? Read its mind,
little devil's got no words, it's still swaddled.
Maybe it wants a bite or a sip of something,
or its bladder pinches—a baby's soft insides
have a will of their own. I had to be a prophet.
Oh I tried, and missed, believe you me, I missed,
and I'd scrub its pretty things until they sparkled.
Washerwoman and wet-nurse shared the shop.
A jack of two trades, that's me,
and an old hand at both . . .
                        and so I nursed Orestes,
yes, from his father's arms I took him once,
and now they say he's dead,
I've suffered it all, and now I'll fetch that man,
the ruination of the house—give him the news,
he'll relish every word.

Translated by Robert Fagles

ORESTES AND HIS MOTHER

The chorus tells the nurse to make sure Aegisthus comes back to the palace alone, without his bodyguard; she does so, and he comes alone. Now the audience hears his death cry and a servant of his runs out on stage to warn Clytemnestra, who, roused by his shouts, comes out herself to find out what has happened.

When Orestes confronts her with drawn sword, she loses no time in confronting him with the full horror of what he intends to do; she bares the breast that suckled him and begs him to have mercy on his mother. Orestes has strong incentives for what he has come to do: the express command of Apollo, his duty as a son to avenge his father—and, as he has frankly told us in the previous scene, his desire to reclaim his inheritance, the throne of Argos. But faced with Clytemnestra's eloquent gesture, his resolution crumbles. He turns to Pylades for advice. What he hears in response is, in effect, the voice of Apollo himself, urging him to do what he must.

Aeschylus had created what we know as drama by adding a second actor to the chorus-plus-actor performance of Thespis. Pylades has to be

*played by a third speaking actor, since Orestes and Clytemnestra have
speaking roles in the same scene. This new resource, a third speaking
actor, had been made available to the tragic poets at the festival of
Dionysus through the initiative of Sophocles; we do not know when, but
it was obviously some time before 458 B.C. Aeschylus used the third actor
to play Cassandra in the first play (she comes on stage in the chariot with
Agamemnon, stands silent through the dialogue of husband and wife,
and then when they go into the palace, breaks into her prophetic song).
In the final play, The Eumenides, he used his three actors to play
Orestes, Athena, and Apollo in the trial scene. But in The Libation
Bearers he gave the third actor, in the role of Pylades, only three lines,
the reply to Orestes' question. In this play Aeschylus reserved this new
resource—introduced by Sophocles to extend the area of dramatic conflict from duo to trio—for one single short speech, which has however
a tremendous theatrical effect: the voice of Apollo speaks through Pylades to nerve Orestes for the matricide from which he has recoiled in
horror.*

FOLLOWER: Ahoy!
   My cry is to the deaf and I babble in vain
   at sleepers to no purpose. Clytaemestra, where
   is she, does what? Her neck is on the razor's edge
   and ripe for lopping, as she did to others before.
   [*Enter* CLYTAEMESTRA.]
CLYTAEMESTRA: What is this, and why are you shouting in the house?
FOLLOWER: I tell you, he is alive and killing the dead.
CLYTAEMESTRA: Ah, so. You speak in riddles, but I read the rhyme.
   We have been won with the treachery by which we slew.
   Bring me quick, somebody, an ax to kill a man
   [*Exit* FOLLOWER.]
   and we shall see if we can beat him before we
   go down—so far gone are we in this wretched fight.
   [*Enter* ORESTES *and* PYLADES *with swords drawn.*]
ORESTES: You next: the other one in there has had enough.
CLYTAEMESTRA: Beloved, strong Aegisthus, are you dead indeed?
ORESTES: You love your man, then? You shall lie in the same grave
   with him, and never be unfaithful even in death.
CLYTAEMESTRA: Hold, my son. Oh take pity, child, before this breast
   where many a time, a drowsing baby, you would feed
   and with soft gums sucked in the milk that made you strong.
ORESTES: What shall I do, Pylades? Be shamed to kill my mother?

PYLADES: What then becomes thereafter of the oracles
declared by Loxias at Pytho? What of sworn oaths?
Count all men hateful to you rather than the gods.
ORESTES: I judge that you win. Your advice is good.
[*To* CLYTAEMESTRA.]

Come here.
My purpose is to kill you over his body.
You thought him bigger than my father while he lived.
Die then and sleep beside him, since he is the man
you love, and he you should have loved got only your hate.
CLYTAEMESTRA: I raised you when you were little. May I grow old with
you?
ORESTES: You killed my father. Would you make your home with me?
CLYTAEMESTRA: Destiny had some part in that, my child.
ORESTES: Why then
destiny has so wrought that this shall be your death.
CLYTAEMESTRA: A mother has her curse, child. Are you not afraid?
ORESTES: No. You bore me and threw me away, to a hard life.
CLYTAEMESTRA: I sent you to a friend's house. This was no throwing
away.
ORESTES: I was born of a free father. You sold me.
CLYTAEMESTRA: So? Where then is the price that I received for you?
ORESTES: I could say. It would be indecent to tell you.
CLYTAEMESTRA: Or if you do, tell also your father's vanities.
ORESTES: Blame him not. He suffered while you were sitting here at
home.
CLYTAEMESTRA: It hurts women to be kept from their men, my child.
ORESTES: The man's hard work supports the women who sit at home.
CLYTAEMESTRA: I think, child, that you mean to kill your mother.
ORESTES: No.
It will be you who kill yourself. It will not be I.
CLYTAEMESTRA: Take care. Your mother's curse, like dogs, will drag
you down.
ORESTES: How shall I escape my father's curse, if I fail here?
CLYTAEMESTRA: I feel like one who wastes live tears upon a tomb.
ORESTES: Yes, this is death, your wages for my father's fate.
CLYTAEMESTRA: You are the snake I gave birth to, and gave the breast.
ORESTES: Indeed, the terror of your dreams saw things to come
clearly. You killed, and it was wrong. Now suffer wrong.
[ORESTES *and* PYLADES *take* CLYTAEMESTRA *inside the house.*]

Translated by Richmond Lattimore

ORESTES SEES THE FURIES

Like his mother before him, Orestes stands on the palace steps—below him the bodies of a man and a woman—and addresses the chorus to justify his action. Unlike Clytemnestra, however, who did not falter in her conviction that right was on her side, Orestes falls prey to doubt and apprehension as he goes on, and ends with an admission that he fears for his sanity: while he still has "some self-control . . . ," he says, he will leave Argos and go to Delphi as Apollo's suppliant. The chorus tries to comfort him.

LEADER: But you've done well. Don't burden yourself
with bad omens, lash yourself with guilt.
You've set us free, the whole city of Argos,
lopped the heads of these two serpents once for all.
[*Staring at the women and beyond,* ORESTES *screams in terror.*]
ORESTES: No, no! Women—look—like Gorgons,
shrouded in black, their heads wreathed,
swarming serpents!
                              —Cannot stay, I must move on.
LEADER: What dreams can whirl you so? You of all men,
you have your father's love. Steady, nothing
to fear with all you've won.
ORESTES: No dreams, these torments,
not to me, they're clear, real—the hounds
of mother's hate.
LEADER: The blood's still wet on your hands.
It puts a kind of frenzy in you . . .
ORESTES: *God Apollo!*
Here they come, thick and fast,
their eyes dripping hate—
LEADER: One thing
will purge you. Apollo's touch will set you free
from all your . . . torments.
ORESTES: You can't see them
I can, they drive me on! I must move on—
[*He rushes out;* PYLADES *follows close behind.*]
LEADER: Farewell then. God look down on you with kindness,
guard you, grant you fortune.
CHORUS: Here once more, for the third time,

the tempest in the race has struck
the house of kings and run its course.
　First the children eaten,
the cause of all our pain, the curse.
And next the kingly man's ordeal,
the bath where the proud commander,
lord of Achaea's armies lost his life.
And now a third has come, but who?
　A third like Saving Zeus?
Or should we call him death?
Where will it end?—
where will it sink to sleep and rest,
　this murderous hate, this Fury?

Translated by Robert Fagles

From THE EUMENIDES

The fearsome creatures Orestes saw at the end of the second play were the Erinyes, to give them their Greek name—Furies, as they are known in English. They are female goddesses, and they are much older than the Olympian gods. The Furies are the overseers and guarantors of a primitive system of justice, the law of blood for blood, of individual retaliation. This is the only system there can be before the community asserts its authority as arbiter and establishes a court to judge cases of homicide. The Furies intervene whenever the widening circle of retaliatory action reaches a limit, and the last victim has no avenger left alive. This is Clytemnestra's case. But the Furies have an extra reason for intervention here: not only are they female themselves, they are also especially wrathful against killers within the immediate family group. And for them no crime could cry more loudly for vengeance than the murder of a mother by her son. From the moment Orestes strikes his mother down, the Furies are at his heels. The third play opens at the Temple of Apollo at Delphi, where Orestes has come as a suppliant for the god's protection.

A priestess enters the temple doors but comes out panic-stricken, crawling on all fours. Inside the shrine, she tells us, she has seen a suppliant clasping the altar, and all around him creatures the like of which she has never seen before—"Are they Gorgons?" she asks, "or Harpies?" They are the Furies, waiting for Orestes to leave the sanctuary of the altar. For the moment they are asleep, immobilized by Apollo,

*who sends Orestes off to seek asylum at Athens, where, he tells him, he
will find judges to try his case. The Furies are awakened by a dream of
Clytemnestra, a dream on stage; she taunts them with their negligence,
urges them on after Orestes. Before they go, they denounce Apollo to his
face and he replies with threats of violence and words of contempt and
loathing. The leader of the chorus of Furies replies to this tirade in calm
and measured terms, stating the case against Orestes, and claiming that
no crime is more heinous than matricide. Apollo in reply assigns the
marriage bond between man and wife a higher value than the blood link
between mother and son. The issue, he says, will be decided at Athens,
where Athena will preside over the trial. The Furies reject any such idea,
and leave in pursuit of Orestes.*

THE BINDING SONG

*The scene changes; we see Orestes at Athens, clinging to the statue of
Athena and calling on her for help. The Furies enter, tracking him by
the scent of blood like hounds; they surround him and dance to what
they call their "binding song." Its purpose is to paralyze him with terror,
so that they can take him and drink his blood. In it they define and
proclaim their functions and privileges.*

Come then, link we our choral. Ours
to show forth the power
and terror of our music, declare
our rights of office, how we conspire
to steer men's lives.
We hold we are straight and just. If a man
can spread his hands and show they are clean,
no wrath of ours shall lurk for him.
Unscathed he walks through his life time.
But one like this man before us, with stained
hidden hands, and the guilt upon him,
shall find us beside him, as witnesses
of the truth, and we show clear in the end
to avenge the blood of the murdered.

Mother, o my mother night, who gave me
birth, to be a vengeance on the seeing
and the blind, hear me. For Leto's
youngling takes my right away,

stealing from my clutch the prey
that crouches, whose blood would wipe
at last the motherblood away.

Over the beast doomed to the fire
this is the chant, scatter of wits,
frenzy and fear, hurting the heart,
song of the Furies
binding brain and blighting blood
in its stringless melody.

This the purpose that the all-involving
destiny spun, to be ours and to be shaken
never: when mortals assume outrage
of own hand in violence,
these we dog, till one goes
under earth. Nor does death
set them altogether free.

Over the beast doomed to the fire
this is the chant, scatter of wits,
frenzy and fear, hurting the heart,
song of the Furies
binding brain and blighting blood
in its stringless melody.

When we were born such lots were assigned for our keeping.
So the immortals must hold hands off, nor is there
one who shall sit at our feasting.
For sheer white robes I have no right and no portion.

I have chosen overthrow
of houses, where the Battlegod
grown within strikes near and dear
down. So we swoop upon this man
here. He is strong, but we wear him down
for the blood that is still wet on him.
Here we stand in our haste to wrench from all others
these devisings, make the gods clear of our counsels
so that even appeal comes
not to them, since Zeus has ruled our blood dripping company
outcast, nor will deal with us.

I have chosen overthrow
of houses, where the Battlegod
grown within strikes near and dear
down. So we swoop upon this man
here. He is strong, but we wear him down
for the blood that is still wet on him.

Men's illusions in their pride under the sky melt
down, and are diminished into the ground, gone
before the onset of our black robes, pulsing
of our vindictive feet against them.

For with a long leap from high
above and dead drop of weight
I bring foot's force crashing down
to cut the legs from under even
the runner, and spill him to ruin.

He falls, and does not know in the daze of his folly.
Such in the dark of man is the mist of infection
that hovers, and moaning rumor tells how his house lies
under fog that glooms above.

For with a long leap from high
above, and dead drop of weight,
I bring foot's force crashing down
to cut the legs from under even
the runner, and spill him to ruin.

All holds. For we are strong and skilled;
we have authority; we hold
memory of evil; we are stern
nor can men's pleadings bend us. We
drive through our duties, spurned, outcast
from gods, driven apart to stand in light
not of the sun. So sheer with rock are ways
for those who see, as upon those whose eyes are lost.

Is there a man who does not fear
this, does not shrink to hear
how my place has been ordained,

granted and given by destiny
and god, absolute? Privilege
primeval yet is mine, nor am I without place
though it be underneath the ground
and in no sunlight and in gloom that I must stand.

Translated by Richmond Lattimore

THE FURIES PREPARE FOR THE TRIAL

*In answer to Orestes' prayer, Athena arrives in time to save him from the
Furies. Unlike Apollo, she treats these dread visitors with respect, maintaining an impartial stance between them and Orestes. Though they had
rejected the idea of a trial when Apollo mentioned it, they agree to abide
by her decision as arbiter. Athena, however, sees the issue as too difficult
for her to judge alone. She proposes to establish a court to try the case; it
will be the first in human history. The Furies, confident of the rightness
of their cause, accept. As they sing in the choral song that follows, a
verdict in favor of Orestes would be, in their view, a signal for anarchy,
an encouragement of the worst crimes humanity can commit. If Orestes
is not found guilty, they will cease to heed the calls of human victims for
justice against their murderers.*

    Here, now, is the overthrow
of every binding law—once his appeal,
    his outrage wins the day,
his matricide! One act links all mankind,
hand to desperate hand in bloody licence.
    Over and over deathstrokes
        dealt by children wait their parents,
    mortal generations still unborn.

    We are the Furies still, yes,
but now our rage that patrolled the crimes of men,
    that stalked their rage dissolves—
we loose a lethal tide to sweep the world!
Man to man foresees his neighbour's torments,
    groping to cure his own—
        poor wretch, there is no cure, no use,
    the drugs that ease him speed the next attack.

Now when the sudden blows come down,
let no one sound the call that once brought help,
"Justice, hear me—Furies throned in power!"
Oh I can hear the father now
or the mother sob with pain
    at the pain's onset . . . hopeless now,
the house of Justice falls.

There is a time when terror helps,
the watchman must stand guard upon the heart.
It helps, at times, to suffer into truth.
Is there a man who knows no fear
in the brightness of his heart,
    or a man's city, both are one,
that still reveres the rights?

            Neither the life of anarchy
        nor the life enslaved by tyrants, no,
            worship neither.
Strike the balance all in all and god will give you power;
    the laws of god may veer from north to south—
        we Furies plead for Measure.
    Violence is Impiety's child, true to its roots,
but the spirit's great good health breeds all we love
        and all our prayers call down,
            prosperity and peace.

            All in all I tell you people,
        bow before the altar of the rights,
            revere it well.
Never trample it underfoot, your eyes set on spoils;
    revenge will hunt the godless day and night—
        the destined end awaits.
So honour your parents first with reverence, I say,
and the stranger guest you welcome to your house,
        turn to attend his needs,
            respect his sacred rights.
        All of your own free will, all uncompelled,
        be just and you will never want for joy,
you and your kin can never be uprooted from the earth.
        But the reckless one—I warn the marauder
dragging plunder, chaotic, rich beyond all rights:

he'll strike his sails,
            harried at long last,
stunned when the squalls of torment break his spars to bits.

He cries to the deaf, he wrestles walls of sea
sheer whirlpools down, down, with the gods' laughter
breaking over the man's hot heart—they see him flailing, crushed.
    The one who boasted never to shipwreck
now will never clear the cape and steer for home,
        who lived for wealth,
                golden his life long,
rams on the reef of law and drowns unwept, unseen.

Translated by Robert Fagles

ORESTES CROSS-EXAMINED

*As the trial begins before the Athenian jury assembled by Athena,
Apollo enters. He comes as a witness for Orestes and one who shares
with him responsibility for what has been done. As in a real Athenian
court of law, the prosecution has the first word; the leader of the chorus
questions Orestes. His questions back Orestes into a corner and he turns
to Apollo to answer for him.*

ATHENA: The trial begins! Yours is the first word—
    the prosecution opens. Start to finish,
    set the facts before us, make them clear.
LEADER: Numerous as we are, we will be brief.
    [*To* ORESTES.]
    Answer count for count, charge for charge.
    First, tell us, did you kill your mother?
ORESTES: I killed her. There's no denying that.
LEADER: Three falls in the match. One is ours already.
ORESTES: You exult before your man is on his back.
LEADER: But *how* did you kill her? You must tell us that.
ORESTES: I will. I drew my sword—more, I cut her throat.
LEADER: And who persuaded you? who led you on?
ORESTES: This god and his command.
    [*Indicating* APOLLO.]
                                He bears me witness.
LEADER: The Seer? He drove you on to matricide?

ORESTES: Yes,
and to this hour I have no regrets.
LEADER: If the verdict
brings you down, you'll change your story quickly.
ORESTES: I have my trust; my father will help me from the grave.
LEADER: Trust to corpses now! You made your mother one.
ORESTES: I do. She had two counts against her, deadly crimes.
LEADER: How? Explain that to your judges.
ORESTES: She killed her husband—killed my father too.
LEADER: But murder set her free, and you live on for trial.
ORESTES: She lived on. You never drove *her* into exile—why?
LEADER: The blood of the man she killed was not her own.
ORESTES: And I? Does mother's blood run in my veins?
LEADER: How could she breed you in her body, murderer?
Disclaim your mother's blood? She gave you life.
ORESTES: [*Turns to* APOLLO.] Bear me witness—show me the way,
Apollo!
Did I strike her down with justice?
Strike I did, I don't deny it, no.
But how does our bloody work impress you now?—
Just or not? Decide.
I must make my case to them. [*Looking to the judges.*]

Translated by Robert Fagles

ATHENA AND THE FURIES

In his argument with the Furies at Delphi, Apollo had proclaimed the priority of the marriage bond over the tie of blood between mother and son, accusing the Furies of showing disrespect for the marriage of Zeus and Hera, the divine model of all earthly unions. In court, he again invokes the authority of Zeus, whose spokesman he claims to be, on the side of Orestes, whose killing of his mother he sees as a lesser offense than Clytemnestra's murder of her husband. The prosecutor, the leader of the chorus, sees a contradiction and seizes his opening. Zeus overthrew and imprisoned his father Cronos; how can he be invoked as heavenly authority for preferring the right to vengeance of a father to that of a mother? Apollo abandons this line of argument and tries another. He proclaims the doctrine that the mother is not a real parent, but merely the receptacle for the male seed; the father is the source of life. As proof of this theory he points to Athena herself, born from the head of Zeus, without need of a mother.

These arguments do not have an overwhelming effect; the votes of the
jury are evenly split, even though Athena casts a vote for Orestes. As in
real Athenian courts, this even tally means that Orestes is acquitted. But
Athena now has to reckon with the Furies. They have been superseded
as ministers of justice by the establishment of the court, but they still
have power to destroy, and they now threaten to use it on Athens and its
citizens. Athena pleads, threatens, and argues with them, offering them
what they have never had—a home—in Athens, a city which is bound
for greatness. They are finally won over and accept her offer. The Furies
now sing a new song, one of blessing on the land and its people, but as
they do so Athena stresses that though they have become kindly god-
desses, they still inspire fear and act as a deterrent to crime. "In the
terror on the faces of these," she says later, "I see great good for our
citizens." For, as the Furies sang before the trial, "There are times when
fear is good . . ."

The play closes with a torchlight procession, as the Furies, now resi-
dent spirits on Athenian soil, are escorted by representatives of the
women of Athens to their new home.

CHORUS: Gods of the younger generation, you have ridden down
the laws of the elder time, torn them out of my hands.
I, disinherited, suffering, heavy with anger
shall let loose on the land
the vindictive poison
dripping deadly out of my heart upon the ground;
this from itself shall breed
cancer, the leafless, the barren
to strike, for the right, their low lands
and drag its smear of mortal infection on the ground.
What shall I do? Afflicted
I am mocked by these people.
I have borne what can not
be borne. Great the sorrows and the dishonor upon
the sad daughters of night.
ATHENE: Listen to me. I would not have you be so grieved.
For you have not been beaten. This was the result
of a fair ballot which was even. You were not
dishonored, but the luminous evidence of Zeus
was there, and he who spoke the oracle was he
who ordered Orestes so to act and not be hurt.
Do not be angry any longer with this land

nor bring the bulk of your hatred down on it, do not
render it barren of fruit, nor spill the dripping rain
of death in fierce and jagged lines to eat the seeds.
In complete honesty I promise you a place
of your own, deep hidden under ground that is yours by right
where you shall sit on shining chairs beside the hearth
to accept devotions offered by your citizens.

CHORUS: Gods of the younger generation, you have ridden down
the laws of the elder time, torn them out of my hands.
I, disinherited, suffering, heavy with anger
shall let loose on the land
the vindictive poison
dripping deadly out of my heart upon the ground;
this from itself shall breed
cancer, the leafless, the barren
to strike, for the right, their low lands
and drag its smear of mortal infection on the ground.
What shall I do? Afflicted
I am mocked by these people.
I have borne what can not
be borne. Great the sorrow and the dishonor upon
the sad daughters of night.

ATHENE: No, not dishonored. You are goddesses. Do not
in too much anger make this place of mortal men
uninhabitable. I have Zeus behind me. Do
we need to speak of that? I am the only god
who know the keys to where his thunderbolts are locked.
We do not need such, do we? Be reasonable
and do not from a reckless mouth cast on the land
spells that will ruin every thing which might bear fruit.
No. Put to sleep the bitter strength in the black wave
and live with me and share my pride of worship. Here
is a big land, and from it you shall win first fruits
in offerings for children and the marriage rite
for always. Then you will say my argument was good.

CHORUS: That they could treat me so!
I, the mind of the past, to be driven under the ground
out cast, like dirt!
The wind I breathe is fury and utter hate.
Earth, ah, earth
what is this agony that crawls under my ribs?
Night, hear me, o Night,

mother. They have wiped me out
and the hard hands of the gods
and their treacheries have taken my old rights away.
ATHENE: I will bear your angers. You are elder born than I
and in that are wiser far than I. Yet still
Zeus gave me too intelligence not to be despised.
If you go away into some land of foreigners,
I warn you, you will come to love this country. Time
in his forward flood shall ever grow more dignified
for the people of this city. And you, in your place
of eminence beside Erechtheus in his house
shall win from female and from male processionals
more than all lands of men beside could ever give.
Only in this place that I haunt do not inflict
your bloody stimulus to twist the inward hearts
of young men, raging in a fury not of wine,
nor, as if plucking the heart from fighting cocks,
engraft among my citizens that spirit of war
that turns their battle fury inward on themselves.
No, let our wars range outward hard against the man
who has fallen horribly in love with high renown.
No true fighter I call the bird that fights at home.
Such life I offer you, and it is yours to take.
Do good, receive good, and be honored as the good
are honored. Share our country, the beloved of god.
CHORUS: That they could treat me so!
I, the mind of the past, to be driven under the ground
out cast, like dirt!
The wind I breathe is fury and utter hate.
Earth, ah, earth
what is this agony that crawls under my ribs?
Night, hear me, o Night,
mother. They have wiped me out
and the hard hands of the gods
and their treacheries have taken my old rights away.
ATHENE: I will not weary of telling you all the good things
I offer, so that you can never say that you,
an elder god, were driven unfriended from the land
by me in my youth, and by my mortal citizens.
But if you hold Persuasion has her sacred place
of worship, in the sweet beguilement of my voice,
then you might stay with us. But if you wish to stay

then it would not be justice to inflict your rage
upon this city, your resentment or bad luck
to armies. Yours the baron's portion in this land
if you will, in all justice, with full privilege.
CHORUS: Lady Athene, what is this place you say is mine?
ATHENE: A place free of all grief and pain. Take it for yours.
CHORUS: If I do take it, shall I have some definite powers?
ATHENE: No household shall be prosperous without your will.
CHORUS: You will do this? You will really let me be so strong?
ATHENE: So we shall straighten the lives of all who worship us.
CHORUS: You guarantee such honor for the rest of time?
ATHENE: I have no need to promise what I cannot do.
CHORUS: I think you will have your way with me. My hate is going.
ATHENE: Stay here, then. You will win the hearts of others, too.
CHORUS: I will put a spell upon the land. What shall it be?
ATHENE: Something that has no traffic with evil success.
Let it come out of the ground, out of the sea's water,
and from the high air make the waft of gentle gales
wash over the country in full sunlight, and the seed
and stream of the soil's yield and of the grazing beasts
be strong and never fail our people as time goes,
and make the human seed be kept alive. Make more
the issue of those who worship more your ways, for as
the gardener works in love, so love I best of all
the unblighted generation of these upright men.
All such is yours for granting. In the speech and show
and pride of battle, I myself shall not endure
this city's eclipse in the estimation of mankind.
CHORUS: I accept this home at Athene's side.
I shall not forget the cause
of this city, which Zeus all powerful and Ares
rule, stronghold of divinities,
glory of Hellene gods, their guarded altar.
So with forecast of good
I speak this prayer for them
that the sun's bright magnificence shall break out wave
on wave of all the happiness
life can give, across their land
ATHENE: Here are my actions. In all good will
toward these citizens I establish in power
spirits who are large, difficult to soften.

To them is given the handling entire
of men's lives. That man
who has not felt the weight of their hands
takes the strokes of life, knows not whence, not why,
for crimes wreaked in past generations
drag him before these powers. Loud his voice
but the silent doom
hates hard, and breaks him to dust.
CHORUS: Let there blow no wind that wrecks the trees.
I pronounce words of grace.
Nor blaze of heat blind the blossoms of grown plants, nor
cross the circles of its right
place. Let no barren deadly sickness creep and kill.
Flocks fatten. Earth be kind
to them, with double fold of fruit
in time appointed for its yielding. Secret child
of earth, her hidden wealth, bestow
blessing and surprise of gods.
ATHENE: Strong guard of our city, hear you these
and what they portend? Fury is a high queen
of strength even among the immortal gods
and the undergods, and for humankind
their work is accomplished, absolute, clear:
for some, singing; for some, life dimmed
in tears; theirs the disposition.
CHORUS: Death of manhood cut down
before its prime I forbid:
girls' grace and glory find
men to live life with them.
Grant, you who have the power.
And o, steering spirits of law,
goddesses of destiny,
sisters from my mother, hear;
in all houses implicate,
in all time heavy of hand
on whom your just arrest befalls,
august among goddesses, bestow.
ATHENE: It is my glory to hear how these
generosities
are given my land. I admire the eyes
of Persuasion, who guided the speech of my mouth

toward these, when they were reluctant and wild.
Zeus, who guides men's speech in councils, was too
strong; and my ambition
for good wins out in the whole issue.

Translated by Richmond Lattimore

THUCYDIDES
Middle 5th Century–399 B.C.?

From THE PELOPONNESIAN WARS

In 458 B.C., Aeschylus gave the actor playing Athena in his play The
Eumenides *some lines that prophesied a great future for the city that
bore the goddess's name: "Time / in his onward flood shall ever grow
more dignified / for the people of this city." By 431 B.C., when the
Peloponnesian War between Athens and the Spartan alliance broke out,
the prophecy had been amply fulfilled. Athens towered over all the other
city-states of Greece and seemed destined to become the power that
would unite under its leadership and eventually control the whole Greek
world. Its fortifications, and its Long Walls connecting them with the
harbor Piraeus, made it impervious both to land assault and blockade; its
formidable navy, superior not only in number of ships but also in the
technical skill of their crews, gave it control of the seas; and its wealth,
much of it in the form of tribute from subject cities on the islands and
coastal cities of the Aegean, gave it the capacity to face a long war.
Athens' power and wealth increased year by year, and the mainland
states of Greece, organized as the Peloponnesian League under the leadership of Sparta, began to feel that if they did not arrest the city's march
to supremacy soon, they might be too late. In the mid-thirties of the
century a series of armed conflicts between Athens and Sparta's wealthiest and most powerful ally, Corinth, resulted in a meeting of the Peloponnesian League at Sparta, at which the Corinthians demanded immediate military action against Athens. In the course of this speech they
delivered a powerful assessment and indictment of the Athenian character as they saw it.*

Thucydides, who reports the speech, was certainly not there to hear it, and it is highly unlikely that he saw a written version. The speeches reported as verbatim in his book are based on oral recollection—his own in the case of Pericles, or that of his informants—but they also contain what he thought should have been said on the occasion he is describing. This he is frank to admit: "As for the speeches made on the eve of the war or during its course, it was hard for me, when I heard them myself, or for any others who reported them to me, to recollect exactly what had been said. I have therefore put into the mouth of each speaker the views that, in my opinion, they would have been most likely to express, as the particular occasion demanded, while keeping as nearly as I could to the general purport of what was actually said." In the case of the three speeches of Pericles, which he certainly heard, we can be more confident of the authenticity of the content than in cases where he could not have been present or in any case where speakers are identified only as "the Corinthians" or "the Plataeans." But clearly, Thucydides is presenting in these speeches his analysis of the political and military background of the historical situation, the conflicting opinions, the alternative courses of action—the material, in fact, that a modern historian presents editorially as his own assessment.

His sketch of fifth-century Athenian history before the outbreak of the war starts exactly where Herodotus left off. But Thucydides is conscious, and proud, of the fact that his idea of history is very different from that of his great predecessor. His interests are as narrow as Herodotus' were wide. He deals only with the power struggles, political and military, of a war in which he himself fought as a general officer, and which dragged on for twenty-seven years as he wrote. Unlike Herodotus, he was severely critical of his sources; he "examined every point with the utmost possible exactness." He realizes that his predecessor may be more entertaining reading—"the lack of romance in my work will perhaps make it seem less agreeable to the ear"—but will be content if the readers of his book consider it "useful." It will be useful because it aims to present "the clear truth about the events which have taken place, and about those which are likely to take place in the future—in the order of human things, they will resemble what has occurred."

THE ATHENIANS, A HOSTILE ESTIMATE

You have never fully considered what manner of men these Athenians are with whom you will have to fight, and how utterly unlike yourselves. They are innovators, equally quick in the conception and in the execution of every plan; while you are careful only to keep what you have and uninventive; in action you do not even go as far as you need. They are audacious beyond their strength; they run risks which policy would condemn; and in the midst of dangers, they are full of hope. Whereas it is your nature to act more feebly than your power allows, in forming your policy not even to rely on certainties, and when dangers arise, to think you will never be delivered from them. They are resolute, and you are dilatory; they are always abroad, and you are always at home. For they think they may gain something by leaving their homes; but you are afraid that any new enterprise may imperil what you have already. When conquerors, they pursue their victory to the utmost; when defeated, they give as little ground as possible. They devote their bodies to their country as though they belonged to other men, and their minds, their dearest possessions, to action in her service. When they do not carry out an intention which they have formed, they seem to themselves to have sustained a personal bereavement; when an enterprise succeeds, they think they have gained a small installment of what is to come; but if they suffer a reverse, they at once conceive new hopes to compensate and supply their wants. For with them alone, to hope is to have, as they lose not a moment in the execution of an idea. In all these activities they wear themselves out with exertions and dangers throughout their entire lives. None enjoy their good things less because they are always seeking for more. To do their duty is their only holiday, and they deem peaceful repose to be no less of a misfortune than incessant fatigue. If a man should say of them, in a word, that it is their nature neither to be at peace themselves nor to allow peace to other men, he would simply speak the truth.

Translated by Benjamin Jowett; revised by P. A. Brunt

PERICLES' FUNERAL SPEECH

Pericles' Funeral Speech is not only a eulogy of the Athenians killed in the battles of the war's first year, it is also a contrast between the Athenian and the Spartan ways of life, and a celebration of the benefits conferred on Athens' citizens by the democratic regime. This part of the speech is one of the classic documents in the history of democratic institutions.

Athenian democracy was a direct, not a representational, democracy. Supreme authority was vested in a popular assembly, a town meeting, so to speak. Business was prepared for the assembly by a council that sat in permanent session; its membership was annually renewed. Administra-

tive officers were elected annually; immediate reelection was possible only for the ten generals who commanded the ten tribal units of the Athenians when mobilized for military or naval action. It was in this office that Pericles, reelected from year to year, presided over Athenian policy for some twenty years prior to the outbreak of the Peloponnesian War.

From the point of view of citizen participation, Athenian democracy was more democratic than ours, but the franchise, the right to hold office and to vote in the meetings of the assembly, was not so widely spread as in modern democracies. Resident aliens were excluded, as were women and, of course, slaves. Greek society was based on slave labor, but in this it conformed to the general pattern of ancient societies, which all depended on some form of forced labor, whether chattel slavery, debt bondage, or serfdom. The modern world, however, is hardly in a position to pass severe judgment on the Athenian restrictions on the franchise. It was not until the nineteenth century that voting rights for the male population were firmly established in the Western European democracies. The same century saw the abolition of slavery in the United States as the result of a prolonged and bloody struggle. As for women, they had to wait for the right to vote until 1920 in the United States, 1928 in England, 1945 in France, and only very recently in Switzerland.

In many times and places Pericles' praise of democracy has served as an inspiration for people oppressed by dictatorial regimes, which have regarded it as a dangerous document. A spectacular example was furnished by modern Greece, where, under the military dictatorship of General Metaxas during the 1930s, a group of students from Athens University were arrested for distributing subversive literature: a modern Greek translation of Pericles' Funeral Speech.

During the same winter, in accordance with traditional custom, the funeral of those who first fell in this war was celebrated by the Athenians at the public charge. The ceremony is as follows: Three days before the celebration they erect a tent in which the bones of the dead are laid out, and every one brings to his own dead any offering which he pleases. At the time of the funeral, the bones are placed in chests of cypress wood, which are conveyed on hearses; there is one chest for each tribe. They also carry a single empty litter decked with a pall for all whose bodies had not been found and recovered. The procession is accompanied by anyone who chooses, whether citizen or foreigner; and the female relatives of the deceased are present at the funeral and make lamentation. The public sepulcher is situated in the most beautiful suburb of the city; there they always bury those who fall in war; only after the battle of Marathon, in recognition of their pre-eminent valor, the dead were interred on the field. When the remains have been laid in the earth, a man, chosen by the city for his reputed sagacity of judgment and eminent prestige, delivers the appropriate eulogy over them; after which the people depart. This is the manner of interment, and the ceremony was repeated from time to time throughout the war. Over the first who were buried, Pericles was chosen to speak. At the fitting moment he advanced from the sepulcher to a lofty stage, which had been erected in order that he might be heard as far away as possible by the crowd, and spoke somewhat as follows:

"Most of those who have spoken here before me commend the lawgiver who added this oration to our other funeral customs, thinking it right for an oration to be delivered at the funeral of those killed in wars. But I would have thought it enough that when men have been brave in action, they should also be publicly honored in action, and with such a ceremony as this state funeral, which you are now witnessing. Then the reputation of many would not have been imperiled by one man and their merits believed or not, as he speaks well or ill. For it is difficult to say neither too little nor too much when belief in the truth is hard to confirm. The friend of the dead who knows the facts may well think that the words of the speaker fall short of his wishes and knowledge; another who is not well informed, when he hears of anything which surpasses his own nature, may be envious and suspect exaggeration. Mankind is tolerant of the praises of others so long as each hearer thinks himself capable of doing anything he has heard; but when the speaker rises above this, jealousy and incredulity are at once aroused. However, since our ancestors have set the seal of their approval upon the practice, I must obey the law and, to the utmost of my power, endeavor to satisfy the wishes and beliefs of you all.

"I will speak of our ancestors first, for it is right and seemly that on such an occasion as this we should also render this honor to their memory. Men of the same stock, ever dwelling in this land, in successive generations to this very day, by their valor handed it down as a free land. They are worthy of praise, and still more are our fathers, who added to their inheritance, and after many a struggle bequeathed to us, their sons, the great empire we possess. Most of it those of our own number who are still in the settled time of life have strengthened further and have richly endowed our city in every way and made her most self-sufficient for both peace and war. Of the military exploits by which our various possessions were acquired or of the energy with which we or our fathers resisted the onslaught of barbarians or Hellenes I will not speak, for the tale would be long and is familiar to you. But before I praise the dead, I shall first proceed to show by what kind of practices we attained to our position, and under what kind of institutions and manner of life our empire became great. For I conceive that it would not be unsuited to the occasion that this should be told, and that this whole assembly of citizens and foreigners may profitably listen to it.

"Our institutions do not emulate the laws of others. We do not copy our neighbors: rather, we are an example to them. Our system is called a democracy, for it respects the majority and not the few; but while the law secures equality to all alike in their private disputes, the claim of excellence is also recognized; and when a citizen is in any way distinguished, he is generally preferred to the public service, not in rotation, but for merit. Nor again is there any bar in poverty and obscurity of rank to a man who can do the state some service. It is as free men that we conduct our public life, and in our daily occupations we avoid mutual suspicions; we are not angry with our neighbor if he does what he likes; we do not put on sour looks at him which, though harmless, are not pleasant. While we give no offense in our private intercourse, in our public acts we are prevented from doing wrong by fear; we respect the authorities and the laws, especially those which are ordained for the protection of the injured as well as those unwritten laws which bring upon the transgressor admitted dishonor.

"Furthermore, none have provided more relaxations for the spirit from toil; we have regular games and sacrifices throughout the year; our homes are furnished with elegance; and the delight which we daily feel in all these things banishes melancholy. Because of the greatness of our city, the fruits of the whole earth flow in upon us so that we enjoy the goods of other countries as freely as our own.

"Then, again, in military training we are superior to our adversaries, as I shall show. Our city is thrown open to the world, and we never expel a foreigner or prevent him from seeing or learning anything which, if not concealed, it might profit an enemy to see. We rely not so much upon preparations or stratagems, as upon our own courage in action. And in the matter of education, whereas from early youth they are always undergoing laborious exercises which are to make them brave, we live at ease and yet are equally ready to face perils to which our strength is equal. And here is the evidence. The Lacedæmonians march against our land not by themselves, but with all their allies: we invade a neighbor's country alone; and although our opponents are fighting for their homes and we are on a foreign soil, we seldom have any difficulty in overcoming them. Our enemies have never yet felt our strength in full; the care of a navy divides our attention, and on land we are obliged to send our own citizens to many parts. But if they meet and defeat some part of our army, they boast of having routed us all, and when defeated, of having been vanquished by our whole force.

"If then we prefer to meet danger with a light heart but without laborious training and with a courage which is instilled by habit more than by laws, we are the gainers; we do not anticipate the pain, although, when the hour comes, we show ourselves no less bold than those who never allow themselves to rest. Nor is this the only cause for marveling at our city. We are lovers of beauty without extravagance and of learning without loss of vigor. Wealth we employ less for talk and ostentation than when there is a real use for it. To avow poverty with us is no disgrace: the true disgrace is in doing nothing to avoid it. The same persons attend at once to the concerns of their households and of the city, and men of diverse employments have a very fair idea of politics. If a man takes no interest in public affairs, we alone do not commend him as quiet but condemn him as useless; and if few of us are originators, we are all sound judges of a policy. In our opinion action does not suffer from discussion but, rather, from the want of that instruction which is gained by discussion preparatory to the action required. For we have an exceptional gift of acting with audacity after calculating the prospects of our enterprises, whereas other men are bold from ignorance but hesitate upon reflection. But it would be right to esteem those men bravest in spirit who have the clearest understanding of the pains and pleasures of life and do not on that account shrink from danger. In doing good, again, we are unlike others; we make our friends by conferring, not by receiving favors. Now a man who confers a favor is the firmer friend because he would keep alive the memory of an obligation by kindness to the recipient; the man who owes an obligation is colder in his feelings because he knows that in recruiting the service, he will not be winning gratitude but only paying a debt. We alone do good to our neighbors, not so much upon a calculation of interest, but in the fearless confidence of freedom.

"To sum up, I say that the whole city is an education for Hellas and that each individual in our society would seem to be capable of the greatest self-reliance and of the utmost dexterity and grace in the widest range of activities. This is no passing boast in a speech, but truth and fact, and verified by the actual power of the city which we have won by this way of life. For when put to the test, Athens alone among her contemporaries is superior to report. No enemy who comes against her is indignant at the reverses which he sustains at the hands of such men; no subject complains that his masters do not deserve to rule. And we shall assuredly not be without witnesses; there are mighty monuments of our power which will make us the wonder of this and of succeeding ages; we shall not need the praises of Homer or of any other whose poetry will please for the moment, but whose reconstruction of the facts the truth will damage. For we have compelled every land and sea to open a path to our daring and have everywhere planted eternal memorials of our triumphs and misfortunes. Such is the city these men fought and died for and nobly disdained to lose, and every one of us who survive would naturally wear himself out in her service.

"This is why I have dwelt upon the greatness of Athens, showing you that we are contending for a higher prize than those who enjoy no like advantages, and establishing by manifest proof the merit of these men whom I am now commemorating. Their loftiest praise has been already spoken; for in descanting on the city, I have honored the qualities which earned renown for them and for men such as they. And of how few Hellenes can it be said as of them, that their deeds matched their fame! In my belief an end such as theirs proves a man's worth; it is at once its first revelation and final seal. For even those who come short in other ways may justly plead the valor with which they have fought for their country; they have blotted out evil with good, and their public services have outweighed the harm they have done in their private actions. None of these men were enervated by wealth or hesitated to resign the pleasures of life; none of them put off the evil day in the hope, natural to poverty, that a man, though poor, may yet become rich. But deeming that vengeance on their enemies was sweeter than any of these things and that they could hazard their lives in no nobler cause, they accepted the risk and resolved on revenge in preference to every other aim. They resigned to hope the obscure chance of success, but in the danger already visible they thought it right to act in reliance upon themselves alone. And when the moment for fighting came, they held it nobler to suffer death than to yield and save their lives; it was the report of dishonor from which they fled, but on the battlefield their feet stood fast; and while for a moment they were in the hands of fortune, at the height, less of terror than of glory, they departed.

"Such was the conduct of these men; they were worthy of Athens. The rest of us must pray for a safer issue to our courage and yet disdain to show any less daring towards our enemies. We must not consider only what words can be uttered on the utility of such a spirit. Anyone might discourse to you at length on all the advantages of resisting the enemy bravely, but you know them just as well yourselves. It is better that you should actually gaze day by day on the power of the city until you are filled with the love of her; and when you are convinced of her greatness, reflect that it was acquired by men of daring who knew their duty and feared dishonor in the hour of action, men who if they ever failed in an enterprise, even then disdained to deprive the city of their prowess but offered themselves up as the finest contribution to the common cause. All alike gave their lives and received praise which grows not old and the most conspicuous of sepulchers—I speak not so much of that in which their remains are laid as of that in which their glory survives to be remembered forever, on every fitting occasion in word and deed. For every land is a sepulcher for famous men; not only are they commemorated by inscriptions on monuments in their own country, but even in foreign lands there dwells an unwritten memorial of them, graven not so much on stone as in the hearts of men. Make them your examples now; and, esteeming courage to be freedom and freedom to be happiness, do not weigh too nicely the perils of war. It is not the unfortunate men with no hope of blessing, who would with best reason be unsparing of their lives, but the prosperous, who, if they survive, are always in danger of a change for the worse, and whose situation would be most transformed by any reverse. To a man of spirit it is more painful to be oppressed like a weakling than in the consciousness of strength and common hopes to meet a death that comes unfelt.

"Therefore I do not now commiserate the parents of the dead who stand here; I shall rather comfort them. They know that their life has been passed amid manifold vicissitudes and that those men may be deemed fortunate who have gained most honor, whether an honorable death, like the men we bury here, or an honorable sorrow like yours, and whose days have been so measured that the term of their happiness is likewise the term of their life. I know how hard it is to make you feel this when the good fortune of others will often remind you of the happiness in which you, like them, once rejoiced. Sorrow is felt at the want not of those blessings which a man never knew, but of those which were a part of his life before they were taken from him. Some of you are of an age at which you may have other children, and that hope should make you bear your sorrow better; not only will the children who may hereafter be born make you forget those you have lost, but the city will be doubly a gainer; she will not be left desolate, and she will be safer. For a man's counsel cannot have equal weight or worth when he has no children like the rest to risk in the general danger. To those of you who have passed their prime, I say: 'Congratulate yourselves that you have been happy during the greater part of your days; remember that what remains will not last long, and let it be lightened by the glory of these men.' For only the love of honor is ever young; and it is not so much profit, as some say, but honor which is the delight of men when they are old and useless.

"To you who are the sons and brothers of the departed, I see that the struggle to emulate them will be arduous. For all men praise the dead, and, however pre-eminent your virtue may be, you would hardly be thought their equals, but somewhat inferior. The living have their rivals and detractors; but when a man is out of the way, the honor and good will which he receives is uncontested. And, if I am also to speak of womanly virtues to those of you who will now be widows, let me sum them up in one short admonition: 'Your glory will be great if you show no more than the infirmities of your nature, a glory that consists in being least the subjects of report among men, for good or evil.'

"I have spoken in obedience to the law, making use of such fitting words as I had. The tribute of deeds has been paid in part, for the dead have been honorably interred; it remains only that their children shall be maintained at the public charge until they are grown up: this is the solid prize with which, as with a garland, Athens crowns these men and those left behind after such contests. For where the rewards of virtue are greatest, there men do the greatest services to their cities. And now, when you have duly lamented, everyone his own dead, you may depart."

Such was the order of the funeral celebrated in this winter, with the end of which ended the first year of this war.

Translated by Benjamin Jowett; revised by P. A. Brunt

THE PLAGUE IN ATHENS

Athens was impregnable behind its fortifications, but the Spartans and their allies invaded Attica, burning and pillaging as they went. Pericles, knowing that Athenian troops could not defeat Sparta in a land battle, refused to go out and fight them. The country people came flooding into the city for refuge, but found no adequate shelter; they lived from hand to mouth in temporary shacks and insanitary conditions. The plague broke out in the summer of 430 B.C.

Thucydides caught the plague, but, unlike most of its victims, he survived. His careful description of the symptoms and course of the disease is reminiscent of the case histories of the contemporary physicians of the Hippocratic School, but his hope that it would enable future generations to identify the disease proved vain. It has been identified as measles, smallpox, bubonic plague, typhus, and typhoid, among other candidates; some scholars have suggested that the bacteria responsible for the disease are not likely to be alive unchanged after some 2,500 years.

Thucydides' skeptical comments about the prophecy that was thought to have predicted the plague are in sharp contrast with the respect Herodotus always shows for prophecies, especially those of the Oracle of Apollo at Delphi. The reason people who remembered Apollo's promise to the Spartans that he would be on their side thought "that they were witnessing the fulfillment of his words" was that Apollo was known as a god who might send plague, as he did at the beginning of the Iliad.

As soon as summer returned [430 B.C.], the Peloponesians and allies, as before with two-thirds of their forces, under the command of the Lacedæmonian king Archidamus the son of Zeuxidamus, invaded Attica, where they established themselves and ravaged the country. They had not been there many days when the plague broke out at Athens for the first time. It is said to have previously smitten many places, particularly Lemnos; but there is no record of so great a pestilence occurring elsewhere, or of so great a destruction of human life. For a while physicians sought to apply remedies in ignorance, but it was in vain, and they themselves were most prone to perish because they came into most frequent contact with it. No other human art was of any avail; and as to supplications in temples, inquiries of oracles, and the like, they were all useless; and at last men were overpowered by the calamity and gave them all up.

The disease is said to have begun south of Egypt in Ethiopia; from there it descended into Egypt and Libya; and after spreading over the greater part of the Persian empire, suddenly fell upon Athens. It first attacked the inhabitants of the Piræus so that it was actually said by them that the Peloponnesians had poisoned the cisterns; no fountains as yet existed there. It afterwards reached the upper city, and then the mortality became far greater. Every man, physician or layman, may declare his own judgment about its probable origin and the causes he thinks sufficient to have produced so great a vicissitude: I shall speak of its actual course and the features by which men may acquire some foreknowledge and be most apt to recognize it, should it ever reappear. I shall describe these clearly as one who was myself attacked, and witnessed the sufferings of others.

The season was universally admitted to have been remarkably free from other sicknesses; and if anybody was already ill of any other disease, it finally turned into this. The other victims who were in perfect health, all in a moment and without any exciting cause, were seized first with violent heats in the head and with redness and burning of the eyes. Internally, the throat and the tongue at once became blood-red, and the breath abnormal and fetid. Sneezing and hoarseness followed; in a short time the disorder, accompanied by a violent cough, reached the chest. And whenever it settled in the heart, it upset it; and there were all the vomits of bile to which physicians have ever given names, and they were accompanied by great distress. An ineffectual retching, producing violent convulsions, attacked most of the sufferers; some, as soon as the previous symptoms had abated, others, not until long afterwards. The body externally was not so very hot to the touch, not yellowish but flushed and livid and breaking out in blisters and ulcers. But the internal fever was intense; the sufferers could not bear to have on them even the lightest linen garment; they insisted on being naked, and there was nothing which they longed for more eagerly than to throw themselves into cold water; many of those who had no one to look after them actually plunged into the cisterns. They were tormented by unceasing thirst, which was not in the least assuaged whether they drank much or little. They could find no way of resting, and sleeplessness attacked them throughout. While the disease was at its height, the body, instead of wasting away, held out amid these sufferings unexpectedly. Thus, most died on the seventh or ninth day of internal fever, though their strength was not exhausted; or, if they survived, then the disease descended into the bowels and there produced violent lesions; at the same time diarrhea set in which was uniformly fluid, and at a later stage caused exhaustion, and this finally carried them off with few exceptions. For the disorder which had originally settled in the head passed gradually through the whole body and, if a person got over the worst, would often seize the extremities and leave its mark, attacking the privy parts, fingers and toes; and many escaped with the loss of these, some with the loss of their eyes. Some again had no sooner recovered than they were seized with a total loss of memory and knew neither themselves nor their friends.

The character of the malady no words can describe, and the fury with which it fastened upon each sufferer was too much for human nature to endure. There was one circumstance in particular which distinguished it from ordinary diseases. Although so many bodies were lying unburied, the birds and animals which feed on human flesh either never came near them or died if they touched them. This is the evidence: there was a manifest disappearance of birds of prey, which were not to be seen either near the bodies or anywhere else; while in the case of the dogs, what happened was even more obvious because they live with man.

Such was the general nature of the disease: I omit many strange peculiarities which variously characterized individual cases. None of the ordinary sicknesses attacked any one while it lasted, or if they did, they ended in the plague. Some died from want of care, but so did others who were receiving the greatest attention. No single remedy was established as a specific; for what did good to one did harm to another. No constitution was noticed of itself strong enough to resist or weak enough to escape the attacks; the disease carried off all alike and defied every mode of treatment. Most appalling was the despondency that seized upon anyone who felt himself sickening; for he instantly abandoned his mind to despair and, instead of holding out, was much more likely to throw away his chance of life. Equally appalling was the fact that men died like sheep, catching the infection if they attended on one another; and this was the principal cause of mortality. When they were afraid to visit one another, the sufferers died in solitude, so that many houses were empty because there had been no one to take care of the sick; or if they ventured, they perished, especially those who made any claim to be good men. Out of a sense of honor, they went to see their friends without thought of themselves at a time when their own relations were at last growing weary and ceasing even to make lamentations over the dead, overwhelmed by the vastness of the calamity. But more often the sick and the dying were tended by the pitying care of those who had recovered, because they knew the course of the disease and were themselves free from apprehension. For no one was ever attacked a second time, or not with a fatal result. All men congratulated them, and they themselves, in the excess of their joy at the moment, had an idle fancy that they could never die thereafter of any other sickness.

The crowding of the people out of the country into the city aggravated the misery, and the newly arrived suffered most. They had no houses of their own but inhabited stifling huts in the height of summer and perished in wild disorder. The dead and the dying lay one upon another, while others hardly alive rolled in the streets and around every fountain craving water. The temples in which they lodged were full of the corpses of those who died in them; for the violence of the calamity was such that men, not knowing where to turn, grew reckless of all law, human and divine. The customs which had hitherto been observed at funerals were universally violated; and they buried their dead, each one as best he could. Many, for lack of what was proper because the deaths had been so numerous already, lost all shame in the burial of the dead. When one man had raised a funeral pile, others would come, put their own dead on it first and set fire to it; or when some other corpse was already burning, they would throw on top the body they brought and be off.

There were other and worse forms of lawlessness which the plague first introduced at Athens. Men who had hitherto concealed that they acted on the dictates of pleasure now grew bolder. They saw the rapid vicissitudes of fortune—how the rich died in a moment, and those who had nothing immediately inherited their property—reflected that life and riches were alike ephemeral, and thought it right to enjoy themselves without a pause and to think only of pleasure. None was eager to exert himself first for an honorable reputation when he esteemed it uncertain if he would not perish before securing it. The pleasure of the moment and everything which conduced to it was established as both honorable and expedient. No fear of gods or law of man deterred. Those who saw all perishing alike thought that the worship or neglect of the gods made no difference; and as for offenses against human law, no one expected to live long enough to be called to account and pay the penalty; already a far heavier sentence had been passed and was suspended over a man's head; before it fell, why should he not take a little pleasure?

Such was the calamity which now afflicted the Athenians; within the walls their people were dying, and without, their country was being ravaged. In their troubles they naturally called to mind a verse which the older men among them declared was current long ago: "A Dorian war will come and with it plague." There was a dispute about the word; some saying that *limos*, a famine, and not *loimos*, a plague, was the original word. Nevertheless, as might have been expected, for men's memories reflected their sufferings, the argument in favor of *loimos* prevailed at the time. But if ever in future years they are in the grip of another Dorian war which happens to be accompanied by a famine, they will probably repeat the verse in the other form. The answer of the oracle to the Lacedæmonians when the god was asked "whether they should go to war or not" and he replied "that if they fought with all their might, they would conquer, and that he himself would take their part" was not forgotten by those who had heard of it, and they quite imagined that they were witnessing the fulfillment of his words. The disease certainly did set in immediately after the invasion of the Peloponnesians and did not spread into the Peloponnese in any degree worth speaking of, while Athens felt its ravages most severely, and next to Athens, the places which were most populous. This was the history of the plague.

Translated by Benjamin Jowett; revised by P. A. Brunt

THE MELIAN DIALOGUE

In 421 b.c., with neither side able to deal the other a decisive blow, Athens and Sparta patched together an agreement that ended the first phase of the war. But it was an uneasy peace; the adversaries continued to fight each other through allies and satellites, and at Mantinea in 418 b.c. Athenian and Spartan troops fought in the opposing battle lines.

Neither side, however, was willing to annul the treaty and proceed to
large-scale offensive operations. These were resumed, by the Spartans,
after the Athenian disaster in Sicily in 415.

Meanwhile Athens decided to add to its Aegean empire the island of
Melos, whose inhabitants, though of Dorian stock and so sympathetic to
the Spartan cause, had so far remained neutral. The Athenians brought
to bear overwhelming force and then summoned the Melian authorities
to a parley. Thucydides' account of the proceedings does not even pre-
tend, this time, to be a report of what was actually said. He does not
name any individual speakers, and although he records short exchanges
elsewhere in his history, only here are the two parties identified by ab-
breviated versions of their names—Ath. and Mel.—at the beginning of
each new speech. It is as if Thucydides wishes to emphasize the fact that
this dialogue deals, to use Aristotle's terms, as much with the universal as
the particular. It is a fundamental analysis of the imperatives of power,
of the law that—as the Athenians put it—"wherever they have the
power, men will rule."

The Brasidas mentioned by the Melians on p. 352 was a Spartan
officer who led a small force to northern Greece in 424 B.C., where his
activity resulted in the rebellion of some of the most important cities
that had been first allies, and then subjects, of Athens.

The Athenians next made an expedition against the island of Melos
with thirty ships of their own, six Chian, and two Lesbian, twelve hundred hoplites and three hundred archers and twenty mounted archers of
their own, and about fifteen hundred hoplites furnished by their allies in
the islands. The Melians are colonists of the Lacedæmonians who would
not submit to Athens like the other islanders. At first they were neutral
and passive. But when the Athenians tried to coerce them by ravaging
their lands, they were driven into open hostilities. The generals, Cleo-
medes the son of Lycomedes and Tisias the son of Tisimachus, en-
camped with the Athenian forces on the island. But before they did the
country any harm, they sent envoys to negotiate with the Melians. Instead of bringing these envoys before the people, the Melians desired
them to explain their errand to the minority who held the magistracies.
They spoke as follows:

"Since we are denied a public audience on the ground that the multitude might be deceived by hearing our seductive arguments without
refutation if they were set forth in a single uninterrupted oration (for we
are perfectly aware that this is what you mean in bringing us before the
select few), we ask you who are seated here to proceed with even further

caution, to reply on each point, instead of speaking continuously yourselves, and to take up at once any statement of ours of which you do not
approve, and so reach your decision. Say first of all how you like our
proposal."

The Melian representatives answered: "The quiet interchange of ex-
planations is reasonable, and we do not object to that. But at this very
time you are actually engaged in acts of war, which obviously belie your
words. We see that you mean to decide the discussion yourselves and
that at the end of it, if (as is likely) the justice of our cause prevail and we
therefore refuse to yield, we may expect war; if we are convinced by you,
slavery."

ATH.: "Of course, if you are going to base your calculations on conjec-
tures of the future or if you meet us with any other purpose than that of
looking your circumstances in the face and thinking how to save your
city, we might as well have done; but if this is your intention, we will
proceed."

MEL.: "It is natural and excusable that men in our position should
resort to many arguments and considerations. But we admit that this
conference has met to consider the question of our preservation; and
therefore let the argument proceed in the manner which you propose, if
you think that best."

ATH.: "Well, then, we Athenians will use no fine words; we will not say
at length, without carrying conviction, that we have a right to rule because we overthrew the Persians or that we are attacking you now because we are suffering any injury at your hands. And you should not
expect to convince us by arguing that, although a colony of the Lacedæmonians, you have taken no part in their expeditions or that you have
never done us any wrong. You must act with realism on the basis of what
we both really think, for we both alike know that in human reckoning
the question of justice only enters where there is equal power to enforce
it and that the powerful exact what they can and the weak grant what
they must."

MEL.: "Well, then, since you thus set aside justice and make expediency the subject of debate, in our judgment it is certainly of advantage
that you respect the common good, that to every man in peril fair treatment be accorded, and that any plea which he has urged, even if failing
of the point a little, should help his cause. Your interest in this principle
is quite as great as ours, since if you fall, you might incur the heaviest
vengeance and be an example to mankind."

ATH.: "The end of our empire, even if it should fall, does not dismay
us; for ruling states such as Lacedæmon are not cruel to their vanquished
enemies. But we are not now contending with the Lacedæmonians; the

real danger is from our subjects, who may of their own motion rise up and overcome their masters. But this is a danger which you may leave to us. We will show that we have come in the interests of our empire and that in what we are about to say, we are only seeking the preservation of your city. We wish to subdue you without effort and to preserve you to our mutual advantage."

MEL.: "It may be your advantage to be our masters, but how can it be ours to be your slaves?"

ATH.: "By submission you would avert the most terrible sufferings, and we should profit from not destroying you."

MEL.: "But must we be your enemies? Would you not receive us as friends if we are neutral and remain at peace with you?"

ATH.: "No, your enmity does not injure us as much as your friendship; for your enmity is in the eyes of our subjects a demonstration of our power, your friendship of our weakness."

MEL.: "But do your subjects think it fair not to distinguish between cities in which you have no connection and those which are chiefly your own colonies, and in some cases have revolted and been subdued?"

ATH.: "Why, they believe that neither lack pleas of right, but that by reason of their power some escape us and that we do not attack them out of fear. So that your subjection would give us security, as well as an extension of empire, all the more as you are islanders, and insignificant islanders."

MEL.: "But do you not think that there is security in our proposal? For, once more, since you drive us from the plea of justice and urge us to submit to you our interest, we must show you what is for our advantage and try to convince you, if it really coincides with yours: Will you not be making enemies of all who are now neutrals? When they see how you are treating us, they will expect you some day to turn against them; and if so, are you not strengthening the enemies whom you already have and bringing upon you others who, if they could help it, would never dream of being your enemies at all?"

ATH.: "We consider that our really dangerous enemies are not any of the peoples inhabiting the mainland who are secure in their freedom and will defer indefinitely any measures of precaution against us, but islanders who, like you, are under no control, and all who are already irritated by the necessity of submission to our empire; for without calculating, they would be most likely to plunge themselves, as well as us, into a danger for all to foresee."

MEL.: "Surely then, if you and your subjects will brave all this danger, you to preserve your empire and they to be quit of it, how base and cowardly would it be for us, as we are still free, not to do and suffer anything rather than be your slaves."

ATH.: "Not if you deliberate with sound sense; you are in an unequal contest; not about your good character and avoiding dishonor: you must think of saving yourselves by not resisting far superior forces."

MEL.: "But we know that the fortune of war is sometimes impartial and not always on the side of numbers. If we yield, hope is at once gone, but if we act, we can still hope to stand unbowed."

ATH.: "Hope comforts men in danger; and when they have ample resources, it may be hurtful, but is not ruinous. But when her spendthrift nature has induced them to stake their all, they see her as she is only in the moment of their ruin; when their eyes are opened, and they would at last take precautions, they are left with nothing. You are weak, and a single turn of the scale may be your ruin: do not desire to be deluded; or to be like the common herd of men; when they still, humanly speaking, have a chance of survival but find themselves, in their extremity, destitute of real grounds for confidence, they resort to illusions, to prophecies and oracles and the like, which ruin men by the hopes which they inspire in them."

MEL.: "You may be sure that we think it hard to struggle against your power and against fortune if she does not mean to be impartial. But still we trust that we shall not have the worst of the fortune that comes from heaven because we stand as righteous men against your injustice, and we are satisfied that our deficiency in power will be compensated by the alliance of the Lacedæmonians; they are bound to help us, if only because we are their kinsmen and for the sake of their own honor. And therefore our confidence is not so utterly unreasonable."

ATH.: "As for the gods, we expect to have quite as much of their favor as you: for we are not claiming or doing anything which goes beyond what men believe of the gods and desire in human relationships. For we believe of the gods by repute, and of men by clear evidence, that by a necessity of nature, wherever they have the power, they will rule. This law was not made by us, and we are not the first who have acted upon it; we did but inherit it, and shall bequeath it to all time; we obey it in the knowledge that you and all mankind, with our strength would act like us. So much for the gods; we have no reason to fear any lack of their favor. And then as to the Lacedæmonians—when you imagine that out of very shame they will assist you, we congratulate you on your blissful ignorance, but we do not admire your folly. No men do each other more services, by their own local standards, than the Lacedæmonians; but as for their conduct to the rest of the world, much might be said, but it could be most clearly expressed in a few words—of all men whom we know, they are the most conspicuous for identifying pleasure with honor and expediency with justice. But how inconsistent is such a character with your present unreasonable hope of deliverance!"

MEL.: "That is the very reason why we are now particularly reliant on them; they will look to their interest, and therefore will not be willing to betray the Melians, their own colonists, lest they should be distrusted by their friends in Hellas and play into the hands of their enemies."

ATH.: "Then you do not think that the path of expediency is safe, whereas justice and honor involve action and danger, which none are more generally averse to facing than the Lacedæmonians."

MEL.: "No, we believe that they would be ready to face dangers for our sake, and will think them safer where we are concerned. If action is required, we are close to the Peloponnese; and they can better trust our loyal feeling because we are their kinsmen."

ATH.: "Yes, but what gives men security in joining in a conflict is clearly not the good will of those who summon help but a decided superiority in real power. To this none look more keenly than the Lacedæmonians; so little confidence have they in their own resources that they only attack their neighbors when they have numerous allies; and therefore they are not likely to find their way by themselves to an island, when we are masters of the sea."

MEL.: "But they might send others; the Cretan sea is a large place, and the masters of the sea will have more difficulty in seizing vessels than those who would elude detection in making their escape. And if the attempt should fail, they might invade Attica itself and find their way to allies of yours whom Brasidas did not reach; and then you will have to make efforts, not for the conquest of a land which is not yours, but nearer home, for the preservation of your confederacy and of your own territory."

ATH.: "Some of this may happen; we have actually experienced it, and you are not unaware that never once have the Athenians retired from a siege through fear of others. You told us that you would deliberate on the safety of your city; but we remark that, in this long discussion, you have uttered not a word which would justify men in expecting deliverance. Your strongest grounds are hopes deferred; and what power you have, compared with that already arrayed against you, is too little to save you. What you have in mind is most unreasonable, unless you ultimately come to a sounder decision after we have withdrawn. For surely you will not fall back on a sense of honor, which has been the ruin of so many, when danger and dishonor were staring them in the face. Many men with their eyes still open to the consequences have found the word *honor* too much for them and have let a mere name lure them on, until with their own acquiescence it has drawn down upon them real and irretrievable calamities; through their own folly they have incurred a worse dishonor than fortune would have inflicted upon them. If you are wise, you will not run this risk; you will think it not unfitting to yield to the greatest of cities, which invites you to become her ally on reasonable terms, keeping your own land and merely paying tribute; you will find no honor, when you have a choice between two alternatives, safety and war, in obstinately preferring the worse. To maintain one's rights against equals, to be politic with superiors and to be moderate toward inferiors is generally the right course. Reflect once more when we have withdrawn, and say to yourselves over and over again that you are deliberating about your one and only country, which a single decision will save or destroy."

The Athenians left the conference; the Melians, after consulting among themselves, resolved to persevere in their refusal and gave the following answer: "Men of Athens, our resolution is unchanged; and we will not in a moment surrender that liberty which our city, founded seven hundred years ago, still enjoys; we will trust to the good fortune which, by the favor of the gods, has hitherto preserved us, and for human help, to the Lacedæmonians; and we will endeavor to save ourselves. We are ready, however, to be your friends and the enemies neither of you nor of the Lacedæmonians and we ask you to leave our country when you have made such a peace as appears to be in the interest of both parties."

This was the substance of the Melian answer; the Athenians said as they quitted the conference: "Well, we must say, judging from the decision at which you have arrived, that you are the only men who find things to come plainer than what lies before their eyes: your wishes make you see the secrets of the future as present realities; you put your faith in the Lacedæmonians, in fortune and in your hopes; none have more than you at stake, and none will be more utterly ruined."

Translated by Benjamin Jowett; revised by P. A. Brunt

[*The Melians decided to fight—and lost. Their city was besieged and finally they surrendered unconditionally to the Athenians, who, so Thucydides tells us, "put to death all men of military age whom they captured and sold the women and children as slaves. Melos itself they took over for themselves, sending out later a colony of 500 men." Thucydides makes no explicit comment on this atrocity, but the next sentence runs: "In the same winter the Athenians resolved again to sail against Sicily. . . ." This is the introduction to his long account of the Sicilian expedition, the greatest land and sea force Athens had ever assembled, which met with total disaster. The Athenians "were utterly defeated at all points, and their sufferings were terrible in every way. Fleet and army perished from the face of the earth, nothing was saved; and of the many who set out, few returned home." The Spartans immediately resumed hostilities, and although the Athenians could hardly hope to win, the war dragged on for another ten years before Athens, like Melos, was besieged and surrended unconditionally in 404 B.C.]*

REVOLUTION IN CORCYRA

The island of Corcyra (modern Corfu), off the west coast of mainland Greece, played a key role in the events that precipitated the outbreak of the war in 431 B.C. Originally a colony of Corinth, Corcyra was embroiled in a bitter dispute with its mother city over territorial rights on the mainland, and turned to Corinth's enemy, Athens, for support. Corcyra was a considerable naval power, strategically located on the trade route to Sicily and southern Italy; in spite of the risk of offending Corinth, Athens became Corcyra's ally.

By 427 B.C., Corcyra was torn by civil war. Democrats supported by Athens were opposed by oligarchic factions supported by Corinth; blood was shed on both sides. Finally, with the arrival of a strong Athenian naval squadron under the command of Eurymedon, the democrats gained the upper hand and proceeded to slaughter their opponents. Thucydides follows his account of the horrors of the massacre with what has ever since been regarded as a classic analysis of what happens to political language, ideas, and action in a revolution.

During the seven days that Eurymedon remained after his arrival with his sixty ships, the Corcyræans continued slaughtering those of their fellow-citizens whom they regarded as enemies; they charged them with designs against the democracy, but some were killed from motives of personal enmity, and some perished at the hands of their debtors because money was owing to them. Every form of death was to be seen; and everything, and more than everything, that commonly happens in revolutions, happened then. Fathers killed their sons, and suppliants were torn from the temples and killed near them; some of them were even walled up in the temple of Dionysus, and perished.

To such extremes of cruelty did revolution go, and this revolution seemed the worse because it was among the first. For afterwards the whole Hellenic world, one may say, was in commotion; in every city the leaders of the people were struggling to bring in the Athenians or the Lacedæmonians. Now in time of peace, they would have had no excuse for introducing either and no desire to do so; but when they were at war, and each party could obtain assistance to injure their opponents and simultaneously to gain new strength for themselves, interventions were easily procured by those with revolutionary designs. And revolution brought many calamities on the cities, which occurred and always will occur so long as human nature remains the same, but which are more or less aggravated and differ in character with every new combination of circumstances. In peace and prosperity both states and individuals act on better principles because they are not involved in necessities which allow them no choice; but war, stealing away the means of providing easily for their daily lives, is a teacher of violence and assimilates the passions of most men to their circumstances.

When civil strife had once begun in the cities, the later outbreaks, doubtless because men had learned of the earlier, far surpassed them in the novelty of the plans, the ingenuity of the enterprises and the enormity of the vengeance taken. And men changed the conventional meaning of words as they chose. Irrational daring was held to be loyal courage; prudent delay, an excuse for cowardice; sound sense, a disguise for unmanly weakness; and men who consider matters in every aspect were thought to be incapable of doing anything. Frantic haste became part of a man's quality; and if anyone made safety the condition for conspiracy, it was a specious pretext for evasion. The lover of violence was always trusted, and his opponent suspected. If anyone succeeded in a plot, he was shrewd; if he detected one, even more clever; but if anyone took measures in advance to make plots or detection superfluous, he was regarded as a man who broke up his own party in terror of the opposition. In a word, it was praiseworthy to strike first, while your enemy was meditating an injury, and to incite a man to strike who was not thinking of it. Furthermore, the tie of party came to be closer than the tie of kinship because the partisan was more audacious and made fewer excuses. For party associations were formed, not for men's good under the existing laws, but in defiance of them, for sheer aggrandizement; and mutual pledges were sealed, not so much in accordance with the divine law as by collaboration in some breach of law. Fair proposals by opponents were received by the stronger party with precautionary actions and not in a generous spirit. Revenge was dearer than self-preservation. And if ever sworn treaties were agreed to, they were granted for the moment when no other course was open and lasted as long as neither party had support from outside; but when opportunity offered, whichever party took courage first, on seeing their adversaries off their guard, they were more delighted by perfidious than by open revenge; they reflected that it was taken in safety and that by a triumph of duplicity they had also gained a prize for superior intelligence. It has generally proved easier to call wicked men clever than to call foolish men good, and men are ashamed of folly and proud of cleverness.

The cause of all these evils was the love of power, originating in avarice and ambition; hence, once engaged in the struggles, men were unsparing of their efforts. The leaders on either side in the cities used specious catchwords; one party preferred "a fair share of political rights for the masses," the other, "the good sense of government by the best men"; they professed devotion to the public interest but rewarded themselves at the public cost. They stopped at nothing in their struggle for victory, did not shrink from the most monstrous crimes and proceeded to even more monstrous acts of revenge, observing no limits of justice or public expediency, but each bounded only by his own pleasure at the time. When an unjust sentence gave them the chance or when force gave them the mastery, they were eager to satiate the enmity of the moment. They had no use for scruples; but when they succeeded in effecting some odious purpose, they were more highly spoken of, if they found a plea that sounded well. The citizens who were of neither party were destroyed by both because they were neutral or because men grudged them survival.

Thus, revolutions gave birth to every form of wickedness in Hellas, and the simplicity which is so large an element in a noble nature was laughed to scorn and disappeared. An attitude of distrustful antagonism widely prevailed, for no words were strong enough and no oaths sufficiently terrible to reconcile opponents; all who obtained the upper hand reasoned that security was not to be hoped for, and were readier to think out precautions against injury than to show a capacity of trusting others. Men of inferior intellect generally succeeded best. Afraid of their own deficiencies and of the shrewdness of their adversaries, fearful that they would get the worst of argument and that the subtle policy of their enemies would find some means of striking at them first, they proceeded boldly to action, whereas the others arrogantly assumed that they would detect their opponents' plans and had no need to take by force what they could get by policy, and were more apt to be taken by surprise and destroyed.

Translated by Benjamin Jowett; revised by P. A. Brunt

◨◨◨◨◨◨◨◨

SOPHOCLES
496–406/5 B.C.

From AJAX

TIME AND CHANGE

Sophocles had a long career as the most admired and successful of the tragic poets; he also distinguished himself in the life of his city, serving Athens in high office in both peace and war. We do not know the date of production of his play Ajax, *though it is probably the earliest of the seven Sophoclean tragedies that have survived. In it the hero, infuriated by the award of Achilles' armor to Odysseus, sets out at night to kill not only Odysseus but also the Atridae—the two kings, Agamemnon and Menelaus—whom he regards as responsible for the award. Athena drives him temporarily mad, so that he tortures and slaughters cattle, mistaking them for his enemies. When he comes to his senses, he sees no recourse except to kill himself rather than wait for a shameful death at the hands of the kings; he brushes aside the entreaties of his wife, the Trojan captive Tecmessa, who had borne him a son, and goes offstage into his tent. The audience must now have expected the entry of a messenger announcing his suicide; instead, it is Ajax who comes on stage, carrying a sword. It is the sword Hector gave him when, after a long, inconclusive duel, they exchanged gifts to show their respect for each other.*

In the speech Ajax now delivers, he seems to have renounced the idea of suicide; as is clear from their later remarks, the chorus and Tecmessa certainly think so. But in fact, after a short choral interlude, the scene changes, and we see Ajax, alone on the seashore, kill himself after a defiant speech in which he curses not only Odysseus and the Atridae but also the whole Achaean army.

Was the speech a deliberate deception, a move to prevent interference with his departure? Ajax, as we know him from Homer and from Sophocles, too, is a man of fearsome violence, but one incapable of

deception. *Does he, then, really mean to submit to the certain and
probably humiliating death that awaits him at the hands of the Atridae?
Many solutions have been proposed but no agreement has been
reached. One possible interpretation is suggested by the form of the
speech. Contrary to Athenian theatrical convention, it opens without
making clear who is the person addressed. (This convention was indispensable in a huge open-air theater in which the actors played in masks.)
This brusque opening line suggests that Ajax is not addressing anyone;
he is thinking out loud, talking to himself. The speech, until the moment when he addresses Tecmessa directly, is a soliloquy. In it we see
how an original feeling of pity for his wife and child weakens his resolve
to kill himself. But as he formulates the consequences of this decision,
his words betray his deep conviction that for Ajax, of all men, the consequences would be intolerable. "Bow before the sons of Atreus . . . learn
place and wisdom . . ."; the harsh phrasing brings to the surface the
revulsion of his fierce pride from such abject surrender. He may, early in
the speech, have sincerely thought that he would bury Hector's sword
"out of sight," but by its end there can have been few in the audience
who did not think of the picture they had seen so often painted on the
surface of their household vases: the swordhilt buried in the ground and
Ajax's body spitted on the upright blade.*

[*Enter* AJAX *from the tent with a sword in his hand.*]
AJAX: Strangely the long and countless drift of time
   Brings all things forth from darkness into light,
   Then covers them once more. Nothing so marvelous
   That man can say it surely will not be—
   Strong oath and iron intent come crashing down.
   My mood, which just before was strong and rigid,
   No dipped sword more so, now has lost its edge—
   My speech is womanish for this woman's sake;
   And pity touches me for wife and child,
   Widowed and lost among my enemies.
   But now I'm going to the bathing place
   And meadows by the sea, to cleanse my stains,
   In hope the goddess' wrath may pass from me.
   And when I've found a place that's quite deserted,
   I'll dig in the ground, and hide this sword of mine,
   Hatefulest of weapons, out of sight. May Darkness
   And Hades, God of Death, hold it in their safe keeping.
   For never, since I took it as a gift
   Which Hector, my great enemy, gave to me,

Have I known any kindness from the Greeks.
I think the ancient proverb speaks the truth:
An enemy's gift is ruinous and no gift.
Well, then,
From now on this will be my rule: Give way
To Heaven, and bow before the sons of Atreus.
They are our rulers, they must be obeyed.
I must give way, as all dread strengths give way,
In turn and deference. Winter's hard-packed snow
Cedes to the fruitful summer; stubborn night
At last removes, for day's white steeds to shine.
The dread blast of the gale slackens and gives
Peace to the sounding sea; and Sleep, strong jailer,
In time yields up his captive. Shall not I
Learn place and wisdom? Have I not learned this,
Only so much to hate my enemy
As though he might again become my friend,
And so much good to wish to do my friend,
As knowing he may yet become my foe?
Most men have found friendship a treacherous harbor.

Enough: this will be well.
                          You, my wife, go in
And fervently and continually pray the gods
To grant fulfilment of my soul's desire.
And you, my friends, heed my instructions too,
And when he comes, deliver this to Teucer:
Let him take care for me and thought for you.
Now I am going where my way must go;
Do as I bid you, and you yet may hear
That I, though wretched now, have found my safety.
    [AJAX *goes out through the wings.*]

Translated by John Moore

ANTIGONE

Sophocles' Antigone, *produced shortly before 441* B.C., *was a great success. The story that this success was responsible for his election to the board of generals for the year 441 almost certainly exaggerates the play's impact on the audience, but it testifies eloquently to its popularity.* Anti-

gone *has also fascinated modern audiences, not only in translations of*
the Sophoclean text but also in modern adaptations; two of the most
famous are that of Jean Anouilh, produced in German-occupied Paris in
1944, and that of Bertolt Brecht, produced at Chur in Switzerland in
1948. George Steiner in his Antigones, *a profound analytic discussion of*
the impact of the play on the modern consciousness, describes it as the
one literary text that expresses "all the principal constants of conflict in
the condition of man. These constants are fivefold: the confrontation of
men and women; of age and of youth; of society and of the individual; of
the living and the dead; of men and of god(s)." And he singles out the
scene between Antigone and Creon (pp. 374–76) as one in which "each
of the five fundamental categories of man's definition and self-definition
through conflict is realized, and . . . all five are at work in a single act of
confrontation."

CHARACTERS

ANTIGONE, *daughter of Oedipus and Jocasta*
ISMENE, *sister of Antigone*
A CHORUS, *of old Theban citizens and their Leader*
CREON, *king of Thebes, uncle of Antigone and Ismene*
A SENTRY
HAEMON, *son of Creon and Eurydice*
TIRESIAS, *a blind prophet*
A MESSENGER
EURYDICE, *wife of Creon*
Guards, attendants, and a boy

TIME AND SCENE: *The royal house of Thebes. It is still night, and the*
invading armies of Argos have just been driven from the city. Fighting
on opposite sides, the sons of Oedipus, Eteocles and Polynices, have
killed each other in combat. Their uncle, CREON, *is now king of Thebes.*

Enter ANTIGONE, *slipping through the central doors of the palace. She*
motions to her sister, ISMENE, *who follows her cautiously toward an altar*
at the center of the stage.

ANTIGONE: My own flesh and blood—dear sister, dear Ismene,
how many griefs our father Oedipus handed down!
Do you know one, I ask you, one grief
that Zeus will not perfect for the two of us
while we still live and breathe? There's nothing,
no pain—our lives are pain—no private shame,

no public disgrace, nothing I haven't seen
in your griefs and mine. And now this:
an emergency decree, they say, the Commander
has just declared for all of Thebes.
What, haven't you heard? Don't you see?
The doom reserved for enemies
marches on the ones we love the most.

ISMENE: Not I, I haven't heard a word, Antigone.
Nothing of loved ones,
no joy or pain has come my way, not since
the two of us were robbed of our two brothers,
both gone in a day, a double blow—
not since the armies of Argos vanished,
just this very night. I know nothing more,
whether our luck's improved or ruin's still to come.
ANTIGONE: I thought so. That's why I brought you out here,
past the gates, so you could hear in private.
ISMENE: What's the matter? Trouble, clearly . . .
you sound so dark, so grim.
ANTIGONE: Why not? Our own brothers' burial!
Hasn't Creon graced one with all the rites,
disgraced the other? Eteocles, they say,
has been given full military honors,
rightly so—Creon's laid him in the earth
and he goes with glory down among the dead.
But the body of Polynices, who died miserably—
why, a city-wide proclamation, rumor has it,
forbids anyone to bury him, even mourn him.
He's to be left unwept, unburied, a lovely treasure
for birds that scan the field and feast to their heart's content.

Such, I hear, is the martial law our good Creon
lays down for you and me—yes, me, I tell you—
and he's coming here to alert the uninformed
in no uncertain terms,
and he won't treat the matter lightly. Whoever
disobeys in the least will die, his doom is sealed:
stoning to death inside the city walls!

There you have it. You'll soon show what you are,
worth your breeding, Ismene, or a coward—
for all your royal blood.

ISMENE: My poor sister, if things have come to this,
who am I to make or mend them, tell me,
what good am I to you?
ANTIGONE: Decide.
Will you share the labor, share the work?
ISMENE: What work, what's the risk? What do you mean?
ANTIGONE: [*Raising her hands.*]
Will you lift up his body with these bare hands
and lower it with me?
ISMENE: What? You'd bury him—
when a law forbids the city?
ANTIGONE: Yes!
He is my brother and—deny it as you will—
your brother too.
No one will ever convict me for a traitor.
ISMENE: So desperate, and Creon has expressly—
ANTIGONE: No,
he has no right to keep me from my own.
ISMENE: Oh my sister, think—
think how our own father died, hated,
his reputation in ruins, driven on
by the crimes he brought to light himself
to gouge out his eyes with his own hands—
then mother . . . his mother and wife, both in one,
mutilating her life in the twisted noose—
and last, our two brothers dead in a single day,
both shedding their own blood, poor suffering boys,
battling out their common destiny hand-to-hand.

Now look at the two of us, left so alone . . .
think what a death we'll die, the worst of all
if we violate the laws and override
the fixed decree of the throne, its power—
we must be sensible. Remember we are women,
we're not born to contend with men. Then too,
we're underlings, ruled by much stronger hands,
so we must submit in this, and things still worse.

I, for one, I'll beg the dead to forgive me—
I'm forced, I have no choice—I must obey
the ones who stand in power. Why rush to extremes?
It's madness, madness.

ANTIGONE: I won't insist,
no, even if you should have a change of heart,
I'd never welcome you in the labor, not with me.
So, do as you like, whatever suits you best—
I will bury him myself.
And even if I die in the act, that death will be a glory.
I will lie with the one I love and loved by him—
an outrage sacred to the gods! I have longer
to please the dead than please the living here:
in the kingdom down below I'll lie forever.
Do as you like, dishonor the laws
the gods hold in honor.
ISMENE: I'd do them no dishonor . . .
but defy the city? I have no strength for that.
ANTIGONE: You have your excuses. I am on my way,
I'll raise a mound for him, for my dear brother.
ISMENE: Oh Antigone, you're so rash—I'm so afraid for you!
ANTIGONE: Don't fear for me. Set your own life in order.
ISMENE: Then don't, at least, blurt this out to anyone.
Keep it a secret. I'll join you in that, I promise.
ANTIGONE: Dear god, shout it from the rooftops. I'll hate you
all the more for silence—tell the world!
ISMENE: So fiery—and it ought to chill your heart.
ANTIGONE: I know I please where I must please the most.
ISMENE: Yes, if you can, but you're in love with impossibility.
ANTIGONE: Very well then, once my strength gives out
I will be done at last.
ISMENE: You're wrong from the start,
you're off on a hopeless quest.
ANTIGONE: If you say so, you will make me hate you,
and the hatred of the dead, by all rights,
will haunt you night and day.
But leave me to my own absurdity, leave me
to suffer this—dreadful thing. I will suffer
nothing as great as death without glory.
       [*Exit to the side.*]
ISMENE: Then go if you must, but rest assured,
wild, irrational as you are, my sister,
you are truly dear to the ones who love you.
       [*Withdrawing to the palace. Enter a* CHORUS, *the old citizens of
       Thebes, chanting as the sun begins to rise.*]
CHORUS: Glory!—great beam of the sun, brightest of all

that ever rose on the seven gates of Thebes,
   you burn through night at last!
        Great eye of the golden day,
mounting the Dirce's banks you throw him back—
the enemy out of Argos, the white shield, the man of bronze—
he's flying headlong now
        the bridle of fate stampeding him with pain!

    And he had driven against our borders,
    launched by the warring claims of Polynices—
    like an eagle screaming, winging havoc
    over the land, wings of armor
    shielded white as snow,
    a huge army massing,
    crested helmets bristling for assault.

He hovered above our roofs, his vast maw gaping
closing down around our seven gates,
   his spears thirsting for the kill
       but now he's gone, look,
before he could glut his jaws with Theban blood
or the god of fire put our crown of towers to the torch.
He grappled the Dragon none can master—Thebes—
       the clang of our arms like thunder at his back!

    Zeus hates with a vengeance all bravado,
    the mighty boasts of men. He watched them
    coming on in a rising flood, the pride
    of their golden armor ringing shrill—
    and brandishing his lightning
    blasted the fighter just at the goal,
    rushing to shout his triumph from our walls.

Down from the heights he crashed, pounding down on the earth!
And a moment ago, blazing torch in hand—
       mad for attack, ecstatic
he breathed his rage, the storm
   of his fury hurling at our heads!
But now his high hopes have laid him low
and down the enemy ranks the iron god of war
      deals his rewards, his stunning blows—Ares
      rapture of battle, our right arm in the crisis.

Seven captains marshaled at seven gates
seven against their equals, gave
their brazen trophies up to Zeus,
god of the breaking rout of battle,
all but two: those blood brothers,
one father, one mother—matched in rage,
spears matched for the twin conquest—
clashed and won the common prize of death.

But now for Victory! Glorious in the morning,
joy in her eyes to meet our joy
    she is winging down to Thebes,
our fleets of chariots wheeling in her wake—
    Now let us win oblivion from the wars,
thronging the temples of the gods
in singing, dancing choirs through the night!
    Lord Dionysus, god of the dance
    that shakes the land of Thebes, now lead the way!
[*Enter* CREON *from the palace, attended by his guard.*]
    But look, the king of the realm is coming,
Creon, the new man for the new day,
whatever the gods are sending now . . .
what new plan will he launch?
Why this, this special session?
Why this sudden call to the old men
summoned at one command?

CREON: My countrymen,
the ship of state is safe. The gods who rocked her,
after a long, merciless pounding in the storm,
have righted her once more.
                Out of the whole city
I have called you here alone. Well I know,
first, your undeviating respect
for the throne and royal power of King Laius.
Next, while Oedipus steered the land of Thebes,
and even after he died, your loyalty was unshakable,
you still stood by their children. Now then,
since the two sons are dead—two blows of fate
in the same day, cut down by each other's hands,
both killers, both brothers stained with blood—
as I am next in kin to the dead,
I now possess the throne and all its powers.

Of course you cannot know a man completely,
his character, his principles, sense of judgment,
not till he's shown his colors, ruling the people,
making laws. Experience, there's the test.
As I see it, whoever assumes the task,
the awesome task of setting the city's course,
and refuses to adopt the soundest policies
but fearing someone, keeps his lips locked tight,
he's utterly worthless. So I rate him now,
I always have. And whoever places a friend
above the good of his own country, he is nothing:
I have no use for him. Zeus my witness,
Zeus who sees all things, always—

I could never stand by silent, watching destruction
march against our city, putting safety to rout,
nor could I ever make that man a friend of mine
who menaces our country. Remember this:
our country *is* our safety.
Only while she voyages true on course
can we establish friendships, truer than blood itself.
Such are my standards. They make our city great.

Closely akin to them I have proclaimed,
just now, the following decree to our people
concerning the two sons of Oedipus.
Eteocles, who died fighting for Thebes,
excelling all in arms: he shall be buried,
crowned with a hero's honors, the cups we pour
to soak the earth and reach the famous dead.

But as for his blood brother, Polynices,
who returned from exile, home to his father-city
and the gods of his race, consumed with one desire—
to burn them roof to roots—who thirsted to drink
his kinsmen's blood and sell the rest to slavery:
that man—a proclamation has forbidden the city
to dignify him with burial, mourn him at all.
No, he must be left unburied, his corpse
carrion for the birds and dogs to tear,
an obscenity for the citizens to behold!

These are my principles. Never at my hands
will the traitor be honored above the patriot.
But whoever proves his loyalty to the state—
I'll prize that man in death as well as life.
LEADER: If this is your pleasure, Creon, treating
our city's enemy and our friend this way . . .
The power is yours, I suppose, to enforce it
with the laws, both for the dead and all of us,
the living.
CREON: Follow my orders closely then,
be on your guard.
LEADER: We're too old.
Lay that burden on younger shoulders.
CREON: No, no,
I don't mean the body—I've posted guards already.
LEADER: What commands for us then? What other service?
CREON: See that you never side with those who break my orders.
LEADER: Never. Only a fool could be in love with death.
CREON: Death is the price—you're right. But all too often
the mere hope of money has ruined many men.
            [*A* SENTRY *enters from the side.*]
SENTRY: My lord,
I can't say I'm winded from running, or set out
with any spring in my legs either—no sir,
I was lost in thought, and it made me stop, often,
dead in my tracks, wheeling, turning back,
and all the time a voice inside me muttering,
"Idiot, why? You're going straight to your death."
Then muttering, "Stopped again, poor fool?
If somebody gets the news to Creon first,
what's to save your neck?"
                            And so,
mulling it over, on I trudged, dragging my feet,
you can make a short road take forever . . .
but at last, look, common sense won out,
I'm here, and I'm all yours,
and even though I come empty-handed
I'll tell my story just the same, because
I've come with a good grip on one hope,
what will come will come, whatever fate—
CREON: Come to the point!
What's wrong—why so afraid?

SENTRY: First, myself, I've got to tell you,
I didn't do it, didn't see who did—
Be fair, don't take it out on me.
CREON: You're playing it safe, soldier,
barricading yourself from any trouble.
It's obvious, you've something strange to tell.
SENTRY: Dangerous too, and danger makes you delay
for all you're worth.
CREON: Out with it—then dismiss!
SENTRY: All right, here it comes. The body—
someone's just buried it, then run off . . .
sprinkled some dry dust on the flesh,
given it proper rites.
CREON: What?
What man alive would dare—
SENTRY: I've no idea, I swear it.
There was no mark of a spade, no pickaxe there,
no earth turned up, the ground packed hard and dry,
unbroken, no tracks, no wheelruts, nothing,
the workman left no trace. Just at sunup
the first watch of the day points it out—
it was a wonder! We were stunned . . .
a terrific burden too, for all of us, listen:
you can't see the corpse, not that it's buried,
really, just a light cover of road-dust on it,
as if someone meant to lay the dead to rest
and keep from getting cursed.
Not a sign in sight that dogs or wild beasts
had worried the body, even torn the skin.

But what came next! Rough talk flew thick and fast,
guard grilling guard—we'd have come to blows
at last, nothing to stop it; each man for himself
and each the culprit, no one caught red-handed,
all of us pleading ignorance, dodging the charges,
ready to take up red-hot iron in our fists,
go through fire, swear oaths to the gods—
"I didn't do it, I had no hand in it either,
not in the plotting, not the work itself!"

Finally, after all this wrangling came to nothing,
one man spoke out and made us stare at the ground,

hanging our heads in fear. No way to counter him,
no way to take his advice and come through
safe and sound. Here's what he said:
"Look, we've got to report the facts to Creon,
we can't keep this hidden." Well, that won out,
and the lot fell to me, condemned me,
unlucky as ever, I got the prize. So here I am,
against my will and yours too, well I know—
no one wants the man who brings bad news.

LEADER: My king,
ever since he began I've been debating in my mind,
could this possibly be the work of the gods?

CREON: Stop—
before you make me choke with anger—the gods!
You, you're senile, must you be insane?
You say—why it's intolerable—say the gods
could have the slightest concern for that corpse?
Tell me, was it for meritorious service
they proceeded to bury him, prized him so? The hero
who came to burn their temples ringed with pillars,
their golden treasures—scorch their hallowed earth
and fling their laws to the winds.
Exactly when did you last see the gods
celebrating traitors? Inconceivable!

No, from the first there were certain citizens
who could hardly stand the spirit of my regime,
grumbling against me in the dark, heads together,
tossing wildly, never keeping their necks beneath
the yoke, loyally submitting to their king.
These are the instigators, I'm convinced—
they've perverted my own guard, bribed them
to do their work.
                    Money! Nothing worse
in our lives, so current, rampant, so corrupting.
Money—you demolish cities, root men from their homes,
you train and twist good minds and set them on
to the most atrocious schemes. No limit,
you make them adept at every kind of outrage,
every godless crime—money!
                              Everyone—
the whole crew bribed to commit this crime,

they've made one thing sure at least:
sooner or later they will pay the price.
[*Wheeling on the* SENTRY.]
                                              You—
I swear to Zeus as I still believe in Zeus,
if you don't find the man who buried that corpse,
the very man, and produce him before my eyes,
simple death won't be enough for you,
not till we string you up alive
and wring the immorality out of you.
Then you can steal the rest of your days,
better informed about where to make a killing.
You'll have learned, at last, it doesn't pay
to itch for rewards from every hand that beckons.
Filthy profits wreck most men, you'll see—
they'll never save your life.
SENTRY: Please,
    may I say a word or two, or just turn and go?
CREON: Can't you tell? Everything you say offends me.
SENTRY: Where does it hurt you, in the ears or in the heart?
CREON: And who are you to pinpoint my displeasure?
SENTRY: The culprit grates on your feelings,
    I just annoy your ears.
CREON: Still talking?
    You talk too much! A born nuisance—
SENTRY: Maybe so,
    but I never did this thing, so help me!
CREON: Yes you did—
    what's more, you squandered your life for silver!
SENTRY: Oh it's terrible when the one who does the judging
    judges things all wrong.
CREON: Well now,
    you just be clever about your judgments—
    if you fail to produce the criminals for me,
    you'll swear your dirty money brought you pain.
    [*Turning sharply, reentering the palace.*]
SENTRY: I hope he's found. Best thing by far.
    But caught or not, that's in the lap of fortune:
    I'll never come back, you've seen the last of me.
    I'm saved, even now, and I never thought,
    I never hoped—

dear gods, I owe you all my thanks!
[*Rushing out.*]
CHORUS: Numberless wonders
terrible wonders walk the world but none the match for man—
that great wonder crossing the heaving gray sea,
              driven on by the blasts of winter
on through breakers crashing left and right,
    holds his steady course
and the oldest of the gods he wears away—
the Earth, the immortal, the inexhaustible—
as his plows go back and forth, year in, year out
    with the breed of stallions turning up the furrows.

And the blithe, lightheaded race of birds he snares,
the tribes of savage beasts, the life that swarms the depths—
              with one fling of his nets
woven and coiled tight, he takes them all,
    man the skilled, the brilliant!
He conquers all, taming with his techniques
the prey that roams the cliffs and wild lairs,
training the stallion, clamping the yoke across
    his shaggy neck, and the tireless mountain bull.

And speech and thought, quick as the wind
and the mood and mind for law that rules the city—
    all these he has taught himself
and shelter from the arrows of the frost
when there's rough lodging under the cold clear sky
and the shafts of lashing rain—
    ready, resourceful man!
              Never without resources
never an impasse as he marches on the future—
only Death, from Death alone he will find no rescue
but from desperate plagues he has plotted his escapes.

Man the master, ingenious past all measure
past all dreams, the skills within his grasp—
    he forges on, now to destruction
now again to greatness. When he weaves in
the laws of the land, and the justice of the gods
that binds his oaths together

    he and his city rise high—
        but the city casts out
that man who weds himself to inhumanity
thanks to reckless daring. Never share my hearth
never think my thoughts, whoever does such things.
    [*Enter* ANTIGONE *from the side, accompanied by the* SENTRY.]
    Here is a dark sign from the gods—
    what to make of this? I know her,
    how can I deny it? That young girl's Antigone!
    Wretched, child of a wretched father,
    Oedipus. Look, is it possible?
    They bring you in like a prisoner—
    why? did you break the king's laws?
    Did they take you in some act of mad defiance?
SENTRY: She's the one, she did it single-handed—
we caught her burying the body. Where's Creon?
    [*Enter* CREON *from the palace.*]
LEADER: Back again, just in time when you need him.
CREON: In time for what? What is it?
SENTRY: My king,
    there's nothing you can swear you'll never do—
    second thoughts make liars of us all.
    I could have sworn I wouldn't hurry back
    (what with your threats, the buffeting I just took),
    but a stroke of luck beyond our wildest hopes,
    what a joy, there's nothing like it. So,
    back I've come, breaking my oath, who cares?
    I'm bringing in our prisoner—this young girl—
    we took her giving the dead the last rites.
    But no casting lots this time; this is *my* luck,
    my prize, no one else's.
                                Now, my lord,
    here she is. Take her, question her,
    cross-examine her to your heart's content.
    But set me free, it's only right—
    I'm rid of this dreadful business once for all.
CREON: Prisoner! Her? You took her—where, doing what?
SENTRY: Burying the man. That's the whole story.
CREON: What?
    You mean what you say, you're telling me the truth?
SENTRY: She's the one. With my own eyes I saw her

bury the body, just what you've forbidden.
There. Is that plain and clear?
CREON: What did you see? Did you catch her in the act?
SENTRY: Here's what happened. We went back to our post,
those threats of yours breathing down our necks—
we brushed the corpse clean of the dust that covered it,
stripped it bare . . . it was slimy, going soft,
and we took to high ground, back to the wind
so the stink of him couldn't hit us;
jostling, baiting each other to keep awake,
shouting back and forth—no napping on the job,
not this time. And so the hours dragged by
until the sun stood dead above our heads,
a huge white ball in the noon sky, beating,
blazing down, and then it happened—
suddenly, a whirlwind!
Twisting a great dust-storm up from the earth,
a black plague of the heavens, filling the plain,
ripping the leaves off every tree in sight,
choking the air and sky. We squinted hard
and took our whipping from the gods.

And after the storm passed—it seemed endless—
there, we saw the girl!
And she cried out a sharp, piercing cry,
like a bird come back to an empty nest,
peering into its bed, and all the babies gone . . .
Just so, when she sees the corpse bare
she bursts into a long, shattering wail
and calls down withering curses on the heads
of all who did the work. And she scoops up dry dust,
handfuls, quickly, and lifting a fine bronze urn,
lifting it high and pouring, she crowns the dead
with three full libations.
                                   Soon as we saw
we rushed her, closed on the kill like hunters,
and she, she didn't flinch. We interrogated her,
charging her with offenses past and present—
she stood up to it all, denied nothing. I tell you,
it made me ache and laugh in the same breath.
It's pure joy to escape the worst yourself,

it hurts a man to bring down his friends.
But all that, I'm afraid, means less to me
than my own skin. That's the way I'm made.
CREON: [*Wheeling on* ANTIGONE.]   You,
with your eyes fixed on the ground—speak up.
Do you deny you did this, yes or no?
ANTIGONE: I did it. I don't deny a thing.
CREON: [*To the* SENTRY.] You, get out, wherever you please—
you're clear of a very heavy charge.

[*He leaves;* CREON *turns back to* ANTIGONE.]
You, tell me briefly, no long speeches—
were you aware a decree had forbidden this?
ANTIGONE: Well aware. How could I avoid it? It was public.
CREON: And still you had the gall to break this law?
ANTIGONE: Of course I did. It wasn't Zeus, not in the least,
who made this proclamation—not to me.
Nor did that Justice, dwelling with the gods
beneath the earth, ordain such laws for men.
Nor did I think your edict had such force
that you, a mere mortal, could override the gods,
the great unwritten, unshakable traditions.
They are alive, not just today or yesterday:
they live forever, from the first of time,
and no one knows when they first saw the light.

These laws—I was not about to break them,
not out of fear of some man's wounded pride,
and face the retribution of the gods.
Die I must, I've known it all my life—
how could I keep from knowing?—even without
your death-sentence ringing in my ears.
And if I am to die before my time
I consider that a gain. Who on earth,
alive in the midst of so much grief as I,
could fail to find his death a rich reward?
So for me, at least, to meet this doom of yours
is precious little pain. But if I had allowed
my own mother's son to rot, an unburied corpse—
that would have been an agony! This is nothing.
And if my present actions strike you as foolish,
let's just say I've been accused of folly
by a fool.

LEADER: Like father like daughter,
   passionate, wild . . .
   she hasn't learned to bend before adversity.
CREON: No? Believe me, the stiffest stubborn wills
   fall the hardest; the toughest iron,
   tempered strong in the white-hot fire,
   you'll see it crack and shatter first of all.
   And I've known spirited horses you can break
   with a light bit—proud, rebellious horses.
   There's no room for pride, not in a slave,
   not with the lord and master standing by.

   This girl was an old hand at insolence
   when she overrode the edicts we made public.
   But once she'd done it—the insolence,
   twice over—to glory in it, laughing,
   mocking us to our face with what she'd done.
   I am not the man, not now: she is the man
   if this victory goes to her and she goes free.

   Never! Sister's child or closer in blood
   than all my family clustered at my altar
   worshiping Guardian Zeus—she'll never escape,
   she and her blood sister, the most barbaric death.
   Yes, I accuse her sister of an equal part
   in scheming this, this burial.
      [*To his attendants.*]
                              Bring her here!
   I just saw her inside, hysterical, gone to pieces.
   It never fails: the mind convicts itself
   in advance, when scoundrels are up to no good,
   plotting in the dark. Oh but I hate it more
   when a traitor, caught red-handed,
   tries to glorify his crimes.
ANTIGONE: Creon, what more do you want
   than my arrest and execution?
CREON: Nothing. Then I have it all.
ANTIGONE: Then why delay? Your moralizing repels me,
   every word you say—pray god it always will.
   So naturally all I say repels you too.
                              Enough.
   Give me glory! What greater glory could I win

than to give my own brother decent burial?
These citizens here would all agree,
   [*To the* CHORUS.]
they'd praise me too
if their lips weren't locked in fear.
   [*Pointing to* CREON.]
Lucky tyrants—the perquisites of power!
Ruthless power to do and say whatever pleases *them.*
CREON: You alone, of all the people in Thebes,
   see things that way.
ANTIGONE: They see it just that way
   but defer to you and keep their tongues in leash.
CREON: And you, aren't you ashamed to differ so from them?
   So disloyal!
ANTIGONE: Not ashamed for a moment,
   not to honor my brother, my own flesh and blood.
CREON: Wasn't Eteocles a brother too—cut down, facing him?
ANTIGONE: Brother, yes, by the same mother, the same father.
CREON: Then how can you render his enemy such honors,
   such impieties in his eyes?
ANTIGONE: He'll never testify to that,
   Eteocles dead and buried.
CREON: He will—
   if you honor the traitor just as much as him.
ANTIGONE: But it was his brother, not some slave that died—
CREON: Ravaging our country!—
   but Eteocles died fighting in our behalf.
ANTIGONE: No matter—Death longs for the same rites for all.
CREON: Never the same for the patriot and the traitor.
ANTIGONE: Who, Creon, who on earth can say the ones below
   don't find this pure and uncorrupt?
CREON: Never. Once an enemy, never a friend,
   not even after death.
ANTIGONE: I was born to join in love, not hate—
   that is my nature.
CREON: Go down below and love,
   if love you must—love the dead! While I'm alive,
   no woman is going to lord it over me.
   [*Enter* ISMENE *from the palace, under guard.*]
CHORUS: Look,
   Ismene's coming, weeping a sister's tears,
   loving sister, under a cloud . . .

her face is flushed, her cheeks streaming.
Sorrow puts her lovely radiance in the dark.
CREON: You—
in my own house, you viper, slinking undetected,
sucking my life-blood! I never knew
I was breeding twin disasters, the two of you
rising up against my throne. Come, tell me,
will you confess your part in the crime or not?
Answer me. Swear to me.
ISMENE: I did it, yes—
if only she consents—I share the guilt,
the consequences too.
ANTIGONE: No,
Justice will never suffer that—not you,
you were unwilling. I never brought you in.
ISMENE: But now you face such dangers . . . I'm not ashamed
to sail through trouble with you,
make your troubles mine.
ANTIGONE: Who did the work?
Let the dead and the god of death bear witness!
I have no love for a friend who loves in words alone.
ISMENE: Oh no, my sister, don't reject me, please,
let me die beside you, consecrating
the dead together.
ANTIGONE: Never share my dying,
don't lay claim to what you never touched.
My death will be enough.
ISMENE: What do I care for life, cut off from you?
ANTIGONE: Ask Creon. Your concern is all for him.
ISMENE: Why abuse me so? It doesn't help you now.
ANTIGONE: You're right—
if I mock you, I get no pleasure from it,
only pain.
ISMENE: Tell me, dear one,
what can I do to help you, even now?
ANTIGONE: Save yourself. I don't grudge you your survival.
ISMENE: Oh no, no, denied my portion in your death?
ANTIGONE: You chose to live, I chose to die.
ISMENE: Not, at least,
without every kind of caution I could voice.
ANTIGONE: Your wisdom appealed to one world—mine, another.
ISMENE: But look, we're both guilty, both condemned to death.

ANTIGONE: Courage! Live your life. I gave myself to death,
long ago, so I might serve the dead.
CREON: They're both mad, I tell you, the two of them.
One's just shown it, the other's been that way
since she was born.
ISMENE: True, my king,
the sense we were born with cannot last forever . . .
commit cruelty on a person long enough
and the mind begins to go.
CREON: Yours did,
when you chose to commit your crimes with her.
ISMENE: How can I live alone, without her?
CREON: Her?
Don't even mention her—she no longer exists.
ISMENE: What? You'd kill your own son's bride?
CREON: Absolutely:
there are other fields for him to plow.
ISMENE: Perhaps,
but never as true, as close a bond as theirs.
CREON: A worthless woman for my son? It repels me.
ISMENE: Dearest Haemon, your father wrongs you so!
CREON: Enough, enough—you and your talk of marriage!
ISMENE: Creon—you're really going to rob your son of Antigone?
CREON: Death will do it for me—break their marriage off.
LEADER: So, it's settled then? Antigone must die?
CREON: Settled, yes—we both know that.
    [*To the guards.*]
Stop wasting time. Take them in.
From now on they'll act like women.
Tie them up, no more running loose;
even the bravest will cut and run,
once they see Death coming for their lives.
    [*The guards escort* ANTIGONE *and* ISMENE *into the palace.* CREON
    remains while the old citizens form their CHORUS.]
CHORUS: Blest, they are the truly blest who all their lives
have never tasted devastation. For others, once
the gods have rocked a house to its foundations
    the ruin will never cease, cresting on and on
from one generation on throughout the race—
like a great mounting tide
driven on by savage northern gales,
    surging over the dead black depths

roiling up from the bottom dark heaves of sand
and the headlands, taking the storm's onslaught full-force,
roar, and the low moaning
                              echoes on and on
                                              and now
as in ancient times I see the sorrows of the house,
the living heirs of the old ancestral kings,
piling on the sorrows of the dead
    and one generation cannot free the next—
some god will bring them crashing down,
the race finds no release.
And now the light, the hope
        springing up from the late last root
in the house of Oedipus, that hope's cut down in turn
by the long, bloody knife swung by the gods of death
by a senseless word
                    by fury at the heart.
                                        Zeus,
yours is the power, Zeus, what man on earth
can override it, who can hold it back?
Power that neither Sleep, the all-ensnaring
    no, nor the tireless months of heaven
can ever overmaster—young through all time,
mighty lord of power, you hold fast
    the dazzling crystal mansions of Olympus.
And throughout the future, late and soon
as through the past, your law prevails:
no towering form of greatness
    enters into the lives of mortals
                            free and clear of ruin.
                                            True,
our dreams, our high hopes voyaging far and wide
bring sheer delight to many, to many others
    delusion, blithe, mindless lusts
and the fraud steals on one slowly . . . unaware
till he trips and puts his foot into the fire.
    He was a wise old man who coined
the famous saying: "Sooner or later
foul is fair, fair is foul
to the man the gods will ruin"—
    He goes his way for a moment only
                        free of blinding ruin.

[*Enter* HAEMON *from the palace.*]
Here's Haemon now, the last of all your sons.
Does he come in tears for his bride,
his doomed bride, Antigone—
bitter at being cheated of their marriage?
CREON: We'll soon know, better than seers could tell us.
[*Turning to* HAEMON.]
Son, you've heard the final verdict on your bride?
Are you coming now, raving against your father?
Or do you love me, no matter what I do?
HAEMON: Father, I'm your *son* . . . you in your wisdom
set my bearings for me—I obey you.
No marriage could ever mean more to me than you,
whatever good direction you may offer.
CREON: Fine, Haemon.
That's how you ought to feel within your heart,
subordinate to your father's will in every way.
That's what a man prays for: to produce good sons—
households full of them, dutiful and attentive,
so they can pay his enemy back with interest
and match the respect their father shows his friend.
But the man who rears a brood of useless children,
what has he brought into the world, I ask you?
Nothing but trouble for himself, and mockery
from his enemies laughing in his face.
                                    Oh Haemon,
never lose your sense of judgment over a woman.
The warmth, the rush of pleasure, it all goes cold
in your arms, I warn you . . . a worthless woman
in your house, a misery in your bed.
What wound cuts deeper than a loved one
turned against you? Spit her out,
like a mortal enemy—let the girl go.
Let her find a husband down among the dead.
Imagine it: I caught her in naked rebellion,
the traitor, the only one in the whole city.
I'm not about to prove myself a liar,
not to my people, no, I'm going to kill her!
That's right—so let her cry for mercy, sing her hymns
to Zeus who defends all bonds of kindred blood.
Why, if I bring up my own kin to be rebels,
think what I'd suffer from the world at large.

Show me the man who rules his household well:
I'll show you someone fit to rule the state.
That good man, my son,
I have every confidence he and he alone
can give commands and take them too. Staunch
in the storm of spears he'll stand his ground,
a loyal, unflinching comrade at your side.

But whoever steps out of line, violates the laws
or presumes to hand out orders to his superiors,
he'll win no praise from me. But that man
the city places in authority, his orders
must be obeyed, large and small,
right and wrong.
                    Anarchy—
show me a greater crime in all the earth!
She, she destroys cities, rips up houses,
breaks the ranks of spearmen into headlong rout.
But the ones who last it out, the great mass of them
owe their lives to discipline. Therefore
we must defend the men who live by law,
never let some woman triumph over us.
Better to fall from power, if fall we must,
at the hands of a man—never be rated
inferior to a woman, never.
LEADER: To us,
    unless old age has robbed us of our wits,
    you seem to say what you have to say with sense.
HAEMON: Father, only the gods endow a man with reason,
    the finest of all their gifts, a treasure.
    Far be it from me—I haven't the skill,
    and certainly no desire, to tell you when,
    if ever, you make a slip in speech . . . though
    someone else might have a good suggestion.

    Of course it's not for you,
    in the normal run of things, to watch
    whatever men say or do, or find to criticize.
    The man in the street, you know, dreads your glance,
    he'd never say anything displeasing to your face.
    But it's for me to catch the murmurs in the dark,
    the way the city mourns for this young girl.

"No woman," they say, "ever deserved death less,
and such a brutal death for such a glorious action.
She, with her own dear brother lying in his blood—
she couldn't bear to leave him dead, unburied,
food for the wild dogs or wheeling vultures.
Death? She deserves a glowing crown of gold!"
So they say, and the rumor spreads in secret,
darkly . . .
                    I rejoice in your success, father—
nothing more precious to me in the world.
What medal of honor brighter to his children
than a father's growing glory? Or a child's
to his proud father? Now don't, please,
be quite so single-minded, self-involved,
or assume the world is wrong and you are right.
Whoever thinks that he alone possesses intelligence,
the gift of eloquence, he and no one else,
and character too . . . such men, I tell you,
spread them open—you will find them empty.
                                                    No,
it's no disgrace for a man, even a wise man,
to learn many things and not to be too rigid.
You've seen trees by a raging winter torrent,
how many sway with the flood and salvage every twig,
but not the stubborn—they're ripped out, roots and all.
Bend or break. The same when a man is sailing:
haul your sheets too taut, never give an inch,
you'll capsize, and go the rest of the voyage
keel up and the rowing-benches under.

Oh give way. Relax your anger—change!
I'm young, I know, but let me offer this:
it would be best by far, I admit,
if a man were born infallible, right by nature.
If not—and things don't often go that way,
it's best to learn from those with good advice.
LEADER: You'd do well, my lord, if he's speaking to the point,
to learn from him,
        [*Turning to* HAEMON.]
                        and you, my boy, from him.
You both are talking sense.
CREON: So,

men our age, we're to be lectured, are we?—
schooled by a boy his age?
HAEMON: Only in what is right. But if I seem young,
look less to my years and more to what I do.
CREON: Do? Is admiring rebels an achievement?
HAEMON: I'd never suggest that you admire treason.
CREON: Oh?—
isn't that just the sickness that's attacked her?
HAEMON: The whole city of Thebes denies it, to a man.
CREON: And is Thebes about to tell me how to rule?
HAEMON: Now, you see? Who's talking like a child?
CREON: Am I to rule this land for others—or myself?
HAEMON: It's no city at all, owned by one man alone.
CREON: What? The city *is* the king's—that's the law!
HAEMON: What a splendid king you'd make of a desert island—
you and you alone.
CREON: [*To the* CHORUS.] This boy, I do believe,
is fighting on her side, the woman's side.
HAEMON: If you are a woman, yes—
my concern is all for you.
CREON: Why, you degenerate—bandying accusations,
threatening me with justice, your own father!
HAEMON: I see my father offending justice—wrong.
CREON: Wrong?
To protect my royal rights?
HAEMON: Protect your rights?
When you trample down the honors of the gods?
CREON: You, you soul of corruption, rotten through—
woman's accomplice!
HAEMON: That may be,
but you'll never find me accomplice to a criminal.
CREON: That's what *she* is,
and every word you say is a blatant appeal for her—
HAEMON: And you, and me, and the gods beneath the earth.
CREON: You will never marry her, not while she's alive.
HAEMON: Then she'll die . . . but her death will kill another.
CREON: What, brazen threats? You go too far!
HAEMON: What threat?
Combating your empty, mindless judgments with a word?
CREON: You'll suffer for your sermons, you and your empty wisdom!
HAEMON: If you weren't my father, I'd say you were insane.
CREON: Don't flatter me with Father—you woman's slave!

HAEMON: You really expect to fling abuse at me
and not receive the same?
CREON: Is that so!
Now, by heaven, I promise you, you'll pay—
taunting, insulting me! Bring her out,
that hateful—she'll die now, here,
in front of his eyes, beside her groom!
HAEMON: No, no, she will never die beside me—
don't delude yourself. And you will never
see me, never set eyes on my face again.
Rage your heart out, rage with friends
who can stand the sight of you.
            [*Rushing out.*]
LEADER: Gone, my king, in a burst of anger.
A temper young as his . . . hurt him once,
he may do something violent.
CREON: Let him do—
dream up something desperate, past all human limit!
Good riddance. Rest assured,
he'll never save those two young girls from death.
LEADER: Both of them, you really intend to kill them both?
CREON: No, not her, the one whose hands are clean—
you're quite right.
LEADER: But Antigone—
what sort of death do you have in mind for her?
CREON: I'll take her down some wild, desolate path
never trod by men, and wall her up alive
in a rocky vault, and set out short rations,
just a gesture of piety
to keep the entire city free of defilement.
There let her pray to the one god she worships:
Death—who knows?—may just reprieve her from death.
Or she may learn at last, better late than never,
what a waste of breath it is to worship Death.
            [*Exit to the palace.*]
CHORUS: Love, never conquered in battle
Love the plunderer laying waste the rich!
Love standing the night-watch
                        guarding a girl's soft cheek,
you range the seas, the shepherds' steadings off in the wilds—
not even the deathless gods can flee your onset,
nothing human born for a day—

whoever feels your grip is driven mad
                 Love—
you wrench the minds of the righteous into outrage,
swerve them to their ruin—you have ignited this,
this kindred strife, father and son at war
              and Love alone the victor—
warm glance of the bride triumphant, burning with desire!
Throned in power, side-by-side with the mighty laws!
Irresistible Aphrodite, never conquered—
Love, you mock us for your sport.
      [ANTIGONE *is brought from the palace under guard.*]
      But now, even I'd rebel against the king,
      I'd break all bounds when I see this—
      I fill with tears, can't hold them back,
      not any more . . . I see Antigone make her way
      to the bridal vault where all are laid to rest.
ANTIGONE: Look at me, men of my fatherland,
    setting out on the last road
looking into the last light of day
the last I'll ever see . . .
the god of death who puts us all to bed
takes me down to the banks of Acheron alive—
    denied my part in the wedding-songs,
no wedding-song in the dusk has crowned my marriage—
I go to wed the lord of the dark waters.
CHORUS: Not crowned with glory, crowned with a dirge,
you leave for the deep pit of the dead.
No withering illness laid you low,
no strokes of the sword—a law to yourself,
alone, no mortal like you, ever, you go down
to the halls of Death alive and breathing.
ANTIGONE: But think of Niobe—well I know her story—
    think what a living death she died,
Tantalus' daughter, stranger queen from the east:
there on the mountain heights, growing stone
binding as ivy, slowly walled her round
and the rains will never cease, the legends say
the snows will never leave her . . .
    wasting away, under her brows the tears
showering down her breasting ridge and slopes—
a rocky death like hers puts me to sleep.
CHORUS: But she was a god, born of gods,

and we are only mortals born to die.
And yet, of course, it's a great thing
for a dying girl to hear, just hear
she shares a destiny equal to the gods,
during life and later, once she's dead.
ANTIGONE: O you mock me!
Why, in the name of all my fathers' gods
why can't you wait till I am gone—
    must you abuse me to my face?
O my city, all your fine rich sons!
And you, you springs of the Dirce,
holy grove of Thebes where the chariots gather,
    you at least, you'll bear me witness, look,
unmourned by friends and forced by such crude laws
I go to my rockbound prison, strange new tomb—
    always a stranger, O dear god,
    I have no home on earth and none below,
    not with the living, not with the breathless dead.
CHORUS: You went too far, the last limits of daring—
smashing against the high throne of Justice!
    Your life's in ruins, child—I wonder . . .
do you pay for your father's terrible ordeal?
ANTIGONE: There—at last you've touched it, the worst pain
the worst anguish! Raking up the grief for father
    three times over, for all the doom
that's struck us down, the brilliant house of Laius.
O mother, your marriage-bed
the coiling horrors, the coupling there—
    you with your own son, my father—doomstruck mother!
Such, such were my parents, and I their wretched child.
I go to them now, cursed, unwed, to share their home—
    I am a stranger! O dear brother, doomed
in your marriage—your marriage murders mine,
    your dying drags me down to death alive!
[*Enter* CREON.]
CHORUS: Reverence asks some reverence in return—
but attacks on power never go unchecked,
    not by the man who holds the reins of power.
Your own blind will, your passion has destroyed you.
ANTIGONE: No one to weep for me, my friends,
no wedding-song—they take me away
in all my pain . . . the road lies open, waiting.

Never again, the law forbids me to see
the sacred eye of day. I am agony!
No tears for the destiny that's mine,
no loved one mourns my death.
CREON: Can't you see?
If a man could wail his own dirge *before* he dies,
he'd never finish.
   [*To the guards.*]
                         Take her away, quickly!
Wall her up in the tomb, you have your orders.
Abandon her there, alone, and let her choose—
death or a buried life with a good roof for shelter.
As for myself, my hands are clean. This young girl—
dead or alive, she will be stripped of her rights,
her stranger's rights, here in the world above.
ANTIGONE: O tomb, my bridal-bed—my house, my prison
cut in the hollow rock, my everlasting watch!
I'll soon be there, soon embrace my own,
the great growing family of our dead
Persephone has received among her ghosts.
                                                 I,
the last of them all, the most reviled by far,
go down before my destined time's run out.
But still I go, cherishing one good hope:
my arrival may be dear to father,
dear to you, my mother,
dear to you, my loving brother, Eteocles—
When you died I washed you with my hands,
I dressed you all, I poured the cups
across your tombs. But now, Polynices,
because I laid your body out as well,
this, this is my reward. Nevertheless
I honored you—the decent will admit it—
well and wisely too.
                         Never, I tell you.
if I had been the mother of children
or if my husband died, exposed and rotting—
I'd never have taken this ordeal upon myself,
never defied our people's will. What law,
you ask, do I satisfy with what I say?
A husband dead, there might have been another.
A child by another too, if I had lost the first.

But mother and father both lost in the halls of Death,
no brother could ever spring to light again.
For this law alone I held you first in honor.
For this, Creon, the king, judges me a criminal
guilty of dreadful outrage, my dear brother!
And now he leads me off, a captive in his hands,
with no part in the bridal-song, the bridal-bed,
denied all joy of marriage, raising children—
deserted so by loved ones, struck by fate,
I descend alive to the caverns of the dead.

What law of the mighty gods have I transgressed?
Why look to the heavens any more, tormented as I am?
Whom to call, what comrades now? Just think,
my reverence only brands me for irreverence!
Very well: if this is the pleasure of the gods,
once I suffer I will know that I was wrong.
But if these men are wrong, let them suffer nothing worse than they
          mete out to me—
these masters of injustice!
LEADER: Still the same rough winds, the wild passion
raging through the girl.
CREON: [*To the guards.*] Take her away.
You're wasting time—you'll pay for it too.
ANTIGONE: Oh god, the voice of death. It's come, it's here.
CREON: True. Not a word of hope—your doom is sealed.
ANTIGONE: Land of Thebes, city of all my fathers—
O you gods, the first gods of the race!
They drag me away, now, no more delay.
Look on me, you noble sons of Thebes—
the last of a great line of kings,
I alone, see what I suffer now
at the hands of what breed of men—
all for reverence, my reverence for the gods!
          [*She leaves under guard: the* CHORUS *gathers.*]
CHORUS: Danaë, Danaë—
even she endured a fate like yours,
     in all her lovely strength she traded
the light of day for the bolted brazen vault—
buried within her tomb, her bridal-chamber,
wed to the yoke and broken.
     But she was of glorious birth
                    my child, my child

and treasured the seed of Zeus within her womb,
the cloudburst streaming gold!
        The power of fate is a wonder,
        dark, terrible wonder—
        neither wealth nor armies
        towered walls nor ships
        black hulls lashed by the salt
        can save us from that force.

The yoke tamed him too
        young Lycurgus flaming in anger
king of Edonia, all for his mad taunts
Dionysus clamped him down, encased
in the chain-mail of rock
        and there his rage
                his terrible flowering rage burst—
sobbing, dying away . . . at last that madman
came to know his god—
        the power he mocked, the power
        he taunted in all his frenzy
        trying to stamp out
        the women strong with the god—
        the torch, the raving sacred cries—
        enraging the Muses who adore the flute.

And far north where the Black Rocks
        cut the sea in half
and murderous straits
split the coast of Thrace
        a forbidding city stands
where once, hard by the walls
the savage Ares thrilled to watch
a king's new queen, a Fury rearing in rage
        against his two royal sons—
                her bloody hands, her dagger-shuttle
stabbing out their eyes—cursed, blinding wounds—
their eyes blind sockets screaming for revenge!

They wailed in agony, cries echoing cries
        the princes doomed at birth . . .
and their mother doomed to chains,
walled off in a tomb of stone—
        but she traced her own birth back

to a proud Athenian line and the high gods
and off in caverns half the world away,
born of the wild North Wind
    she sprang on her father's gales,
        racing stallions up the leaping cliffs—
child of the heavens. But even on her the Fates
the gray everlasting Fates rode hard
my child, my child.
    [*Enter* TIRESIAS, *the blind prophet, led by a boy.*]
TIRESIAS: Lords of Thebes,
    I and the boy have come together,
    hand in hand. Two see with the eyes of one . . .
    so the blind must go, with a guide to lead the way.
CREON: What is it, old Tiresias? What news now?
TIRESIAS: I will teach you. And you obey the seer.
CREON: I will,
    I've never wavered from your advice before.
TIRESIAS: And so you kept the city straight on course.
CREON: I owe you a great deal, I swear to that.
TIRESIAS: Then reflect, my son: you are poised,
    once more, on the razor-edge of fate.
CREON: What is it? I shudder to hear you.
TIRESIAS: You will learn
    when you listen to the warnings of my craft.
    As I sat on the ancient seat of augury,
    in the sanctuary where every bird I know
    will hover at my hands—suddenly I heard it,
    a strange voice in the wingbeats, unintelligible,
    barbaric, a mad scream! Talons flashing, ripping,
    they were killing each other—that much I knew—
    the murderous fury whirring in those wings
    made that much clear!
                              I was afraid,
    I turned quickly, tested the burnt-sacrifice,
    ignited the altar at all points—but no fire,
    the god in the fire never blazed.
    Not from those offerings . . . over the embers
    slid a heavy ooze from the long thighbones,
    smoking, sputtering out, and the bladder
    puffed and burst—spraying gall into the air—
    and the fat wrapping the bones slithered off
    and left them glistening white. No fire!

The rites failed that might have blazed the future
with a sign. So I learned from the boy here:
he is my guide, as I am guide to others.
                              And it's you—
your high resolve that sets this plague on Thebes.
The public altars and sacred hearths are fouled,
one and all, by the birds and dogs with carrion
torn from the corpse, the doomstruck son of Oedipus!
And so the gods are deaf to our prayers, they spurn
the offerings in our hands, the flame of holy flesh.
No birds cry out an omen clear and true—
they're gorged with the murdered victim's blood and fat.

Take these things to heart, my son, I warn you.
All men make mistakes, it is only human.
But once the wrong is done, a man
can turn his back on folly, misfortune too,
if he tries to make amends, however low he's fallen,
and stops his bullnecked ways. Stubbornness
brands you for stupidity—pride is a crime.
No, yield to the dead!
Never stab the fighter when he's down.
Where's the glory, killing the dead twice over?

I mean you well. I give you sound advice.
It's best to learn from a good adviser
when he speaks for your own good:
it's pure gain.
CREON: Old man—all of you! So,
you shoot your arrows at my head like archers at the target—
I even have *him* loosed on me, this fortune-teller.
Oh his ilk has tried to sell me short
and ship me off for years. Well,
drive your bargains, traffic—much as you like—
in the gold of India, silver-gold of Sardis.
You'll never bury that body in the grave,
not even if Zeus' eagles rip the corpse
and wing their rotten pickings off to the throne of god!
Never, not even in fear of such defilement
will I tolerate his burial, that traitor.
Well I know, we can't defile the gods—
no mortal has the power.

No,
reverend old Tiresias, all men fall,
it's only human, but the wisest fall obscenely
when they glorify obscene advice with rhetoric—
all for their own gain.
TIRESIAS: Oh god, is there a man alive
who knows, who actually believes . . .
CREON: What now?
What earth-shattering truth are you about to utter?
TIRESIAS: . . . just how much a sense of judgment, wisdom
is the greatest gift we have?
CREON: Just as much, I'd say,
as a twisted mind is the worst affliction going.
TIRESIAS: You are the one who's sick, Creon, sick to death.
CREON: I am in no mood to trade insults with a seer.
TIRESIAS: You have already, calling my prophecies a lie.
CREON: Why not?
You and the whole breed of seers are mad for money!
TIRESIAS: And the whole race of tyrants lusts to rake it in.
CREON: This slander of yours—
are you aware you're speaking to the king?
TIRESIAS: Well aware. Who helped you save the city?
CREON: You—
you have your skills, old seer, but you lust for injustice!
TIRESIAS: You will drive me to utter the dreadful secret in my heart.
CREON: Spit it out! Just don't speak it out for profit.
TIRESIAS: Profit? No, not a bit of profit, not for you.
CREON: Know full well, you'll never buy off my resolve.
TIRESIAS: Then know this too, learn this by heart!
The chariot of the sun will not race through
so many circuits more, before you have surrendered
one born of your own loins, your own flesh and blood,
a corpse for corpses given in return, since you have thrust
to the world below a child sprung for the world above,
ruthlessly lodged a living soul within the grave—
then you've robbed the gods below the earth,
keeping a dead body here in the bright air,
unburied, unsung, unhallowed by the rites.

You, you have no business with the dead,
nor do the gods above—this is violence

you have forced upon the heavens.
And so the avengers, the dark destroyers late
but true to the mark, now lie in wait for you,
the Furies sent by the gods and the god of death
to strike you down with the pains that you perfected!

There. Reflect on that, tell me I've been bribed.
The day comes soon, no long test of time, not now,
that wakes the wails for men and women in your halls.
Great hatred rises against you—
cities in tumult, all whose mutilated sons
the dogs have graced with burial, or the wild beasts
or a wheeling crow that wings the ungodly stench of carrion
back to each city, each warrior's hearth and home.

These arrows for your heart! Since you've raked me
I loose them like an archer in my anger,
arrows deadly true. You'll never escape
their burning, searing force.
    [*Motioning to his escort.*]
Come, boy, take me home.
So he can vent his rage on younger men,
and learn to keep a gentler tongue in his head
and better sense than what he carries now.
    [*Exit to the side.*]
LEADER: The old man's gone, my king—
  terrible prophecies. Well I know,
  since the hair on this old head went gray,
  he's never lied to Thebes.
CREON: I know it myself—I'm shaken, torn.
  It's a dreadful thing to yield . . . but resist now?
  Lay my pride bare to the blows of ruin?
  That's dreadful too.
LEADER: But good advice,
  Creon, take it now, you must.
CREON: What should I do? Tell me . . . I'll obey.
LEADER: Go! Free the girl from the rocky vault
  and raise a mound for the body you exposed.
CREON: That's your advice? You think I should give in?
LEADER: Yes, my king, quickly. Disasters sent by the gods
  cut short our follies in a flash.

CREON: Oh it's hard,
giving up the heart's desire . . . but I will do it—
no more fighting a losing battle with necessity.
LEADER: Do it now, go, don't leave it to others.
CREON: Now—I'm on my way! Come, each of you,
take up axes, make for the high ground,
over there, quickly! I and my better judgment
have come round to this—I shackled her,
I'll set her free myself. I am afraid . . .
it's best to keep the established laws
to the very day we die.
          [*Rushing out, followed by his entourage. The* CHORUS *clusters
          around the altar.*]
CHORUS: God of a hundred names!
                         Great Dionysus—
          Son and glory of Semele! Pride of Thebes—
Child of Zeus whose thunder rocks the clouds—
Lord of the famous lands of evening—
King of the Mysteries!
                         King of Eleusis, Demeter's plain
her breasting hills that welcome in the world—
Great Dionysus!
                    Bacchus, living in Thebes
the mother-city of all your frenzied women—
                                        Bacchus
          living along the Ismenus' rippling waters
standing over the field sown with the Dragon's teeth!

You—we have seen you through the flaring smoky fires,
          your torches blazing over the twin peaks
where nymphs of the hallowed cave climb onward
                         fired with you, your sacred rage—
we have seen you at Castalia's running spring
and down from the heights of Nysa crowned with ivy
the greening shore rioting vines and grapes
          down you come in your storm of wild women
                    esctatic, mystic cries—
                                   Dionysus—
down to watch and ward the roads of Thebes!
First of all cities, Thebes you honor first
you and your mother, bride of the lightning—

come, Dionysus! now your people lie
in the iron grip of plague,
come in your racing, healing stride
                    down Parnassus' slopes
or across the moaning straits.
                                Lord of the dancing
dance, dance the constellations breathing fire!
Great master of the voices of the night!
Child of Zeus, God's offspring, come, come forth!
Lord, king, dance with your nymphs, swirling, raving
arm-in-arm in frenzy through the night
they dance you, Iacchus—
                    Dance, Dionysus
giver of all good things!
      [*Enter a* MESSENGER *from the side.*]
MESSENGER: Neighbors,
friends of the house of Cadmus and the kings,
there's not a thing in this mortal life of ours
I'd praise or blame as settled once for all.
Fortune lifts and Fortune fells the lucky
and unlucky every day. No prophet on earth
can tell a man his fate. Take Creon:
there was a man to rouse your envy once,
as I see it. He saved the realm from enemies,
taking power, he alone, the lord of the fatherland,
he set us true on course—he flourished like a tree
with the noble line of sons he bred and reared . . .
and now it's lost, all gone.
                          Believe me,
when a man has squandered his true joys,
he's good as dead, I tell you, a living corpse.
Pile up riches in your house, as much as you like—
live like a king with a huge show of pomp,
but if real delight is missing from the lot,
I wouldn't give you a wisp of smoke for it,
not compared with joy.
LEADER: What now?
What new grief do you bring the house of kings?
MESSENGER: Dead, dead—and the living are guilty of their death!
LEADER: Who's the murderer? Who is dead? Tell us.
MESSENGER: Haemon's gone, his blood spilled by the very hand—

LEADER: His father's or his own?
MESSENGER: His own . . .
   raging mad with his father for the death—
LEADER: Oh great seer,
   you saw it all, you brought your word to birth!
MESSENGER: Those are the facts. Deal with them as you will.
   [*As he turns to go,* EURYDICE *enters from the palace.*]
LEADER: Look, Eurydice. Poor woman, Creon's wife,
   so close at hand. By chance perhaps,
   unless she's heard the news about her son.
EURYDICE: My countrymen,
   all of you—I caught the sound of your words
   as I was leaving to do my part,
   to appeal to queen Athena with my prayers.
   I was just loosing the bolts, opening the doors,
   when a voice filled with sorrow, family sorrow,
   struck my ears, and I fell back, terrified,
   into the women's arms—everything went black.
   Tell me the news, again, whatever it is . . .
   sorrow and I are hardly strangers.
   I can bear the worst.
MESSENGER: I—dear lady,
   I'll speak as an eye-witness. I was there.
   And I won't pass over one word of the truth.
   Why should I try to soothe you with a story,
   only to prove a liar in a moment?
   Truth is always best.
                                    So,
   I escorted your lord, I guided him
   to the edge of the plain where the body lay,
   Polynices, torn by the dogs and still unmourned.
   And saying a prayer to Hecate of the Crossroads,
   Pluto too, to hold their anger and be kind,
   we washed the dead in a bath of holy water
   and plucking some fresh branches, gathering . . .
   what was left of him, we burned them all together
   and raised a high mound of native earth, and then
   we turned and made for that rocky vault of hers,
   the hollow, empty bed of the bride of Death.
   And far off, one of us heard a voice,
   a long wail rising, echoing
   out of that unhallowed wedding-chamber,

he ran to alert the master and Creon pressed on,
closer—the strange, inscrutable cry came sharper,
throbbing around him now, and he let loose
a cry of his own, enough to wrench the heart,
"Oh god, am I the prophet now? going down
the darkest road I've ever gone? My son—
it's *his* dear voice, he greets me! Go, men,
closer, quickly! Go through the gap,
the rocks are dragged back—
right to the tomb's very mouth—and look,
see if it's Haemon's voice I think I hear,
or the gods have robbed me of my senses."

The king was shattered. We took his orders,
went and searched, and there in the deepest,
dark recesses of the tomb we found her . . .
hanged by the neck in a fine linen noose,
strangled in her veils—and the boy,
his arms flung around her waist,
clinging to her, wailing for his bride,
dead and down below, for his father's crimes
and the bed of his marriage blighted by misfortune.
When Creon saw him, he gave a deep sob,
he ran in, shouting, crying out to him,
"Oh my child—what have you done? what seized you,
what insanity? what disaster drove you mad?
Come out, my son! I beg you on my knees!"
But the boy gave him a wild burning glance,
spat in his face, not a word in reply,
he drew his sword—his father rushed out,
running as Haemon lunged and missed!—
and then, doomed, desperate with himself,
suddenly leaning his full weight on the blade,
he buried it in his body, halfway to the hilt.
And still in his senses, pouring his arms around her,
he embraced the girl and breathing hard,
released a quick rush of blood,
bright red on her cheek glistening white.
And there he lies, body enfolding body . . .
he has won his bride at last, poor boy,
not here but in the houses of the dead.

Creon shows the world that of all the ills
afflicting men the worst is lack of judgment.
  [EURYDICE *turns and reenters the palace.*]
LEADER: What do you make of that? The lady's gone,
  without a word, good or bad.
MESSENGER: I'm alarmed too
  but here's my hope—faced with her son's death
  she finds it unbecoming to mourn in public.
  Inside, under her roof, she'll set her women
  to the task and wail the sorrow of the house.
  She's too discreet. She won't do something rash.
LEADER: I'm not so sure. To me, at least,
  a long heavy silence promises danger,
  just as much as a lot of empty outcries.
MESSENGER: We'll see if she's holding something back,
  hiding some passion in her heart.
  I'm going in. You may be right—who knows?
  Even too much silence has its dangers.
    [*Exit to the palace. Enter* CREON *from the side, escorted by
    attendants carrying* HAEMON*'s body on a bier.*]
LEADER: The king himself! Coming toward us,
  look, holding the boy's head in his hands.
  Clear, damning proof, if it's right to say so—
  proof of his own madness, no one else's,
    no, his own blind wrongs.
CREON: Ohhh,
  so senseless, so insane . . . my crimes,
  my stubborn, deadly—
  Look at us, the killer, the killed,
  father and son, the same blood—the misery!
  My plans, my mad fanatic heart,
  my son, cut off so young!
  Ai, dead, lost to the world,
  not through your stupidity, no, my own.
LEADER: Too late,
  too late, you see what justice means.
CREON: Oh I've learned
  through blood and tears! Then, it was then,
  when the god came down and struck me—a great weight
  shattering, driving me down that wild savage path,
  ruining, trampling down my joy. Oh the agony,
    the heartbreaking agonies of our lives.
    [*Enter the* MESSENGER *from the palace.*]

MESSENGER: Master,
  what a hoard of grief you have, and you'll have more.
  The grief that lies to hand you've brought yourself—
  [*Pointing to* HAEMON's *body.*]
  the rest, in the house, you'll see it all too soon.
CREON: What now? What's worse than this?
MESSENGER: The queen is dead.
  The mother of this dead boy . . . mother to the end—
  poor thing, her wounds are fresh.
CREON: No, no,
  harbor of Death, so choked, so hard to cleanse!—
  why me? why are you killing me?
  Herald of pain, more words, more grief?
  I died once, you kill me again and again!
  What's the report, boy . . . some news for me?
  My wife dead? O dear god!
  Slaughter heaped on slaughter?
      [*The doors open; the body of* EURYDICE *is brought out on her bier.*]
MESSENGER: See for yourself:
  now they bring her body from the palace.
CREON: Oh no,
  another, a second loss to break the heart.
  What next, what fate still waits for me?
  I just held my son in my arms and now,
  look, a new corpse rising before my eyes—
  wretched, helpless mother—O my son!
MESSENGER: She stabbed herself at the altar,
  then her eyes went dark, after she'd raised
  a cry for the noble fate of Megareus, the hero
  killed in the first assault, then for Haemon,
  then with her dying breath she called down
  torments on your head—you killed her sons.
CREON: Oh the dread,
  I shudder with dread! Why not kill me too?—
  run me through with a good sharp sword?
  Oh god, the misery, anguish—
  I, I'm churning with it, going under.
MESSENGER: Yes, and the dead, the woman lying there,
  piles the guilt of all their deaths on you.
CREON: How did she end her life, what bloody stroke?
MESSENGER: She drove home to the heart with her own hand,
  once she learned her son was dead . . . that agony.
CREON: And the guilt is all mine—

can never be fixed on another man,
no escape for me. I killed you,
I, god help me, I admit it all!
[*To his attendants.*]
Take me away, quickly, out of sight.
I don't even exist—I'm no one. Nothing.
LEADER: Good advice, if there's any good in suffering.
Quickest is best when troubles block the way.
CREON: [*Kneeling in prayer.*]
Come, let it come!—that best of fates for me
that brings the final day, best fate of all.
Oh quickly, now—
so I never have to see another sunrise.
LEADER: That will come when it comes;
we must deal with all that lies before us.
The future rests with the ones who tend the future.
CREON: That prayer—I poured my heart into that prayer!
LEADER: No more prayers now. For mortal men
there is no escape from the doom we must endure.
CREON: Take me away, I beg you, out of sight.
A rash, indiscriminate fool!
I murdered you, my son, against my will—
you too, my wife . . .
                            Wailing wreck of a man,
whom to look to? where to lean for support?
[*Desperately turning from* HAEMON *to* EURYDICE *on their biers.*]
Whatever I touch goes wrong—once more
a crushing fate's come down upon my head!
[*The* MESSENGER *and attendants lead* CREON *into the palace.*]
CHORUS: Wisdom is by far the greatest part of joy,
and reverence toward the gods must be safeguarded.
The mighty words of the proud are paid in full
with mighty blows of fate, and at long last
those blows will teach us wisdom.
[*The old citizens exit to the side.*]

Translated by Robert Fagles

From OEDIPUS AT COLONUS

The two choral songs which follow both come from Sophocles' last play,
Oedipus at Colonus. *He must have written it fairly soon before he died,
in 406 B.C., at the age of ninety. It was produced in the theater of
Dionysus by his son in 401 B.C., after the restoration of the democracy,
which had been suppressed in 404, when with Spartan support the so-
called "Thirty Tyrants" established a short-lived oligarchic regime.*

This is the sequel to Sophocles' most famous play, Oedipus Tyrannus,
*which had been performed some twenty years earlier. Oedipus, now old
as well as blind, is a beggar on the roads of Greece, attended by his
daughter Antigone. He comes to the village of Colonus, near Athens
(Sophocles' birth-place), and after being ordered to leave by the old men
of the chorus, is welcomed by Theseus, Athens' king. He has to endure
the threats and violence of Creon, who comes to take him to Thebes,
because of a prophecy that his grave would be the site of victory over a
foreign invader. Rescued by Theseus, Oedipus promises this gift of future victory to Athens. In the final scene, summoned by the gods, he
goes off with Theseus to a mysterious end.*

*The shorter ode, a lament for the sorrows and indignities of old age,
takes as its exemplar the blind, ragged old man who after confronting
Creon now awaits the arrival of his son Polynices, who will attempt to
enlist his aid for an attack on Thebes, but who will be met by a tremendous curse and a prophecy of death at his brother's hand. The other
choral song, a celebration of the glories of Athens, is sung immediately
after the scene in which Theseus accepts Oedipus as a citizen of Athens.
When Sophocles wrote these marvelous lines, he must have known that
the war was almost over and that Athens might not survive its end. The
olive trees he praises as immortal had long since been hacked down or
burned by the invading Spartan armies; the young cavalrymen whose
images Phidias carved on the frieze of the Parthenon had long since
perished on the many battlefields of the war or in the quarries of Syracuse; and the Athenian "mastery of the ocean roads" was a thing of the
past: within months of Sophocles' death, Athens' last fleet was destroyed
at Aegospotami and the blockade of Athens began.*

*To represent the lyric meters of this second ode, the translator has
used a brilliant English adaptation of the Sapphic stanza.*

PRAISE OF ATHENS

Come, let us praise this haven of strong horses,
unmatched, brilliant Kolonos, white with sunlight,
where the shy one, the nightingale, at evening
        flutes in the darkness,

the ivy dark, so woven of fruit and vine-leaves
no winter storms nor light of day can enter
this sanctuary of the dancing revels
        of Dionysos.

Here, under heaven's dew, blooms the narcissus,
crown of life's mother and her buried daughter,
of Earth and the Dark below; here, too, the sunburst
        flares of the crocus.

The river's ample springs, cool and unfailing,
rove and caress this green, fair-breasted landscape.
Here have the Muses visited with dances,
        and Aphrodite

has reined her chariot here. And here is something
unheard of in the fabulous land of Asia,
unknown to Doric earth—a thing immortal;
        gift of a goddess,

beyond the control of hands, tough, self-renewing,
an enduring wealth, passing through generations,
here only: the invincible grey-leafed olive.
        Agèd survivor

of all vicissitudes, it knows protection
of the All-Seeing Eye of Zeus, whose sunlight
always regards it, and of Grey-Eyed Athena.
        I have another

tribute of praise for this city, our mother:
the greatest gift of a god, a strength of horses,
strength of young horses, a power of the ocean,
        strength and a power.

O Lord Poseidon, you have doubly blessed us
with healing skills, on these roads first bestowing
the bit that gentles horses, the controlling
    curb and the bridle,

and the carved, feathering oar that skims and dances
like the white nymphs of water, conferring mastery
of ocean roads, among the spume and wind-blown
    prancing of stallions.

OLD AGE

What is unwisdom but the lusting after
Longevity: to be old and full of days!
For the vast and unremitting tide of years
Casts up to view more sorrowful things than joyful;
And as for pleasures, once beyond our prime,
They all drift out of reach, they are washed away.
And the same gaunt bailiff calls upon us all,
Summoning into Darkness, to those wards
Where is no music, dance, or marriage hymn
That soothes or gladdens. To the tenements of Death.

Not to be born is, past all yearning, best.
And second best is, having seen the light,
To return at once to deep oblivion.
When youth has gone, and the baseless dreams of youth,
What misery does not then jostle man's elbow,
Join him as a companion, share his bread?
Betrayal, envy, calumny and bloodshed
Move in on him, and finally Old Age—
Infirm, despised Old Age—joins in his ruin,
The crowning taunt of his indignities.

So is it with that man, not just with me.
He seems like a frail jetty facing North
Whose pilings the waves batter from all quarters;
From where the sun comes up, from where it sets,
From freezing boreal regions, from below,
A whole winter of miseries now assails him,
Thrashes his sides and breaks over his head.

Translated by Anthony Hecht

EURIPIDES
485–406 B.C.

We have seven complete plays of Aeschylus, the same number for Sophocles, but under Euripides' name nineteen have come down to us (though in the case of one of them, the Rhesus, *Euripidean authorship is doubtful). Ten of his plays were, like the seven of the other two, selected for educational use during the early Byzantine centuries and so were continuously copied. During the revival of interest in classical literature that occurred in the thirteenth to the fifteenth centuries, a manuscript containing nine more plays of Euripides was discovered and recopied. It is clear from the titles of these plays that the manuscript contained part of what had once been a complete edition of the plays of Euripides arranged in roughly alphabetical order (hence the designation of the nine plays as "alphabetic").*

Not all nine plays are masterpieces, but taken together with the canonical ten, they give us a broad overview of the work of a versatile dramatist, whose plays exhibit the many different facets of his talent. Aristotle called him "the most tragic of the poets," and he could indeed arouse pity and fear with such themes as the revenge of Medea, the destruction of Phaedra and Hippolytus, or the destruction and enslavement of a whole city, as in Trojan Women. *He could also write wartime patriotic plays, like* Suppliants *and* Children of Heracles, *in which Athens, represented by Theseus or his son Demophon, appears as the protector of the weak and oppressed. Euripides seems to have been the inventor of what was to become a standard melodrama, the play or story in which representatives of a higher civilization escape from captivity among the barbarians by cunning manipulation of their superstitions; two of the alphabetic plays,* Helen *and* Iphigenia in Tauris, *belong to this category. In* Ion, *another alphabetic play, Euripides foreshadows the comedies of Menander in his tale of an abandoned son restored to his mother and his kingdom after a series of hair-raising developments that bring them to the verge of killing each other; catastrophe is averted when the mother recognizes and identifies the objects contained in a box* she had left with the child when she exposed it. *In* The Bacchae, *Euripides recreated on stage the wild fury and the ecstatic bliss of primitive Dionysiac worship in a play that ends with a human sacrifice of unprecedented horror. And in the* Alcestis, *he dramatizes a fairy-tale plot in which a wife gives her life to save her husband's, but is restored to life and to him by the efforts of a friend he had welcomed into the house. The fairy-tale atmosphere is poisoned, however, by the long speeches of the husband (after all, what can he say in such a situation?), and by the insertion of a scene in which the husband reviles his father for not offering to die in his place and is told some home truths in return. One of the father's lines—"You love the light. What makes you think your father doesn't like it too?"—became proverbial.*

Though he was often granted a chorus (appointed one of the three tragic poets to compete in the festival), Euripides rarely won first prize— only three times in his lifetime, and once posthumously, for the group of plays containing Bacchae *and* Iphigenia in Aulis. *The contrast with Sophocles, who won first prize twenty-four times, and though often second, never came in third, is striking. Euripides seems to have had a knack for setting his audience's teeth on edge, for raising questions they would rather not have to think about. He has often been compared to such abrasive dramatists as Ibsen and Shaw, but the comparison does not do him justice, for, unlike them, he was a great poet as well as a great dramatist. His lyric choral odes were famous all over the Greek world. Some of the Athenian prisoners in the quarries of Syracuse in 412 B.C. gained their freedom by singing for their captors Euripidean lyrics that had not reached Syracuse during the war. And Plutarch tells us that after the surrender of Athens in 404, there were voices raised among Sparta's allies in favor of selling the Athenians as slaves and even for razing Athens to the ground. But at a banquet, someone sang a lyric excerpt from Euripides'* Electra *and all those present were deeply moved, feeling that "it would be an atrocity to destroy a city that was so famous and could raise such men."*

From MEDEA

MEDEA'S SPEECH TO THE CHORUS

The Medea *of Euripides' play is no longer the lovesick princess of the epic tale of Jason and the Golden Fleece. She has borne Jason two sons; she has committed murder for him in his home city of Iolcos in a vain*

attempt to win the throne for him; and she now shares his exile in
Corinth. But he has won the love of the daughter of Creon, king of
Corinth, and plans to marry her. His union with Medea, a non-Greek, he
evidently does not regard as binding. Medea, we learn from her old
nurse, who opens the play, is in a tremendous rage, even turning her
passionate resentment, in a hint of things to come, against the children.
The nurse's report is fully confirmed by Medea's offstage laments and
curses. But when she comes out of the house to speak to the chorus,
young women of Corinth, she has mastered her rage, and appeals diplo-
matically—and successfully—for their support in her plans for revenge.

MEDEA: Women of Corinth, I have come outside to you
   Lest you should be indignant with me; for I know
   That many people are overproud, some when alone,
   And others when in company. And those who live
   Quietly, as I do, get a bad reputation.
   For a just judgement is not evident in the eyes
   When a man at first sight hates another, before
   Learning his character, being in no way injured;
   And a foreigner especially must adapt himself.
   I'd not approve of even a fellow-countryman
   Who by pride and want of manners offends his neighbours.
   But on me this thing has fallen so unexpectedly,
   It has broken my heart. I am finished. I let go
   All my life's joy. My friends, I only want to die.
   It was everything to me to think well of one man,
   And he, my own husband, has turned out wholly vile.
   Of all things which are living and can form a judgement
   We women are the most unfortunate creatures.
   Firstly, with an excess of wealth it is required
   For us to buy a husband and take for our bodies
   A master; for not to take one is even worse.
   And now the question is serious whether we take
   A good or bad one; for there is no easy escape
   For a woman, nor can she say no to her marriage.
   She arrives among new modes of behaviour and manners,
   And needs prophetic power, unless she has learnt at home,
   How best to manage him who shares the bed with her.
   And if we work out all this well and carefully,
   And the husband lives with us and lightly bears his yoke,

Then life is enviable. If not, I'd rather die.
A man, when he's tired of the company in his home,
Goes out of the house and puts an end to his boredom
And turns to a friend or companion of his own age.
But we are forced to keep our eyes on one alone.
What they say of us is that we have a peaceful time
Living at home, while they do the fighting in war.
How wrong they are! I would very much rather stand
Three times in the front of battle than bear one child.
Yet what applies to me does not apply to you.
You have a country. Your family home is here.
You enjoy life and the company of your friends.
But I am deserted, a refugee, thought nothing of
By my husband,—something he won in a foreign land.
I have no mother or brother, nor any relation
With whom I can take refuge in this sea of woe.
This much then is the service I would beg from you:
If I can find the means or devise any scheme
To pay my husband back for what he has done to me,—
Him and his father-in-law and the girl who married him,—
Just to keep silent. For in other ways a woman
Is full of fear, defenceless, dreads the sight of cold
Steel; but, when once she is wronged in the matter of love,
No other soul can hold so many thoughts of blood.
CHORUS: This I will promise. You are in the right, Medea,
In paying your husband back. I am not surprised at you
For being sad.

Translated by Rex Warner

IN PRAISE OF WOMEN

Creon, rightly, regards Medea as a dangerous woman, and comes to pronounce a sentence of exile on her; she must leave Corinth at once. She manages to wring from him a concession: she may remain one more day, to make her preparations for exile. After Creon's exit, Medea deliberates about the revenge she will take, hesitates at the thought of the consequences—who will give her refuge after the murder of a royal family?—but then, in heroic terms, reaffirms her resolution to punish her enemies. The chorus, sharing her indignation and inspired by her courage, sings a new song, one in which "Women are paid their due."

Flow backward to your sources, sacred rivers,
And let the world's great order be reversed.
It is the thoughts of *men* that are deceitful,
Their pledges that are loose.
Story shall now turn my condition to a fair one,
Women are paid their due.
No more shall evil-sounding fame be theirs.

Cease now, you muses of the ancient singers,
To tell the tale of my unfaithfulness;
For not on us did Phoebus, lord of music,
Bestow the lyre's divine
Power, for otherwise I should have sung an answer
To the other sex. Long time
Has much to tell of us, and much of them.

You sailed away from your father's home,
With a heart on fire you passed
The double rocks of the sea.
And now in a foreign country
You have lost your rest in a widowed bed,
And are driven forth, a refugee
In dishonour from the land.

Good faith has gone, and no more remains
In great Greece a sense of shame.
It has flown away to the sky.
No father's house for a haven
Is at hand for you now, and another queen
Of your bed has dispossessed you and
Is mistress of your home.

Translated by Rex Warner

MEDEA AND JASON

*In the fierce altercation that takes place when Jason comes with an offer
to "make some provision" for Medea and his sons as they go into exile,
Medea reminds him how much he owes her and denounces his ingratitude in a passionate speech. Of his reply, at equal length, the chorus
remarks: "you have made this speech of yours look well." He has in fact
used many of the techniques taught by the Sophists as rhetorical aids*

toward making *"the weaker cause appear the stronger." This was the*
phrase of Protagoras, the most famous of the Sophists; it so happens that
the Greek words for "weaker" and "stronger" can also mean "worse"
and "better."
 Up to this point Medea's plan has been to kill Creon, his daughter,
and Jason. It is only much later that she decides to leave Jason alive but
kill his sons. In this scene, Jason's complacent satisfaction with the num-
ber of his sons—"I am quite content"—and his solicitude for their fu-
ture play a role in the birth in her mind of a new and more terrible plan
for revenge: to deprive Jason not only of the sons he expects from the
new marriage but also of those he already has.

[*Enter* JASON, *with attendants.*]
JASON: This is not the first occasion that I have noticed
  How hopeless it is to deal with a stubborn temper.
  For, with reasonable submission to our ruler's will,
  You might have lived in this land and kept your home.
  As it is you are going to be exiled for your loose speaking.
  Not that I mind myself. You are free to continue
  Telling everyone that Jason is a worthless man.
  But as to your talk about the king, consider
  Yourself most lucky that exile is your punishment.
  I, for my part, have always tried to calm down
  The anger of the king, and wished you to remain.
  But you will not give up your folly, continually
  Speaking ill of him, and so you are going to be banished.
  All the same, and in spite of your conduct, I'll not desert
  My friends, but have come to make some provision for you,
  So that you and the children may not be penniless
  Or in need of anything in exile. Certainly
  Exile brings many troubles with it. And even
  If you hate me, I cannot think badly of you.
MEDEA: O coward in every way,—that is what I call you,
  With bitterest reproach for your lack of manliness,
  You have come, you, my worst enemy, have come to me!
  It is not an example of over-confidence
  Or of boldness thus to look your friends in the face,
  Friends you have injured,—no, it is the worst of all
  Human diseases, shamelessness. But you did well
  To come, for I can speak ill of you and lighten
  My heart, and you will suffer while you are listening.

And first I will begin from what happened first.
I saved your life, and every Greek knows I saved it,
Who was a ship-mate of yours aboard the Argo,
When you were sent to control the bulls that breathed fire
And yoke them, and when you would sow that deadly field.
Also that snake, who encircled with his many folds
The Golden Fleece and guarded it and never slept,
I killed, and so gave you the safety of the light.
And I myself betrayed my father and my home,
And came with you to Pelias' land of Iolcos.
And then, showing more willingness to help than wisdom,
I killed him, Pelias, with a most dreadful death
At his own daughters' hands, and took away your fear.
This is how I behaved to you, you wretched man,
And you forsook me, took another bride to bed
Though you had children; for, if that had not been,
You would have had an excuse for another wedding.
Faith in your word has gone. Indeed I cannot tell
Whether you think the gods whose names you swore by then
Have ceased to rule and that new standards are set up,
Since you must know you have broken your word to me.
O my right hand, and the knees which you often clasped
In supplication, how senselessly I am treated
By this bad man, and how my hopes have missed their mark!
Come, I will share my thoughts as though you were a friend,—
You! Can I think that you would ever treat me well?
But I will do it, and these questions will make you
Appear the baser. Where am I to go? To my father's?
Him I betrayed and his land when I came with you.
To Pelias' wretched daughters? What a fine welcome
They would prepare for me who murdered their father!
For this is my position,—hated by my friends
At home, I have, in kindness to you, made enemies
Of others whom there was no need to have injured.
And how happy among Greek women you have made me
On your side for all this! A distinguished husband
I have,—for breaking promises. When in misery
I am cast out of the land and go into exile,
Quite without friends and all alone with my children,
That will be a fine shame for the new-wedded groom,
For his children to wander as beggars and she who saved him.
O God, you have given to mortals a sure method

Of telling the gold that is pure from the counterfeit;
Why is there no mark engraved upon men's bodies,
By which we could know the true ones from the false ones?
CHORUS: It is a strange form of anger, difficult to cure
When two friends turn upon each other in hatred.
JASON: As for me, it seems I must be no bad speaker.
But, like a man who has a good grip of the tiller,
Reef up his sail, and so run away from under
This mouthing tempest, woman, of your bitter tongue.
Since you insist on building up your kindness to me,
My view is that Cypris was alone responsible
Of men and gods for the preserving of my life.
You are clever enough,—but really I need not enter
Into the story of how it was love's inescapable
Power that compelled you to keep my person safe.
On this I will not go into too much detail.
In so far as you helped me, you did well enough.
But on this question of saving me, I can prove
You have certainly got from me more than you gave.
Firstly, instead of living among barbarians,
You inhabit a Greek land and understand our ways,
How to live by law instead of the sweet will of force.
And all the Greeks considered you a clever woman.
You were honoured for it; while, if you were living at
The ends of the earth, nobody would have heard of you.
For my part, rather than stores of gold in my house
Or power to sing even sweeter songs than Orpheus,
I'd choose the fate that made me a distinguished man.
There is my reply to your story of my labours.
Remember it was you who started the argument.
Next for your attack on my wedding with the princess:
Here I will prove that, first, it was a clever move,
Secondly, a wise one, and, finally, that I made it
In your best interest and the children's. Please keep calm.
When I arrived here from the land of Iolcos,
Involved, as I was, in every kind of difficulty,
What luckier chance could I have come across than this,
An exile to marry the daughter of the king?
It was not,—the point that seems to upset you—that I
Grew tired of your bed and felt the need of a new bride;
Nor with any wish to outdo your number of children.
We have enough already. I am quite content.

But,—this was the main reason—that we might live well,
And not be short of anything. I know that all
A man's friends leave him stone-cold if he becomes poor.
Also that I might bring my children up worthily
Of my position, and, by producing more of them
To be brothers of yours, we would draw the families
Together and all be happy. You need no children.
And it pays me to do good to those I have now
By having others. Do you think this a bad plan?
You wouldn't if the love question hadn't upset you.
But you women have got into such a state of mind
That, if your life at night is good, you think you have
Everything; but, if in that quarter things go wrong,
You will consider your best and truest interests
Most hateful. It would have been better far for men
To have got their children in some other way, and women
Not to have existed. Then life would have been good.

CHORUS: Jason, though you have made this speech of yours look well,
   Still I think, even though others do not agree,
   You have betrayed your wife and are acting badly.

MEDEA: Surely in many ways I hold different views
   From others, for I think that the plausible speaker
   Who is a villain deserves the greatest punishment.
   Confident in his tongue's power to adorn evil,
   He stops at nothing. Yet he is not really wise.
   As in your case. There is no need to put on the airs
   Of a clever speaker, for one word will lay you flat.
   If you were not a coward, you would not have married
   Behind my back, but discussed it with me first.

JASON: And you, no doubt, would have furthered the proposal,
   If I had told you of it, you who even now
   Are incapable of controlling your bitter temper.

MEDEA: It was not that. No, you thought it was not respectable
   As you got on in years to have a foreign wife.

JASON: Make sure of this: it was not because of a woman
   I made the royal alliance in which I now live,
   But, as I said before, I wished to preserve you
   And breed a royal progeny to be brothers
   To the children I have now, a sure defence to us.

MEDEA: Let me have no happy fortune that brings pain with it,
   Or prosperity which is upsetting to the mind!

JASON: Change your ideas of what you want, and show more sense.

Do not consider painful what is good for you,
Nor, when you are lucky, think yourself unfortunate.
MEDEA: You can insult me. You have somewhere to turn to.
But I shall go from this land into exile, friendless.
JASON: It was what you chose yourself. Don't blame others for it.
MEDEA: And how did I choose it? Did I betray my husband?
JASON: You called down wicked curses on the king's family.
MEDEA: A curse, that is what I am become to your house too.
JASON: I do not propose to go into all the rest of it;
But, if you wish for the children or for yourself
In exile to have some of my money to help you,
Say so, for I am prepared to give with open hand,
Or to provide you with introductions to my friends
Who will treat you well. You are a fool if you do not
Accept this. Cease your anger and you will profit.
MEDEA: I shall never accept the favours of friends of yours,
Nor take a thing from you, so you need not offer it.
There is no benefit in the gifts of a bad man.
JASON: Then, in any case, I call the gods to witness that
I wish to help you and the children in every way,
But you refuse what is good for you. Obstinately
You push away your friends. You are sure to suffer for it.
MEDEA: Go! No doubt you hanker for your virginal bride,
And are guilty of lingering too long out of her house.
Enjoy your wedding. But perhaps,—with the help of God—
You will make the kind of marriage that you will regret.
[JASON *goes out with his attendants.*]

Translated by Rex Warner

From HIPPOLYTUS

PHAEDRA'S NURSE

Phaedra, the wife of Theseus, king of Athens, has fallen in love with Theseus' son by a former wife, Hippolytus. This is the work of the goddess Aphrodite (Cypris); it is part of her plan to destroy Hippolytus, who scorns her deity, remains chaste, and worships exclusively the virgin goddess Artemis. Theseus is away from home, and Phaedra, afraid that she will surrender to her passion and approach Hippolytus, starts to

starve herself to death. Her old nurse, who brought her up from child-
hood and is devoted to her, finally extorts her secret from her, and when
she hears the truth she goes offstage in despair. But she returns, deter-
mined now to save Phaedra's life: she urges her to give way to her passion
and declare her love to Hippolytus.

The arguments she brings to bear against Phaedra's resolution in her
opening speech are typical of sophistic rhetoric at its most cynical; the
claim for instance that Aphrodite-Cypris is irresistible resembles one
famous sophistic argument, that physis, *the force of nature, is more*
powerful than human reason or morality—a plea that could be used in
court to excuse violent action, and the basis for the idea of the superman,
a superior being whose natural force and genius cannot, and should not,
be restrained by mere laws established by lesser men.

Phaedra resists, but the nurse, sensing weakness, presses her case. In
the end Phaedra gives her permission to proceed with her plan—which
the nurse describes in the vaguest of terms. Phaedra is afraid the nurse
intends to tell Hippolytus of her feelings but is fobbed off with an ambig-
uous reply, which, however, she accepts. The nurse does of course tell
Hippolytus of Phaedra's passion, and so brings about the death not only
of Hippolytus but of Phaedra as well.

NURSE: My mistress, as you saw, just now the news of your
    predicament filled me with sudden dreadful fear.
    But now I think that I was silly. Among men
    one's second thoughts are in a way the wiser ones.
    To you nothing outrageous or unheard-of has
    happened. It is the goddess' anger strikes at you.
    You are in love. What's strange in that? Most people are.
    And then because of love will you destroy your life?
    There'll be no point in loving those who are close to us
    now or in future, if one has to die for it.
    Cypris is irresistible when in full force,
    but gently visits those whose spirits yield to her;
    and when she finds a man who's proud and arrogant,
    of course she seizes him and makes a mock of him.
    She ranges through the air, and in the surge of sea
    there Cypris is, and everything proceeds from her.
    And she it is who plants in us and gives desire
    from which all we inhabitants of earth are born.
    Indeed those people who possess the books of old
    writers and are themselves great readers of their works

know how Zeus once desired to have the joys of love
with Semele, and know how once fair-shining Dawn
snatched up to heaven Cephalus to join the gods,
and all this out of passion; and yet, all the same,
they dwell in heaven, do not shun the paths of gods,
and are, I think, quite pleased to yield to what has passed.
Will you object? Your father then should have made you
on special terms, or else controlled by other gods,
if you will not consent to follow these known laws.
How many men, and wise ones, are there, do you think,
who see their beds defiled, and pretend not to see?
How many fathers who assist their erring sons
in finding love affairs? Amongst the wise this is
a general rule,—to hide what is not fair to see.
Nor should men try to be too strict about their lives.
They cannot even make the roofs, with which their homes
are covered, absolutely right. And you, fallen
to such a state, how can you hope to swim out clear?
No, if the good in you is greater than the bad,
you, being only human, will do very well.
So, please, my dear child, give up these bad thoughts of yours.
Give up your arrogance, for it is nothing else
but arrogance to wish to have more strength than gods.
Love, and be bold. It is a god that willed all this.
You may be ill, but find a way to come out well.
Charms do exist and words that soothe and sway the mind.
We shall discover medicine for this ill of yours.
Indeed it's true that men would still be looking for it,
unless it was we women could find out the way.

CHORUS: Phaedra, she tells you things that are more useful too you
in your present distress. Yet I think *you* are right.
And you will find this view of mine more hard to bear
than are her words, more painful too to listen to.

PHAEDRA: This is the thing that ruins the well-ordered towns
and homes of men,—words spoken too persuasively.
For people should not say what charms the listener's ear
but what will bring to those who hear it good report.

NURSE: Why this grand language? What you need is not fine words
but to find out as fast as possible about
the man, and us to tell him the straight story of you.
For if it was not that your life was in this state
of peril, if you were a woman more controlled,

I never would, because of love and your delights,
have urged you on so far; but now the struggle is
to save your life, and I cannot be blamed for this.
PHAEDRA: What awful things you say! Will you please keep your
    mouth
shut, and never again speak such disgraceful words.
NURSE: Disgraceful, yes, but better for you than your fine
words, and a better deed if I can save your life
than save your name, to glory in which name you'd die.
PHAEDRA: Please, not to me, I beg you (you speak well, but foully)
go any further now. My heart is well prepared
by love, and, if you speak so well of shameful things,
I shall be swept away by what I fly from now.
NURSE: If this is what you think, you ought not to have sinned.
You have. Then listen to me, for the next best thing
is to give way. I have at home some soothing draughts
for love,—the thought has only just occurred to me,—
and these, without dishonour, doing no harm to your wits,
will free you from your sickness, if you will be brave.
But I must have something from him whom you desire,
some mark, either a lock of hair or piece of clothing,
so from the two of you to make consentment one.
PHAEDRA: Is this a drug to drink or ointment to put on?
NURSE: I do not know. Be happy and never mind, my child.
PHAEDRA: I am afraid that you may be too clever in all this.
NURSE: Be sure you would fear everything. What do you fear?
PHAEDRA: That you might tell some word of this to Theseus' son.
NURSE: Leave me alone, my child. I shall arrange things well.
    [*She turns to go into the palace but first addresses the statue
    of Aphrodite.*]
Only be you my helper, lady of the sea,
Cypris! As for what else I have within my mind
it will be enough to tell it to our friends indoors.
    [*She goes into the palace.*]

                                    Translated by Rex Warner

                        THE POWER OF LOVE

*As the nurse goes off on her fatal errand, the chorus sings a hymn to Eros
(Love), personification of the overpowering force of sexual passion. The
hymn speaks of the delight brought by Eros, but the dominant theme is*

love's destructiveness. The chorus wonders why men sacrifice to Zeus by the Alpheus River at Olympia and to Apollo at Delphi but take no measures to placate the dangerous power, Eros. They allude to two stories that tell of this destructive power in action. The hero Heracles, son of Alcmene, won the hand of Iole, princess of Oechalia, with whom he was in love, in an archery contest. Denied his prize, he captured and sacked the city, carrying Iole off to his home, where, as the audience knew well without being reminded of it, her arrival led to his own death. Semele, daughter of King Cadmus of Thebes, was loved by Zeus himself, who visited her by night and in human form. Pregnant by the god, she asked to see him in his divine shape; she did, and was blasted by the thunderbolt. Zeus rescued his child, however, and gave it a second womb in his thigh; in the fullness of time it was born—Dionysus, the Twice-born.

Love, O Love, you that make well to the eyes
drops of desire, you that bring sweet delight
into the hearts that you with your force invade,
never to me appear in catastrophe,
never in discord come!
Since there exists no bolt of the fire and no
weightier bolt of the stars than that
arrow of Aphrodite hurled
out of the hands of Love,
Love, the child of the Highest.

Useless it is that still by Alpheus' stream,
Useless it is by Phoebus' Pythian shrines
for the land of Hellas to sacrifice more and more
blood of oxen, when we neglect to give
the honour that's due to Love,
Love, the ruler of men, he who keeps the keys
of Aphrodite's pleasantest dwelling-place,
he who ravages on his way,
bringing to mortals all
catastrophes at his coming.

The girl in Oichalia,
a maiden unyoked to love,
unmarried as yet and husbandless, Cypris took
and loosed her from home in ships,

and, a fugitive thing, like a nymph or Bacchante, she gave her,
with blood and with fire
and murder for wedding hymns,
to Alcmene's child.
Poor wretch she was in her marriage!

O holy fortress of Thebes,
O fountain of Dirce, you
well could witness the force of Cypris' coming.
For with thunder and lightning flash
she brought to her bed the mother of Bacchus, the Zeus-born,
and gave her a wedding
with death for a fate. She breathes
in terror on all
and flies on her way like a bee.

Translated by Rex Warner

From THE BACCHAE

DIONYSIAC ECSTASY

In the Bacchae—*one of the last plays Euripides wrote and which was not staged in Athens until after his death—the god Dionysus, in the form of a human celebrant of his cult, comes from Asia, with a chorus of female Asian devotees, to Thebes, where he was born. The Theban king, Pentheus, resists the introduction of his orgiastic rites; in reprisal, Dionysus inflicts the women of Thebes with madness (they become Maenads, literally, "mad women"), and they leave the city for the pine forests on the mountains, where they live a wild life in close communion with nature. Among the Maenads is Pentheus' mother, Agave. Pentheus sets out to hunt them down with troops and to capture the foreigner who has brought the worship of this new god to Thebes; but before he can start, Dionysus, in human form, is brought before him, a captive. He has an effeminate look, is dressed in Oriental clothes, and wears a smiling mask. The king interrogates him, mocks him, and consigns him to prison. But the god is freed when an earthquake brings the prison down in ruins.*

King and god now confront each other for a second time, but this time it is Dionysus who is the dominant partner. Divining the king's prurient curiosity about what he thinks are obscene rites celebrated by the women in the mountains, he proposes to lead Pentheus to a place where he can spy on them. Pentheus is unable to resist temptation, even though he is told that to escape detection he will have to dress up as a woman. He goes offstage into the palace, and Dionysus, before he follows to help him dress for his part, tells the chorus: "The man is in the trap. He will go to the Maenads, where he will pay with his life." The choral song which follows combines the two poles of Dionysiac possession, bliss and violence.

—When shall I dance once more
with bare feet the all-night dances,
tossing my head for joy
in the damp air, in the dew,
as a running fawn might frisk
for the green joy of the wide fields,
free from fear of the hunt,
free from the circling beaters
and the nets of woven mesh
and the hunters hallooing on
their yelping packs? And then, hard pressed,
she sprints with the quickness of wind,
bounding over the marsh, leaping
to frisk, leaping for joy,
gay with the green of the leaves,
to dance for joy in the forest,
to dance where the darkness is deepest,
    where no man is.

—What is wisdom? What gift of the gods
is held in honor like this:
to hold your hand victorious
over the heads of those you hate?
Honor is precious forever.

—Slow but unmistakable
the might of the gods moves on.
It punishes that man,
infatuate of soul
and hardened in his pride,
who disregards the gods.
The gods are crafty:

they lie in ambush
a long step of time
to hunt the unholy.
Beyond the old beliefs,
no thought, no act shall go.
Small, small is the cost
to believe in this:
whatever is god is strong;
whatever long time has sanctioned,
that is a law forever;
the law tradition makes
is the law of nature.

—What is wisdom? What gift of the gods
is held in honor like this:
to hold your hand victorious
over the heads of those you hate?
Honor is precious forever.

—Blessèd is he who escapes a storm at sea,
    who comes home to his harbor.
—Blessèd is he who emerges from under affliction.
—In various ways one man outraces another in the
    race for wealth and power.
—Ten thousand men possess ten thousand hopes.
—A few bear fruit in happiness; the others go awry.
—But he who garners day by day the good of life,
    he is happiest. Blessèd is he.

Translated by William Arrowsmith

THE DEATH OF PENTHEUS

*Before Pentheus is killed, he is to be mocked, as he had mocked
Dionysus when he held him prisoner earlier in the play. He comes out of
the palace dressed as a woman, his mind possessed by the god; he sees
double—two suns, two cities of Thebes—and his previous reluctance to
put on women's dress has been replaced by a simpering pride in his
appearance, as Dionysus plays handmaid, adjusting his coiffure and his
skirt length. As the god leads him off to his ghastly fate, the chorus sings
a savage hymn calling for the punishment of the man who has mocked
the god. And as the closing strains of their song die away, a messenger
comes from the mountains to tell them what has happened to Pentheus.*

MESSENGER: There were three of us in all: Pentheus and I,
attending my master, and that stranger who volunteered
his services as guide. Leaving behind us
the last outlying farms of Thebes, we forded
the Asopus and struck into the barren scrubland
of Cithaeron.
                There in a grassy glen we halted,
unmoving, silent, without a word,
so we might see but not be seen. From that vantage,
in a hollow cut from the sheer rock of the cliffs,
a place where water ran and the pines grew dense
with shade, we saw the Maenads sitting, their hands
busily moving at their happy tasks. Some
wound the stalks of their tattered wands with tendrils
of fresh ivy; others, frisking like fillies
newly freed from the painted bridles, chanted
in Bacchic songs, responsively.
                                    But Pentheus—
unhappy man—could not quite see the companies
of women. "Stranger," he said, "from where I stand,
I cannot see these counterfeited Maenads.
But if I climbed that towering fir that overhangs
the banks, then I could see their shameless orgies
better."
          And now the stranger worked a miracle.
Reaching for the highest branch of a great fir,
he bent it down, down, down to the dark earth,
till it was curved the way a taut bow bends
or like a rim of wood when forced about the circle
of a wheel. Like that he forced that mountain fir
down to the ground. No mortal could have done it.
Then he seated Pentheus at the highest tip
and with his hands let the trunk rise straightly up,
slowly and gently, lest it throw its rider.
And the tree rose, towering to heaven, with my master
huddled at the top. And now the Maenads saw him
more clearly than he saw them. But barely had they seen,
when the stranger vanished and there came a great voice
out of heaven—Dionysus', it must have been—
crying: "Women, I bring you the man who has mocked
at you and me and at our holy mysteries.
Take vengeance upon him." And as he spoke
a flash of awful fire bound earth and heaven.

The high air hushed, and along the forest glen
the leaves hung still; you could hear no cry of beasts.
The Bacchae heard that voice but missed its words,
and leaping up, they stared, peering everywhere.
Again that voice. And now they knew his cry,
the clear command of god. And breaking loose
like startled doves, through grove and torrent,
over jagged rocks, they flew, their feet maddened
by the breath of god. And when they saw my master
perching in his tree, they climbed a great stone
that towered opposite his perch and showered him
with stones and javelins of fir, while the others
hurled their wands. And yet they missed their target,
poor Pentheus in his perch, barely out of reach
of their eager hands, treed, unable to escape.
Finally they splintered branches from the oaks
and with those bars of wood tried to lever up the tree
by prying at the roots. But every effort failed.
Then Agave cried out: "Maenads, make a circle
about the trunk and grip it with your hands.
Unless we take this climbing beast, he will reveal
the secrets of the god." With that, thousands of hands
tore the fir tree from the earth, and down, down
from his high perch fell Pentheus, tumbling
to the ground, sobbing and screaming as he fell,
for he knew his end was near. His own mother,
like a priestess with her victim, fell upon him
first. But snatching off his wig and snood
so she would recognize his face, he touched her cheeks,
screaming, *"No, no Mother! I am Pentheus,*
your own son, the child you bore to Echion!
Pity me, spare me, Mother! I have done a wrong,
but do not kill your own son for my offense."
But she was foaming at the mouth, and her crazed eyes
rolling with frenzy. She was mad, stark mad,
possessed by Bacchus. Ignoring his cries of pity,
she seized his left arm at the wrist; then, planting
her foot upon his chest, she pulled, wrenching away
the arm at the shoulder—not by her own strength,
for the god had put inhuman power in her hands.
Ino, meanwhile, on the other side, was scratching off
his flesh. Then Autonoë and the whole horde

of Bacchae swarmed upon him. Shouts everywhere,
he screaming with what little breath was left,
they shrieking in triumph. One tore off an arm,
another a foot still warm in its shoe. His ribs
were clawed clean of flesh and every hand
was smeared with blood as they played ball with scraps
of Pentheus' body.
              The pitiful remains lie scattered,
one piece among the sharp rocks, others
lying lost among the leaves in the depths
of the forest. His mother, picking up his head,
impaled it on her wand. She seems to think it is
some mountain lion's head which she carries in triumph
through the thick of Cithaeron. Leaving her sisters
at the Maenad dances, she is coming here, gloating
over her grisly prize. She calls upon Bacchus:
he is her "fellow-huntsman," "comrade of the chase,
crowned with victory." But all the victory
she carries home is her own grief.
                    Now,
before Agave returns, let me leave
this scene of sorrow. Humility,
a sense of reverence before the sons of heaven—
of all the prizes that a mortal man might win,
these, I say, are wisest; these are best.
    [*Exit* MESSENGER.]
CHORUS: —We dance to the glory of Bacchus!
We dance to the death of Pentheus,
the death of the spawn of the dragon!
    He dressed in woman's dress;
    he took the lovely thyrsus;
    it waved him down to death,
        led by a bull to Hades.
Hail, Bacchae! Hail, women of Thebes!
Your victory is fair, fair the prize,
    this famous prize of grief!
Glorious the game! To fold your child
in your arms, streaming with his blood!
CORYPHAEUS: But look: there comes Pentheus' mother, Agave,
running wild-eyed toward the palace.
                    —Welcome,
welcome to the reveling band of the god of joy!

[*Enter* AGAVE *with other Bacchantes. She is covered with blood and carries the head of* PENTHEUS *impaled upon her thyrsus.*]

AGAVE: Bacchae of Asia—
CHORUS: Speak, speak.
AGAVE: We bring this branch to the palace,
   this fresh-cut spray from the mountains.
   Happy was the hunting.
CHORUS: I see.
   I welcome our fellow-reveler of god.
AGAVE: The whelp of a wild mountain lion,
   and snared by me without a noose.
   Look, look at the prize I bring.
CHORUS: Where was he caught?
AGAVE: On Cithaeron—
CHORUS: On Cithaeron?
AGAVE: Our prize was killed.
CHORUS: Who killed him?
AGAVE: I struck him first.
   The Maenads call me "Agave the blest."
CHORUS: And then?
AGAVE: Cadmus'—
CHORUS: Cadmus'?
AGAVE: Daughters.
   After me, they reached the prey.
   After me. Happy was the hunting.
CHORUS: Happy indeed.
AGAVE: Then share my glory,
   share the feast.
CHORUS: Share, unhappy woman?
AGAVE: See, the whelp is young and tender.
   Beneath the soft mane of its hair,
   the down is blooming on the cheeks.
CHORUS: With that mane he *looks* a beast.
AGAVE: Our god is wise. Cunningly, cleverly,
   Bacchus the hunter lashed the Maenads
   against his prey.
CHORUS: Our king is a hunter.
AGAVE: You praise me now?
CHORUS: I praise you.
AGAVE: The men of Thebes—
CHORUS: And Pentheus, your son?

AGAVE: Will praise his mother. She caught
a great quarry, this lion's cub.

Translated by William Arrowsmith

[*Cadmus, who meanwhile has collected the miserable remains of Pentheus' corpse, comes on stage and restores Agave to her senses. As she
realizes the full horror of what she has done, Dionysus appears, this time
not in human form but in divine glory, to pronounce sentence of exile
from Thebes on Agave and her sisters.*

*Plutarch tells the story of a spectacular performance of this play,
which took place some 250 years after its premiere, at the court of the
Parthian king Hyrodes in 53 B.C. His general Surena had just defeated an
invading Roman army; its commander Crassus, the third member of the
First Triumvirate together with Pompey and Caesar, had been killed in
the battle. Surena despatched a messenger carrying Crassus' head to
Hyrodes; he arrived toward the end of a performance of the Euripidean
play, "just before the entrance of Agave." The messenger threw the
head into the middle of the audience. The principal actor of the Greek
troupe on stage, one Jason of Tralles, seized up the head and, acting the
role of Agave, sang the lines: "We bring this branch to the palace / this
fresh-cut spray from the mountains . . ." The audience went wild.*]

From IPHIGENIA IN TAURIS

ORESTES RECOGNIZES IPHIGENIA

The Tauris *of the play's title is not the name of a country but of a
people—in* Tauris *in Latin means "among the Taurians." They were a
tribe living in what is now the Crimean Peninsula, who worshipped a
statue of the goddess Artemis, to whom they sacrificed all strangers who
arrived in their country. The priestess who, all unwilling, presided over
these sacrifices was Iphigenia, daughter of Agamemnon, king of Argos.
In Aeschylus'* Agamemnon *she was killed, but in this version of the
legend she was saved from the knife at the last moment by Artemis (who
had demanded her sacrifice in the first place) and spirited away to serve
as priestess of the goddess among the Taurians. What Agamemnon
actually sacrificed was a deer, but no one realized what had happened*

*and no one in Greece knows, at the time of this play, that Iphigenia is
still alive.*

*Her brother Orestes, an exile in penance for his murder of his mother,
is sent by Apollo to the Taurian land; he is to steal and bring back
to Greece the statue of Artemis and so put an end to the sacrificial cult.
He and his friend Pylades are captured and brought before Iphigenia.
She finds out that they are Greeks from Argos and offers to spare Orestes' life if he will take a letter there and deliver it to her family; his
companion Pylades will be sufficient sacrifice for the goddess. Orestes
refuses, insisting that Pylades should take the letter; he himself is ready
to die. Iphigenia goes inside to bring the letter. Her reentry is the beginning of one of the most skillfully engineered recognition scenes in Greek
tragedy.*

*After the recognition, it is Iphigenia who thinks of a plan to rescue
them all and take the statue back to Greece. She will persuade the
barbarian king Thoas that the statue has been polluted by the presence
of a matricide and must be purified by washing it in the sea. While all
the Taurians stand with eyes averted, she will carry the image down to
the shore where Orestes' ship is moored and off they will sail to Greece.
In the event they do launch the ship but then run aground, forced ashore
by a gigantic wave. Thoas and his men rush to capture them, but the
goddess Athena appears to order Thoas to let them go. What is more, he
is to let the chorus of captive Greek maidens go with them.*

IPHIGENIA: Here is my letter, safe within these folds.
But I have wondered. A man who has been in danger
When he comes out of it forgets his fears,
And sometimes he forgets his promises.
Might it not happen that your friend, intent
Upon his own concerns again, forget
How very much this letter means to me?
ORESTES: And what would you suggest, to ease your mind?
IPHIGENIA: His solemn vow to take this where I say.
ORESTES: And will you make a vow balancing his?
IPHIGENIA: To do what, or undo what?
ORESTES: To make sure
He be allowed to leave this deathly place.
IPHIGENIA: How could he keep his vow, unless he leave?
ORESTES: What makes you think the king will let him sail?
IPHIGENIA: I can persuade the king and will myself
Go to the ship and see your friend aboard.

ORESTES: Then word the vow as you would have him make it.
IPHIGENIA: You promise the delivery of my letter?
PYLADES: I promise the delivery of your letter.
IPHIGENIA: I promise you the king will let you leave.
PYLADES: In whose name do you swear?
IPHIGENIA: By Artemis,
   Here in Her Temple—and implore Her help.
PYLADES: And I by Zeus Himself, by Heaven's King.
IPHIGENIA: And what if you should fail to keep your word?
PYLADES: Then may I never again set eyes on Argos.
   And what if you should fail in keeping yours?
IPHIGENIA: Then may I never again set foot in Argos.
PYLADES: But we forget one possibility.
IPHIGENIA: Which might affect the keeping of your vow?
PYLADES: How could I keep my vow if this should happen—
   If we were wrecked by a storm, torn by a reef,
   If we were sunk and everything went down,
   And if my life were saved but not the letter.
   If that should happen, how could I keep my word?
IPHIGENIA: In any plan, two ways improve on one.
   So I will tell you, slowly, line by line,
   The contents of my letter, which, if need be,
   You are to tell my friend. Then he will know.
   For either you will place it in his hand
   And the written words will speak to him or else,
   If they are lost, your voice will be their echo.
PYLADES: That is a surer way, for both of us.
   So whom am I to find for you in Argos?
   What shall I say to him?
IPHIGENIA: Say this to him.
   Say to Orestes, son of Agamemnon,
   "A greeting comes from one you think is dead."
   Tell him, "Your sister is not dead at Aulis
   But is alive."
ORESTES: Alive? Iphigenia?
   Oh, no! Unless the dead come back again!
IPHIGENIA: You are looking at her now, for I am she.
   But let me finish what I ask of him.
   "O brother, come and save me from a life
   As priestess in a loathsome ritual—
   Save me from dying in this lonely land."
ORESTES: Where am I, Pylades? What am I hearing?

IPHIGENIA: "Lest memory of me should always haunt you."
The name, you must repeat it, is Orestes.
ORESTES: I hear a God!
IPHIGENIA: You hear only a woman.
ORESTES: I hear a woman—and I hear a God!
Let me hear more! I hear a miracle!
IPHIGENIA: Then tell him, "Artemis put out Her hand
And spared my life at Aulis, leaving a deer
To bleed instead." And tell him this, "My father,
Not looking when he struck, believed me dead.
Artemis brought me here." The letter ends.
PYLADES: No word was ever easier to keep!
Lady, keep yours or not, I keep mine now!
I give you this, Orestes, from your sister!
ORESTES: How can I look at letters! Let me look—
Oh let me stare at you whom I had lost!
Oh let me touch you with my hands and prove
That you are real and hold you close, close!

Translated by Witter Bynner

From THE TROJAN WOMEN

POSEIDON AND ATHENA

*The Prologue sets the stage for a series of harrowing scenes which show
us the fate of a conquered city, or rather of its women and children—for
all its men, as in the case of Melos, have been killed. Two great Olympian gods who were opposed, one favoring the Trojans, the other the
Achaeans, now unite to punish the victors as they make their way home.
Athena, who nursed a deadly hatred for Troy and helped the Achaeans
from the start, now turns on them because Ajax (not the great Ajax, son
of Telamon, but a lesser hero) has raped Priam's daughter Cassandra in
her temple, where the girl had taken refuge. "And the Achaeans," says
the goddess, "did nothing."*

*The play begins by telling us that the Achaeans' homecoming will be
disastrous and it also tells us why. The rest of the play shows us a series of
atrocities they inflict on the women and children of Troy, culminating in
the cold-blooded murder of Astyanax, Hector's infant son. But all this,*

*Euripides' ironic juxtaposition of the divine and human planes suggests,
has nothing to do with their punishment; the gods are concerned, not
with man's inhumanity to man but with their own worship, honor, and
prestige. Yet Poseidon's last words are a warning to all conquerors: "His
own turn must come."*

[*Enter* POSEIDON.]

POSEIDON: I am Poseidon. I come from the Aegean depths
of the sea beneath whose waters Nereid choirs evolve
the intricate bright circle of their dancing feet.
For since that day when Phoebus Apollo and I laid down
on Trojan soil the close of these stone walls, drawn true
and straight, there has always been affection in my heart
unfading, for these Phrygians and for their city;
which smolders now, fallen before the Argive spears,
ruined, sacked, gutted. Such is Athene's work, and his,
the Parnassian, Epeius of Phocis, architect
and builder of the horse that swarmed with inward steel,
that fatal bulk which passed within the battlements,
whose fame hereafter shall be loud among men unborn,
the Wooden Horse, which hid the secret spears within.
Now the gods' groves are desolate, their thrones of power
blood-spattered where beside the lift of the altar steps
of Zeus Defender, Priam was cut down and died.
The ships of the Achaeans load with spoils of Troy
now, the piled gold of Phrygia. And the men of Greece
who made this expedition and took the city, stay
only for the favoring stern-wind now to greet their wives
and children after ten years' harvests wasted here.

The will of Argive Hera and Athene won
its way against my will. Between them they broke Troy.
So I must leave my altars and great Ilium,
since once a city sinks into sad desolation
the gods' state sickens also, and their worship fades.
Scamander's valley echoes to the wail of slaves,
the captive women given to their masters now,
some to Arcadia or the men of Thessaly
assigned, or to the lords of Athens, Theseus' strain; .
while all the women of Troy yet unassigned are here

beneath the shelter of these walls, chosen to wait
the will of princes, and among them Tyndareus' child
Helen of Sparta, named—with right—a captive slave.

Nearby, beside the gates, for any to look upon
who has the heart, she lies face upward, Hecuba
weeping for multitudes her multitude of tears.
Polyxena, one daughter, even now was killed
in secrecy and pain beside Achilles' tomb.
Priam is gone, their children dead; one girl is left,
Cassandra, reeling crazed at King Apollo's stroke,
whom Agamemnon, in despite of the gods' will
and all religion, will lead by force to his secret bed.
O city, long ago a happy place, good-bye;
good-bye, hewn bastions. Pallas, child of Zeus, did this.
But for her hatred, you might stand strong-founded still.
        [ATHENE *enters.*]
ATHENE: August among the gods, O vast divinity,
    closest in kinship to the father of all, may one
    who quarreled with you in the past make peace, and speak?
POSEIDON: You may, lady Athene; for the strands of kinship
    close drawn work no weak magic to enchant the mind.
ATHENE: I thank you for your gentleness, and bring you now
    questions whose issue touches you and me, my lord.
POSEIDON: Is this the annunciation of some new word spoken
    by Zeus, or any other of the divinities?
ATHENE: No; but for Troy's sake, on whose ground we stand, I come
    to win the favor of your power, and an ally.
POSEIDON: You hated Troy once; did you throw your hate away
    and change to pity now its walls are black with fire?
ATHENE: Come back to the question. Will you take counsel with me
    and help me gladly in all that I would bring to pass?
POSEIDON: I will indeed; but tell me what you wish to do.
    Are you here for the Achaeans' or the Phrygians' sake?
ATHENE: For the Trojans, whom I hated this short time since,
    to make the Achaeans' homecoming a thing of sorrow.
POSEIDON: This is a springing change of sympathy. Why must
    you hate too hard, and love too hard, your loves and hates?
ATHENE: Did you not know they outraged my temple, and shamed me?
POSEIDON: I know that Ajax dragged Cassandra there by force.
ATHENE: And the Achaeans did nothing. They did not even speak.
POSEIDON: Yet Ilium was taken by your strength alone.

ATHENE: True, therefore help me. I would do some evil to them.
POSEIDON: I am ready for anything you ask. What will you do?
ATHENE: Make the home voyage a most unhappy coming home.
POSEIDON: While they stay here ashore, or out on the deep sea?
ATHENE: When they take ship from Ilium and set sail for home
Zeus will shower down his rainstorms and the weariless beat
of hail, to make black the bright air with roaring winds.
He has promised my hand the gift of the blazing thunderbolt
to dash and overwhelm with fire the Achaean ships.
Yours is your own domain, the Aegaean crossing. Make
the sea thunder to the tripled wave and spinning surf,
cram thick the hollow Euboean fold with floating dead;
so after this Greeks may learn how to use with fear
my sacred places, and respect all gods beside.
POSEIDON: This shall be done, and joyfully. It needs no long
discourse to tell you. I will shake the Aegaean Sea.
Myconos' nesses and the swine-back reefs of Delos,
the Capherean promontories, Scyros, Lemnos
shall take the washed up bodies of men drowned at sea.
Back to Olympus now, gather the thunderbolts
from your father's hands, then take your watcher's post, to wait
the chance, when the Achaean fleet puts out to sea.

That mortal who sacks fallen cities is a fool,
who gives the temples and the tombs, the hallowed places
of the dead to desolation. His own turn must come.

Translated by Richmond Lattimore

THE BURIAL OF ASTYANAX

*Talthybius, the Achaean herald, brings the corpse of Astyanax to
Hecuba, his grandmother, for burial. It is carried on the great shield of
his father Hector. The corpse is mangled; the child has been thrown
down from the high walls of Troy. Hecuba makes her funeral lament
over the body as she and the chorus of Trojan women wait for the
soldiers to come and take them to the ships, bound for Greece and
slavery.*

HECUBA: Lay down the circled shield of Hector on the ground:
a hateful thing to look at; it means no love to me.
[TALTHYBIUS *and his escort leave. Two soldiers wait.*]

Achaeans! All your strength is in your spears, not in
the mind. What were you afraid of, that it made you kill
this child so savagely? That Troy, which fell, might be
raised from the ground once more? Your strength meant nothing,
   then.
When Hector's spear was fortunate, and numberless
strong hands were there to help him, we were still destroyed.
Now when the city is fallen and the Phrygians slain,
this baby terrified you? I despise the fear
which is pure terror in a mind unreasoning.

O darling child, how wretched was this death. You might
have fallen fighting for your city, grown to man's
age, and married, and with the king's power like a god's,
and died happy, if there is any happiness here.
But no. You grew to where you could see and learn, my child,
yet your mind was not old enough to win advantage
of fortune. How wickedly, poor boy, your father's walls,
Apollo's handiwork, have crushed your pitiful head
tended and trimmed to ringlets by your mother's hand,
and the face she kissed once, where the brightness now is blood
shining through the torn bones—too horrible to say more.
O little hands, sweet likenesses of Hector's once,
now you lie broken at the wrists before my feet;
and mouth beloved whose words were once so confident,
you are dead; and all was false, when you would lean across
my bed, and say: "Mother, when you die I will cut
my long hair in your memory, and at your grave
bring companies of boys my age, to sing farewell."
It did not happen; now I, a homeless, childless, old
woman must bury your poor corpse, which is so young.
Alas for all the tendernesses, my nursing care,
and all your slumbers gone. What shall the poet say,
what words will he inscribe upon your monument?
Here lies a little child the Argives killed, because
they were afraid of him. That? The epitaph of Greek shame.
You will not win your father's heritage, except
for this, which is your coffin now: the brazen shield.

O shield, who guarded the strong shape of Hector's arm:
the bravest man of all, who wore you once, is dead.
How sweet the impression of his body on your sling,

and at thc true circle of your rim the stain of sweat
where in the grind of his many combats Hector leaned
his chin against you, and the drops fell from his brow!

Take up your work now; bring from what is left some robes
to wrap the tragic dead. The gods will not allow us
to do it right. But let him have what we can give.

That mortal is a fool who, prospering, thinks his life
has any strong foundation; since our fortune's course
of action is the reeling way a madman takes,
and no one person is ever happy all the time.
  [HECUBA's *handmaidens bring out from the shelter a basket of robes
  and ornaments. During the scene which follows, the body of*
  ASTYANAX *is being made ready for burial.*]
CHORUS: Here are your women, who bring you from the Trojan spoils
  such as is left, to deck the corpse for burial.
HECUBA: O child, it is not for victory in riding, won
  from boys your age, not archery—in which acts our people
  take pride, without driving competition to excess—
  that your sire's mother lays upon you now these treasures
  from what was yours before; though now the accursed of God,
  Helen, has robbed you, she who has destroyed as well
  the life in you, and brought to ruin all our house.
CHORUS: My heart,
  you touched my heart, you who were once
  a great lord in my city.
HECUBA: These Phrygian robes' magnificence you should have worn
  at your marriage to some princess uttermost in pride
  in all the East, I lay upon your body now.
  And you, once so victorious and mother of
  a thousand conquests, Hector's huge beloved shield:
  here is a wreath for you, who die not, yet are dead
  with this body; since it is better far to honor you
  than the armor of Odysseus the wicked and wise.
CHORUS: Ah me.
  Earth takes you, child;
  our tears of sorrow.
  Cry aloud, our mother.
HECUBA: Yes.
CHORUS: The dirge of the dead.
HECUBA: Ah me.

CHORUS: Evils never to be forgotten.
HECUBA: I will bind up your wounds with bandages, and be
  your healer: a wretched one, in name alone, no use.
  Among the dead your father will take care of you.
CHORUS: Rip, tear your faces with hands
  that beat like oars.
  Alas.
HECUBA: Dear women. . . .
CHORUS: Hecuba, speak to us. We are yours. What did you cry aloud?
HECUBA: The gods meant nothing except to make life hard for me,
  and of all cities they chose Troy to hate. In vain
  we sacrificed. And yet had not the very hand
  of God gripped and crushed this city deep in the ground,
  we should have disappeared in darkness, and not given
  a theme for music, and the songs of men to come.
  You may go now, and hide the dead in his poor tomb;
  he has those flowers that are the right of the underworld.
  I think it makes small difference to the dead, if they
  are buried in the tokens of luxury. All this
  is an empty glorification left for those who live.

Translated by Richmond Lattimore

From ION

TOURISTS AT DELPHI

Near the start of Ion, *a chorus of young Athenian women arrive—
accompanying their queen, Creusa—at Delphi, where her husband
wishes to consult the Oracle of Apollo about his childlessness and Creusa
secretly intends to ask Apollo about the fate of the child she bore him
many years ago and exposed on the Acropolis of Athens. The reactions
of the chorus to the temple art suggest that a suitable title for this
excerpt would be: "Tourists at Delphi." The young women excitedly
point out to each other the sculptural groups (or perhaps paintings) that
represent Heracles and the Hydra, his helper Iolaus, Bellerophon on the
winged horse Pegasus killing the Chimaera, and the Battle of the Gods
and Giants. Ion, the temple attendant who gives the ladies such unen-
thusiastic, official answers to their questions, will eventually be recognized—but only after a series of highly dramatic incidents—as Creusa's
long-lost son.*

CHORUS: Not only in holy Athens after all
  Are there courts of the gods
  With fair columns, and homage paid
  To Apollo who protects the streets.
  Here too on this temple
  Of Leto's son shows
  The bright-eyed beauty of twin façades.

  Look, look at this: Zeus' son
  Is killing the Lernaean Hydra
  With a golden sickle,
  Look there, my dear.

  Yes—and near him another is raising
  On high a flaming torch.
  Can it be he whose story I hear
  As I sit at my weaving,
  Iolaus the shield-bearer,
  Companion of Heracles,
  Whom he helped to endure his labors?

  And look at this one
  On a horse with wings.
  He is killing the mighty three-bodied
  Fire-breathing monster.

  My eyes dart everywhere.
  See! The battle of the giants
  On the marble walls.

  Yes we are looking.

  Can you see her, brandishing
  Her Gorgon shield against Enceladus—?

  I can see my goddess Pallas Athene.

  Oh! The terrible thunderbolt
  With fire at each end which Zeus holds
  Ready to throw.

  Yes I see. Raging Mimas
  Is burnt up in the flames.

And Bacchus, the boisterous god,
With unwarlike wand of ivy is killing
Another of Earth's giant sons.
[ION *enters through the central doors of the temple.*]
CHORUS LEADER: You there by the temple,
May we with naked feet
Pass into this sanctuary?
ION: You may not, strangers.
CHORUS LEADER: Perhaps you would tell me—?
ION: Tell me, what do you want?
CHORUS LEADER: Is it true that Apollo's temple
Really contains the world's center?
ION: Yes, wreathed in garlands, flanked by Gorgons.
CHORUS LEADER: That is the story we have heard.
ION: If you have offered sacrificial food
In front of the temple, and you have a question
For Apollo to answer, come to the altar steps.

But do not pass into the inner shrine
Unless you have slaughtered a sheep.
CHORUS LEADER: I understand.
We are not for transgressing Apollo's law.
The outside charms us enough.
ION: Look where you please at what is lawful.

Translated by Ronald Frederick Willetts

From ALCESTIS

FATHER AND SON

*Admetos, king of Thessaly, was fated to die young, but Apollo won for
him the privilege of living a full term if he could find someone to die for
him. He went to his aged parents, but they declined; only his wife
Alcestis loved him enough to give her life for his. Admetos' father Pheres
comes bringing gifts to honor Alcestis at the funeral ceremony, and
father and son proceed to revile each other in one of Euripides' most
painful and realistic scenes.*
*The scene perhaps has a more realistic base for us than it did for him.
For Euripides and his audience, the idea of dying in place of someone*

else was a fairy-tale motif, no more. *But modern techniques of organ transplants are bringing closer the day when parents may in fact face the possibility that they could give their own lives to save those of their children.*

LEADER: Wait, Admetos.
I see your father Pheres on his way, and servants with him
bringing gifts to offer to the gods below.
 [*Enter* PHERES *dressed in mourning black. His shorn hair is white
 and he is stooped with age; he walks slowly up the ramp to the bier
 of* ALCESTIS; ADMETOS *faces him on the other side of the bier.*]
PHERES: Son,
I have come to help you bear the burden of your grief.
You have lost a good wife: a decent, loving,
humble wife. A hard and bitter loss, but bear it
you must.
 [*He motions to his servants to come forward with the funeral gifts.*]
Accept these tokens of my respect,
and let her take them with her to the world below.
We must honor her in death as she deserves;
she gave her life to let you keep the light. No,
she would not let this poor old man drag out
his dying years deprived of all he had—his one,
his only, son. And by her bravery in death,
she has been a credit—no, a glory—to her sex.
 [*Formally addressing the body on the bier.*]
—Lady,
rest in peace.
By your courage you have been the savior of my son.
Your generosity restored the fortunes
of my broken house, when it was down. Alcestis,
fare you well, even in the world below.
And rest in peace.
                    —Mark my words, son.
Marriage is for most of us a losing proposition.
But this wife of yours was pure gold, and no mistake.
And gold is what I give her now.
 [*He signals to his servants to lay their gifts upon the bier, while
 ADMETOS angrily steps forward to intercept them.*]
ADMETOS: Who asked you to come? Who invited you?
Not I. Not her.

Love? *What* love? Your love's a lie: all words.
So keep your gold. She'll never wear your trinket
love.
She'll be buried as she is. Without your gifts.
Or you. Leave. Who needs you anyway?
Who needs you *now?*
You came, you say, to bring me sympathy and help.
The time for you to help was when I had to die
or find a substitute. Where were you *then?*
Vanished. Nowhere. Like your love. You disappeared
and let another take your place in death.
You were old, and she was young.
And now you have the gall to come here with your mock
sorrow and your hypocrisy of love!
You never gave a damn for me!
Where was your love when I needed you? Why,
for all you cared, I might have been some slave's bastard
smuggled in the house and set to suckle at the breast
of that barren bitch who calls herself my mother.

No, when courage was required,
when dying was the issue and the test,
you showed us what you really are.
Not my father, but a cheap coward!
Gods, is there any coward in this world like you?
There you were, a withered bag of bones, tottering
into eternity. But still you wouldn't die! Not you.
You didn't dare to die. So you let a woman,
no blood of yours, do your duty for you.
To her and her alone I owe the tenderness and love
I would have lavished on my parents in their age,
had they loved me like a son.
If I were you,
I would have fought—yes, *fought!*—for the privilege
of dying for my son. Besides,
your time was short. A few brief years at best.
So what had you to lose?
Every happiness a man could have, you had.
You inherited a kingdom when you were still a boy.
You had a son, so your succession was secure
and you could die in peace, knowing there would be
no rival claimants for your throne, no wars.
You cannot say that you abandoned me

because of my neglect: I showed you all the honor
a son could give. I was always good to you
in your old age. And how have you repaid my love?
You would have let me die.
Well, now your time is running out, old man.
So hurry. Use what little time you've got to breed
another son to care for you in your old age and stuff you
in the ground.
   [*Raising his hand.*]
                     So help me gods,
I will never lift a hand to bury you!
You refused to lift a finger for my life.
I disown you both.

If I still live and see the light,
everything I might have owed to you as son,
I pledge to her who gave me life.

Gods, how I hate them,
all these aging hypocrites, tottering around,
telling you how much they want to die,
stuffed with self-pity, whining about old age
and its indignities, their long, slow, crawling passage
to the grave.
But let them get the slightest glimpse of Death
and suddenly they stick like leeches to the light
and tell you life is not so bad.
LEADER: Stop it, both of you.
   Haven't you sorrows enough without this too?
                                        Boy,
why must you exasperate your father?
PHERES: Boy,
   who in god's name do you think you are?
   Are you my master now, and I some poor, bought,
   cringing Asiatic slave that you dare dress me down
   like this? I am a free man, Thessalian born,
   a prince of Thessaly. And I will not be bullied
   by the likes of you, arrogant boy.
      [ADMETOS *turns angrily away.*]
                              Hear me out.
   Don't think you'll pelt me, boy, with your abuse
   and then just turn your back.

Damn you, boy,
I made you lord and master of this house of mine.
I gave you life, I raised you.
I am not obliged to die for you as well.
Or do you think my father died for me?
There is no law, no precedent, in Greece
that children have a claim upon their fathers' lives.
A man is born to happiness, or otherwise.
He is born for himself.
Everything you had the right to get from me, you got.
I made you ruler of a rich and populous country.
And I intend to leave you all the vast domain
my father left to me.
So how have I hurt you? What *more* do I owe you?
Life?
No. You live yours, and I'll live mine.
Do your own dying. I'll do mine.
You love the light.
What makes you think your father doesn't love it too?
The time we spend beneath the earth, I think, is very long.
And life is short, but what there is of it is good,
good and sweet.
                        As for fighting, boy, you fought all right.
You fought like hell to live—life at any price!—
beyond your destined time. You only live
because you took her life. You *murdered* her.
And you dare talk about *my* cowardice—
you, who let a woman outdo you in bravery,
let her give her life to keep her gigolo
alive?
But you're clever, I admit.
Immortality is yours, yours for the asking.
All you have to do is wheedle your latest wife
into dying in your place.
And then, like the cheap coward that you are,
you accuse the rest of us of failing in our duty!
ADMETOS: Listen—
PHERES: You listen, boy. Remember this.
You love your life. Well, so does every man alive.
And if you call us names for that,
worse things will be said of you. They won't be pretty,
and they'll all be true.

LEADER: There have been too many ugly words, too much abuse,
  already.
          —Old man, stop provoking your son.
ADMETOS: Let him talk, and then I'll have my say.
                                            —You see?
  The truth hurts. Your cowardice was your mistake.
  You didn't dare to die.
PHERES: That was no mistake.
  The mistake would have been dying for you.
ADMETOS: And dying young is just the same as dying old?
PHERES: One life is all we have. Not two.
ADMETOS: The way you clutch at that one life of yours,
  you'll outlive Zeus.
PHERES: How have I hurt you
  that you should hate me so?
ADMETOS: Old age
  has made you greedy. Greedy to live!
PHERES: Greedy, am I?
  Who killed that girl whose corpse you're burying?
  And you talk to me of greed!
ADMETOS: It was your cowardice that killed her.
PHERES: You took her life. You killed her.
ADMETOS: O gods, I hope
  I live to see the day when you come crawling to me
  for help!
PHERES: That's your style, not mine.
  Find some woman to help you live. Marry her,
  then let her die.
ADMETOS: Your fault. You wouldn't die.
PHERES: No, I wouldn't.
  This god's light is sweet, I tell you, sweet.
ADMETOS: You cheap coward, you don't deserve to live!
PHERES: Go bury your dead.
  Whether you like it or not, *I'm* still alive.
  You won't gloat over my dead body. Not today,
  boy.
ADMETOS: Don't expect the world to praise you when you die—
  if you ever do.
PHERES: What the hell do I care what people say of me
  after I'm dead?
ADMETOS: Gods,
  what shabby, shameless cowards these old men are!

PHERES: *She* wasn't shabby, was she? No, she was brave.
   Brave enough—stupid enough—to die for you.
ADMETOS: Leave. Let me bury my dead.
PHERES: I'm leaving.
   Let the murderer bury his victim in peace.
   [*Exit* PHERES, *followed by his servants with the rejected gifts.*]
ADMETOS: Go and be damned to you,
   you and that woman I used to call my mother.
   You have no son.
   Grow old, both of you, as you deserve—
   childless, heirless, alone.
   Never let me see you in this house again.
   So help me god,
   if I had heralds here to proclaim
   that I disown you both and ban you from my house,
   I'd do it.

                                    Translated by William Arrowsmith

From ELECTRA

BROTHER AND SISTER

As in Aeschylus' The Libation Bearers, *the corpses of Aegisthus and Clytemnestra are brought out of the house and laid on the steps. But whereas in Aeschylus Orestes alone follows, to stand over them and speak, here brother and sister come, not to speak but to sing—the lyric meters mark their highly emotional state. And unlike Orestes, they make no attempt to justify their action.*

The whole play is a deliberate contrast with what had become the classic Aeschylean original. Aegisthus is cut down treacherously at a ceremony of sacrifice; his body is brought on stage and Electra makes a speech over it, hurling at it all the reproaches and insults, which, as she tells us, she had rehearsed often in the night when Aegisthus was alive. When she proceeds to plan the murder of Clytemnestra, Orestes balks. This time it is not Pylades but Electra who stiffens his resolve. She has lured Clytemnestra into the trap with a false report of her pregnancy by the farmer Aegisthus has forced her to marry. Her mother, once arrived, turns out not to be the demonic creature of the Aeschylean trilogy, but a woman who listens patiently to her daughter's reproaches and can even admit that she was wrong. And now brother and sister face the full horror of what they have just done.

CHORUS: Behold them coming from the house in robes of blood
   newly stained by a murdered mother, walking straight,
   living signs of triumph over her frightful cries.
   There is no house, nor has there been, more suffering
   or more at war than this, the house of Tantalus.
ORESTES: O Earth and Zeus who watch all work
   men do, look at this work of blood
   and corruption, two bodies in death
   lying battered along the dirt
   under my hands, only to pay
   for my pain.
ELECTRA: Weep greatly for me, my brother, I am guilty.
   A girl flaming in hurt I marched against
      the mother who bore me.
CHORUS: Weep for destiny; destiny yours
   to mother unforgettable wrath,
   to suffer unforgettable pain
   beyond pain at your children's hands.
   You paid for their father's death as the law asks.
ORESTES: Phoebus, you hymned the law in black
   melody, but the deed has shone
   white as a scar. You granted us rest
   as murderers rest—to leave the land
   of Greece. But where else can I go?
   What state, host, god-fearing man
   will look steady upon my face,
      who killed my mother?
ELECTRA: O weep for me. Where am I now? What dance—
   what wedding may I come to? What man will take
      me bride to his bed?
CHORUS: Circling, circling, your wilful mind
   veers in the blowing wind and turns;
   you think piously now, but then
   thoughtless you wrought an impious thing,
   dear girl, when your brother's will was against you.
ORESTES: You saw her agony, how she threw aside her dress,

how she was showing her breast there in the midst of death?
   My god, how she bent to earth
the legs which I was born through? and her hair—I touched it—
CHORUS: I know, I understand; you have come
   through grinding torment hearing her cry
   so hurt, your own mother.
ORESTES: She cracked into a scream then, she stretched up her hand
   toward my face: "My son! Oh, be pitiful my son!"
   She clung to my face,
   suspended, hanging; my arm dropped with the sword—
CHORUS: Unhappy woman—how could your eyes
   bear to watch her blood as she fought
   for her breath and died there?
ORESTES: I snatched a fold of my cloak to hood my eyes, and, blind,
   took the sword and sacrificed
   my mother—sank steel to her neck.
ELECTRA: I urged you on, I urged you on,
   I touched the sword beside your hand.
CHORUS: Working a terrible pain and ruin.
ORESTES: Take it! shroud my mother's dead flesh in my cloak,
   clean and close the sucking wounds.
   You carried your own death in your womb.
ELECTRA: Behold! I wrap her close in the robe,
   the one I loved and could not love.
CHORUS: Ending your family's great disasters.

Translated by Emily Townsend Vermeule

From HECUBA

TROY'S LAST NIGHT

The chorus of captive Trojan women in Hecuba, *another play about the
victims of the Trojan War, sing of their memory of the night Troy fell to
the invaders.*

O Ilium! O my country,
whose name men speak no more
among unfallen cities!
So dense a cloud of Greeks

came, spear on spear, destroying!
Your crown of towers shorn away,
and everywhere the staining fire,
most pitiful. O Ilium,
whose ways I shall not walk again!

At midnight came my doom.
Midnight when the feast is done
and sleep falls sweetly on the eyes.
The songs and sacrifice,
the dances, all were done.
My husband lay asleep,
his spear upon the wall,
forgetting for a while
the ships drawn up on Ilium's shore.

I was setting my hair
in the soft folds of the net,
gazing at the endless light
deep in the golden mirror,
preparing myself for bed,
when tumult broke the air
and shouts and cries
shattered the empty streets:—
Onward, onward, you Greeks!
Sack the city of Troy
and see your homes once more!

Dressed only in a gown
like a girl of Sparta,
I left the bed of love
and prayed to Artemis.
But no answer came.
I saw my husband lying dead,
and they took me over sea.
Backward I looked at Troy,
but the ship sped on
and Ilium slipped away,
and I was dumb with grief.

A curse on Helen,
sister of the sons of Zeus,

and my curse on him,
disastrous Paris
whose wedding wasted Troy!
O adulterous marriage!
Helen, fury of ruin!
Let the wind blow
and never bring her home!
Let there be no landing
for Helen of Troy!

Translated by William Arrowsmith

ARISTOPHANES

455?–c. 385 B.C.

From THE CLOUDS

Eleven complete plays of the comic poet Aristophanes have come down to us. The Clouds, produced in 423 B.C., was awarded third prize for comedy in the festival of Dionysus. Aristophanes was much put out by this rejection of what he regarded as his finest play so far. We know this because in the text we have (which is a much revised second edition of the 423 original), he addresses the audience on the subject. "Firmly convinced," he says, through the chorus leader, his spokesman, "that this play The Clouds *was the finest of my comedies to date, / I submitted an earlier version, expecting your pleasure and approval. / It cost me enormous anguish and and labor, and yet I was forced to withdraw, / ignobly defeated by cheap and vulgar rivals . . ." Evidently Aristophanes considered, rightly or wrongly, that his* Clouds *was intellectually a cut above the low comic capers of his rivals. And it is true that the play did tackle, in broad comic style, a serious theme—the higher education offered to Athenians who could pay for it by the so-called "Sophists," who claimed to prepare men for civic life in a democracy by training them in the art of public speaking and also the general curriculum we know as the liberal arts.*

In the play, Strepsiades, a solid Athenian farmer who has married above his station, has a son, Pheidippides, who frequents aristocratic circles, raises and trains racehorses, and has saddled his father with enormous debts in the process. The old man sees only one way to avoid ruin from the lawsuits for non-payment that now threaten him—to send his son to the "Thinkery" run by Socrates, where they teach you, for a fee, not only modern secular humanism but also the technique of winning lawsuits even when you are manifestly in the wrong.

This is of course a gross misrepresentation of Socrates, who did not offer courses in rhetoric or in anything else, who took no fees, and who was philosophically an opponent of the Sophists (who did make a fortune by teaching rhetorical skills and much else besides). But the great Sophists—Protagoras, Prodicus, Hippias, Gorgias, and the rest—were, so to speak, visiting professors, foreigners who came to Athens for a while and then moved on to fresh markets. Socrates was very much a homebody, leaving Athens only when obliged to do so on military service. And he had infuriated many of his fellow citizens by his apparently simple-minded questions, which always led to the revelation that his interlocutor had no idea whatsoever of the meaning of the fine words—justice, piety, courage—that he had been using. Socrates described himself as the gadfly on the lazy Athenian horse; it was not a recipe for widespread popularity. So he was fair game for a comic poet who needed a figure of fun to represent the intellectual fashions of the younger generation. And his poverty, his ugliness of feature, and his habit of going barefoot were all extra grist for the Aristophanic comic mill.

STREPSIADES' INITIATION

Pheidippides refuses indignantly to have anything to do with Socrates and the Thinkery, so Strepsiades presents himself to Socrates as an applicant for training. He is introduced to the Clouds, patron goddesses of "chiropractors, prophets, longhairs, quacks, fops, charlatans, / fairies, dithyrambic poets, scientists, dandies, astrologers" and other people who "walk with their heads in the clouds." The Clouds are the chorus of the play. (In this translation, the chorus leader is given his Greek name— Koryphaios.)

STREPSIADES: Welcome then, august Ladies!
    Welcome, queens of heaven!
            If ever you spoke to mortal man,

I implore you, speak to me!

[*A great burst of thunder.* STREPSIADES *cowers with fright.*]

KORYPHAIOS: Hail, superannuated man!
Hail, old birddog of culture!

[*To* SOKRATES.]

                          And hail to you, O Sokrates,
high priest of poppycock!

                          Inform us what your wishes are.
For of all the polymaths on earth, it's you we most prefer—
you and Prodikos. Him we love for wisdom's sake, but you, sir,
for your swivel-eyes, your barefoot swagger down the street,
because you're poor on our account and terribly affected.

STREPSIADES: Name of Earth, what a voice! Solemn and holy and
    awful!

SOKRATES: These are the only gods there are. The rest are but figments.

STREPSIADES: Holy name of Earth! Olympian Zeus is a figment?

SOKRATES: Zeus?
                          What Zeus?
                          Nonsense.
                          There is no Zeus.

STREPSIADES: No Zeus?
Then *who* makes it rain? Answer me that.

SOKRATES: Why, the Clouds,
    of course.
                          What's more, the proof is incontrovertible.
                          For instance,
have you ever yet seen rain when you didn't see a cloud?
But if your hypothesis were correct, Zeus could drizzle from an
    empty sky
while the clouds were on vacation.

STREPSIADES: By Apollo, you're right. A pretty
    proof.
And to think I always used to believe the rain was just Zeus
pissing through a sieve.
                          All right, *who* makes it thunder?
Brrr. I get goosebumps just saying it.

SOKRATES: The Clouds again,
    of course. A simple process of Convection.

STREPSIADES: I admire you,
    but I don't follow you.

SOKRATES: Listen. The Clouds are a saturate
    water-solution.

Tumescence in motion, of necessity, produces precipitation.
When these distended masses collide—*boom*!
                                        Fulmination.
STREPSIADES: But who makes them move before they collide? Isn't that
    Zeus?
SOKRATES: Not Zeus, idiot. The Convection-principle!
STREPSIADES: Convection?
    That's a new one.
Just think. So Zeus is out and convection-principle's in.
Tch, tch.
                    But wait: you haven't told me who makes it thunder.
SOKRATES: But I just *finished* telling you! The Clouds are
    water-packed;
they collide with each other and explode because of the pressure.
STREPSIADES: Yeah?
And what's your proof for *that*?
SOKRATES: Why, take yourself as example.
You know that meat-stew the vendors sell at the Panathenaia?
How it gives you the cramps and your stomach starts to rumble?
STREPSIADES: By Apollo! I remember. What an awful feeling! You feel
    sick
and your belly churns and the fart rips loose like thunder.
First just a gurgle, *pappapax;* then louder, *pappaPAPAXapaX,*
and finally like thunder, *PAPAPAPAXAPAXAPPAPAXapap!*
SOKRATES: Precisely.
First think of the tiny fart that your intestines make.
Then consider the heavens: their infinite farting is thunder.
For thunder and farting are, in principle, one and the same.
STREPSIADES: Then where does lightning come from? And when it
    strikes
why is it that some men are killed and others aren't even touched.
Clearly it's *got* to be Zeus. He's behind it, blasting the liars
with bolts of lightning.
SOKRATES: Look, you idiotic Stone-Age relic,
if Zeus strikes the liars with lightning, then why on earth
is a man like Simon still alive? Or Kleonymos? Or Theoros?
They're liars ten times over.
                            But no. Instead of doing that,
he shatters his own shrines, blasts the holiest place names
in Homer and splinters the great oaks. And why, I ask you
Have you ever heard of an oak tree committing perjury?
STREPSIADES: Say,

you know, you've got something there. But how do you explain
the lightning?

SOKRATES: Attend.

[*Illustrating his lecture by means of the potbellied-stove Model of
the Universe.*]

                              Let us hypothesize a current of arid air
ascending heavenwards. Now then, as this funnelled flatus
slowly invades the limp and dropsical sacks of the Clouds,
they, in turn, begin to belly and swell, distended with gas
like a child's balloon when inflated with air. Then, so prodigious
become the pressures within that the cloud-casings burst apart,
exploding with that celestial ratatat called thunder and therein
     releasing
the winds. These, in turn, whizz out at such incalculable velocities
that they catch on fire.

                              Result: lightning.

STREPSIADES: The very same thing that
     happened to me
at the great feast of Zeus!

                              I was roasting myself a sausage
and forgot to slit the skin. Well, suddenly it bloated up
and SPLAT!

                    —singed my eyebrows off and splattered my face with
     guts.

CHORUS: —Ah, how he hungers after learning!

     [*To* STREPSIADES.]

                              —Sir, if you can pass
     our test,
we guarantee that you shall be

                              —the cynosure of Hellas.

—Our requirements are these:

                              —First, is your memory keen?

—Do you hanker for researching?

                              —Are you subject to fatigue
from standing up or walking?

                              —Does winter weather daunt you?

—Can you go without a meal?

                              —Abstain from wine and exercise?

—And keep away from girls?

                              —Last, do you solemnly swear
adherence to our code?

                    —*To wrangle*
                        —*niggle*
                            —*haggle*
                                —*battle*
—*a loyal soldier of the Tongue, conducting yourself always
like a true philosopher.*
STREPSIADES: Ladies, if all you require
is hard work, insomnia, worry, endurance, and a stomach
that eats anything, why, have no fear. For I'm your man
and as hard as nails.
SOKRATES: And you promise to follow faithfully in my path,
acknowledging no other gods but mine, to wit, the Trinity—
GREAT CHAOS, THE CLOUDS, and BAMBOOZLE?
STREPSIADES: If I met another god,
I'd cut him dead, so help me. Here and now I swear off
sacrifice and prayer forever.
KORYPHAIOS: Then, Sir, inform us boldly
what you wish. Providing you honor and revere the Clouds
and faithfully pursue the Philosophical Life, you shall not fail.
STREPSIADES: Ladies, I'll tell you.
                    My ambition is modest, a trifling
        favor.
Just let my muscular tongue outrace the whole of Hellas
by a hundred laps.
KORYPHAIOS: Sir, you may consider your wishes granted.
Never, from this time forth, shall any politician in Athens
introduce more bills than you.
STREPSIADES: *But I don't want to be a Senator!*
Listen, ladies: all I want is to escape the clutches
of my creditors.
KORYPHAIOS: Your wishes are modest; we grant them.
And now, Candidate, boldly commit yourself to the hands
of our ministers.
STREPSIADES: Ladies, you've convinced me completely. Anyway,
        thanks to my thoroughbreds, my son, and my wife, I have no
        choice.

            So I hereby bequeath you my body,
                for better, dear girls, or worse.
            You can shrink me by slow starvation;
                or shrivel me dry with thirst.

You can freeze me or flay me skinless;
  thrash me as hard as you please.
Do any damn thing you've a mind to—
  my only conditions are these:

that when the ordeal is completed,
  a new Strepsiades rise,
renowned to the world as a WELSHER,
  famed as a TELLER OF LIES,

a CHEATER,
            a BASTARD,
                    a PHONEY,
                            a BUM,
SHYSTER,
        MOUTHPIECE,
                TINHORN,
                        SCUM,
STOOLIE,
        CON-MAN,
                WINDBAG,
                        PUNK,
OILY,
     GREASY,
            HYPOCRITE,
                    SKUNK,
DUNGHILL,
        SQUEALER,
                SLIPPERY SAM,
FAKER,
     DIDDLER,
            SWINDLER,
                    SHAM,
—or just plain Lickspittle.

And then, dear ladies, for all I care,
  Science can have the body,
to experiment, as it sees fit,
  or serve me up as salami.

Yes, you can serve me up as salami!

                         Translated by William Arrowsmith

PHEIDIPPIDES WINS THE ARGUMENT

Strepsiades is taken in hand by Socrates, but is so inept a pupil that he is finally flunked and thrown out of the Thinkery. The Clouds suggest that he enroll his son, and he eventually drags Pheidippides, protesting vigorously, to the Thinkery and hands him over to Socrates for training. Pheidippides emerges as a graduate magna cum laude, *with what his overjoyed father calls a "negative and disputatious look." Tutored by his son, Strepsiades baffles the creditors who have come for their money with sophistical distinctions and philosophical pseudo-scientific analogies and drives them away. But at the banquet he puts on to celebrate his success, he runs into trouble. He comes on stage pursued by Pheidippides, who is beating him with a stick. His protests are met with a claim that a son has a right to beat his father; what is more, Pheidippides offers to give a "logical demonstration" of the rightness of his case. The Clouds ask Strepsiades to explain what happened. Following old Athenian custom, he says, he had called on the young man to sing, suggesting a famous old song of Simonides. But his son denounced the old custom as obsolete—"strictly for grandmothers . . ."*

PHEIDIPPIDES: You damn well got what you deserved.
Asking me to sing on an empty stomach! What is this anyway?
A banquet or a cricket-concert?
STREPSIADES: You hear that?
A cricket-concert!
His exact words.
And then he started sneering at Simonides!
Called him—get this—Puny Pipsqueak Hack!
Was I *sore?*
Brother!
Well, somehow I counted to ten, and then I asked him
to sing me some Aischylos.
Please.
And you know what he replied?
That he considered Aischylos "a poet of colossal stature."—
Yup,
"the most colossal, pretentious, pompous, spouting, bombastic bore
in poetic history."
I was so damn mad I just about went through the
roof.

But I gritted my teeth together, mustered up a sick smile
and somehow managed to say, "All right, son, if that's how you feel,
then sing me a passage from one of those highbrow modern plays
you're so crazy about."
                              So he recited—you can guess—Euripides!
One of those slimy tragedies where, so help me, there's a brother
who screws his own sister!
                              Well, Ladies, *that* did it!
                                             I jumped up,
blind with rage, started cursing at him and calling him names,
and he started screaming and cursing back and before I knew it,
he hauled off and—*wham!*—he biffed me and bashed me and
    clipped me
and poked me and choked me and—
PHEIDIPPIDES: And, by god, you had it coming!
Knocking a genius like Euripides!
STREPSIADES: Euripides!
                                    A GENIUS??
                                             That . . .
That . . . that . . . !
    [PHEIDIPPIDES *raises his stick threateningly.*]
                    HALP! He's hitting me!
PHEIDIPPIDES: You've got it coming,
    Dad!
STREPSIADES: *Got it coming,* do I?
                              Why, you ungrateful brat, I *raised*
    you!
When you were a baby I pampered you! I waited on you hand and
    foot!
I understood your babytalk. You babbled GOO and I obeyed. Why,
when you whimpered WAWA DADA, who brought your water?
    DADA did.
When you burbled BABA, who brought your Baby Biscuits?
    DADA did.
And when you cried GOTTA GO KAKA DADA, who saved his
    shitty darling?
Who rushed you to the door? Who held you while you did it? Damn
    you,
    DADA did!
                    And in return you choked me.
                    and when I shat in terror,
                    would you give your Dad a hand,

would you help me to the door?
No, you left me there alone
to do it on the floor!

Yes, to do it on the floor!
CHORUS: YOUR ATTENTION, PLEASE!
Pheidippides
now makes his demonstration—

a proof which will,
I'm certain, thrill
the younger generation.

For if this lad
defeats his Dad,
there's not an older man

or father in
this town, whose skin
is worth a Tinker's Damn!
KORYPHAIOS: And now that Doughty Champion of Change, that
Golden-Tongued Attorney
for Tomorrow, that Harbinger of Progress
—PHEIDIPPIDES!
[*To* PHEIDIPPIDES.]
Remember, Sir,
we want the truth
—or a reasonable facsimile.
PHEIDIPPIDES: Gentlemen, Eloquence
is sweet, sweeter than I ever dreamed! This utter bliss of speech!
This rapture of articulation! But oh, the sheer Attic honey
of subverting the Established Moral Order!
And yet when I look back
on those benighted days of pre-Sokratic folly, upon the boy
I used to be, whose only hobby was horses, who could not speak
three words of Greek without a blunder, why . . .
words fail me.
But *now*, now that Sokrates has made a fresh Pheidippides of me,
now that my daily diet is Philosophy, Profundity, Subtlety,
and Science, I propose to prove beyond the shadow of a doubt
the philosophical propriety of beating my Father.
STREPSIADES: For the love of Zeus,

go back to your damn horses! I'd rather be stuck with a stable
than be battered by a stick.

PHEIDIPPIDES: I ignore these childish interruptions
and proceed with my demonstration.

Now then, answer my question:
did you lick me when I was a little boy?

STREPSIADES: Of course I licked you.
For your own damn good. Because I loved you.

PHEIDIPPIDES: Then *ipso facto,*
since you yourself admit that loving and lickings are synonymous,
it's only fair that I—for your own damn good, you understand?—
whip you in return.

In any case, by what right do you whip me
but claim exemption for yourself?

What do you think I am? A slave?
Wasn't I born as free a man as you?

Well?

STREPSIADES: But . . .

PHEIDIPPIDES: But what?
Spare the Rod and Spoil the Child?

Is that your argument?

If so,
then I can be sententious too. *Old Men Are Boys Writ Big,*
as the saying goes.

A fortiori then, old men logically deserve
to be beaten more, since at their age they have clearly less excuse
for the mischief that they do.

STREPSIADES: But it's unnatural! It's . . . *illegal!*
Honor your father and mother.

That's the law.

Everywhere.

PHEIDIPPIDES: The *law?*
And who made the law?

An ordinary man. A man like you or me.
A man who lobbied for his bill until he persuaded the people
to make it law.

By the same token then, what prevents me now
from proposing new legislation granting sons the power to inflict
corporal punishment upon wayward fathers?

Nothing vindictive,
of course.

In fact, I would personally insist on adding a rider,
a Retroactive Amnesty for Fathers, waiving our right to
  compensation
for any whippings we received prior to the passage of the new law.
However, if you're still unconvinced, look to Nature for a sanction.
Observe the roosters, for instance, and what do you see?
                                                        A society
whose pecking-order envisages a permanent state of open warfare
between fathers and sons. And how do roosters differ from men,
except for the trifling fact that human society is based upon law
and rooster society isn't?

STREPSIADES: Look, if you want to imitate the roosters,
why don't you go eat shit and sleep on a perch at night?

PHEIDIPPIDES: Why? Er . . .
because the analogy doesn't hold, that's why. If you don't believe
  me,
then go ask Sokrates.

STREPSIADES: Well, whatever your roosters happen to do,
you'd better not lick me. It's your neck if you do.

PHEIDIPPIDES: *My* neck?
How so?

STREPSIADES: Because look: I lick you. All right, someday you'll have a
  son
and you can even the score with me by licking the hell out of him.
But if you lick me, then your son will follow your precedent
by licking you. If you have a son.

PHEIDIPPIDES: And if I don't have a son?
You've licked me, but where am I? I'm left holding the bag,
and you'll go to your grave laughing at me.
    [*There is a long tense silence as the full force of this crushing
    argument takes its effect upon* STREPSIADES.]

STREPSIADES: What?
                                    But how . . . ?
                                                Hmm,
by god, you're right!
    [*To the audience.*]
                      —Speaking for the older generation, gentlemen,
I'm compelled to admit defeat. The kids have proved their point:
naughty fathers should be flogged.

PHEIDIPPIDES: Of course, I nearly forgot.
One final matter.

STREPSIADES: The funeral?
PHEIDIPPIDES: Far from it. In fact,
it may even soothe your feelings.
STREPSIADES: How to be licked and like it, eh?
Go on. I'm listening.
PHEIDIPPIDES: Well now, Misery Loves Company, they say.
So I'll give you some company:
                I'll horsewhip Mother.
STREPSIADES: You'll
    WHAT???
    HORSEWHIP YOUR OWN MOTHER?
                But this is worse! Ten
        thousand times worse!
PHEIDIPPIDES: Is that so? And suppose I prove by Sokratic logic the
    utter propriety
of horsewhipping Mother?
                What would you say to that?
STREPSIADES: What would
    I *say?*
                By god, if you prove *that,*
                then for all I care, you heel,
                you can take your stinking Logics
                and your Thinkery as well
                with Sokrates inside it
                and damn well go to hell!

                Translated by William Arrowsmith

From THE FROGS

SONG OF THE FROGS

The Frogs *was first performed in 405 B.C. Sophocles and Euripides had died the previous year. In the play, Dionysus, the patron god of the theater, disgusted with the tragic poets who remain alive, decides to go down to Hades and bring back Euripides, his favorite poet. He has to cross a lake on the boat steered by Charon, the ferryman of the dead.*

The second stanza of the choral song refers to the ceremonies of the Anthesteria, celebrated in February at the precinct of Dionysus in the Marshes. Barrels of the new wine were opened on the first day and on

*the second a great deal of it was drunk in contests to see who could drink
the most. As a result, many of the participants in the ceremonies of the
last day (called "Pots" because lttle pots full of cereal were offered to the
dead) had a bad hangover.*

[DIONYSOS *climbs, awkwardly, into the boat.*]
CHARON: You, sit to your oar.
  [DIONYSOS *sits on his oar.*]
                       Anyone else going? Hurry it up.
  [*A few extras (the ones who carried the corpse) get into the boat,
  each taking an oar.*]
  Hey, *you* there. What d'you think you're doing?
DIONYSOS: [*With dignity.*]   *I* am sitting
  to my oar. Exactly what you told me to do.
CHARON: [*Rearranging him.*] Well, sit *here*, fatso. Sit like this. Got it?
DIONYSOS: Okay.
CHARON: Now get your hands away and bring them back.
DIONYSOS: Okay.
CHARON: Stop being such an ass, will you? Bring your weight forward.
  Get your back into it.
DIONYSOS: What do you want? I never rowed before.
  I'm no Old Navy Man. I didn't make the First Crew.
  How'm I supposed to row?
CHARON: Easily. Just begin to do it,
  and you'll get a pretty song to give you the time.
DIONYSOS: Who's singing?
CHARON: It's a swan song, but the swans are lovely frogs.
DIONYSOS: Go ahead.
  Give me the stroke.
CHARON: OO-pah, oo-pah.
  [*If he cares to,* CHARON *can go on doing this all during the
  following chorus.*]
  [*The* CHORUS *appears, in green masks and tights, as Frogs. They
  are Frogs only in this rowing-scene. They dance around the boat.*]
CHORUS: Brekekekex ko-ax ko-ax,
  Brekekekex ko-ax ko-ax,
  children of freshwater ponds and springs,
  gather we all together now
  and swell our lofty well-becroaken chorus,
  ko-ax ko-ax

Dionysos' Nysos-song
we sing to the son of Zeus,
Dionysos-in-the-marshes,
when with morning-frog-in-the-throat
the hangover-haggard procession
staggers to the holy Pot-Feast through my dominion,
brekekekex ko-ax ko-ax.
DIONYSOS: I think that I'm beginning to fail,
I'm raising blisters on my tail,
ko-ax ko-ax, I think I am,
but possibly you don't care a damn.
CHORUS: Brekekekex ko-ax ko-ax.
DIONYSOS: I can't hear anything but ko-ax,
go 'way, I'd like to give you the axe.
CHORUS: Of course, you fool, you can't hear anything else,
for the sweet Muses have gifted me with their lyres,
and Pan the horned walker, voice of reed in the woods,
and lyric Apollo himself goes glad for my singing
when with the music of piping my lyrical
song is heard in the pondy waters.
Brekekekex ko-ax ko-ax.
DIONYSOS: My bloody blisters refuse to heal.
My anguished bottom's beginning to squeal.
When I bend over it joins the attack.
CHORUS: Brekekekex ko-ax ko-ax.
DIONYSOS: Oh ah ye songful tribe, will you
shut up?
CHORUS: Exactly what we won't do.
Longer stronger
sing in the sunny daytime
as we wriggle and dive in the marsh-
flowers blithe on the lily pads
and dive and duck as we sing,
and when Zeus makes it rain
in green escape to the deep
water our song still pulses
and bubbles up from below.
DIONYSOS: Brepepepeps ko-aps ko-aps
I'm picking the rhythm up from you chaps.
CHORUS: We're sorry for us if *you* join in.
DIONYSOS: I'm sorry for *me* if I begin
to split in two from bottom to chin.

CHORUS: Brekekekcx ko-ax ko-ax.
DIONYSOS: And the hell with you. I don't *care* what you do.
CHORUS: Whatever you say we'll croak all day
  as long as we're stout
  and our throats hold out.
DIONYSOS: Brekekekex ko-ax ko-ax.
  There, I can do it better than you.
CHORUS: No, *we* can do it better than *you.*
DIONYSOS: No, *I* can do it better than *you.*
  I'll croak away
  if it takes all day,
  brekekekex ko-ax ko-ax,
  and I'll croak you down in the grand climax
  brekekekex ko-ax ko-ax.
  [*Frogs slink away. Silence.*]
  Ha ha. I knew I could beat you. You and your ko-ax!

Translated by Richmond Lattimore

AESCHYLUS AND EURIPIDES

Dionysus arrives in Hades to find the place in an uproar. Ever since he arrived Aeschylus has held the place of honor at the table of Pluto, the ruler of the Underworld. But Euripides no sooner appears on the scene than he begins claiming the place for himself, as the better tragic poet. The two of them are just about to state their case and criticize each other; what better judge of the contest than Dionysus in person?

At the end of the contest, Dionysus awards the place of honor to Aeschylus, and also decides that it is Aeschylus, not Euripides, that he will take back to Athens with him.

In the long and hilarious literary duel, some of the allusions that were instantly intelligible to the original audience need a word of explanation. Phrynichus was one of the earliest tragic poets, a contemporary of Thespis; Euripides cites him as hopelessly old-fashioned. The "roosterhorse" that so puzzled Dionysus was an emblem painted on war galleys, a winged horse with the tail of a fighting cock. Eryxis and Piloxenos are just names to us, but no doubt Aristophanes' audience caught the joke. Cephisophon was an Athenian living in Euripides' house; elsewhere Aristophanes suggests (1) that he helped write Euripides' plays; and (2) that he was the lover of Euripides' wife. Dionysus' reaction to Euripides' claim that he made tragedy more democratic is addressed, in our transla-

tion, to Aeschylus; others have thought it aimed at Euripides, who had aristocratic friends. Manes and Megainetos we know nothing about, but Phormisios was a right-wing politician, and Theramenes, the "Trimmer," was famous for his ability to change sides at the most advantageous moment.

The female heroines of Euripides who—so Aeschylus says—have ruined the morals of Athenian wives are Phaedra, who fell in love with her stepson Hippolytus, and Stheneboia, who in a lost Euripidean play tried to seduce the hero Bellerophon, who had come to her husband's royal palace. When her advances were rejected, she accused Bellerophon of attempting to rape her. Dionysus' objection to Aeschylus' play Seven Against Thebes is natural in light of the fact that the Thebans were bitterly hostile to Athens and fighting on Sparta's side in the war. Aeschylus' play The Persians had been produced in 472 B.C. Lamachos was one of the generals who lost his life in Sicily. It was a duty of rich Athenian citizens to provide money for public needs—to finance the production of tragedy or the outfitting of a warship. Aeschylus claims that the sight of Euripidean heroes in rags has given them ideas on how to avoid paying up. "Is life life?" is a quotation from a lost Euripidean play.

AESCHYLUS: I would have preferred not to have the match down
    here.
It isn't fair. We don't start even.
DIONYSOS: What do you mean?
AESCHYLUS: I mean my poetry didn't die with me, but his
    did die with him; so he'll have it here to quote. Still,
    if this is your decision, then we'll have to do it.
DIONYSOS: All right, bring on the incense and the fire, while I
    in the presence of these great intelligences pray
    that I may judge this match most literarily.
You, chorus, meanwhile, sing an anthem to the Muses.
CHORUS: Daughters of Zeus, nine maidens immaculate,
  Muses, patronesses of subtly spoken, acute brains
  of men, forgers of idiom, when to the contest they hasten, with
    care—
sharpened wrestling-hooks and holds for their disputations,
come, o Muses, to watch and bestow
potency on these mouths of magnificence,
figures and jigsaw patterns of words.
Now the great test of artistic ability goes into action.

DIONYSOS: Both of you two pray also, before you speak your lines.
AESCHYLUS: [*Putting incense on the fire.*]
   Demeter, mistress, nurse of my intelligence,
   grant me that I be worthy of thy mysteries.
DIONYSOS: Now you put your incense on, too.
EURIPIDES: Excuse me, please.
   Quite other are the gods to whom I sacrifice.
DIONYSOS: You mean, you have private gods? New currency?
EURIPIDES: Yes, I have.
DIONYSOS: Go ahead, then, sacrifice to your private gods.
EURIPIDES: Bright upper air, my foodage! Socket of the tongue!
   Oh, comprehension, sensitory nostrils, oh
   grant I be critical in all my arguments.
CHORUS: We're all eager to listen
   to the two great wits debating
   and stating
   the luminous course of their wissen-
   schaft. Speech bitter and wild,
   tough hearts, nothing mild.
   Neither is dull.
   From one we'll get witty designs
   polished and filed.
   The other can pull
   up trees by the roots for his use,
   goes wild, cuts loose
   stampedes of lines.
DIONYSOS: Get on with it, get on with it, and put your finest wit in all
   you say, and be concrete, and be exact; and, be original.
EURIPIDES: I'll make my self-analysis a later ceremony
   after having demonstrated that my rival is a phony.
   His audience was a lot of louts and Phrynichus was all they knew.
   He gypped and cheated them with ease, and here's one thing he
      used to do.
   He'd start with one veiled bundled muffled character plunked down
      in place,
   Achilleus, like, or Niobe, but nobody could see its face.
   It looked like drama, sure, but not one syllable would it mutter.
DIONYSOS: By Jove, they didn't, and that's a fact.
EURIPIDES: The chorus then
      would utter
   four huge concatenations of verse. The characters just sat there
      mum.

DIONYSOS: You know, I liked them quiet like that. I'd rather have them
   deaf and dumb
than yak yak yak the way they do.
EURIPIDES: That's because you're an idiot too.
DIONYSOS: Oh, by all means, and to be sure, and what was Aeschylus
   trying to do?
EURIPIDES: Phony effects. The audience sat and watched the panorama
   breathlessly. *"When will Niobe speak?"* And that was half the
   drama.
DIONYSOS: It's the old shell game. I've been had. Aeschylus, why this
   agitation?
You're looking cross and at a loss.
EURIPIDES: He doesn't like investigation.
   Then after a lot of stuff like this, and now the play was half-way
   through,
   the character would grunt and moo a dozen cow-sized lines or two,
   with beetling brows and hairy crests like voodoo goblins all got up,
   incomprehensible, of course.
AESCHYLUS: You're killing me.
DIONYSOS: Will you shut up?
EURIPIDES: Not one word you could understand . . .
DIONYSOS: No, Aeschylus,
   don't grind your teeth . . .
EURIPIDES: . . . but battles of Skamandros, barbicans with ditches
   underneath,
   and hooknosed eagles bronze-enwrought on shields, verse armed like
   infantry,
   not altogether easy to make out the sense.
DIONYSOS: You're telling me?
   Many a night I've lain awake and puzzled on a single word.
   A fulvid roosterhorse is please exactly just what kind of bird?
AESCHYLUS: It was a symbol painted on the galleys, you illiterate block.
DIONYSOS: I thought it was Eryxis, our Philoxenos's fighting-cock.
EURIPIDES: Well, should a rooster—vulgah bird!—get into tragedy at
   all?
AESCHYLUS: Tell me of *your* creations, you free-thinker, if you have the
   gall.
EURIPIDES: No roosterhorses, bullmoosegoats, nor any of the millions
   of monsters that the Medes and Persians paint on their pavilions.
   When I took over our craft from you, I instantly became aware
   that she was gassy from being stuffed with heavy text and noisy air,

so I cased her aches and reduced the swelling and took away the
weights and heats
with neat conceits and tripping feets, with parsnips, radishes, and
beets.
I gave her mashed and predigested baby-food strained from my
books,
then fed her on solo-arias.
DIONYSOS: Kephisophon had you in his hooks.
EURIPIDES: My openings were never confused or pitched at random.
They were not
difficult. My first character would give the background of the plot
at once.
DIONYSOS: That's better than giving away your personal background,
eh, what, what?
EURIPIDES: Then, from the opening lines, no person ever was left with
nothing to do.
They all stepped up to speak their piece, the mistress spoke, the slave
spoke too,
the master spoke, the daughter spoke, and grandma spoke.
AESCHYLUS: And tell
me why
you shouldn't be hanged for daring that.
EURIPIDES: No, cross my heart and hope
to die,
I made the drama *democratic.*
DIONYSOS: [*To* AESCHYLUS.]   You'd better let that one pass, old
sport;
you never were such a shining light in that particular line of thought.
EURIPIDES: Then I taught natural conversational dialogue.
AESCHYLUS: I'll say you
did.
And before you ever taught them that, I wish you could have split in
middle.
EURIPIDES: [*Going right on.*]
Taught them delicate tests and verbalized commensuration,
and squint and fraud and guess and god and loving application,
and always how to think the worst of everything.
AESCHYLUS: So I believe.
EURIPIDES: I staged the life of everyday, the way we live. I couldn't
deceive
my audience with the sort of stuff they knew as much about as I.

They would have spotted me right away. I played it straight and
   didn't try
to bind a verbal spell and hypnotize and lead them by the nose
with Memnons and with Kyknoses with rings on their fingers and
   bells on their toes.
Judge both of us by our influence on followers. Give him Manes,
Phormisios and Megainetos and sundry creeps and zanies,
the big moustachio bugleboys, the pinetreebenders twelve feet high,
but Kleitophon is mine, and so's Theramenes, a clever guy.
DIONYSOS: I'll grant your Theramenes. Falls in a puddle and comes out
   dry.
The man is quick and very slick, a true Euripidean.
When Chians are in trouble he's no Chian, he's a Keian.
EURIPIDES: So that's what my plays are about,
   and these are my contributions,
   and I turn everything inside out
   looking for new solutions
   to the problems of today,
   always critical, giving
   suggestions for gracious living,
   and they come away from seeing a play
   in a questioning mood, with "where are we at?"
   and "who's got my this?" and "who took my that?"
DIONYSOS: So now the Athenian hears a pome
   of yours, and watch him come stomping home
   to yell at his servants every one:
   "where oh where are my pitchers gone?—
   where is the maid who hath betrayed
   my heads of fish to the garbage trade?
   Where are the pots of yesteryear?
   Where's the garlic of yesterday?
   Who hath ravished my oil away?"
   Formerly they sat like hicks
   fresh out of the sticks
   with their jaws hung down in a witless way.
CHORUS: [*To* AESCHYLUS.] *See you this, glorious*
   Achilleus? What have you got to say?
   Don't let your rage
   sweep you away,
   or you'll never be victorious.
   This cynical sage
   hits hard. Mind the controls.

Don't lead with your chin.
Take skysails in.
Scud under bare poles.
Easy now. Keep him full in your sights.
When the wind falls, watch him,
then catch him
dead to rights.

DIONYSOS: O mighty-mouthed inventor of harmonies, grand old
  bulwark of balderdash,
frontispiece of Hellenic tragedy, open the faucets and let 'er splash.

AESCHYLUS: The whole business gives me a pain in the middle, my rage
  and resentment are heated
at the idea of having to argue with *him*. But so he can't say I'm
  defeated,
here, answer me, you. What's the poet's duty, and why is the poet
  respected?

EURIPIDES: Because he can write, and because he can think, but mostly
  because he's injected
some virtue into the body politic.

AESCHYLUS: What if you've broken your trust,
  and corrupted good sound right-thinking people and filled them with
    treacherous lust?
  If poets do that, what reward should they get?

DIONYSOS: The axe. That's what
  we should do with 'em.

AESCHYLUS: Then think of the people *I* gave him, and think of the
  people when he got through with 'em.
I left him a lot of heroic six-footers, a grand generation of heroes,
unlike our new crop of street-corner loafers and gangsters and
  decadent queer-os.
Mine snorted the spirit of spears and splendor, of white-plumed
  helmets and stricken fields,
of warrior heroes in shining armor and greaves and sevenfold-oxhide
  shields.

DIONYSOS: And that's a disease that never dies out. The
  munition-makers will kill me.

EURIPIDES: Just what did you do to make them so noble? Is that what
  you're trying to tell me?

DIONYSOS: Well, answer him, Aeschylus, don't withdraw into injured
  dignity. That don't go.

AESCHYLUS: I made them a martial drama.

DIONYSOS: Which?

AESCHYLUS: *Seven Against*
   Thebes, if you want to know.
   Any man in an audience sitting through that would aspire to heroic
     endeavor.
DIONYSOS: That was a mistake, man. Why did you make the Thebans
     more warlike than ever
   and harder to fight with? By every right it should mean a good
     beating for you.
AESCHYLUS: [*To the audience.*]
   Well, *you* could have practiced austerity too. It's exactly what *you*
     wouldn't *do.*
   Then I put on my *Persians,* and anyone witnessing that would
     promptly be smitten
   with longing for victory over the enemy. Best play I ever have
     written.
DIONYSOS: Oh, yes, I loved that, and I thrilled where I sat when I
     heard old Dareios was dead
   and the chorus cried "wahoo" and clapped with their hands. I tell
     you, it went to my head.
AESCHYLUS: There, there is work for poets who also are MEN. From
     the earliest times
   incitement to virtue and useful knowledge have come from the
     makers of rhymes.
   There was Orpheus first. He preached against murder, and showed
     us the heavenly way.
   Musaeus taught divination and medicine; Hesiod, the day-after-day
   cultivation of fields, the seasons, and plowings. Then Homer,
     divinely inspired,
   is a source of indoctrination to virtue. Why else is he justly admired
     than for teaching how heroes armed them for battle?
DIONYSOS: He didn't teach
   Pantakles, though.
   He can't get it right. I watched him last night. He was called to
     parade, don't you know,
   and he put on his helmet and tried to tie on the plume when the
     helm was on top of his head.
AESCHYLUS: Ah, many have been my heroic disciples; the last of them,
     Lamachos (recently dead).
   The man in the street simply has to catch something from all my
     heroics and braveries.
   My Teucers and lion-hearted Patrokloses lift him right out of his
     knaveries

and make him thrill to the glory of war and spring to the sound of
  the trumpet.
But I never regaled you with Phaidra the floozie—or Sthenoboia the
  strumpet.
I think I can say that a lovesick woman has never been pictured by
  me.
EURIPIDES: Aphrodite never did notice you much.
AESCHYLUS: Aphrodite can go
  climb a tree.
But you'll never have to complain that she didn't bestow her
  attentions on you.
She got you in person, didn't she?
DIONYSOS: Yes, she did, and your stories came
  true.
The fictitious chickens came home to roost.
EURIPIDES: But tell me, o man
  without pity:
suppose I did write about Sthenoboia. What harm has she done to
  our city?
AESCHYLUS: Bellerophon-intrigues, as given by you, have caused the
  respectable wives
of respectable men, in shame and confusion, to do away with their
  lives.
EURIPIDES: But isn't my story of Phaidra a story that really has
  happened?
AESCHYLUS: So be it.
It's true. But the poet should cover up scandal, and not let anyone
  see it.
He shouldn't exhibit it out on the stage. For the little boys have their
  teachers
to show them example, but when they grow up we poets must act as
  their preachers,
and what we preach should be useful and good.
EURIPIDES: But you, with your
  massive construction,
huge words and mountainous phrases, is that what you call useful
  instruction?
You ought to make people talk like people.
AESCHYLUS: Your folksy style's for the
  birds.
For magnificent thoughts and magnificent fancies, we must have
  magnificent words.

It's appropriate too for the demigods of heroic times to talk bigger
than we. It goes with their representation as grander in costume and
figure.
I set them a standard of purity. You've corrupted it.
EURIPIDES: How did I do it?
AESCHYLUS: By showing a royal man in a costume of rags, with his skin
showing through it.
You played on emotions.
EURIPIDES: But why should it be so wrong to awaken
their pity?
AESCHYLUS: The rich men won't contribute for warships. You can't
find one in the city
who's willing to give. He appears in his rags, and howls, and
complains that he's broke.
DIONYSOS: But he always has soft and expensive underwear under the
beggarman's cloak.
The liar's so rich and he eats so much that he has to feed some to the
fishes.
AESCHYLUS: You've taught the young man to be disputatious. Each
argues as long as he wishes.
You've emptied the wrestling yards of wrestlers. They all sit around
on their fannies
and listen to adolescent debates. The sailormen gossip like grannies
and question their officers' orders. In my time, all that they knew
how to do
was to holler for rations, and sing "yeo-ho," and row, with the rest of
the crew.
DIONYSOS: And blast in the face of the man behind, that's another
thing too that they knew how to do.
And how to steal from the mess at sea, and how to be robbers ashore.
But now they argue their orders. We just can't send them to sea any
more.
AESCHYLUS: That's what he's begun. What hasn't he done?
His nurses go propositioning others.
His heroines have their babies in church
or sleep with their brothers
or go around murmuring: *"Is* life life?"
So our city is rife
with the clerk and the jerk,
the altar-baboon, the political ape,
and our physical fitness is now a disgrace

with nobody in shape
to carry a torch in a race.

Translated by Richmond Lattimore

From LYSISTRATA

Lysistrata *was first performed in 411* B.C., *two years after the disaster in Sicily. The war was still going on, and it was not going well for Athens; the Spartans had established a permanent base at Decelea in Attica and, with Persian help, had built a fleet that in numbers at any rate was superior to that of Athens.*

LYSISTRATA AND THE MAGISTRATE

In the play, Lysistrata (her name means "Disbander of Armies") organizes a sex strike of all the women of Greece to force their husbands to make peace. She seizes the Acropolis in Athens, where the reserves of the Athenian treasury are held. In the following excerpt, she and her friends Kleonike and Myrrhine deal with an Athenian Commissioner, an elderly man who is a member of the emergency committee set up after the disaster in Sicily to guide Athenian policy. Lysistrata explains to him the reasons for the action the women have taken.

Her quotation from Homer is represented by the translator in a parody of medieval English in order to suggest the effect of the contrast in the original between the lively tone of the rest of her speech and the archaic solemnity of Homeric diction. The words come from Hector's speech to Andromache in Book VI of the Iliad; *on p. 68 they appear in the form: "the men must see to the fighting."*

LYSISTRATA: When the War began, like the prudent, dutiful wives
    that we are,
we tolerated you men, and endured your actions in silence. (Small
    wonder—
you wouldn't let us say boo.)
                      You were not precisely the answer
to a matron's prayer—we knew you too well, and found out more.
Too many times, as we sat in the house, we'd hear that you'd
    done it
again—manhandled another affair of state with your usual

staggering incompetence. Then, masking our worry with a nervous
  laugh,
we'd ask you, brightly, "How was the Assembly today, dear?
  Anything
in the minutes about Peace?" And my husband would give
  his stock reply.
"What's that to you? Shut up!" And I did.
KLEONIKE: [*Proudly.*]   *I* never shut up!
COMMISSIONER: I trust you were shut up. Soundly.
LYSISTRATA: Regardless, *I* shut up.
And then we'd learn that you'd passed another decree, fouler
than the first, and we'd ask again: "Darling, how *did* you manage
anything so idiotic?" And my husband, with his customary glare,
would tell me to spin my thread, or else get a clout on the head.
And of course he'd quote from Homer:
                                          Yᵉ menne must husband yᵉ
        warre.
COMMISSIONER: Apt and irrefutably right.
LYSISTRATA: *Right,* you miserable misfit?
To keep us from giving advice while you fumbled the City away
in the Senate? Right, indeed!
                                But this time was really too much:
Wherever we went, we'd hear you engaged in the same conversation:

"What Athens needs is a Man."
                                "But there isn't a Man in the
        country."
"You can say that again."
                                There was obviously no time to lose.
We women met in immediate convention and passed a unanimous
resolution: To work in concert for safety and Peace in Greece.
We have valuable advice to impart, and if you can possibly
deign to emulate our silence, and take your turn as audience,
we'll rectify you—we'll straighten you out and set you right.
COMMISSIONER: *You'll* set *us* right? You go too far. I cannot permit
such a statement to . . .
LYSISTRATA: Shush.
COMMISSIONER: I categorically decline to shush
for some confounded woman, who wears—as a constant reminder
of congenital inferiority, an injunction to public silence—a veil!
Death before such dishonor!
LYSISTRATA: [*Removing her veil.*] If that's the only obstacle . . .

I feel you need a new panache,
so take the veil, my dear Commiss-
ioner, and drape it thus—
and SHUSH!
[*As she winds the veil around the startled* COMMISSIONER *'s head,*
KLEONIKE *and* MYRRHINE, *with carding-comb and wool-basket,*
rush forward and assist in transforming him into a woman.]
KLEONIKE: Accept, I pray, this humble comb.
MYRRHINE: Receive this basket of fleece as well.
LYSISTRATA: Hike up your skirts, and card your wool,
and gnaw your beans—and stay at home!
While we rewrite Homer:
Yᵉ WOMEN must WIVE yᵉ warre!
[*To the* CHORUS OF WOMEN, *as the* COMMISSIONER *struggles to*
remove his new outfit.]
Women, weaker vessels, arise!
Put down your pitchers.
It's our turn, now. Let's supply our friends with some moral support.
CHORUS OF WOMEN:
[*Singly.*]
Oh, yes! I'll dance to bless their success.
Fatigue won't weaken my will. Or my knees.
I'm ready to join in any jeopardy,
with girls as good as *these*!
[*Tutte.*]
A tally of their talents
convinces me they're giants
of excellence. To commence:
there's Beauty, Duty, Prudence, Science,
Self-Reliance, Compliance, Defiance,
and Love of Athens in balanced alliance
with Common Sense!
KORYPHAIOS OF WOMEN: [*To the women from the Akropolis.*]
Autochthonous daughters of Attika, sprung from the soil that bore
your mothers, the spiniest, spikiest nettles known to man,
prove your mettle and attack! Now is no time to dilute your
anger. You're running ahead of the wind!
LYSISTRATA: We'll wait for the wind
from heaven. The gentle breath of Love and his Kyprian mother
will imbue our bodies with desire, and raise a storm to tense
and tauten these blasted men until they crack. And soon
we'll be on every tongue in Greece—the *Pacifiers.*

COMMISSIONER: That's quite
a mouthful. How will you win it?
LYSISTRATA: First, we intend to withdraw
that crazy Army of Occupation from the downtown shopping
section.
KLEONIKE: Aphrodite be praised!
LYSISTRATA: The pottery shop and the grocery stall
are overstocked with soldiers, clanking around like those maniac
    Korybants,
armed to the teeth for a battle.
COMMISSIONER: A Hero is Always Prepared!
LYSISTRATA: I suppose he is. But it does look silly to shop for sardines
from behind a shield.
KLEONIKE: I'll second that. I saw
a cavalry captain buy vegetable soup on horseback. He carried
the whole mess home in his helmet.
                              And then that fellow from
    Thrace,
shaking his buckler and spear—a menace straight from the stage.
The saleslady was stiff with fright. He was hogging her ripe
    figs—free.
COMMISSIONER: I admit, for the moment, that Hellas' affairs are in one
    hell of
a snarl. But how can you set them straight?
LYSISTRATA: Simplicity itself.
COMMISSIONER: Pray demonstrate.
LYSISTRATA: It's rather like yarn. When a hank's
    in a tangle,
we lift it—*so*—and work out the snarls by winding it up
on spindles, now this way, now that way.
                                That's how we'll wind up
    the War,
if allowed: We'll work out the snarls by sending Special
    Commissions—
back and forth, now this way, now that way—to ravel these tense
international kinks.
COMMISSIONER: I lost your thread, but I know there's a hitch.
Spruce up the world's disasters with spindles—typically woolly
    female logic.
LYSISTRATA: If *you* had a scrap of logic, you'd adopt
our wool as a master plan for Athens.

COMMISSIONER: What course of action
does the wool advise?
LYSISTRATA: Consider the City as fleece, recently
shorn. The first step is Cleansing: Scrub it in a public bath,
and remove all corruption, offal, and sheepdip.
Next, to the couch
for Scutching and Plucking: Cudgel the leeches and similar vermin
loose with a club, then pick the prickles and cockleburs out.
As for the clots—those lumps that clump and cluster in knots
and snarls to snag important posts—you comb these out,
twist off their heads, and discard.
Next, to raise the City's
nap, you card the citizens together in a single basket
of common weal and general welfare. Fold in our loyal
Resident Aliens, all Foreigners of proven and tested friendship,
and any Disenfranchised Debtors. Combine these closely with the
rest.
Lastly, cull the colonies settled by our own people:
these are nothing but flocks of wool from the City's fleece,
scattered throughout the world. So gather home these far-flung
flocks, amalgamate them with the others.
Then, drawing this blend
of stable fibers into one fine staple, you spin a mighty
bobbin of yarn—and weave, without bias or seam, a cloak
to clothe the City of Athens!
COMMISSIONER: This is too much! The City's
died in the wool, worsted by the distaff side—by women
who bore no share in the War. . . .
LYSISTRATA: None, you hopeless hypocrite?
The quota we bear is double. First, we delivered our sons
to fill out the front lines in Sicily . . .
COMMISSIONER: Don't tax me with that memory.
LYSISTRATA: Next, the best years of our lives were levied. Top-level
strategy
attached our joy, and we sleep alone.
But it's not the matrons
like us who matter. I mourn for the virgins, bedded in single
blessedness, with nothing to do but grow old.
COMMISSIONER: Men *have* been known
to age, as well as women.
LYSISTRATA: No, not as well as—better.

A man, an absolute antique, comes back from the war, and he's
barely
doddered into town before he's married the veriest nymphet.
But a woman's season is brief; it slips, and she'll have no husband,
but sit out her life groping at omens—and finding no men.

COMMISSIONER: Lamentable state of affairs. Perhaps we can rectify
matters:
[*To the audience.*]
TO EVERY MAN JACK, A CHALLENGE:

ARISE!

Provided you can . . .

LYSISTRATA: Instead, Commissioner, why not simply curl up and *die?*
Just buy a coffin; here's the place.
[*Banging him on the head with her spindle.*]
I'll knead you a cake for the wake—and *these*
[*Winding the threads from the spindle around him.*]
make excellent wreaths. So Rest In Peace.

KLEONIKE: [*Emptying the chamber pot over him.*] Accept these tokens
of deepest grief.

MYRRHINE: [*Breaking her lamp over his head.*] A final garland for the
dear deceased.

LYSISTRATA: May I supply any last request?
Then run along. You're due at the wharf:
Charon's anxious to sail—
you're holding up the boat for Hell!

COMMISSIONER: This is monstrous—maltreatment of a public official—
maltreatment of ME!
I must repair directly
to the Board of Commissioners, and present my colleagues concrete
evidence of the sorry specifics of this shocking attack!
[*He staggers off left.* LYSISTRATA *calls after him.*]

LYSISTRATA: You won't haul us into court on a charge of neglecting
the dead, will you? (How like a man to insist
on his rights—even his last ones.) Two days between death
and funeral, that's the rule.
Come back here early
day after tomorrow, Commissioner:
We'll lay you out.
[LYSISTRATA *and her women re-enter the Akropolis.*]

Translated by Douglass Parker

PLATO

427–341 B.C.

Plato was a young aristocrat with literary ambitions when, probably about 407 B.C., he became an admirer of Socrates and turned his attention to philosophy. In a series of dramatic dialogues written after Socrates' execution in 399 B.C., Plato recreated the personality of his beloved teacher and the method—question and answer—that was characteristic of his search for ethical definitions.

From PHAEDRUS

SOCRATES BY THE ILISSUS

The opening section of the Phaedrus *presents us with a Socrates who, contrary to his usual custom, goes for a walk in the country, together with the young man after whom the dialogue is named.*

Phaedrus was a young associate of Socrates who also frequented the Sophist teachers—in fact he appears among their admiring audience in another Platonic dialogue, the Protagoras. *The Lysias whose speech on love Phaedrus is so excited about was one of the sons of Cephalus, a wealthy Syracusan who had settled in Athens and owned a prosperous factory that made shields. After the fall of the Thirty Tyrants and the restoration of democracy in Athens, Lysias became famous as a writer of speeches for clients who faced prosecution (or acted as prosecutor) in the law courts. Many of these survive; they show a gift for characterization as well as persuasive argument and were considered models of Attic prose style. The speech Socrates is so curious about, however, is of a different kind; it is what the rhetoricians called an "epideictic," literally, "display" speech, one designed to show off the author's talents or one suited to a public occasion such as a state funeral. This one would obviously demand some ingenuity of argument since its paradoxical message is that the handsome boy should "surrender . . . to one who is not in love with him rather than one who is."*

Love, in this case, as generally in Plato's dialogues (and especially in The Symposium*), is not heterosexual love. Athenian upper-class culture encouraged erotic relationships between male adolescents and fully grown men; they were viewed as a sort of initiation for the younger partner, his entry into the adult male world under the tutelage of an older, but still young, man. This was perhaps a not unsurprising product of an exclusively male culture that placed a heavy emphasis on athletic and military training and male companionship, a world from which women, at least respectable women, were excluded.*

SOCRATES: Where do you come from, Phaedrus my friend, and where are you going?

PHAEDRUS: I've been with Lysias, Socrates, the son of Cephalus, and I'm off for a walk outside the wall, after a long morning's sitting there. On the instructions of our common friend Acumenus I take my walks on the open roads, he tells me that is more invigorating than walking in the colonnades.

SOCRATES: Yes, he's right in saying so. But Lysias, I take it, was in town.

PHAEDRUS: Yes, staying with Epicrates, in that house where Morychus used to live, close to the temple of Olympian Zeus.

SOCRATES: Well, how were you occupied? No doubt Lysias was giving the company a feast of eloquence.

PHAEDRUS: I'll tell you, if you can spare time to come along with me and listen.

SOCRATES: What? Don't you realise that I should account it, in Pindar's words, "above all business" to hear how you and Lysias passed your time?

PHAEDRUS: Lead on then.

SOCRATES: Please tell me.

PHAEDRUS: As a matter of fact the topic is appropriate for your ears, Socrates; for the discussion that engaged us may be said to have concerned love. Lysias, you must know, has described how a handsome boy was tempted, but not by a lover: that's the clever part of it: he maintains that surrender should be to one who is not in love rather than to one who is.

SOCRATES: Splendid! I wish he would add that it should be to a poor man rather than a rich one, an elderly man rather than a young one, and, in general, to ordinary folk like myself. What an attractive democratic theory that would be! However, I'm so eager to hear about it that I vow I won't leave you even if you extend your walk as far as Megara, up to the walls and back again as recommended by Herodicus.

PHAEDRUS: What do you mean, my good man? Do you expect an amateur like me to repeat by heart, without disgracing its author, the work of the ablest writer of our day, which it took him weeks to compose at his leisure? That is far beyond me; though I'd rather have had the ability than come into a fortune.

SOCRATES: I know my Phaedrus; yes indeed, I'm as sure of him as of my own identity. I'm certain that the said Phaedrus didn't listen just once to Lysias' speech: time after time he asked him to repeat it to him, and Lysias was very ready to comply. Even that would not content him: in the end he secured the script and began poring over the parts that specially attracted him; and thus engaged he sat there the whole morning, until he grew weary and went for a walk. Upon my word, I believe he had learnt the whole speech by heart, unless it was a very long one; and he was going into the country to practise declaiming it. Then he fell in with one who has a passion for listening to discourses; and when he saw him he was delighted to think he would have someone to share his frenzied enthusiasm; so he asked him to join him on his way. But when the lover of discourses begged him to discourse, he became difficult, pretending he didn't want to, though he meant to do so ultimately, even if he had to force himself on a reluctant listener. So beg him, Phaedrus, to do straightway what he will soon do in any case.

PHAEDRUS: Doubtless it will be much my best course to deliver myself to the best of my ability, for I fancy you will never let me go until I have given you some sort of a speech.

SOCRATES: You are quite right about my intention.

PHAEDRUS: Then here's what I will do: it really is perfectly true, Socrates, that I have not got the words by heart; but I will sketch the general purport of the several points in which the lover and the non-lover were contrasted, taking them in order one by one, and beginning at the beginning.

SOCRATES: Very well, my dear fellow: but you must first show me what it is that you have in your left hand under your cloak; for I surmise that it is the actual discourse. If that is so, let me assure you of this, that much as I love you I am not altogether inclined to let you practise your oratory on me when Lysias himself is here present. Come now, show it me.

PHAEDRUS: Say no more, Socrates; you have dashed my hope of trying out my powers on you. Well, where would you like us to sit for our reading?

SOCRATES: Let us turn off here and walk along the Ilissus: then we can sit down in any quiet spot you choose.

PHAEDRUS: It's convenient, isn't it, that I chance to be bare-footed: you of course always are so. There will be no trouble in wading in the stream, which is especially delightful at this hour of a summer's day.

SOCRATES: Lead on then, and look out for a place to sit down.

PHAEDRUS: You see that tall plane-tree over there?

SOCRATES: To be sure.

PHAEDRUS: There's some shade, and a little breeze, and grass to sit down on, or lie down if we like.

SOCRATES: Then make for it.

PHAEDRUS: Tell me, Socrates, isn't it somewhere about here that they say Boreas seized Oreithuia from the river?

SOCRATES: Yes, that is the story.

PHAEDRUS: Was this the actual spot? Certainly the water looks charmingly pure and clear; it's just the place for girls to be playing beside the stream.

SOCRATES: No, it was about a quarter of a mile lower down, where you cross to the sanctuary of Agra: there is, I believe, an altar dedicated to Boreas close by.

PHAEDRUS: I have never really noticed it; but pray tell me, Socrates, do you believe that story to be true?

SOCRATES: I should be quite in the fashion if I disbelieved it, as the men of science do: I might proceed to give a scientific account of how the maiden, while at play with Pharmaceia, was blown by a gust of Boreas down from the rocks hard by, and having thus met her death was said to have been seized by Boreas: though it may have happened on the Areopagus, according to another version of the occurrence. For my part, Phaedrus, I regard such theories as no doubt attractive, but as the invention of clever, industrious people who are not exactly to be envied, for the simple reason that they must then go on and tell us the real truth about the appearance of Centaurs and the Chimaera, not to mention a whole host of such creatures, Gorgons and Pegasuses and countless other remarkable monsters of legend flocking in on them. If our sceptic, with his somewhat crude science, means to reduce every one of them to the standard of probability, he'll need a deal of time for it. I myself have certainly no time for the business: and I'll tell you why, my friend: I can't as yet "know myself," as the inscription at Delphi enjoins; and so long as that ignorance remains it seems to me ridiculous to inquire into extraneous matters. Consequently I don't bother about such things, but accept the current beliefs about them, and direct my inquiries, as I have just said, rather to myself, to dis-

cover whether I really am a more complex creature and more puffed
up with pride than Typhon, or a simpler, gentler being whom heaven
has blessed with a quiet, un-Typhonic nature. By the way, isn't this
the tree we were making for?

PHAEDRUS: Yes, that's the one.

SOCRATES: Upon my word, a delightful resting-place, with this tall,
spreading plane, and a lovely shade from the high branches of the
agnus: now that it's in full flower, it will make the place ever so
fragrant. And what a lovely stream under the plane-tree, and how cool
to the feet! Judging by the statuettes and images I should say it's
consecrated to Achelous and some of the Nymphs. And then too, isn't
the freshness of the air most welcome and pleasant: and the shrill
summery music of the cicada-choir! And as crowning delight the
grass, thick enough on a gentle slope to rest your head on most comfortably. In fact, my dear Phaedrus, you have been the stranger's
perfect guide.

PHAEDRUS: Whereas you, my excellent friend, strike me as the oddest of
men. Anyone would take you, as you say, for a stranger being shown
the country by a guide instead of a native: never leaving town to cross
the frontier nor even, I believe, so much as setting foot outside the
walls.

SOCRATES: You must forgive me, dear friend; I'm a lover of learning, and
trees and open country won't teach me anything, whereas men in the
town do. Yet you seem to have discovered a recipe for getting me out.
A hungry animal can be driven by dangling a carrot or a bit of green
stuff in front of it: similarly if you proffer me volumes of speeches I
don't doubt you can cart me all round Attica, and anywhere else you
please. Anyhow, now that we've got here I propose for the time being
to lie down, and you can choose whatever posture you think most
convenient for reading, and proceed.

PHAEDRUS: Here you are then.

Translated by R. Hackforth

From THE SYMPOSIUM

ALCIBIADES

Writing in the first quarter of the fourth century B.C., *Plato chose as the
scene of his dialogue* The Symposium *a party given by the tragic poet
Agathon to celebrate his first victory; he had won first prize at the*

Lenaea, the earlier of the two annual festivals of Dionysus celebrated in Athens. The year was 416 B.C., one year before the Athenian assembly, yielding to the persuasion and promises of Alcibiades, would make the fatal decision to send a large expeditionary force to Sicily.

Plato, who of course was not present at this banquet (he was born in 427), presents his brilliant narrative as the report of one Apollodorus, who was not present either, but had heard about it from Aristodemus, who was. Both men were close associates of Socrates; Apollodorus was present at his death (p. 506). But there can be no doubt that even if in fact the guests at the party were those named in the dialogue (and in view of the travesty of Socrates in The Clouds, *the presence of Aristophanes seems strange), the speeches reported are the work of Plato.*

Besides Socrates and Aristodemus (who was not invited but is brought along by Socrates), the party consists of Aristophanes, Phaedrus, Pausanias (the lover of Agathon), and Eryximachus, a doctor. Early in the evening, after the company has been fed and serious drinking is about to begin (the literal meaning of symposium *is "drinking together"), Eryximachus proposes that instead of drinking heavily and listening to the flute-girl, they should send her away to entertain the women in the separate part of the house reserved for them, drink lightly, and entertain one another with speeches. Most of the guests had in any case drunk too much the night before; the proposal is accepted. The subject agreed on for the speeches is Eros, passionate love—not, of course, that between men and women, but that of male lovers.*

Each of them in turn, including Agathon the host, produces an impromptu speech in praise of Eros (that of Aristophanes is a comic gem but is not without profundity), and Socrates has the last word. The others have all been speaking throughout of earthly love, sexual passion, but Socrates tells the company what he claims to have learned from a woman, a sort of prophet named Diotima, about the nature of Eros. Its true worshipper may begin with earthly love, a passionate attachment to another human being. But he is really in search of an ideal beauty which is not of the senses. Socrates starts from this tangible world and uses examples of beauty as steps to ascend continually in search of absolute beauty until he finds at last "absolute beauty in its essence, pure and unalloyed . . . instead of a beauty tainted by human flesh and color and a mass of perishable rubbish. . . ."

Socrates has just finished speaking when "there was a loud knocking at the street door" and in comes Alcibiades, the personification of earthly love in all its splendor—the handsome, brilliant man who was the darling (and the evil genius) of Athenian democracy. He enters crowned with the ivy of Dionysus and the violets of Aphrodite.

... suddenly there was a loud knocking at the street door. It sounded like a party of drunks; one could hear a girl playing the flute.

"Go and see who it is," Agathon said to the servants, "and if it is any of our friends ask them in. Otherwise say that my party is over and that we are going to bed."

A moment later they heard the voice of Alcibiades in the courtyard, very tipsy and shouting, wanting to know where Agathon was and demanding to be taken to Agathon. He was helped in by the flute-girl and some of his other companions; he stood in the doorway crowned with a thick wreath of ivy and violets, from which a number of ribands hung about his head, and said:

"Good evening, gentlemen. Will you welcome into your company a man who is already drunk, utterly drunk, or shall we just put a garland on Agathon, which is what we came for, and go away? I couldn't be at the celebration yesterday, but I've come now with this wreath to have the pleasure of transferring it from my own head to the head of this paragon of beauty and cleverness. You'll laugh at me, will you, because I'm drunk? Well, you may laugh, but I know that what I say is true. But tell me at once, am I to join your party on the conditions stated? Will you drink with me or not?"

There was a unanimous cry that he should come in, and Agathon joined in the invitation. So in he came, supported by the people with him, and trying to take off the wreath with which he meant to crown Agathon. It was tilted over his eyes, and so he did not see Socrates, but sat down next to Agathon, with Socrates, who moved so as to make room for him, on his other side. As he took his place he embraced Agathon and crowned him.

"Take off Alcibiades' shoes," ordered Agathon, "so that he can put his feet up and make a third at this table."

"Splendid," said Alcibiades, "but who is our table companion?" With these words he twisted himself round and saw Socrates, then leapt to his feet, and said: "Good God, what have we here? Socrates? Lying there in wait for me again? How like you to make a sudden appearance just when I least expect to find you. What are you doing here? And why have you taken this place? You ought to be next to Aristophanes or some other actual or would-be buffoon, and instead you've managed to get yourself next to the handsomest person in the room."

"Be ready to protect me, Agathon," said Socrates, "for I find that the love of this fellow has become no small burden. From the moment when I first fell in love with him I haven't been able to exchange a glance or a word with a single good-looking person without his falling into a passion of jealousy and envy, which makes him behave outrageously and abuse me and practically lay violent hands on me. See to it that he doesn't commit some excess even here, or if he attempts to do anything violent protect me; I am really quite scared by his mad behaviour and the intensity of his affection."

"There can be no peace between you and me," said Alcibiades, "but I'll settle accounts with you for this presently. For the moment, Agathon, give me some of those ribands to make a wreath for his head too, for a truly wonderful head it is. Otherwise he might blame me for crowning you and leaving him uncrowned, whose words bring him victory over all men at all times, not merely on single occasions, like yours the day before yesterday." So saying he took some of the ribands, made a wreath for Socrates, and lay back.

As soon as he had done so he exclaimed: "Come, sirs, you seem to me to be quite sober; this can't be allowed; you must drink; it's part of our agreement. So as master of the revels, until you are in adequate drinking order, I appoint—myself. Let them bring a big cup, Agathon, if you've got one. No, never mind, bring that wine-cooler," he went on, seeing one that held more than half a gallon. He had this filled, and first of all drained it himself, and then told them to fill it again for Socrates, adding as he did so: "Not that my scheming will have the slightest effect on Socrates, my friends. He will drink any quantity that he is bid, and never be drunk all the same." The servant refilled the vessel for Socrates, and he drank.

Then Eryximachus began: "This is no way for us to be going on, Alcibiades. Are we to have neither conversation nor songs over our wine, but just to sit drinking as men do when they are thirsty?"

"Ah, Eryximachus," replied Alcibiades, "best of sons of the best and soberest of fathers, my compliments to you."

"And mine to you," said Eryximachus. "But how are we to amuse ourselves?"

"However you like; we must obey your orders. 'One man of healing shall a host outweigh.' So prescribe for us whatever you choose."

"Listen then," said Eryximachus. "Before you came we had resolved that each of us in turn, going from left to right, should make the best speech he could in praise of Love. The rest of us have already spoken, so it is clearly right that you, who have not yet spoken, but have finished your wine, should deliver a speech, and then prescribe whatever task you like to Socrates, and he to his right-hand neighbour, and so on."

"An excellent idea, Eryximachus, but it can't be fair to make a man who is drunk compete in speaking with men who are sober. Besides, my good friend, you surely don't believe a word of what Socrates has just said? You know that the truth is quite the opposite? If I praise any person but him in his presence, be it god or man, he won't be able to keep his hands off me."

"Be quiet," said Socrates.

"It's no good your protesting," Alcibiades said. "I won't make a speech in praise of any other person in your presence."

"Very well," said Eryximachus, "adopt that course, if you like, and make a speech in praise of Socrates."

"What?" said Alcibiades. "Do you think I ought, Eryximachus? Shall I set about the fellow and pay him out in the presence of you all?"

"Here, I say!" said Socrates; "what have you in mind? Are you going to make fun of me by a mock-panegyric? Or what?"

"I shall tell the truth. Do you allow that?"

"Oh yes, I'll allow you to tell the truth; I'll even invite you to do so."

"Very well then," said Alcibiades. "And here is what you can do. If I say anything untrue, pull me up in the middle of my speech, if you like, and tell me that I'm lying. I certainly shan't do so intentionally. But don't be surprised if I get into a muddle in my reminiscences; it isn't easy for a man in my condition to sum up your extraordinary character in a smooth and orderly sequence.

"I propose to praise Socrates, gentlemen, by using similes. He will perhaps think that I mean to make fun of him, but my object in employing them is truth, not ridicule. I declare that he bears a strong resemblance to those figures of Silenus in statuaries' shops, represented holding pipes or flutes; they are hollow inside, and when they are taken apart you see that they contain little figures of gods. I declare also that he is like Marsyas the satyr. You can't deny yourself, Socrates, that you have a striking physical likeness to both of these, and you shall hear in a moment how you resemble them in other respects. For one thing you're a bully, aren't you? I can bring evidence of this if you don't admit it. But you don't play the flute, you will say. No, indeed; the performance you give is far more remarkable. Marsyas needed an instrument in order to charm men by the power which proceeded out of his mouth, a power which is still exercised by those who perform his melodies (I reckon the tunes ascribed to Olympus to belong to Marsyas, who taught him); his productions alone, whether executed by a skilled male performer or by a wretched flute-girl, are capable, by reason of their divine origin, of throwing men into a trance and thus distinguishing those who yearn to enter by initiation into union with the gods. But you, Socrates, are so far superior to Marsyas that you produce the same effect by mere words without any instrument. At any rate, whereas we most of us pay little or no attention to the words of any other speaker, however accomplished, a speech by you or even a very indifferent report of what you have said stirs

us to the depths and casts a spell over us, men and women and young lads
alike. I myself, gentlemen, were it not that you would think me absolutely drunk, would have stated on oath the effect which his words have
had on me, an effect which persists to the present time. Whenever I
listen to him my heart beats faster than if I were in a religious frenzy, and
tears run down my face, and I observe that numbers of other people have
the same experience. Nothing of this kind ever used to happen to me
when I listened to Pericles and other good speakers; I recognized that
they spoke well, but my soul was not thrown into confusion and dismay
by the thought that my life was no better than a slave's. That is the
condition to which I have often been reduced by our modern Marsyas,
with the result that it seems impossible to go on living in my present
state. You can't say that this isn't true, Socrates. And even at this moment, I know quite well that, if I were prepared to give ear to him, I
should not be able to hold out, but the same thing would happen again.
He compels me to realize that I am still a mass of imperfections and yet
persistently neglect my own true interests by engaging in public life. So
against my real inclination I stop up my ears and take refuge in flight, as
Odysseus did from the Sirens, otherwise I should sit here beside him till I
was an old man. He is the only person in whose presence I experience a
sensation of which I might be thought incapable, a sensation of shame;
he, and he alone, positively makes me ashamed of myself. The reason is
that I am conscious that there is no arguing against the conclusion that
one should do as he bids, and yet that, whenever I am away from him, I
succumb to the temptations of popularity. So I behave like a runaway
slave and take to my heels, and when I see him the conclusions which he
has forced upon me make me ashamed. Many a time I should be glad for
him to vanish from the face of the earth, but I know that, if that were to
happen, my sorrow would far outweigh my relief. In fact, I simply do not
know what to do about him.

"This is the effect which the 'piping' of this satyr has had on me and
on many other people. But listen and you shall hear how in other respects too he resembles the creatures to which I compared him; and how
marvellous is the power which he possesses. You may be sure that none
of you knows his true nature, but I will reveal him to you, now that I have
begun. The Socrates whom you see has a tendency to fall in love with
good-looking young men, and is always in their society and in an ecstasy
about them. (Besides, he is, to all appearances, universally ignorant and
knows nothing.) But this is exactly the point in which he resembles
Silenus; he wears these characteristics superficially, like the carved figure, but once you see beneath the surface you will discover a degree of
self-control of which you can hardly form a notion, gentlemen. Believe

me, it makes no difference to him whether a person is good-looking—he despises good looks to an almost inconceivable extent—nor whether he is rich nor whether he possesses any of the other advantages that rank high in popular esteem; to him all these things are worthless, and we ourselves of no account, be sure of that. He spends his whole life pretending and playing with people, and I doubt whether anyone has ever seen the treasures which are revealed when he grows serious and exposes what he keeps inside. However, I once saw them, and found them so divine and precious and beautiful and marvellous that, to put the matter briefly, I had no choice but to do whatever Socrates bade me.

"Believing that he was serious in his admiration of my charms, I supposed that a wonderful piece of good luck had befallen me; I should now be able, in return for my favours, to find out all that Socrates knew; for you must know that there was no limit to the pride that I felt in my good looks. With this end in view I sent away my attendant, whom hitherto I had always kept with me in my encounters with Socrates, and left myself alone with him. I must tell you the whole truth; attend carefully, and do you, Socrates, pull me up if anything I say is false. I allowed myself to be alone with him, I say, gentlemen, and I naturally supposed that he would embark on conversation of the type that a lover usually addresses to his darling when they are *tête-à-tête*, and I was glad. Nothing of the kind; he spent the day with me in the sort of talk which is habitual with him, and then left me and went away. Next I invited him to train with me in the gymnasium, and I accompanied him there, believing that I should succeed with him now. He took exercise and wrestled with me frequently, with no one else present, but I need hardly say that I was no nearer my goal. Finding that this was no good either, I resolved to make a direct assault on him, and not to give up what I had once undertaken; I felt that I must get to the bottom of the matter. So I invited him to dine with me, behaving just like a lover who has designs upon his favourite. He was in no hurry to accept this invitation, but at last he agreed to come. The first time he came he rose to go away immediately after dinner, and on that occasion I was ashamed and let him go. But I returned to the attack, and this time I kept him in conversation after dinner far into the night, and then, when he wanted to be going, I compelled him to stay, on the plea that it was too late for him to go.

"So he betook himself to rest, using as a bed the couch on which he had reclined at dinner, next to mine, and there was nobody sleeping in the room but ourselves. Up to this point my story is such as might be told to anybody, but you would not have heard the sequel from me but for two reasons. In the first place there is, as the proverb says, truth in

Plato

wine—whether one adds 'and in children' or not is of no significance—and in the second it would be wrong, when one is setting out to compose a panegyric, to allow so proud an exploit on the part of Socrates to remain unknown. Besides, I am in much the same state as a man suffering from snake-bite. They say that such a man cannot endure to reveal his sufferings except to those who have experienced the like; they are the only people who will understand and make allowances if his agony drives him to outrageous speech and behaviour. Now I have suffered a bite more painful than that in the most sensitive part in which one can be bitten; I have been wounded and stung in my heart or soul or whatever you like to call it by philosophical talk which clings more fiercely than a snake when it gets a hold on the soul of a not ill-endowed young man. Seeing too that your company consists of people like Phaedrus, Agathon, Eryximachus, Pausanias, Aristodemus, as well as Aristophanes, not to mention Socrates himself, people who have all had your share in the madness and frenzy of philosophy—well, you shall all hear what happened. You will make allowances both for my actions then and for my words now. As for the servants and any other vulgar and uninitiated persons who may be present, they must shut their ears tight against what I am going to say.

"Well, gentlemen, when the light was out and the servants had withdrawn, I decided not to beat about the bush with him, but to tell him my sentiments boldly. I nudged him and said: 'Are you asleep, Socrates?' 'Far from it,' he answered. 'Do you know what I think?' 'No, what?' 'I think that you are the only lover that I have ever had who is worthy of me, but that you are afraid to mention your passion to me. Now, what I feel about the matter is this, that it would be very foolish of me not to comply with your desires in this respect as well as in any other claim that you might make either on my property or on that of my friends. The cardinal object of my ambition is to come as near perfection as possible, and I believe that no one can give me such powerful assistance towards this end as you. So the disapproval of wise men, which I should incur if I refused to comply with your wishes, would cause me far more shame than the condemnation of the ignorant multitude if I yielded to you."

"He listened to what I had to say, and then made a thoroughly characteristic reply in his usual ironical style: 'You must be a very sharp fellow, my dear Alcibiades, if what you say about me is true, and I really have a power which might help you to improve yourself. You must see in me a beauty which is incomparable and far superior to your own physical good looks, and if, having made this discovery, you are trying to get a share of it by exchanging your beauty for mine, you obviously mean to get much the better of the bargain; you are trying to get true beauty in return for sham; in fact, what you are proposing is to exchange dross for gold. But look more closely, my good friend, and make quite sure that you are not mistaken in your estimate of my worth. A man's mental vision does not begin to be keen until his physical vision is past its prime, and you are far from having reached that point.' "

" 'Well,' I said, 'I have done my part; what I have said represents my real sentiments and it is now for you to decide what you think best for me and for yourself.'

" 'Quite right,' he answered, 'we will consider hereafter, and do whatever seems to be best in this as in other matters.'

"I had now discharged my artillery, and from the answer which he made I judged that I had wounded him; so, without allowing him to say anything further, I got up and covered him with my own clothes—for it was winter—and then laid myself down under his worn cloak, and threw my arms round this truly superhuman and wonderful man, and remained thus the whole night long. Here again, Socrates, you cannot deny that I am telling the truth. But in spite of all my efforts he proved completely superior to my charms and triumphed over them and put them to scorn, insulting me in the very point on which I piqued myself, gentlemen of the jury—I may well call you that, since you have the case of Socrates' disdainful behaviour before you. I swear by all the gods in heaven that for anything that had happened between us when I got up after sleeping with Socrates, I might have been sleeping with my father or elder brother.

"What do you suppose to have been my state of mind after that? On the one hand I realized that I had been slighted, but on the other I felt a reverence for Socrates' character, his self-control and courage; I had met a man whose like for wisdom and fortitude I could never have expected to encounter. The result was that I could neither bring myself to be angry with him and tear myself away from his society, nor find a way of subduing him to my will. It was clear to me that he was more completely proof against bribes than Ajax against sword-wounds, and in the one point in which I had expected him to be vulnerable he had eluded me. I was utterly disconcerted, and wandered about in a state of enslavement to the man the like of which has never been known.

"It was after these events that we served in the campaign against Potidaea together, and were mess-mates there. Of this I may say first that in supporting hardship he showed himself not merely my superior but the whole army's. Whenever we were cut off, as tends to happen on service, and compelled to go without food, the rest of us were nowhere in the matter of endurance. And again, when supplies were abundant, no one enjoyed them more; at drinking especially, though he drank only when he was forced to do so, he was invincible, and yet, what is most remarkable of all, no human being has ever seen Socrates drunk. You will see the proof of this very shortly if I am not mistaken. As for the hardships of winter—and the winters there are very severe—he performed prodigies; on one occasion in particular, when there was a tremendous frost, and everybody either remained indoors or, if they did go out, muffled themselves up in a quite unheard-of way, and tied and swathed their feet in felt and sheepskin, Socrates went out with nothing on but his ordinary clothes and without anything on his feet, and walked over the ice barefoot more easily than other people in their boots. The soldiers viewed him with suspicion, believing that he meant to humiliate them.

"So much for this subject, but 'another exploit that the hero dared' in the course of his military service is worth relating. A problem occurred to him early one day, and he stood still on the spot to consider it. When he couldn't solve it he didn't give up, but stood there ruminating. By the time it was midday people noticed him, and remarked to one another with wonder that Socrates had been standing wrapped in thought since early morning. Finally in the evening after dinner, some Ionians brought their bedding outside—it was summertime—where they could take their rest in the cool and at the same time keep an eye on Socrates to see if he would stand there all night as well. He remained standing until it was dawn and the sun rose. Then he made a prayer to the sun and went away.

"Now, if you please, we will consider his behaviour in battle; we ought to do him justice on this score as well. When the action took place in which I won my decoration for valour, it was entirely to Socrates that I owed my preservation; he would not leave me when I was wounded, but succeeded in rescuing both me and my arms. That was the time too when I recommended the generals to confer the decoration on you, Socrates; here at any rate you cannot find any handle for criticism or contradiction. But the generals were influenced in my favour by the fact that I was well-connected, and their desire to confer the distinction on me was surpassed by your own eagerness that I should receive it rather than yourself. In addition, gentlemen, let me tell you that Socrates was a sight well worth seeing when the army made its disorderly retreat from Delium. I was then serving in the cavalry, whereas he was an infantryman, and after the rout had begun I came upon him marching along in company with Laches, and called out to them not to be down-hearted, and assured them that I would not desert them. And here I had an even better chance of observing Socrates than at Potidaea, because being mounted I had less occasion to be frightened myself. In the first place I noticed that he was far cooler than Laches, and next, if I may borrow an expression from you, Aristophanes, that he was using just the same gait as he does in Athens, 'strutting along with his head in the air and casting side-long glances,' quietly observing the movements of friend and foe, and making it perfectly plain even at a distance that he was prepared to put up a strong resistance to any attack. That is how both he and his companion got off safe; those who show a bold front in war are hardly ever molested; the attention of the pursuers is concentrated on those who are in headlong rout.

"One might find many other remarkable qualities to praise in Socrates, but a description of his general way of life would perhaps be equally applicable to some other people; the really wonderful thing about him is that he is like no other human being, living or dead. If you are looking for a parallel for Achilles, you can find it in Brasidas and others; if Pericles is your subject you can compare him to Nestor and Antenor (and they do not exhaust the possibilities); and you can make similar comparisons in other cases. But our friend here is so extraordinary, both in his person and in his conversation, that you will never be able to find anyone remotely resembling him either in antiquity or in the present generation, unless you go beyond humanity altogether, and have recourse to the images of Silenus and satyr which I am using myself in this speech. They are as applicable to his talk as to his person; I forgot to say at the beginning that his talk too is extremely like the Silenus-figures which take apart. Anyone who sets out to listen to Socrates talking will probably find his conversation utterly ridiculous at first, it is clothed in such curious words and phrases, the hide, so to speak, of a hectoring satyr. He will talk of pack-asses and blacksmiths, cobblers and tanners, and appear to express the same ideas in the same language over and over again, so that any inexperienced or foolish person is bound to laugh at his way of speaking. But if a man penetrates within and sees the content of Socrates' talk exposed, he will find that there is nothing but sound sense inside, and that this talk is almost the talk of a god, and enshrines countless representations of ideal excellence, and is of the widest possible application; in fact that it extends over all the subjects with which a man who means to turn out a gentleman needs to concern himself.

"That is what I have to say, gentlemen, in praise of Socrates. I have included in my speech the grievance which I have against him, and told you how he has insulted me. I may add that I am not the only sufferer in this way; Charmides the son of Glaucon and Euthydemus the son of Diocles and many others have had the same treatment; he has pretended to be in love with them, when in fact he is himself the beloved rather than the lover. So I warn you, Agathon, not to be deceived by him; learn from my experience and be on your guard, and do not be like the child in the proverb, who learns to dread the fire by being burnt."

When Alcibiades had finished, the freedom with which he had spoken raised a general laugh, because he seemed still to be amorously inclined towards Socrates. The latter took up the conversation and said: "You seem to me quite sober, Alcibiades. Otherwise you wouldn't try to conceal your real object with such an apparatus of artful circumlocution, and then slip it in at the end by way of afterthought and as if the main motive of your whole speech were not to make trouble between Agathon and me. You think that I ought to be in love with nobody but you, and that nobody but you ought to be in love with Agathon. But we've seen through you; the object of your little play of satyr and Silenus is perfectly clear. Don't let him succeed, my dear Agathon; take steps to prevent anybody from setting you and me at variance."

"You are very likely right, Socrates," replied Agathon; "no doubt that was why he sat down between us, in order to keep us apart. But he shan't succeed; I will come and take the place on your other side."

"Do," said Socrates; "come and sit here, beyond me."

"My God," said Alcibiades, "look how the fellow treats me. He thinks that he must always get the better of me. If you won't be content otherwise, you extraordinary man, you might at least let Agathon sit between us."

"Quite impossible," said Socrates. "You have just spoken in praise of me, and now it is my turn to speak in praise of my right-hand neighbour. If Agathon sits next to you, it will fall to him to speak in praise of me all over again, instead of my speaking in praise of him. Let it be as I propose, my good friend, and don't grudge the lad his tribute of praise from me, especially as I have a strong desire to eulogize him."

"Hurrah, hurrah," cried Agathon. "You see I can't stay here; I simply must change my place so as to have the privilege of being praised by Socrates."

"That's just what always happens," said Alcibiades. "If Socrates is there no one else has a chance with anybody who is good-looking. See how readily he has found a plausible excuse for getting Agathon beside him."

Agathon got up, intending to move to the place on the other side of Socrates. But at that moment a crowd of revellers came to the door, and finding it left open by somebody who had just gone out, made their way into the dining-room and installed themselves there. There was a general uproar, all order was abolished, and deep drinking became the rule.

Aristodemus reported that Eryximachus and Phaedrus and some others went away at this point. He himself fell asleep and slept for some timc, as the nights weie long at that time of year. Towards daybreak, when the cocks were already crowing, he woke up, and found that the rest of the party had either fallen asleep or gone away, and that the only people still awake were Agathon and Aristophanes and Socrates. They were drinking from a largc cup which they passed round from left to right, and Socrates was holding forth to the others. Aristodemus did not remember most of what passed—he had not been conscious at the beginning of the conversation and was still nodding with sleep—but the main point was that Socrates was compelling them to admit that the man who knew how to write a comedy could also write a tragedy, and that a skilful tragic writer was capable of being also a comic writer. They were giving way to his arguments, which they didn't follow very well, and nodding. Aristophanes fell asleep first, and when it was fully light Agathon followed him.

Then Socrates, having put both his interlocutors to sleep, got up and went away, followed by Aristodemus, as usual. He went to the Lyceum and washed, and spent the day as he would any other, and finally towards evening went home to bed.

Translated by Walter Hamilton

From THE APOLOGY

THE MISSION OF SOCRATES

The Greek word apologia *means "a speech for the defense"; Plato's* Apology *is his version of the speech Socrates made in court in 399 B.C. In that year, three Athenian citizens, Anytus, Meletus, and Lycon, brought charges against him of impiety and corruption of the young. The charges were vaguely formulated and it was not hard for Socrates to counter them effectively, but it was much harder for him to deal with the widespread prejudice against him that fueled the legal action in the first place. The source of one such prejudice, which is not explicitly referred to in the proceedings, was political. Among the many aristocratic young men who had been fascinated associates of Socrates were Alcibiades, who had gone over to the Spartan side when threatened with prosecution for alleged impiety, and had given the Spartans invaluable advice on how to prosecute the war against his own city; Charmides, Plato's uncle, who was one of the Thirty Tyrants; and Critias, who was their leader.*

The civil war between the democrats and the supporters of the Thirty (referred to by Socrates in the following extract as "the recent expulsion and restoration") had been brought to an end in *403* with an amnesty, which prohibited prosecution for any action connected with the civil war, except in the case of the Thirty and their hatchet men. Consequently a charge that Socrates was, so to speak, the éminence grise of the counterrevolution of *404* could only be formulated in some such vague phrase as "corrupting the youth"—but it was an undoubted factor in the decision to prosecute. Some fifty years later, the Athenian orator and statesman Aeschines asked a jury: "Didn't you put to death the Sophist Socrates, because he was proved to be the teacher of Critias, who overthrew the democracy?" As for the other source of his unpopularity, Socrates deals with it in the following extract from the speech.

Here perhaps one of you might interrupt me and say "But what is it that you do, Socrates? How is it that you have been misrepresented like this? Surely all this talk and gossip about you would never have arisen if you had confined yourself to ordinary activities, but only if your behaviour was abnormal. Tell us the explanation, if you do not want us to invent it for ourselves. "This seems to me to be a reasonable request, and I will try to explain to you what it is that has given me this false notoriety; so please give me your attention. Perhaps some of you will think that I am not being serious; but I assure you that I am going to tell you the whole truth.

I have gained this reputation, gentlemen, from nothing more or less than a kind of wisdom. What kind of wisdom do I mean? Human wisdom, I suppose. It seems that I really am wise in this limited sense. Presumably the geniuses whom I mentioned just now are wise in a wisdom that is more than human; I do not know how else to account for it. I certainly have no knowledge of such wisdom, and anyone who says that I have is a liar and wilful slanderer. Now, gentlemen, please do not interrupt me if I seem to make an extravagant claim; for what I am going to tell you is not my own opinion; I am going to refer you to an unimpeachable authority. I shall call as witness to my wisdom (such as it is) the god at Delphi.

You know Chaerephon, of course. He was a friend of mine from boyhood, and a good democrat who played his part with the rest of you in the recent expulsion and restoration. And you know what he was like; how enthusiastic he was over anything that he had once undertaken. Well, one day he actually went to Delphi and asked this question of the god—as I said before, gentlemen, please do not interrupt—he asked whether there was anyone wiser than myself. The priestess replied that there was no one. As Chaerephon is dead, the evidence for my statement will be supplied by his brother, who is here in court.

Please consider my object in telling you this. I want to explain to you how the attack upon my reputation first started. When I heard about the oracle's answer, I said to myself "What does the god mean? Why does he not use plain language? I am only too conscious that I have no claim to wisdom, great or small; so what can he mean by asserting that I am the wisest man in the world? He cannot be telling a lie; that would not be right for him."

After puzzling about it for some time, I set myself at last with considerable reluctance to check the truth of it in the following way. I went to interview a man with a high reputation for wisdom, because I felt that here if anywhere I should succeed in disproving the oracle and pointing out to my divine authority "You said that I was the wisest of men, but here is a man who is wiser than I am."

Well, I gave a thorough examination to this person—I need not mention his name, but it was one of our politicians that I was studying when I had this experience—and in conversation with him I formed the impression that although in many people's opinion, and especially in his own, he appeared to be wise, in fact he was not. Then when I began to try to show him that he only thought he was wise and was not really so, my efforts were resented both by him and by many of the other people present. However, I reflected as I walked away: "Well, I am certainly wiser than this man. It is only too likely that neither of us has any knowledge to boast of; but he thinks that he knows something which he does not know, whereas I am quite conscious of my ignorance. At any rate it seems that I am wiser than he is to this small extent, that I do not think that I know what I do not know."

After this I went on to interview a man with an even greater reputation for wisdom, and I formed the same impression again; and here too I incurred the resentment of the man himself and a number of others.

From that time on I interviewed one person after another. I realized with distress and alarm that I was making myself unpopular, but I felt compelled to put my religious duty first; since I was trying to find out the meaning of the oracle, I was bound to interview everyone who had a reputation for knowledge. And by Dog, gentlemen! (for I must be frank with you) my honest impression was this: it seemed to me, as I pursued my investigation at the god's command, that the people with the greatest reputations were almost entirely deficient, while others who were supposed to be their inferiors were much better qualified in practical intelligence.

I want you to think of my adventures as a sort of pilgrimage under-

taken to establish the truth of the oracle once for all. After I had finished
with the politicians I turned to the poets, dramatic, lyric, and all the rest,
in the belief that here I should expose myself as a comparative ignora-
mus. I used to pick up what I thought were some of their most perfect
works and question them closely about the meaning of what they had
written, in the hope of incidentally enlarging my own knowledge. Well,
gentlemen, I hesitate to tell you the truth, but it must be told. It is
hardly an exaggeration to say that any of the bystanders could have
explained those poems better than their actual authors. So I soon made
up my mind about the poets too: I decided that it was not wisdom that
enabled them to write their poetry, but a kind of instinct or inspiration,
such as you find in seers and prophets who deliver all their sublime
messages without knowing in the least what they mean. It seemed clear
to me that the poets were in much the same case; and I also observed
that the very fact that they were poets made them think that they had a
perfect understanding of all other subjects, of which they were totally
ignorant. So I left that line of inquiry too with the same sense of advantage that I had felt in the case of the politicians.

Last of all I turned to the skilled craftsmen. I knew quite well that I
had practically no technical qualifications myself, and I was sure that
I should find them full of impressive knowledge. In this I was not disappointed; they understood things which I did not, and to that extent they
were wiser than I was. But, gentlemen, these professional experts
seemed to share the same failing which I had noticed in the poets; I
mean that on the strength of their technical proficiency they claimed a
perfect understanding of every other subject, however important; and
I felt that this error more than outweighed their positive wisdom. So I
made myself spokesman for the oracle, and asked myself whether I
would rather be as I was—neither wise with their wisdom nor stupid
with their stupidity—or possess both qualities as they did. I replied
through myself to the oracle that it was best for me to be as I was.

The effect of these investigations of mine, gentlemen, has been to
arouse against me a great deal of hostility, and hostility of a particularly
bitter and persistent kind, which has resulted in various malicious
suggestions, including the description of me as a professor of wisdom.
This is due to the fact that whenever I succeed in disproving another
person's claim to wisdom in a given subject, the bystanders assume that I
know everything about that subject myself. But the truth of the matter,
gentlemen, is pretty certainly this: that real wisdom is the property of
God, and this oracle is his way of telling us that human wisdom has little
or no value. It seems to me that he is not referring literally to Socrates,
but has merely taken my name as an example, as if he would say to us

"The wisest of you men is he who has realized, like Socrates, that in respect of wisdom he is really worthless."

That is why I still go about seeking and searching in obedience to the divine command, if I think that anyone is wise, whether citizen or stranger; and when I think that any person is not wise, I try to help the cause of God by proving that he is not. This occupation has kept me too busy to do much either in politics or in my own affairs; in fact, my service to God has reduced me to extreme poverty.

[*The jury of 501 Athenian citizens (Athenian juries were always an odd number, to avoid verdicts like that which acquitted Orestes) split surprisingly favorably for Socrates: 221 for acquittal, 280 against. The procedure in case of condemnation was for the prosecution to propose one penalty, the defense another; the jury had to choose between them. The prosecution proposed death. They almost certainly expected Socrates to propose exile, a possibility, however, which he emphatically rejects in his speech. What he proposed was not calculated to win him votes: that he should be given free meals in the Prytaneum, the meeting place of the Council of the Assembly, a privilege granted to public benefactors and victors at the Olympic Games. He finally offered to pay a fine; the money was promised by friends present in court—Plato, Crito, Critobulus, and Apollodorus. But the vote is for death, this time 360 to 141. Socrates makes a final address to the court.*

In it he mentions a "voice" or "divine sign." He had referred to this phenomenon earlier in his speech. "I am subject," he said there, "to a divine or supernatural experience. . . . It began in my early childhood—a sort of voice which comes to me; and when it comes it always dissuades me from what I am proposing to do, and never urges me on."

The "Great King" is the ruler of the Persian Empire. Socrates' vision of the next world (if there is indeed life after death, for he contemplates both possibilities) includes conversation with (and perhaps questioning of) the judges of the Underworld, the poets Orpheus, Musaeus, Homer, and Hesiod, and also the great heroic figures who, like him, have been unjustly condemned. Ajax, who according to Homer was the bravest man at Troy next to Achilles, was denied the armor of Achilles, the prize of valor, by judges who awarded it to Odysseus. Palamedes, who proposed making a compromise peace with the Trojans, was executed for treason, a charge based on false testimony and faked evidence provided by Odysseus. Sisyphus was a legendary trickster (some accounts make him the father of Odysseus) who actually managed to return from the Underworld to life.]

Well, gentlemen, for the sake of a very small gain in time you are
going to earn the reputation—and the blame from those who wish to
disparage our city—of having put Socrates to death, "that wise man"—
because they will say I am wise even if I am not, these people who want
to find fault with you. If you had waited just a little while, you would
have had your way in the course of nature. You can see that I am well on
in life and near to death. I am saying this not to all of you but to those
who voted for my execution, and I have something else to say to them as
well.

No doubt you think, gentlemen, that I have been condemned for lack
of the arguments which I could have used if I had thought it right to
leave nothing unsaid or undone to secure my acquittal. But that is very
far from the truth. It is not a lack of arguments that has caused my
condemnation, but a lack of effrontery and impudence, and the fact that
I have refused to address you in the way which would give you most
pleasure. You would have liked to hear me weep and wail, doing and
saying all sorts of things which I regard as unworthy of myself, but which
you are used to hearing from other people. But I did not think then that
I ought to stoop to servility because I was in danger, and I do not regret
now the way in which I pleaded my case; I would much rather die as the
result of this defence than live as the result of the other sort. In a court of
law, just as in warfare, neither I nor any other ought to use his wits to
escape death by any means. In battle it is often obvious that you could
escape being killed by giving up your arms and throwing yourself upon
the mercy of your pursuers; and in every kind of danger there are plenty
of devices for avoiding death if you are unscrupulous enough to stick at
nothing. But I suggest, gentlemen, that the difficulty is not so much to
escape death; the real difficulty is to escape from doing wrong, which is
far more fleet of foot. In this present instance, I, the slow old man, have
been overtaken by the slower of the two, but my accusers, who are clever
and quick, have been overtaken by the faster: by iniquity. When I leave
this court I shall go away condemned by you to death, but they will go
away convicted by Truth herself of depravity and wickedness. And they
accept their sentence even as I accept mine. No doubt it was bound to
be so, and I think that the result is fair enough.

Having said so much, I feel moved to prophesy to you who have given
your vote against me; for I am now at that point where the gift of
prophecy comes most readily to men: at the point of death. I tell you, my
executioners, that as soon as I am dead, vengeance shall fall upon you
with a punishment far more painful than your killing of me. You have
brought about my death in the belief that through it you will be delivered from submitting your conduct to criticism; but I say that the result

will be just the opposite. You will have more critics, whom up till now I have restrained without your knowing it; and being younger they will be harsher to you and will cause you more annoyance. If you expect to stop denunciation of your wrong way of life by putting people to death, there is something amiss with your reasoning. This way of escape is neither possible nor creditable; the best and easiest way is not to stop the mouths of others, but to make yourselves as good men as you can. This is my last message to you who voted for my condemnation.

As for you who voted for my acquittal, I should very much like to say a few words to reconcile you to the result, while the officials are busy and I am not yet on my way to the place where I must die. I ask you, gentlemen, to spare me these few moments; there is no reason why we should not exchange fancies while the law permits. I look upon you as my friends, and I want you to understand the right way of regarding my present position.

Gentlemen of the jury—for *you* deserve to be so called—I have had a remarkable experience. In the past the prophetic voice to which I have become accustomed has always been my constant companion, opposing me even in quite trivial things if I was going to take the wrong course. Now something has happened to me, as you can see, which might be thought and is commonly considered to be a supreme calamity; yet neither when I left home this morning, nor when I was taking my place here in the court, nor at any point in any part of my speech did the divine sign oppose me. In other discussions it has often checked me in the middle of a sentence; but this time it has never opposed me in any part of this business in anything that I have said or done. What do I suppose to be the explanation? I will tell you. I suspect that this thing that has happened to me is a blessing, and we are quite mistaken in supposing death to be an evil. I have good grounds for thinking this, because my accustomed sign could not have failed to oppose me if what I was doing had not been sure to bring some good result.

We should reflect that there is much reason to hope for a good result on other grounds as well. Death is one of two things. Either it is annihilation, and the dead have no consciousness of anything; or, as we are told, it is really a change: a migration of the soul from this place to another. Now if there is no consciousness but only a dreamless sleep, death must be a marvellous gain. I suppose that if anyone were told to pick out the night on which he slept so soundly as not even to dream, and then to compare it with all the other nights and days of his life, and then were told to say, after due consideration, how many better and happier days and nights than this he had spent in the course of his life—well, I think that the Great King himself, to say nothing of any private person, would find these days and nights easy to count in comparison with the rest. If death is like this, then, I call it gain; because the whole of time, if you look at it in this way, can be regarded as no more than one single night. If on the other hand death is a removal from here to some other place, and if what we are told is true, that all the dead are there, what greater blessing could there be than this, gentlemen? If on arrival in the other world, beyond the reach of our so-called justice, one will find there the true judges who are said to preside in those courts, Minos and Rhadamanthys and Aeacus and Triptolemus and all those other half-divinities who were upright in their earthly life, would that be an unrewarding journey? Put it in this way: how much would one of you give to meet Orpheus and Musaeus, Hesiod and Homer? I am willing to die ten times over if this account is true. It would be a specially interesting experience for me to join them there, to meet Palamedes and Ajax the son of Telamon and any other heroes of the old days who met their death through an unfair trial, and to compare my fortunes with theirs—it would be rather amusing, I think—; and above all I should like to spend my time there, as here, in examining and searching people's minds, to find out who is really wise among them, and who only thinks that he is. What would one not give, gentlemen, to be able to question the leader of that great host against Troy, or Odysseus, or Sisyphus, or the thousands of other men and women whom one could mention, to talk and mix and argue with whom would be unimaginable happiness? At any rate I presume that they do not put one to death there for such conduct; because apart from the other happiness in which their world surpasses ours, they are now immortal for the rest of time, if what we are told is true.

You too, gentlemen of the jury, must look forward to death with confidence, and fix your minds on this one belief, which is certain: that nothing can harm a good man either in life or after death, and his fortunes are not a matter of indifference to the gods. This present experience of mine has not come about mechanically; I am quite clear that the time had come when it was better for me to die and be released from my distractions. That is why my sign never turned me back. For my own part I bear no grudge at all against those who condemned me and accused me, although it was not with this kind intention that they did so, but because they thought that they were hurting me; and that is culpable of them. However, I ask them to grant me one favour. When my sons grow up, gentlemen, if you think that they are putting money or anything else before goodness, take your revenge by plaguing them as I plagued you; and if they fancy themselves for no reason, you must scold them just as I scolded you, for neglecting the important things and thinking that they are good for something when they are good for nothing. If you do this, I shall have had justice at your hands, both I myself and my children.

Now it is time that we were going, I to die and you to live; but which of us has the happier prospect is unknown to anyone but God.

Translated by Hugh Trederrick

From CRITO

SOCRATES AND THE LAWS

In Athens, execution usually followed immediately on condemnation, but in Socrates' case there was a long delay. During the visit of the State galley to the island of Delos to commemorate Theseus' rescue of the Athenian victims from the Minotaur, no executions could be carried out, and Socrates' condemnation coincided with the absence of the State galley on this mission. But it has now been sighted off the southern coast of Attica on its way back; Socrates' time is almost up. Crito, a rich friend, has organized an escape (and it seems likely that the Athenian authorities would not have interfered), but when he urges Socrates to take this last opportunity to escape death, he is met with a firm refusal. Socrates justifies that refusal in the following excerpt.

SOCRATES: Look at it in this way. Suppose that while we were preparing to run away from here (or however one should describe it) the Laws and Constitution of Athens were to come and confront us and ask this question: "Now, Socrates, what are you proposing to do? Can you deny that by this act which you are contemplating you intend, so far as you have the power, to destroy us, the Laws, and the whole State as well? Do you imagine that a city can continue to exist and not be turned upside down, if the legal judgments which are pronounced in it have no force but are nullified and destroyed by private persons?"— how shall we answer this question, Crito, and others of the same kind? There is much that could be said, especially by a professional advocate, to protest against the invalidation of this law which enacts that judgments once pronounced shall be binding. Shall we say "Yes, I do intend to destroy the laws, because the State wronged me by passing a faulty judgment at my trial"? Is this to be our answer, or what?

CRITO: What you have just said, by all means, Socrates.

SOCRATES: Then what supposing the Laws say "Was there provision for this in the agreement between you and us, Socrates? Or did you undertake to abide by whatever judgments the State pronounced?" If we expressed surprise at such language, they would probably say: "Never mind our language, Socrates, but answer our questions; after all, you are accustomed to the method of question and answer. Come now, what charge do you bring against us and the State, that you are trying to destroy us? Did we not give you life in the first place? was it not through us that your father married your mother and begot you? Tell us, have you any complaint against those of us Laws that deal with marriage?" "No, none," I should say." Well, have you any against the laws which deal with children's upbringing and education, such as you had yourself? Are you not grateful to those of us Laws which were instituted for this end, for requiring your father to give you a cultural and physical education?" "Yes," I should say. "Very good. Then since you have been born and brought up and educated, can you deny, in the first place, that you were our child and servant, both you and your ancestors? And if this is so, do you imagine that what is right for us is equally right for you, and that whatever we try to do to you, you are justified in retaliating? You did not have equality of rights with your father, or your employer (supposing that you had had one), to enable you to retaliate; you were not allowed to answer back when you were scolded or to hit back when you were beaten, or to do a great many other things of the same kind. Do you expect to have such license against your country and its laws that if we try to put you to death in the belief that it is right to do so, you on your part will try your hardest to destroy your country and us its Laws in return? and will you, the true devotee of goodness, claim that you are justified in doing so? Are you so wise as to have forgotten that compared with your mother and father and all the rest of your ancestors your country is something far more precious, more venerable, more sacred, and held in greater honour both among gods and among all reasonable men? Do you not realize that you are even more bound to respect and placate the anger of your country than your father's anger? that if you cannot persuade your country you must do whatever it orders, and patiently submit to any punishment that it imposes, whether it be flogging or imprisonment? And if it leads you out to war, to be wounded or killed, you must comply, and it is right that you should do so; you must not give way or retreat or abandon your position. Both in war and in the law-courts and everywhere else you must do whatever your city and your country commands, or else persuade it in accordance with universal justice; but violence is a sin even against your parents, and it is a far greater sin against your country."—What shall we say to this, Crito?—that what the Laws say is true, or not?

CRITO: Yes, I think so.

SOCRATES: "Consider, then, Socrates," the Laws would probably continue, "whether it is also true for us to say that what you are now trying to do to us is not right. Although we have brought you into the world and reared you and educated you, and given you and all your fellow-citizens a share in all the good things at our disposal, nevertheless by the very fact of granting our permission we openly proclaim this principle: that any Athenian, on attaining to manhood and seeing for himself the political organization of the State and us its Laws, is permitted, if he is not satisfied with us, to take his property and go away wherever he likes. If any of you chooses to go to one of our colonies, supposing that he should not be satisfied with us and the State, or to emigrate to any other country, not one of us Laws hinders or prevents him from going away wherever he likes, without any loss of property. On the other hand, if any one of you stands his ground when he can see how we administer justice and the rest of our public organization, we hold that by so doing he has in fact undertaken to do anything that we tell him; and we maintain that anyone who disobeys is guilty of doing wrong on three separate counts: first because we are his parents, and secondly because we are his guardians; and thirdly because, after promising obedience, he is neither obeying us not persuading us to change our decision if we are at fault in any way; and although all our orders are in the form of proposals, not of savage commands, and we give him the choice of either persuading us or doing what we say, he is actually doing neither. These are the charges, Socrates, to which we say that you will be liable if you do what you are contemplating; and you will not be the least culpable of your fellow-countrymen, but one of the most guilty." If I said "Why do you say that?" they would no doubt pounce upon me with perfect justice and point out that there are very few people in Athens who have entered into this agreement with them as explicitly as I have. They would say "Socrates, we have substantial evidence that you are satisfied with us and with the State. You would not have been so exceptionally reluctant to cross the borders of your country if you had not been exceptionally attached to it. You have never left the city to attend a festival or for any other purpose, except on some military expedition; you have never travelled abroad as other people do, and you have never felt the impulse to acquaint yourself with another country or constitution; you have been content with us and with our city. You have definitely chosen us, and undertaken to observe us in all your activities as a citizen; and as the crowning proof that you are satisfied with our city, you have begotten children in it. Furthermore, even at the time of your trial you could have proposed the penalty of banishment, if you had chosen to do so; that is, you could have done then with the sanction of the State what you are now trying to do without it. But whereas at that time you made a noble show of indifference if you had to die, and in fact preferred death, as you said, to banishment, now you show no respect for your earlier professions, and no regard for us, the Laws, whom you are trying to destroy; you are behaving like the lowest type of menial, trying to run away in spite of the contracts and undertakings by which you agreed to live as a member of our State. Now first answer this question: Are we or are we not speaking the truth when we say that you have undertaken, in deed if not in word, to live your life as a citizen in obedience to us?" What are we to say to that, Crito? Are we not bound to admit it?

CRITO: We cannot help it, Socrates.

SOCRATES: "It is a fact, then," they would say, "that you are breaking covenants and undertakings made with us, although you made them under no compulsion or misunderstanding, and were not compelled to decide in a limited time; you had seventy years in which you could have left the country, if you were not satisfied with us or felt that the agreements were unfair. You did not choose Sparta or Crete—your favourite models of good government—or any other Greek or foreign state; you could not have absented yourself from the city less if you had been lame or blind or decrepit in some other way. It is quite obvious that you stand by yourself above all other Athenians in your affection for this city and for us its Laws;—who would care for a city without laws? And now, after all this, are you not going to stand by your agreement? Yes, you are, Socrates, if you will take our advice; and then you will at least escape being laughed at for leaving the city.

"We invite you to consider what good you will do to yourself or your friends if you commit this breach of faith and stain your conscience. It is fairly obvious that the risk of being banished and either losing their citizenship or having their property confiscated will extend to your friends as well. As for yourself, if you go to one of the neighbouring states, such as Thebes or Megara, which are both well governed, you will enter them as an enemy to their constitution, and all good patriots will eye you with suspicion as a destroyer of law and order. Incidentally you will confirm the opinion of the jurors who tried you that they gave a correct verdict; a destroyer of laws might very well be supposed to have a destructive influence upon young and foolish human beings. Do you intend, then, to avoid well governed states and the higher forms of human society? and if you do, will life be worth living? Or will you approach these people and have the impudence to converse with them? What arguments will you use, Socrates? The same which you used here, that goodness and integrity, institutions and laws, are the most precious possessions of mankind? Do you not think that Socrates and everything about him will appear in a disreputable light? You certainly ought to think so. But perhaps you will retire from this part of the world and go to Crito's friends in Thessaly? That is the home of indiscipline and laxity, and no doubt they would enjoy hearing the amusing story of how you managed to run away from prison by arraying yourself in some costume or putting on a shepherd's smock or some other conventional runaway's disguise, and altering your personal appearance. And will no one comment on the fact that an old man of your age, probably with only a short time left to live, should dare to cling so greedily to life, at the price of violating the most stringent laws? Perhaps not, if you avoid irritating anyone. Otherwise, Socrates, you will hear a good many humiliating comments. So you will live as the toady and slave of all the populace, literally 'roistering in Thessaly,' as though you had left this country for Thessaly to attend a banquet there; and where will your discussions about goodness and uprightness be then, we should like to know? But of course you want to live for your children's sake, so that you may be able to bring them up and educate them. Indeed! by first taking them off to Thessaly and making foreigners of them, so that they may have that additional enjoyment? Or if that is not your intention, supposing that they are brought up here with you still alive, will they be better cared for and educated without you, because of course your friends will look after them? Will they look after your children if you go away to Thessaly, and not if you go away to the next world? Surely if those who profess to be your friends are worth anything, you must believe that they would care for them.

"No, Socrates; be advised by us your guardians, and do not think more of your children or of your life or of anything else than you think of what is right; so that when you enter the next world you may have all this to plead in your defence before the authorities there. It seems clear that if you do this thing, neither you nor any of your friends will be the better for it or be more upright or have a cleaner conscience here in this world, nor will it be better for you when you reach the next. As it is, you will leave this place, when you do, as the victim of a wrong done not by us, the Laws, but by your fellow-men. But if you leave in that dishonourable way, returning wrong for wrong and evil for evil, breaking your agreements and covenants with us, and injuring those whom you least ought to injure—yourself, your friends, your country, and us—then you will have to face our anger in your lifetime, and in that place beyond when the laws of the other world know that you have tried, so far as you could, to destroy even us their brothers, they will not receive you with a kindly welcome. Do not take Crito's advice, but follow ours."

That, my dear friend Crito, I do assure you, is what I seem to hear them saying, just as a mystic seems to hear the strains of music; and the sound of their arguments rings so loudly in my head that I cannot hear the other side. I warn you that, as my opinion stands at present, it will be useless to urge a different view. However, if you think that you will do any good by it, say what you like.

CRITO: No, Socrates, I have nothing to say.

SOCRATES: Then give it up, Crito, and let us follow this course, since God points out the way.

Translated by Hugh Tredennick

From PHAEDO

THE DEATH OF SOCRATES

Phaedo, *the dialogue in which Plato gives an account of Socrates' last day on earth, is named after a young devotee of Socrates who was present (as Plato was not) at Socrates' execution and who tells the story to his friend Echecrates. The bulk of the dialogue consists of an argument between Socrates and two young admirers from Thebes, Simmias and Cebes, about the immortality of the soul, an idea which Socrates maintains against the doubts and objections of the two young men. His presentation of his case ends with a description of the life after death, in which "those who have purified themselves sufficiently by philosophy live thereafter altogether without bodies" in a paradisal state that he does not, he says, have time to describe more exactly. His last words, just before he dies—a reminder to Crito to sacrifice a cock to Asclepius on his behalf—reflect this belief, for Asclepius was the healing god, to whom the invalid sacrificed a cock when he regained his health.*

"There is one way, then, in which a man can be free from all anxiety about the fate of his soul; if in life he has abandoned bodily pleasures and adornments, as foreign to his purpose and likely to do more harm than good, and has devoted himself to the pleasures of acquiring knowledge;

and so by decking his soul not with a borrowed beauty but with its own—with self-control, and goodness, and courage, and liberality, and truth—has fitted himself to await his journey to the next world. You, Simmias and Cebes and the rest, will each make this journey some day in the future; but 'for me the fated hour' (as a tragic character might say) 'calls even now.' In other words, it is about time that I took my bath. I prefer to have a bath before drinking the poison, rather than give the women the trouble of washing me when I am dead."

When he had finished speaking, Crito said "Very well, Socrates. But have you no directions for the others or myself about your children or anything else? What can we do to please you best?"

"Nothing new, Crito," said Socrates; "just what I am always telling you. If you look after yourselves, whatever you do will please me and mine and you too, even if you don't agree with me now. On the other hand, if you neglect yourselves and fail to follow the line of life as I have laid it down both now and in the past, however fervently you agree with me now, it will do no good at all."

"We shall try our best to do as you say," said Crito. "But how shall we bury you?"

"Any way you like," replied Socrates, "that is, if you can catch me and I don't slip through your fingers." He laughed gently as he spoke, and turning to us went on: "I can't persuade Crito that I am this Socrates here who is talking to you now and marshalling all the arguments; he thinks that I am the one whom he will see presently lying dead; and he asks how he is to bury me! As for my long and elaborate explanation that when I have drunk the poison I shall remain with you no longer, but depart to a state of heavenly happiness, this attempt to console both you and myself seems to be wasted on him. You must give an assurance to Crito for me—the opposite of the one which he gave to the court which tried me. He undertook that I should stay; but you must assure him that when I am dead I shall not stay, but depart and be gone. That will help Crito to bear it more easily, and keep him from being distressed on my account when he sees my body being burned or buried, as if something dreadful were happening to me; or from saying at the funeral that it is Socrates whom he is laying out or carrying to the grave or burying. Believe me, my dear friend Crito: misstatements are not merely jarring in their immediate context; they also have a bad effect upon the soul. No, you must keep up your spirits and say that it is only my body that you are burying; and you can bury it as you please, in whatever way you think is most proper."

With these words he got up and went into another room to bathe; and Crito went after him, but told us to wait. So we waited, discussing and reviewing what had been said, or else dwelling upon the greatness of the calamity which had befallen us; for we felt just as though we were losing a father and should be orphans for the rest of our lives. Meanwhile, when Socrates had taken his bath, his children were brought to see him—he had two little sons and one big boy—and the women of his household— you know—arrived. He talked to them in Crito's presence and gave them directions about carrying out his wishes; then he told the women and children to go away, and came back himself to join us.

It was now nearly sunset, because he had spent a long time inside. He came and sat down, fresh from the bath; and he had only been talking for a few minutes when the prison officer came in, and walked up to him. "Socrates," he said, "at any rate I shall not have to find fault with you, as I do with others, for getting angry with me and cursing when I tell them to drink the poison—carrying out Government orders. I have come to know during this time that you are the noblest and the gentlest and the bravest of all the men that have ever come here, and now especially I am sure that you are not angry with me, but with them; because you know who are responsible. So now—you know what I have come to say— goodbye, and try to bear what must be as easily as you can." As he spoke he burst into tears, and turning round, went away.

Socrates looked up at him and said "Goodbye to you, too; we will do as you say." Then addressing us he went on "What a charming person! All the time I have been here he has visited me, and sometimes had discussions with me, and shown me the greatest kindness; and how generous of him now to shed tears for me at parting! But come, Crito, let us do as he says. Someone had better bring in the poison, if it is ready prepared; if not, tell the man to prepare it."

"But surely, Socrates," said Crito, "the sun is still upon the mountains; it has not gone down yet. Besides, I know that in other cases people have dinner and enjoy their wine, and sometimes the company of those whom they love, long after they receive the warning; and only drink the poison quite late at night. No need to hurry; there is still plenty of time."

"It is natural that these people whom you speak of should act in that way, Crito," said Socrates, "because they think that they gain by it. And it is also natural that I should not; because I believe that I should gain nothing by drinking the poison a little later—I should only make myself ridiculous in my own eyes if I clung to life and hugged it when it has no more to offer. Come, do as I say and don't make difficulties."

At this Crito made a sign to his servant, who was standing nearby. The servant went out and after spending a considerable time returned with the man who was to administer the poison; he was carrying it ready prepared in a cup. When Socrates saw him he said "Well, my good fellow, you understand these things; what ought I to do?"

"Just drink it," he said, "and then walk about until you feel a weight in your legs, and then lie down. Then it will act of its own accord."

As he spoke he handed the cup to Socrates, who received it quite cheerfully, Echecrates, without a tremor, without any change of colour or expression, and said, looking up under his brows with his usual steady gaze, "What do you say about pouring a libation from this drink? Is it permitted, or not?"

"We only prepare what we regard as the normal dose, Socrates," he replied.

"I see," said Socrates. "But I suppose I am allowed, or rather bound, to pray the gods that my removal from this world to the other may be prosperous. This is my prayer, then; and I hope that it may be granted." With these words, quite calmly and with no sign of distaste, he drained the cup in one breath.

Up till this time most of us had been fairly successful in keeping back our tears; but when we saw that he was drinking, that he had actually drunk it, we could do so no longer; in spite of myself the tears came pouring out, so that I covered my face and wept broken-heartedly—not for him, but for my own calamity in losing such a friend. Crito had given up even before me, and had gone out when he could not restrain his tears. But Apollodorus, who had never stopped crying even before, now broke out into such a storm of passionate weeping that he made everyone in the room break down, except Socrates himself, who said:

"Really, my friends, what a way to behave! Why, that was my main reason for sending away the women, to prevent this sort of disturbance; because I am told that one should make one's end in a tranquil frame of mind. Calm yourselves and try to be brave."

This made us feel ashamed, and we controlled our tears. Socrates walked about, and presently, saying that his legs were heavy, lay down on his back—that was what the man recommended. The man (he was the same one who had administered the poison) kept his hand upon Socrates, and after a little while examined his feet and legs; then pinched his foot hard and asked if he felt it. Socrates said no. Then he did the same to his legs; and moving gradually upwards in this way let us see that he was getting cold and numb. Presently he felt him again and said that when it reached the heart, Socrates would be gone.

The coldness was spreading about as far as his waist when Socrates uncovered his face—for he had covered it up—and said (they were his last words): "Crito, we ought to offer a cock to Asclepius. See to it, and don't forget."

"No, it shall be done," said Crito. "Are you sure that there is nothing else?"

Socrates made no reply to this question, but after a little while he stirred; and when the man uncovered him, his eyes were fixed. When Crito saw this, he closed the mouth and eyes.

Such, Echecrates, was the end of our comrade, who was, we may fairly say, of all those whom we knew in our time, the bravest and also the wisest and most upright man.

Translated by Hugh Tredennick

From EPISTLE VII

PLATO AND POLITICS

One of Plato's closest friends and devoted students at the Academy was Dion, a close relative of Dionysius I, who had established himself as tyrant at Syracuse in Sicily in the last years of the fifth century. Dion and Plato, who made two visits to Syracuse, attempted (but failed miserably) to turn Dionysius' successor Dionysius II, who succeeded his father in 367 B.C., into a philosopher-king. In 357, Dion, an exile in Athens, led a small expedition to Syracuse while Dionysius was on campaign and seized the city. But in the struggles that followed (Dionysius carried on hostilities from other bases) Dion was eventually murdered by the leader of a rival faction in Syracuse. Plato's Seventh Letter is addressed to the followers of the murdered Dion in Syracuse; it is a report of his own dealings with Dionysius II and of Dion's whole career. But it begins with this account of his reaction to the execution of Socrates.

The constitution he refers to as "anathema to many" was the Athenian democracy that had launched the disastrous expedition to Sicily, and in the final desperate years of the war had several times rejected concessions that would have brought peace with a war-weary Sparta.

When I was a young man I had the same ambition as many others: I thought of entering public life as soon as I came of age. And certain happenings in public affairs favored me, as follows. The constitution we then had, being anathema to many, was overthrown; and a new government was set up consisting of fifty-one men, two groups—one of eleven and another of ten—to police the market place and perform other necessary duties in the city and the Piraeus respectively, and above them thirty other officers with absolute powers. Some of these men happened to be relatives and acquaintances of mine, and they invited me to join

them at once in what seemed to be a proper undertaking. My attitude
toward them is not surprising, because I was young. I thought that they
were going to lead the city out of the unjust life she had been living and
establish her in the path of justice, so that I watched them eagerly to see
what they would do. But as I watched them they showed in a short time
that the preceding constitution had been a precious thing. Among their
other deeds they named Socrates, an older friend of mine whom I should
not hesitate to call the wisest and justest man of that time, as one of a
group sent to arrest a certain citizen who was to be put to death illegally,
planning thereby to make Socrates willy-nilly a party to their actions. But
he refused, risking the utmost danger rather than be an associate in their
impious deeds. When I saw all this and other like things of no little
consequence, I was appalled and drew back from that reign of injustice.
Not long afterwards the rule of the Thirty was overthrown and with it
the entire constitution; and once more I felt the desire, though this time
less strongly, to take part in public and political affairs. Now many deplorable things occurred during those troubled days, and it is not surprising that under cover of the revolution too many old enmities were
avenged; but in general those who returned from exile acted with great
restraint. By some chance, however, certain powerful persons brought
into court this same friend Socrates, preferring against him a most
shameless accusation, and one which he, of all men, least deserved. For
the prosecutors charged him with impiety, and the jury condemned and
put to death the very man who, at the time when his accusers were
themselves in misfortune and exile, had refused to have a part in the
unjust arrest of one of their friends.

The more I reflected upon what was happening, upon what kind of
men were active in politics, and upon the state of our laws and customs,
and the older I grew, the more I realized how difficult it is to manage a
city's affairs rightly. For I saw it was impossible to do anything without
friends and loyal followers; and to find such men ready to hand would be
a piece of sheer good luck, since our city was no longer guided by the
customs and practices of our fathers, while to train up new ones was
anything but easy. And the corruption of our written laws and our customs was proceeding at such amazing speed that whereas at first I had
been full of zeal for public life, when I noted these changes and saw how
unstable everything was, I became in the end quite dizzy; and though I
did not cease to reflect how an improvement could be brought about in
our laws and in the whole constitution, yet I refrained from action,
waiting for the proper time. At last I came to the conclusion that all
existing states are badly governed and the condition of their laws practically incurable, without some miraculous remedy and the assistance of

fortune; and I was forced to say, in praise of true philosophy, that from
her height alone was it possible to discern what the nature of justice is,
either in the state or in the individual, and that the ills of the human race
would never end until either those who are sincerely and truly lovers of
wisdom come into political power, or the rulers of our cities, by the grace
of God, learn true philosophy.

Translated by Glenn R. Morrow

MENANDER

342–c. 292 B.C.

*Menander was a prolific writer of what is known, to emphasize its radical
departure from the boisterous license of the comedy of Aristophanes and
his peers, as New Comedy. We know the titles of close to one hundred
of his plays. Yet, in spite of his great fame in the ancient world, we had
little evidence on which to judge his importance before the publication
of the papyrus finds of the nineteenth and twentieth centuries; what we
did have were fragments quoted in anthologies, like those printed on pp.
520–21. We now have most of* The Girl from Samos, *a considerable
portion of* The Shield, *and all of* Dyskolos (The Bad-Tempered Man),
which was first published in 1958.

From THE BAD-TEMPERED MAN

ACT I

*The first act (all we have room for here) opens with a speech by the god
Pan, the lord of the wild, uncultivated land. The cave he speaks of is still
there, set in the pinewoods and defiles of Mount Parnes on the northern
frontier of Attica. Needless to say, the play ends happily, with a double
betrothal and a celebration to which the protagonist, bad-tempered to
the last, is dragged against his will.*

[*Enter* PAN *from the shrine.*]
PAN: Imagine that this place is Phyle in Attica;
That this cave from which I have come is a shrine of the Nymphs,
A well-known holy place belonging to the people of Phyle—
Those of them who manage to cultivate these rocks.
This farm on my right is the home of Cnemon, an old man
Who prefers his own to anyone else's company;
Surly-tempered to everybody; detests crowds.
Crowds, did I say? He has never yet in all his life—
And that's a good many years—uttered a pleasant word
To a single soul; never opened a conversation;
Except that, being my neighbour, he will speak in passing
To me, Pan, because he's obliged to; but I'm sure
A moment later he wishes he hadn't.
                            Yet this man,
This surly creature, married a widow, whose first husband
Had newly died, leaving her with one little boy.
Joined to her in the state of holy acrimony
He spent his days, and a great part of his nights as well,
In quarrelling—an unhappy life. When a girl was born
Things became worse; until at last they reached a point
Where misery beggared all comparison, and the woman,
Finding her life intolerable, left him and went back
To live with her son by her first marriage, Gorgias.
He, now grown up, has this little farm next door, where he keeps
His mother and one faithful slave who belonged to his father.
They are poor; but the lad has common sense beyond his years;
For hard experience quickly matures a man.
Old Cnemon, with his daughter, and an aged crone
To serve them, lives a lonely life, fetching in logs,
Digging, toiling away; and loathing every soul
Without exception, from his own wife and his neighbours here
To the villagers of Cholargos further down the valley.
But the girl does honour to her simple upbringing;
She is pure, good-hearted; serves with devoted piety
The Nymphs, who are my companions. So she inspires in us
A wish to help her.
                    Not far from here a wealthy man
Farms an estate worth many talents. This man's son,
A town-bred youth, happened to come here with a friend
Hunting. He saw Cnemon's daughter. I made him fall
Madly in love. So that's the outline of the plot;

The details you can hear if you choose—and please do choose!
I think I see him coming, this lover—and his friend,
Both deep in conversation about this very thing.
[*Exit* PAN. *Enter* SOSTRATOS *and* CHAEREAS.]

CHAEREAS: What was it you said, Sostratos? You saw a girl,
A free-born girl here, bringing garlands for the Nymphs,
And you fell in love at once?

SOSTRATOS: At once.

CHAEREAS: Fast work. Surely
You'd made your mind up, when you first set out from home,
To fall in love with someone?

SOSTRATOS: You laugh, Chaereas;
But I'm in a bad way.

CHAEREAS: I believe you.

SOSTRATOS: And that's why
I've brought you here to help me. You're my friend, I'm sure;
And you always know what to do.

CHAEREAS: In such matters, Sostratos,
This is the way I go to work. Say, one of my friends
Is keen on a girl, asks me to help. If she's one of that sort,
I act in a flash—I simply allow no argument;
I get drunk, burn her door down, swoop and carry her off.
Before I even ask who she is, she must be had.
The longer he waits, you see, the more he falls in love;
While if he enjoys her soon he soon gets over it.
But if it's marriage he talks of, with a free-born girl,
I take a different line; enquire about her family,
Her life, the sort of girl she is; for in this case
I leave my friend a souvenir for the rest of his life
Of my own efficiency in these matters.

SOSTRATOS: Excellent—
[*Aside.*] But not exactly what I wanted.

CHAEREAS: Now I must hear
The whole story.

SOSTRATOS: You know Pyrrhias, the boy who hunts with us?

CHAEREAS: Yes.

SOSTRATOS: Well, early this morning I sent him off with a message.

CHAEREAS: A message—yes, who for?

SOSTRATOS: I told him to see her father,
Or whatever man's in charge of the house—

CHAEREAS: Oh, Heracles!
You didn't do *that*?

SOSTRATOS: It was a mistake. It's hardly the thing
To send a *slave* on such a business. When you're in love
It isn't easy to know what's best. I wonder, now,
What can have kept Pyrrhias all this time. I told him
To find out how the land lay there, and come straight back.
[*Enter* PYRRHIAS, *running and breathless.*]
PYRRHIAS: Look out! Get away quick, everyone clear out! He's mad,
There's a madman after me.
SOSTRATOS: What's all this?
PYRRHIAS: Get out of his way!
SOSTRATOS: Whose way?
PYRRHIAS: I'm being pelted with sods and rocks. I'm wrecked.
SOSTRATOS: Who's pelting you?—Here, where are you off to?
[SOSTRATOS *seizes* PYRRHIAS, *who thus has time to look round and
see that he is not being pursued.*]
PYRRHIAS: Perhaps
he isn't
Chasing me any longer.
SOSTRATOS: He isn't.
PYRRHIAS: [*Mopping his brow.*] I thought he was.
SOSTRATOS: What *are* you talking about?
PYRRHIAS: [*Nervously.*] Look here, now—let's get
away.
SOSTRATOS: Where to?
PYRRHIAS: Away from that door, as far as possible.
He's a son of mischief, the devil's in him, he's lunatic—
The man who lives there, in that house you sent me to.
The brute! O gods, my toes! I've pretty near broken them all
On these rocks.
SOSTRATOS: Chaereas, he must have been rude to the man.
PYRRHIAS: I'm sure he's coming back here to set on me again.
By Zeus, I tell you, Sostratos, we'll all be murdered.
SOSTRATOS: You won't be murdered. Now just tell me carefully
Exactly what you said when you spoke to him.
PYRRHIAS: I can't.
I'm shaking, and I'm out of breath.
SOSTRATOS: [*Getting hold of him.*] You'll tell me now.
PYRRHIAS: Well, first I knocked at the door, and said I wished to see
The master. A wretched hag came out, and stood over there,
Where I was talking just now, and pointed him out to me
Up on that hillside, prowling round his blasted pear-trees
Collecting wood enough for a gallows made to measure.

SOSTRATOS: How terrifying! Go on, go on.

PYRRHIAS: Well, then I went
Into the field and walked towards him. And I thought
I'd show him I was a really friendly, capable sort
Of chap; so I called out to him—still quite a long way off—
"I've come to see you on urgent business, sir," I said,
"Of moment to yourself, sir," I said. "Damn you," says he,
"Who told you to walk into my field?" With that he picks up
A lump of turf and slings it slap into my face.

CHAEREAS: Hell! To the crows with him!

PYRRHIAS: And as I blinked, and yelled
"Poseidon drown you!" he picked up a stick this time, and beat me
With it, and bellowed, "What business have you got with me?"
At the top of his voice, and, "Don't you know the public road?"

CHAEREAS: [*To* SOSTRATOS.] This farmer friend of yours is a plain
    lunatic.

PYRRHIAS: In the finish, I ran. He chased me best part of two miles,
Right round the hill, then down here through the thorn-bushes,
Pelting me first with sods and stones, then with his pears
When he hadn't anything else. He's a proper old savage,
A holy terror. Come away, plea . . . se!

SOSTRATOS: I'm not afraid of him.

PYRRHIAS: You don't know what a beast he is. He'll eat us raw.

CHAEREAS: Perhaps he's feeling a bit upset today. I think
    You might do well to put off meeting him, Sostratos.
    There's always a right time for everything; and that's
    A good practical rule, you take my word for it.

PYRRHIAS: [*Fervently.*] You're so right.

CHAEREAS: Penniless peasants are almost all
    like that—
    Vicious tempered; he's not the only one. Tomorrow,
    First thing, I'll come here alone, now that I know the house,
    And talk to him. Now I'm off home; you go home, too,
    And wait a bit, see? Everything's going to be all right.
    [*Exit* CHAEREAS.]

PYRRHIAS: Yes, let's go home.

SOSTRATOS: Ha! Chaereas jumped at the excuse.
    It was obvious he disliked coming here with me,
    And disapproved my plan to marry. As for you, Pyrrhias,
    You wretch, may all the gods blast you as you deserve!

PYRRHIAS: What, *me?* What have *I* done, Sostratos? Eh? What have I
    done?

I didn't do any damage in the man's field, or steal—
Not a single thing.
SOSTRATOS: No? So the man was beating you
For doing nothing?
PYRRHIAS: Look! He's coming! That's the man!
I'm going, I am, sir! You talk to him yourself.
[*Exit* PYRRHIAS.]
SOSTRATOS: Oh, but I can't. I never make a good impression
When I start talking. What do you *say* to a man like this?
He certainly looks anything but kind. By Zeus,
What a rage he's in! Here, I'll stand back from the door a bit—
That's better. Why, as he walks he's mumbling to himself.
He doesn't look sane to me. Apollo and all the gods!
I'm frightened—that's the truth, I may as well confess it.
[*Enter* CNEMON.]
CNEMON: Now Perseus was a famous man. What luck he had!
First, he had wings—could fly about in the air. That meant
He never had to meet a soul that walks on earth.
Second, he had an invaluable possession, with which
He could turn everyone who annoyed him into stone.
If only I had that power now! There'd be nothing
More plentiful anywhere than fine stone statues.
As it is—by Asclepios, life grows impossible.
People come trespassing on my ground and chat to me.
I've taken to spending my days on the public highway, have I?
Why, I don't even work this bit of land any more,
I've given it up, to avoid the people who pass by;
And now—they hunt me up to the hill-tops. Curse them all,
There are too many *people!*—Oh, for pity's sake, there's another,
Standing at my front door!
SOSTRATOS: Is he going to hit me now?
CNEMON: Where can one get away from *people?* Even if a man
Wanted to hang himself he couldn't do it in private.
SOSTRATOS: It's me he's angry with.—Excuse me, sir, I'm waiting
For someone here; I've made an appointment.
CNEMON: [*Choking with rage.*]   Didn't I say so?
Do you take this for a public square or a market-place?
[*He advances on* SOSTRATOS, *who retreats.*]
Go on, then! If there's anyone you want to see,
Come to my door—why not? Do all your business here!
While you're about it, bring your favourite arm-chair!
Build a committee-room, just here at my front door!

[*He leaves* SOSTRATOS *and turn back to his house.*]
Sheer, shouting rudeness—that's the trouble nowadays.
[*Exit* CNEMON *to his house.* PYRRHIAS *creeps back, but keeps out of*
SOSTRATOS' *way.*]
SOSTRATOS: It seems I've taken on no ordinary job;
This plainly calls for special measures. Should I go
And fetch my father's slave Getas? By God, I will.
There's a spark about him; and he's seen a lot of the world.
Let the old man rave—Getas will be a match for him.
I don't believe in wasting time; a lot can happen
In one day.—Why, here's someone coming out of his house.
[*Enter* MYRRHINE *from* CNEMON's *house.*]
MYRRHINE: Oh, what shall I do now? Isn't that just my luck?
Nurse dropped the bucket down the well!
SOSTRATOS: O Father Zeus!
Saviour Apollo, and Heavenly Twins! What loveliness!
She's ravishing!
MYRRHINE: Father told us when he left the house
To get hot water ready.
SOSTRATOS: [*Appealing to audience.*] Athenians! Did you ever . . . ?
MYRRHINE: If he finds out, he'll beat her terribly. Oh, dear!
By the two goddesses, there's not a moment to lose—
[*She turns towards the shrine, hesitating.*]
Dear Nymphs, I'll have to take some water from your spring.
[*She sees* SOSTRATOS.]
There's someone in there making an offering. I daren't
Disturb him.
SOSTRATOS: Please, give *me* your jug; I'll dip it in
And bring it to you.
MYRRHINE: [*Handing him the jug.*] Will you? Very well, please do.
SOSTRATOS: [*Aside.*] What charm, what breeding!—and a country girl!
MYRRHINE: [*Turning suddenly round.*] Oh, gods!
What sound was that? Is it father coming? How terrible!
He'll beat me if he finds me here.
[*The door of the house on the left opens and* DAOS *comes out.*
MYRRHINE, *relieved, turns to the shrine to look for* SOSTRATOS.]
DAOS: [*Speaking back into the house, addressing Gorgias' mother*
inside.] Now look: I know
That you're my mistress; but I've stayed in long enough
Doing chores for you, while your son Gorgias is out
In the field digging, single-handed. I'm going to help him.

[*He slams the door.*]
Oh, hateful, damnable Poverty, why did we get
So large a share of you? Why have you come to stay
So many years in our house, a guest who never leaves?
SOSTRATOS: [*To* MYRRHINE.] Here's your jug. Come nearer, take it.
[MYRRHINE *takes it and goes towards her door.*]
DAOS: [*Looking from one to the other.*] What's *he* doing there?
SOSTRATOS: [*To* MYRRHINE.] Good-bye now, and attend to your father.
[*Exit* MYRRHINE.]

Oh, she's gone,
And I'm in misery.
[PYRRHIAS *comes forward.*]
PYRRHIAS: Now stop moaning, Sostratos.
SOSTRATOS: Oh, *you've come back.*
PYRRHIAS: Everything'll turn out all right.
SOSTRATOS: Turn out all right? How?
PYRRHIAS: Never worry. Simply do
What you were going to do: find Getas, and explain
The whole thing to him clearly; and then come back here.
[*Exeunt* SOSTRATOS *and* PYRRHIAS *together.*]
DAOS: Now, what the mischief? I don't like the look of this.
A young man making up to Myrrhine? Most improper.
Cnemon, may the gods punish you for the fool you are!
This innocent girl—instead of keeping guard on her,
You leave her alone out here, with no one else about.
This fellow, I'll bet, as soon as he heard the coast was clear,
Blessed his good luck, and flew straight to her. Well, I'd best
Tell Gorgias immediately what's going on;
Then we can both keep a more careful eye on her.
I think I'll go and talk to him now.
[*Voices are heard approaching, talking and singing.*]
There are people coming,
With offerings for Pan. They've had a drop to drink;
This is no time to get involved with *them.* I'm off.
[*Exit* DAOS.]

Translated by Philip Vellacott

From THE CHANGELING, OR THE RUSTIC

THE HAPPIEST LIFE

I'll tell you, Parmenon,
Who seems to me to have the happiest life: the man
Who takes a steady look at the majestic sights
Our world offers—the common sun, stars, water, clouds,
Fire; and having seen them, and lived free from pain, at once
Goes back to where he came from. These same sights will be,
If you live to a hundred, always there, always the same;
And equally if you die young; but you will never
See more majestic sights than these. Think of this time
I speak of as a people's festival, or as
A visit to some city, where you stand and watch
The crowds, the streets, the thieves, the gamblers, and the way
People amuse themselves. If you go back early
To your lodging, you'll have money in your pocket, and
No enemies. The man who stays too long grows tired,
Loses what he once had, gets old, wretched, and poor,
Wanders about, makes enemies, or falls a prey
To plotters; till at last an ignominious death
Sends him off home.

Translated by Philip Vellacott

From AN UNIDENTIFIED PLAY

SHOPPING FOR A WIFE

The right way to go marrying, by Saviour Zeus,
Is the same way you go shopping. You shouldn't haggle over
Irrelevant details—who was the girl's grandfather,
Or grandmother—while giving never a thought or look
To the character of the bride herself, the woman you mean
To live with; and what's the use of hurrying off to the Bank
With her dowry-money, to get the Banker to test the coin—
Which won't stay in the house five months—if you don't apply
A single test to the woman who's going to settle down

In your house for the rest of your life, but take haphazard
An inconsiderate, quarrelsome, difficult wife, who even
May be a talker.
                    I shall take my own daughter round
The whole city: "You who want to marry this girl," I'll say,
"Just chat with her; find out beforehand the true measure
Of the pest that you're acquiring. A woman *is* a pest—
That can't be helped; the luckiest man's the one who gets
The least unbearable pest."

Translated by Philip Vellacott

From AN UNIDENTIFIED PLAY

The Anacharsis mentioned in the following fragment was a prince of the royal family of the Scythians, a nomadic people located in the area of the Crimea and the Don River. According to Herodotus and other Greek writers, this prince traveled widely in the Greek world of the sixth century B.C., *and won a reputation among the Greeks for wisdom.*

DAUGHTER TO MOTHER

Family? I'm fed up with this talk of "family."
Mother, don't—if you love me—every time I mention
A man, start talking about his family. People who
Haven't a single good quality to call their own—
They are the ones who talk like that of family,
Or titles, or decorations; reel off grandfathers
One after the other, and that's all they've got. Can you
Tell me of a man who hasn't got grandfathers? or how
A man could be born without them? People who, for one
Reason or another—living abroad, or losing friends—
Can't name their grandfathers—are they any worse born than those
Who can? Mother, if a man has a noble character
Which prompts him to a good life, then he's of noble birth,
Even if he's a black African. And you "don't like
Scythians"? To hell! Wasn't Anacharsis a Scythian?

Translated by Philip Vellacott

THEOPHRASTUS

c. 370–287 B.C.

From CHARACTERS

Theophrastus succeeded Aristotle as head of the Peripatetic school of philosophy in Athens and was the author of many scientific and philosophical studies—among the survivors are two books on plants. But he also produced a book called Characters. *Written probably in the last quarter of the fourth century B.C., these lively sketches need no introduction; the bores and nuisances they bring so startlingly to life are not confined to ancient Athens.*

The "parasite" mentioned by the tiresome man is a professional dinner guest whose function is to praise the host, ask his opinion, and introduce his best stories. And the Antipater mentioned by the boaster was the Macedonian general who ruled Macedonia for Alexander when he went east and after his death kept the Greek cities subject to Macedon.

THE CHATTERER

The chatterer is the sort of man who sits down beside someone he doesn't know and begins by delivering a panegyric on his own wife; continues with an account of his dream of the night before; then describes in detail what he had for supper. Next, getting into his stride, he remarks how far inferior men of the present day are to the ancients; how reasonable wheat is now in the shops; how full of foreigners Athens is getting. He observes that since the Dionysia it has been good sailing weather; and that if only Zeus would send more rain it would be better for the farmers. Then he tells you what part of his land he will put down to crops next year; and how difficult it is to live; and that Damippus has set up an enormous torch at the Mysteries; and "How many columns has the Odeion?" and "I was violently sick yesterday"; and "What day of the month is it today?" Then he tells you that the Mysteries are in September, the Apaturia in October, and the Rural Dionysia in December. In fact, if you put up with him, he will never stop.

ANXIETY TO PLEASE

The ingratiating man is, shall we say, the sort who greets you from fifty yards off with "My dear man," gazes at you full of admiration, holds you by both hands and won't let go, and then after accompanying you a little way and asking when he is to see you next, finally departs on a note of eulogy. When he is called in to an arbitration he is anxious to please not only the man he is supporting but also his opponent, so as to appear impartial. In a dispute between foreigners and Athenians he will say the foreigners are in the right. When invited out to dinner he will ask his host to call the children; and when they come in he will say they are as like their father as so many peas in a pod. Then he pulls them towards him, kisses them and makes them stand by him. Then he romps with them, and sings the words of the game himself—

> *Atishoo, atishoo,*
> *We all fall down!*

—and he lets some of them fall asleep on his stomach, in spite of the cramp it gives him.

THE TALKER

The talker is the sort of man who, when you meet him, if you make any remark to him, will tell you that you are quite wrong; that he himself knows all the facts, and if you listen to him you shall learn what they are. When you reply, he interrupts you with. "You've already told me, remember, what you're just going to say"; or "What a good thing you reminded me!" or, "It's so valuable to have a talk"; or, "Oh, I just forgot to mention—" or, "You saw the point at once"; or, "Yes, I've been watching you to see if you'd come round to my view." He gives himself openings like this, one after the other, so that you never have time to take breath. Then, when he has talked the hind legs off individual victims, nothing will stop him advancing on groups and gatherings, and making them leave their business in the middle and take to flight. He will even walk into schools or sports-grounds, and hinder boys in their exercises, by talking in this endless way to their trainers and teachers. When people say, "We must go now," he likes to keep them company on the way and see them safely home. When he hears what has happened in the Assembly, he tells you about it; and adds, for good measure, the story of the battle in Aristophon's year, and of the Spartan victory under Lysander; and of the speech he himself once made, which drew some applause from the Assembly; at the same time throwing into his discourse some derogatory remarks about "the masses." The result is that his audience either let their attention wander, or drop off to sleep, or desert him in mid-course and vanish. When he is on a jury he prevents his fellow-jurors from reaching a verdict; in a theatre he won't let you follow the play, at a dinner he won't let you eat." "A talker finds it hard to stop," he says; and adds that his tongue runs on of itself, and he couldn't stop it, even if people thought him worse than a nest of swallows. He is actually ready to let his own children make fun of him, when they are feeling sleepy and say to him, "Daddy, talk to us and send us to sleep!"

THE SKINFLINT, OR STINGY MAN

The stingy man is the sort who will come to your house in the middle of the month and ask you for half a month's interest on his loan. When he is at table with others, he will count how many cups each person has drunk; and of the whole company at dinner, he will pour the smallest libation to Artemis. If you buy anything from him, however cheaply, he will say, when you send in your account, that it has taken his last penny. If a servant breaks a jug or a dish, he stops the price of it out of his allowance. If his wife has dropped a threepenny-bit, he is the sort of person to start moving the furniture, shifting couches and cupboards, rummaging among rugs. If he has anything to sell, he will only let it go at a price which means a bad bargain for the buyer. He would never let you eat a fig out of his garden, or walk through his land, or pick up one of his windfall olives or dates. Every single day he inspects his boundaries to see if they have been tampered with. He is a terror, too, for enforcing the right of distraint, and for charging compound interest. When it is his turn to give the parish dinner, he cuts the meat into tiny slices to serve out. He goes off to market, and comes home again without buying anything. He forbids his wife to lend salt, or lamp-wick, or herbs, or barley-grains, or garlands, or holy-cakes. "These things all mount up, you know," he says, "in a twelvemonth."

THE TIRESOME MAN

The tiresome man is the kind who will walk in when you have just dozed off and wake you up to have a chat with you. When people are on the point of setting sail he will hinder their departure. He will arrive for an appointment, and then ask you to wait till he has taken a walk. He will take his child from its nurse, bite up its food and feed it himself, cooing and clucking at it and calling it "Daddy's little imp." When you sit next to him at a meal he will describe to you how he took a dose of hellebore which gave him a thorough clean-out; "You should have seen the colour of the bile in my excreta," he says, "darker than that gravy you've got." He's a terror for asking his mother, in front of relations, "Tell me, Mummy, when you were in labour with me, was it an easy birth?" Then he answers for her, and says that childbirth is pleasurable, but that it is not easy to conceive a human being without experiencing both pleasure and pain. He tells you that in his house he has cold water laid on from a reservoir; that he has a garden with many kinds of vegetables, young and tender; that he has a cook who is very clever with fish; that his house is a regular hotel, and his friends are like the proverbial sieve: "The more you do for them, the less they're satisfied." When he gives a dinner, he draws his guests' attention to his parasite, commenting on the man's personal qualities. And as he stands over the wine-bowl he announces encouragingly that provision has been made for the pleasure of those present: they have only to ask and his slave will fetch her at once from the agency. "Then," he says, "she will supply us all with music and merriment."

THE BOASTER

The boaster is a man who will stand on the jetty talking to foreigners about the vast sums he has at sea; describing the wide extent of his investment in overseas trade, with details of his own gains and losses; and while shooting a great line on this topic, he will send off his boy to the Bank, where his balance is one drachma. If you travel with him, he has you at his mercy; he loves to tell you how he campaigned with Alexander; how he got on with him; how many jewel-encrusted cups he brought home. Then he talks about Asiatic craftsmen, maintaining that they are better than the European; and all this he will say, without having ever travelled outside Attica. He will tell you he has had letters—three in succession—from Antipater inviting him to Macedonia; that he has been offered a licence for tax-free export of timber from Macedonia, but he refused it, so that no one may cast aspersions on him as a pro-Macedonian. In the famine, he says, his outlay in gifts to distressed citizens amounted to more than five talents—"I never could say No." Then, though the men sitting next to him are strangers, he tells one of them to work it out in writing; and reckoning in sums of six hundred drachmae or one mina, and speciously assigning a name to each gift, he finally makes it as much as ten talents. He points out that this is the amount contributed by himself to charities, mentioning that it does not include the trierarchies or other public expenses he has undertaken. He will go up to a dealer in horses of quality, and pretend that he wants to buy. He will go into a clothing-store, and ask to see clothing priced at anything up to two talents, and then browbeat his slave for coming without his money. And when he is living in a rented house he will assert, to someone who doesn't know this, that it is the family residence; but he intends to sell it. "It's a bit small," he says; "I do a lot of entertaining."

THE AUTHORITARIAN

The authoritarian is the sort of person who, when the Assembly is discussing what men to appoint as assistants to the Archon in organizing the procession at the Great Dionysia, will come forward and state his opinion that those appointed should be given unconditional powers; and if someone else proposes ten assistants, he will answer, "One is enough, but he must be a *man*." Of the poems of Homer there is one single line he has made his own:

From many rulers no good comes; let one man rule.

Of all the rest of Homer he knows nothing. Typical of him are utterances like this: "We must get together by ourselves and discuss these matters, out of reach of the rabble and the street-corner. It's time we stopped kow-towing to every jack-in-office, and ourselves accepting kicks or compliments from them. Either they or we must run this city. "He will go out about midday, with his cloak thrown well back, his hair tastefully trimmed, his nails precisely pared, and strut about declaiming statements like this: "These blackmailers make Athens impossible to live in"; or, "In the law-courts we are simply slapped down by corrupt juries"; or, "People who meddle in politics—I can't imagine what they want"; or, "The working classes—they're always the same: ungrateful, and ready to obey anyone who offers a bribe or a bonus." Or he will tell you how ashamed he feels in the Assembly, when some mean-looking, scruffy citizen sits down next to him. "The rich are being bled to death," he says, "with subsidizing the navy, the theatre, the festivals, and everything else. When is it going to end? Democratic agitators—how I detest them!" Then he names Theseus as the original cause of the country's deterioration; for it was he who concentrated the twelve small States in one, thus elevating the lower classes, putting power into the hands of the majority, and destroying the monarchy. He adds that Theseus got his deserts; for he was himself the first victim of democracy. And many other such assertions he bestows on foreigners and on Athenians whose temperament and policies are similar to his.

Translated by Philip Vellacott

CALLIMACHUS

c. 310–240 B.C.

From THE AITIA

Callimachus came from the Greek city of Cyrene in what is now Libya to Alexandria, where King Ptolemy II of Egypt assigned him the job of making a catalogue of the great library; when complete, it ran to 120 volumes. But Calllimachus was also a poet, and an influential one. The Roman poets of the first century B.C. all expressed their indebtedness to him.

The Aitia (literally, Causes) was one of Callimachus' major works. It was some 7,000 lines long, and explored the mythic origins ("causes") of contemporary customs and religious rites. We have only fragments of it, most of them on scraps of papyrus from Egypt, but it is clear that the length of the poem does not violate the Callimachean program of keeping poems short, since the Aitia consists of a large number of different stories, none of them told at great length.

PROLOGUE

The "Prologue" is a programmatic poem written for a second edition of the Aitia. *Like much Alexandrian poetry, it is packed with literary allusions, some of them no longer fully clear to us.* Demeter's Cornucopia *is possibly a long poem by Philetas of Cos that is contrasted unfavorably with his shorter poems, and the "fat* Lady *poem" may be a reference to Mimnermus'* Nanno, *a long poem that, again, is dismissed in favor of his shorter efforts. (Hardly any of the work of these two poets has survived.) The flight of the cranes (a reference to Homer) and the long shots of the Massagetae (a reference to Herodotus?) are two images for long poems, and a* parasang *(as anyone knows who was dragged at a slow pace through Xenophon's* Anabasis *at school) is a Persian measure of distance, about three and one-third miles.*

The malignant gnomes who write reviews in Rhodes
    are muttering about my poetry again
tone-deaf ignoramuses out of touch with the Muse—
because I have not consummated a continuous epic
    of thousands of lines on heroes and lords
but turn out minor texts as if I were a child
    although my decades of years are substantial.
To which brood of cirrhotic adepts
I, Callimachus, thus:

A few distichs in the pan outweigh *Deméter's Cornucopia,*
    and Mimnermos is sweet for a few subtle lines,
not that fat *Lady* poem. Let "cranes fly south to Egypt"
    when they lust for pygmy blood,
and "the Masságetai arch arrows long distance"
    to lodge in a Mede,
but nightingales are honey-pale
    and small poems are sweet.
So evaporate, Green-Eyed Monsters,
or learn to judge poems by the critic's art
    instead of by the parasang,
and don't snoop around here for a poem that rumbles:
    not I but Zeus owns the thunder.

When I first put a tablet on my knees, the Wolf-God
    Apollo appeared and said:

"Fatten your animal for sacrifice, poet,
    but keep your muse slender."
And
"follow trails unrutted by wagons,
don't drive your chariot down public highways,
    but keep to the back roads though the going is narrow.
We are the poets for those who love
    the cricket's high chirping, not the noise of the jackass."

A long-eared bray for others, for me delicate wings,
    dewsip in old age and bright air for food,

mortality dropping from me like Sicily shifting
    its triangular mass from Enkélados' chest.
No nemesis here:
the Muses do not desert the gray heads
of those on whose childhood
their glance once brightened.

> *Translated by Stanley Lombardo and Diane Rayor*

From HYMN V

THE BLINDING OF TIRESIAS

The Fifth Hymn of Callimachus, "The Bath of Pallas," is a fictional recreation of a ritual enacted at Argos, the bath of the statue of Athena. There was a similar ceremony at Athens, the Plynteria, *literally, "Washing," for Athens' patron divinity Pallas Athena. The statue was taken down to the sea and washed (as in Euripides' play* Iphigenia in Tauris*). Here the voice, presumably that of a priestess of the goddess, addresses the women engaged in the ceremony—"My dears"—and tells the story of the blinding of Tiresias, who saw Athena naked as she bathed in the waters of the spring Hippocrene on Mount Helicon. To see a goddess naked was a great misfortune. Actaeon, the great hunter and favorite of the goddess Artemis, saw the goddess bathing in a stream; she drove his hounds mad and they tore their master to pieces.*

There was a time in Thebes, my dears, Athena
    loved a nymph, loved her to distraction,

loved her more than any other, the mother
   of Tirésias, Kháriklo by name.
And they were always together: when Athena
   drove her horses to ancient Théspiai
or to Plataîa or Haliártos,
   riding through the farmlands of Boiótia,
or on to Koroneîa, where her grove is heavy
   with incense, and her altars lie close
to the river Kuríalos, it was goddess and nymph
   in one chariot together.
No party or dance was ever complete
   without Kháriklo there: then it was sweet.

But even for Kháriklo there were tears in store,
   dear as she was to Athena's heart.
One day these two unbuckled their robes.
   It was by Horse Spring, on Hélikon,
and the two were bathing in the beautiful creek.
   It was noon on the hill, dead calm, silent heat,
and they were bathing together. High noon. The hillside
   was steeped in awesome quiet,
and Tirésias was hunting, alone with his dogs,
   roaming that eerie hill.
                              He was young,
just bearded. Dry thirst led him down to the creek.
   And he stumbled upon the forbidden scene.
Controlling her anger, Athena spoke evenly:
   "Some god—which one, son of Evéres?—
has led you a rough road
   with an eyeless return."
And with her words night took the boy's eyes.
   He stood there, speechless, pain gluing his knees,
his voice paralyzed with shock. But the nymph screamed:

"What have you done to my boy?
Is this how goddesses
show their friendship?
You've blinded him! O my poor baby,
you've seen the breast and thighs
   of Pallas Athena
but never the sunlight again.
Mountain of my sorrow, O Hélikon,

never will I set foot on you again.
You trade too hard,
  my son's eyes
for a few roe and deer!"

As she said this she cradled her son in her arms,
  mourning over him like a nightingale,
and led him away. But the goddess Athena
  pitied her friend and said this to her:

"You've spoken in anger, divine woman. Take back your words.
  It was not I who struck your son blind.
Putting out your eyes is not sweet to Athena,
  but the laws of Kronos demand
that whoever sees an immortal against the god's will
  must pay for the sight, and pay dearly.
What is done, divine woman, cannot be undone;
  this is the thread the Moirai spun
when you brought him to light. Now, son of Evéres,
  accept like a man what is only your due.
How many sacrifices would Autónoê burn,
  how many would Aristasîos, her husband,
to see their son Aktaion merely go blind?
  He will run in the company of great Artemis,
but neither their hunts in the hills together
  nor all of the arrows they'll shoot
will save him when he sees the bath of the goddess,
  not wanting to, mind you, but still his hounds
will chew their master to bits, and his mother will gather
  his bones from bushes all over the hill.
She will think you lucky and a fortunate woman
  to have your son home from the hills only blind.

"You mustn't grieve so, darling. Your son will be honored,
  all for your sake, by divine gift to him.
I'll make him a prophet, his fame will be mythic,
  the greatest prophet that ever has been:
He'll know all the birds in the sky, those of good omen
  and those whose flight presages doom.
He'll give oracles to the Boiótians, oracles to Kadmos,
  oracles to the mighty descendants of Lábdakos.

I will give him a great staff to guide his footsteps,
and I will give him time, a long term of life,
and he alone,when he dies, will walk among the dead,
wits intact, honored by Agesiláos, host of the dead."

When she had finished speaking Athena nodded her head,
ensuring fulfillment of all that she said.
Pallas alone of all Zeus' daughters
has received paternal prerogatives,
for no mother bore her, but the high brow of Zeus,
and neither brow bends to affirm what is false,

Translated by Stanley Lombardo and Diane Rayor

EPIGRAMS

*For a poet who proclaimed the supremacy of the short poem the epi-
gram was a natural form, and Callimachus was a master of the genre.
The third specimen presented here is a courtly compliment to Berenice,
the wife of the reigning monarch of Egypt, Ptolemy II. The fourth and
fifth are two versions of tribute to a fellow poet, Heraclitus, one the
classic Victorian translation of Henry Cory, the other a spare (Callimachean) version by Kenneth Rexroth. The sixth is the shortest and perhaps the most moving epigram in the whole enormous range of the
genre.*

1

"Is Kháridas beneath this stone?"
"Yes, if you mean Arrímas's son
From Kyréne, I'm his tomb."

"Kháridas, what's it like below?"
"Dark." "Are there exits?" "None."
"And Pluto?" "He's a myth." "Oh, no!"

"All that I'm telling you is true,
But if you want the bright side too,
The cost of living here is low."

2

He stooped to put flowers on his stepmother's tomb,
Thinking she'd changed since meeting her doom.

He died when her gravestone fell on his head.
Stepmothers are dangerous even when dead.

3

Four Graces now, for to the Three
One has been added, just modeled
And still wet with perfume:
   Blest, radiant Bereníkê,
Without whom the very Graces are graceless.

   Translated by Stanley Lombardo and Diane Rayor

4

Somebody told me you were dead,
Herakleitos, and I wept when
I remembered how many times
The sun had set as we gossiped
Together when you came to see
Me once from Halikarnassos.
Where are you now? Long, long ago
Ashes. But your "Nightingales" still
Live. Death snatches everything, but
He shall not lay his hand on them.

   Translated by Kenneth Rexroth

5

They told me, Heraclitus, they told me you were dead,
They brought me bitter news to hear and bitter tears to shed.
I wept as I remember'd how often you and I
Had tired the sun with talking and sent him down the sky.

And now that thou art lying, my dear old Carian guest,
A handful of grey ashes, long, long ago at rest,

Still are thy pleasant voices, thy nightingales, awake;
For Death, he taketh all away, but them he cannot take.

Translated by Henry Cory

6

His father Philip laid here the twelve-year-old boy
Nikotelês:
his dearest hope.

Translated by Dudley Fitts

APOLLONIUS RHODIUS

c. 295–215 B.C.

From ARGONAUTICA

Like Callimachus, Apollonius of Rhodes worked in the Alexandrian Library; he was in fact at one time head librarian. But, unlike Callimachus, he turned to the long poem, the epic. Though his Argonautica *is nowhere near as long as the* Iliad *or the* Odyssey, *he uses Homer's hexameter line and, in the main, his epic dialect. But he avoids the Homeric use of fixed epithets and typical scenes. And in other respects too he is worlds away from Homer's heroic sagas. Jason is a less than heroic figure on more than one occasion throughout the poem, and Medea is treated with a psychological depth that is unlike anything to be found in Homer. In addition, Apollonius' epic gods are very different from the formidable presences that people Homer's Olympus. The three goddesses who appear in the opening scenes of Book III—Hera, Athena, and Aphrodite (Cypris)—are more like great ladies of an eighteenth-century royal court; the scene between Aphrodite and her naughty child Eros seems to call for the brush of Fragonard or Boucher.*

THREE GODDESSES

The story begins in Iolcos, the chief city of Thessaly in central Greece. Its king, Pelias, had been told by a prophet that he would meet his death through the agency of a man who came wearing one sandal. Jason, his nephew, who was the rightful heir to the throne Pelias sat on, happened to lose a sandal while crossing a stream in flood on his way to the palace of Pelias. The king decided to get rid of him by sending him off to bring back to Greece the Golden Fleece, which was in the possession of King Aietes of Colchis, a land at the far eastern end of the Black Sea. The first ship, the Argo, *is built with the aid of Athena, and Jason and his Argonauts, after many adventures on the way, finally arrive in Colchis, where they bed down for the night by the bank of a river. At this point two goddesses, Athena, Jason's protector, and Hera, who has been insulted by Pelias and so wants Jason to get safely home, decide to ask for help from Aphrodite. They beg her to make Medea fall in love with Jason, so that she will use her magic powers to enable him to deal with the formidable guardians of the Golden Fleece. Apollonius begins by invoking Erato, one of the Nine Muses, whose name signals the dominant theme of what is to follow.*

Now come, Erató, stand by me, and tell me how Jason
brought the fleece back from Kolchis to Iolkos
through the love of Medeia: for you yourself belong
to Kypris' team, you bewitch with the cares of passion
virginal maidens, your very name's erotic!

So the heroes stayed out of sight, waited in ambush
among the clustering reed-beds; but they'd been spotted
by Hera and Athena, who retired to a chamber
well apart from Zeus himself and the other immortals
and took counsel together. First Hera sounded out
Athena: "Daughter of Zeus, let's begin with your opinion—
what's to be done? Will you work out some trick that lets them
get the golden fleece from Aiëtes and take it back
to Hellas? It seems unlikely they could deceive and sweet-talk him
into agreement, he's so appallingly arrogant—yet
no possible line of approach should be left untested."
  So she spoke, and instantly Athena made answer:

Apollonius Rhodius

"I too, Hera, was debating such matters in my mind
when you put your blunt question to me; but as yet,
though I've weighed up numerous plans to boost the heroes'
spirits, I still don't feel I've hit upon the right one."
With that, eyes fixed on the ground before their feet,
both sat there, each brooding in private, till Hera quickly
came up with a new proposal, and broke the silence:
"Let's both go and call on Kypris: when we've found her
let's urge her to tell her son (if only he'll obey her!)
to aim one of his shafts at Aiëtes' drug-wise daughter,
charm *her* into love for Jason. If he follows
her suggestions, I reckon he'll get that fleece back to Hellas."
Such her words; the shrewd suggestion pleased Athena,
who once more made her an accommodating answer:
"Hera, my father bore me to know nothing of such pangs,
nor do I feel that need which can charm a man's desires;
but if this project pleases you, then I'd be willing
to follow—but you, when we meet her, must do the talking."
    So she spoke, and up they both got, and made their way
to Kypris' big house, that her lame husband built for her
when first he brought her home from Zeus as his bride.
Entering through the courtyard, they stood in the colonnade
of the chamber where the goddess tended Hephaistos' bed.
He himself had gone off early to his forge and anvils
in a roomy recess on the wandering island, where with fireblast
he wrought all manner of intricate objects; but herself was sitting
alone in the house, by the door, on a well-turned chair.
She'd let her hair tumble loose on each white shoulder
and was teasing it out with a golden comb, about to braid it
into long plaits; but when she saw them there before her
she stopped, and invited them in, and got up from her chair
and made them sit down on recliners; then settled herself too,
gathered up her mane of hair, still uncombed, with a ribbon,
and smiling, ironic, addressed them thus: "Dear ladies,
what occasion, what purpose is it that brings you here
after so long an absence? Why both of you? Hitherto
I've had few visits from you, high goddesses that you are."
To her Hera delivered this reply: "You will have your joke,
But what concerns us here is a serious problem.
Already Aison's son and his crew, in hot pursuit of
the fleece, have their ship at anchor in the Phasis river.
For all of them, since the moment of action's at hand,

but above all for Aison's son, our anxiety's terrible.
Him, even should he voyage to the nether regions
of Hades, to free Ixion from his brazen chains,
I will protect, with all my limbs' innate strength,
so that Pelias, who in his arrogance left me unhonoured
with sacrifice, may not make mock of me by escaping
his evil fate. Besides, long before this Jason had won my
great love, ever since at the estuary of the flooded
Anauros he met me (I was testing men's righteousness)
on his way home from hunting: all the mountains and lofty
peaks were powdered with snow, while down their gulleys
water cascaded in thunderous torrents. I'd taken
the likeness of an old woman: he felt sorry for me,
heaved me up on his shoulders, bore me through the rapids.
Hence the unfailing high honour in which I hold him. Nor will
Pelias pay for his outrage, unless you grant Jason
a safe homecoming." This speech left Kypris dumbfounded,
awestruck at the sight of Hera entreating her,
so now it was with gentle words she made answer:
"Revered goddess, may you encounter nothing more vile than
Kypris, if I make light of your most urgent appeal
either in word or deed, whatever can be effected
by these weak hands of mine—and I ask no favour back."
Thus she spoke, and Hera gave a considered response:
"It's no lack of force or hands has brought us to you—
relax, don't fret, just tell that boy of yours to charm
Aiëtes' virgin daughter with passion for Aison's son.
For if she wishes him well and gives him good counsel,
I think he'll easily capture the golden fleece
and get back to Iolkos, for she's guile incarnate."
Thus she spoke, and Kypris now addressed them both:
"Athena and Hera, he'd certainly do *your* bidding
rather than mine: for you, despite his shamelessness,
there'll be some faint glimmer of shame in his eye, but for me
he cares nothing, but always provokes me, treats me with contempt.
And indeed, thus plagued with his naughtiness, I was minded
to smash up his bow and nasty-sounding arrows
in public! The threats he uttered when he was angry!—
that if I don't keep my hands right off him while he's still
in control of his temper, later I'll have only myself to blame."
    Thus she spoke, and the goddesses smiled, exchanged glances
one with the other. Much chagrined, she went on:

"Others find my troubles a joke, and I certainly can't tell them
to everyone: bad enough that I know them myself.
But now, since this is a plan that you both cherish,
I'll do my best to coax him: he won't refuse me."
Thus she spoke; and Hera clasped her slender hand,
and with a fleeting smile responded slily:
"Just so, Kythereia: in this business, as you yourself say,
act with dispatch—and don't be cross, don't wrangle
with your boy in your anger: he'll change his ways hereafter."
    So saying she rose from her chair, and Athena likewise,
and both hurried off back home. But Kypris
went checking the nooks of Olympos in search of Eros.
She found him some way off, in Zeus's tree-rich orchard,
not alone: he had Ganymede with him, whom earlier Zeus
had set up in heaven, a hearthmate to the immortals,
being entranced by his beauty. The two of them were playing
at knucklebones—golden ones—as boys in the same house will;
and already greedy Eros was clutching a fistful
in his left hand, holding them tight, close under his breast
as he stood erect there, a sweet blush mantling
the bloom of his cheeks. But Ganymede was crouched down
beside him, silent, dejected; just two dice left, and he threw them
one after the other, maddened by Eros' snickering,
and losing both in a trice, like all their predecessors,
took himself off, empty-handed and hopeless, failed
to notice Kypris approaching. She stopped before her son,
chucked him under the chin, and sharply addressed him:
"What are you grinning at, you unspeakable little horror?
Did you cheat him again, win unfairly, cash in on his innocence?
Listen now: if you're willing to do the job I tell you,
I'll give you one of Zeus' most beautiful playthings,
that his dear nurse Adrasteia fashioned for him
when he was still a mere infant in that cave on Ida:
a well-rounded ball, than which you'll get no better
toy, not even from Hephaistos' hands. Its rings
have been fashioned of gold, and over each are basted
twin segment-edges, all the way round, their seams
camouflaged, since over each one runs a spiral
pattern of cobalt. If you toss this ball up to catch it
like a meteor it unleashes a gleaming airy trail.
This I will give you—if you will shoot Aiëtes' virgin
daughter full of desire for Jason. And don't you loiter,

otherwise my gratitude will be much diminished." Thus
she spoke, and Eros, hearing them, welcomed her words.
He tossed aside all his playthings, and, two-fisted,
seized the goddess's robe on both sides, hugged her close,
begged her to give it him *now*, on the spot. She countered
with gentle words, pinching his cheeks, then drew him
towards her, kissed him, and replied as follows:
"Your dearest head, and my own, now be my witness
that, yes, I'll give you this present, I won't cheat you,
so long as you put a shaft into Aiëtes' daughter."
Such her words. He collected his knucklebones, dropped them—
after counting them carefully—in his mother's dazzling lap,
then slung from a golden baldric the quiver he'd left leaning
against a tree-trunk, took up his curved bow, hurried
on his way out of great Zeus's rich fruit-laden orchard,
and then passed on, out through the airy portals
of Olympos. From there a vertiginous skyborne path
runs downward: the peaks of two high-towering mountains,
roof to the world, support this vault of heaven
where the rising sun's first rays glow blushing-red.
Down below he could see, in the course of his long flight,
now fertile stretches of farmland, teeming cities,
the lines of rivers; now mountains and the surrounding sea.

Translated by Peter Green

JASON AND MEDEA

*A miraculous flying ram rescued Phrixus and his sister Helle, children of
Aeolus, king of Thebes, from their cruel stepmother Ino, who planned to
kill them. As the ram flew over the straits that separate Europe from
Asia, Helle felt giddy and fell off into the sea (which took its name, the
Hellespont, from her). Phrixus was carried on to Colchis, where he was
welcomed by King Aeetes and married Chalciope, the king's daughter,
elder sister of Medea. The ram was sacrificed; its golden fleece was hung
up in a sacred precinct, guarded by a dragon. Phrixus had four sons by
Chalciope. When they grew up, they decided to go to Greece to claim
their inheritance. But they were shipwrecked on an island from which
they were rescued by Jason, on his way to Colchis, and so came home
with the Argonauts.*

*When Jason goes to ask Aeetes for the fleece, he takes the sons of
Phrixus with him. As they all appear at the palace, Chalciope recognizes*

her sons and Medea sees Jason for the first time; as she does, Eros shoots
his arrow and she falls in love. Meanwhile Argus, one of the sons of
Phrixus, explains Jason's mission to the king, but Aeetes angrily rejects
the request for the fleece. When Jason appeals in person, Aeetes tells
him he can have the fleece provided he can yoke two fire-breathing bulls,
plow a field with them, sow the ground with serpent's teeth that grow
into armed men, and kill the men as they spring out of the ground. Jason
accepts the challenge and goes back to his ship to give his companions
the news. Argus suggests that Jason should enlist the support of Medea,
whose skill with magic herbs enables her to work miracles. He returns to
the palace and urges his mother Chalciope to speak to Medea. She does
so, and Medea, madly in love with Jason, agrees to help him. But as night
falls she agonizes over her decision to betray her father.

Night soon darkened the earth, and out on ocean
sailors looked up from their ships to the stars of Orion
and the Great Bear, while travellers and gate-porters
longed for a chance to sleep, and a profound torpor
enveloped some mother whose children had all perished:
throughout the city even the dogs ceased their barking,
human voices fell silent: stillness possessed the deepening gloom.
But on Medeia sleep sweet could get no hold, kept
wakeful as she was by worrying over Jason
in her longing for him, and dreading the great might of the bulls
that would bring him an ill fate there on Ares' ploughland.
Close and quick now beat the heart in her bosom,
as a shaft of sunlight will dance along the housewall
when flung up from water new-poured into pail or cauldron:
hither and thither the swiftly circling ripples
send it darting, a *frisson* of brightness; in just such a way
her virgin heart now beat a tattoo on her ribs,
her eyes shed tears of pity, constant anguish
ran smouldering through her flesh, hotwired her finespun
nerve-ends, needled into the skull's base, the deep spinal
cord where pain pierces sharpest when the unresting
passions inject their agony into the senses.
Her mind veered: now she thought she'd give him the magic stuff
to quell the bulls; now not, but would herself die with him;
then the next moment that she'd neither help him nor perish,
but rather just stay put, and bear her fate in silence.
Finally, indecisive, she sat herself down and said:

"Wretch that I am, I'm for trouble, one way or the other—
my mind lacks any resource, there's no sure remedy
for this pain of mine, it burns without cess: how I wish
I'd been killed already by the swift shafts of Artemis
before I'd ever set eyes on him, before Chalkiope's sons
had gone to Achaia: it was a god or some Fury
brought them thence hither, for us sore grief and weeping.
Let the contest destroy him, then, if it's his destiny
to die on that ploughland! For how could I set up my magic
drugs and my parents not know it? What tale can I tell them?
What deception, what crafty scheme will there be to help me?
How catch him alone, approach him, away from his companions?
And suppose him dead—not even thus can I hope, with my
bad luck, for relief from my sorrows: it's then, when bereft of life,
that he'd do me most grievous harm. . . . Ah, let modesty go hang,
and my good name with it! Saved by my intervention
let him take off, unharmed, for anywhere he chooses—
and then, the very day that he triumphs in his contest,
may I find death, either stretching my neck from a roofbeam
or swallowing drugs that destroy the human spirit.
Yet even so, when I'm dead, there'll be nods and winks, reproaches
at my expense, the whole city will broadcast my fate
far and wide, my name will be common coin, bandied
to and fro, with vile insults, on the lips of our Kolchian
women—"This girl who cared so much for some foreign
man that she died, this girl who shamed home and parents,
overcome by sheer lust—' What reproach will I not suffer?
With my blind infatuation would it not be better
this very night to slough life off, here in my chamber,
a sudden end, unexplained, and so escape all censure,
before committing such deeds, unspeakable, infamous?"
With that she fetched out a casket, in which were stored
drugs of all kinds, some healing, others destructive,
and setting it on her knees she wept, raining endless
tears down over her bosom, a flood, a torrent,
as she bitterly mourned her fate. A yearning seized her
to select some lethal drug, and then to drink it,
and she actually started to lift the hasps of the casket,
poor girl, in her eagerness; but then, on a sudden,
a deathly fear gripped her heart of loathsome Hades,
and long she froze, numb and speechless, while around her
all life's delectable cares caressed her vision.

She remembered the many delights that exist among the living,
she remembered her happy companions, as a young girl will,
and the sun grew sweeter to look on than ever before
once she truly reached out to all these things with her mind.
The casket she raised from her lap and put away once more,
transformed by the promptings of Hera, wavering no longer
between decisions, but impatient for dawn to break
quickly, that moment, so she could give him the spellbinding
charms as she'd covenanted, and meet him face to face.
Time and again she unbolted and opened her door
watching for first light, and happy she was when daybreak
brightened the sky, and folk began stirring in the city.

[*The next morning, Medea, with her young women in attendance, sets
off for the Temple of Hecate to await Jason's arrival. While waiting she
and her attendants dance and play, a scene reminiscent of Nausicaa and
her maids in the* Odyssey. *The girls have been ordered to withdraw when
Jason approaches.*

*Jason's mention of Ariadne (who in rescuing Theseus from the Mino-
taur betrayed her father and her own people, sailing off with him for
Greece) and Medea's questions about this episode strike a grim ironic
note. The fact is not mentioned, but Apollonius' readers knew that
Theseus, on the way home, abandoned Ariadne—as Jason later, in Corinth, will abandon Medea.*]

Medeia could not remove her thoughts to other matters
whatever games she might play: not a one that she embarked on
caught her attention for long. She quickly found them boring,
kept helplessly chopping and changing. She couldn't hold
her eyes quietly on her attendants, but was forever
looking round up the road, peering into the distance.
The times her heart stopped in her breast, when she couldn't be
    sure
if the sound that scampered by her was wind or footfall!
But soon enough he appeared to her in her longing
like Sirius, springing high into heaven out of Ocean,
a star most bright and splendid to observe in
its ascent, yet to flocks an unspeakable disaster:
in such splendour did Jason appear to her eager gaze,
yet his coming started the sickening miseries of passion.
The heart dropped out of her breast, of their own accord

her eyes misted over, a warm blush mantled her cheeks.
Her knees she lacked strength to shift, forward or backward,
while her feet were nailed to the ground. Her attendants meanwhile
had all retired to a distance, away from them both.
Silent and speechless the two were left face to face
like oaks or tall pine-trees, side by side in the mountains
standing deep-rooted and quiet, while a calm
stillness prevails, but then a breeze comes blowing
and stirs them to endless murmuring converse: so these two,
stirred by the winds of love, talked on to one another.
Perceiving that she'd been made the victim of some heaven-sent
twist to the mind, with comforting flattery Jason addressed her:
"Young lady, why so in awe of me? Because I'm alone?
I'm not like some of those other loudmouthed braggarts
you'll find around, nor was I before, when still dwelling
in my own country. So, girl, no need for such modesty—
feel free to ask or tell me whatever you've a mind to.
No, since we've come together with friendly motives,
on holy ground, where deception's unthinkable,
speak openly, ask what you will—only do not beguile me
with sweet-sounding talk, since at the beginning you promised
your own sister to give me the drugs to enhance my strength.
By your parents I implore you, by Hekate herself,
by Zeus, who extends his hand to guests and to suppliants;
both as suppliant and as guest I come before you here,
kneeling perforce through my need, since without your assistance
I'll never come out on top in this grievous contest.
And to you I'll make return later for your assistance,
as is right and proper for distant dwellers to do,
promoting your fame and good name; so too will the other
heroes spread your renown when they're back in Hellas,
with those heroes' wives and mothers, who maybe already
are sitting there on the seastrand, and making lament for us:
their weary load of sorrow you could scatter to the winds.
Indeed, Theseus too once was saved from a nasty ordeal
by the kindness of Ariadne, Minos' maiden daughter,
whom Pasiphaë, child of the Sun, bore to him; but Ariadne,
once Minos had calmed his anger, boarded a vessel
with Theseus and fled her country. Her even the immortals
loved dearly, and as witness to her in mid-heaven
a starry crown, that men now speak of as Ariadne's,
orbits all night long among the sky's constellations.

So to you too gratitude will accrue from the gods, should you rescue
such a great crew, heroes all; for your appearance
suggests that you're of a sweet and friendly disposition."
Thus he spoke, flattering her; and she, with lowered gaze,
smiled sweet as nectar, and the heart within her melted,
she soared on his praise, looked up directly at him,
yet couldn't decide how to begin their discussion
but felt the urge to blurt out everything at once.
First, though, without hesitation she took from her fragrant
      breast-band
the drug, and he quickly laid hands on it, rejoicing.
And indeed she'd have gladly drawn out all the soul from her breast
and given it to him, exulting in his great need for her:
such the sweet flame that Eros sent flashing forth
from Jason's fair head, and ravished away her eyes'
bright glances: melting, it warmed the heart within her
just as dewdrops, a necklace around rose-trees,
melt and dissolve when warmed by morning sunlight.
Both of them now kept their eyes downcast on the ground
out of modesty, now again stole glances at one another,
from beneath bright brows exchanged their smiles of yearning.
Finally, with great effort, the maiden greeted him thus:
"Listen carefully. This is the way I'll work your rescue.
When you go to my father, and he furnishes you
with the deadly teeth from the dragon's jaws for your sowing,
then wait for the midpoint that divides the passing night,
and after washing yourself in the flow of the tireless river,
alone, apart from the others, wrapped in a dark cloak,
dig a round pit, and over it cut the throat of
a ewe and sacrifice it, burning the carcass whole
on a pyre that you've stacked up high at the pit's brink,
and sweeten with offerings Hékate, Perses' only daughter,
pouring out from a cup the bees' hive-garnered produce.
Then, when you've appeased the goddess, forgetting nothing,
turn away and retreat from the pyre. You must not let the sound
of footsteps impel you to turn, to look behind you,
no, nor dogs barking, lest you abort the spell
and yourself fail to return in good order to your comrades.
Then, at dawn, steep this drug in water, strip off naked,
and rub it all over your body like oil: within it
there'll be great strength and unlimited prowess—it's not men
you'd think of matching yourself with, but the immortal gods.

On top of this, see that your spear and shield are sprinkled,
and your sword too: then you'll be proof against the spear-points
of the earthborn men, against the irresistible onrush
of flame from the deadly bulls. Yet you'll not stay immunc
for long, but for one day only: still, never back off
from the contest. And I'll tell you something else to help you:
As soon as you've yoked the tough oxen, and speedily
with might and main ploughed over that stubborn fallow,
when along the furrows the giants come sprouting up
from the serpent's teeth that are sown in the black glebe,
the moment you see a mass of them rise from the ploughland,
then covertly toss a big stone among them: like ravening
hounds that fight over food, they'll kill each other over
the stone; and then do you with all haste betake yourself
to the battle. As for the fleece—win the contest, and you'll carry it
off back from Aia to Hellas, a long, long haul. Still, after
you leave here you'll go where you choose, where your pleasure takes
  you."
So she spoke, and silently, gaze lowered groundwards,
she let the hot tears drop wet on her sweet fair cheeks
in sorrow that he would soon be gone far away from her,
wandering over the deep. Then with sad words she once more
addressed him, but face to face, for the shame had left her eyes:
"If you one day accomplish your homeward journey, then remember
Medeia's name, as surely as I'll remember yours
far away though you'll be. And tell me, please, just where
is your home? Along what sea-route will you now steer
your vessel? Will you come near wealthy Orchómenos
or skirt the isle of Aiaia? And tell me, who's this maiden
you spoke of before, this bright and famous daughter
of my father's sister Pasiphaë?" So she spoke,
and over him too, as the girl's tears moved his heart,
stole Love the destroyer, and with hidden meaning he said:
"Too true it is, I think, that neither at night nor by day
will I ever forget you, if I but cheat fate, if I really
escape unscathed to Achaea, and there's no further
worse challenge that Aiëtes flings down before us.
But if it's your pleasure to learn about my country
I'll tell you, for indeed my own heart's minded
to do just that. There's a land ringed with lofty mountains,
teeming with sheep and cattle, where Prometheus,
Iápetos' scion, engendered noble Deukálion,

who was the first to build cities and raise up temples
to the immortal gods, first to be king among men:
and those dwelling along the marches call it Haimónia,
and in it there lies Iolkos, my city, and many others
besides, where men have not even heard the name
of the isle of Aiaia: yet there's a story that Minyas
set out thence—Minyas, Aiolos' son—and founded
Orchómenos, that city that marches with the Kadmeians.
But why am I telling you all this idle gossip
about our home and about the daughter of Minos,
the far-famed—that's the splendid title they gave
to the lovely maiden whom you're asking about—Ariadne?
I could wish that, just as Minos then came to terms with Theseus
on her account, so your father might be a friend of ours."
So he spoke, caressing her with his sweet proposals.
But her heart was rubbed raw by the bitterest pangs of anguish,
and grieving, she embraced him with her urgent words:
"In Hellas perhaps it's fine to hold by your covenants:
but Aiëtes is not such a man as, so you assure me,
is Minos, Pasiphaë's husband, nor can I match myself
with Ariadne; so, no talk, please, of guest-friendship.
No: all I ask is, when you get back to Iolkos,
remember me, just as I, in despite of my parents,
will remember you. And from far off may there reach me,
when—if—you forget me, some divine voice, some winged courier—
or else may tearing storm-winds snatch *me* up skyward
and carry me to Iolkos, far out over the deep,
to reproach you face to face, remind you it was by *my*
favour that you escaped. Ah yes, it's *then* I'd desire,
out of the blue, to make claim on your hearth and home!"
So she spoke, while the piteous tears ran streaming
down her cheeks; and he then guilefully answered her:
"Silly girl, let the storm-winds blow themselves out wherever,
and your winged courier too: you're talking airy
nonsense! If you come our way, to the land of Hellas,
honoured among women and by men respected
shall you be: indeed, they'll honour you as a goddess,
since it was thanks to you that their sons accomplished the journey
home once more, that their brothers and other kinsmen
and a passel of hearty husbands were saved from disaster;
and our bed in the bridal chamber shall be tended
by you, and no other barrier shall keep us from our love
till the death decreed by fate enfolds us about."

So he spoke, and at those words the heart within her melted,
yet shuddered to contemplate such deeds of destruction.
Unhappy creature! Not for long was she destined to refuse
a dwelling-place in Hellas, for this way Hera planned it,
that Aiaian Medeia, forsaking her native land,
might come to sacred Iolkos as trouble for Pelias.

Translated by Peter Green

THEOCRITUS
1st Half of 3rd Century B.C.

Callimachus and Apollonius of Rhodes both worked at the Alexandrian Library—Callimachus as the author of the 120-volume catalogue, Apollonius as chief librarian. But Theocritus, who came to Alexandria from Syracuse in Sicily, held no such official position; he seems to have relied on a helping hand from rich and powerful patrons. One of his poems is in fact a lamentation for the lot of poets dependent on miserly patrons. It ends with praise of Hiero II of Syracuse and a hope that he will reward the bard who stands ready to hymn his victories in the coming war against the Carthaginians. Another is a celebration of the royal, indeed divine, stature of Ptolemy II of Egypt as well as of his martial power and his generosity to poets. Theocritus' most famous poems, however, are the pastoral idylls that, through their imitation in Virgil's Eclogues, served as the model for Dante's Latin idylls and the vernacular pastoral poetry of the Italian, French, and English Renaissance.

IDYLL I

DAPHNIS

This First Idyll of Theocritus assembles most of the conventions that characterize pastoral poetry throughout its long history. Its people are shepherds, neatherds, and goatherds who are all musicians playing on the syrinx, the reed pipe of Pan, or poets singing of their loves and sorrows; its landscape is the pastureland beyond the cultivated fields, in the hills where there are trees and flowing streams. Theocritus deploys, if he did not invent, all the literary affectations that would later appear in Virgil's Eclogues, Spenser's Shepheardes Calender, Milton's Lycidas (whose "Where were ye Nymphs . . ." is a quotation from this Idyll), and—from the sublime to the ridiculous—of Marie Antoinette's court ladies dressed as milkmaids in the Petit Trianon.

The song Thyrsis sings to earn the handsome cup so lovingly described by the goatherd is a lament for Daphnis, the mythical inventor of pastoral song. His condition is a puzzle: why is Daphnis wasting away? Hermes' lines suggest that the cause is unrequited love, whereas the reproaches of Priapus suggest the opposite—abstention, love refused. And this would explain the wrath of Cypris; Daphnis is another Hippolytus. In one version of the myth preserved by ancient commentators, Daphnis vowed eternal fidelity to a nymph and, breaking his promise, resolved to die. In that case, the girl mentioned by Hermes may be one who seeks to console him, whom he avoids.

His angry answer to the taunts of Cypris depends for its effect on the readers' knowledge of mythological events. Cypris herself had twice fallen deeply in love with a mortal man—once with Anchises, the father of Aeneas, who was tending cattle at the time, and again with Adonis, a handsome youth who was a hunter (but is here made into a shepherd as well). Both of them came to bad ends; Anchises was crippled by a thunderbolt sent by Zeus, and Adonis was killed by a wild boar. Diomedes is the Achaean champion who dominates the field of battle at Troy when Achilles withdraws from the fighting. At one point the gods come down to join the fray; Cypris faces Diomedes, but he gives her a wound that sends her weeping back to her mother Dione on Olympus to be healed.

A syrinx is a reed pipe and a peplos a long robe. When Thyrsis asks the nymphs where they were when Daphnis was wasting away, the places he suggests—Tempe, the Peneios River, the Pindos mountain range—are all in northern Greece; he is asking them if they had deserted their usual Sicilian haunts—the Anapos River at Syracuse, Mount Etna, and the Acis River. Priapus was a minor deity whose ithyphallic statue was often placed in gardens to warn trespassers off. After dismissing Cypris, Daphnis bids farewell to the Sicilian landscape (Arethusa was a spring at Syracuse and Thybris a Sicilian valley) and asks Pan, the patron deity of shepherds, to leave his usual haunts in Arcadia, a mountainous region of central Greece, for Sicily. The stream to which Daphnis went was presumably the Acheron, one of the rivers of the land of the dead.

THYRSIS: Sweet is the whisper of wind as it plays in that pine
Near the spring, O goatherd, and sweet, too, is your piping;
In a contest with Pan you would win second prize.
If he took the horned he-goat, you'd win the dam,
But should his prize be the dam, the kid would be yours,
And a kid before it gives milk is delectable eating.
GOATHERD: Sweeter, O shepherd, pours forth the song from your lips
Than the water tumbling down from those rocks overhead.
Should the Muses bear away a ewe as their gift,
The cosset lamb would be your prize; but if the lamb
Should content them, you next would be awarded the ewe.
THYRSIS: By the nymphs, goatherd, would it please you to sit down
On this sloping hillock here where the tamarisks grow
And play your syrinx, while I meanwhile look after your goats?
GOATHERD: Custom forbids, O shepherd, that at noontime we play
     on the syrinx,
For we go in fear of great Pan. At this time of day,
Weary, he rests from the chase. He has an irascible temper,
And bitter gall perches forever over his nostrils.
But you, Thyrsis, sing of the sorrows of Daphnis
And are skilled in the pastoral song of the Muses.
Let us sit down here under the elm tree facing Priapos
And the nymphs of the spring, where stand the oaks
And the bench of the shepherds, and if you sing as you did
When vying in song once with Chromis of Libya,
I will let you have a twin-bearing goat for three milkings,
Who, besides feeding two kids, yields up two milk pails,
And a deep ivywood drinking cup coated with sweet-scented wax,
Two-handled and newly wrought, and from the chisel still
     fragrant.
Ivy twines high along the lip of the cup,
And scattered among the ivy leaves are helichryse blossoms,
And the spiraling tendrils below are glorious with golden fruit.
Inside the cup a woman, carved as by one of the gods,
Wearing a peplos and headband; two men stand beside her
With fine long hair, contending with speeches, first one,
Then the other in turn, but they cannot kindle her heart.
At one moment, laughing, she looks on this man,
The next moment turns her mind to the other, while they,
Long heavy-eyed from love's suffering, labor in vain.
Near them is engraved a fisherman on a rough rock,
An old man who visibly strains as he gathers up

His great net for a cast, like a man worn out with hard work.
You might say he was fishing with all the strength of his limbs
From the swollen sinews that stand out all over his neck,
But gray-haired though he is, his strength is that of a youth.
And not far away from this seaworn old man is a vineyard
Heavily laden with ripening clusters of grapes,
Where on a dry-stone wall a small boy sits on guard.
Two foxes flank him: one prowls up and down the vine rows,
Pilfering the already ripe fruit, while the other
Directs all her cunning toward the boy's wallet, and vows not to
  rest
Until she has left him lean fare for his breakfast.
But he, plaiting with asphodel stalks a fine cage for locusts,
Fits in a reed and thinks not at all of his wallet
Or of the vines, so great is his joy in his weaving.
And all over the cup is spread the wavy acanthus—
A sight for goatherds! The marvelous thing will amaze you!
I gave the Calydnian boatman a she-goat in payment
And a great wheel of white cheese. Never so far
Has it been touched by my lips, but still lies unsullied.
It would be a pleasure indeed, my friend, to give it to you
If you would sing for me that beautiful song.
I do not mock you. Come, sir, for to hoard it
Will not serve you at all in Hades' realm where all is forgotten.
THYRSIS: *Begin the pastoral song, dear Muses, begin the song.*

Thyrsis of Etna am I, and this is the sweet voice of Thyrsis.
Where were you, nymphs, where were you when Daphnis was
  wasting?
In Tempe, the lovely vale of Peneios, or off on the slopes of the
  Pindos?
For not then did you haunt the great stream of the river Anapos
Or Etna's high peak or the holy waters of Acis.

Begin the pastoral song, dear Muses, begin the song.

For him the jackals lamented, for him the wolves howled,
For him, dead, the lion mourned in the oak wood.

Begin the pastoral song, dear Muses, begin the song.

Around him cows without number and bulls made lament,
Many a heifer and many a calf too bewailed him.

Begin the pastoral song, dear Muses, begin the song.

Hermes came from the hill first of all and said, "Daphnis,
Who wastes away your life thus? For whom, good man, such
    desire?"

Begin the pastoral song, dear Muses, begin the song.

The cowherds came, the shepherds came, and the goatherds,
And all of them asked why he suffered. Priapos came too
And said, "Daphnis, poor wretch, why are you pining? The girl
On hastening feet goes to every spring, every grove searching.

Begin the pastoral song, dear Muses, begin the song.

"A laggard in love are you and helpless indeed!
Cowherd you were called, but now you resemble a goatherd—
A goatherd, forsooth, who when he sees nannies mounted
Pines, teary-eyed, because he was not born a he-goat.

Begin the pastoral song, dear Muses, begin the song.

"And you, whenever you chance to see maidens laughing,
Pine, teary-eyed, because you cannot dance among them."
To all of this the herdsman made no reply,
But endured his bitter love, bore it out to the end preordained.

Begin the song, Muses, begin again the pastoral song.

Cypris came too, sweetly laughing but laughing falsely,
Holding back the wrath deep in her heart,
And said, "Daphnis, you vowed to wrestle Love to a fall,
But have not you yourself been thrown by mischievous Eros?"

Begin the song, Muses, begin again the pastoral song.

And to her then Daphnis replied, "Hardhearted Cypris,
Cypris the terrible, Cypris hateful to mortals,
Are you so sure that all my suns have already set?
Even in Hades will Daphnis be bitter trouble for Eros.

Begin the song, Muses, begin again the pastoral song.

"Is it not said that with Cypris a cowherd once—? Creep off to Ida,
Crawl to Anchises; oak trees grow there and galingale,
And bees murmurously hum in swarms round the hives.

Begin the song, Muses, begin again the pastoral song.

"Adonis, too, in the prime of his youth pastures his flocks,
And shoots hares and hunts every wild beast in the chase.

Begin the song, Muses, begin against the pastoral song.

"Or go take up your stand again before Diomedes
And say, 'I overcame Daphnis the herdsman, but come on and fight
    me.'

Begin the song, Muses, begin again the pastoral song.

"O wolves, O jackals, O bears lurking in dens in the mountains,
Farewell. No more will I, Daphnis the herdsman, pass through your
    forest,
No more through your oak woods or groves. Farewell, Arethusa,
And rivers whose rushing water pours down from Thybris.

Begin the song, Muses, begin again the pastoral song.

"I, that Daphnis who here pastured his cattle,
The Daphnis who here watered his bulls and his calves.

Begin the song, Muses, begin again the pastoral song.

"O Pan, Pan, whether you range the lofty peaks of Lycaios
Or busy yourself on high Mainalos, come to the island
Of Sicily, leaving Helike's mound and the tall tomb
Of the son of Lycaon's daughter, at which even the blessed ones
    marvel.

Cease the song, Muses, cease now the pastoral song.

"Come, lord, and take this sweet-breathing syrinx smelling of honey
And beeswax, and bound securely around the fine lip,
For now, defeated by Eros, I go down to Hades.

Cease the song, Muses, cease now the pastoral song.

"Now you brambles, you thornbushes, may you bear violets,
May the lovely narcissus on junipers bloom,
Let all be confounded, and pears grow on pine trees,
Since Daphnis is dying; may deer drag down dogs,
And may owls from the mountains to nightingales sing."

Cease the song, Muses, cease now the pastoral song.

So much he said, then was silent. Willingly would Aphrodite
Have spared him but the whole thread of his fate had run out,
And Daphnis went to the stream. The swirling waters washed over
The man dear to the Muses, the man not abhorred by the nymphs.

Cease the song, Muses, cease now the pastoral song.

Now give me the goat and the cup, so I may milk her
And pour out to the Muses an offering. Muses, farewell,
Many times farewell, but I will sing you a sweeter song later.
GOATHERD: May your lovely mouth be filled with honey, Thyrsis,
Filled too with honeycomb, and may you munch the sweet figs
Of Aigilia, for you sing to surpass the cicada.
See, here is the cup; notice, my friend, its fine fragrance.
It would make you think it was dipped in the spring of the Hours.
Come here, Cissaitha!—you milk her. Don't frisk around,
You other nannies! Calm down lest the billy goat mount you.

                            Translated by Thelma Sargent

IDYLL II

THE LOVE CHARM

*Theocritus' scene is not always pastoral; here and in Idyll XV we are in
Alexandria. Simaetha practices magic in an attempt to win back the love
of Delphis who has abandoned her. It is a night scene; Simaetha addresses Selene, the moon goddess. The magic wheel she calls on in the
refrain that punctuates the incantation (the first half of the poem) is a
small bronze wheel with cords threaded between holes in it, which can*

*be made to revolve very fast as the cords are twisted and then untwist
again. In the second half of the poem, Simaetha tells the story of her
meeting with and passion for Delphis.*

    Where are my bay leaves? Bring them, Thestylis, and the love
       charms,
And wreathe the caldron with fine crimson wool,
That I may bind to myself that man I love, cruel though he be.
For the twelfth day now the wretch has not come to my house,
Nor does he know if I am dead or alive, or, heartless one.
Rattle my door. Surely to some other love he has gone,
His fickle heart in thrall to Aphrodite and Eros.
To Timagetos' wrestling school I will go in the morning
And see him and reproach him for the way that he treats me;
But now I will bind him fast to me with a spell, and, Selene.
Shine brightly, for I will softly sing to you, goddess,
And to Hecate under the earth, before whom whelps tremble
As she comes up through the tombs of the dead and the black
       blood.
Hail, terrible Hecate! Attend me to the end,
That this charm may work no worse than any of Circe's
Or those of Medea or yellow-haired Perimede.

   Spin, magic wheel, and draw that man to my house.

Let barley first be consumed in the fire. Scatter it,
Thestylis! Wretched girl, where have your wits flown to?
Or have I become, horrid creature, a laughingstock even to you?
Sprinkle it, saying these words: "The bones of Delphis I scatter."

   Spin, magic wheel, and draw that man to my house.

Delphis has wronged me; for Delphis I burn this laurel.
How loudly it crackles as it catches fire,
And, suddenly blazing up, leaves no ash behind it.
So in flame may Delphis's flesh be completely destroyed.

   Spin, magic wheel, and draw that man to my house.

This wax I now melt with the goddess's aid;
So may Delphis the Myndian melt at once under love;

And as by Aphrodite's power spins this whirling bronze shape,
So may he irresistibly spin to my door.

    Spin, magic wheel, and draw that man to my house.

Now I will offer the bran. And, Artemis, you who can move
Even the adamant gates of Hades, and whatever else is unyielding—
Thestylis, the dogs howl through the city!
The goddess is at the triple crossways! Sound the bronze quickly!

    Spin, magic wheel, and draw that man to my house.

Look: the sea lies in silence; the winds too are hushed;
But the torment with in my breast is not still.
I am all on fire for that man who has made me so wretched
And left me not only no wife but no longer a virgin.

    Spin, magic wheel, and draw that man to my house.

Three times do I pour out wine to you, mistress, and three times I cry:
Whether it is a woman who lies with him now or a man,
May he forget his love as thoroughly as once they say
Theseus on Dia forgot lovely-haired Ariadne.

    Spin, magic wheel, and draw that man to my house.

In Arcadia there is a plant called horse-madness, and for it
All of the colts and swift horses go mad on the mountains;
May I see Delphis in just such a frenzy
Come to this house from his oily wrestling arena.

    Spin, magic wheel, and draw that man to my house.

Here is a fringe Delphis once lost from his cloak,
And I now, shredding it, throw it into the ravening fire.
Oh, unfeeling Eros, why do you cling to me thus,
Like some leech of the marsh, drinking all the dark blood from my
    body?

    Spin, magic wheel, and draw that man to my house.

Tomorrow I'll grind up a lizard and send him a poisonous brew,
But now, Thestylis, take these herbs to his house

And smear them high up on his doorposts, while it's still night,
And mutter meanwhile: "The bones of Delphis I splatter."

Spin, magic wheel, and draw that man to my house.

Now I am alone whence shall I weep for this love?
Where should I begin? Who brought this trouble upon me?
As basket-bearer, our servant Anaxo, Eubolos' daughter,
Went to Artemis' grove, and to honor the goddess that day
There was a procession of many wild beasts, a lioness among them.

Consider whence, mistress Selene, this love of mine came.

And Theumaridas' Thracian nurse—blessed soul, now departed—
Who was living next door, begged and implored me to go
And watch the procession. And I, most wretched of women,
Accompanied her, trailing a beautiful gown of fine linen,
Clearista's magnificent cloak gathered around me.

Consider whence, mistress Selene, this love of mine came.

When halfway along the highway leading past Lycon's,
I saw Delphis and Eudamippos walking together,
The beards on their faces more golden than helichryse blossoms,
Their breasts gleaming even more brightly, Selene, than you,
For they had just come away from the gym and their manly exertions.

Consider whence, mistress Selene, this love of mine came.

I went mad when I saw him; my unlucky heart caught on fire,
My looks faded away. I had no further thought
For that procession, and how I got home again I don't know.
But I was suddenly shaken by some parching fever,
And forced to lie abed for ten days and ten nights.

Consider whence, mistress Selene, this love of mine came.

And oftentimes my skin grew as yellow as fustic,
And all my hair began to fall out of my head;
What was left of me was just skin and bones. To whom didn't I go?
What old crone's house did I not seek out if she knew magic?
But nothing gave me relief, and time was fast flying.

Consider whence, mistress Selene, this love of mine came.

And so I finally told my slave girl the truth.
"Come, Thestylis, find me some cure for this tiresome illness.
The Myndian, alas, altogether possesses my soul.
Go and keep watch at Timagetos' palaestra,
For he frequents the place, and finds it pleasant to sit there.

Consider whence, mistress Selene, this love of mine came.

"And when you know he is alone, secretly give him a nod
And say, 'Simaitha summons you'; then bring him here."
So I said. And she went and brought Delphis, all shiny of skin,
To my house. But as soon as I was aware
Of his light step at my door as he crossed the threshold—

Consider whence, mistress Selene, this love of mine came—

I grew colder than snow all over, and from my forehead
Beads of sweat streamed down like wet dew;
Not a word could I say, not even so much as the whimper
Children make in sleep calling for their dear mother,
But my whole beautiful body froze as stiff as a doll's.

Consider whence, mistress Selene, this love of mine came.

He glanced at me, heartless brute, and with his eyes fixed on the
    ground,
Sat down on the couch and, sitting there, uttered these words:
"Truly, Simaitha, your calling me to your house
Outdistanced my coming by only so much as I
Not long ago outdistanced in running the charming Philinos.

Consider whence, mistress Selene, this love of mine came.

"For I would have come—yes, by sweet Eros, I would have come—
With two friends or three just as soon as night fell,
Bearing apples of Dionysos within the folds of my tunic,
And on my head a garland of Heracles' sacred white poplar,
The spray wound all about with bands of deep crimson.

Consider whence, mistress Selene, this love of mine came.

"And if you had received me, that would have been pleasant
(For I am known among all the young men for my swiftness and
     beauty),
And I would have slept if I had but kissed your beautiful lips;
But if you had sent me away and put up the bar on your door,
Then axes and torches would have come promptly against you.

Consider whence, mistress Selene, this love of mine came.

"But now I declare I owe my thanks first to Cypris,
And after Cypris, dear lady, to you, for you snatched me,
Already half consumed, out of the fire ·
By calling me here to your home; for very often
Eros kindles a hotter blaze than Hephaistos on Lipara,

Consider whence, mistress Selene, this love of mine came.

"And with ruinous madness drives the maid from her virginal chamber
And the bride from her bridegroom's bed while it's still warm."
So he spoke. And I, one all too quickly persuaded,
Took his hand and pulled him down beside me upon the soft couch.
And soon body warmed against body and faces glowed
With more heat than before, and we whispered sweetly together.
So as not to babble on about love for too long, Selene,
All came about, and we both assuaged our desire.
And until yesterday he had no fault to find with me,
Nor I with him. But early today, at the time
When her chariot bears rosy Eos swiftly to heaven from Ocean,
The mother of Melixo and of Philista our flute girl
Came and told me among other things that Delphis had fallen in love.
Whether his passion was for a woman or for a man
She claimed not exactly to know, but only this: Always to Eros
He poured out unmixed libations, and afterward
Left in a rush, vowing to deck that house with bright garlands.
So my guest told me, and I believe she is truthful.
He used to come to my house three or four times a day,
And often left in my keeping his Dorian oil flask,
But now it has been twelve days since I had seen him.
Must he not have another sweetheart that he forgets me?
But now I will bind him with a spell, and if he still grieves me,
Then—yes, by the Fates!—may he knock at the entrance of Hades!
For I keep lethal drugs of that sort, I swear, in my casket for him,

Having learned this lore, mistress, from an Assyrian stranger.
But farewell to you, lady; turn your colts back toward Ocean,
And I will endure my longing as I have endured it.
Farewell, bright-throned Selene, and farewell to you other
Stars, attendants upon the car of calm Night.

Translated by Thelma Sargent

Idyll III

THE SERENADE

The lovesick swain, the faithful shepherd that Theocritus introduces in his Third Idyll, was to have a long line of descendants in the European pastoral tradition, and the name of his cruel lady love, Amaryllis, was to become the standard name for the shepherd's nymph, from Guarini's Pastor Fido *and Monteverdi's madrigal to Milton's "sport with Amaryllis in the shade." The "leaf of love-in-absence" is used like the flowers from which the modern country lover picks the petals to the refrain of "She loves me, she loves me not."*

The shepherd, in typical Alexandrian style, cites a series of learned mythical allusions to lovers who, unlike him, finally won their loves. Hippomenes (Milanion in the usual version) distracted Atalanta from winning the race by dropping golden apples in her path and so won her hand. The second example is abstruse enough to have caused even some of Theocritus' original readers to scratch their heads. Bias was in love with Pero, whose father Neleus, king of Pylos, would permit her marriage only with the suitor who would restore to him the herd of cattle stolen by Phylacus, who lived on Mount Orthrys. Bias' brother Melampus undertook to get the cattle and, after initial failure and imprisonment, succeeded, bringing the herd back to Pylos. So Bias married Pero, who bore him a daughter, Alphesiboea. The following mythical examples, however, seem to point rather to the shepherd's final death wish than a happy ending. Adonis was killed by a wild boar and died in the arms of Cytherea (Venus). Endymion was married to the moon goddess Selene, but was sunk in everlasting sleep. Iasion, the lover of the goddess Demeter, was blasted by the thunderbolt of Zeus. This last story seems to have played some part in the celebration of mystery cults associated with Demeter; hence the shepherd's reference to Amaryllis as "profane," i.e., not initiated.

I'm off to serenade Amaryllis.
Tityrus grazes my goats on the hill.
Feed them, good Tityrus, lead them to water.
And watch that ram, the yellow Libyan,
or he'll be butting you.

My Amaryllis, my beauty, why can it be
you no longer seek me out from your cave
and call me in? Me, your lover?
Do you hate me? Or is it, perhaps,
at closer range, I seem snub-nosed?
My chin's too long? I'll hang myself,
for you one day. I will, I know.
I've brought you, see, ten apples,
picked just where you asked me;
tomorrow I promise I'll fetch you some more.
But look, I'm in pain. My heart's in a turmoil.
How I wish I were that buzzing bee
that I might so easily fly into your cave
through the ivy and fern you hide behind.
Now I know Love. He's a formidable god.
A lioness suckled him, brought him up
deep in the woods. And now I'm tortured
to the very bones by his slow fires.
Your bewitching glances are solid stone,
my Nymph, my love, my dark-browed beauty;
come to my arms, your goatherd's arms,
for he longs, he longs to give you his kiss.
Even in empty kisses there is fond delight.
You will make me tear this garland to pieces,
Amaryllis, my love, this crown I made you
of ivy, of rosebuds and sweet celery.
What lies ahead for me? What but pain?
You are deaf to my every complaint.
At the cliff where Olpis the fisherman
watches for tunny, I shall bare my back
and throw myself off into the waves:
if I die, you at least will be satisfied.

It was not long ago I learnt the truth.
You were on my mind; I was wondering
if you loved me, so I slapped the leaf
of love-in-absence firmly on my arm—

but no, it didn't stick; uselessly
it shrivelled up on my smooth skin.
Agroeo, too, the prophet of the sieve,
told me a truth the other day
as we were harvesting side by side:
I loved you, she said, with all my heart,
but you took not a moment's notice of me.
Look, I've kept you a snow-white goat,
with two kids, which Memnon's dusky girl
keeps asking for. And she shall have them
since you persist in showing me such disdain.
My right eye twitched. Can she be coming?
I'll lean here, beneath this pine, awhile,
and sing for her. Perhaps she'll notice me;
she cannot be made all of adamant.

Hippomenes, to win his bride,
dropped apples as he ran.
Atalanta saw, was overcome,
fell deep in love with him.

From Othrys down to Pylus
wise Melampus drove his herd.
Alphesiboa's mother thus
fell into Bias' arms.

Adonis, as he grazed his sheep,
drove Cytherea mad
with love, and even as he died
she held him to her breast.

I would I were Endymion
who sleeps unending sleep,
or Iasion, whose luck, my love,
you profane may never know.

My head aches, but that's nothing to you.
I will sing no more. I'll just lie here,
here where I've fallen, till the wolves devour me.
Let's hope you'll find that as sweet as honey.

Translated by Anthony Holden

Idyll XV

GORGO AND PRAXINOA

*Gorgo, accompanied by her maid Eutychis, comes to call on her friend
Praxinoa. The two ladies, each with their maid (Praxinoa's is called
Eonoa), go off to the palace of Ptolemy II to hear a singer perform the
dirge for Adonis at the festival of the Adonia.*

GORGO: Is Praxinoa at home?
PRAXINOA: She is, Gorgo dear!
    Such a time since I saw you:
    it's quite a surprise to have you here!
    A chair for her, Eunoa, and a cushion.
GORGO: Don't worry. I'm fine as I am.
PRAXINOA: Do sit down.
GORGO: Silly me! What a day to try and come!
    I scarcely got through alive, Praxinoa,
    what with all the people, all their chariots,
    knee-boots everywhere, men in uniform—
    that street is endless; and I'm sure,
    every time I come, you've moved further away.
PRAXINOA: That's that crazy husband of mine.
    He comes here, to the ends of the earth,
    and buys this cowshed—call it a home?—
    just to stop you and me being neighbours.
    All out of pure spite, the jealous brute—
    he was always the same.
GORGO: Now you mustn't talk of your Dinon
    like that, my dear—not in front of the child.
    See how he's staring at you, woman.
    There, Zopyrion darling, never mind.
    She wasn't talking about Daddy.
PRAXINOA: Good God, the child understands.
GORGO: *Nice* Daddy! Good old Daddy!
PRAXINOA: Well, that *nice* Daddy the other day . . .
    Just the other day, I said to him:
    "Dad, get me some soap and some rouge
    from the shops." He came back, did Daddy,
    that giant of a man, carrying a pack of salt.

GORGO: Mine's just the same. Old Diocleidas
  is a financial wizard. Just yesterday
  he paid seven drachmas for five fleeces—
  five motheaten dogskins, more like,
  pickings from faded old purses,
  nothing but filth, just work and more work.
  But come, get your dress and cloak on,
  and let's go to King Ptolemy's palace
  and take a look at this Adonis.
  The Queen, I hear, is doing things in style.
PRAXINOA: Oh, nothing but the best. Well, they can keep it.
GORGO: But when you've seen it, just think,
  you can tell those who haven't all about it.
  Come on, it's time we were off.
PRAXINOA: Every day's a holiday for the idle.
  Eunoa, pick that spinning up. Leave it
  lying around once more, and you'll regret it.
  The cat would love so soft a bed.
  Now get a move on. Bring me water quickly.
  I ask for water, and she brings soap.
  Never mind, let's have it. Not that much,
  you robber. Now pour the water. Idiot!
  You've spilt it all over my slip.
  That's quite enough. I must be thankful,
  I suppose, I've got that much washed.
  Now where's the key of the big wardrobe?
  Bring it here.
GORGO: Oh, Praxinoa, that dress. So full. It's just you.
  Tell me, what did you pay for the cloth?
PRAXINOA: Oh don't remind me, Gorgo. I paid
  more than two whole minas of good money.
  And I put my very soul into making it.
GORGO: Well, it's a triumph. And that's the truth.
PRAXINOA: Bring me my cloak and hat, Eunoa.
  And put them on properly this time.
  No, baby, I can't take you.
  Boo hoo! The bogey man would catch you!
  You can cry as much as you like;
  I'm not having you crippled for life.
  Let's go.
  Phrygia, take baby and play with him.
  Call the dog in and lock the front door.

[*Out in the street.*]
Ye Gods, what a crowd! The crush!
How on earth are we going to get through it?
They're like ants! Swarms of them, beyond counting!
Well, you've done us many favours, Ptolemy,
since your father went to heaven.
We don't get those no-goods now, sliding up to us
in the street and playing their Egyptian tricks.
What they used to get up to, those rogues!
A bunch of villains, each as bad
as the next, and all utterly cursed!

Gorgo dear, what will become of us?
Here are the king's horses! Take care,
my good man, don't tread on me.
That brown one's reared right up!
Look how wild he is! He'll kill his groom!
Eunoa, you fool, get back!
Thank God I left that child at home.
GORGO: Don't worry, Praxinoa.
We've got behind them now.
They're back in their places.
PRAXINOA: I'm all right now.
Ever since I was a girl, two things
have always terrified me—horses,
and long, cold snakes. Let's hurry.
This great crowd will drown us.
GORGO: You coming from the palace, grandma?
OLD WOMAN: I am, children.
GORGO: Then we'll get in all right?
OLD WOMAN: By trying, my dears, the Greeks took Troy.
Try hard enough, and you can manage anything.
GORGO: The old girl's vanished—
she just spoke her oracles and went.
PRAXINOA: Women, Gorgo, know everything.
Even the story of Zeus and Hera.
GORGO: Look, Praxinoa! What a crowd at the door!
PRAXINOA: Fantastic! Gorgo, give me your hand.
And you, Eunoa, hold on to Eutychis.
Take care you don't lose each other.
We must all go in together. Stay close by us.
Oh no! Gorgo! My coat! It's been ripped

clean in two! My God, sir, as you hope
for heaven, mind my coat!
STRANGER: It wasn't my fault. But I'll be careful.
PRAXINOA: What a herd! They push like pigs.
STRANGER: Don't worry, madam, we'll be all right.
PRAXINOA: And may you, sir, be all right
   forever and beyond, for looking after us.
   What a charming man! Where's Eunoa?
   She's getting squashed! Come on, girl, push!
   That's it. "All safely in,"
   as the bridegroom said when he locked the door.
GORGO: Praxinoa, come here! You must look
   at these tapestries before anything else.
   What grace! What delicacy!
   The work of a god, don't you think?
PRAXINOA: By Athena, what craftsmen they must have been
   to make these, what artists to draw such lines.
   Those figures stand, they move around,
   like living things! They can't be just figures.
   What a marvellous creature man is!
   And there's Adonis; how superb he looks,
   lying there in his silver chair,
   the first down spreading from his temples—
   thrice-loved Adonis, adored even in Hades!
ANOTHER STRANGER: Oh do be quiet, you stupid woman.
   Stop that ceaseless pattling.
   Like two turtle doves! I swear
   their oohs and aahs will be the end of me.
PRAXINOA: Well! Where did he spring from?
   What concern is it of yours, pray,
   if we do prattle? You must buy
   your slaves before you order them about.
   And it's to Syracusans you're giving your orders.
   If you must know, we're of Corinthian descent,
   like Bellerophon himself. We speak Peloponnesian.
   Dorians, I presume, may speak Dorian?
   We have one master, by Persephone,
   let's have no more. Don't waste your time on us.

Translated by Anthony Holden

EPIGRAMS

1

Look on this statue, traveller; look well,
and then, when back at home, "In Teos," say,
"I saw an image of Anacreon,
the greatest of the songmakers of old."
And, if you seek the essence of the man,
then say of him "He gave joy to the young."

2

This bank makes welcome citizen and foreigner
alike. Deposits and withdrawals strictly depend
upon the state of your account. No haggling here.
Caicus will change your money even after dark.

Translated by Anthony Holden

HERODAS

c. 300–250 B.C.

From MIMIAMBOI

AUNTIE DROPS BY

Before 1889, Herodas of Cos was little more than a name for us, and even that name was variously reported as Herodas, Herondas, and Herodes. But in that year the British Museum acquired a papyrus roll which, when combined with other fragments, gives us the text (complete in some cases) of eight of Herodas' Mimes (Mimiamboi), short dramatic sketches, in iambic verse, of Alexandrian life. Most of it is pretty low life: Mime I (which follows) is about a procuress and Mime II a panderer; Mimes V and VI deal with sexual activities that reflect little credit on the participants.

Unlike Gorgo and Praxinoa, whose Doric dialect so offended the by-stander in the palace, Herodas' people speak a brand of literary Ionic. The translator has attempted to represent it by a mixture of southern and southwestern regional American accents.

SCENE: The third-century B.C. equivalent of an appartement meublé. It contains, at the moment, METRICHE, a young professional woman who has left general practice to specialize, and TRESSY, a slattern slave. They will shortly be joined by GYLLIS, an entrepreneuse of advanced years who formerly managed METRICHE's career.

METRICHE: Tressy! There goes a thump at the doah. Go see if someone's here from the farm to visit.
Well, go!
TRESSY: Whoozat who's at the door?
GYLLIS: It's me.
TRESSY: Who're you?
Scared to come close?
GYLLIS: So here I am, up close.
TRESSY: So who are you?
GYLLIS: I'm Gyllis. Philainis' mama.
(You know Philainis. Everybody knows Philainis.)
You git in there and announce my presence to Metriche.
TRESSY: She says . . .
METRICHE: Who is it?
TRESSY: Gyllis.
METRICHE: Why, Auntie Gyllis!
(Gal, you find somethin to do.)
It must be fate,
you droppin by!
Ah wonder why.
Well, Gyllis!
Why this epiphany for us mere mo'tals?
Gyllis!
It's gotta be, lemme think now, five whole months
since anyone even halLUcinated that you'd
be standin befoah this doah!

GYLLIS: It's quite a piece
to my place, honey, and the mud and muck in these alleys
comes up over my *knees,* and, you know me, I got
no more zip than a *fly.* It's Old Age, that's what's
draggin me down. Sticks to me like my shadow.
METRICHE: Tut tut, Auntie. Let's not go bad-mouthin Time.
'Sides, look at you. There's many a good bout left
in that—uh—shapely frame: All-in, catch-as-catch-can . . .
GYLLIS: Go on, make cracks. Wisht I was young. You girls
got nothin better to do . . .
METRICHE: Come ON, now, really!
All hot an bothered at a friendly observation?
[*They sit. A short but pregnant pause.*]
GYLLIS: [*Brightly.*] Well, now, dearie, how long's it going to be?
This solitary life, this single blessedness,
this makin the bed creak all by yourself . . . how long?
Mandris, that man of yours, it's been ten months
since he set out for Egypt, and nary a letter,
not even an alpha, from Mandris' fine white hand.
He has for-got-ten you; he drinks to forget,
he gulps his wine these days from a fine new goblet
(not like some weaker vessels I could mention) . . .
and nacherly so:
Why, he's in the Land where Love lives—
Egypt the Gorgeous! Birthplace and homeland of, oh,
jest everythin there is in this world! You name it:
Riches, an Physical Fitness, an Power, an Peace,
an Pee-rades, an Pageants, an Terribly Serious Thinkers,
an Spring All Year, an Glory, an Fine Young Studs,
an the Holy Holy Home of the Sacred Siblings,
an a King who's top-drawer, first-class, A-double-plus,
an the Great State University, home of the Muses,
an Wine, an evry blessin you could want,
an WIMMIN!
                          Yes, wimmin!
                                    So many, the sky's ashamed
to boast about her double handful of stars . . .
And lookers?
                          Not mentionin any names, but all
them goddesses that trotted over to Ida to enter
that beauty contest, well, they better look out.
(An I better look out, too. No offense, up there!)

Anyway, what do you mean by spendin these
best years of your life jist keepin your chair warm? Huh?
You stick with that, and before you know it, you're *old*,
yes, OLD, and your bloomtime's swallowed up in ashes!

You need new vistas. Set yourself some bran-new goals . . .
jist for two-three days: Like Joy,
                              or Love . . .
Might take a look-see at somebody new. Male.
You know what they say:
                    A ship that's hitched
to only one single anchor goes down with all hands.
Once Death comes by in his bright bathrobe, aint no one
gonna bring us around again.
                         The wild winds blow,
and away we go.
                    Dont none of us know the future.
There's nothin certain about tomorrow.
                              So listen . . .
    [*Looking around.*]
We havent got compny, have we?
METRICHE: Nobody here.
GYLLIS: That's good.
                    Now, listen close, an I'll tell you the matter
of Mutual Profit that brought me here today:
You know Pataikion's daughter Matakínê?
                              Well, she's
got a son, name of Gryllos. A real winner.
At the Games, *five times*!
                    He was jist a tad at Delphi,
then twicet at Korinth while he was still all peach-fuzz,
but up at Olympia, now that he's a man,
he won the boxin, yes, he did, TWO TIMES,
by knock-outs!
                    And he's *rich* (but tasteful, of course),
and *manners*? He walks so nice the grass don't rustle.
PLUS: When it comes to lovin, he's not jist merely
untouched . . . this boy is still in the *wrapper!*
                              (Trainin.)
Well, Gryllos saw you in church the second day
of the hallowtide celebration, and then and there
his insides went flip-*flop*, love needled his heart,

an he's been over to my place ever since,
both day an night, jes' buglin at my front door,
an callin me granny and generly dyin by inches
of un-re-qui-ted passion!
                          Well, now, dearie,
might that suggest goin back on the active list?
Can't you stretch your ethics a little, jist once?
In a holy cause?
    [*Piously.*]
                          It's all for Aphrodite.
Reededicate yourself to the Goddess's service,
Metriche honey . . .
    [*Savagely.*]
                          Cause if you don't, but keep on
playin OLD, you'll be it before you see it!
    [*Cooing.*]
I might point out that you're gonna profit twice over:
the thrill of the sport—or joy of lovin, PLUS
    [*Chinking coins.*]
a little somethin on the side. Let's call it a gift.
See, now? You know you can trust me. I'm your friend,
so-help-me-Fate-and-may-she-drive-me-up-
to-my-neck-in-the-ground-if-I-aint.
METRICHE: My goodness, Gyllis,
Ah do believe that white hair saps the brain.
As Ah expect to see Mandris' sail swoosh safe into harbor,
as Ah reveah the love of the goddess Demetah,
Ah sweah Ah wouldnt have stood an *effusion* like that
from any woman else. Why, by the tahm
Ah'd taught her a lesson, her legs 'd be as lame
as her logic, and she'd 've conceived a propuh distaste
for the mat at my doah.
                          So don't you go bringin a story
like that around to my place ever again, heah?
You peddle your granny-tales to lil-bitty gals,
but Metriche, Pythias' daughter, you leave her keep her
chair warm.
                  There isnt nobody goin to sass
    [*Savage.*]
my Mandris!
    [*Cooing.*]

But that's not hardly polite, not nice
conversation like Gyllis is used to.
                                    —You! Tressy!
Wipe the mug clean an poah out, oh, three fingers
of winc from the bottle, with just a *splash* of water,
an give our guest a drink.
    [TRESSY *complies and offers the mug.*]
GYLLIS: I really couldnt . . .
METRICHE: [*Grabbing the mug from* TRESSY *and shoving it in*
    GYLLIS' *face*]
Here, Gyllis. Drink up!
GYLLIS: [*Groping*]   Where is it?
                                    Oh, thanks.
                                            I didnt
drop by to lead you astray. I reckoned it was
my duty as a good religious woman. You know, the rites
of Aphrodite. And that's the reason . . .
METRICHE: Give it up, Gyllis.
    [*Drinking.*] Down the hatch!
GYLLIS: [*Drinks, then.*]   But, dearie . . .
                            Oh, well, anyway,
it *is* good wine. Yes. Damn me Demeter, old Gyllis
hasnt imbibed a tastier slug than this in, oh,
how long's it been?
                    An so goodbye, sweet thang,
an DO take care of yourself, now, wont you?
                                    'Bove all,
dont you grow OLD . . .
a fate that's only reserved
for naughty girls what dont stick by their Auntie.
I'll remember you in my prayers, missy.
                        'Bye now!

                            Translated by Douglass Parker

ERINNA
4th Century B.C.?

From THE DISTAFF

*About Erinna of Telos (a small island near Rhodes) we know very little;
not even her date is certain. Some ancient notices make her a contemporary of Sappho, but a date in the fourth century B.C. is more likely. She
wrote only one poem,* The Distaff; *it consisted of 300 hexameter lines, of
which we have about 20, and some fragments of a few others. They
come from a papyrus that was published in 1929.*

*The poem is a lament for the death of Erinna's girlfriend Baucis, who
died very soon after her marriage. It recalls their childhood games, one of
which, as we know from the ancient encyclopedia of Pollux, was called
"the Tortoise." Girls ran in a circle round a seated girl (the Tortoise) and
asked her: "What was your child doing when he died?" The Tortoise
answered: "From white horses into the sea he leapt." On that last word
she jumped up to tag one of the running girls, who became the Tortoise
in her turn. Mormo is one of the many childhood bogeys Greek children
were afraid of. Erinna cannot leave her house to mourn at her friend's
funeral; it has been suggested that she is a priestess of some cult that
made it unlawful for her to come in contact with the dead.*

*The last nine lines of the translation are based on scraps of papyrus
that do not yield continuous sense; they should and must be regarded as
a hypothetical reconstruction. We do have information, from other
sources, that Erinna died young, at nineteen years of age.*

For Antipater of Sidon's epigram on Erinna, see p. 578.

. . . Deep into the wave you raced,
Leaping from white horses,
Whirling the night on running feet.
But loudly I shouted, "Dearest,
You're mine!" Then you, the Tortoise,
Skipping, ran to the rutted garth

Of the great court. These things I
Lament and sorrow, sad Baucis.
These are for me, O Maiden,
Warm trails back through my heart:
Joy, once filled, smoulders in ash;
Young, in rooms without a care,
We held our miming dolls—girls
In the pretense of young brides
(And the toward-dawn-mother
Lotted wool to tending women,
Calling Baucis to salt the meat);
O, what trembling when we were small
And fear was brought by MORMO—
Huge of ear up on her head,
With four feet walking, always
Changing from face to other.
But mounted in the bed of
Your husband, dearest Baucis,
You forgot things heard from mother,
While still the littler child.
Fast Aphrodite set your
Forgetful heart. So I lament,
Neglecting though your obsequies:
Unprofaned, my feet may not leave
And my naked hair's not loosed abroad,
No lighted eye may disgrace your corpse
And in this house, O my Baucis,
Purpling shame grips me about.
Wretched Erinna! Nineteen,
I moan with a blush to grieve. . . .
Old women voice the mortal bloom. . . .
One cries out the lamenting flame. . . .
Hymen! . . . O Hymenaeus! . . .
While the night whirls unvoiced
Darkness is on my eyes . . .

Translated by Daniel Haberman

From THE GREEK
ANTHOLOGY

The Greek Anthology *is the modern title of a collection of over four thousand poems ranging in date from those of Archilochus (seventh century B.C.) to those of Christian poets in the Byzantine Empire, writing up to A.D. 1000 and later. They are in a variety of meters, but the elegiac couplet is far and away the most frequent form chosen for these short poems. It is a meter which, as J. W. Mackail put it in the introduction to his famous* Select Epigrams from the Greek Anthology, *"solved the problem . . . of a metre which would refuse nothing, which could rise to the occasion and sink with it, and be equally suited to the epitaph of a hero or the verses accompanying a birthday present, a light jest or a profound moral idea, the sigh of a lover or the lament over a perished Empire."*

Many of the authors are little more than names to us, and many of the attributions to known authors are suspect; few scholars now believe, for example, that the exquisite poems attributed to Plato were really from his hand. Anyte of Tegea in the Peloponnese was active in the third century B.C.; other Hellenistic poets represented here are Diotimos, Asclepiades of Samos, Leonidas of Tarentum, Dioscorides, Erucius, and Meleager, who made the first collection of epigrams, the "Garland of Meleager," in the first century B.C. In that century Greek poets were welcome at Rome. Philodemus, the Epicurean philosopher (no. 25), won high praise from Cicero, and Pompeius and Crinagoras were attached to court circles in the time of Augustus. Antipater of Thessalonica was also active in this period. Nikarchos and Lucilius came later, in the days of the philhellenic emperor Nero, and Marcus Argentarius also lived in the first century A.D. Automedon and Glaukos belong to the second century, and Paulus Silentiarius wrote his love poems in Byzantium, under the emperor Justinian, in the sixth century A.D.

ANONYMOUS

The monument of Phrasikleia:

For ever shall I be called virgin,
The gods having granted me this instead of marriage.

PLATO

1

I Laïs whose laughter was scornful in Hellas,
Whose doorways were thronged daily with young lovers,
I dedicate my mirror to Aphroditê:

For I will not see myself as I am now,
And can not see myself as once I was.

Translated by Dudley Fitts

2

THOU wert the morning star among the living,
  Ere thy fair light had fled;
Now, having died, thou art as Hesperus, giving
  New splendor to the dead.

Translated by Percy Bysshe Shelley

3

You were the morning star among the living:
But now in death your evening lights the dead.

Translated by Peter Jay

ANYTE

Early 4th Century B.C.?

1

Idle now in Athenê's shining house,
Brass tip no longer red with enemy blood,
Stand, lance of Echekratidas,
            a witness
To all men that this soldier of Crete was brave.

Translated by Dudley Fitts

2

When this man, Manes, lived, he was a slave;
Dead, he is worth as much as Darius the Great.

Translated by Sally Purcell

ANTIPATER OF SIDON
2nd Century B.C.

1

—Lysidice, I'm anxious to find out the meaning
of the carvings Agis has made on your gravestone,
for the reins, the muzzle and the bird of Tanagra
famous for owls that rouse men to battle,
are not what we normally expect to be pleasing
to stay-at-home housewives, but spindles and looms.

—The nightbird proclaims me an early riser,
the reins show how I managed a household,
the horse's muzzle that I wasn't a gossip
but a woman of beautiful silence.

Translated by Tony Harrison

2

Where is your famous beauty,
Corinth of the Dorians?
Where is your crown of towers?
Where are your ancient treasures?
Where are the temples of the
Immortals, and where are the
Houses and the wives of the
Lineage of Sisyphos,
All your myriad people?
Most unhappy city, not
A trace is left of you. War
Has seized and eaten it all.
Only the inviolate
Sea nymphs, the daughters of the

Ocean, remain, crying like
Sea birds over your sorrows.

Translated by Kenneth Rexroth

3

This piece of Lydian earth holds Amyntor,
Philip's son, hardened by battles to iron war.

No lingering disease dragged him off to his end,
killed, with his shield held high above his friend.

Translated by Tony Harrison

4

Who hung these shields here still all shiny,
these spears with no blood on, these helmets undented,
dedicating to Ares arms as ornaments only?
Will no one clear this rubbish from my house?

The banqueting halls of unbellicose softies
are fitter for those than the walls of the War God.

I want hacked trophies, the blood of the dying,
or else I'm not Ares, the plague of mankind.

Translated by Tony Harrison

5

More than the Pleiadês' setting
More than the yammering surf at the point of the jetty
More than the frenzied lightning that scores the vast arch of the sky
I fear the man who drinks water
And so remembers this morning what the rest of us said last night.

Translated by Dudley Fitts

6

Short in measure, narrow in theme, Erinna
Took this little epic from the Muses

And she is still remembered, is not shuttered
In the shadows, under night's murky wing.
And we, friend, we hordes of later poets?
—Here we are, lying in heaps, rotting,
Forgotten.
                    Better a swan's low song
Than the cackling of crows
Echoing through spring clouds.

Translated by Peter Jay

DIOTIMOS

Homeward at evening through the drifted snow
The cows plod back to shelter from the hill
But ah, the long strange sleep
Of the cow-herd Therimachos lying beneath the oak,
Struck still, still, by the fire that falls from heaven!

Translated by Dudley Fitts

NIKARCHOS

Yesterday Dr. Marcus went to see the statue of Zeus.
Though Zeus,
                    & though marble,
We're burying the statue today.

Translated by Dudley Fitts

ASCLEPIADES OF SAMOS

c. 320–? B.C.

1

Although she's a girl, Dorkion
Is wise to the ways of the boys.
Like a chubby kid, she knows how
To throw over her shoulder, from
Under her broadbrimmed hat, the quick
Glance of Public Love, and let her
Cape show a glimpse of her bare butt.

2

Didyme waved her wand at me.
I am utterly enchanted.
The sight of her beauty makes me
Melt like wax before the fire. What
Is the difference if she is black?
So is coal, but alight, it shines like roses.

Translated by Kenneth Rexroth

LEONIDAS OF TARENTUM

1st Half of 3rd Century B.C.

1

Philokles offers his bouncing
Ball to Hermes, along

With the other toys of his
Boyhood, his boxwood rattle,
The knuckle bones he once was
So crazy about, and his
Spinning top.

Translated by Kenneth Rexroth

2

These were my end: a fierce down-squall from the east,
And night, and the waves of Oriôn's stormy setting:
And I, Kallaischros, yielded my life
Far on the waste of the lonely Libyan sea.

And now I roll with drifting currents, the prey
Of fishes:
            and this gravestone lies
If it says that it marks the place of my burial.

Translated by Dudley Fitts

3

Theris, whose hands were cunning,
Gives to Pallas, now the years
Of craftsmanship are over,
His stiff saw with curved handle,
His bright axe, his plane, and his
Revolving auger.

Translated by Kenneth Rexroth

ALEXANDER AETOLUS

You who will die, watch over your life; don't set sail
    at the wrong season, for at best no man lives long.
Poor Cleonicus, so impatient to reach
    bright Thasos, trading out of hollow Syria,

trading, Cleonicus, sailing just as the Pleiades
were setting, so that you and the Pleiades sank together.

Translated by W. S. Merwin

DIOSKORIDES

Hiero's former Nurse
Silenis, who liked wine
Straight & plentiful
Rests in these vine-fields,
May her old body
Buried amid vines
Feed in death the vats
She loved in life.

Translated by Peter Whigham

MELEAGER

c. 100 B.C.

Whose the hand unloosed Clearista's zone
at bride-night, in her bride-room?
Death, in guise of the bridegroom.

Evening, & flutes & clapping hands
clamour at bridal door.
At dawn the funeral wail. No more

the Hymen song. The very lights
that lit the bridal bed
light now Clearista's journey to the dead.

Translated by Peter Whigham

GLAUKOS

Time was when once upon a time, such toys
As balls or pet birds won a boy, or dice.
Now it's best china, or cash. Lovers of boys,
Try something else next time. Toys cut no ice.

Translated by Peter Jay

ANONYMOUS

1

You too, Clenorides, homesickness drove
deathwards, braving an icy, southerly squall.
Treacherous weather held you, the wringing swell
rinses right out of you the youth I love.

Translated by Tony Harrison

2

Boy, hold my wreath for me.
The night is black,
                                  the path is long,
And I am completely and beautifully drunk.

Nevertheless I will go
To Themison's house and sing beneath his window.
You need not come with me:
                                though I may stumble,
He is a steady lamp for the feet of love.

Translated by Dudley Fitts

PHILODEMOS

1

In the middle of the night
I stole from my husband's bed
And came to you, soaked with rain.
And now, are we going to
Sit around, and not get down
To business, and not bill and coo,
And love like lovers ought to love?

Translated by Kenneth Rexroth

2

Here it's rose-time again, chick-peas in season,
cabbages, Sosylus, first heads of the year,
fillets of smelt, fresh-salted cheese,
tender and furled up lettuce leaves . . .
but we don't go way out to the point, Sosylus,
or picnic, as we used to, on the overlook.
Antigenes and Bacchios had the old party spirit,
but today we dump them in their graves.

Translated by William Moebius

KRINAGORAS

Back from the west, back from the war, Marcellus,
carrying his loot, at the rocky frontier post
first shaved his tawny beard—as the fatherland
had wished: it sent a boy, got back a man.

Translated by Alistair Elliot

AUTOMEDON

Yesterday I ate tough mutton
and a cabbage ten days old;
I won't say where I went to dinner,
for my host is of a cold
revengeful temper, and he might
invite me back another night.

Translated by Robin Skelton

ANONYMOUS

At sixty I, Dionysios of Tarsos, lie here,
Never having married:
                    and I wish my father had not.

Translated by Dudley Fitts

ERUCIUS

Even though he lies underground
pour pitch on dirty-tongued Parthenios
who vomited such spit at the Muses,
such foul linen of filthy elegies:
he was so mad he said the *Odyssey*
was mud and the *Iliad* was shit.
Therefore the dark Furies have him
in middle Kokytos with his neck
in a collar like a dog's.

Translated by Peter Levi

ANTIPATER OF SALONICA
1st Century B.C.–1st Century A.D.

1

Europa (in Athens) does business
at truly reasonable rates.
You needn't fear interruption
or the gainsaying of whims;
also, she offers irreproachable
sheets, and—in winter—
a coal-fire. This time, Zeus,
come as you are. No bull.

Translated by Andrew Miller

2

Astrologers foretold to me
I'd live till I was thirty-six,
but I will settle for the three
decades and then be glad to quit;
for thirty years is the proper
limit of our mortal span;
Nestor may have lasted longer,
but he went to Hades then!

Translated by Robin Skelton

MARCUS ARGENTARIUS
1st Century B.C.–1st Century A.D.?

1

Welcome, old friend, long-necked bottle,
Dearest companion of my table
And of the winejar, with your soft gurgle
And your sweetly chuckling mouth: welcome;
You secret witness of my poverty
(Which you've done little enough to aid)
At last I hold you in my hand again.
But I wish you had come to me undiluted,
Pure as a virgin to her bridegroom's bed.

Translated by Fleur Adcock

2

Lately thumbing the pages of *Works and Days*,
I saw my Pyrrhê coming.
                    Goodbye book!
"Why in the world should I cobweb my days," I cried,
"With the works of Old Man Hesiod?"

3

It was this way:

I'd been going for weeks with this girl,
Alkippê her name was; well, so
One night I manage to get her up to my room.
That's all right,
Though our hearts are cloppety-clopping like mad
For fear we'll be caught together.
                                    Well,
Everything's fine, you know what I mean, when
All of a sudden the door pops
And in pokes her old mother's sheep-head:
"Remember, daughter," she bleats, "you and I go halves!"

Translated by Dudley Fitts

POMPEIUS

Even if I am only more dust
piled on this desert & even

if I am plainer than a common
stone you just happen to look at—

look again at that other famous
city Ilium whose walls I broke

underfoot to empty Priam's house
& you will know how mighty young

Mycenae was—if my old age wronged
me I still have Homer's testimony

Translated by Dennis Schmitz

LUCILIUS

Doubly unfortunate are those who dwell in Hell—
Eutychides the Lyric Poet,
out of breath at last, has had burned with him
twelve lyres and twenty-five
albums of songs, which poor Charon will have to
ferry over the charcoal waters.
Alas, where will music-lovers take refuge now
Eutychides will be singing for eternity?

Translated by Peter Porter

NIKARCHOS

Agelaus was kind to Acestorides,
who, if he'd lived, would have been lame.
Agelaus decided to operate.

Translated by Peter Porter

PAULUS SILENTIARIUS
6th Century A.D.

1

My name is—What does it matter?—*My*
Country was—Why speak of it?—*I*
Was of noble birth—Indeed? And if
You had been of the lowest?—*Moreover, my life*
Was decorous—And if it had not been so,
What then?
　　　　　—and I lie here now beneath you—

Who are you that speak?
To whom do you speak?

Translated by Dudley Fitts

2

I saw them, caught them in the act.
　　They could not slake, though lip
was fixed on feverish lip in fury,
　　their tyrannous thirst. They longed
each to invade the other's heart:
　　exchanging clothes, they eased
the ache of impossibility.
　　So he like young Achilles
among the girls of Skyros, she,
　　bare-kneed, a counterfeit
of Artemis at hunt, fell to,
　　love-ravened, hunger-racked.
Simpler to separate two vines
　　plaited in ancient growth

than them, intent in their embrace.
Thrice blest the man, my love,
who in such chains is snared & locked
while *we* burn apart.

Translated by Andrew Miller

ROME

LUCRETIUS

98–c. 55 B.C.

From ON THE NATURE OF THINGS

Titus Lucretius Carus is the author of a poem in six books called De
Rerum Natura—On the Nature of Things. *Though it is written in the
hexameter line that had been adapted from Homer for Latin epic poetry, Lucretius' work is a philosophical treatise. It is a full-scale exposition for Roman readers of the system of the Greek philosopher Epicurus
(341–270 B.C.), who accepted the atomic theory of the fifth-century
philosopher Democritus and taught the rejection of superstitious fears
and the cultivation of a tranquil mind.*

THE FEAR OF DEATH

*The selection that follows is the culmination of a long argument de-
signed to banish from the reader's consciousness all trace of fear—fear of
the gods, of death, and of life (and punishment) after death. The argument itself is a demonstration that the soul or spirit is as material as the
body and perishes with it, or rather dissolves, like the body, into its
constituent atoms, which rearrange themselves in fresh combinations.
This atomic theory of the nature of matter was developed by two Greek
philosophers of the fifth century B.C., Democritus and Leucippus: It was
adopted by Epicurus in the fourth century as the scientific base for his
moral philosophy, which advocated the attainment of* ataraxia *(literally,
"freedom from turmoil"), a mental tranquility based on an understanding of nature and a consequent absence of fear. Epicurus is Lucretius'
master and model, hailed as such in the opening lines of the book that
contains the argument:*

O glory of the Greeks, the first to raise
The shining light out of tremendous dark
Illumining the blessings of our life,
You are the one I follow . . .

    The passage that mentions the "Carthaginian hordes" recalls for the Roman reader the epic events of the third and second centuries B.C., the three Punic Wars the Romans fought on land and sea against the Phoenician empire of Carthage, a great trading city on what is now the Tunisian shore. In the second of these wars the Carthaginian general Hannibal invaded Italy, starting from his base in Spain and crossing the Alps. From 218 to 203 B.C. he stayed in Italy, defeating one Roman army after another, but in the end, unable either to take Rome by assault or to detach Rome's Italian allies from their allegiance, he retired to Carthage, where in 202 he was defeated at Zama by the Roman general Scipio, who then took the title "Africanus."

    Democritus is mentioned toward the end of the extract as one who "gave himself to death." This refers to a tradition that he starved himself to death when he grew too old and feeble to enjoy life any more.

Death

Is nothing to us, has no relevance
To our condition, seeing that the mind
Is mortal. Just as, long ago, we felt
Not the least touch of trouble when the wars
Were raging all around the shaken earth
And from all sides the Carthaginian hordes
Poured forth to battle, and no man ever knew
Whose subject he would be in life or death,
Which doom, by land or sea, would strike him down,
So, when we cease to be, and body and soul,
Which joined to make us one, have gone their ways,
Their separate ways, nothing at all can shake
Our feelings, not if earth were mixed with sea
Or sea with sky. Perhaps the mind or spirit,
After its separation from our body,
Has some sensation; what is that to us?
Nothing at all, for what we knew of being,
Essence, identity, oneness, was derived
From body's union with spirit, so, if time,
After our death, should some day reunite

All of our present particles, bring them back
To where they now reside, give us once more
The light of life, this still would have no meaning
For us, with our self-recollection gone.
As we are now, we lack all memory
Of what we were before, suffer no wound
From those old days. Look back on all that space
Of time's immensity, consider well
What infinite combinations there have been
In matter's ways and groupings. How easy, then,
For human beings to believe we are
Compounded of the very selfsame motes,
Arranged exactly in the selfsame ways
As once we were, our long-ago, our now
Being identical. And yet we keep
No memory of that once-upon-a-time,
Nor can we call it back; somewhere between
A break occurred, and all our atoms went
Wandering here and there and far away
From our sensations. If there lies ahead
Tough luck for any man, he must be there,
Himself, to feel its evil, but since death
Removes this chance, and by injunction stops
All rioting of woes against our state,
We may be reassured that in our death
We have no cause for fear, we cannot be
Wretched in nonexistence. Death alone
Has immortality, and takes away
Our mortal life. It does not matter a bit
If we once lived before.
                              So, seeing a man
Feel sorry for himself, that after death
He'll be a rotting corpse, laid in a tomb,
Succumb to fire, or predatory beasts,
You'll know he's insincere, just making noise,
With rancor in his heart, though he believes,
Or tries to make us think so, that death ends all.
And yet, I'd guess, he contradicts himself,
He does not really see himself as gone,
As utter nothingness, but does his best—
Not really understanding what he's doing—
To have himself survive, for, in his life,

He will project a future, a dark day
When beast or bird will lacerate his corpse.
So he feels sorry for himself; he fails
To make the real distinction that exists
Between his castoff body, and the man
Who stands beside it grieving, and imputes
Some of his sentimental feelings to it.
Resenting mortal fate, he cannot see
That in true death he'll not survive himself
To stand there as a mourner, stunned by grief
That he is burned or mangled. If in death
It's certainly no pleasure to be mauled
By beak of bird or fang of beast, I'd guess
It's no voluptuous revel to be laid
Over the flames, or packed in honey and ice,
Stiff on the surface of a marble slab,
Or buried under a great mound of earth.

And men behave the same way at a banquet,
Holding the cups or garlanding the brows,
And sighing from the heart, "Ah, life is short
For puny little men, and when it goes
We cannot call it back," as if they thought
The main thing wrong, after their death, will be
That they are very thirsty, or may have
A passionate appetite for who knows what.
"No longer will you happily come home
To a devoted wife, or children dear
Running for your first kisses, while your heart
Is filled with sweet unspoken gratitude.
You will no longer dwell in happy state,
Their sword and shield. Poor wretch," men tell themselves,
"One fatal day has stolen all your gains."
But they don't add, "And all your covetings."
If they could see this clearly, follow it
With proper reasoning, their minds would be
Free of great agony and fear, "As now
You lie asleep in death, forevermore
You will be quit of any sickening pain,
While we, who stood beside your funeral pyre,
Have, with no consolation, mourned your death
In sorrow time will never heal." Well, then,

Ask of your dead what bitterness he finds
In sleep and quiet; why should anyone
Wear himself out in everlasting grief?
No man, when body and soul are lost in sleep,
Finds himself missing, or conducts a search
For his identity; for all we know,
For all we care, that sleep might last forever
And we would never list ourselves as missing.
Yet, all this while, our motes, our atoms, wander
Not far from sense-producing shift and stir,
And suddenly we come to wakefulness.
So we must think of death as being nothing,
As less than sleep, or less than nothing, even,
Since our array of matter never stirs
To reassemble, once the chill of death
Has taken over.

        Hark! The voice of Nature
Is scolding us: "What ails you, little man,
Why this excess of self-indulgent grief,
This sickliness? Why weep and groan at death?
If you have any sense of gratitude
For a good life, if you can't claim her gifts
Were dealt you in some kind of riddled jar
So full of cracks and holes they leaked away
Before you touched them, why not take your leave
As men go from a banquet, fed to the full
On life's good feast, come home, and lie at ease,
Free from anxiety? Alas, poor fool,
If, on the other hand, all of your joys
Are gone, and life is only wretchedness,
Why try to add more to it? Why not make
A decent end? There's nothing, it would seem,
My powers can contrive for your delight.
The same old story, always. If the years
Don't wear your body, don't corrode your limbs
With lassitude, if you keep living on
For centuries, if you never die at all,
What's in it for you but the same old story
Always, and always?" How could we reply
To this, except to say that Nature's case
Is argued to perfection? Now suppose

Some older man, a senior citizen,
Were plaintiff, wretcheder than he ought to be,
Lamenting death, would Nature not be right
To cry him down, with even sharper voice,
"Why, you old scoundrel, take those tears of yours
Somewhere away from here, cut out the whining.
You have had everything from life, and now
You find you're going to pieces. You desire,
Always, what isn't there; what is, you scorn,
So life has slipped away from you, incomplete,
Unsatisfactory, and here comes death,
An unexpected summoner, to stand
Beside you, long before you want to leave,
Long, long, before you think you've had enough.
Let it all go, act as becomes your age,
Be a great man, composed; give in; you must."
Such a rebuke from Nature would be right,
For the old order yields before the new,
All things require refashioning from others.
No man goes down to Hell's black pit; we need
Matter for generations yet to come,
Who, in their turn, will follow you, as men
Have died before you and will die hereafter.
So one thing never ceases to arise
Out of another; life's a gift to no man
Only a loan to him. Look back at time—
How meaningless, how unreal!—before our birth.
In this way Nature holds before our eyes
The mirror of our future after death.
Is this so grim, so gloomy? Is it not
A rest more free from care than any sleep?
Now all those things which people say exist
In Hell, are really present in our lives.
The story says that Tantalus, the wretch,
Frozen in terror, fears the massive rock
Balanced in air above him. It's not true.
What happens is that in our lives the fear,
The silly, vain, ridiculous fear of gods,
Causes our panic dread of accident.
No vultures feed on Tityos, who lies
Sprawled out for them in Hell; they could not find
In infinite eternities of time

What they are searching for in that great bulk,
Nine acres wide, or ninety, or the spread
Of all the globe. No man can ever bear
Eternal pain, nor can his body give
Food to the birds forever. We do have
A Tityos in ourselves, and lie, in love,
Torn and consumed by our anxieties,
Our fickle passions. Sisyphus, too, is here
In our own lives; we see him as the man
Bent upon power and office, who comes back
Gloomy and beaten after every vote.
To seek for power, such an empty thing,
And never gain it, suffering all the while,
This is to shove uphill the stubborn rock
Which over and over comes bouncing down again
To the flat levels where it started from.
Or take another instance: when we feed
A mind whose nature seems unsatisfied,
Never content, with all the blessings given
Through season after season, with all the charms
And graces of life's harvest, this, I'd say,
Is to be like those young and lovely girls,
The Danaids, trying in vain to fill
Their leaky jars with water. Cerberus,
The Furies, and the dark, and the grim jaws
Of Tartarus, belching blasts of heat—all these
Do not exist at all, and never could.
But here on earth we do fear punishment
For wickedness, and in proportion dread
Our dreadful deeds, imagining all too well
Being cast down from the Tarpeian Rock,
Jail, flogging, hangmen, brands, the rack, the knout;
And even though these never touch us, still
The guilty mind is its own torturer
With lash and rowel, can see no end at all
To suffering and punishment, and fears
These will be more than doubled after death.
Hell does exist on earth—in the life of fools.

You well might think of saying to yourself:
"Even good Ancus closed his eyes on the light—
A better man than you will ever be,

You reprobate—and many lords and kings
Rulers of mighty nations, all have died.
Even that monarch, who once paved the way
Making the sea a highway for his legions
Where foot and horse alike could march dry-shod
While the deep foamed and thundered at the outrage,
Even he, great Xerxes, died and left the light,
And Scipio, the thunderbolt of war,
Terror of Carthage, gave his bones to earth
As does the meanest lackey. Add to these
Philosophers and artists, all the throng
Blessed by the Muses; Homer's majesty
Lies low in the same sleep as all the rest.
Democritus, warned by a ripe old age
That, with his memory, his powers of mind
Were also failing, gave himself to death;
And Epicurus perished, that great man
Whose genius towered over all the rest,
Making their starry talents fade and die
In his great sunlight. Who are you, forsooth,
To hesitate, resent, protest your death?
Your life is death already, though you live
And though you see, except that half your time
You waste in sleep, and the other half you snore
With eyes wide open, forever seeing dreams,
Forever in panic, forever lacking wit
To find out what the trouble is, depressed,
Or drunk, or drifting aimlessly around."

Men seem to feel some burden on their souls,
Some heavy weariness; could they but know
Its origin, its cause, they'd never live
The way we see most of them do, each one
Ignorant of what he wants, except a change,
Some other place to lay his burden down.
One leaves his house to take a stroll outdoors
Because the household's such a deadly bore,
And then comes back, in six or seven minutes—
The street is every bit as bad. Now what?
He has his horses hitched up for him, drives,
Like a man going to a fire, full-speed,
Off to his country-place, and when he gets there

Is scarcely on the driveway, when he yawns,
Falls heavily asleep, oblivious
To everything, or promptly turns around,
Whips back to town again. So each man flees
Himself, or tries to, but of course that pest
Clings to him all the more ungraciously.
He hates himself because he does not know
The reason for his sickness; if he did,
He would leave all this foolishness behind,
Devote his study to the way things are,
The problem being his lot, not for an hour,
But for all time, the state in which all men
Must dwell forever and ever after death.
Finally, what's this wanton lust for life
To make us tremble in dangers and in doubt?
All men must die, and no man can escape.
We turn and turn in the same atmosphere
In which no new delight is ever shaped
To grace our living; what we do not have
Seems better than everything else in all the world
But should we get it, we want something else.
Our gaping thirst for life is never quenched.
We have to know what luck next year will bring,
What accident, what end. But life, prolonged,
Subtracts not even one second from the term
Of death's continuance. We lack the strength
To abbreviate that eternity. Suppose
You could contrive to live for centuries,
As many as you will. Death, even so,
Will still be waiting for you; he who died
Early this morning has as many years
Interminably before him, as the man,
His predecessor, has, who perished months
Or years, or even centuries ago.

Translated by Rolfe Humphries

CATULLUS

c. 84–c. 54 B.C.

Gaius Valerius Catullus was born at Verona and came to Rome, where he soon became a member of a circle of young poets who were strongly influenced by the Greek poets of the Alexandrian school. He also seems (we have only the evidence of his poems) to have carried on a passionate and in the end unhappy love affair with a married woman whom he calls "Lesbia."

The numbers here assigned to the poems are those found in all modern editions; they represent the order in which the poems appeared in the one manuscript copy on which our text is based. Although no. 1 is clearly designed to introduce a collection, it seems doubtful that the text we have is what Catullus published; it contains unfinished poems and some that look like rejected first drafts. It is generally supposed that after his death, a friend put the volume together by adding to a previously published, smaller collection (for which no. 1 was the first item) whatever poems Catullus had later circulated or left behind in manuscript. The poems in the basic manuscript and in all modern editions text are arranged roughly by meter: nos. 1–60 use a variety of meters, with hendecasyllable and iambic predominating; nos. 65–116, elegiac couplets; and nos. 61–64 are longer poems, mostly in hexameter. The poems to and about Lesbia are scattered throughout; their position in the collection is not consonant with a chronological account of the love affair.

Apuleius, writing in the second century A.D., claims that the name Lesbia was a metrical substitute for Clodia. Modern scholars have identified Clodia with the sister of Publius Clodius Pulcher—a gangster politician in the service of Julius Caesar and a violent enemy of Cicero. If so, Clodia was member of one of Rome's oldest and most distinguished families, a married woman, and one notorious for her love affairs.

1

To whom will I give this sophisticated,
abrasively accomplished new collection?
To you, Cornelius! You had the habit

of making much of my poetic little,
when you, the first in Italy, were boldly
unfolding all past ages in three volumes,
a monument of scholarship & labor!
And so it's yours; I hand this slim book over,
such as it is—for the sake of its patron
may it survive a century or better.

5

Lesbia, let us live only for loving,
and let us value at a single penny
all the loose flap of senile busybodies!
Suns when they set are capable of rising,
but at the setting of our own brief light
night is one sleep from which we never waken.
Give me a thousand kisses, then a hundred,
another thousand next, another hundred,
a thousand without pause & then a hundred,
until when we have run up our thousands
we will cry bankrupt, hiding our assets
from ourselves & any who would harm us,
knowing the volume of our trade in kisses.

7

My Lesbia, you ask how many kisses
would be enough to satisfy, to sate me!
—As many as the sandgrains in the desert
near Cyrene, where silphium is gathered,
between the shrine of Jupiter the sultry
& the venerable sepulchre of Battus!
—As many as the stars in the tacit night
that watch as furtive lovers lie embracing:
only to kiss you with that many kisses
would satisfy, could sate your mad Catullus!
A sum to thwart the reckoning of gossips
& baffle the spell-casting tongues of envy.

8

Wretched Catullus! You have to stop this nonsense,
admit that what you see has ended is over!

Once there were days which shone for you with rare brightness,
when you would follow wherever your lady led you,
the one we once loved as we will love no other;
there was no end in those days to our pleasures,
when what you wished for was what she also wanted.
Yes, there were days which shone for you with rare brightness.
Now she no longer wishes; you mustn't want it,
you've got to stop chasing her now—cut your losses,
harden your heart & hold out firmly against her.
Goodbye now, lady. Catullus' heart is hardened,
he will not look to you nor call against your wishes—
how you'll regret it when nobody comes calling!
So much for you, bitch—your life is all behind you!
Now who will come to see you, thinking you lovely?
Whom will you love now, and whom will you belong to?
Whom will you kiss? And whose lips will you nibble?
But *you*, Catullus! *You* must hold out now, firmly!

13

You will dine well with me, my dear Fabullus,
in a few days or so, the gods permitting.
—Provided you provide the many-splendored
feast, and invite your fair-complected lady,
your wine, your salt & all the entertainment!
Which is to say, my dear, if you bring dinner
you will dine well, for these days your Catullus
finds that his purse is only full of cobwebs.
But in return, you'll have from me Love's Essence,
—or what (if anything) is more delicious:
I'll let you sniff a certain charming fragrance
which Venuses & Cupids gave my lady;
one whiff of it, Fabullus, and you'll beg the
gods to transform you into nose, completely!

22

Varus, you know Suffenus as well as any;
the man is charming, witty, sophisticated—
nevertheless, he's written reams of bad verses.
I'm sure he must have churned out more than ten thousand,
and not just jotted down on scraps of papyrus,

as we do—no, they're copied out on good new rolls
wound up on ivory, with red parchment wrappers,
lead-ruled, smoothed with pumice: what a grand production!
And when you *read* his stuff, this darling man, our
sophisticated Suffenus seems a perfect
goatsucker, miles away from his urbane brilliance.
Who can explain this? A man brighter than diamonds
or what (if anything) is even more polished,
becomes less clever than the least clever rustic
when he turns to verse. At the same time, he's never
more beatific than when he's busy writing—
pleased and even astounded by his own talent.
Conceited? Yes, but show me a man who isn't:
someone who doesn't seem like Suffenus in something.
A glaring fault? It must be somebody else's:
I carry mine in my backpack & ignore them.

43

Greetings to you, girl of the nose not tiny,
the feet not pretty, eyes not darkly-shadowed,
stubby fat fingers, mouth forever spraying
language that shows us your lack of refinement,
whore of that bankrupt wastrel from Formiae!
Is it your beauty they praise in the province?
Do they compare you to our Lesbia?
Mindless, this age. And insensitive, really.

45

Septimius, with his beloved Acme
curled on his lap, moans, "Acme, dear, my darling,
unless I love you, Love, unto perdition,
now & forever after, with a frenzy
as fierce as any fabled frenzied lover's,
may I be savaged by a green-eyed lion,
in Libya or India the torrid!"
(As Cupid heard, he sneezed in approbation,
rapidly first on one side then the other.)
—But Acme coyly tilted back her head, and
covered her lover's swimming eyes with kisses
fresh from her mouth as luscious as a berry:

"Septimius," she said, "my life, my darling,
forever may we both serve this one master,
as now I swear by Love's consuming fire—
from which I suffer rather more than you do."
(As Cupid heard, he sneezed in approbation,
rapidly first on one side then the other.)
They start from so fortuitous an omen,
their loving & beloved souls entangled:
Septimius would rather have his Acme
than a great heap of Syrias & Britains.
And in Septimius, his faithful Acme
finds nothing less than total satisfaction!
Who's ever witnessed a more beatific
couple, or known sweet Venus more auspicious?

55 & 58B

Tell us, if it isn't too much trouble,
where it is that you've been lurking lately.
We've looked all over for you—at the racetrack,
at the Circus, in the Forum's bookstalls,
the sacred temple of great Jupiter!
I went as far as Pompey's portico,
questioning every hooker who approached me:
what a lot of innocent expressions!
Unconvinced, I finally exploded,
"Give me Camerius, you bargain baggage!"
One answered me with a complete disclosure:
"He's hiding here, between my blushing titties. . . ."
You think I'm Hercules? I'm not. Even
if I were changed into the Cretan Giant,
and had the wings of Pegasus for soaring,
and were as fast as Perseus or Ladas,
or the white horses of the Thracian King;
add all flying fowl of every feather,
and have the winds rush in from every quarter;
order them all, Camerius, to aid me
and still I'd be worn down to a frazzle,
suffer fainting spells & palpitations,
and God knows what, my friend, from chasing you!
It really isn't nice to be so distant.
Come on now, tell us where we can reach you,

put an end to this absurd deception!
Are your little blondes holding you captive?
If you remain obstinately tongue-tied,
the rewards of love will all escape you:
Venus likes nothing more than juicy gossip.
But if you must, keep it from the others,
so long as I can share your little secret!

76

If any pleasure can come to a man through recalling
    decent behavior in his relations with others,
not breaking his word, and never, in any agreement,
    deceiving men by abusing vows sworn to heaven,
then countless joys will await you in old age, Catullus,
    as a reward for this unrequited passion!
For all of those things which a man could possibly say or
    do have all been said & done by you already,
and none of them counted for anything, thanks to her vileness!
    Then why endure your self-torment any longer?
Why not abandon this wretched affair altogether,
    spare yourself pain the gods don't intend you to suffer!
It's hard to break off with someone you've loved such a long time:
    it's hard, but you have to do it, somehow or other.
Your only chance is to get out from under this sickness,
    no matter whether or not you think you're able.
O gods, if pity is yours, or if ever to any
    who lay near death you offered the gift of your mercy,
look on my suffering: if my life seems to you decent,
    then tear from within me this devouring cancer,
this heavy dullness wasting the joints of my body,
    completely driving every joy from my spirit!
Now I no longer ask that she love me as I love her,
    or—even less likely—that she give up the others:
all that I ask for is health, an end to this foul sickness!
    O gods, grant me this in exchange for my worship.

92

Lesbia never avoids a good chance to abuse me
    in public, yet I'll be damned if she doesn't love me!

How can I tell? Because I'm exactly the same: I malign her
always—yet I'll be damned if I don't really love her!

101

Driven across many nations, across many oceans,
    I am here, my brother, for this final parting,
to offer at last those gifts which the dead are given
    and to speak in vain to your unspeaking ashes,
since bitter fortune forbids you to hear me or answer,
    O my wretched brother, so abruptly taken!
But now I must celebrate grief with funeral tributes
    offered the dead in the ancient way of the fathers;
accept these presents, wet with my brotherly tears, and
    now & forever, my brother, hail & farewell.

                                 Translated by Charles Martin

11

Furius and Aurelius, Catullus' comrades,
Whether he penetrate the ultimate Indies,
Where the rolling surf on the shores of Morning
    Beats and again beats,
Or in the land of Bedouin, the soft Arabs,
Or Parthians, the ungentlemanly archers,
Or where the Nile with seven similar streamlets
    Colors the clear sea;
Or if he cross the loftier Alpine passes
And view the monuments of almighty Caesar—
The Rhine, and France, and even those remotest
    Shuddersome British—
Friends, prepared for all of these, whatever
Province the celestial ones may wish me,
Take a little bulletin to my girl friend,
    Brief but not dulcet:
Let her live and thrive with her fornicators,
Of whom she hugs three hundred in an evening,
With no true love for any, leaving them broken-
    Winded the same way.
She need not look, as once she did, for my love.
By her own fault it died, like a tumbling flower

At the field's edge, after the passing harrow
Clipped it and left it.

Translated by Robert Fitzgerald

6

Your most recent acquisition, Flavius,
must be as unattractive as
                    (doubtless) she is unacceptable
or you would surely have told us about her.
You are wrapped up with a whore to end all whores
and ashamed to confess it.
                    You do not spend bachelor nights.
Your divan, reeking of Syrian unguents,
draped with bouquets & blossoms etc.
                    proclaims it,
the pillows & bedclothes indented in several places,
a ceaseless jolting & straining of the framework
the shaky accompaniment to your sex parade.
Without more discretion your silence is pointless.
Attenuated thighs betray your preoccupation.
Whoever, whatever she is, good or bad,
                    tell us, my friend—
Catullus will lift the two of you & your love-acts into the heavens
in the happiest of his hendecasyllables.

26

Your cottage, Furius, sheltered
from the dry Scirocco,
from Zephyrus,
                    from Apeliota,
from the bitter North-East draughts
is exposed to an *over*draft of a different sort—
£1,250:
          ghastly . . . ruinous.

31

Apple of islands, Sirmio, & bright peninsulas, set
in our soft-flowing lakes or in the folds of ocean,

with what delight delivered, safe & sound,
from Thynia
from Bithynia
    you flash incredibly upon the darling eye.
What happier thought
    than to dissolve
the mind of cares
    the limbs from sojourning,
and to accept the down of one's own bed
under one's own roof
    —held so long at heart . . .

and that one moment paying for all the rest.

So, Sirmio, with a woman's loveliness, gladly
echoing Garda's rippling lake-laughter,
and, laughing there, Catullus' house
catching the brilliant echoes!

49

Silver-tongued among the sons of Rome
the dead, the living & the yet unborn,
Catullus, least of poets, sends
Marcus Tullius his warmest thanks:

—as much the least of poets
as he a prince of lawyers.

58

Lesbia, our Lesbia, the same old Lesbia,
Caelius, she whom Catullus loved once
more than himself and more than all his own,
loiters at the cross-roads
and in the backstreets
ready to toss-off the "magananimous" sons of Rome.

70

Lesbia says she'd rather marry me
than anyone,
though Jupiter himself came asking

or so she says,
              but what a woman tells her lover in desire
should be written out on air & running water.

83

Lesbia is extraordinarily vindictive
about me in front of her husband
who is thereby moved to fatuous laughter—
a man mulishly insensitive, failing to grasp
that a mindless silence (about me) spells safety
while to spit out my name in curses, baring
her white teeth, means she remembers me, and
what is more pungent still, is scratching the wound
ripening herself while she talks.

84

*"H*advantageous" breathes Arrius heavily
                              when he means
        "advantageous,"
intending "artificial" he labours *"h* artificial,"
convinced he is speaking impeccably while
he blows his h's about most *"h* artificially."
One understands that his mother—his uncle—
his family, in fact, on the distaff side
spoke so.
              Fortunately he was posted to Syria
and our ears grew accustomed to normal speech again,
unapprehensive for a while of such words
until suddenly the grotesque news reaches us
that the Ionian Sea has become
                              since the advent of Arrius
no longer Ionian
              but (inevitably) *H*ionian.

85

I hate and I love. And if you ask me how,
I do not know: I only feel it, and I'm torn in two.

86

We have heard of Quintia's beauty. To me she is tall, slender
and of a white "beauty." Such things I freely admit;
but such things do not constitute beauty.
                In her there is nothing of Venus,
not a pinch of love spice in her long body.
While Lesbia, Lesbia is loveliness indeed.
                Herself of particular beauty
has she not plundered womanhead of all its graces,
                flaunting them as her adornment?

107

If ever anyone anywhere, Lesbia, is looking
                        for what he knows will not happen
and then unexpectedly it happens—
the soul is astonished,
as we are now in each other,
                        an event dearer than gold,
for you have restored yourself, Lesbia, desired
restored yourself, longed for, unlooked for,
                        brought yourself back
to me. White day in the calendar!
                        Who happier than I?
What more can life offer
than the longed for unlooked for event when it happens?

Translated by Peter Whigham

HORACE

65–8 B.C.

*Quintus Horatius Flaccus was the son of a former slave, who prospered
financially once he obtained his freedom, and was able to give his son a
good education. Young Horace (as he is known familiarly in English)*

studied at the University of Athens, where he joined the republican army that fought against the man who was to become the emperor Augustus. Later, however, he became a member of Augustus' inner circle of literary figures who gave a cultural luster to the new imperial regime. Horace wrote in many different genres (for a specimen of his Satires, see pp. 635–39), but his greatest achievement was to adapt for the Latin language the meters of Greek lyric poetry.

ODES

The four books of Horace's Odes contain 103 short lyric poems in a bewildering variety of moods and meters, all of them distinguished by that verbal felicity for which Horace was famous. The following short selection—a mere nineteen—attempts to give some idea of the variety and of the poetic achievement.

From BOOK I

4

Winter to Spring: the west wind melts the frozen rancour,
    The windlass drags to sea the thirsty hull;
Byre is no longer welcome to beast or fire to ploughman,
    The field removes the frost-cap from his skull.

Venus of Cythera leads the dances under the hanging
    Moon and the linked line of Nymphs and Graces
Beat the ground with measured feet while the busy Fire-God
    Stokes his red-hot mills in volcanic places.

Now is the time to twine the spruce and shining head with myrtle,
    Now with flowers escaped the earthy fetter,
And sacrifice to the woodland god in shady copses
    A lamb or a kid, whichever he likes better.

Equally heavy is the heel of white-faced Death on the pauper's
    Shack and the towers of kings, and O my dear
The little sum of life forbids the ravelling of lengthy
    Hopes. Night and the fabled dead are near

And the narrow house of nothing, past whose lintel
You will meet no wine like this, no boy to admire
Like Lycidas, who today makes all young men a furnace
And whom tomorrow girls will find a fire.

Translated by Louis MacNeice

5

The last stanza of this poem refers to a religious thanksgiving made by
survivors from shipwreck: a picture of the event was hung on the temple
wall and the wet clothes were dedicated to the god of the sea. Soracte
(no. 9)—now Soratte—is a mountain about 20 miles north of Rome that
is visible from high points in the city.

What slim youth, Pyrrha, drenched in perfumed oils,
Lying in an easy grotto among roses, roses,
    Now woos, and watches you
    Gathering back your golden hair,

With artless elegance? How many a time
Will he cry out, seeing all changed, the gods, your promise,
    And stare in wondering shock
    At winds gone wild on blackening seas!

Now fondling you, his hope, his perfect gold,
He leans on love's inviolable constancy, not dreaming
    How false the breeze can blow.
    Ah, pity all those who have not found

Your glossy sweetness out! My shipwreck's tale
Hangs, told in colors, on Neptune's temple wall, a votive
    Plaque, with salvaged clothes
    Still damp, vowed to the sea's rough lord.

Translated by Cedric Whitman

7

Others can praise in their verse Mitylene, Rhodes and its glories,
    Great Ephesus, high-walled, twin-harboured Corinth,
Bacchus's home town Thebes, or Delphi, haunt of Apollo,
    Or Tempe up in Thessaly. Some poets

Concentrate all their lives on a long-drawn epic extolling
  Virgin Athene's city, plucking sprigs of
Olive from Attica's history, wreaths to adorn their foreheads;
  And some, to honour Juno's reputation,
Celebrate Argos, country for horses, and rich Mycenae.
  But, as for me, neither the sturdy Spartan
Hills nor the low lush fields of Larissa can knock at the heart as
  My Tibur does, the Sibyl's booming grotto,
Anio's fine cascade, Tiburnus' grove and the orchards
  Whose rivulets weave a dance of irrigation.
Winds from the south blow clear; they sweep clouds out of a dark
    sky
  And never breed long rains: remember, Plancus,
Good wine does just that for the wise man—chases away all
  The stresses and distresses of existence.
Hold to this truth in the camp, hemmed round by the glittering
    standards,
  And, when you come home soon to Tibur's leafy
Privacy, keep it in mind. When Teucer was sent into exile
  From Salamis by his father, undismayed he
Set on his wine-flushed brow, they say, brave garlands of poplar
  And cried to his dispirited companions:
"Fortune will prove more kind than a parent. Wherever she takes us,
  Thither, my friends and comrades, we shall follow.
Teucer shall lead and his star shall preside. No cause for despair,
    then
  Phoebus, who never lies, has pledged a second
Salamis, rival in name, to arise in a new-found country.
  You who have stayed by me through worse disasters,
Heroes, come, drink deep, let wine extinguish our sorrows.
  We take the huge sea on again tomorrow."

Translated by James Michie

9

You see how deep Soracte stands in snow,
A hoary blaze, the laboring forests cringing
    Under the load, the rivers standing
    Pinned in their course by piercing ice.

Heap logs in plenty on the grate, melt off
The cold, and tilt the crock up by both handles,

Good revel master, pour the four year
Vintage out with freer hand.

Leave all the rest to the gods; once they have laid
Asleep these winds that now go brawling over
    The boiling sea, no more will cypress
    Shiver and flail, nor aged ash.

Let be what comes tomorrow, reckoning
Pure gain whatever gift of days your fortune
    Yields, and in youth be not disdainful
    Of love in all its sweetness; dance,

While yet no sorry white head nods upon
Your springtime shoulders; look to the piazza,
    The pleasure walks, the hushed whisper
    By nightfall at the trysting hour;

When a girl's laughter happily betrays
Her hiding place, lurked in a secret corner;
    Then plunder a trinket from her finger,
    Or languidly protesting arm.

                                    Translated by Cedric Whitman

                                   11

Do not, Leúconoé, seek to inquire what is forbidden, what
End the gods have assigned to you or to me; nor do you meddle
    with
Astrological numbers. What shall arise count to your balance if
God marks down to you more winters—or perhaps this very one is
    the
Last which now on the rocks wears out the fierce Mediterranean
Sea; but be wise and have wine, wine on the board, prune to a
    minimum
Long-drawn hopes. While we chat, envious time threatens to give us
    the
Slip; so gather the day, never an inch trusting futurity.

                                    Translated by Louis MacNeice

22

The poem is addressed to Aristius Fuscus, a teacher and critic who was a close friend of Horace. Like Socrates, he had no use for the countryside, so Horace tells us elsewhere; the mock-epic account of his encounter with a wolf on his country farm may be a humorous compliment to Fuscus' prejudice.

The good man innocent of sin,
Fuscus, may walk the world unharmed.
He has no need to travel armed
With bow or Moorish javelin

Or clanking, poison-arrowed quiver
To cross the Syrtes' burning sands,
The hostile Caucasus or the lands
Washed by that legendary river,

Hydaspes. Proof: quite unconcerned,
Singing of Lalage in my grounds,
I wandered unarmed out of bounds
And when I met a wolf it turned

And fled! Apulia, whose scions
Are soldiers, in broad oakwoods feeds
No beast that size; Numidia breeds,
Parched nurse of monsters, lesser lions.

Banish me to a lifeless plain
Where no tree ever is renewed
By summer's breeze, some latitude
Of louring weather and long rain,

Or where the sun steers close and mile
On mile is uninhabited heat,
I'll still love Lalage, my sweet
Chatterer with the charming smile.

Translated by James Michie

24

We are not sure who this Quintilian was, but Horace mentions him elsewhere as a friendly but incisive critic of his own poetry.

When somebody as dear as he is dead,
Grief must be huge and uninhibited.
Melpomene, to whom, God-given, belong
Lyre and clear voice, teach me a funeral song.
So, now Quintilius sleeps the sleep which men
Never recover from and who knows when
Honour, Good Faith, and naked Truth will find
His parallel again among mankind?
He's dead: good men in plenty mourn his end,
But none of them as bitterly, my friend
Virgil, as you, who even now still strain
The power of prayer demanding back, in vain,
Life, which the gods on their terms lend and take.
Though you were Thracian Orpheus and could make
The woods hang listening on your lute, would music
Conjure the blood back to his veins or physic
The sickly ghost once it has passed the gate
Which Mercury, stern officer of Fate,
Shuts against all entreaty, and been made
Of that grim-wanded shepherd's flock a shade?
Loss hurts. Yet patience helps us to endure
The ills no human should presume to cure.

Translated by James Michie

37

This is a drinking song in celebration of the suicide of Cleopatra in Alexandria in 30 B.C. Antony had taken his life some time previously. The victor, Octavian, who later took the title "Augustus," intended to have Cleopatra led in chains in his triumphal procession in Rome (where she would have been strangled in an underground prison at the exact moment Augustus started up the hill to the Capitol). But she killed herself with the help of some poisonous snakes. It is remarkable that Horace's poem starts out with a Cleopatra who is a "queen of half-men, girt by her crew / Of sickly shame . . ." but ends with a heroic figure who "had loftier thoughts, / To find out death . . ."

Drink, comrades, drum the ground, now it is time
For freedom's dance; and call on all the gods
    To come, lay out their gorgeous couches,
    And let them recline at the feast of Mars.

It had been crime till now to pour good wine
From crypts of our forefathers, while ruin poised
    Over the Capitol, and fevered madness
    Was winding cerecloth round our realm—

Dreams of the queen of half-men, girt by her crew
Of sickly shame, and drunk with delirious hopes
    Grown fat and reckless on easy fortune!
    But all that glare of frenzy waned

When scarce one vessel of her fleet sailed home
Unscorched by flame; her mind, long tranced and dazed
    On heady Egypt's wine, now waking
    To terror's truth, found Caesar's oars

Hard pressing on her flight from Italy,
Swift hawk on downy dove, hunter on hare
    In snowy fields of Thrace, and ready
    To fling her into chains, a beast

Of ominous wonder. But she had loftier thoughts,
To find out death; blades could not make her check
    Blanch like a girl's, or drive her flying
    With huddled sails to lurking shores.

Her courage soared; with placid face she scanned
Her fallen palace, and valorously reached
    Her hands to rasping snakes, sucking
    Their venom's blackness through her limbs.

Once death was fixed, the fiercer grew her mind:
Indeed, she scorned his cruel galleys, and men
    Who would have had her walk uncrowned,
    No spiritless woman, in triumph's pride.

                    Translated by Cedric Whitman

From BOOK II

3

A level mind in crooked times
Preserve, preserve; nor in better fortune
    Dash into rash self-glory,
    My brother bound for death—

Whether your life be a string of doldrums
Or whether you loll on days of festa
    At a private fête champêtre
    With a bottle of vintage wine.

Towering pine and silver poplar—
Why do they intermingle their friendly
    Shade? And why do these cantering waters
    Jockey their way through winding banks?

Here is the place for wine and perfume
And the too fleeting bloom of the rose
    While Time and Chance and the black threads
    Of the three Fates give chance and time.

You must leave the estates you bought, the house
You built, which yellow Tiber washes,
    Leave them—and all that pinnacled wealth,
    Your work, will fall to another master.

If rich and of ancient lineage, it makes
No odds; no odds if born a beggar
    You lived your life in the foulest slum,
    Victims all of the pitiless Reaper.

All of us briefed the same; for all of us
Our lot is rattled like dice and sooner
    Or later will fall and embark our souls
    On the packet boat to eternal exile.

Translated by Louis MacNeice

7

Pompeius was evidently a fellow officer with Horace in the republican
army of Brutus and Cassius that fought, unsuccessfully, against Antony
and Octavian in the two bloody battles at Philippi in 42 B.C. Horace was
allowed to make his way back to Rome after the victory of Antony and
Octavian, though he was deprived of the property inherited from his
father. Pompeius, however, remained in opposition, first with Sextus
Pompeius, who challenged Octavian and Antony in the western Medi-
terranean, and later, after the rift between the two triumvirs, with An-
tony in the East. His return to Rome, here celebrated by Horace, may
have been made possible by the amnesty declared by Octavian after his
decisive victory at Actium in 31 B.C.

Horace's claim that the god Mercury carried him out of battle in a
cloud is of course a joking reference to the many passages in the Iliad
where a god rescues a favored hero from danger by hiding him in a mist
and whisking him away.

O my friend and oldest comrade,
with whom I have often seen out
the vinous, lagging day,
with Syrian myrrh in my hair;

Pompeius, so often led with me
into extremity by our general
Brutus; who has restored you
to citizenship, your native

Gods and Italian skies? With you I knew
the rout at Philippi and my shield,
to my shame, left behind
where manhood failed and words

were eaten. Luckily Mercury
bore me away, in my fright, in a cloud:
but the undertow sucked you back
to the weltering straits of war.

Now render to Jove the banquet pledged:
lay your corse, fatigued with long
campaigns, beneath my laurel nor spare
the jars set aside for this day.

Fill the bright cups with Massic
oblivion, pour scent from capacious
shells. Who will contrive our
crowns of myrtle and moist

parsley? Whom will the dice make master
of wine? I shall drink deep
as Edonians do: it is sweet
to rave for a friend restored.

Translated by W. G. Shepherd

14

*Postumus cannot be securely identified. Hadria is the Adriatic Sea. The
cypress was planted in cemeteries (as it still is in Italy) and cypress
branches were strewn on the coffin at a funeral. Caecuban was a choice
Italian wine. The pontiffs were priests of the gods; their banquets were
noted for their opulence.*

Ah, how they glide by, Postumus, Postumus,
The years, the swift years! Wrinkles and imminent
    Old age and death, whom no one conquers—
        Piety cannot delay their onward

March; no, my friend, not were you to sacrifice
Three hundred bulls each day to inflexible
    Pluto, whose grim moat holds the triple
        Geryon jailed with his fellow Giants—

Death's lake that all we sons of mortality
Who have the good earth's fruits for the picking are
    Foredoomed to cross, no matter whether
        Rulers of kingdoms or needy peasants.

In vain we stay unscratched by the bloody wars,
In vain escape tumultuous Hadria's
    Storm-waves, in vain each autumn dread the
        Southern sirocco, our health's destroyer.

We must at last set eyes on the scenery
Of Hell: the ill-famed daughters of Danaus,

Cocytus' dark, slow, winding current,
Sisyphus damned to his endless labour.

Farewell to lands, home, dear and affectionate
Wife then. Of all those trees that you tended well
Not one, a true friend, save the hated
Cypress shall follow its short-lived master.

An heir shall drain those cellars of Caecuban
You treble-locked (indeed he deserves it more)
And drench the stone-flagged floor with prouder
Wine than is drunk at the pontiffs' banquet.

Translated by James Michie

16

Grosphus, the addressee of the poem, was a rich landowner with property in Sicily.

Peace, Grosphus, is what the man on the open
Aegean requires of the Gods when black cloud
obscures the moon and no fixed star can
    flash for the sailors.

Peace for the Thracians enraged with war,
peace for the Medes with their stylish quivers,
is not to be bought with gems or gold
    or gleaming fabrics.

Neither Persian treasure nor the consul's
lictor can disperse the wretched mob
of the mind or the cares that flit about
    your coffered ceilings.

He lives well on a little whose family
salt-cellar shines amid a modest
table, whose gentle sleep is not dispelled
    by fear or base greed.

Why do we aim so high, so bravely,
so briefly? Why hanker for countries scorched

by an alien sun? What exile from home
can avoid himself?

Care clambers aboard the armoured ships,
keeps pace with the cavalry squadrons, comes
swift as East-Wind-driven rain, comes
swift as any stag.

The soul content with the present
is not concerned with the future and tempers
dismay with an easy laugh. No
blessing is unmixed.

An early death snatched bright Achilles;
long senility reduced Tithonus:
this hour will offer to me, maybe, the good
it denies to you.

For you a hundred herds of Sicilian
cattle moo; for you are bred
neighing mares apt for the chariot;
you dress in twice-dyed

Tyrian purple wool: to me honest Fate
has given a little farm, the delicate breath
of the Grecian Muse, and disdain
for the jealous mob.

Translated by W. G. Shepherd

From BOOK III

5

*This is one of the so-called "Roman Odes," the first six of Book III; they
are all couched in the solemn Alcaic meter and all address themes of
high seriousness—political, moral, and religious. This fifth ode is concerned with the apparent decay of the Roman military morale.*

*In 53 B.C. Marcus Licinius Crassus, the third member of the First
Triumvirate with Julius Caesar and Pompey, set off to earn a military
reputation and acquire an army that would put him on an equal footing*

*with his partners in power. His invasion of Parthia, Rome's permanent
enemy on its eastern frontier, ended in disaster at Carrhae. Crassus was
killed, Roman legionary standards were captured and displayed in Parthian temples, and, worse still, captured Roman soldiers settled down,
married Parthian wives, and served the Parthian king. Such degeneration, Horace says, had been foreseen by Regulus, a general in the First
Punic War, who had been captured with his men in 255 b.c. He was sent
to Rome by his captors to propose the release of the captives in exchange
for humiliating concessions. Once there he warned his fellow countrymen against any such bargain, thus sealing his own fate—death and
torture when he returned to Carthage.*

    *The first stanza of the poem refers to an Augustan plan (which never
got beyond the drawing board) to follow up Julius Caesar's two landings
in Britain in 55 and 54 b.c. with a full-scale invasion. (It took place under
Claudius in a.d. 43.) There was also talk in Rome of a new invasion of
Parthia, but in the end all that happened was a diplomatic settlement of
the frontier dispute and the return of the legionary standards to Rome.*

    *Venafrum was a prosperous country town southeast of Rome, and
Tarentum (Taranto) was a seaside resort in the far south of Italy which
had originally been founded by Spartan colonists.*

> His thunder confirms our belief that Jove
> is lord of heaven; Augustus shall be held
> an earthly God for adding to the Empire
> the Britons and redoubtable Parthians.

> Did Crassus' troops live in scandalous
> marriage to barbarians (o Senate,
> and custom perverted), grow old
> bearing arms for alien fathers-in-law;

> did Marsians, Apulians, under a Parthian
> king, forget the sacred shields,
> the name, the toga, and immortal Vesta;
> while Jove and his city Rome were unharmed?

> The provident mind of Regulus was ware
> of this when he rejected shameful terms,
> extrapolating catastrophe in time
> to come from such a precedent

unless the captured youths should
perish unpitied. "I myself have seen
our standards affixed to Punic shrines,"
he said, "with the weapons wrested

from our soldiers and no blood split; I myself
have seen the arms of free men, citizens,
twisted back, the gates of Carthage open,
the fields we ravaged worked again.

Ransomed with gold our cohorts will, of course,
re-form with heightened morale . . . To shame
you add expense. The wool that's treated with dye
will never resume the colours it lost;

nor does manhood, once it has lapsed,
consent to lodge in less than men.
When the doe disentangled from close-
meshed nets puts up a fight, then will he

be brave who entrusted himself to treacherous foes;
and he will trample Carthage in another war
who has tamely felt the thongs
on his pinioned arms, and dreaded death.

Not knowing whence he draws his life, he
has confounded peace and war. Obscene!
O mighty Carthage, more sublime
by Rome's opprobrious downfall!"

They say that like an outlaw
he put aside his chaste wife's kiss
and little children and sternly lowered
his manly gaze to the ground,

hoping to steady the vacillating Senate
by counsel never given before,
and hurried out among his grieving
friends an unexampled exile.

He knew very well what the alien
torturers proposed. Nevertheless,

he parted the kinsmen blocking his path
and the crowd delaying his going,

as though, some tedious law-suit settled,
he were leaving his clients' affairs
in order to travel amid Venafran fields
or perhaps to Spartan Tarentum.

Translated by W. G. Shepherd

6

In 28 B.C., three years after his final victory over Antony and Cleopatra at Actium, Augustus launched a program of rebuilding and renovating Rome's temples, many of which had been neglected or damaged during the civil wars. He claimed, in the famous inscription commemorating his achievements, to have restored eighty-two old temples and built twelve new ones. Horace in III .6 blames past generations' neglect of the gods for the evils inflicted on Hesperia (Italy), among them two defeats on the eastern frontier at the hands of the Parthian commanders Monaeses and Pacorus. He adds to this Rome's near escape from disaster at Actium (adopting the official line that this was a victory not in a civil war but against a foreign enemy, Egypt) and Roman defeats on the Balkan frontier in battles against the Dacians. From Roman neglect of the gods, he proceeds to the degeneration of Roman morals and the decay of the family values—values that had produced, in earlier centuries, the tough citizen-soldiers who defeated Pyrrhus (the Hellenistic Macedonian invader of southern Italy), Carthage in three separate wars, and Antiochus, the Hellenistic ruler of Syria. This gloomy analysis of Roman moral decadence is in part a plea for Augustus' legislative program for restoring the sanctity of marriage and encouraging—and even, by taxation, trying to enforce—the propagation of children.

Though innocent you shall atone for the crimes
of your fathers, Roman, until you have restored
the temples and crumbling shrines of the Gods
and their statues grimy with smoke.

Acknowledge the rule of the Gods—and rule:
hence all things begin, to this ascribe the outcome.
Contemned, the Gods have visited many
evils on grieving Hesperia.

Already twice Monaeses and Pacorus' band
have crushed our ill-starred offensive
and preen themselves on having added
Roman spoils to their paltry gauds.

Our city busied with sedition has almost
suffered destruction by Egypt allied to Dacia,
the former renowned for her fleet, the latter
rather for hurtling arrows.

Teeming with sin, the times have sullied
first marriage, our children, our homes:
sprung from that source disaster has whelmed
our fatherland and our people.

The grown girl loves to be taught to be
artful and dance oriental dances,
obsessed to her dainty fingernails
with illicit amours.

She sniffs out young philand'rers at her
husband's feast, nor is she nice to choose
to whom she (hurriedly) grants her favours
when the lamps are removed,

but brazenly stands when called—with her
husband's assent—though some travelling
salesman or Spanish ship's captain
may be the agent of Shame.

The generation that dyed the Punic
sea with blood and laid low Pyrrhus,
Antiochus and Hannibal was not born
of parents such as these,

but of manly comrades, yeoman soldiers
taught to turn the soil with Sabine hoes
and carry cut firewood at a strict
mother's bidding when the Sun

advanced the shadows of the hills
and lifted the yokes from weary steers,

his departing chariot leading in
the hours of comfort.

What does corrupting time not diminish?
Our grandparents brought forth feebler heirs;
we are further degen'rate; and soon will beget
progeny yet more wicked.

9, 13

*The two odes that follow show Horace in a lighter vein: a lovers' quarrel
and reconciliation, and an address to the spring outside his country
house on the occasion of the* Fontinalia *(October 13), a day on which
the Romans made thank-offerings to springs and wells.*

"When I was dear to you
and no more favoured rival put his arms
about your snowy neck,
I flourished then as bless'd as Persia's king."

"When you burned for no one
more than for me and Lydia came before Chloe,
Lydia's reputation
flourished as bright as Roman Ilia's name."

"But Thracian Chloe rules
me now (a clever lyrist, skilled in seductive modes), for whom I would
not fear to die if the Fates would let her live."

"But Thurian Calais
kindles me now with a torch of mutual love,
for whom I would die twice
if the Fates would agree to let my love live."

"What if our love should
come again and Venus yoke her strays with bronze,
blonde Chloe be jilted,
the door thrown open for disregarded Lydia?"

"Though he is fair as a star
and you are light as cork and bad-tempered

as Adriatic, I'd love
to live with you, with you would gladly die."

Translated by W. G. Shepherd

Fountain of Bandusia, glassy waters gleaming,
You call to us for gifts, sweet wine and flowers today,
 Tomorrow a spruce goat,
 Pride of the lusty herd,

With young horns just swelling, ready for fight and rut.
But no, his destiny is here, to consecrate
 His blood, and tinge with winding
 Red your cooling brooks.

You stream untouched by summer and Dogstar fire, your gift
Of freshness long desired sets free the wearied oxen
 From under plough, and flocks
 From long days' wandering;

From this hour you are counted among the springs of fame,
And here am I, singing to the oak that overslants
 Your hollowed rocks, your leaping
 Waters, full of voices.

Translated by Cedric Whitman

26

The "sea-born deity" is of course Venus, who had a famous shrine at Paphos in Cyprus and a lesser known one at Memphis on the Nile. "Sithonian" is a fancy term for Thracian.

In love's wars I have long maintained
Good fighting trim and even gained
 Some glory; but now lyre
 And veteran sword retire

And the left wall in the temple of
The sea-born deity of love
 Shall house them. Come, lay here,
 Lay down the soldier's gear—

The crowbar, the tar-blazing torch,
The bow for forcing past the porch.
    This is my last request:
    Goddess, ruler of blest

Cyprus and Memphis, shrine that knows
No shiver of Sithonian snows,
    Whose whip bends proud girls' knees—
    One flick for Chloe, please.

Translated by James Michie

From BOOK IV

1

Paulus Maximus was a friend of Augustus, and of Ovid. The Salii were dancing worshippers of Mars, the war god.

    Must it be war again
After so long a truce? Venus, be kind, refrain,
    I beg you. The time's over
When Cinara was my gracious queen and I her lover.
    Fifty years, pitiless
Mother of the sweet Loves, weigh hard. You must not press
    This old tough-jointed horse
To run to your cajoling order round the course.
    Leave me. Go back to where
The young men call for you with a persuasive prayer.
    To Paulus Maximus' house
Pilot your lustrous swans, in proper style carouse,
    And, seeing you desire
A hot and likely heart, choose his to set on fire.
    Handsome, blue-blooded, young,
He for his nervous clients wields a ready tongue;
    He knows a hundred arts
To spread your army's banners to remotest parts;
    And when some rival, free
With lavish presents, fails, grateful and jubilant he
    Shall by the Alban lake

Beneath a cedar roof your image in marble make.
  Thick incense you'll inhale,
Sweet to your nostrils, there, and music shall regale
  Your ears—concerted lute
And curly Berecynthian pipe and shepherd's flute.
  With the sun's earliest rays
And latest, boys and girls shall give your godhead praise,
  Flashing their snow-white feet,
Dancing the Salian dance, treading the triple beat.
  These days I take no joy
In the naïve hope of mutual love with woman or boy,
  Or drinking bouts with men,
Or garlanding my temples with fresh flowers. Why then,
  My Ligurinus, why
Should the reluctant-flowing tears surprise these dry
  Cheeks, and my fluent tongue
Stumble in unbecoming silences among
  Syllables? In dreams at night
I hold you in my arms, or toil behind your flight
  Across the Martian Field,
Or chase through yielding waves the boy who will not yield.

Translated by James Michie

7

Ancus and Tullus are two legendary kings of early Rome. Diana (Artemis) could not rescue her devotee Hippolytus from the land of the dead, nor could Theseus save Pirithous, his companion on the ill-fated expedition to abduct Persephone, the queen of the dead.

Snows have fled, the grass returns now to the meadows,
  And long locks to the trees;
Earth runs her course of change, and streams no longer swollen
  Flow tamely past their banks.
Thalia and her two sisters, with all the nymphs, take heart
  And lead the naked dance.
The season warns us, and time, as it steals the nurturing day,
  Bids dream no deathless dreams.
West winds temper the chill, but summer jostles spring,
  Herself to die, at once
Turned autumn, apple-bearer, bringer of fruits; and soon
  The rigid frost returns.

But hastening moons redeem their ebbings in the skies;
    We, when we go down
Where good Aeneas is gone, with lordly Tullus and Ancus,
    We lapse to dust and shade.
Who knows if the lofty gods will add a span of tomorrows
    To what is summed today?
Your heir's turn comes, when only the gifts that ripen your soul
    Will slip his hungry grasp.
When once you die, and Minos hands down upon your life
    His judgment's instant flash,
Not birth, nor eloquent tongue, my friend, nor upright mind
    Will bear you back to us.
Diana never has freed her chaste Hippolytus
    From that infernal dark,
Nor mighty Theseus broken oblivion's chain that binds
    Pirithous, whom he loved.

Translated by Cedric Whitman

From SATIRES

II.6

Horace here records his happiness in the Sabine farm given him by Maecenas and his relief at escape from the pressures of life in Rome. The "son of Maia" whom he addresses in line 5 is Mercury, a god of the marketplace, to whom people prayed for wealth and profit. In his second example of the folly of asking too much, Horace is referring, rather elliptically, to an Italian folktale. A day laborer in the fields continually begged Hercules for help; Hercules took him to Mercury, who arranged for him to find a buried treasure. With the money he bought the fields he had always plowed and went on working just as hard as before.

Janus is the god of beginnings (hence January). The word translated as "guarantor" means someone who stands surety for a friend at a trial; to do so for someone influential would earn favor that would prove useful— hence the admonition to hurry up. The Esquiline, one of the Seven Hills of Rome, was the site of Maecenas' house, but also of old cemeteries, hence the epithet "grim." The "Thracian Chick" and "the Arab" are gladiators. Beans are "relatives of Pythagoras" because his disciples were forbidden to eat them—they might contain souls of the dead. The phrase "house-boy's duty" is ironical: the town mouse is sneaking a bite

from the plate he serves, like Leporello in the last act of Mozart's Don
Giovanni.

This is what I prayed for. A piece of land—not so very big,
with a garden and, near the house, a spring that never fails,
and a bit of wood to round it off. All this and more
the gods have granted. So be it. I ask for nothing else,
O son of Maia, except that you make these blessings last.

If I haven't increased my assets by any dishonest trick
and don't intend to fritter them away by extravagance or neglect,
if I'm not such a fool as to pray: I wish my little farm
could take in that corner of my neighbour's, which at present spoils
        its shape;

I wish I could stumble on a pot of silver and be like the fellow
who on finding some treasure bought and ploughed the very field
in which he had worked as a hired hand; it was thanks to Hercules
he became rich; if I'm pleased and content with what I have, this
is my prayer: make fat the flocks I own and everything else
except my head, and remain as ever my chief protector.

Well then, now that I've left town for my castle in the hills
what can I better celebrate in the satires of my lowland muse?
Here I am not worried by the rat-race or the leaden sirocco,
which in the unhealthy autumn makes a grim profit for the
        undertaker.

O father of the dawn, or Janus if you would rather have that name,
you watch over the beginning of man's working day,
for such is the will of heaven. So let me begin my song
with you. In Rome you dispatch me to act as a guarantor.
"Hurry up, or someone else will answer the call before you!"
The north wind may be rasping the earth, or winter may be drawing
the snowy day into a smaller circle, but go I must.

Later, after saying something loud and clear to my own
        disadvantage,
I have to barge through the crowd, injuring the slow movers.
"What do you want, you idiot, and what are you doing?" says a
        lout,
cursing angrily. "Do you think you can kick everything aside

just because you're dashing back to keep an appointment with
Maecenas?"

I like that, I admit, and it's sweet music in my ears.
But as soon as I reach the grim Esquiline, a hundred items
of other people's business start buzzing through my head and
jumping round my legs.
"Roscius would like you to meet him at the Wall by eight
tomorrow."
"The Department said be sure to come in today, Quintus;
an important matter of common concern has just cropped up."
"Get Maecenas' signature on these documents."
"I'll try,"
you say.
"You can if you want to," he replies, refusing to be put off.

Time flies. It's now seven, in fact almost eight,
years since Maecenas came to regard me as one of his friends—
or at least he was willing to go so far as to take me with him
when making a journey in his carriage and to risk casual remarks
like "What time do you make it?" "Is the Thracian Chick a match
for the Arab?"
"These frosty mornings are quite nippy; you've got to be careful,"
and other observations which might be entrusted to a leaky ear.
All this time, every day and hour, yours truly has become
a more frequent target for jealous comment. Suppose he has sat
beside you in the grandstand or played with you in the Park, there's
an immediate chorus
of "Lucky dog!" If a chilling rumour runs through the streets
from the city centre, everyone I meet asks me for details.
"Excuse me, sir, but you must know, for you're so close
to the supreme power—you haven't by any chance heard some news
about the Dacians?"
"No, none at all."
"Teasing as usual!"
"I swear it; I don't know a thing."
"No? Well what about the land
Caesar has promised to give his ex-servicemen? Will it be in Italy
or Triangleland?"
When I protest my ignorance, they regard me with
amazement
as a deep man, if you please, of quite unusual reticence!

That's how the day is wasted. In exasperation I murmur:
"When shall I see that place in the country, when shall I be free
to browse among my old books or laze in sleep and idleness,
drinking in a blissful oblivion of life's troubles?
When shall I sit down to a plate of beans, those relatives of
        Pythagoras,
and cabbage with just some fat bacon to make it tasty?"

Ah, those evenings and dinners. What heaven! My friends and I
have our meal at my own fireside. Then, after making an offering,
I hand the rest to the cheeky servants. Each guest
drinks from whatever glass he likes, big or small.
We have no silly regulations. One goes for the stronger stuff
like a hero, another mellows more happily on a milder blend.
And so the conversation begins—not about other people's
town and country houses, nor the quality of Mr Grace's dancing;
we discuss things which affect us more nearly and which one ought
        to know about:
what is the key to happiness, money or moral character?
In making friends are we motivated by self-interest or idealism?
What is the nature of goodness, and what is its highest form?

From time to time our neighbour Cervius comes out with a story
which is old but apt. Suppose someone envies Arellius' money
without considering his worries, he begins: Once upon a time
a country mouse is said to have welcomed to his humble hole
a mouse from the city—a friend and guest of long standing.
He was a rough fellow, who kept a tight hand on his savings,
though he didn't mind relaxing when it came to a party. Anyhow,
he drew generously on his store of vetch and long oats,
he brought a raisin in his mouth and bits of half-eaten bacon,
hoping that by varying the menu he might please his finicky guest.
The latter would barely touch each item with his fastidious teeth,
whereas the master of the house, reclining on a couch of fresh straw
ate coarse grain and darnel, avoiding the choicer dishes.
Finally the city-dweller said: "Look old man, why on earth
do you want to eke out a living on a cliff edge in the woods?
You ought to give up this wild forest in favour of the city
and its social life. Come on back with me now; I mean it.
All earthly creatures have been given mortal souls;
large or small they have no means of escaping death.
So my dear chap, while there's still time, enjoy the good things
of life, and never forget your days are numbered."

His words
prodded the countryman into action. He hopped nimbly from his
    house,
and then the pair completed the journey as planned, taking care
to creep within the city wall under cover of darkness. Night
had reached the mid-point of her journey across the heavens
when they made their way into a wealthy house. Covers steeped
in scarlet dye shimmered expensively on ivory couches,
and close by, piled in baskets, were several courses
left over from a great dinner held earlier that evening.
Inviting the countryman to relax on the red material, the host
bustled about, like a waiter in a short jacket, serving
one course after another, not forgetting the house-boy's
duty of testing everything he brought with a preliminary nibble.
The other was lying there, thoroughly enjoying his change of
    circumstance
and playing the happy guest surrounded by good cheer,
when suddenly the doors crashed open and sent them scuttling from
    their places.
They dashed in fright down the long hall, their fear turning
to utter panic when they heard the sound of mastiffs baying
through the great house. Then the countryman said: "This isn't the
    life
for me. Good-bye: my hole in the woods will keep me safe
from sudden attack, and simple vetch will assuage my hunger."

Translated by Niall Rudd

VIRGIL
70–19 B.C.

From GEORGICS

*Publius Virgilius Maro came, like Catullus, from the north of Italy (he
was born near Mantova). His first published work, the* Eclogues, *a Latin
adaptation of the pastoral idylls of Theocritus, brought him to the atten-*

tion of Maecenas, the patron of poets and a close associate of Augustus. In 29 B.C. Virgil published the Georgics, *and dedicated the work to Maecenas.*

The Georgics *(a name derived from the Greek word* georgos, *"farmer") is a hexameter poem of some 2,000 lines which presents itself as a didactic treatise on agriculture, its literary model the* Works and Days *of Hesiod. The first book deals with cereal crops, the second with trees, mainly the olive and the vine, the third with cattle, and the fourth with beekeeping. (This was more important for the ancient world than for ours, since sugar was unknown in Europe until the Middle Ages.) But the* Georgics, *like the* Works and Days, *is much less and at the same time much more than a practical guide to work on the land; it is a poet's hymn to the glories of the Italian earth and, like Hesiod's poem, a celebration of the unrelenting work,* labor improbus, *that the earth demands.*

ORPHEUS AND EURYDICE

The story of Orpheus' quest for Eurydice and his fatal look back at her has, as far as we know, no precedent; Virgil may have invented it. The reason (or pretext) for its appearance at the end of a long and fascinating account of bees and beekeeping is that it gives a mythical explanation of bugonia, *literally, "generation from cattle"—a method of creating a swarm of bees discussed by many ancient writers (though not by Aristotle) that has more to do with folklore than reality. A two-year-old bullock is beaten to death (no blood spilt) and the corpse enclosed in a small shed; after some months a new swarm of bees emerges from the corruption of the flesh. The famous riddle of Samson in* Judges XIV— *"out of the strong came forth sweetness . . ."—is based on a similar belief.*

In Virgil's poem, the shepherd Aristaeus, losing his bees to some incurable sickness, goes to seek help from his goddess mother Cyrene. She tells him to find Proteus, the old man of the sea who can change his shape, to hold on to him until he tires of trying to escape, and force him to reveal the reason why the swarm of bees died. Our extract begins with the opening of Proteus' reply. After this, Aristaeus' mother tells him to propitiate the Dryads, forest nymphs who were the companions of Eurydice, by a sacrifice of bulls and to leave the carcasses to rot. From them will emerge a new swarm of bees.

"The anger that pursues you is divine,
Grievous the sin you pay for. Piteous Orpheus
It is that seeks to invoke this penalty
Against you—did the Fates not interpose—
Far less than you deserve, for bitter anguish
At the sundering of his wife. You were the cause:
To escape from your embrace across a stream
Headlong she fled, nor did the poor doomed girl
Notice before her feet, deep in the grass,
The watcher on the bank, a monstrous serpent.
Then with their cries the Dryad band, her peers,
Filled the high mountain-tops. Mount Rhodope
Wailed, and Pangaea's peaks, and warlike Thrace,
The land of Rhesus, the Getae and the Hebrus
And Attic Orithuia. He himself
Sought with his lyre of hollow tortoiseshell
To soothe his love-sick heart, and you, sweet wife,
You on the desolate shore alone he sang,
You at return, you at decline of day.
Even the jaws of Taenarum he braved,
Those lofty portals of the Underworld,
And entering the gloomy grove of terror
Approached the shades and their tremendous king,
Hard hearts no human prayer can hope to soften.
His music shook them: drawn from the very depths
Of Erebus came insubstantial shades,
The phantoms of the lightless. Thick as birds
That hide themselves in thousands in the leaves
When evening or a wintry shower has brought them
Down from the mountains. Mothers were there and men,
And forms of great-heart heroes who had run
Their course; boys and unwedded girls, and youths
Laid on the pyre before their parents' eyes.
All these Cocytus circling round about
Hemmed in with pitchy mire and ugly sedge
And sluggish, hateful pools, and Styx itself
With nine-fold moat imprisoned. More than this,
The very halls of Death and inmost dens
Of Tartarus were awestruck, and the Furies,
Their dark-blue locks entwined with writhing snakes;
Cerberus stood with his three mouths agape,
And the gale that drives Ixion's wheel was stilled.

At last, having evaded every hazard,
He was returning, and Eurydice
Restored to him and following behind
(So Proserpine's stern ruling had demanded)
Was coming back into the world above,
When suddenly a madness overcame
The unwary lover—pardonable indeed
Did Hell know any pardoning: he halted
And on the very brink of light, alas,
Forgetful, yielding in his will, looked back
At his own Eurydice. At that same instant
All his endeavour foundered, void the pact
Made with the ruthless tyrant; and three times
Thunder resounded over the pools of Avernus.
"Orpheus," she cried, "we are ruined, you and I!
What utter madness is this? See, once again
The cruel Fates are calling me back and darkness
Falls on my swimming eyes. Goodbye for ever.
I am borne away wrapped in an endless night,
Stretching to you, no longer yours, these hands,
These helpless hands." She finished, and suddenly
Out of his sight, like smoke into thin air,
Vanished away, unable any more
To see him as he vainly grasped at shadows
With so much more to say; and the ferryman
Of Orcus would not let him pass again
Over the sundering marsh. What should he do,
Where turn, bereft a second time of her?
Would any weeping move the powers below
Or prayer the powers above? She all the while,
Now cold, was crossing in the Stygian barque.
    For seven whole months on end, they say, he wept
Beneath a lofty crag beside the Strymon
Alone in the wild, under the chilly stars,
And sang his tale of woe, entrancing tigers
And drawing oak-trees; as the nightingale
Mourning beneath the shade of a poplar-tree
Laments lost young ones whom a heartless ploughman
Has spied unfledged in the nest and plundered. She
Weeps all night long and perched upon a bough
Repeats her piteous plaint, and far and wide

Fills all thc air with grief. No thought of love
Could touch his heart, no thought of marriage rites.
Alone he wandered over icy stppes
Of the farthest north, the snowy river Don
And those Rhipacan fields for ever wedded
To frost, lamenting for Eurydice
And Pluto's cancelled boon. But Thracian women,
Deeming themselves despised by such devotion,
Amid their Bacchic orgies in the night
Tore him apart, this youth, and strewed his limbs
Over the countryside. And so it was
That as the river of his fatherland,
The Hebrus, bore in the middle of its current
His head, now severed from his marble neck,
"Eurydice!" the voice and frozen tongue
Still called aloud, "Ah, poor Eurydice!"
As life was ebbing away, and the river banks
Echoed across the flood, "Eurydice!"

Translated by L. P. Wilkinson

THE AENEID

The myth that underlies Virgil's national Roman epic, the Aeneid, *is not as old as the* Iliad, *though it tells the story of a hero who does appear in that poem, where it is predicted by Poseidon that he will maintain the Trojan presence in the world even though Troy and most of its people will perish. As early as the fifth century B.C. a Greek writer, Hellanicus of Lesbos, mentioned Aeneas' journey to the West and may even have identified his goal as Italy. In the next century, the Sicilian Greek historian Timaeus speaks of Aeneas as the founder of the city of Lavinium in Latium, the coastal plain through which the Tiber River makes its way to the sea. Later, according to legend, settlers from Lavinium founded Alba Longa, about 20 miles from the future site of Rome—and from that city in the fullness of time came Romulus and Remus, the founders of what was to become the capital of the world. The legend was adopted and refined by the Romans as they moved toward dominance in the Hellenistic world, and it was given epic treatment in the* Annales *of Ennius in the second century B.C.*

PROLOGUE

Virgil's Prologue introduces Juno (the Roman equivalent of Hera), who hates the Trojans, as she did in the Iliad, *because of the Judgment of Paris and her husband Jupiter's love for the Trojan prince Ganymede. She is intent on winning the future empire of the world for a city that is just being founded on the North African shore by Dido, a Phoenician refugee queen. The founders of Carthage came from the Phoenician cities of Tyre and Sidon on the Palestinian coast; Dido's people are often called Tyrians, as in our text.*

Opposed to Juno and her schemes is Venus, the Roman Aphrodite. She is the mother of Aeneas by Anchises; and Aeneas' son Ascanius has another name: Iulus. He was claimed as their ancestor by the patrician Roman family, the gens Iulia, *the family of Julius Caesar and his great-nephew and adopted son Octavian—Augustus. Venus has on her side the supreme deity Jupiter, the Roman Zeus, who knows that the Fates, the* Parcae, *have decreed world domination not for Carthage, but for Rome.*

I sing of warfare and a man at war.
From the sea-coast of Troy in early days
He came to Italy by destiny,
To our Lavinian western shore,
A fugitive, this captain, buffeted
Cruelly on land as on the sea
By blows from powers of the air—behind them
Baleful Juno in her sleepless rage.
And cruel losses were his lot in war,
Till he could found a city and bring home
His gods to Latium, land of the Latin race,
The Alban lords, and the high walls of Rome.
Tell me the causes now, O Muse, how galled
In her divine pride, and how sore at heart
From her old wound, the queen of gods compelled him—
A man apart, devoted to his mission—
To undergo so many perilous days
And enter on so many trials. Can anger
Black as this prey on the minds of heaven?
Tyrian settlers in that ancient time
Held Carthage, on the far shore of the sea,

Set against Italy and Tiber's mouth,
A rich new town, warlike and trained for war.
And Juno, we are told, cared more for Carthage
Than for any walled city of the earth,
More than for Samos, even. There her armor
And chariot were kept, and, fate permitting,
Carthage would be the ruler of the world.
So she intended, and so nursed that power.
But she had heard long since
That generations born of Trojan blood
Would one day overthrow her Tyrian walls,
And from that blood a race would come in time
With ample kingdoms, arrogant in war,
For Libya's ruin: so the Parcae spun.
In fear of this, and holding in memory
The old war she had carried on at Troy
For Argos' sake (the origins of that anger,
That suffering, still rankled: deep within her,
Hidden away, the judgment Paris gave,
Snubbing her loveliness; the race she hated;
The honors given ravished Ganymede),
Saturnian Juno, burning for it all,
Buffeted on the waste of sea those Trojans
Left by the Greeks and pitiless Achilles,
Keeping them far from Latium. For years
They wandered as their destiny drove them on
From one sea to the next: so hard and huge
A task it was to found the Roman people.

Translated by Robert Fitzgerald

From BOOK I

AENEAS AT CARTHAGE

*When Aeneas and his fleet reach western waters between Sicily and
North Africa, Juno arranges for a violent storm that scatters the ships far
and wide. Aeneas lands on the North African shore. Leaving his crew
with the ship, he goes, with his companion Achates, to reconnoiter.
What they find is the new city of Carthage, under construction.*

*The scenes represented on the walls of the new temple to Juno stem
partly from the* Iliad, *partly from the later poems of the so-called "Epic
Cycle." Rhesus, a Thracian king who came to the aid of the Trojans, was*

killed, and his white horses captured, by Diomedes and Odysseus in a daring night raid on the Trojan lines. This story is told in Book X of the Iliad, *which does not, however, contain the prophecy, obliquely referred to here, that Troy would not fall if the horses of Rhesus once tasted Trojan grass and water. Troilus, a young son of Priam, is mentioned in the* Iliad *as one of Achilles' numerous victims, but the prophecy that Troy would not fall if Troilus reached his twentieth year is a later legend (and the story of his love for Cressida is later still—a medieval creation). In the* Iliad, *the corpse of Hector is not dragged round the walls of Troy even once, only round the corpse of Patroclus. Memnon, king of Ethiopia, came to fight for Troy, but was killed by Achilles, as was Penthesilea, queen of the Amazons. Both legends are post-Iliadic.*

             . . . Meanwhile
The two men pressed on where the pathway led,
Soon climbing a long ridge that gave a view
Down over the city and facing towers.
Aeneas found, where lately huts had been,
Marvelous buildings, gateways, cobbled ways,
And din of wagons. There the Tyrians
Were hard at work: laying courses for walls,
Rolling up stones to build the citadel,
While others picked out building sites and plowed
A boundary furrow. Laws were being enacted,
Magistrates and a sacred senate chosen.
Here men were dredging harbors, there they laid
The deep foundation of a theatre,
And quarried massive pillars to enhance
The future stage—as bees in early summer
In sunlight in the flowering fields
Hum at their work, and bring along the young
Full-grown to beehood; as they cram their combs
With honey, brimming all the cells with nectar,
Or take newcomers' plunder, or like troops
Alerted, drive away the lazy drones,
And labor thrives and sweet thyme scents the honey.
Aeneas said: "How fortunate these are
Whose city walls are rising here and now!"

He looked up at the roofs, for he had entered,
Swathed in cloud—strange to relate—among them,

Mingling with men, yet visible to none.
In mid-town stood a grove that cast sweet shade
Where the Phoenicians, shaken by wind and sea,
Had first dug up that symbol Juno showed them,
A proud warhorse's head: this meant for Carthage
Prowess in war and ease of life through ages.
Here being built by the Sidonian queen
Was a great temple planned in Juno's honor,
Rich in offerings and the godhead there.
Steps led up to a sill of bronze, with brazen
Lintel, and bronze doors on groaning pins.
Here in this grove new things that met his eyes
Calmed Aeneas' fear for the first time.
Here for the first time he took heart to hope
For safety, and to trust his destiny more
Even in affliction. It was while he walked
From one to another wall of the great temple
And waited for the queen, staring amazed
At Carthaginian promise, at the handiwork
Of artificers and the toil they spent upon it:
He found before his eyes the Trojan battles
In the old war, now known throughout the world—
The great Atridae, Priam, and Achilles,
Fierce in his rage at both sides. Here Aeneas
Halted, and tears came.
               "What spot on earth,"
He said, "what region of the earth, Achatës,
Is not full of the story of our sorrow?
Look, here is Priam. Even so far away
Great valor has due honor; they weep here
For how the world goes, and our life that passes
Touches their hearts. Throw off your fear. This fame
Insures some kind of refuge."
               He broke off
To feast his eyes and mind on a mere image,
Sighing often, cheeks grown wet with tears,
To see again how, fighting around Troy,
The Greeks broke here, and ran before the Trojans,
And there the Phrygians ran, as plumed Achilles
Harried them in his warcar. Nearby, then,
He recognized the snowy canvas tents
Of Rhesus, and more tears came: these, betrayed

In first sleep, Diomedes devastated,
Swording many, till he reeked with blood,
Then turned the mettlesome horses toward the beachhead
Before they tasted Trojan grass or drank
At Xanthus ford.
                        And on another panel
Troilus, without his armor, luckless boy,
No match for his antagonist, Achilles,
Appeared pulled onward by his team: he clung
To his warcar, though fallen backward, hanging
On to the reins still, head dragged on the ground,
His javelin scribbling S's in the dust.
Meanwhile to hostile Pallas' shrine
The Trojan women walked with hair unbound,
Bearing the robe of offering, in sorrow,
Entreating her, beating their breasts. But she,
Her face averted, would not raise her eyes.
And there was Hector, dragged around Troy walls
Three times, and there for gold Achilles sold him,
Bloodless and lifeless. Now indeed Aeneas
Heaved a mighty sigh from deep within him,
Seeing the spoils, the chariot, and the corpse
Of his great friend, and Priam, all unarmed,
Stretching his hands out.
                        He himself he saw
In combat with the first of the Achaeans,
And saw the ranks of Dawn, black Memnon's arms;
Then, leading the battalion of Amazons
With half-moon shields, he saw Penthesilëa
Fiery amid her host, buckling a golden
Girdle beneath her bare and arrogant breast,
A girl who dared fight men, a warrior queen.
Now, while these wonders were being surveyed
By Aeneas of Dardania, while he stood
Enthralled, devouring all in one long gaze,
The queen paced toward the temple in her beauty,
Dido, with a throng of men behind.

Translated by Robert Fitzgerald

From BOOK II

THE DEATH OF PRIAM

Aeneas and Achates are invisible in a protective cloud provided by Venus; as they watch Dido approach, they see the crews of the vessels they thought lost appear and ask the queen for hospitality. It is freely granted, and when the cloud disperses, Aeneas is recognized by his comrades and presented to the queen as their leader. Dido is impressed by his royal mien and heroic past, but Venus decides to make her fall in love with him. Venus substitutes her child Cupido (she also addresses him as "Amor") for Ascanius; when Dido embraces the child, she is at once consumed with love for Aeneas. At the banquet that night she makes him tell her the story of the fall of Troy and his wanderings—the encounter with the Cyclops, the death of Anchises in Sicily.

A high point of the second book, the story of the fall of Troy, is the death of Priam at the hand of Achilles' son Pyrrhus, who is also called Neoptolemus, a name that means "New War." As so often in the Aeneid, the mythic events resonate with echoes of Roman history. The last lines of the extract—"he that in other days . . ."—would recall to the Roman reader the fate of Gnaeus Pompeius, the opponent of Caesar in the civil war that began in 49 B.C. Pompey, as he is commonly known in English, had to abandon Italy to Caesar, and, like Antony after him, mobilized the forces of the Eastern half of the empire—"the power of Asia." Defeated at Pharsalus in Greece in 48 B.C., Pompey took refuge in Egypt, but the Egyptians, hoping for Caesar's favor, killed him and presented his head to Caesar. "On the distant shore / The vast trunk headless lies without a name."

What was the fate of Priam, you may ask.
Seeing his city captive, seeing his own
Royal portals rent apart, his enemies
In the inner rooms, the old man uselessly
Put on his shoulders, shaking with old age,
Armor unused for years, belted a sword on,
And made for the massed enemy to die.
Under the open sky in a central court
Stood a big altar; near it, a laurel tree
Of great age, leaning over, in deep shade
Embowered the Penatës. At this altar
Hecuba and her daughters, like white doves

Blown down in a black storm, clung together,
Enfolding holy images in their arms.
Now, seeing Priam in a young man's gear,
She called out:
        "My poor husband, what mad thought
Drove you to buckle on these weapons?
Where are you trying to go? The time is past
For help like this, for this kind of defending,
Even if my own Hector could be here.
Come to me now: the altar will protect us,
Or else you'll die with us."
                She drew him close,
Heavy with years, and made a place for him
To rest on the consecrated stone.
                   Now see
Politës, one of Priam's sons, escaped
From Pyrrhus' butchery and on the run
Through enemies and spears, down colonnades,
Through empty courtyards, wounded. Close behind
Comes Pyrrhus burning for the death-stroke: has him,
Catches him now, and lunges with the spear.
The boy has reached his parents, and before them
Goes down, pouring out his life with blood.
Now Priam, in the very midst of death,
Would neither hold his peace nor spare his anger.
"For what you've done, for what you've dared," he said,
"If there is care in heaven for atrocity,
May the gods render fitting thanks, reward you
As you deserve. You forced me to look on
At the destruction of my son: defiled
A father's eyes with death. That great Achilles
You claim to be the son of—and you lie—
Was not like you to Priam, his enemy;
To me who threw myself upon his mercy
He showed compunction, gave me back for burial
The bloodless corpse of Hector, and returned me
To my own realm."
            The old man threw his spear
With feeble impact; blocked by the ringing bronze,
It hung there harmless from the jutting boss.
Then Pyrrhus answered:
            "You'll report the news

To Pelidës, my father; don't forget
My sad behavior, the degeneracy
Of Neoptolemus. Now die."
                    With this,
To the altar step itself he dragged him trembling,
Slipping in the pooled blood of his son,
And took him by the hair with his left hand.
The sword flashed in his right; up to the hilt
He thrust it in his body.
                    That was the end
Of Priam's age, the doom that took him off,
With Troy in flames before his eyes, his towers
Headlong fallen—he that in other days
Had ruled in pride so many lands and peoples,
The power of Asia.
                    On the distant shore
The vast trunk headless lies without a name.

Translated by Robert Fitzgerald

BOOK IV

THE PASSION OF THE QUEEN

Dido (also known as Elissa) is a widow. In Tyre she was married to a wealthy man named Sychaeus, whom her brother Pygmalion, the tyrannical ruler of Tyre, murdered. He concealed his responsibility for her husband's death, but Dido learned the truth through dream visitations from her dead husband. Sychaeus revealed to her the whereabouts of his buried treasure and urged her to gather the opponents of Pygmalion together and set sail to found a new city. It is to her appropriation of the treasure that she is referring when she says on her deathbed: "I . . . made my hostile brother / Pay for his crime." In Carthage she has rejected offers of marriage from many of the local chieftains, prominent among them Iarbas, king of the Gaetuli, and taken a vow of chastity. But now she is passionately in love with Aeneas.

Dido's sister Anna persuades her that she should win Aeneas' hand in marriage and enlist the Trojans' help in the building and defense of the new city. She makes offerings to the gods: to Ceres (Demeter), the goddess of the crops; to Lyaeus, a title of Dionysus; to Phoebus Apollo; and to Juno, patron of Carthage but also, as the wife of Jupiter, the goddess of the marriage rites—she "has the bonds of marriage in her keeping." Dido also tries to ascertain the future through the Roman (originally Etruscan) system of divination based on the state of the entrails of the sacrificial victims.

The union of Dido and Aeneas in a cave during a storm is thought of as a marriage by Dido, but the absence of the usual ceremonies enables Aeneas to claim that it was not so. He did not, he says, hold "the torches of a bridegroom" or enter "upon the pact of marriage."

Mercury (the Roman Hermes) is called "progeny of Cyllene" because he was born to the nymph Maia and to Jupiter on Mount Cyllene in Arcadia. Maia's father was the rebel Titan Atlas, now transformed into a mountain near the straits of Gibraltar, a connection referred to in the phrase "on the wing from his maternal grandsire."

Teucer was the founder of the royal line of Troy, hence Teucrians for Trojans; another name for them—Dardan, Dardanians—comes from Dardanus, son-in-law of Teucer. Next to last of the line was Laomedon, father of Priam. Hesperia and Ausonia are alternative names for Italy.

Dido's prayer to Jupiter to inflict suffering on Aeneas will be fulfilled. Though he will reach Italy and start the long process that will culminate in the greatness of Rome, the last six books of the Aeneid show him "beset in war by a brave people" (the Rutulians under their prince Turnus). At one point he has to leave Iulus behind in the beleaguered Trojan camp and beg help from Evander, a neighboring Italian king; later he will be present at the death in battle of Pallas, Evander's young son, killed by Turnus. And in the end he has to accept "peace on unjust terms": a bargain struck by Jupiter and Juno denies him complete victory. Trojans and Italians are to coalesce and the name of Troy will vanish. "Ausonian folk," says Jupiter later, "will keep / Their fathers' language and their way of life / And, that being so, their name. The Teucrians / Will mingle and be submerged, incorporated" (p. 702). And Aeneas will die in battle well before his time; his body will never be found.

In this fourth book, as everywhere in the Aeneid, there are echoes of Roman history, not only in Dido's curse that evokes the memory of over a century of war against Carthage, but also of more recent events. No contemporary of Virgil could read Jupiter's stern condemnation of Aeneas' prolonged stay in Carthage, his union with Dido, and his busy engagement of the building of her city, without thinking of Mark Antony in Alexandria, enchanted by Cleopatra and—so Octavian's propaganda had suggested—helping her build an Eastern Hellenistic empire that would challenge Rome's supremacy.

The queen, for her part, all that evening ached
With longing that her heart's blood fed, a wound

Or inward fire eating her away.
The manhood of the man, his pride of birth,
Came home to her time and again; his looks,
His words remained with her to haunt her mind,
And desire for him gave her no rest.
                                        When Dawn
Swept earth with Phoebus' torch and burned away
Night-gloom and damp, this queen, far gone and ill,
Confided to the sister of her heart:
"My sister Anna, quandaries and dreams
Have come to frighten me—such dreams!
                                        Think what a stranger
Yesterday found lodging in our house:
How princely, how courageous, what a soldier.
I can believe him in the line of gods,
And this is no delusion. Tell-tale fear
Betrays inferior souls. What scenes of war
Fought to the bitter end he pictured for us!
What buffetings awaited him at sea!
Had I not set my face against remarriage
After my first love died and failed me, left me
Barren and bereaved—and sick to death
At the mere thought of torch and bridal bed—
I could perhaps give way in this one case
To frailty. I shall say it: since that time
Sychaeus, my poor husband, met his fate,
And blood my brother shed stained our hearth gods,
This man alone has wrought upon me so
And moved my soul to yield. I recognize
The signs of the old flame, of old desire.
But O chaste life, before I break your laws,
I pray that Earth may open, gape for me
Down to its depth, or the omnipotent
With one stroke blast me to the shades, pale shades
Of Erebus and the deep world of night!
That man who took me to himself in youth
Has taken all my love; may that man keep it,
Hold it forever with him in the tomb."

At this she wept and wet her breast with tears.
But Anna answered:
                        "Dearer to your sister
Than daylight is, will you wear out your life,

Young as you are, in solitary mourning,
Never to know sweet children, or the crown
Of joy that Venus brings? Do you believe
This matters to the dust, to ghosts in tombs?
Granted no suitors up to now have moved you,
Neither in Libya nor before, in Tyre—
Iarbas you rejected, and the others,
Chieftains bred by the land of Africa
Their triumphs have enriched—will you contend
Even against a welcome love? Have you
Considered in whose lands you settled here?
On one frontier the Gaetulans, their cities,
People invincible in war—with wild
Numidian horsemen, and the offshore banks,
The Syrtës, on the other, desert sands,
Bone-dry, where fierce Barcaean nomads range.
Or need I speak of future wars brought on
From Tyre, and the menace of your brother?
Surely by dispensation of the gods
And backed by Juno's will, the ships from Ilium
Held their course this way on the wind.
                                        Sister,
What a great city you'll see rising here,
And what a kingdom, from this royal match!
With Trojan soldiers as companions in arms
By what exploits will Punic glory grow!
Only ask the indulgence of the gods,
Win them with offerings, give your guests ease,
And contrive reasons for delay, while winter
Gales rage, drenched Orion storms at sea,
And their ships, damaged still, face iron skies."

   This counsel fanned the flame, already kindled,
Giving her hesitant sister hope, and set her
Free of scruple. Visiting the shrines
They begged for grace at every altar first,
Then put choice rams and ewes to ritual death
For Ceres Giver of Laws, Father Lyaeus,
Phoebus, and for Juno most of all
Who has the bonds of marriage in her keeping.
Dido herself, splendidly beautiful,
Holding a shallow cup, tips out the wine

On a white shining heifer, between the horns,
Or gravely in the shadow of the gods
Approaches opulent altars. Through the day
She brings new gifts, and when the breasts are opened
Pores over organs, living still, for signs.
Alas, what darkened minds have soothsayers!
What good are shrines and vows to maddened lovers?
The inward fire eats the soft marrow away,
And the internal wound bleeds on in silence.

Unlucky Dido, burning, in her madness
Roamed through all the city, like a doe
Hit by an arrow shot from far away
By a shepherd hunting in the Cretan woods—
Hit by surprise, nor could the hunter see
His flying steel had fixed itself in her;
But though she runs for life through copse and glade
The fatal shaft clings to her side.
                              Now Dido
Took Aeneas with her among her buildings,
Showed her Sidonian wealth, her walls prepared,
And tried to speak, but in mid-speech grew still.
When the day waned she wanted to repeat
The banquet as before, to hear once more
In her wild need the throes of Illium,
And once more hung on the narrator's words.
Afterward, when all the guests were gone,
And the dim moon in turn had quenched her light,
And setting stars weighed weariness to sleep,
Alone she mourned in the great empty hall
And pressed her body on the couch he left:
She heard him still, though absent—heard and saw him.
Or she would hold Ascanius in her lap,
Enthralled by him, the image of his father,
As though by this ruse to appease a love
Beyond all telling.
                    Towers, half-built, rose
No farther; men no longer trained in arms
Or toiled to make harbors and battlements
Impregnable. Projects were broken off,
Laid over, and the menacing huge walls
With cranes unmoving stood against the sky.

As soon as Jove's dear consort saw the lady
Prey to such illness, and her reputation
Standing no longer in the way of passion,
Saturn's daughter said to Venus:
                              "Wondrous!
Covered yourself with glory, have you not,
You and your boy, and won such prizes, too.
Divine power is something to remember
If by collusion of two gods one mortal
Woman is brought low.
                        I am not blind.
Your fear of our new walls has not escaped me,
Fear and mistrust of Carthage at her height.
But how far will it go? What do you hope for,
Being so contentious? Why do we not
Arrange eternal peace and formal marriage?
You have your heart's desire: Dido in love,
Dido consumed with passion to her core.
Why not, then, rule this people side by side
With equal authority? And let the queen
Wait on her Phrygian lord, let her consign
Into your hand her Tyrians as a dowry."

Now Venus knew this talk was all pretense,
All to divert the future power from Italy
To Libya; and she answered:
                              "Who would be
So mad, so foolish as to shun that prospect
Or prefer war with you? That is, provided
Fortune is on the side of your proposal.
The fates here are perplexing: would one city
Satisfy Jupiter's will for Tyrians
And Trojan exiles? Does he approve
A union and a mingling of these races?
You are his consort: you have every right
To sound him out. Go on, and I'll come, too."

But regal Juno pointedly replied:
"That task will rest with me. Just now, as to
The need of the moment and the way to meet it,
Listen, and I'll explain in a few words.
Aeneas and Dido in her misery

Plan hunting in the forest, when the Titan
Sun comes up with rays to light the world.
While beaters in excitement ring the glens
My gift will be a black raincloud, and hail,
A downpour, and I'll shake heaven with thunder.
The company will scatter, lost in gloom,
As Dido and the Trojan captain come
To one same cavern. I shall be on hand,
And if I can be certain you are willing,
There I shall marry them and call her his.
A wedding, this will be."
　　　　　　　Then Cytherëa,
Not disinclined, nodded to Juno's plea,
And smiled at the stratagem now given away.

Dawn came up meanwhile from the Ocean stream,
And in the early sunshine from the gates
Picked huntsmen issued: wide-meshed nets and snares,
Broad spearheads for big game, Massylian horsemen
Trooping with hounds in packs keen on the scent.
But Dido lingered in her hall, as Punic
Nobles waited, and her mettlesome hunter
Stood nearby, cavorting in gold and scarlet,
Champing his foam-flecked bridle. At long last
The queen appeared with courtiers in a crowd,
A short Sidonian cloak edged in embroidery
Caught about her, at her back a quiver
Sheathed in gold, her hair tied up in gold,
And a brooch of gold pinning her scarlet dress.
Phrygians came in her company as well,
And Iulus, joyous at the scene. Resplendent
Above the rest, Aeneas walked to meet her,
To join his retinue with hers. He seemed—
Think of the lord Apollo in the spring
When he leaves wintering in Lycia
By Xanthus torrent, for his mother's isle
Of Delos, to renew the festival;
Around his altars Cretans, Dryopës,
And painted Agathyrsans raise a shout,
But the god walks the Cynthian ridge alone
And smooths his hair, binds it in fronded laurel,
Braids it in gold; and shafts ring on his shoulders.

So elated and swift, Aeneas walked
With sunlit grace upon him.
                          Soon the hunters,
Riding in company to high pathless hills,
Saw mountain goats shoot down from a rocky peak
And scamper on the ridges; toward the plain
Deer left the slopes, herding in clouds of dust
In flight across the open lands. Alone,
The boy Ascanius, delightedly riding
His eager horse amid the lowland vales,
Outran both goats and deer. Could he only meet
Amid the harmless game some foaming boar,
Or a tawny lion down from the mountainside!

Meanwhile in heaven began a rolling thunder,
And soon the storm broke, pouring rain and hail.
Then Tyrians and Trojans in alarm—
With Venus' Dardan grandson—ran for cover
Here and there in the wilderness, as freshets
Coursed from the high hills.
                          Now to the self-same cave
Came Dido and the captain of the Trojans.
Primal Earth herself and Nuptial Juno
Opened the ritual, torches of lightning blazed,
High Heaven became witness to the marriage,
And nymphs cried out wild hymns from a mountain top.
That day was the first cause of death, and first
Of sorrow. Dido had no further qualms
As to impressions given and set abroad;
She thought no longer of a secret love
But called it marriage. Thus, under that name,
She hid her fault.
                  Now in no time at all
Through all the African cities Rumor goes—
Nimble as quicksilver among evils. Rumor
Thrives on motion, stronger for the running,
Lowly at first through fear, then rearing high,
She treads the land and hides her head in cloud.
As people fable it, the Earth, her mother,
Furious against the gods, bore a late sister
To the giants Coeus and Enceladus,
Giving her speed on foot and on the wing:

Monstrous, deformed, titanic. Pinioned, with
An eye beneath for every body feather,
And, strange to say, as many tongues and buzzing
Mouths as eyes, as many pricked-up ears,
By night she flies between the earth and heaven
Shrieking through darkness, and she never turns
Her eye-lids down to sleep. By day she broods,
On the alert, on rooftops or on towers,
Bringing great cities fear, harping on lies
And slander evenhandedly with truth.
In those days Rumor took an evil joy
At filling countrysides with whispers, whispers,
Gossip of what was done, and never done:
How this Aeneas landed, Trojan born,
How Dido in her beauty graced his company,
Then how they reveled all the winter long
Unmindful of the realm, prisoners of lust.

These tales the scabrous goddess put about
On men's lips everywhere. Her twisting course
Took her to King Iarbas, whom she set
Ablaze with anger piled on top of anger.
Son of Jupiter Hammon by a nymph,
A ravished Garamantean, this prince
Had built the god a hundred giant shrines,
A hundred altars, each with holy fires
Alight by night and day, sentries on watch,
The ground enriched by victims' blood, the doors
Festooned with flowering wreaths. Before his altars
King Iarbas, crazed by the raw story,
Stood, they say, amid the Presences,
With supplicating hands, pouring out prayer:
"All powerful Jove, to whom the feasting Moors
At ease on colored couches tip their wine,
Do you see this? Are we then fools to fear you
Throwing down your bolts? Those dazzling fires
Of lightning, are they aimless in the clouds
And rumbling thunder meaningless? This woman
Who turned up in our country and laid down
A tiny city at a price, to whom
I gave a beach to plow—and on my terms—
After refusing to marry me has taken

Aeneas to be master in her realm.
And now Sir Paris with his men, half-men,
His chin and perfumed hair tied up
In a Maeonian bonnet, takes possession.
As for ourselves, here we are bringing gifts
Into these shrines—supposedly your shrines—
Hugging that empty fable."
                                        Pleas like this
From the man clinging to his altars reached
The ears of the Almighty. Now he turned
His eyes upon the queen's town and the lovers
Careless of their good name; then spoke to Mercury,
Assigning him a mission:
                                        "Son, bestir yourself,
Call up the Zephyrs, take to your wings and glide.
Approach the Dardan captain where he tarries
Rapt in Tyrian Carthage, losing sight
Of future towns the fates ordain. Correct him,
Carry my speech to him on the running winds:
No son like this did his enchanting mother
Promise to us, nor such did she deliver
Twice from peril at the hands of Greeks.
He was to be the ruler of Italy,
Potential empire, armorer of war;
To father men from Teucer's noble blood
And bring the whole world under law's dominion.
If glories to be won by deeds like these
Cannot arouse him, if he will not strive
For his own honor, does he begrudge his son,
Ascanius, the high strongholds of Rome?
What has he in mind? What hope, to make him stay
Amid a hostile race, and lose from view
Ausonian progeny, Lavinian lands?
The man should sail: that is the whole point.
Let this be what you tell him, as from me."

He finished and fell silent. Mercury
Made ready to obey the great command
Of his great father, and he first tied on
The golden sandals, winged, that high in air
Transport him over seas or over land
Abreast of gale winds; then he took the wand

With which he summons pale souls out of Orcus
And ushers others to the undergloom,
Lulls men to slumber or awakens them,
And opens dead men's eyes. This wand in hand,
He can drive winds before him, swimming down
Along the stormcloud. Now aloft, he saw
The craggy flanks and crown of patient Atlas,
Giant Atlas, balancing the sky
Upon his peak—his pine-forested head
In vapor cowled, beaten by wind and rain.
Snow lay upon his shoulders, rills cascaded
Down his ancient chin and beard a-bristle,
Caked with ice. Here Mercury of Cyllenë
Hovered first on even wings, then down
He plummeted to sea-level and flew on
Like a low-flying gull that skims the shallows
And rocky coasts where fish ply close inshore.
So, like a gull between the earth and sky,
The progeny of Cyllenë, on the wing
From his maternal grandsire, split the winds
To the sand bars of Libya.
                          Alighting tiptoe
On the first hutments, there he found Aeneas
Laying foundations for new towers and homes.
He noted well the swordhilt the man wore,
Adorned with yellow jasper; and the cloak
Aglow with Tyrian dye upon his shoulders—
Gifts of the wealthy queen, who had inwoven
Gold thread in the fabric. Mercury
Took him to task at once:
                          "Is it for you
To lay the stones for Carthage's high walls,
Tame husband that you are, and build their city?
Oblivious of your own world, your own kingdom!
From bright Olympus he that rules the gods
And turns the earth and heaven by his power—
He and no other sent me to you, told me
To bring this message on the running winds:
What have you in mind? What hope, wasting your days
In Libya? If future history's glories
Do not affect you, if you will not strive
For your own honor, think of Ascanius,

Think of the expectations of your heir,
Iulus, to whom the Italian realm, the land
Of Rome, are due."
                              And Mercury, as he spoke,
Departed from the visual field of mortals
To a great distance, ebbed in subtle air.
Amazed, and shocked to the bottom of his soul
By what his eyes had seen, Aeneas felt
His hackles rise, his voice choke in his throat.
As the sharp admonition and command
From heaven had shaken him awake, he now
Burned only to be gone, to leave that land
Of the sweet life behind. What can he do? How tell
The impassioned queen and hope to win her over?
What opening shall he choose? This way and that
He let his mind dart, testing alternatives,
Running through every one. And as he pondered
This seemed the better tactic: he called in
Mnestheus, Sergestus and stalwart Serestus,
Telling them:
                              "Get the fleet ready for sea,
But quietly, and collect the men on shore.
Lay in ship stores and gear."
                              As to the cause
For a change of plan, they were to keep it secret,
Seeing the excellent Dido had no notion,
No warning that such love could be cut short;
He would himself look for the right occasion,
The easiest time to speak, the way to do it.
The Trojans to a man gladly obeyed.

The queen, for her part, felt some plot afoot
Quite soon—for who deceives a woman in love?
She caught wind of a change, being in fear
Of what had seemed her safety. Evil Rumor,
Shameless as before, brought word to her
In her distracted state of ships being rigged
In trim for sailing. Furious, at her wits' end,
She traversed the whole city, all aflame
With rage, like a Bacchanté driven wild
By emblems shaken, when the mountain revels
Of the odd year possess her, when the cry

Of Bacchus rises and Cithaeron calls
All through the shouting night. Thus it turned out
She was the first to speak and charge Aeneas:

"You even hoped to keep me in the dark
As to this outrage, did you, two-faced man,
And slip away in silence? Can our love
Not hold you, can the pledge we gave not hold you,
Can Dido not, now sure to die in pain?
Even in winter weather must you toil
With ships, and fret to launch against high winds
For the open sea? Oh, heartless!
                      Tell me now,
If you were not in search of alien lands
And new strange homes, if ancient Troy remained,
Would ships put out for Troy on these big seas?
Do you go to get away from me? I beg you,
By these tears, by your own right hand, since I
Have left my wretched self nothing but that—
Yes, by the marriage that we entered on,
If ever I did well and you were grateful
Or found some sweetness in a gift from me,
Have pity now on a declining house!
Put this plan by, I beg you, if a prayer
Is not yet out of place.
Because of you, Libyans and nomad kings
Detest me, my own Tyrians are hostile;
Because of you, I lost my integrity
And that admired name by which alone
I made my way once toward the stars.
                     To whom
Do you abandon me, a dying woman,
Guest that you are—the only name now left
From that of husband? Why do I live on?
Shall I, until my brother Pygmalion comes
To pull my walls down? Or the Gaetulan
Iarbas leads me captive? If at least
There were a child by you for me to care for,
A little one to play in my courtyard
And give me back Aeneas, in spite of all,
I should not feel so utterly defeated,
Utterly bereft."

She ended there.
The man by Jove's command held fast his eyes
And fought down the emotion in his heart.
At length he answered:
                    "As for myself, be sure
I never shall deny all you can say,
Your majesty, of what you meant to me.
Never will the memory of Elissa
Stale for me, while I can still remember
My own life, and the spirit rules my body.
As to the event, a few words. Do not think
I meant to be deceitful and slip away.
I never held the torches of a bridegroom,
Never entered upon the pact of marriage.
If Fate permitted me to spend my days
By my own lights, and make the best of things
According to my wishes, first of all
I should look after Troy and the loved relics
Left me of my people. Priam's great hall
Should stand again; I should have restored the tower
Of Pergamum for Trojans in defeat.
But now it is the rich Italian land
Apollo tells me I must make for: Italy,
Named by his oracles. There is my love;
There is my country. If, as a Phoenician,
You are so given to the charms of Carthage,
Libyan city that it is, then tell me,
Why begrudge the Teucrians new lands
For homesteads in Ausonia? Are we not
Entitled, too, to look for realms abroad?
Night never veils the earth in damp and darkness,
Fiery stars never ascend the east,
But in my dreams my father's troubled ghost
Admonishes and frightens me. Then, too,
Each night thoughts come of young Ascanius,
My dear boy wronged, defrauded of his kingdom,
Hesperian lands of destiny. And now
The gods' interpreter, sent by Jove himself—
I swear it by your head and mine—has brought
Commands down through the racing winds! I say
With my own eyes in full daylight I saw him
Entering the building! With my very ears

I drank his message in! So please, no more
Of these appeals that set us both afire.
I sail for Italy not of my own free will."

   During all this she had been watching him
With face averted, looking him up and down
In silence, and she burst out raging now:

"No goddess was your mother. Dardanus
Was not the founder of your family.
Liar and cheat! Some rough Caucasian cliff
Begot you on flint. Hyrcanian tigresses
Tendered their teats to you. Why should I palter?
Why still hold back for more indignity?
Sigh, did he, while I wept? Or look at me?
Or yield a tear, or pity her who loved him?
What shall I say first, with so much to say?
The time is past when either supreme Juno
Or the Saturnian father viewed these things
With justice. Faith can never be secure.
I took the man in, thrown up on this coast
In dire need, and in my madness then
Contrived a place for him in my domain,
Rescued his lost fleet, saved his shipmates' lives.
Oh, I am swept away burning by furies!
Now the prophet Apollo, now his oracles,
Now the gods' interpreter, if you please,
Sent down by Jove himself, brings through the air
His formidable commands! What fit employment
For heaven's high powers! What anxieties
To plague serene immortals! I shall not
Detain you or dispute your story. Go,
Go after Italy on the sailing winds,
Look for your kingdom, cross the deepsea swell!
If divine justice counts for anything,
I hope and pray that on some grinding reef
Midway at sea you'll drink your punishment
And call and call on Dido's name!
From far away I shall come after you
With my black fires, and when cold death has parted
Body from soul I shall be everywhere
A shade to haunt you! You will pay for this,

Unconscionable! I shall hear! The news will reach me
Even among the lowest of the dead!"

At this abruptly she broke off and ran
In sickness from his sight and the light of day,
Leaving him at a loss, alarmed, and mute
With all he meant to say. The maids in waiting
Caught her as she swooned and carried her
To bed in her marble chamber.
                                    Duty-bound,
Aeneas, though he struggled with desire
To calm and comfort her in all her pain,
To speak to her and turn her mind from grief,
And though he sighed his heart out, shaken still
With love of her, yet took the course heaven gave him
And went back to the fleet. Then with a will
The Teucrians fell to work and launched the ships
Along the whole shore: slick with tar each hull
Took to the water. Eager to get away,
The sailors brought oar-boughs out of the woods
With leaves still on, and oaken logs unhewn.
Now you could see them issuing from the town
To the water's edge in streams, as when, aware
Of winter, ants will pillage a mound of spelt
To store it in their granary; over fields
The black battalion moves, and through the grass
On a narrow trail they carry off the spoil;
Some put their shoulders to the enormous weight
Of a trundled grain, while some pull stragglers in
And castigate delay; their to-and-fro
Of labor makes the whole track come alive.
At that sight, what were your emotions, Dido?
Sighing how deeply, looking out and down
From your high tower on the seething shore
Where all the harbor filled before your eyes
With bustle and shouts! Unconscionable Love,
To what extremes will you not drive our hearts!
She now felt driven to weep again, again
To move him, if she could, by supplication,
Humbling her pride before her love—to leave
Nothing untried, not to die needlessly.

"Anna, you see the arc of waterfront
All in commotion: they come crowding in
From everywhere. Spread canvas calls for wind,
The happy crews have garlanded the sterns.
If I could brace myself for this great sorrow,
Sister, I can endure it, too. One favor,
Even so, you may perform for me.
Since that deserter chose you for his friend
And trusted you, even with private thoughts,
Since you alone know when he may be reached,
Go, intercede with our proud enemy.
Remind him that I took no oath at Aulis
With Danaans to destroy the Trojan race;
I sent no ship to Pergamum. Never did I
Profane his father Anchisës' dust and shade.
Why will he not allow my prayers to fall
On his unpitying ears? Where is he racing?
Let him bestow one last gift on his mistress:
This, to await fair winds and easier flight.
Now I no longer plead the bond he broke
Of our old marriage, nor do I ask that he
Should live without his dear love, Latium,
Or yield his kingdom. Time is all I beg,
Mere time, a respite and a breathing space
For madness to subside in, while my fortune
Teaches me how to take defeat and grieve.
Pity your sister. This is the end, this favor—
To be repaid with interest when I die."

She pleaded in such terms, and such, in tears,
Her sorrowing sister brought him, time and again.
But no tears moved him, no one's voice would he
Attend to tractably. The fates opposed it;
God's will blocked the man's once kindly ears.
And just as when the north winds from the Alps
This way and that contend among themselves
To tear away an oaktree hale with age,
The wind and tree cry, and the buffeted trunk
Showers high foliage to earth, but holds
On bedrock, for the roots go down as far
Into the underworld as cresting boughs

Go up in heaven's air: just so this captain,
Buffeted by a gale of pleas
This way and that way, dinned all the day long,
Felt their moving power in his great heart,
And yet his will stood fast; tears fell in vain.

On Dido in her desolation now
Terror grew at her fate. She prayed for death,
Being heartsick at the mere sight of heaven.
That she more surely would perform the act
And leave the daylight, now she saw before her
A thing one shudders to recall: on altars
Fuming with incense where she placed her gifts,
The holy water blackened, the spilt wine
Turned into blood and mire. Of this she spoke
To no one, not to her sister even. Then, too,
Within the palace was a marble shrine
Devoted to her onetime lord, a place
She held in wondrous honor, all festooned
With snowy fleeces and green festive boughs.
From this she now thought voices could be heard
And words could be made out, her husband's words,
Calling her, when midnight hushed the earth;
And lonely on the rooftops the night owl
Seemed to lament, in melancholy notes,
Prolonged to a doleful cry. And then, besides,
The riddling words of seers in ancient days,
Foreboding sayings, made her thrill with fear.
In nightmare, fevered, she was hunted down
By pitiless Aeneas, and she seemed
Deserted always, uncompanioned always,
On a long journey, looking for her Tyrians
In desolate landscapes—
                              as Pentheus gone mad
Sees the oncoming Eumenidës and sees
A double sun and double Thebes appear,
Or as when, hounded on the stage, Orestës
Runs from a mother armed with burning brands,
With serpents hellish black,
And in the doorway squat the Avenging Ones.

So broken in mind by suffering, Dido caught
Her fatal madness and resolved to die.

She pondered time and means, then visiting
Her mournful sister, covered up her plan
With a calm look, a clear and hopeful brow.

"Sister, be glad for me! I've found a way
To bring him back or free me of desire.
Near to the Ocean boundary, near sundown,
The Aethiops' farthest territory lies,
Where giant Atlas turns the sphere of heaven
Studded with burning stars. From there
A priestess of Massylian stock has come;
She had been pointed out to me: custodian
Of that shrine named for daughters of the west,
Hesperidës, and it is she who fed
The dragon, guarding well the holy boughs
With honey dripping slow and drowsy poppy.
Chanting her spells she undertakes to free
What hearts she wills, but to inflict on others
Duress of sad desires; to arrest
The flow of rivers, make the stars move backward,
Call up the spirits of deep Night. You'll see
Earth shift and rumble underfoot and ash trees
Walk down mountainsides. Dearest, I swear
Before the gods and by your own sweet self,
It is against my will that I resort
For weaponry to magic powers. In secret
Build up a pyre in the inner court
Under the open sky, and place upon it
The arms that faithless man left in my chamber,
All his clothing, and the marriage bed
On which I came to grief—solace for me
To annihilate all vestige of the man,
Vile as he is: my priestess shows me this."

While she was speaking, cheek and brow grew pale.
But Anna could not think her sister cloaked
A suicide in these unheard-of rites;
She failed to see how great her madness was
And feared no consequence more grave
Than at Sychaeus' death. So, as commanded,
She made the preparations. For her part,
The queen, seeing the pyre in her inmost court

Erected huge with pitch-pine and sawn ilex,
Hung all the place under the sky with wreaths
And crowned it with funeral cypress boughs.
On the pyre's top she put a sword he left
With clothing, and an effigy on a couch,
Her mind fixed now ahead on what would come.
Around the pyre stood altars, and the priestess,
Hair unbound, called in a voice of thunder
Upon three hundred gods, on Erebus,
On Chaos, and on triple Hecatë,
Three-faced Diana. Then she sprinkled drops
Purportedly from the fountain of Avernus.
Rare herbs were brought out, reaped at the new moon
By scythes of bronze, and juicy with a milk
Of dusky venom; then the rare love-charm
Or caul torn from the brow of a birthing foal
And snatched away before the mother found it.
Dido herself with consecrated grain
In her pure hands, as she went near the altars,
Freed one foot from sandal straps, let fall
Her dress ungirdled, and, now sworn to death,
Called on the gods and stars that knew her fate.
She prayed then to whatever power may care
In comprehending justice for the grief
Of lovers bound unequally by love.

   The night had come, and weary in every land
Men's bodies took the boon of peaceful sleep.
The woods and the wild seas had quieted
At that hour when the stars are in mid-course
And every field is still; cattle and birds
With vivid wings that haunt the limpid lakes
Or nest in thickets in the country places
All were asleep under the silent night.
Not, though, the agonized Phoenician queen:
She never slackened into sleep and never
Allowed the tranquil night to rest
Upon her eyelids or within her heart.
Her pain redoubled; love came on again,
Devouring her, and on her bed she tossed
In a great surge of anger.

So awake,
She pressed these questions, musing to herself:

"Look now, what can I do? Turn once again
To the old suitors, only to be laughed at—
Begging a marriage with Numidians
Whom I disdained so often? Then what? Trail
The Ilian ships and follow like a slave
Commands of Trojans? Seeing them so agreeable,
In view of past assistance and relief,
So thoughtful their unshaken gratitude?
Suppose I wished it, who permits or takes
Aboard their proud ships one they so dislike?
Poor lost soul, do you not yet grasp or feel
The treachery of the line of Laömedon?
What then? Am I to go alone, companion
Of the exultant sailors in their flight?
Or shall I set out in their wake, with Tyrians,
With all my crew close at my side, and send
The men I barely tore away from Tyre
To sea again, making them hoist their sails
To more sea-winds? No: die as you deserve,
Give pain quietus with a steel blade.
                                        Sister,
You are the one who gave way to my tears
In the beginning, burdened a mad queen
With sufferings, and thrust me on my enemy.
It was not given me to lead my life
Without new passion, innocently, the way
Wild creatures live, and not to touch these depths.
The vow I took to the ashes of Sychaeus
Was not kept."
                    So she broke out afresh
In bitter mourning. On his high stern deck
Aeneas, now quite certain of departure,
Everything ready, took the boon of sleep.
In dream the figure of the god returned
With looks reproachful as before: he seemed
Again to warn him, being like Mercury
In every way, in voice, in golden hair,
And in the bloom of youth.

"Son of the goddess,
Sleep away this crisis, can you still?
Do you not see the dangers growing round you,
Madman, from now on? Can you not hear
The offshore westwind blow? The woman hatches
Plots and drastic actions in her heart,
Resolved on death now, whipping herself on
To heights of anger. Will you not be gone
In flight, while flight is still within your power?
Soon you will see the offing boil with ships
And glare with torches; soon again
The waterfront will be alive with fires,
If Dawn comes while you linger in this country.
Ha! Come, break the spell! Woman's a thing
Forever fitful and forever changing."

At this he merged into the darkness. Then
As the abrupt phantom filled him with fear,
Aeneas broke from sleep and roused his crewmen:
"Up, turn out now! Oarsmen, take your thwarts!
Shake out sail! Look here, for the second time
A god from heaven's high air is goading me
To hasten our break away, to cut the cables.
Holy one, whatever god you are,
We go with you, we act on your command
Most happily! Be near, graciously help us,
Make the stars in heaven propitious ones!"

He pulled his sword aflash out of its sheath
And struck at the stern hawser. All the men
Were gripped by his excitement to be gone,
And hauled and hustled. Ships cast off their moorings,
And an array of hulls hid inshore water
As oarsmen churned up foam and swept to sea.

Soon early Dawn, quitting the saffron bed
Of old Tithonus, cast new light on earth,
And as air grew transparent, from her tower
The queen caught sight of ships on the seaward reach
With sails full and the wind astern. She knew
The waterfront now empty, bare of oarsmen.
Beating her lovely breast three times, four times,

And tearing her golden hair,
                    "O Jupiter,"
She said, "will this man go, will he have mocked
My kingdom, stranger that he was and is?
Will they not snatch up arms and follow him
From every quarter of the town? and dockhands
Tear our ships from moorings? On! Be quick
With torches! Give out arms! Unship the oars!
What am I saying? Where am I? What madness
Takes me out of myself? Dido, poor soul,
Your evil doing has come home to you.
Then was the right time, when you offered him
A royal scepter. See the good faith and honor
Of one they say bears with him everywhere
The hearthgods of his country! One who bore
His father, spent with age, upon his shoulders!
Could I not then have torn him limb from limb
And flung the pieces on the sea? His company,
Even Ascanius could I not have minced
And served up to his father at a feast?
The luck of battle might have been in doubt—
So let it have been! Whom had I to fear,
Being sure to die? I could have carried torches
Into his camp, filled passage ways with flame,
Annihilated father and son and followers
And given my own life on top of all!
O Sun, scanning with flame all works of earth,
And thou, O Juno, witness and go-between
Of my long miseries; and Hecatë,
Screeched for at night at crossroads in the cities;
And thou, avenging Furies, and all gods
On whom Elissa dying may call: take notice,
Overshadow this hell with your high power,
As I deserve, and hear my prayer!
If by necessity that impious wretch
Must find his haven and come safe to land,
If so Jove's destinies require, and this,
His end in view, must stand, yet all the same
When hard beset in war by a brave people,
Forced to go outside his boundaries
And torn from Iulus, let him beg assistance,
Let him see the unmerited deaths of those

Around and with him, and accepting peace
On unjust terms, let him not, even so,
Enjoy his kingdom or the life he longs for,
But fall in battle before his time and lie
Unburied on the sand! This I implore,
This is my last cry, as my last blood flows.
Then, O my Tyrians, besiege with hate
His progeny and all his race to come:
Make this your offering to my dust. No love,
No pact must be between our peoples; No,
But rise up from my bones, avenging spirit!
Harry with fire and sword the Dardan countrymen
Now, or hereafter, at whatever time
The strength will be afforded. Coast with coast
In conflict, I implore, and sea with sea,
And arms with arms: may they contend in war,
Themselves and all the children of their children!"

Now she took thought of one way or another,
At the first chance, to end her hated life,
And briefly spoke to Barcë, who had been
Sychaeus' nurse; her own an urn of ash
Long held in her ancient fatherland.
                                    "Dear nurse,
Tell Sister Anna to come here, and have her
Quickly bedew herself with running water
Before she brings our victims for atonement.
Let her come that way. And you, too, put on
Pure wool around your brows. I have a mind
To carry out that rite to Stygian Jove
That I have readied here, and put an end
To my distress, committing to the flames
The pyre of that miserable Dardan."

At this with an old woman's eagerness
Barcë hurried away. And Dido's heart
Beat wildly at the enormous thing afoot.
She rolled her bloodshot eyes, her quivering cheeks
Were flecked with red as her sick pallor grew
Before her coming death. Into the court
She burst her way, then at her passion's height
She climbed the pyre and bared the Dardan sword—

A gift desired once, for no such need.
Her eyes now on the Trojan clothing there
And the familiar bed, she paused a little,
Weeping a little, mindful, then lay down
And spoke her last words:
                    "Remnants dear to me
While god and fate allowed it, take this breath
And give me respite from these agonies.
I lived my life out to the very end
And passed the stages Fortune had appointed.
Now my tall shade goes to the under world.
I built a famous town, saw my great walls,
Avenged my husband, made my hostile brother
Pay for his crime. Happy, alas, too happy,
If only the Dardanian keels had never
Beached on our coast." And here she kissed the bed.
"I die unavenged," she said, "but let me die.
This way, this way, a blessed relief to go
Into the undergloom. Let the cold Trojan,
Far at sea, drink in this conflagration
And take with him the omen of my death!"

Amid these words her household people saw her
Crumpled over the steel blade, and the blade
Aflush with red blood, drenched her hands. A scream
Pierced the high chambers. Now through the shocked city
Rumor went rioting, as wails and sobs
With women's outcry echoed in the palace
And heaven's high air gave back the beating din,
As though all Carthage or old Tyre fell
To storming enemies, and, out of hand,
Flames billowed on the roofs of men and gods.
Her sister heard and trembling, faint with terror,
Lacerating her face, beating her breast,
Ran through the crowd to call the dying queen:

"It came to this, then, sister? You deceived me?
The pyre meant this, altars and fires meant this?
What shall I mourn first, being abandoned? Did you
Scorn your sister's company in death?
You should have called me out to the same fate!
The same blade's edge and hurt, at the same hour,

Should have taken us off. With my own hands
Had I to build this pyre, and had I to call
Upon our country's gods, that in the end
With you placed on it there, O heartless one,
I should be absent? You have put to death
Yourself and me, the people and the fathers
Bred in Sidon, and your own new city.
Give me fresh water, let me bathe her wound
And catch upon my lips any last breath
Hovering over hers."
                          Now she had climbed
The topmost steps and took her dying sister
Into her arms to cherish, with a sob,
Using her dress to stanch the dark blood flow.
But Dido trying to lift her heavy eyes
Fainted again. Her chest-wound whistled air.
Three times she struggled up on one elbow
And each time fell back on the bed. Her gaze
Went wavering as she looked for heaven's light
And groaned at finding it. Almighty Juno,
Filled with pity for this long ordeal
And difficult passage, now sent Iris down
Out of Olympus to set free
The wrestling spirit from the body's hold.
For since she died, not at her fated span
Nor as she merited, but before her time
Enflamed and driven mad, Prosperina
Had not yet plucked from her the golden hair,
Delivering her to Orcus of the Styx.
So humid Iris through bright heaven flew
On saffron-yellow wings, and in her train
A thousand hues shimmered before the sun.
At Dido's head she came to rest.
                                   "This token
Sacred to Dis I bear away as bidden
And free you from your body."
                                   Saying this,
She cut a lock of hair. Along with it
Her body's warmth fell into dissolution,
And out into the winds her life withdrew.

Translated by Robert Fitzgerald

From BOOK V

PALINURUS

After the Trojans leave Carthage, bad weather interrupts their north-
ward passage to Italy. They put in at Eryx in Sicily, where they had been
welcomed, before the storm drove them to Carthage, by its king Acestes,
who is of Trojan lineage. It was there that Aeneas' father Anchises had
died and now, on the anniversary of his death, Aeneas holds funeral
games for him. Anchises appears to him in a vision and tells him that on
arrival in Italy he is to visit the Underworld of the dead. There he will
meet Anchises and be shown the great future of his race and the city that
his descendants are to found.

Meanwhile, Venus approaches Neptune (the Roman Poseidon) and
appeals to him to give Aeneas fair wind and weather on his voyage to
Italy. Neptune agrees, but informs her that Aeneas and his men will
arrive safely, all except one. "One shall be lost, / But only one to look
for, lost at sea; / One life given for many." That one is the helmsman of
Aeneas' ship, Palinurus.

Aeneas later meets the shade of Palinurus in the Underworld. There
are some serious discrepancies between the account given here (in Book
V) and the story of his death as Palinurus himself tells it in Book VI.
They are due to the fact that when Virgil died suddenly in 19 B.C. on his
return from a visit to Greece, the Aeneid *was unfinished. This is clear*
from, among other things, the considerable number of uncompleted
hexameter lines it contains. Virgil, a perfectionist if ever there was one
(he took seven years to produce the 2,000 lines of the Georgics*), told his*
friend Varius to destroy the manuscript. Augustus, however, who had
heard Virgil reading from the finished portions of it, ordered that it be
preserved and published.

The seamen as one man hauled on the sheets
Now port, now starboard, set the bellying canvas
Evenly to the wind, and took the braces,
Veering, this way and that, yard arms aloft
Until the freshening stern-wind filled the sails
And bore them onward. On the leading ship
Palinurus guided the close formation,
All under orders to set course by him.
Now dewy Night had touched her midway mark
Or nearly, and the crews, relaxed in peace

On their hard rowing benches, took their rest,
When Somnus, gliding softly from the stars
Put the night air aside, parted the darkness,
Palinurus, in quest of you. He brought
Bad dreams to you, in all your guiltlessness.
Upon the high poop deck the god sat down
In Phorbas' guise, and said:
                              "Son of Iasius,
Palinurus, the very sea itself
Moves the ships onward. There's a steady breeze.
The hour for rest has come. Put down your head
And steal a respite for your tired eyes.
I'll man your tiller for a while."
                              But Palinurus
Barely looked around. He said:

"Forget my good sense for this peaceful face
The sea puts on, the calm swell? Put my trust
In that capricious monster? Or hand over
Aeneas to the tricky winds, when I
Have been deceived so often by clear weather?"

With this response he held fast to the helm
And would not give it up, but kept his eyes
Upon the stars. Now see the god, his bough
A-drip with Lethe's dew, and slumberous
With Stygian power, giving it a shake
Over the pilot's temples, to unfix,
Although he fought it, both his swimming eyes.
His unexpected drowse barely begun,
Somnus leaned over him and flung him down
In the clear water, breaking off with him
A segment of the stern and steering oar.
Headfirst he went down, calling in vain on friends.
The god himself took flight into thin air,
But still the fleet ran safely on its course,
Serene in Father Neptune's promises.
Borne onward, now it neared the Sirens' reef,
That oldtime peril, white with many bones,
Now loud far off with trample of surf on rock.
Here the commander felt a loss of way
As his ship's head swung off, lacking a helmsman,

And he himself took over, holding course
In the night waves. Hard hit by his friend's fate
And sighing bitterly, he said:
                "For counting
Overmuch on a calm world, Palinurus,
You must lie naked on some unknown shore."

Translated by Robert Fitzgerald

From BOOK VI

ENTRY INTO THE LOWER WORLD

Once on Italian soil Aeneas, following his father's instructions, goes to see the Sybil, the prophetic priestess inspired by Apollo, to ask her to guide him to the lower world through which he must pass to see his father in Elysium. First, she tells him, he must find a golden bough in the forest and bring it with him as an offering to Proserpina (Greek Persephone), the queen of the Underworld. He finds the bough, and the Sybil leads him down into the darkness.

Dis and Orcus are Latin names for the lord of the Underworld. Styx, Acheron, Cocytus, and Phlegethon are names of the rivers of the land of the dead. Milton in Paradise Lost *explains the meaning of the names by their Greek etymology:*

> *Abhorred Styx, the flood of deadly hate;*
> *Sad Acheron of sorrow, black and deep;*
> *Cocytus, named of lamentation loud*
> *Heard on the rueful stream; fierce Phlegethon,*
> *Whose waves of torrent fire inflame with rage.*

Palinurus' phrase "Phoebus' caldron" refers to the fact that the priestess of Apollo delivered his prophecies at Delphi seated on what the Greeks called a tripod—a three-legged metal caldron that could be used for cooking by lighting a fire under it.

The Sybil's promise to Palinurus still holds good; there is a Capo Palinuro on the west coast of southern Italy.

Gods who rule the ghosts; all silent shades;
And Chaos and infernal Fiery Stream,
And regions of wide night without a sound,
May it be right to tell what I have heard,

May it be right, and fitting, by your will,
That I describe the deep world sunk in darkness
Under the earth.
           Now dim to one another
In desolate night they walked on through the gloom,
Through Dis' homes all void, and empty realms,
As one goes through a wood by a faint moon's
Treacherous light, when Jupiter veils the sky
And black night blots the colors of the world.

Before the entrance, in the jaws of Orcus,
Grief and avenging Cares have made their beds,
And pale Diseases and sad Age are there,
And Dread, and Hunger that sways men to crime,
And sordid Want—in shapes to affright the eyes—
And Death and Toil and Death's own brother, Sleep,
And the mind's evil joys; on the door sill
Death-bringing War, and iron cubicles
Of the Eumenidës, and raving Discord,
Viperish hair bound up in gory bands.
In the courtyard a shadowy giant elm
Spreads ancient boughs, her ancient arms where dreams,
False dreams, the old tale goes, beneath each leaf
Cling and are numberless. There, too,
About the doorway forms of monsters crowd—
Centaurs, twiformed Scyllas, hundred-armed
Briareus, and the Lernaean hydra
Hissing horribly, and the Chimaera
Breathing dangerous flames, and Gorgons, Harpies,
Huge Geryon, triple-bodied ghost.
Here, swept by sudden fear, drawing his sword,
Aeneas stood on guard with naked edge
Against them as they came. If his companion,
Knowing the truth, had not admonished him
How faint these lives were—empty images
Hovering bodiless—he had attacked
And cut his way through phantoms, empty air.

The path goes on from that place to the waves
Of Tartarus' Acheron. Thick with mud,
A whirlpool out of a vast abyss
Boils up and belches all the silt it carries

Into Cocytus. Here the ferryman,
A figure of fright, keeper of waters and streams,
Is Charon, foul and terrible, his beard
Grown wild and hoar, his staring eyes all flame,
His sordid cloak hung from a shoulder knot.
Alone he poles his craft and trims the sails
And in his rusty hull ferries the dead,
Old now—but old age in the gods is green.

Here a whole crowd came streaming to the banks,
Mothers and men, the forms with all life spent
Of heroes great in valor, boys and girls
Unmarried, and young sons laid on the pyre
Before their parents' eyes—as many souls
As leaves that yield their hold on boughs and fall
Through forests in the early frost of autumn,
Or as migrating birds from the open sea
That darken heaven when the cold season comes
And drives them overseas to sunlit lands.
There all stood begging to be first across
And reached out longing hands to the far shore.

But the grim boatman now took these aboard,
Now those, waving the rest back from the strand.
In wonder at this and touched by the commotion,
Aeneas said:
          "Tell me, Sister, what this means,
The crowd at the stream. Where are the souls bound?
How are they tested, so that these turn back,
While those take oars to cross the dead-black water?"

Briefly the ancient priestess answered him:

"Cocytus is the deep pool that you see,
The swamp of Styx beyond, infernal power
By which the gods take oath and fear to break it.
All in the nearby crowd you notice here
Are pauper souls, the souls of the unburied.
Charon's the boatman. Those the water bears
Are souls of buried men. He may not take them
Shore to dread shore on the hoarse currents there
Until their bones rest in the grave, or till

They flutter and roam this side a hundred years;
They may have passage then, and may return
To cross the deeps they long for."
                                        Anchises' son
Had halted, pondering on so much, and stood
In pity for the souls' hard lot. Among them
He saw two sad ones of unhonored death,
Leucaspis and the Lycian fleet's commander,
Orontës, who had sailed the windy sea
From Troy together, till the Southern gale
Had swamped and whirled them down, both ship and men.
Of a sudden he saw his helmsman, Palinurus,
Going by, who but a few nights before
On course from Libya, as he watched the stars,
Had been pitched overboard astern. As soon
As he made sure of the disconsolate one
In all the gloom, Aeneas called:
                                    "Which god
Took you away from us and put you under,
Palinurus? Tell me. In this one prophecy
Apollo, who had never played me false,
Falsely foretold you'd be unharmed at sea
And would arrive at the Ausonian coast.
Is the promise kept?"
                        But the shade said:
                                    "Phoebus' caldron
Told you no lie, my captain, and no god
Drowned me at sea. The helm that I hung on to,
Duty bound to keep our ship on course,
By some great shock chanced to be torn away,
And I went with it overboard. I swear
By the rough sea, I feared less for myself
Than for your ship: with rudder gone and steersman
Knocked overboard, it might well come to grief
In big seas running. Three nights, heavy weather
Out of the South on the vast water tossed me.
On the fourth dawn, I sighted Italy
Dimly ahead, as a wave-crest lifted me.
By turns I swam and rested, swam again
And got my footing on the beach, but savages
Attacked me as I clutched at a cliff-top,
Weighted down by my wet clothes. Poor fools,

They took me for a prize and ran me through.
Surf has me now, and sea winds, washing me
Close inshore.
                    By heaven's happy light
And the sweet air, I beg you, by your father,
And by your hopes of Iulus' rising star,
Deliver me from this captivity,
Unconquered friend! Throw earth on me—you can—
Put in to Velia port! Or if there be
Some way to do it, if your goddess mother
Shows a way—and I feel sure you pass
These streams and Stygian marsh by heaven's will—
Give this poor soul your hand, take me across,
Let me at least in death find quiet haven."
When he had made his plea, the Sibyl said:
"From what source comes this craving, Palinurus?
Would you though still unburied see the Styx
And the grim river of the Eumenidës,
Or even the river bank, without a summons?
Abandon hope by prayer to make the gods
Change their decrees. Hold fast to what I say
To comfort your hard lot: neighboring folk
In cities up and down the coast will be
Induced by portents to appease your bones,
Building a tomb and making offerings there
On a cape forever named for Palinurus."

Translated by Robert Fitzgerald

DIDO'S GHOST

*Aeneas and the Sibyl reach the Styx, where the infernal ferryman
Charon challenges Aeneas, a living man, but, shown the golden bough,
allows Aeneas and the Sibyl aboard and takes them to the far bank. They
come to a region reserved for children who died in infancy, people
executed on false charges, suicides, and those who perished victims of
love. In this last category are Phaedra; Procris, whose husband Cephalus
killed her by mistake; Eriphyle, who, bribed by Polynices, sent her husband Amphiaraus to his death in the attack of the Seven on Thebes and
was killed by her son Alcmeon; Evadne, the wife of Capaneus, another
of the Seven against Thebes, who threw herself to her death on his
funeral pyre; Pasiphae, wife of Minos, king of Crete, who fell in love*

with a sacred bull and bore the Minotaur, the monster that guarded the Labyrinth; Laodamia, who begged the gods for a three-hour reunion with her husband, killed at Troy, and at the end of the appointed time killed herself in his arms; Caeneus, once Caenis, a girl who, seduced by the god Poseidon, asked him to change her sex, became a famous warrior, and is now, in death, a girl once more. Last of all is Dido, not only a victim of love, but also a suicide.

Now voices crying loud were heard at once—
The souls of infants wailing. At the door
Of the sweet life they were to have no part in,
Torn from the breast, a black day took them off
And drowned them all in bitter death. Near these
Were souls falsely accused, condemned to die.
But not without a judge, or jurymen,
Had these souls got their places: Minos reigned
As the presiding judge, moving the urn,
And called a jury of the silent ones
To learn of lives and accusations. Next
Were those sad souls, benighted, who contrived
Their own destruction, and as they hated daylight,
Cast their lives away. How they would wish
In the upper air now to endure the pain
Of poverty and toil! But iron law
Stands in the way, since the drear hateful swamp
Has pinned them down here, and the Styx that winds
Nine times around exerts imprisoning power.
Not far away, spreading on every side,
The Fields of Mourning came in view, so called
Since here are those whom pitiless love consumed
With cruel wasting, hidden on paths apart
By myrtle woodland growing overhead.
In death itself, pain will not let them be.
He saw here Phaedra, Procris, Eriphylë
Sadly showing the wounds her hard son gave;
Evadnë and Pasiphaë, at whose side
Laodamia walked, and Caeneus,
A young man once, a woman now, and turned
Again by fate into the older form.
Among them, with her fatal wound still fresh,
Phoenician Dido wandered the deep wood.

The Trojan captain paused nearby and knew
Her dim form in the dark, as one who sees,
Early in the month, or thinks to have seen, the moon
Rising through cloud, all dim. He wept and spoke
Tenderly to her:
                    "Dido, so forlorn,
The story then that came to me was true,
That you were out of life, had met your end
By your own hand. Was I, was I the cause?
I swear by heaven's stars, by the high gods,
By any certainty below the earth,
I left your land against my will, my queen.
The gods' commands drove me to do their will,
As now they drive me through this world of shades,
These mouldy waste lands and these depths of night.
And I could not believe that I would hurt you
So terribly by going. Wait a little.
Do not leave my sight.
Am I someone to flee from? The last word
Destiny lets me say to you is this."

Aeneas with such pleas tried to placate
The burning soul, savagely glaring back,
And tears came to his eyes. But she had turned
With gaze fixed on the ground as he spoke on,
Her face no more affected than if she were
Immobile granite or Marpesian stone.
At length she flung away from him and fled,
His enemy still, into the shadowy grove
Where he whose bride she once had been, Sychaeus,
Joined in her sorrows and returned her love.
Aeneas still gazed after her in tears,
Shaken by her ill fate and pitying her.

                              Translated by Robert Fitzgerald

The Vision of Rome's Future

Aeneas and the Sybil come to a fork in the road: to the right is their goal, Elysium; to the left, Tartarus, the deep hell of punishment. The Sybil, who was appointed guardian of Avernus (the lake at the entrance to the lower world) by Hecate, one of the identities of Apollo's sister Diana

(Artemis), was shown the secrets of Tartarus and now tells Aeneas what she saw.

The Titans were the older generation of gods, who fought against the new rule of Jupiter (Zeus). Some, like Atlas, were assigned special punishments, but most of them, like Milton's rebel angels, were condemned to the realms of darkness for ever. The twin sons of Aloeus were Otus and Ephialtes, who attempted to storm Olympus by piling Mount Pelion on Mount Ossa. Tityos, a giant like the sons of Aloeus, tried to assault Leto, who bore Apollo and Artemis to Zeus. Ixion tried to rape Juno-Hera, and his son (or son-in-law) Pirithous, who became king of the Lapiths in Thessaly, helped Theseus in his unsuccessful attempt to abduct Proserpina, the queen of the Underworld. To these two, Virgil assigns penalties usually associated with Tantalus. Theseus was imprisoned in his seat, the flesh fused with the marble. Phlegyas, in revenge for Apollo's rape of Coronis, set fire to Apollo's temple.

At the end of the Sybil's account, Aeneas dedicates the golden bough to Proserpina, and the two proceed to the Elysian Fields. For his description of them, Virgil draws on Pindar, Plato, and poetic traditions current among Orphic and Pythagorean mystics. Orpheus and Musaeus were the supposed authors of religious texts that contained Orphic doctrines of transmigration of souls, ritual purifications, and rules of dietary abstinence. Aeneas finds his father at the bank of the Lethe (Oblivion) River, reviewing the souls that, purified after long penance, are about to drink the water and embark on a new existence, forgetting their previous incarnation. They are the souls of the great Romans of the centuries to come. Aeneas asks for an explanation and his father Anchises expounds the doctrine of the World Spirit (a Stoic conception) and the Orphic tradition (drawn on by Plato) of reincarnation.

The procession of future Romans begins with the kings of Alba Longa, the city that is to be founded by young Ascanius. These kings will found the cities—Nomentum, Gabii, and the rest—that will be Rome's closest and staunchest allies. Next comes Romulus; he is of the blood line of Assaracus, Aeneas' great-grandfather. The focus now shifts several centuries, to Augustus, adopted son of the deified Julius Caesar, whose wide empire, great feats and conquests are rated above those of Heracles (Alcides) and Bacchus, who conquered Greece and the East for his worship.

From Augustus, Anchises returns to early days, the legendary kings of Rome: Numa the lawgiver; Tullus Hostilius, a warrior king, as his name suggests, and conqueror of Alba Longa; and Ancus, whose lust for popularity may be a Virgilian invention. The Tarquin kings, Priscus and

Superbus, were tyrants (and the traditions about them disguise the fact, clear from the archeological record, that early Rome was for a considerable period under Etruscan domination, if not rule). Tarquinius Superbus, the last king of Rome, was overthrown by Roman aristocrats led by Brutus, who established the republic, he was notable for his stern application of the letter of the law, even in a case where his son was the victim. The Decii and Drusi are typical of the great patrician families that provided Rome with leaders in peace and war for many generations. Torquatus, like Brutus, is an example of stern discipline maintained in spite of kindred blood—he executed his own son for closing with the enemy against orders. Camillus recovered from the Gauls who captured Rome in 390 B.C. the ransom in gold they had exacted and (presumably) some legionary standards; these are obviously mentioned with the contemporary concern for the standards captured by the Parthians in mind. The "pair" are Julius Caesar and Pompey, father-in-law and son-in-law, whose political rivalry turned into civil war in 49 B.C. when Caesar came down into Italy from his conquests in Gaul. Anchises' passionate appeal to stop is of course addressed to Caesar, "child of my own blood."

Mummius was the conqueror (and destroyer) of Corinth in 146 B.C. He and Aemilius Paulus, who defeated Perseus, king of Macedon, in 168 B.C., are hailed as avengers of the destruction of Troy by the Greeks. Cato, known as the Censor, was a stern conservative, who hounded his countrymen to launch a third Punic War against Carthage by ending every speech he made in the Senate with the famous formula: Delenda est Carthago—*"Carthage must be destroyed." Cossus was one of the only three Romans to dedicate the* spolia opima, *the spoils won from the enemy general killed in single combat; the other two were Romulus and Claudius Marcellus (who will be mentioned further on). The Gracchi, sons of a famous father, were statesmen who tried, unsuccessfully, to reform the Roman political system along lines that might have avoided the civil wars of the first century B.C. The two Scipios are the victor over Hannibal at Zama in 202 and the destroyer of Carthage in 146 B.C. Fabricius was famous for his honesty and austerity, a model of old Roman virtues; Serranus was sowing the fields of his farm when messengers came to tell him he had been elected consul. From the long line of distinguished Romans who bore the name Fabius, Anchises singles out the one who saved the republic after the disastrous defeat of the Roman Army by Hannibal at Cannae in 216 B.C.; he constantly harassed Hannibal but always avoided battle, "waiting out the enemy."*

Last comes Claudius Marcellus, four times consul, victor over the Gauls in 222 B.C., where he personally killed the enemy commander in combat and dedicated the spolia opima. *Next to him walks a figure of sorrow, the young Marcellus, a nephew whom Augustus was grooming as his successor. But the young man died at the age of twenty, in 23 B.C. We are told that when Virgil read these lines to Augustus and his family, Octavia, the young man's mother, "fainted and was only with difficulty brought back to consciousness."*

Now of a sudden Aeneas looked and saw
To the left, under a cliff, wide buildings girt
By a triple wall round which a torrent rushed
With scorching flames and boulders tossed in thunder,
The abyss's Fiery River. A massive gate
With adamantine pillars faced the stream,
So strong no force of men or gods in war
May ever avail to crack and bring it down,
And high in air an iron tower stands
On which Tisiphonë, her bloody robe
Pulled up about her, has her seat and keeps
Unsleeping watch over the entrance way
By day and night. From the interior, groans
Are heard, and thud of lashes, clanking iron,
Dragging chains. Arrested in his tracks,
Appalled by what he heard, Aeneas stood.

"What are the forms of evil here? O Sister,
Tell me. And the punishments dealt out:
Why such a lamentation?"
                                        Said the Sibyl:
"Light of the Teucrians, it is decreed
That no pure soul may cross the sill of evil.
When, however, Hecatë appointed me
Caretaker of Avernus wood, she led me
Through heaven's punishments and taught me all.
This realm is under Cretan Rhadamanthus'
Iron rule. He sentences. He listens
And makes the souls confess their crooked ways,
How they put off atonements in the world
With foolish satisfaction, thieves of time,
Until too late, until the hour of death.
At once the avenger girdled with her whip,
Tisiphonë, leaps down to lash the guilty,
Vile writhing snakes held out on her left hand,

And calls her savage sisterhood. The awaited
Time has come, hell gates will shudder wide
On shrieking hinges. Can you see her now,
Her shape, as doorkeeper, upon the sill?
More bestial, just inside, the giant Hydra
Lurks with fifty black and yawning throats.
Then Tartarus itself goes plunging down
In darkness twice as deep as heaven is high
For eyes fixed on etherial Olympus.
Here is Earth's ancient race, the brood of Titans,
Hurled by the lightning down to roll forever
In the abyss. Here, too, I saw those giant
Twins of Aloeus who laid their hands
Upon great heaven to rend it and to topple
Jove from his high seat, and I saw, too,
Salmoneus paying dearly for the jape
Of mimicking Jove's fire, Olympus' thunder:
Shaking a bright torch from a four-horse car
He rode through Greece and his home town in Elis,
Glorying, claiming honor as a god—
Out of his mind, to feign with horses' hoofs
On bronze the blast and inimitable bolt.
The father almighty amid heavy cloud
Let fly his missile—no firebrand for him
Nor smoky pitchpine light—and spun the man
Headlong in a huge whirlwind.
                          One had sight
Of Tityos, too, child of all-mothering Earth,
His body stretched out over nine whole acres
While an enormous vulture with hooked beak
Forages forever in his liver,
His vitals rife with agonies. The bird,
Lodged in the chest cavity, tears at his feast,
And tissues growing again get no relief.
As for the Lapiths, need I tell: Ixion,
Pirithoüs, and the black crag overhead
So sure to fall it seems already falling.
Golden legs gleam on the feasters' couches,
Dishes in royal luxury prepared
Are laid before them—but the oldest Fury
Crouches near and springs out with her torch,
Her outcry, if they try to touch the meal.

Here come those who as long as life remained
Held brothers hateful, beat their parents, cheated
Poor men dependent on them; also those
Who hugged their newfound riches to themselves
And put nothing aside for relatives—
A great crowd, this—then men killed for adultery,
Men who took arms in war against the right,
Not scrupling to betray their lords. All these
Are hemmed in here, awaiting punishment.
Best not inquire what punishment, what form
Of suffering at their last end overwhelms them.
Some heave at a great boulder, or revolve,
Spreadeagled, hung on wheel-spokes. Theseus
Cleaves to his chair and cleaves to it forever.
Phlegyas in his misery teaches all souls
His lesson, thundering out amid the gloom:
"Be warned and study justice, not to scorn
The immortal gods.' Here's one who sold his country,
Foisted a tyrant on her, set up laws
Or nullified them for a price; another
Entered his daughter's room to take a bride
Forbidden him. All these dared monstrous wrong
And took what they dared try for. If I had
A hundred tongues, a hundred mouths, a voice
Of iron, I could not tell of all the shapes
Their crimes had taken, or their punishments."

All this he heard from her who for long years
Had served Apollo. Then she said:
                                        "Come now,
Be on your way, and carry out your mission.
Let us go faster. I can see the walls
The Cyclops' forges built and, facing us,
The portico and gate where they command us
To leave the gifts required."
                                        On this the two
In haste strode on abreast down the dark paths
Over the space between, and neared the doors.
Aeneas gained the entrance, halted there,
Asperged his body with fresh water drops,
And on the sill before him fixed the bough.

Now that at last this ritual was performed,
His duty to the goddess done, they came
To places of delight, to green park land,
Where souls take ease amid the Blessed Groves.
Wider expanses of high air endow
Each vista with a wealth of light. Souls here
Possess their own familiar sun and stars.
Some train on grassy rings, others compete
In field games, others grapple on the sand.
Feet moving to a rhythmic beat, the dancers
Group in a choral pattern as they sing.
Orpheus, the priest of Thrace, in his long robe
Accompanies, plucking his seven notes
Now with his fingers, now with his ivory quill.
Here is the ancient dynasty of Teucer,
Heroes high of heart, beautiful scions,
Born in greater days: Ilus, Assaracus,
And Dardanus, who founded Troy. Aeneas
Marvels to see their chariots and gear
Far off, all phantom: lances fixed in earth,
And teams unyoked, at graze on the wide plain.
All joy they took, alive, in cars and weapons,
As in the care and pasturing of horses,
Remained with them when they were laid in earth.
He saw, how vividly! along the grass
To right and left, others who feasted there
And chorused out a hymn praising Apollo,
Within a fragrant laurel grove, where Po
Sprang up and took his course to the world above,
The broad stream flowing on amid the forest.
This was the company of those who suffered
Wounds in battle for their country; those
Who in their lives were holy men and chaste
Or worthy of Phoebus in prophetic song;
Or those who bettered life, by finding out
New truths and skills; or those who to some folk
By benefactions made themselves remembered.
They all wore snowy chaplets on their brows.
To these souls, mingling on all sides, the Sibyl
Spoke now, and especially to Musaeus,
The central figure, toward whose towering shoulders

All the crowd gazed:
                    "Tell us, happy souls,
And you, great seer, what region holds Anchises,
Where is his resting place? For him we came
By ferry across the rivers of Erebus."
And the great soul answered briefly:
                                        "None of us
Has one fixed home. We walk in shady groves
And bed on riverbanks and occupy
Green meadows fresh with streams. But if your hearts
Are set on it, first cross this ridge; and soon
I shall point out an easy path."
                                So saying,
He walked ahead and showed them from the height
The sweep of shining plain. Then down they went
And left the hilltops.
                        Now Aeneas' father
Anchises, deep in the lush green of a valley,
Had given all his mind to a survey
Of souls, till then confined there, who were bound
For daylight in the upper world. By chance
His own were those he scanned now, all his own
Descendants, with their futures and their fates,
Their characters and acts. But when he saw
Aeneas advancing toward him on the grass,
He stretched out both his hands in eagerness
As tears wetted his cheeks. He said in welcome:

"Have you at last come, has that loyalty
Your father counted on conquered the journey?
Am I to see your face, my son, and hear
Our voices in communion as before?
I thought so, surely; counting the months I thought
The time would come. My longing has not tricked me.
I greet you now, how many lands behind you,
How many seas, what blows and dangers, son!
How much I feared the land of Libya
Might do you harm."
                        Aeneas said:
                                        "Your ghost,
Your sad ghost, father, often before my mind,
Impelled me to the threshold of this place.

My ships ride anchored in the Tuscan sca.
But let me have your hand, let me embrace you,
Do not draw back."
                    At this his tears brimmed over
And down his cheeks. And there he tried three times
To throw his arms around his father's neck,
Three times the shade untouched slipped through his hands,
Weightless as wind and fugitive as dream.
Aeneas now saw at the valley's end
A grove standing apart, with stems and boughs
Of woodland rustling, and the stream of Lethe
Running past those peaceful glades. Around it
Souls of a thousand nations filled the air,
As bees in meadows at the height of summer
Hover and home on flowers and thickly swarm
On snow-white lilies, and the countryside
Is loud with humming. At the sudden vision
Shivering, at a loss, Aeneas asked
What river flowed there and what men were those
In such a throng along the riverside.
His father Anchises told him:
                            "Souls for whom
A second body is in store: their drink
Is water of Lethe, and it frees from care
In long forgetfulness. For all this time
I have so much desired to show you these
And tell you of them face to face—to take
The roster of my children's children here,
So you may feel with me more happiness
At finding Italy."
                  "Must we imagine,
Father, there are souls that go from here
Aloft to upper heaven, and once more
Return to bodies' dead weight? The poor souls,
How can they crave our daylight so?"
                                     "My son,
I'll tell you, not to leave you mystified,"
Anchises said, and took each point in order:

"First, then, the sky and lands and sheets of water,
The bright moon's globe, the Titan sun and stars,
Are fed within by Spirit, and a Mind

Infused through all the members of the world
Makes one great living body of the mass.
From Spirit come the races of man and beast,
The life of birds, odd creatures the deep sea
Contains beneath her sparkling surfaces,
And fiery energy from a heavenly source
Belongs to the generative seeds of these,
So far as they are not poisoned or clogged
By mortal bodies, their free essence dimmed
By earthiness and deathliness of flesh.
This makes them fear and crave, rejoice and grieve.
Imprisoned in the darkness of the body
They cannot clearly see heaven's air; in fact
Even when life departs on the last day
Not all the scourges of the body pass
From the poor souls, not all distress of life.
Inevitably, many malformations,
Growing together in mysterious ways,
Become inveterate. Therefore they undergo
The discipline of punishments and pay
In penance for old sins: some hang full length
To the empty winds, for some the stain of wrong
Is washed by floods or burned away by fire.
We suffer each his own shade. We are sent
Through wide Elysium, where a few abide
In happy lands, till the long day, the round
Of Time fulfilled, has worn our stains away,
Leaving the soul's heaven-sent perception clear,
The fire from heaven pure. These other souls,
When they have turned Time's wheel a thousand years,
The god calls in a crowd to Lethe stream,
That there unmemoried they may see again
The heavens and wish re-entry into bodies."
Anchises paused. He drew both son and Sibyl
Into the middle of the murmuring throng,
Then picked out a green mound from which to view
The souls as they came forward, one by one,
And to take note of faces.
                              "Come," he said,
"What glories follow Dardan generations
In after years, and from Italian blood
What famous children in your line will come,

Souls of the future, living in our name,
I shall tell clearly now, and in the telling
Teach you your destiny. That one you see,
The young man leaning on a spear unarmed,
Has his allotted place nearest the light.
He will be first to take the upper air,
Silvius, a child with half Italian blood
And an Alban name, your last born, whom your wife,
Lavinia, late in your great age will rear
In forests to be king and father of kings.
Through him our race will rule in Alba Longa.
Next him is Procas, pride of the Trojan line,
And Capys, too, then Numitor, then one
Whose name restores you: Silvius Aeneas,
Both in arms and piety your peer,
If ever he shall come to reign in Alba.
What men they are! And see their rugged forms
With oakleaf crowns shadowing their brows. I tell you,
These are to found Nomentum, Gabii,
Fidenae town, Collatia's hilltop towers,
Pometii, Fort Inuus, Bola, Cora—
Names to be heard for places nameless now.
Then Romulus, fathered by Mars, will come
To make himself his grandfather's companion,
Romulus, reared by his mother, Ilia,
In the blood-line of Assaracus. Do you see
The double plume of Mars fixed on his crest,
See how the father of the gods himself
Now marks him out with his own sign of honor?
Look now, my son: under his auspices
Illustrious Rome will bound her power with earth,
Her spirit with Olympus. She'll enclose
Her seven hills with one great city wall,
Fortunate in the men she breeds. Just so
Cybelë Mother, honored on Berecynthus,
Wearing her crown of towers, onward rides
By chariot through the towns of Phrygia,
In joy at having given birth to gods,
And cherishing a hundred grandsons, heaven
Dwellers with homes on high.
                         Turn your two eyes
This way and see this people, your own Romans.

Here is Caesar, and all the line of Iulus,
All who shall one day pass under the dome
Of the great sky: this is the man, this one,
Of whom so often you have heard the promise,
Caesar Augustus, son of the deified,
Who shall bring once again an Age of Gold
To Latium, to the land where Saturn reigned
In early times. He will extend his power
Beyond the Garamants and Indians,
Over far territories north and south
Of the zodiacal stars, the solar way,
Where Atlas, heaven-bearing, on his shoulder
Turns the night-sphere, studded with burning stars.
At that man's coming even now the realms
Of Caspia and Maeotia tremble, warned
By oracles, and the seven mouths of Nile
Go dark with fear. The truth is, even Alcidës
Never traversed so much of earth—I grant
That he could shoot the hind with brazen hoofs
Or bring peace to the groves of Erymanthus,
Or leave Lerna affrighted by his bow.
Neither did he who guides his triumphal car
With reins of vine-shoots twisted, Bacchus, driving
Down from Nysa's height his tiger team.
Do we lag still at carrying our valor
Into action? Can our fear prevent
Our settling in Ausonia?
                              Who is he
So set apart there, olive-crowned, who holds
The sacred vessels in his hands? I know
That snowy mane and beard: Numa, the king,
Who will build early Rome on a base of laws,
A man sent from the small-town poverty
Of Curës to high sovereignty. After him
Comes Tullus, breaker of his country's peace,
Arousing men who have lost victorious ways,
Malingering men, to war. Near him is Ancus,
Given to boasting, even now too pleased
With veering popularity's heady air.
Do you care to see now, too, the Tarquin kings
And the proud soul of the avenger, Brutus,
By whom the bundled *fasces* are regained?

Consular power will first be his, and his
The pitiless axes. When his own two sons
Plot war against the city, he will call
For the death penalty in freedom's name—
Unhappy man, no matter how posterity
May see these matters. Love of the fatherland
Will sway him—and unmeasured lust for fame.
Now see the Decii and the Drusi there,
And stern Torquatus, with his axe, and see
Camillus bringing the lost standards home.
That pair, however, matched in brilliant armor,
Matched in their hearts' desire now, while night
Still holds them fast, once they attain life's light
What war, what grief, will they provoke between them—
Battle-lines and bloodshed—as the father
Marches from the Alpine ramparts, down
From Monaco's walled height, and the son-in-law,
Drawn up with armies of the East, awaits him.
Sons, refrain! You must not blind your hearts
To that enormity of civil war,
Turning against your country's very heart
Her own vigor of manhood. You above all
Who trace your line from the immortals, you
Be first to spare us. Child of my own blood,
Throw away your sword!
                              Mummius there,
When Corinth is brought low, will drive his car
As victor and as killer of Achaeans
To our high Capitol. Paulus will conquer
Argos and Agamemnon's old Mycenae,
Defeating Perseus, the Aeacid,
Heir to the master of war, Achilles—thus
Avenging his own Trojan ancestors
And the defilement of Minerva's shrine.
Great Cato! Who would leave you unremarked,
Or, Cossus, you, or the family of Gracchi,
Or the twin Scipios, bright bolts of war,
The bane of Libya, or you, Fabricius,
In poverty yet powerful, or you,
Serranus, at the furrow, casting seed?
Where, though I weary, do you hurry me,
You Fabii? Fabius Maximus,

You are the only soul who shall restore
Our wounded state by waiting out the enemy.
Others will cast more tenderly in bronze
Their breathing figures, I can well believe,
And bring more lifelike portraits out of marble;
Argue more eloquently, use the pointer
To trace the paths of heaven accurately
And accurately foretell the rising stars.
Roman, remember by your strength to rule
Earth's peoples—for your arts are to be these:
To pacify, to impose the rule of law,
To spare the conquered, battle down the proud."
Anchises paused here as they gazed in awe,
Then added:
                 "See there, how Marcellus comes
With spoils of the commander that he killed:
How the man towers over everyone.
Cavalry leader, he'll sustain the realm
Of Rome in hours of tumult, bringing to heel
The Carthaginians and rebellious Gaul,
And for the third time in our history
He'll dedicate an enemy general's arms
To Father Romulus."
                         But here Aeneas
Broke in, seeing at Marcellus' side
A young man beautifully formed and tall
In shining armor, but with clouded brow
And downcast eyes:
                        "And who is that one, Father,
Walking beside the captain as he comes:
A son, or grandchild from the same great stock?
The others murmur, all astir. How strong
His presence is! But night like a black cloud
About his head whirls down in awful gloom."

His father Anchises answered, and the tears
Welled up as he began:
                            "Oh, do not ask
About this huge grief of your people, son.
Fate will give earth only a glimpse of him,
Not let the boy live on. Lords of the sky,
You thought the majesty of Rome too great

If it had kept these gifts. How many groans
Will be sent up from that great Field of Mars
To Mars' proud city, and what sad rites you'll see,
Tiber, as you flow past the new-built tomb.
Never will any boy of Ilian race
Exalt his Latin forefathers with promise
Equal to his; never will Romulus' land
Take pride like this in any of her sons.
Weep for his faithful heart, his old-world honor,
His sword arm never beaten down! No enemy
Could have come through a clash with him unhurt,
Whether this soldier went on foot or rode,
Digging his spurs into a lathered mount.
Child of our mourning, if only in some way
You could break through your bitter fate. For you
Will be Marcellus. Let me scatter lilies,
All I can hold, and scarlet flowers as well,
To heap these for my grandson's shade at least,
Frail gifts and ritual of no avail."

So raptly, everywhere, father and son
Wandered the airy plain and viewed it all.
After Anchises had conducted him
To every region and had fired his love
Of glory in the years to come, he spoke
Of wars that he must fight, of Laurentines,
And of Latinus' city, then of how
He might avoid or bear each toil to come.

Translated by Robert Fitzgerald

From BOOK XII

THE FUTURE OF ITALY

The first six books of Virgil's epic poem are the Odyssey *of Aeneas, but
the last six are his* Iliad; *for as the Sibyl prophesied, Italy will be like
Troy:*

> *Wars, vicious wars*
> *I see ahead, and Tiber foaming blood.*
> *Timois, Xanthus, Dorians encamped—*

You'll have them all again, with an Achilles
Child of Latium, he, too, goddess-born.

The new Achilles is Turnus, son of the nymph Venilia; he is king of
the Rutulians, a powerful Italian people. He is the most prominent of
the suitors for the hand of Lavinia, the daughter of Latinus, king of
Latium, but the king offers her to Aeneas, because of a prophecy that she
must marry a stranger from overseas. Juno incites Turnus and the Rutulians to war, and although the Trojan situation often seems desperate,
they finally emerge as the predominant power. A truce is arranged:
Aeneas and Turnus will decide the issue of Lavinia's hand in single
combat. But Juno incites Turnus' sister, the nymph Juturna, to disrupt
the proceedings and provoke a general engagement. In the course of the
renewed fighting, Aeneas is hit by an arrow. But, healed with the help of
his mother Venus, he goes in pursuit of Turnus and eventually catches
up with him. At this point Jupiter addresses Juno and they make their
pact.

On Earth Aeneas disarms Turnus, and would have spared his life had
he not suddenly caught sight of the belt of Pallas, Evander's young son,
clasped around his waist. Carried away by rage, he kills Turnus. The epic
ends not on the conciliatory note of the dialogue between Jupiter and
Juno, but with a final killing—a reminder, perhaps, that the great empire
of Aeneas' descendants will, as Anchises prescribed, "impose the rule of
peace," but will do so by incessant war.

    Omnipotent Olympus' king meanwhile
Had words for Juno, as she watched the combat
Out of a golden cloud. He said:
                       "My consort,
What will the end be? What is left for you?
You yourself know, and say you know, Aeneas
Born for heaven, tutelary of this land,
By fate to be translated to the stars.
What do you plan? What are you hoping for,
Keeping your seat apart in the cold clouds?
Fitting, was it, that a mortal archer
Wound an immortal? That a blade let slip
Should be restored to Turnus, and new force
Accrue to a beaten man? Without your help
What could Juturna do? Come now, at last
Have done, and heed our pleading, and give way.
Let yourself no longer be consumed

Without relief by all that inward burning;
Let care and trouble not forever come to me
From your sweet lips. The finish is at hand.
You had the power to harry men of Troy
By land and sea, to light the fires of war
Beyond belief, to scar a family
With mourning before marriage. I forbid
Your going further."
                So spoke Jupiter,
And with a downcast look Juno replied:

"Because I know that is your will indeed,
Great Jupiter, I left the earth below,
Though sore at heart, and left the side of Turnus.
Were it not so, you would not see me here
Suffering all that passes, here alone,
Resting on air. I should be armed in flames
At the very battle-line, dragging the Trojans
Into a deadly action. I persuaded
Juturna—I confess—to help her brother
In his hard lot, and I approved her daring
Greater difficulties to save his life,
But not that she should fight with bow and arrow.
This I swear by Styx' great fountainhead
Inexorable, which high gods hold in awe.
I yield now and for all my hatred leave
This battlefield. But one thing not retained
By fate I beg for Latium, for the future
Greatness of your kin: when presently
They crown peace with a happy wedding day—
So let it be—and merge their laws and treaties,
Never command the land's own Latin folk
To change their old name, to become new Trojans,
Known as Teucrians; never make them alter
Dialect or dress. Let Latium be.
Let there be Alban kings for generations,
And let Italian valor be the strength
Of Rome in after times. Once and for all
Troy fell, and with her name let her lie fallen."

The author of men and of the world replied
With a half-smile:
                "Sister of Jupiter

Indeed you are, and Saturn's other child,
To feel such anger, stormy in your breast.
But come, no need; put down this fit of rage.
I grant your wish. I yield, I am won over
Willingly. Ausonian folk will keep
Their fathers' language and their way of life,
And, that being so, their name. The Teucrians
Will mingle and be submerged, incorporated.
Rituals and observances of theirs
I'll add, but make them Latin, one in speech.
The race to come, mixed with Ausonian blood,
Will outdo men and gods in its devotion,
You shall see—and no nation on earth
Will honor and worship you so faithfully."

To all this Juno nodded in assent
And, gladdened by his promise, changed her mind.

Translated by Robert Fitzgerald

LIVY

59 B.C.–A.D. 17

*Livy, or Titus Livius, was the author of an enormous history of Rome
from its foundation (the traditional date was, in our notation, 753 B.C.)
to the Augustan settlement of which he was a witness. Of the 192 books
of the original, only 35 survive intact—those dealing with the legendary
days of the kings and the early republic, and those covering the first two
wars against Carthage and the campaigns in Macedonia and Greece.*

*Livy certainly welcomed the Augustan settlement that had brought
peace after a century of civil wars, but his heart was with the republic,
whose heroes, legendary and historical, he celebrated with compelling
narrative style. When Augustus read the final volumes on the recent civil
war between his adoptive father Julius Caesar and Pompey, he told Livy
that he was a "Pompeian." But their relations remained friendly.*

Our selections come from the first two books and present some of the legends, which, unlike the Greek stories of gods and men that the Roman poets adopted wholesale, constitute the real Roman mythology. We begin with Livy's starting point.

From THE HISTORY OF ROME

THE BEGINNING

Aeneas' son Ascanius had founded the city of Alba Longa, and a long line of his descendants, many of whom bore the name Silvius, ruled the city as kings and succeeded each other peacefully until the death of King Proca.

Proca, the next king, had two sons, Numitor and Amulius, to the elder of whom, Numitor, he left the hereditary realm of the Silvian family; that, at least, was his intention, but respect for seniority was flouted, the father's will ignored and Amulius drove out his brother and seized the throne. One act of violence led to another; he proceeded to murder his brother's male children, and made his niece, Rhea Silvia, a Vestal, ostensibly to do her honour, but actually by condemning her to perpetual virginity to preclude the possibility of issue.

But (I must believe) it was already written in the book of fate that this great city of ours should arise, and the first steps be taken to the founding of the mightiest empire the world has known—next to God's. The Vestal Virgin was raped and gave birth to twin boys. Mars, she declared, was their father—perhaps she believed it, perhaps she was merely hoping by the pretence to palliate her guilt. Whatever the truth of the matter, neither gods nor men could save her or her babes from the savage hands of the king. The mother was bound and flung into prison; the boys, by the king's order, were condemned to be drowned in the river. Destiny, however, intervened; the Tiber had overflowed its banks; because of the flooded ground it was impossible to get to the actual river, and the men entrusted to do the deed thought that the flood-water, sluggish though it was, would serve their purpose. Accordingly they made shift to carry out the king's orders by leaving the infants on the edge of the first flood-water they came do. . . .

In those days the country thereabouts was all wild and uncultivated, and the story goes that when the basket in which the infants had been exposed was left high and dry by the receding water, a she-wolf, coming down from the neighbouring hills to quench her thirst, heard the children crying and made her way to where they were. She offered them her teats to suck and treated them with such gentleness that Faustulus, the king's herdsman, found her licking them with her tongue. Faustulus took them to his hut and gave them to his wife Larentia to nurse. Some think that the origin of this fable was the fact that Larentia was a common whore and was called Wolf by the shepherds.

Such, then, was the birth and upbringing of the twins. By the time they were grown boys, they employed themselves actively on the farm and with the flocks and began to go hunting in the woods; their strength grew with their resolution, until not content only with the chase they took to attacking robbers and sharing their stolen goods with their friends the shepherds. Other young fellows joined them, and they and the shepherds would fleet the time together, now in serious talk, now in jollity.

[*Romulus and Remus eventually restored Numitor to the throne Amulius had usurped and were recognized as of royal blood in Alba Longa. But they were not content.*]

  Romulus and Remus, after the control of Alba had passed to Numitor in the way I have described, were suddenly seized by an urge to found a new settlement on the spot where they had been left to drown as infants and had been subsequently brought up. There was, in point of fact, already an excess of population at Alba, what with the Albans themselves, the Latins, and the addition of the herdsmen: enough, indeed, to justify the hope that Alba and Lavinium would one day be small places compared with the proposed new settlement. Unhappily the brothers' plans for the future were marred by the same source which had divided their grandfather and Amulius—jealousy and ambition. A disgraceful quarrel arose from a matter in itself trivial. As the brothers were twins and all question of seniority was thereby precluded, they determined to ask the tutelary gods of the countryside to declare by augury which of them should govern the new town once it was founded, and give his name to it. For this purpose Romulus took the Palatine hill and Remus the Aventine as their respective stations from which to observe the auspices. Remus, the story goes, was the first to receive a sign—six vultures; and no sooner was this made known to the people than double the number of birds appeared to Romulus. The followers of each promptly saluted their master as king, one side basing its claim upon priority, the other upon number. Angry words ensued, followed all too soon by blows, and in the course of the affray Remus was killed. There is another story, a commoner one, according to which Remus, by way of jeering at his brother, jumped over the half-built walls of the new settlement, whereupon Romulus killed him in a fit of rage, adding the threat, "So perish whoever else shall overleap my battlements."

This, then, was how Romulus obtained the sole power. The newly built city was called by its founder's name. . . .

Meanwhile Rome was growing. More and more ground was coming within the circuit of its walls. Indeed, the rapid expansion of the enclosed area was out of proportion to the actual population, and evidently indicated an eye to the future. In antiquity the founder of a new settlement, in order to increase its population, would as a matter of course shark up a lot of homeless and destitute folk and pretend that they were "born of earth" to be his progeny; Romulus now followed a similar course: to help fill his big new town, he threw open, in the ground—now enclosed—between the two copses as you go up the Capitoline hill, a place of asylum for fugitives. Hither fled for refuge all the rag-tag-and-bobtail from the neighbouring peoples: some free, some slaves, and all of them wanting nothing but a fresh start. That mob was the first real addition to the City's strength, the first step to her future greatness. . . .

Rome was now strong enough to challenge any of her neighbours; but, great though she was, her greatness seemed likely to last only for a single generation. There were not enough women, and that, added to the fact that there was no intermarriage with neighbouring communities, ruled out any hope of maintaining the level of population. Romulus accordingly, on the advice of his senators, sent representatives to the various peoples across his borders to negotiate alliances and the right of intermarriage for the newly established state. The envoys were instructed to point out that cities, like everything else, have to begin small; in course of time, helped by their own worth and the favour of heaven, some, at least, grow rich and famous, and of these Rome would assuredly be one: Gods had blessed her birth, and the valour of her people would not fail in the days to come. The Romans were men, as they were; why, then, be reluctant to intermarry with them?

Romulus' overtures were nowhere favourably received; it was clear that everyone despised the new community, and at the same time feared, both for themselves and for posterity, the growth of this new power in their midst. More often than not his envoys were dismissed with the question of whether Rome had thrown open her doors to female, as well as to male, runaways and vagabonds, as that would evidently be the most suitable way for Romans to get wives. The young Romans naturally resented this jibe, and a clash seemed inevitable. Romulus, seeing it must come, set the scene for it with elaborate care. Deliberately hiding his resentment, he prepared to celebrate the Consualia, a solemn festival in honour of Neptune, patron of the horse, and sent notice of his intention all over the neighbouring countryside. The better to advertise it, his people lavished upon their preparations for the spectacle all the resources—such as they were in those days—at their command. On the appointed day crowds flocked to Rome, partly, no doubt, out of sheer curiosity to see the new town. The majority were from the neighbouring settlements of Caenina, Crustumium, and Antemnae, but all the Sabines were there too, with their wives and children. Many houses offered hospitable entertainment to the visitors; they were invited to inspect the fortifications, layout, and numerous buildings of the town, and expressed their surprise at the rapidity of its growth. Then the great moment came; the show began, and nobody had eyes or thoughts for anything else. This was the Romans' opportunity: at a given signal all the able-bodied men burst through the crowd and seized the young women. Most of the girls were the prize of whoever got hold of them first, but a few conspicuously handsome ones had been previously marked down for leading senators, and these were brought to their houses by special gangs. There was one young woman of much greater beauty than the rest; and the story goes that she was seized by a party of men belonging to the household of someone called Thalassius, and in reply to the many questions about whose house they were taking her to, they, to prevent anyone else laying hands upon her, kept shouting, "Thalassius, Thalassius!" This was the origin of the use of this word at weddings.

By this act of violence the fun of the festival broke up in panic. The girls' unfortunate parents made good their escape, not without bitter comments on the treachery of their hosts and heartfelt prayers to the God to whose festival they had come in all good faith in the solemnity of the occasion, only to be grossly deceived. The young women were no less indignant and as full of foreboding for the future.

Romulus, however, reassured them. Going from one to another he declared that their own parents were really to blame, in that they had been too proud to allow intermarriage with their neighbours; nevertheless, they need not fear; as married women they would share all the fortunes of Rome, all the privileges of the community, and they would be bound to their husbands by the dearest bond of all, their children. He urged them to forget their wrath and give their hearts to those to whom chance had given their bodies. Often, he said, a sense of injury yields in the end to affection, and their husbands would treat them all the more kindly in that they would try, each one of them, not only to fulfil their own part of the bargain but also to make up to their wives for the homes and parents they had lost. The men, too, played their part: they spoke honeyed words and vowed that it was passionate love which had prompted their offence. No plea can better touch a woman's heart.

Translated by Aubrey de Sélincourt

THE FALL OF THE MONARCHY

Romulus was followed on the throne by six other kings; the last of them, Tarquinius Superbus (his second name means "Arrogant"), was driven out of Rome in 510 B.C. The republic was established. It was governed by a Senate and two annually elected magistrates called consuls; the first two were Collatinus and Lucius Junius Brutus.

Tarquinius, like a Greek tyrant, had launched a huge program of public building; he had also confiscated the property of the Roman aristocrats and put many of them to death. He had three sons—Titus, Arruns, and Sextus. It was Sextus who committed a crime that was to lead to the expulsion of the royal house from Rome and the birth of the republic.

About this time an alarming and ominous event occurred: a snake slid out from a crack in a wooden pillar in the palace. Everyone ran from it in a fright; even the king was scared, though in his case it was not fear so much as foreboding. About signs and omens of public import the custom had always been to consult only Etruscan sooth-sayers; this, however, was a different matter: it was in the king's own house that the portentous sight had been seen; and that, Tarquin felt, justified the unusual step of sending to Delphi, to consult the most famous oracle in the world. Unwilling to entrust the answer of the oracle to anybody else, he sent on the mission two of his sons, Titus and Arruns, who accordingly set out for Greece through country which Roman feet had seldom trod and over seas which Roman ships had never sailed. With them went Lucius Junius Brutus, son of the king's sister Tarquinia.

Now Brutus had deliberately assumed a mask to hide his true character. When he learned of the murder by Tarquin of the Roman aristocrats, one of the victims being his own brother, he had come to the conclusion that the only way of saving himself was to appear in the king's eyes as a person of no account. If there were nothing in his character for

Tarquin to fear, and nothing in his fortune to covet, then the sheer contempt in which he was held would be a better protection than his own rights could ever be. Accordingly he pretended to be a half-wit and made no protest at the seizure by Tarquin of everything he possessed. He even submitted to being known publicly as the "Dullard" (which is what his name signifies), that under cover of that opprobrious title the great spirit which gave Rome her freedom might be able to bide its time. On this occasion he was taken by Arruns and Titus to Delphi less as a companion than as a butt for their amusement; and he is said to have carried with him, as his gift to Apollo, a rod of gold inserted into a hollow stick of cornel-wood—symbolic, it may be, of his own character.

The three young men reached Delphi, and carried out the king's instructions. That done, Titus and Arruns found themselves unable to resist putting a further question to the oracle. Which of them, they asked, would be the next king of Rome? From the depths of the cavern came the mysterious answer: "He who shall be the first to kiss his mother shall hold in Rome supreme authority." Titus and Arruns were determined to keep the prophecy absolutely secret, to prevent their other brother, Tarquin, who had been left in Rome, from knowing anything about it. Thus he, at any rate, would be out of the running. For themselves, they drew lots to determine which of them, on their return, should kiss his mother first.

Brutus, however, interpreted the words of Apollo's priestess in a different way. Pretending to trip, he fell flat on his face, and his lips touched the Earth—the mother of all living things.

Back in Rome, they found vigorous preparations in progress for war with the Rutuli. The chief town of the Rutuli was Ardea, and they were a people, for that place and period, of very considerable wealth. Their wealth was, indeed, the reason for Tarquin's preparations: he needed money to repair the drain on his resources resulting from his ambitious schemes of public building and he knew, moreover, that the commons were growing ever more restive, not only in view of his tyrannical behaviour generally but also, and especially, because they had been so long employed in manual labour such as belonged properly to slaves, and the distribution of plunder from a captured town would do much to soften their resentment.

The attempt was made to take Ardea by assault. It failed; siege operations were begun, and the army settled down into permanent quarters. With little prospect of any decisive action, the war looked like being a long one, and in these circumstances leave was granted, quite naturally, with considerable freedom, especially to officers. Indeed, the young princes, at any rate, spent most of their leisure enjoying themselves in entertainments on the most lavish scale. They were drinking one day in the quarters of Sextus Tarquinius—Collatinus, son of Egerius, was also present—when someone chanced to mention the subject of wives. Each of them, of course, extravagantly praised his own; and the rivalry got hotter and hotter, until Collatinus suddenly cried: "Stop! What need is there of words, when in a few hours we can prove beyond doubt the incomparable superiority of my Lucretia? We are all young and strong: why shouldn't we ride to Rome and see with our own eyes what kind of women our wives are? There is no better evidence, I assure you, than what a man finds when he enters his wife's room unexpectedly."

They had all drunk a good deal, and the proposal appealed to them; so they mounted their horses and galloped off to Rome. They reached the city as dusk was falling; and there the wives of the royal princes were found enjoying themselves with a group of young friends at a dinner-party, in the greatest luxury. The riders then went on to Collatia, where they found Lucretia very differently employed: it was already late at night, but there, in the hall of her house, surrounded by her busy maid-servants, she was still hard at work by lamplight upon her spinning. Which wife had won the contest in womanly virtue was no longer in doubt.

With all courtesy Lucretia rose to bid her husband and the princes welcome, and Collatinus, pleased with his success, invited his friends to sup with him. It was at that fatal supper that Lucretia's beauty, and proven chastity, kindled in Sextus Tarquinius the flame of lust, and determined him to debauch her.

Nothing further occurred that night. The little jaunt was over, and the young men rode back to camp.

A few days later Sextus, without Collatinus' knowledge, returned with one companion to Collatia, where he was hospitably welcomed in Lucretia's house, and, after supper, escorted, like the honoured visitor he was thought to be, to the guest-chamber. Here he waited till the house was asleep, and then, when all was quiet, he drew his sword and made his way to Lucretia's room determined to rape her. She was asleep. Laying his left hand on her breast, "Lucretia," he whispered, "not a sound! I am Sextus Tarquinius. I am armed—if you utter a word, I will kill you." Lucretia opened her eyes in terror; death was imminent, no help at hand. Sextus urged his love, begged her to submit, pleaded, threatened, used every weapon that might conquer a woman's heart. But all in vain; not even the fear of death could bend her will. "If death will not move you," Sextus cried, "dishonour shall. I will kill you first, then cut the throat of a slave and lay his naked body by your side. Will they not believe that you have been caught in adultery with a servant—and paid the price?" Even the most resolute chastity could not have stood against this dreadful threat.

Lucretia yielded. Sextus enjoyed her, and rode away, proud of his success.

The unhappy girl wrote to her father in Rome and to her husband in Ardea, urging them both to come at once with a trusted friend—and quickly, for a frightful thing had happened. Her father came with Valerius, Volesus' son, her husband with Brutus, with whom he was returning to Rome when he was met by the messenger. They found Lucretia sitting in her room, in deep distress. Tears rose to her eyes as they entered, and to her husband's question, "Is it well with you?" she answered, "No. What can be well with a woman who has lost her honour? In your bed, Collatinus, is the impress of another man. My body only has been violated. My heart is innocent, and death will be my witness. Give me your solemn promise that the adulterer shall be punished—he is Sextus Tarquinius. He it is who last night came as my enemy disguised as my guest, and took his pleasure of me. That pleasure will be my death—and his, too, if you are men."

The promise was given. One after another they tried to comfort her. They told her she was helpless, and therefore innocent; that he alone was guilty. It was the mind, they said, that sinned, not the body: without intention there could never be guilt.

"What is due to *him,*" Lucretia said, "is for you to decide. As for me I am innocent of fault, but I will take my punishment. Never shall Lucretia provide a precedent for unchaste women to escape what they deserve." With these words she drew a knife from under her robe, drove it into her heart, and fell forward, dead.

Her father and husband were overwhelmed with grief. While they stood weeping helplessly, Brutus drew the bloody knife from Lucretia's body, and holding it before him cried: "By this girl's blood—none more chaste till a tyrant wronged her—and by the gods, I swear that with sword and fire, and whatever else can lend strength to my arm, I will pursue Lucius Tarquinius the Proud, his wicked wife, and all his children, and never again will I let them or any other man be King in Rome."

He put the knife into Collatinus' hands, then passed it to Lucretius, then to Valerius. All looked at him in astonishment: a miracle had happened—he was a changed man. Obedient to his command, they swore their oath. Grief was forgotten in the sudden surge of anger, and when Brutus called upon them to make war, from that instant, upon the tyrant's throne, they took him for their leader.

Lucretia's body was carried from the house into the public square. Crowds gathered, as crowds will, to gape and wonder—and the sight was unexpected enough, and horrible enough, to attract them. Anger at the criminal brutality of the king's son and sympathy with the father's grief stirred every heart; and when Brutus cried out that it was time for deeds not tears, and urged them, like true Romans, to take up arms against the tyrants who had dared to treat them as a vanquished enemy, not a man amongst them could resist the call. The boldest spirits offered themselves at once for service; the rest soon followed their lead. Lucretia's father was left to hold Collatia; guards were posted to prevent news of the rising from reaching the palace, and with Brutus in command the armed populace began their march on Rome.

In the city the first effect of their appearance was alarm and confusion, but the sight of Brutus, and others of equal distinction, at the head of the mob, soon convinced people that this was, at least, no mere popular demonstration. Moreover the horrible story of Lucretia had had hardly less effect in Rome than in Collatia. In a moment the Forum was packed, and the crowds, by Brutus' order, were immediately summoned to attend the Tribune of Knights—an office held at the time by Brutus himself. There, publicly throwing off the mask under which he had hitherto concealed his real character and feelings, he made a speech painting in vivid colours the brutal and unbridled lust of Sextus Tarquinius, the hideous rape of the innocent Lucretia and her pitiful death, and the bereavement of her father, for whom the cause of her death was an even bitterer and more dreadful thing than the death itself. He went on to speak of the king's arrogant and tyrannical behaviour; of the sufferings of the commons condemned to labour underground clearing or constructing ditches and sewers; of gallant Romans—soldiers who had beaten in battle all neighbouring peoples—robbed of their swords and turned into stone-cutters and artisans. He reminded them of the foul murder of Servius Tullius, of the daughter who drove her carriage over her father's corpse, in violation of the most sacred of relationships—a crime which God alone could punish. Doubtless he told them of other, and worse, things, brought to his mind in the heat of the moment and by the sense of this latest outrage, which still lived in his eye and pressed upon his heart; but a mere historian can hardly record them.

The effect of his words was immediate: the populace took fire, and were brought to demand the abrogation of the king's authority and the exile of himself and his family.

Translated by Aubrey de Sélincourt

Livy

HEROES OF THE REPUBLIC

Tarquinius appealed for help to the powerful Etruscan king, Porsena,
who marched on Rome with a huge army.

On the approach of the Etruscan army, the Romans abandoned their
farmsteads and moved into the city. Garrisons were posted. In some
sections the city walls seemed sufficient protection, in others the barrier
of the Tiber. The most vulnerable point was the wooden bridge, and the
Etruscans would have crossed it and forced an entrance into the city,
had it not been for the courage of one man, Horatius Cocles—that great
soldier whom the fortune of Rome gave to be her shield on that day of
peril. Horatius was on guard at the bridge when the Janiculum was
captured by a sudden attack. The enemy forces came pouring down the
hill, while the Roman troops, throwing away their weapons, were behaving more like an undisciplined rabble than a fighting force. Horatius
acted promptly: as his routed comrades approached the bridge, he
stopped as many as he could catch and compelled them to listen to him.
"By God," he cried, "can't you see that if you desert your post escape is
hopeless? If you leave the bridge open in your rear, there will soon be
more of them in the Palatine and the Capitol than on the Janiculum."
Urging them with all the power at his command to destroy the bridge by
fire or steel or any means they could muster, he offered to hold up the
Etruscan advance, so far as was possible, alone. Proudly he took his stand
at the outer end of the bridge; conspicuous amongst the rout of fugitives,
sword and shield ready for action, he prepared himself for close combat,
one man against an army. The advancing enemy paused in sheer astonishment at such reckless courage. Two other men, Spurius Lartius and
Titus Herminius, both aristocrats with a fine military record, were
ashamed to leave Horatius alone, and with their support he won through
the first few minutes of desperate danger. Soon, however, he forced
them to save themselves and leave him; for little was now left of the
bridge, and the demolition squads were calling them back before it was
too late. Once more Horatius stood alone; with defiance in his eyes he
confronted the Etruscan chivalry, challenging one after another to single
combat, and mocking them all as tyrants' slaves who, careless of their
own liberty, were coming to destroy the liberty of others. For a while
they hung back, each waiting for his neighbour to make the first move,
until shame at the unequal battle drove them to action, and with a fierce

cry they hurled their spears at the solitary figure which barred their way. Horatius caught the missiles on his shield and, resolute as ever, straddled the bridge and held his ground. The Etruscans moved forward, and would have thrust him aside by the sheer weight of numbers, but their advance was suddenly checked by the crash of the falling bridge and the simultaneous shout of triumph from the Roman soldiers who had done their work in time. The Etruscans could only stare in bewilderment as Horatius, with a prayer to Father Tiber to bless him and his sword, plunged fully armed into the water and swam, through the missiles which fell thick about him, safely to the other side where his friends were waiting to receive him. It was a noble piece of work—legendary, maybe, but destined to be celebrated in story through the years to come. . . .

The siege nonetheless continued; food in the city was scarce and dear, and Porsena's hopes rose of being able to starve it into submission without risking an assault. It was in these circumstances that the young aristocrat Gaius Mucius performed his famous act of heroism. In the days of her servitude under the monarchy Rome had never, in any war, suffered the humiliation of a siege, and Mucius was so deeply conscious of the shame of the present situation, when, after winning their liberty, the Romans were blockaded by—of all people—the Etruscans, whom they had so often defeated in the field, that he determined to vindicate the national pride by a bold stroke. His first thought was to make his way, on his own initiative, into the enemy lines; but there was a risk, if he attempted this without anybody's knowledge and without the authorization of the consuls, of being arrested by the guards as a deserter—a charge only too plausible, conditions in Rome being what they were. Accordingly he changed his mind, and presented himself in the Senate. "I wish," he said, "to cross the river and to enter, if I can, the enemy's lines. My object is neither plunder nor reprisals, but, with the help of God, something more important than either."

The Senate granted him permission to proceed and he started on his way, a dagger concealed in his clothing. Arrived at the Etruscan camp, he took his stand, in the crowd, close to the raised platform where the king was sitting. A great many people were present, as it was pay-day for the army. By the side of the king sat his secretary, very busy; he was dressed much like his master, and, as most of the men addressed themselves to him, Mucius could not be sure which was the secretary and which the king. Fearing to inquire, lest his ignorance should betray him, he took a chance—and stabbed the secretary. There was a cry of alarm; he was seized by the guards as he tried to force hsi way through the crowd with his blood-stained dagger, and dragged back to where Porsena was sitting. Help there was none, and his situation was desperate indeed: but he never flinched and, when he spoke, his proud words were those of a man who inspires fear, but feels none. "I am a Roman," he said to the king; "my name is Gaius Mucius. I came here to kill you—my enemy. I have as much courage to die as to kill. It is our Roman way to do and to suffer bravely. Nor am I alone in my resolve against your life; behind me is a long line of men eager for the same honour. Gird yourself, if you will, for the struggle—a struggle for your life from hour to hour, with an armed enemy always at your door. That is the war we declare against you: you need fear no action in the field, army against army; it will be fought against you alone, by one of us at a time."

Porsena in rage and alarm ordered the prisoner to be burnt alive unless he at once divulged the plot thus obscurely hinted at, whereupon Mucius, crying: "See how cheap men hold their bodies when they care only for honour!" thrust his right hand into the fire which had been kindled for a sacrifice, and let it burn there as if he were unconscious of the pain. Porsena was so astonished by the young man's almost superhuman endurance that he leapt to his feet and ordered his guards to drag him from the altar. "Go free," he said; "you have dared to be a worse enemy to yourself than to me. I should bless your courage, if it lay with my country to dispose of it. But, as that cannot be, I, as an honourable enemy, grant you pardon, life, and liberty."

"Since you respect courage," Mucius replied, as if he were thanking him for his generosity, "I will tell you in gratitude what you could not force from me by threats. There are three hundred of us in Rome, all young like myself, and all of noble blood, who have sworn an attempt upon your life in this fashion. It was I who drew the first lot; the rest will follow, each in his turn and time, until fortune favour us and we have got you."

The release of Mucius (who was afterwards known as Scaevola, or the Left-Handed Man, from the loss of his right hand) was quickly followed by the arrival in Rome of envoys from Porsena. The first attempt upon his life, foiled only by a lucky mistake, and the prospect of having to face the same thing again from every one of the remaining conspirators, had so shaken the king that he was coming forward with proposals for peace. The proposals contained a demand for the restoration of the Tarquins. Porsena knew well enough that it would be refused—as indeed it was— but out of deference to the Tarquin family he could hardly avoid making it. He was successful, however, in obtaining the return of captured territory to Veii, and in forcing the Romans to give hostages if they wanted the Etruscan garrison withdrawn from the Janiculum. Peace was made on these terms: Porsena withdrew his troops from the Janiculum and evacuated Roman territory. Caius Mucius was rewarded by the Senate with a grant of land west of the river; it was known subsequently as the Mucian Meadows.

The public recognition of Mucius' heroism inspired even the women of Rome to emulate him. A notable instance is the story of Cloelia. Cloelia, an unmarried girl, was one of the hostages, held, as it happened, in the Etruscan lines not far from the Tiber; one day with a number of other girls who had consented to follow her, she eluded the guards, swam across the river under a hail of missiles, and brought her company safe to Rome, where they were all restored to their families. Porsena was furious, and sent to Rome to demand Cloelia's return—adding that the loss of the other girls did not trouble him; soon, however, his anger gave way to admiration of her more than masculine courage: Horatius and Mucius, he declared, were not to be compared with her, and he made it clear that though he would regard the treaty as broken if she were not returned, he would nevertheless, if the Romans surrendered her, himself restore her safe and sound to her family. Both sides acted honourably: the Romans, as the terms of the treaty required, sent the hostage back, and Porsena not only protected the brave girl but praised her publicly, and marked his appreciation of her exploit by handing over to her discretion a certain number of the other hostages, to be chosen by herself. She is said to have chosen the young boys, a choice in accordance with her maiden modesty: the other hostages, moreover, agreed that in liberating them from the enemy those should be first considered who were most subject to injurious treatment. Friendly relations were thus restored, and the Romans paid tribute to Cloelia's courage, unprecedented in a woman, by an equally unprecedented honour: a statue representing her on horseback was set up at the top of the Sacred Way.

Translated by Aubrey de Sélincourt

⊡⊡⊡⊡⊡⊡⊡

PROPERTIUS

c. 50 B.C.–After 16 B.C.

ELEGIES

Sextus Propertius was a protégé of Maecenas like Horace and Virgil, but unlike them, he seems to have been, if not skeptical about the blessings of the Augustan settlement, at least indifferent to them. In his poems, the conventional stance of the love elegist—that his poetic gifts are not great enough to sound the imperial theme—has a deeper resonance than in the protestations of Horace and Ovid. In one poem (II.15) he opposes the joys of love to the horrors of war and refers to the Battle of Actium in terms more appropriate to a lament for the Roman dead than a celebration of Augustus' victory; furthermore, he implicitly contradicts the official propaganda that tried to make Actium a victory over a foreign enemy rather than the culminating battle of a civil war. And in his letter to his friend Tullus (I.6), explaining why he cannot accompany him on his journey to take up official functions in the East (Cynthia won't let him go), he sees in his friend one whose "love always has been the business of the nation's wars," and himself as one "Born unfit for action (even citation)," whose wish is to be listed in the company of those "who were glad / to die in the extremity of length of love."

Love, in Propertius, is no light matter. His Eros is not the pretty boy of Apollonius, but a demonic power that enslaves him. Yet his celebration of love's dominion over him is often combined with visions of death, and it may be this ambivalence, in combination with his wit, that appealed to such modern poets as Pound and Lowell—two of whose adaptations of Propertius are printed here, side by side with more faithful versions.

From BOOK I

6

In this era, Tullus, and in your company,
I have no fear of learning an unknown ocean
(leaving on Adriatic salt or the Aegean).
We could mount the mountains of the utmost north together
and saunter beyond the domes of Ethiopia.
But blenching, blushing, beseeching, she plaits
me around with words and again I remain.

Whole night after night she argues, argues: heat, heat, heat.
Forlorn, and God-forsaken, and there are no Gods;
denying she is mine, or was sometime, or will
be next; she makes the customary menaces to me
(to master in anger from mistress in distress).
I can't hold out an hour: Damn the man
who could be that indifferently in love.

Are knowledge of Athens' sophistications
and a glance at costly Asian antiques
worth so much to me when their price is Cynthia
devising curses against me as my launch withdraws?
and she marks her face, her hands gone crazy, and says
her kisses will belong to the wind that comes against me,
and nothing is harder to bear than betrayal.

Try to surpass your uncle's honored reign.
Restore their ancient rights (forgotten by now)
to our allies. You are the man. Your youth never
has lain negligent for the yen of love: Your love
always has been the business of the nation's wars.
Never may the Boy God bring upon you labors like mine,
nor the universe of particulars my tears know.

Allow me meanwhile, whose luck has always been to lie
beaten, to offer my soul finally to sinful
idleness. Many have been the men who were glad
to die in the extremity of length of love: May I too,
when loam houses me, be listed in that company.

Born unfit for action (even citation)
Fate has impressed me into Love's Service.

You, whether where plush Ionia extends, whether
where Pactólus tints Lydian ploughlands moist-dark,
Whether you pedal on those lands or paddle over
the deep, you will have your share in a welcome New Regime.
If in that future an hour not unpermissive
of reminiscence comes to you, Tullus,
you will know, if I live, under what hard star.

Translated by Richard E. Braun

From BOOK II

15

No man more blest! O night, not dark for me,
beloved bed, scene of such dear delight!
To lie and talk there in the lamp's soft flickering,
and then to learn ourselves by touch, not sight—
to have her hold me with her breasts uncovered,
or, slipping on her tunic, balk my hand;
to have her kiss my eyes awake and murmur,
Why must you sleep? and make her sweet demand.
Shifting our arms, moving to new embraces,
we kissed a thousand kisses multiplied;
then, with the lamp rekindled, fed our senses
on new delights—the eye is love's best guide.
For Paris himself, they say, seeing Helen naked
on Menelaus' bed, loved at first sight;
Endymion, naked, roused the cold Diana,
naked to lie with her throughout the night.
Put on your tunic if you will, my Cynthia;
these furious hands will rip it into shreds.
You'll have bruised arms to show your mother, sweetheart;
when did frustration ever cool hot heads?
Youth's in those light ripe breasts, not yet gone flabby
as women's do when they have borne a child.
O let us love until we are each other—
we on whom Fate these few swift hours has smiled.
It will not be for long. A night will take us

which must refuse to brighten into dawn.
Strain closer to me, lock me in a nearness
that will not fail when time would have it gone.
Remember doves, how they are one in passion,
yoked, as we are, the male and female one?
Love is a frenzy, and it has no limit;
no love, if it is true, is ever done.
Let earth bear winter fruit and shock the farmer,
or let the sun god drive the steeds of night,
rivers run backward, or the seas be shrivelled,
fish dead in unaccustomed air and light—
these things will chance before I love another.
Living, I'll praise her; dead, dream of no other.

A single year of such nights, should she grant it—
for this I'd give up three-score-and-ten.
If there were many, I would be immortal;
if there were even one, a god again.
Ah, men are fools who do not pass their life so,
limbs languorous and heavy with much wine.
Did they, there'd be no need for swords and warships,
for sailors' bones to steep in Actium's brine;
no need for Rome to break her heart with Romans
die in the shambles of a civil war.
No god was ever outraged by our wine cups—
men can say this for us, if nothing more.
Do not renounce life while its light is in you.
Given all your kisses, still I'd have too few.
See how the withering wreath lets fall its petals
to float within the cup—O Cynthia, you
and I are lovers blest and hopeful, but
who knows what day may see that last door shut?

From BOOK III

14

The Spartan wrestlers and their rules amaze me—
but, more, the school in which their women train,
where they may exercise their naked bodies
on the same ground on which those wrestlers strain,

and where the swift ball tricks the hand stretched for it
and the hooked rod guides the hoop's rolling flight.
That dusty figure at the goal's a woman;
a woman's in this rough-and-tumble fight!
Another binds her eager hands for boxing;
a fourth girl whirls the discus overhead,
or, with the hoarfrost on her hair, goes racing
after her father's hounds, where they have sped;
puts a horse through his paces, slings a sword on
her white thigh, or a helmet on her head,
fierce as the Amazonian warriors bathing
barebreasted in Thermodon's river bed,
like Helen, when with Castor and with Pollux
she carried arms (so the report persists)
nor blushed before her brothers, one the horseman
and one the champion who fought with fists.
This is that Sparta that indulges lovers,
where couples hand-in-hand in public walk,
no girl goes guarded, no one rants of honor,
none dreads a husband's wrath or threatening talk.
All unannounced, there you may state your business
with neither deputy nor long delay;
a lover's not beguiled by nonessentials,
his dear does not arrange her hair all day.
But here where Cynthia walks are people, people—
I cannot even reach her through that crowd.
I don't know what to wear or how to hail her.
The path I tread what doubts and darkness shroud!

Rome, learn from Sparta's healthy point of view.
Yield! Give us further cause to honor you!

Translated by Constance Carrier

16

Midnight: a letter came from my mistress to me:
She ordered me, without delay, to be at Tibur,
Where gleam-white peaks display twin towers,
And Anio's waters fall to spreading pools.
What shall I do? Trust myself to occluding
Darkness and fear for my limbs at insolent hands?

Yet if I should defer her commission from fear,
Her weeping would be more cruel than mugging at night.
I offended once—was thrust off one whole year:
She does not manage me with gentle hands.

Yet no one would harm a consecrated lover:
He may go down the middle of Sciron's road.
Whoever's in love, though he stroll on Scythian shores,
No one will be so savage as to harm him.
The moon attends his way, stars point out the potholes,
Love himself shakes up the lighted torch ahead.
Mad raging watchdogs turn aside their gaping bites:
For such as him the road is safe at any time.
Who so unfeeling as to spatter his hands with a lover's
Little blood? Venus herself befriends the man kept off.

And yet if certain murder attended my mischance,
Such a death would be well bought at the price:
She will bring me perfumes and deck my tomb
With wreaths, sitting and watching by my grave.
Gods, make her not place my bones in crowded earth,
Where the rabble forever walks along the paths!—
Thus after death are lovers' mounds disgraced.
Let a leafy tree shade me in secluded ground,
Or may I be interred walled in by unknown dunes:
I'd not be pleased to have my name inscribed on the road.

Translated by W. G. Shepherd

16

Midnight, and a letter comes to me from our mistress:
    Telling me to come to Tibur, *At* once!!
"Bright tips reach up from twin towers,
    Anienan spring water falls into flat-spread pools."
What *is* to be done about it?
    Shall I entrust myself to entangled shadows,
Where bold hands may do violence to my person?

Yet if I postpone my obedience
                        because of this respectable terror
I shall be prey to lamentations worse than a nocturnal assailant.

And I shall be in the wrong,
                    and it will last a twelve-month,
For her hands have no kindness me-ward,

Nor is there anyone to whom lovers are not sacred at midnight
    And in the Via Sciro.
If any man would be a lover
                  he may walk on the Scythian coast,
No barbarism would go to the extent of doing him harm,
The moon will carry his candle,
    the stars will point out the stumbles,
Cupid will carry lighted torches before him
                  and keep mad dogs off his ankles.
Thus all roads are perfectly safe
                and at any hour;
Who so indecorous as to shed the pure gore of a suitor?!
    Cypris is his cicerone.

What if undertakers follow my track,
                such a death is worth dying.
She would bring frankincense and wreaths to my tomb,
    She would sit like an ornament on my pyre.

Gods' aid, let not my bones lie in a public location
    with crowds too assiduous in their crossing of it;
For thus are tombs of lovers most desecrated.

May a woody and sequestered place cover me with its foliage
Or may I inter beneath the hummock
of some as yet uncatalogued sand;
At any rate I shall not have my epitaph in a high road.

                            Translated by Ezra Pound

                  From BOOK IV

                    7

Ghosts do exist. Death does not finish all.
The colourless shade escapes the burnt-out pyre.
Though lately buried beside the rumbling road,
Yet Cynthia seemed to lean above my bed

When after love's last rites my sleep hung back
And I grieved that my bed was now a chilly realm.
She had the selfsame hair and eyes as on
Her bier, her shroud was burned into her side,
The fire had gnawed at her favourite beryl ring,
And Lethe's water had wasted away her lips.
She breathed out living passion, and spoke,
Yet her brittle hands rattled their thumb-bones.

"Forsworn (although no girl should hope for better
From you), can sleep already possess your faculties?
Had waking Suburan secrets, the window-sill worn
By nightly intrigue, already slipped your mind?—
From which for you I've often hung on a rope
And descended hand over hand to your arms!
Often our love was joined in the very street,
Heart to heart: our cloaks warmed up the path.
Alas, the secret oaths whose lying words
The South has torn apart and will not heed!

"Why, no one cried out at my glazing eyes:
Your calling me back would have gained one day!
No watchman rattled split reeds on my account,
My head was bruised by the intervening tile.
In short, who saw you stooping by my corpse,
Your mourning-toga grow warm with tears?
If you could not bear to pass the gate, you could
Have had my litter go more slow thus far.
Why didn't you pray for a breeze to fan my pyre,
Ingrate, why weren't my flames perfumed with nard?
Was it too much to strew cheap hyacinths,
Propitiate my tomb by breaking a jar?

"Burn Lygdamus—white-hot irons for a slave—
I knew him when I drank the spiked and pallid wine—
And Nomas—let her slyly hide her secret spittles,
A fiery sherd shall declare her criminal hands.
Who was lately on view for inexpensive nights,
The same now marks the dirt with her golden train.
And if some chatterbox mentions my beauty, she pays
Her back with unfair heavier loads of sewing.
Because Petale brought some flowers to my tomb,

The old woman is chained to a filthy log.
Lalage's hung by her twisted hair and whipped
For daring to make a request in my name.
With your permission she's melted my bust in gold—
She'd get a dowry from my burning pyre!

"However, I'll not carp, though you deserve it,
Propertius: my reign in your books was long.
By the irreversible chant of the Fates I swear—
As may Cerberus softly growl for me—
I have kept faith. If I prove false, may vipers
Hiss on my grave and couch above my bones.

"Beyond the ugly Stream twin mansions are allotted,
The whole host rows on the flood opposing ways.
The one bears Clytemnestra's taint, another
Conveys the monstrous wooden mimic-cow of Crete.
Observe these others swept along in a garlanded hoy,
Where happy airs caress Elysian roses,
And many strings and Cybebe's rounded bronze
And turbaned choirs with Lydian plectra sound.
Andromeda and Hypermestra, guileless wives,
Narrate the tales of their egregious times:
The one bewails arms bruised by a mother's chains,
Her hands that did not merit freezing rock;
Hypermestra tells how her sisters greatly dared,
But she had not the stomach for such crime.
With tears in death we ratify life's loves—
But I conceal your myriad perfidies.

"Now I charge you, if you are moved perhaps,
And not entirely bound by Chloris' drug:
Let my nurse Parthenie lack for nothing
In shaking age: she could, but did not, wheedle you.
And let my sweet Servante, named for her work,
Not hold the mirror up for some new mistress.
Whatever poems you made in my name, burn them;
For me: cease to enjoy my reputation.
Pull from my tomb the ivy, proliferating
Berries, which binds with twisting stems my crumbling bones.
Where fruit-bearing Anio falls in his branchy fields
And ivory never yellows, by Hercules' will,

Indite on a column these verses worthy of me,
But brief, that travellers from the town may read:
'Here golden Cynthia lies in Tibur's soil,
Whereby your praises, Anio, more abound.'

"Don't spurn the dreams that come by the holy gate:
When holy dreams come, they have some pith.
Night frees the shades, by night we appear at large:
His bolt withdrawn, Cerberus himself may roam.
At dawn, Law sounds a return to Lethe's mere:
We are freight, the ferryman counts his freighted load.

"For now, let others possess you: soon I alone
Shall have you: you shall be with me,
And I shall grind down bone entwined with bones."

Having brought to a close her complaint and suit,
Her shadow fell away from my embrace.

Translated by W. G. Shepherd

7

A ghost is someone: death has left a hole
For the lead-coloured soul to beat the fire:
    Cynthia leaves her dirty pyre
    And seems to coil herself and roll
        Under my canopy,
Love's stale and public playground, where I lie
And fill the run-down empire of my bed.
I see the street, her potter's field, is red
And lively with the ashes of the dead;

She no longer sparkles off in smoke:
It is the body carted to the gate
    Last Friday, when the sizzling grate
    Left its charred furrows on her smock
        And ate into her hip.
A black nail dangles from a finger tip
And Lethe oozes from her neither lip.
Her thumb-bones rattle on her brittle hands,
As Cynthia stamps and hisses and demands:

Sextus, has sleep already washed away
Your manhood? You forget the window-sill
    My sliding wore to slivers? Day
    Would break before the Seven Hills
        Saw Cynthia retreat
And climb your shoulders to the knotted sheet.
You shouldered me and galloped on bare feet
To lay me by the crossroads. Have no fear:
Notus, who snatched your promise, has no ear.

But why did no one call in my deaf ear?
Your calling would have gained me one more day.
    Sextus, although you ran away
    You might have called and stopped my bier
        A second by your door.
No tears drenched a black toga for your whore
When broken tilestones bruised her face before
The Capitol. Would it have strained your purse
To scatter ten cheap roses on my hearse?

The State will make Pompilia's Chloris burn:
I knew her secret when I kissed the skull
    Of Pluto in the tainted bowl.
    Let Nomas burn her books and turn
        Her poisons into gold;
The finger-prints upon the potsherd told
Her love. You let a slut, whose body sold
To Thracians, liquefy my golden bust
In the coarse flame that crinkled me to dust.

If Chloris' bed has left you with your head,
Lover, I think you'll answer my arrears:
    My nurse is getting on in years,
    See that she gets a little bread—
        She never clutched your purse;
See that my little humpback hears no curse
From her close-fisted friend. But burn the verse
You bellowed half a life time in my name:
Why should you feed me to the fires of fame?

I will not hound you, much as you have earned
It, Sextus: I shall reign in your four books—

I swear this by the Hag who looks
Into my heart where it was burned:
Propertius, I kept faith;
If not, may serpents suck my ghost to death
And spit it with their forked and killing breath
Into the Styx where Agamemnon's wife
Founders in the green circles of her life.

Beat the sycophant ivy from my urn,
That twists its binding shoots about my bones
    Where apple-sweetened Anio drones
    Through orchards that will never burn
        While honest Herakles,
My patron, watches. Anio, you will please
Me if you whisper upon sliding knees:
"Propertius, Cynthia is here:
She shakes her blossoms when my waters clear."

You cannot turn your back upon a dream,
For phantoms have their reasons when they come:
    We wander midnights: then the numb
    Ghost wades from the Lethaean stream:
        Even the foolish dog
Stops its hell-raising mouth and casts its clog;
At cock-crow Charon checks us in his log.
Others can have you, Sextus; I alone
Hold: and I grind your manhood bone on bone.

                              Translated by Robert Lowell

OVID

43 B.C.–A.D. 17

Ovid (Publius Ovidius Naso) was not, like the older poets of the Augustan age, a member of the circle of Maecenas. He was associated, like another young poet who composed love elegies, Tibullus, with a differ-

ent patron of the arts and letters, Corvinus Messala. This was a man who
had, like Horace, fought on the republican side against Octavian and
Antony. He then sided with Antony, but later abandoned him for Octavian, fighting against Sextus Pompeius in the West and against Antony at Actium. It was he who later proposed that Augustus be granted
the title pater patriae, "Father of his Country."

AMORES

The poems of Ovid's first publication, Amores, like those of the later Ars
Amatoria, are written in elegiac couplets. Guy Lee, our translator, experiments with witty free-verse couplets that owe more than a little to
Pound's Homage to Sextus Propertius.
   There is little that calls for explanation in these poems. Readers of I.4
should remember that the Romans, like the Greeks, did not sit down to
dinner; they reclined on couches. In I.4 the phrase "Even Mars was
caught . . ." refers to a story told by the Phaeacian singer Demodocus in
the Odyssey. Aphrodite, wife of the lame smith god Hephaestus, was
carrying on a love affair with Ares (Mars to the Romans). Hephaestus
contrived a golden net that trapped the lovers in bed, and then invited
all the gods to come and see them.

From BOOK I

4

Your husband? Going to the same dinner as us?
I hope it chokes him.

So I'm only to gaze at you, darling? Play gooseberry
while another man enjoys your touch?

You'll lie there snuggling up to him? He'll put his arm
round your neck whenever he wants?

No wonder Centaurs fought over Hippodamia
when the wedding wine began to flow.

I don't live in the forest nor am I part horse
but I find it hard to keep my hands off you.

However here's my plan. Listen carefully.
Don't throw my words of wisdom to the winds.

Arrive before him—not that I see what good
arriving first will do but arrive first all the same.

When he takes his place on the couch and you go to join him
looking angelic, secretly touch my foot.

Watch me for nods and looks that talk
and unobserved return my signals

in the language of eyebrows and fingers
with annotations in wine.

Whenever you think of our love-making
stroke that rosy cheek with your thumb.

If you're cross with me, darling,
press the lobe of your ear

but turn your ring round if you're pleased
with anything I say or do.

When you feel like cursing your fool of a husband
touch the table as if you were praying.

If he mixes you a drink, beware—tell him to drink it himself,
then quietly ask the waiter for what you want.

I'll intercept the glass as you hand it back
and drink from the side you drank from.

Refuse all food he has tasted first—
it has touched his lips.

Don't lean your gentle head against his shoulder
and don't let him embrace you

or slide a hand inside your dress
or touch your breasts. Above all don't kiss him.

If you do I'll cause a public scandal,
grab you and claim possession.

I'm bound to see all this. It's what I shan't see
that worries me—the goings on under your cloak.

Don't press your thigh or your leg against his
or touch his coarse feet with your toes.

I know all the tricks. That's why I'm worried.
I hate to think of him doing what I've done.

We've often made love under your cloak, sweetheart,
in a glorious race against time.

You won't do that, I know. Still,
to avoid all doubt don't wear one.

Encourage him to drink but mind—no kisses.
Keep filling his glass when he's not looking.

If the wine's too much for him and he drops off
we can take our cue from what's going on around us.

When you get up to leave and we all follow
move to the middle of the crowd.

You'll find me there—or I'll find you
so touch me anywhere you can.

But what's the good? I'm only temporizing.
Tonight decrees our separation.

Tonight he'll lock you in and leave me
desolated at your door.

Then he'll kiss you, then go further,
forcing his right to our secret joy.

But you *can* show him you're acting under duress.
Be mean with your love—give grudgingly—in silence.

He won't enjoy it if my prayers are answered.
And if they're not, at least assure me you won't.

But whatever happens tonight tell me tomorrow
you didn't sleep with him—and stick to that story.

5

Siesta time in sultry summer.
I lay relaxed on the divan.

One shutter closed, the other ajar,
made sylvan semi-darkness,

a glimmering dusk, as after sunset,
or between night's end and day's beginning—

the half light shy girls need
to hide their hesitation.

At last—Corinna. On the loose in a short dress,
long hair parted and tumbling past the pale neck—

lovely as Lais of the many lovers,
Queen Semiramis gliding in.

I grabbed the dress; it didn't hide much,
but she fought to keep it,

only half-heartedly though.
Victory was easy, a self-betrayal.

There she stood, faultless beauty
in front of me, naked.

Shoulders and arms challenging eyes and fingers.
Nipples firmly demanding attention.

Breasts in high relief above the smooth belly.
Long and slender waist. Thighs of a girl.

Why list perfection?
I hugged her tight.

The rest can be imagined—we fell asleep.
Such afternoons are rare.

9

Yes, Atticus, take it from me—
lovers are all soldiers, in Cupid's private army.

Military age equals amatory age—
fighting and making love don't suit the old.

Commanders expect gallantry of their men—
and so do pretty girls.

Lovers too keep watch, bivouac, mount guard—
at their mistress' door instead of H.Q.

They have their forced marches,
tramping miles for love,

crossing rivers, climbing mountains,
trudging through the snow.

Ordered abroad they brave the storm
and steer by winter stars.

Hardened to freezing nights,
to showers of hail and sleet,

they go out on patrol,
observe their rivals' movements,

lay siege to rebel mistresses
and batter down front doors.

Tacticians recommend the night attack,
use of the spearhead, catching the foe asleep.

These tactics wiped out Rhesus and his Thracians,
capturing the famous horses.

Lovers use them too—to exploit a sleeping husband,
thrusting hard while the enemy snores,

eluding guards and night patrols,
moving under cover.

If war's a gamble, love's a lottery. Both have ups and downs.
In both apparent heroes can collapse.

So think again if you think of love as a soft option—
it calls for enterprise and courage.

Achilles loved Briseis, sulked when he lost her—
Trojans, now's your chance to hammer the Greeks!

Andromache strapped Hector's helmet on
and sent him into battle with a kiss.

Great Agamemnon fell in love at first sight—
with Cassandra's wind-swept hair.

Even Mars was caught. Trapped in the blacksmith's net
he caused an epic scandal in the sky.

And what about me? I was soft—born in a dressing-gown.
A reading-couch in the shade had sapped my morale.

But a pretty girl soon put me on my feet—
Fall in she ordered, *follow me.*

And look at me now—alive and alert, the night-fighter.
Yes, if you want an active life try love.

From BOOK II

7

So that's my role—the professional defendant?
I'm sick of standing trial—though I always win.

At the theatre I've only to glance at the back rows
and your jealous eye pin-points a rival.

A pretty girl need only look at me
and you're sure the look is a signal.

I compliment another woman—you grab my hair.
I criticize her—and you think I've something to hide.

If I'm looking well I don't love you.
If pale, I'm pining for someone else.

I wish to God I had been unfaithful—
the guilty can take their punishment.

As it is you accuse me blindly, believing anything.
It's your own fault your anger cuts no ice.

Remember the donkey, putting his long ears back—
the more he's beaten the slower he goes.

So that's the latest count against me—
I'm carrying on with your maid Cypassis?

Good God, if I wanted variety
is it likely I'd pick on a drudge like her?

What man of breeding would sleep with a slave
or embrace a body scarred by the lash?

Besides, she's your coiffeuse—her skill
makes her a favourite of yours.

I'd be mad to ask a maid so devoted to you.
She'd only turn me down and tell.

By Venus and Cupid's bow,
I'm innocent—I swear it!

8

Cypassis, incomparable coiffeuse
who should start a *salon* on Olympus,

no country lass, as I know from our encounters,
but Corinna's treasure and my treasure-hunt—

who was it told her about *us?*
How does she know we slept together?

I didn't blush though, did I? Said nothing by mistake
to betray our secret?

I may have argued no one in his right mind
would have an affair with a maid,

but Achilles adored his maid Briseis
and Agememnon fell for his slave Cassandra.

I can't claim to be greater than those two.
What goes for royalty is good enough for me.

Corinna looked daggers at *you* though.
And how you blushed! I saw you.

But I saved the day, you must admit,
by swearing my Venus oath.

—Dear goddess, bid the warm south winds
blow that white lie over the ocean!—

So in return, my black beauty,
reward me today with your sweet self.

Why shake your head? The danger's over.
Don't be ungrateful. Remember your duty to *me.*

If you're stupid enough to refuse I'll have to confess
and betray myself for betraying her.

I'll tell your mistress where and when we met, Cypassis,
and what we did and how many times and how we did it.

9b

Offered a sexless heaven I'd say *No thank you*—
women are such sweet hell.

Of course one gets bored, and passion cools, but always
desire begins to spiral again.

Like a horse bolting, with helpless rider
tugging at the reins,

or a gust catching a yacht about to tie up
and driving her out to sea,

Cupid's erratic air-stream hits me,
announcing love's target practice.

Then shoot, boy! I can't resist you.
Your aim strikes home in my heart.

Love's missiles lodge there automatically now—
they hardly know your quiver.

I pity the man whose idea of bliss
is eight hours' sleep.

Poor fool—what's sleep but death warmed up?
Resting in peace comes later.

Lead me astray, beguiling female voices.
Feed me on hope,

cooing today, cursing tomorrow,
locking me out and letting me in.

The fortunes of love. Cupid, Mars takes after you—
like stepson, like stepfather.

You're unpredictable, far more flightly than your wings,
giving delight, denying delight, evading question.

But maybe you and your lovely mother will hear this prayer:
be king of my heart for ever,

let women, those floating voters, crowd into the kingdom
and both sexes join there in your worship.

From BOOK III

8

Does anyone these days respect the artist
or value elegiac verse?

Time was when imagination meant more than money
but today *poor* and *boor* mean the same thing.

"I adore your poetry" she says,
and allows it in where I can't follow.

After the compliments the door curtly closes
and I, her poet, moon about humiliated,

displaced by a new-rich upstart, a bloody soldier
who butchered his way to wealth and a knighthood.

Him in your lovely arms! You in his clutches!
Light of my life, how could you?

That head wore a helmet, remember—
that obliging flank a sword.

His left hand, flashing the new equestrian ring,
once gripped a shield. His right has killed.

How can you hold hands with a killer?
Have you no sensibility?

Look at his scars, marks of a brutal trade—
that body earned him all he has.

I expect he even brags about his killings.
How can you touch him after that, gold-digger,

and allow me, the priest of Phoebus and the Muses,
to serenade your locked door in vain?

No man of taste should waste his time on art—
he'd better enlist and rough it under canvas.

Don't turn out couplets, turn out on parade.
Homer, join up if you want a date!

Jove Almighty realized gold's omnipotence
when he cashed himself to seduce a girl.

Before the transaction father looked grim, daughter prudish,
her turret steely, the doorposts coppered.

But when the crafty lecher arrived in cash
she opened her lap and gave as golden as she got.

Long ago, when Saturn ruled in the kingdom of heaven,
Earth sank all her capital in darkness—

stowed bronze and silver, gold and heavy iron in hell.
Ingots were not yet known:

she had better things to offer—crops without cultivation,
fruit on the bough, honey in the hollow oak.

No one tore the ground with ploughshares
or parcelled out the land

or swept the sea with dipping oars—
the shore was the world's end.

Clever human nature, victim of your inventions,
disastrously creative,

why cordon cities with towered walls?
Why arm for war?

Why take to the sea—as if happiness were far away?
Why not annex the sky too?

We have, in a modest way—by deifying Bacchus
and Hercules and Romulus and now Caesar.

We dig for gold instead of food.
Our soldiers earn blood-money.

The Senate's barred to the poor. Capital is king,
creates the solemn judge and the censorious knight.

Let them own the world—knights controlling Campus and Forum,
Senate dictating peace and war,

but hands off love! Sweethearts shouldn't be up for auction.
Leave the poor man his little corner.

As it is, if my girl were chaste as a Sabine prude
she'd crawl for anyone with money.

So I am locked out. When I'm around she's scared of her husband.
He'd vanish quick enough if I could pay.

O for a god in heaven to right a lover's wrongs
and turn those fat pickings to a pile of dust!

Translated by Guy Lee

THE ART OF LOVE

*This practical handbook of seduction (Ovid is discreetly mocking the
didactic pose of such poems as Hesiod's* Works and Days *and Virgil's*
Georgics) *was the poem* (carmen) *that Ovid later named as one of the
reasons for the sentence of banishment that Augustus handed down in
A.D. 8. Though it cannot have been the main reason (the first two books
of the* Ars Amatoria *had been in circulation for some ten years at the
time), we can be sure that Augustus, the self-proclaimed reformer of
Rome's decadent morals, was deeply offended by it. In 18 B.C. he had
promulgated the* lex Iulia de adulteriis coercendis, *the Julian law re-
straining adultery, which made it a criminal offense with harsh penalties.
In the Prologue to Book I, Ovid warns married women that this book is
not for them; "safe love" and "legitimate liaisons" will be his theme. By
this formula, as he later explained in the poems written from exile, he
meant relationships with* meretrices—*women who, though socially far
above the level of the prostitutes who worked in brothels, were the
equivalent of the Greek* hetaira *or the Japanese* geisha, *a cultivated
professional mistress. It is doubtful that anyone in Rome could have
been deceived by this; the* Amores, *for example, clearly celebrate adulterous love, with the husband the butt of the joke, and as for* meretrices,
*there would surely be little need for the elaborate campaigns of seduc-
tion recommended in the first two books of the* Ars, *nor would these
professionals have needed the advice Ovid offers them in Book III. It is
of course true that a love affair with a married woman is a conventional*

theme of Latin love elegy, but there could hardly have been such a convention without some base in contemporary social relations.

In his translation of Ovid's elegiac couplets, Peter Green has worked out a brilliant metrical equivalent of the Latin qualitative meter that runs smoothly as English verse.

From BOOK I

The story of the rape of the Sabine women was part of Rome's legendary past, the era of the kings. When Romulus founded his city, he attracted settlers by proclaiming it a place of refuge for men on the run—from family feuds, from avengers for murder, refugees from conquest or persecution, outlaws of all kinds. He soon had a population, but it was entirely male. So he proclaimed a festival day of games and invited the neighboring tribe, the Sabines. At a signal from Romulus, the Romans seized the daughters of the Sabines and carried them off to be married. A war with the Sabines followed but was concluded with a treaty, according to one version, as a result of the intercession of the Sabine newlyweds. (Livy's account of the rape of the Sabine women can be found on pp. 706–7.)

WHERE TO FIND A WOMAN

Should anyone here in Rome lack finesse at love-making, let him
    try me—read my book, and results are guaranteed!
Technique is the secret. Charioteer, sailor, oarsman,
    All need it. Technique can control
Love himself. As Automedon was charioteer to Achilles,
    And Tiphys Jason's steersman, so I,
By Venus' appointment, am made Love's artificer, shall be known as
    The Tiphys, the very Automedon of Love.
He's a wild handful, will often rebel against me,
    But still just a child—
Malleable, easily disciplined. Chiron made young Achilles
    A fine musician, hammered that fierce heart
On the anvil of peaceful artistry. So this future terror
    To friend and foe alike went in awe, it's said,
Of his elderly teacher, at whose bidding the hand that in after-
    Time bore down Hector was held out for the tawse.
As Chiron taught Achilles, so I am Love's preceptor:
    Wild boys both, both goddess-born—and yet
Even bulls can be broken to plough, or spirited horses
    Subdued with bridle and bit.

So Love shall likewise own my mastery, though his bowshots
  Skewer my breast, though his torch
Flicker and sear me. The worse the wounds, the deeper the
    branding,
  That much keener I to avenge
Such outrage. Nor shall I falsely ascribe my arts to Apollo:
  No airy bird comes twittering advice
Into *my* ear, *I* never had a vision of the Muses
  Herding sheep in Ascra's valleys. This work is based
On experience: what I write, believe me, I have practised.
  My poem will deal in truth.

* * *

Aid my enterprise, Venus! Respectable ladies, the kind who
  Wear hairbands and ankle-length skirts,
Are hereby warned off. Safe love, legitimate liaisons
  Will be my theme. This poem breaks no taboos.
First, then, you fledgling troopers in passion's service,
  Comes the task of finding an object for your love.
Next, you must labour to woo and win your lady;
  Thirdly, ensure that the affair will last.
Such are my limitations, such the ground I will cover,
  The race I propose to run.
While you are fancy-free still, and can drive at leisure,
  Pick a girl, tell her, "You're the one I love.
And only you." But this search means using your eyes: a mistress
  Won't drop out of the sky at your feet.
A hunter's skilled where to spread his nets for the stag, senses
  In which glen the wild boar lurks.
A fowler's familiar with copses, an expert angler
  Knows the richest shoaling-grounds for fish.
You too, so keen to establish some long-term relationship,
  Must learn, first, where girl is to be found.
Your search need not take you—believe me—on an overseas voyage:
  A short enough trek will bring you to your goal.
True, Perseus fetched home Andromeda from the coloured Indies,
  While Phrygian Paris abducted Helen in Greece,
But Rome can boast of so many and such dazzling beauties
  You'd swear the whole world's talent was gathered here.
The girls of your city outnumber Gargara's wheatsheaves,
  Methymna's grape-clusters, all
Birds on the bough, stars in the sky, fish in the ocean:
  Venus indeed still haunts

Her son Aeneas' foundation. If you like budding adolescents
    Any number of (guaranteed) maidens are here to delight
Your roving eye. You prefer young women? They'll charm you
    By the thousand, you won't know which to choose.
And if you happen to fancy a more mature, experienced
    Age-group, believe me, *they* show up in droves.

Here's what to do. When the sun's on the back of Hercules'
    Lion, stroll down some shady colonnade,
Pompey's, say, or Octavia's (for her dead son Marcellus:
    Extravagant marble facings, R.I.P.),
Or Livia's, with its gallery of genuine Old Masters,
    Or the Danaids' Portico (note
The artwork: Danaus' daughters plotting mischief for their cousins,
    Father attitudinizing with drawn sword).
Don't miss the shrine of Adonis, mourned by Venus,
    Or the synagogue—Syrian Jews
Worship there each Sabbath—or the linen-clad heifer-goddess's
    Memphian temple: Io makes many a maid what *she*
Was to Jove. The very courts are hunting-grounds for passion;
    Amid lawyers' rebuttals love will often be found.
Here, where under Venus' marble temple the Appian
    Fountain pulses its jets high in the air,
Your jurisconsult's entrapped by Love's beguilements—
    Counsel to others, he cannot advise himself.
Here, all too often, words fail the most eloquent pleader,
    And a new sort of case comes on—his own. He must
Defend *himself* for a change, while Venus in her nearby
    Temple snickers at this reversal of roles.

But the theatre's curving tiers should form your favourite
    Hunting-ground: here you are sure to find
The richest returns, be your wish for lover or playmate,
    A one-night stand or a permanent affair.
As ants hurry to and fro in column, mandibles
    Clutching grains of wheat
(Their regular diet), as bees haunt fragrant pastures
    And meadows, hovering over the thyme,
Flitting from flower to flower, so our fashionable ladies
    Swarm to the games in such crowds, I often can't
Decide which I like. As spectators they come, come to be inspected:
    Chaste modesty doesn't stand a chance.

Such incidents at the games go back to Romulus—
   Men without women, Sabine rape.
No marble theatre then, no awnings, no perfumed saffron
   To spray the stage red:
The Palatine woods supplied a leafy backdrop (nature's
   Scenery, untouched by art),
While the tiers of seats were plain turf, and spectators shaded
   Their shaggy heads with leaves.
Urgently brooding in silence, the men kept glancing
   About them, each marking his choice
Among the girls. To the skirl of Etruscan flutes' rough triple
   Rhythm, the dancers stamped
And turned. Amid cheers (applause then lacked discrimination)
   The king gave the sign for which
They'd so eagerly watched. Project Rape was on. Up they sprang then
   With a lusty roar, laid hot hands on the girls.
As timorous doves flee eagles, as a lambkin
   Runs when it sees the hated wolf,
So this wild charge of men left the girls all panic-stricken,
   Not one had the same colour in her cheeks as before—
The same nightmare for all, though terror's features varied:
   Some tore their hair, some just froze
Where they sat; some, dismayed, kept silence, others vainly
   Yelled for Mamma; some wailed; some gaped;
Some fled, some just stood there. So they were carried off as
   Marriage-bed plunder; even so, many contrived
To make panic look fetching. Any girl who resisted her pursuer
   Too vigorously would find herself picked up
And borne off regardless. "Why spoil those pretty eyes with weeping?"
   She'd hear, "I'll be all to you
That your Dad ever was to your Mum." (You alone found the proper
   Bounty for soldiers, Romulus: give me that,
And I'll join up myself!) Ever since that day, by hallowed custom,
   Our theatres have always held dangers for pretty girls.
Don't forget the races, either: the spacious Circus offers
   Chances galore. No need,
Here, of private finger-talk, or secret signals,
   Nods conveying messages: you'll sit
Right beside your mistress, without let or hindrance,
   So be sure to press against her wherever you can—
An easy task: the seating-divisions restrict her,
   Regulations facilitate contact. Now find

Some excuse to engage in friendly conversation,
    Casual small-talk at first—
Ask, with a show of interest, whose are those horses
    Just coming past: find out
Her favourite, back it yourself. When the long procession of ivory
    Deities approaches, be sure you give
A big hand to Lady Venus. If some dust should settle
    In your girl's lap, flick it away
With your fingers; and if there's no dust, still flick away—nothing:
    Let any excuse serve to prove your zeal.
If her cloak's trailing, gather it up, make a great business
    Of rescuing it from the dirt—
Instant reward for your gallantry, a licensed peep at
    Delectable ankles, and more.
Keep an eye on whoever may be sitting behind you,
    Don't let him rub his knee
Against her smooth back. Light minds are captivated by trifles:
    Plumping out a cushion can often help,
Or fanning the lady, or slipping a little footstool
    Under her dainty feet.

GET ACQUAINTED WITH HER MAID

Why doubt that you can conquer
    Any girl in sight? Few indeed
Will turn you down—and (willing or not) a male proposition
    Is something they all enjoy. Draw a blank,
Rejection brings no danger. But why should you be rejected
    When new thrills delight, when what's not ours
Has more allure than what is? The harvest's always richer
    In another man's fields, the herd
Of our neighbour has fuller udders.

                                But first you must get acquainted
    With your quarry's maid—she can help
In the early stages. Make sure she enjoys the full confidence
    Of her mistress: make sure you can trust
Her with your secret liaison. Corrupt her with promises,
    Corrupt her with prayers. If
She's willing, you'll get what you want. She'll await the propitious
    Time (like a doctor) when her mistress is in

A receptive, seducible mood, when she's bursting out all over
    With cheerfulness, like a wheat-crop in rich soil.
When hearts are rejoicing, and have no sorrow to constrict them,
    They're wide open, Venus can steal
In by persuasive guile. Grim Troy long faced her besiegers,
    But a light-hearted change of mood
Fell for that troop-gravid horse.
                                    Another time to try her
    Is when she's been miffed by a rival. Make it your job
To ensure she gets her revenge. Prime her maid to egg her on while
    Combing her hair each morning, put an oar in
To boost Ma'am's plain sailing, sigh to herself, and murmur
    "What a pity it is you can't just pay him out
With a tit-for-tat," then talk about *you* in persuasive
    Language, swear you're dying of mad
Passion. But lose no time, don't let the wind subside or
    The sails drop slack. Fury, like brittle ice,
Melts with delay. You may ask, does it pay to seduce the
    Maid herself? Such a gambit involves great risk.
Bed makes one girl jealous, takes the edge off another: will she
    Want you for her mistress—or for *her?*
It can go either way. Though the situation calls for
    Bold risks, my advice is, *Don't.* I'm not the sort
To climb precipitous paths, sharp peaks. With me for leader
    No young man will be caught. But if,
While she carries your letters back and forth, it's not just
    Her zeal but her figure that tickles your fancy, then make
Mistress first, maid second. Never *begin* your wooing
    With the lady's companion. And here's one piece of advice
(If you trust in my skill at all, if the greedy winds don't
    Blow my words out to sea):
Lay off—*or make sure of her.* Once she's involved, and guilty,
    There's no longer any fear
That she'll turn informer against you. What's the use of liming
    A bird's wings if it escapes? A loose-netted boar
That breaks free is no good. Play your fish on the hook she's taken,
    Press home your assault, don't give up till victory's won.
But keep such relationships secret: with a secret informer
    You'll always know every move your mistress makes.

                                    Translated by Peter Green

From BOOK II

KEEP CLEAR OF ALL QUARRELS

This disquisition on the duties incumbent on a seducer contains two
mythical examples of patient, obsequious lovers: Milanion and Hercules.
Milanion was in love with Atalanta, a virgin huntress who scorned men
and marriage. Milanion in his pursuit of her accompanied her on her
expeditions through the woods as her servant, and on one occasion was
wounded by an arrow from the bow of the centaur Hylaeus, from whose
assault he had rescued her. The end of the story, not told here, is a happy
one—for Milanion, at least. Atalanta challenged her many suitors to run
a footrace with her; if they failed to reach the winning post before her,
their lives were forfeit. Carrying a spear, she would give them a head
start, then easily overtake them and kill them. Milanion, however,
started on the race carrying a bunch of golden apples, which he dropped
from time to time as he ran. Atalanta stopped to pick them up and
Milanion won the race.

Hercules was told by the Oracle of Apollo at Delphi that to expiate his
treacherous murder of Eurytus of Oechalia, he must be sold into slavery
for three years. His buyer was Omphale, queen of Lydia; she put on his
lionskin and carried his club, making him dress as a woman and work
with the distaff.

Nothing works on a mood like tactful tolerance: harshness
    Provokes hatred, makes nasty rows.
We detest the hawk and the wolf, those natural hunters,
    Always preying on timid flocks;
But the gentle swallow goes safe from man's snares, we fashion
    Little turreted houses for doves.
Keep clear of all quarrels, sharp-tongued recriminations—
    Love's sensitive, needs to be fed
With gentle words. Leave nagging to wives and husbands,
    Let *them*, if they want, think it a natural law,
A permanent state of feud. Wives thrive on wrangling,
    That's their dowry. A mistress should always hear
What she wants to be told. You don't share one bed by legal
    Fiat, with you love substitutes for law.
Use tender blandishments, language that caresses
    The ear, make her glad you came.

I'm not here as preceptor of loving to the wealthy; a suitor
    With gifts doesn't need my skills—
Anyone attractive who says "Here's something for you,"
    Has genius of his own. To such a one
I give place: he's got my tricks beat. I'm the poor man's poet,
    Was poor myself as a lover, couldn't afford
Gifts, so spun words. Poor suitors must woo with caution,
    Watch their tongues, bear much that the rich
Would never put up with. I recall how once in anger
    I pulled my girl's hair. The days I lost through that
Little outburst! I don't think I tore her dress, I wasn't conscious
    Of doing so—but *she* said I did, and the bill
Was paid for at my expense. Avoid (if you're wise) your teacher's
    Errors, shun what may cost you dear.
Fight Parthians, but keep peace with a civilized mistress,
    Have fun together, do all that induces love.

If the girl's curt and unreceptive to your wooing,
    Persist, be obdurate: the time will come
When she's more welcoming. Go with the bough, you'll bend it;
    Use brute force, it'll snap.
Go with the current: that's how to swim across rivers—
    Fighting upstream's no good.
Go easy with lions or tigers if you aim to tame them;
    The bull gets inured to the plough by slow degrees.
Was there ever a girl more prickly than Atalanta?
    Yet tough as she was, she went down
Before a man's prowess. Milanion, roaming the forest,
    Kept bewailing his lot, and the girl's
Unkindness. She made him hump hunting-nets on his back, he
    Was for ever spearing wild boars;
His wounded flesh learnt the strength of Hylaeus the Centaur's
    Taut bow—yet his keener pangs
Came from another bow, Cupid's. I'm not suggesting
    You have to go lugging nets up mountain glens
Or play the hunter, or bare your breast to flying arrows—
    A cautious lover will find the rules of my art
Undemanding enough. So, yield if she shows resistance:
    That way you'll win in the end. Just be sure to play
The part she allots you. Censure the things she censures,
    Endorse her endorsements, echo her every word,

Pro or con, and laugh whenever she laughs; remember,
    If she weeps, to weep too: take your cue
From her every expression. Suppose she's playing a board-game,
    Then throw the dice carelessly, move
Your pieces all wrong. At knucklebones, when you beat her,
    Exact no forfeit, roll low throws yourself
As often as you can manage. If you're playing halma, permit her
    Glass piece to take yours. Open up
Her parasol, hold it over her when she's out walking,
    Clear her a path through the crowd.
When she's on her chaise-longue, make haste to find a footstool
    For those dainty feet of hers, help her on and off
With her slippers. At times she'll feel cold: then (though you're
        shivering
    Yourself) warm her tiny hand
In your bosom. Don't jib at a slavish task like holding
    Her mirror: slavish or not, such attentions please.
When his stepmother Hera tired of sending him monsters
    To vanquish, then the hero who won a place
In the sky he'd formerly shouldered took to the distaff
    And basket, spun wool among Ionian girls.
If Hercules, then, obeyed *his* mistress's orders, will you
    Flinch from enduring what he endured?
She says you've a date in town? Be sure you always get there
    Ahead of time; don't give her up
Till it's *really* late. If she asks you to meet her somewhere,
    Put everything off, elbow your way through the crowd
At the double. When she comes home, late at night, from a party,
    You still must attend, like her slave,
If she summons you. It's the same when she's in the country:
    Love detests laggards. You've no transport? Walk.
Don't be put off by bad weather, or a heatwave,
    Or snowdrifts blocking your road.

Translated by Peter Green

From BOOK III

*Ovid opens Book III, his advice to the ladies, with a drumroll of mytho-
logical allusions, all of them crystal clear to his sophisticated Roman
audience, and many of them probably, by now, familiar to the readers of
this book. But Phyllis and the Nine Ways demand a word of explana-*

tion. Nine Ways was an important road junction in Thrace. Phyllis, daughter of the king of Thrace, was betrothed to Demophoon, son of Theseus. When he had to go off to Crete, Phyllis, remembering perhaps that his father had deserted Ariadne, convinced herself that he had abandoned her; she committed suicide and was changed into an almond tree. Ovid, in another poem, says that the Nine Ways got its name from the fact that Phyllis, in despair, walked nine times along a track to the seashore before she resolved to hang herself.

Stesichorus, a Greek Sicilian poet of the sixth century B.C., wrote a long poem, The Sack of Troy, in which he followed the usual story, blaming Helen for the loss of all those lives. We are told that he then went blind and, attributing this affliction to Helen (who was worshipped as a goddess at Sparta), wrote the first palinode, taking it all back. The opening lines (all we have) were: "This story is not true. You did not go in the well-benched ships, nor did you reach Troy's citadel . . ." Instead, according to Stesichorus' new version, Helen went to Egypt and the gods sent a clone Helen to Troy, a version later dramatized by Euripides in his play Helen. Stesichorus regained his sight.

"Lemnian swords" refers to a strange legend about the women of the island of Lemnos in the northern Aegean. They neglected the worship of Aphrodite, and she punished them by giving them a repulsive odor. Their husbands turned way from them, taking concubines from the Thracian mainland, so the Lemnian women slaughtered the entire male population of the island (except that their queen Hypsipyle spared her father).

In the famous story of Cephalus and Procris, the word "Aura," which sounds like a girl's name, means simply "Breeze."

LESSONS FOR THE LADIES

I've armed Greeks against Amazons: now I must fashion weapons
    For Penthesilea and her girls.
A well matched fight is best, with victory granted
    Through the favour of kind
Venus, and Venus' earth-girdling son. Unfair for naked
    Ladies to meet armed troops: a victory gained that way
Would disgrace our gallants. "But why lend venom to serpents?"
    I hear you ask, "why betray a fold of sheep
To the ravening she-wolf?" Don't pin the evil reputation
    Of one or two on them all, judge each girl by
Her own proper merits. It's true that Helen and Clytemnestra
    Must face sisterly charges from both

The sons of Atreus; it's true that what Eriphyle plotted
  Sent Amphiaraus and his horses down,
Still living, to Styx; yet Penelope stayed constant
  For ten years, while her husband was at the wars,
And ten more of his wanderings. Look at Protesilaus
  And Laodameia—who cut short her span on earth
To follow the man she loved. Alcestis redeemed Admetus'
  Life by pledging her own, was borne to the grave
In his stead, Evadne cried, "Ah take me, Capaneus!
  We'll mingle our ashes," and sprang
On to the pyre. Virtue herself, by name and fashion,
  Is a lady: naturally she has her own
Followers to please, though my art doesn't call for such strict
  Principles—my little craft
Can manage with smaller sails. Only wanton passions
  Are learnt through me, I'll teach
How a woman should be courted. You seldom see the ladies
  Using bows and flaming arrows on their men—
Men are often deceivers, girls hardly ever: inquiries
  Will prove the feminine cheat
A rare bird indeed. Medea, already a mother, was dumped by
  Perfidious Jason for another bride,
And as far as Theseus knew, deserted Ariadne
  Had long been food for gulls
On that lonely beach. How did Nine Ways get its title?
  How did the very woods come to shed their leaves
And weep for Phyllis? Remember that guest with the reputation
  For *piety? He* left poor Dido a sword—
And a motive for suicide. What ruined all these ladies?
  Erotic ineptitude, lack of technique. It takes
Technique to make love last—and they'd *still* be inept, had Venus
  Not appeared to me in a vision, made it clear
That my job was to teach them. "Poor girls," she said, "what have
    they done,
  Weak defenceless lot, to be thrown
To the armed male wolves? Two books you've written instructing
  Men in the game: high time the opposite sex
Got benefit from your counsels. Stesichorus cursed Helen
  To begin with, but ended—better luck for him—
Singing her praises. If I know you, you'll be seeking their favour
  Till the day you die—so don't go mean on them now."

With that she gave me a leaf from the garland of myrtle
    Binding her hair, and a few
Of the berries. Taking them, I sensed her numinous
    Power: air shone more brightly, my heart
Rose bouyant and carefree. While my inspiration lasts, then,
    Take lessons from me, girls (those of you whom the law,
And modesty, and your code, will permit): be mindful of creeping
    Old age, don't waste precious time—
Have fun while you can, in your salad days; the years glide
    Past like a moving stream,
And the water that's gone can never be recovered,
    The lost hour never returns.

CEPHALUS AND PROCRIS

I remember once complaining that you had to watch out for
    Your friends: it's not men alone
To whom this applies. If you show yourself over-trustful,
    Other women will reap your pleasures: the hare
You started, they'll hunt. Watch that girl with the spare bedroom
    Who's so eager to help you—believe me, I've
Been in there more than once. And don't have a maid who's too
        pretty—
    She's often usurped her mistress's role with me—
I must be crazy going on like this. Why charge bare-breasted
    Against the foe? Why testify to my own
Betrayal? Game birds don't notify the fowler
    Where he can take them; no hind sets a savage pack
On her own trail—
                Damn advantage! I'll stick to my purpose,
    Arm the girls with Lemnian swords, expose my heart
To their thrusts. Just make us believe we're loved—a simple
    Assignment: desire is quick to kindle faith
In what it seeks. Let a woman glance sweetly at her lover,
    Sigh deeply, ask him why he's so late,
Then start crying, pretend to be cross about some rival,
    Claw his face with her nails—
That'll convince him in no time, he'll soon start feeling
    Sorry for her, say "Why, the poor little thing,
She's just crazy about me!" And if he's smart, if his mirror
    Flatters his profile, then (he thinks) goddesses too

Will compete for his favours. But however badly he wrongs you,
  Don't look put out. When there's talk of some other girl,
Keep calm, don't jump to conclusions: just how dangerous snap
      judgments
  Can be, the story of Procris should demonstrate.

High under flowery Hymettus' violet hillside
  Flows a sacred spring: soft earth,
Lush turf, a little spinney of trailing arbutus,
  Dark myrtle, rosemary, scented bay,
Thick-burgeoning boxwood, the brittle tamarisk, slender
  Lucerne, domestic pines, a gentle stir
And rustle of warm spring breezes through that variegated
  Leafage, an airy caress blown over the grass.
Here Cephalus came to enjoy his siesta, hounds and huntsmen
  Abandoned, here he'd stretch out
When weary. "Come hither," he'd cry, "come, changeable Aura,
  Come to my bosom, relieve my sultry heat!"
Some stupid tattling busybody remembered this utterance,
  Told it to Cephalus' wife.
Poor Procris thought "Aura" was the name of a rival—
  She fainted, struck dumb with sudden grief,
Turned pale as late vine-leaves, caught by winter's onset
  When the clustering grapes have been picked,
Or ripe quinces, bending the bough they hang from, or cornel-
  Berries while they're still unfit to eat.
When she came round, she rent her flimsy garments,
  Raked nails down her innocent cheeks,
And at once rushed out down the street, hair all dishevelled,
  Like a thyrsus-crazed Maenad. When
She got near the spot, she left her companions in the valley
  And tiptoed bravely into the wood, alone.
What went on in your mind as you lurked there, jealous-crazy,
  Procris? What fire consumed your frantic heart?
Any moment she'd come now, this Aura, you thought, whoever
  She might be, and you'd see their shame
With your own eyes. Now you regretted coming (you never
  Wanted to catch him at it), now you were glad,
As love spun you every which way. Name, place, informer,
  All urged belief; and always, what the mind
Fears may be true it thinks is true.

When she saw the flattened
Grass where a body had lain, her heart beat fast
In her trembling bosom. By now it was noon, the shadows shrunken
At the midpoint between dawn and dusk,
And—look!—mercurial Cephalus came back through the woodlands,
Rinsed his hot face at the spring, while Procris lay
Hidden, taut, anxious. He settled down in his usual
Grassbed. "Soft Zephyrs, gentle Aura, blow
On me!" he called. Poor girl, when she grasped her more-than-welcome
Misunderstanding, the colour flowed back to her face
And the sense to her brain: up she sprang, thrashed through the foliage,
A wife making a beeline for her beloved's arms.
He—thinking the movement a beast's—with youthful swiftness
Jack-knifed to his feet, spear poised. *You fool,*
What are you at? That's no beast, hold back your weapon!—
Too late, ah God, you've hit her, the shaft's
Through your girl!
                    "My love," she whispered, "you've pierced this loving
Heart of mine yet again, the last
Of so many wounds from Cephalus! Though I pass untimely,
No rival's displaced me: *that* will make the earth
Lie light on my bones. Now the breeze that I mistrusted
Gathers my yielding spirit: I faint, I'm gone—
Close my eyes with your dear hand—"
                                        He clasped her dying
Body to his, rained tears on the cruel wound,
And as the last breath ebbed from her (poor rash lady!)
The lips of her sad lover gathered it in.

SOME TECHNICAL INSTRUCTIONS

What's left I blush to tell you; but kindly Venus
Claims as uniquely hers
All that raises a blush. Each woman should know herself, pick
methods
To suit her body: one fashion won't do for all.
Let the girl with a pretty face lie supine, let the lady
Who boasts a good back be viewed
From behind. Milanion bore Atalanta's legs on
His shoulders: nice legs should always be used this way.

The petite should ride horse (Andromache, Hector's Theban
    Bride, was too tall for these games: no jockey she);
If you're built like a fashion model, with willowy figure,
    Then kneel on the bed, your neck
A little arched; the girl who has perfect legs and bosom
    Should lie sideways on, and make her lover stand.
Don't blush to unbind your hair like some ecstatic maenad
    And tumble long tresses about
Your upcurved throat. If childbirth's seamed your belly
    With wrinkles, then offer a rear
Engagement, Parthian style. Sex has countless positions—
    An easy and undemanding one is to lie
On your right side, half-reclining. Neither Delphi nor Ammon
    Will tell you more truth than my Muse:
Long experience, if anything, should establish credit: trust my
    Art, and let these verses speak for themselves!
A woman should melt with passion to her very marrow,
    The act should give equal pleasure to them both:
Keep up a flow of seductive whispered endearments,
    Use sexy taboo words while you're making love,
And if nature's denied you the gift of achieving a climax,
    Moan as though you were coming, put on an act!
(The girl who can't feel down there is really unlucky,
    Missing out on what both sexes should enjoy.)
Only take care that you make your performance convincing,
    Thrash about in a frenzy, roll your eyes,
Let your cries and gasping breath suggest what pleasure
    You're getting (that part has its own private signs).
After the pleasures of sex, though, *don't* try to dun your lover
    For a present: such habits defeat
Their own ends. And don't open all the bedroom windows:
    Much of your body is better left unseen.

Our sport is ended: high time to quit this creative venture,
    Turn loose the swans that drew my poet's car.
As once the young men, so now let my girl-disciples
    Inscribe their trophies: *Ovid was my guide.*

                                    Translated by Peter Green

THE METAMORPHOSES

This long poem (longer than the Aeneid) is composed not in the elegiac couplets Ovid used for the Amores and the Ars Amatoria, but in hexameters, the meter of epic narrative. It is narrative poetry all right, but of an unusual form. Instead of tracing the passions and actions of a few great heroic figures, it contains over 250 separate stories, with a correspondingly huge cast of characters. The stories, drawn from the rich mine of Greek, and in the later books Roman, mythology, all feature a change of shape. They are told some by Ovid, some by characters in the poem, some at great length, some in a nutshell, and they are connected in a bewildering variety of ways, most of them quite unpredictable, many of them subtly witty. Ovid's version of these tales has in most cases become the classic one; he was widely read in the Middle Ages and much admired by the poets of the Renaissance. Shakespeare obviously knew the Metamorphoses well, in Golding's 1565 translation if not in the Latin too, and a contemporary critic wrote, in 1598, that "the sweet witty soul of Ovid lives in mellifluous and honey-tongued Shakespeare. . . ."

From BOOK I

The opening of the poem describes the original metamorphosis of chaotic atoms into the ordered structure of the universe—the globe, the land and sea, the air—and culminates in the appearance of humankind. Ovid's account relies on Stoic cosmology, but is more concerned with poetic effect than with philosophical consistency.

My intention is to tell of bodies changed
To different forms; the gods, who made the changes,
Will help me—or I hope so—with a poem
That runs from the world's beginning to our own days.

THE CREATION

Before the ocean was, or earth, or heaven,
Nature was all alike, a shapelessness,
Chaos, so-called, all rude and lumpy matter,
Nothing but bulk, inert in whose confusion
Discordant atoms warred: there was no sun

To light the universe; there was no moon
With slender silver crescents filling slowly;
No earth hung balanced in surrounding air;
No sea reached far along the fringe of shore.
Land, to be sure, there was, and air, and ocean,
But land on which no man could stand, and water
No man could swim in, air no man could breathe,
Air without light, substance forever changing,
Forever at war: within a single body
Heat fought with cold, wet fought with dry, the hard
Fought with the soft, things having weight contended
With weightless things.
                              Till God, or kindlier Nature,
Settled all argument, and separated
Heaven from earth, water from land, our air
From the high stratosphere, a liberation.
So things evolved, and out of blind confusion
Found each its place, bound in eternal order.
The force of fire, that weightless element,
Leaped up and claimed the highest place in heaven;
Below it, air; and under them the earth
Sank with its grosser portions; and the water,
Lowest of all, held up, held in, the land.
Whatever god it was, who out of chaos
Brought order to the universe, and gave it
Division, subdivision, he molded earth,
In the beginning, into a great globe,
Even on every side, and bade the waters
To spread and rise, under the rushing winds,
Surrounding earth; he added ponds and marshes,
He banked the river-channels, and the waters
Feed earth or run to sea, and that great flood
Washes on shores, not banks. He made the plains
Spread wide, the valleys settle, and the forest
Be dressed in leaves; he made the rocky mountains
Rise to full height, and as the vault of Heaven
Has two zones, left and right, and one between them
Hotter than these, the Lord of all Creation
Marked on the earth the same design and pattern.
The torrid zone too hot for men to live in,
The north and south too cold, but in the middle
Varying climate, temperature and season.

Above all things the air, lighter than earth,
Lighter than water, heavier than fire,
Towers and spreads; there mist and cloud assemble,
And fearful thunder and lightning and cold winds,
But these, by the Creator's order, held
No general dominion; even as it is,
These brothers brawl and quarrel; though each one
Has his own quarter, still, they come near tearing
The universe apart. Eurus is monarch
Of the lands of dawn, the realms of Araby,
The Persian ridges under the rays of morning.
Zephyrus holds the west that glows at sunset,
Boreas, who makes men shiver, holds the north,
Warm Auster governs in the misty southland,
And over them all presides the weightless either,
Pure without taint of earth.
                              These boundaries given,
Behold, the stars, long hidden under darkness,
Broke through and shone, all over the spangled heaven,
Their home forever, and the gods lived there,
And shining fish were given the waves for dwelling
And beasts the earth, and birds the moving air.
                    *   *   *
But something else was needed, a finer being,
More capable of mind, a sage, a ruler,
So Man was born, it may be, in God's image,
Or Earth, perhaps, so newly separated
From the old fire of Heaven, still retained
Some seed of the celestial force which fashioned
Gods out of living clay and running water.
All other animals look downward; Man,
Alone, erect, can raise his face toward Heaven.

[*Humanity, however, does not start out very well. Through the four ages familiar from Hesiod—gold, silver, bronze, and iron—it goes morally downhill to utter depravity. Jupiter decides to visit the Earth to see with his own eyes how bad things are and arrives in Arcadia, the kingdom of Lycaon. He proclaims his divinity and the people begin to worship, but Lycaon decides to put him to the test, to see if he is really a god. He kills a prisoner and serves up the cooked flesh to Jupiter at a banquet. Jupiter blasts the palace of Lycaon with a thunderbolt and as Lycaon runs for the safety of the woods, he turns into a wolf.*

Ovid

758

Jupiter decides that things have gone too far; this race of men must perish and he will then create a new one. He organizes a worldwide flood. Ovid goes on to tell the story of the two survivors, Deucalion and Pyrrha (the Greek Noah and his wife), and the metamorphosis by means of which the Earth was repeopled. Through a series of skillful transitions this leads to the story of Apollo and Daphne, daughter of the river god Peneus. (It should be remembered that the Greek word daphne *means* "laurel.")]*

THE FLOOD

So, in the cave of Aeolus, he prisoned
The North-wind, and the West-wind, and such others
As ever banish cloud, and he turned loose
The South-wind, and the South-wind came out streaming
With dripping wings, and pitch-black darkness veiling
His terrible countenance. His beard is heavy
With rain-cloud, and his hoary locks a torrent,
Mists are his chaplet, and his wings and garments
Run with the rain. His broad hands squeeze together
Low-hanging clouds, and crash and rumble follow
Before the cloudburst, and the rainbow, Iris,
Draws water from the teeming earth, and feeds it
Into the clouds again. The crops are ruined,
The farmers' prayers all wasted, all the labor
Of a long year, comes to nothing.
                                  And Jove's anger,
Unbounded by his own domain, was given
Help by his dark-blue brother. Neptune called
His rivers all, and told them, very briefly,
To loose their violence, open their houses,
Pour over embankments, let the river horses
Run wild as ever they would. And they obeyed him.
His trident struck the shuddering earth; it opened
Way for the rush of waters. The leaping rivers
Flood over the great plains. Not only orchards
Not only men and houses, but altars, temples,
And shrines with holy fires. If any building
Stands firm, the waves keep rising over its roof-top,
Its towers are under water, and land and ocean
Are all alike, and everything is ocean,
An ocean with no shore-line.

Some poor fellow
Seizes a hill-top; another, in a dinghy,
Rows where he used to plough, and one goes sailing
Over his fields of grain or over the chimney
Of what was once his cottage. Someone catches
Fish in the top of an elm-tree, or an anchor
Drags in green meadow-land, or the curved keel brushes
Grape-arbors under water. Ugly sea-cows
Float where the slender she-goats used to nibble
The tender grass, and the Nereids come swimming
With curious wonder, looking, under water,
At houses, cities, parks, and groves. The dolphins
Invade the woods and brush against the oak-trees;
The wolf swims with the lamb; lion and tiger
Are borne along together; the wild boar
Finds all his strength is useless, and the deer
Cannot outspeed that torrent; wandering birds
Look long, in vain, for landing-place, and tumble,
Exhausted, into the sea. The deep's great license
Has buried all the hills, and new waves thunder
Against the mountain-tops. The flood has taken
All things, or nearly all, and those whom water,
By chance, has spared, starvation slowly conquers.

DEUCALION AND PYRRHA

Phocis, a fertile land, while there was land,
Marked off Oetean from Boeotian fields.
It was ocean now, a plain of sudden waters.
There Mount Parnassus lifts its twin peaks skyward,
High, steep, cloud-piercing. And Deucalion came there
Rowing his wife. There was no other land,
The sea had drowned it all. And here they worshipped
First the Corycian nymphs and native powers,
Then Themis, oracle and fate-revealer.
There was no better man than this Deucalion,
No one more fond of right; there was no woman
More scrupulously reverent than Pyrrha.
So, when Jove saw the world was one great ocean,
Only one woman left of all those thousands,
And only one man left of all those thousands,
Both innocent and worshipful, he parted

The clouds, turned loose the North-wind, swept them off,
Showed earth to heaven again, and sky to land,
And the sea's anger dwindled, and King Neptune
Put down his trident, calmed the waves, and Triton,
Summoned from far down under, with his shoulders
Barnacle-strewn, loomed up above the waters,
The blue-green sea-god, whose resounding horn
Is heard from shore to shore. Wet-bearded, Triton
Set lip to that great shell, as Neptune ordered,
Sounding retreat, and all the lands and waters
Heard and obeyed. The sea has shores; the rivers,
Still running high, have channels; the floods dwindle,
Hill-tops are seen again; the trees, long buried,
Rise with their leaves still muddy. The world returns.
Deucalion saw that world, all desolation,
All emptiness, all silence, and his tears
Rose as he spoke to Pyrrha: "O my wife,
The only woman, now, on all this earth,
My consort and my cousin and my partner
In these immediate dangers, look! Of all the lands
To East or West, we two, we two alone,
Are all the population. Ocean holds
Everything else; our foothold, our assurance,
Are small as they can be, the clouds still frightful.
Poor woman—well, we are not all alone—
Suppose you had been, how would you bear your fear?
Who would console your grief? My wife, believe me,
Had the sea taken you, I would have followed.
If only I had the power, I would restore
The nations as my father did, bring clay
To life with breathing. As it is, we two
Are all the human race, so Heaven has willed it,
Samples of men, mere specimens."
                                        They wept,
And prayed together, and having wept and prayed,
Resolved to make petition to the goddess
To seek her aid through oracles. Together
They went to the river-water, the stream Cephisus,
Still far from clear, but flowing down its channel,
And they took river-water, sprinkled foreheads,
Sprinkled their garments, and they turned their steps
To the temple of the goddess, where the altars

Stood with the fires gone dead, and ugly moss
Stained pediment and column. At the stairs
They both fell prone, kissed the chill stone in prayer:
"If the gods' anger ever listens
To righteous prayers, O Themis, we implore you,
Tell us by what device our wreck and ruin
May be repaired. Bring aid, most gentle goddess,
To sunken circumstance."
                And Themis heard them,
And gave this oracle: "Go from the temple,
Cover your heads, loosen your robes, and throw
Your mother's bones behind you!" Dumb, they stood
In blank amazement, a long silence, broken
By Pyrrha, finally: she would not do it!
With trembling lips she prays whatever pardon
Her disobedience might merit, but this outrage
She dare not risk, insult her mother's spirit
By throwing her bones around. In utter darkness
They voice the cryptic saying over and over,
What can it mean? They wonder. At last Deucalion
Finds the way out: "I might be wrong, but surely
The holy oracles would never counsel
A guilty act. The earth is our great mother,
And I suppose those bones the goddess mentions
Are the stones of earth; the order means to throw them,
The stones, behind us."
                She was still uncertain,
And he by no means sure, and both distrustful
Of that command from Heaven; but what damage,
What harm, would there be in trying? They descended,
Covered their heads, loosened their garments, threw
The stones behind them as the goddess ordered.
The stones—who would believe it, had we not
The unimpeachable witness of Tradition?—
Began to lose their hardness, to soften, slowly,
To take on form, to grow in size, a little,
Become less rough, to look like human beings,
Or anyway as much like human beings
As statues do, when the sculptor is only starting,
Images half blocked out. The earthy portion,
Damp with some moisture, turned to flesh, the solid
Was bone, the veins were as they always had been.

The stones the man had thrown turned into men,
The stones the woman threw turned into women,
Such being the will of God. Hence we derive
The hardness that we have, and our endurance
Gives proof of what we have come from.
                                        Other forms
Of life came into being, generated
Out of the earth: the sun burnt off the dampness,
Heat made the slimy marshes swell; as seed
Swells in a mother's womb to shape and substance,
So new forms came to life. When the Nile river
Floods and recedes and the mud is warmed by sunshine,
Men, turning over the earth, find living things,
And some not living, but nearly so, imperfect,
On the verge of life, and often the same substance
Is part alive, part only clay. When moisture
Unites with heat, life is conceived; all things
Come from this union. Fire may fight with water,
But heat and moisture generate all things,
Their discord being productive. So when earth,
After that flood, still muddy, took the heat,
Felt the warm fire of sunlight, she conceived,
Brought forth, after their fashion, all the creatures,
Some old, some strange and monstrous.
                                        One, for instance,
She bore unwanted, a gigantic serpent,
Python by name, whom the new people dreaded,
A huge bulk on the mountain-side. Apollo,
God of the glittering bow, took a long time
To bring him down, with arrow after arrow
He had never used before except in hunting
Deer and the skipping goats. Out of the quiver
Sped arrows by the thousand, till the monster,
Dying, poured poisonous blood on those black wounds.
In memory of this, the sacred games,
Called Pythian, were established, and Apollo
Ordained for all young winners in the races,
On foot or chariot, for victorious fighters,
The crown of oak. That was before the laurel,
That was before Apollo wreathed his forehead
With garlands from that tree, or any other.

APOLLO AND DAPHNE

Now the first girl Apollo loved was Daphne,
Whose father was the river-god Peneus,
And this was no blind chance, but Cupid's malice.
Apollo, with pride and glory still upon him
Over the Python slain, saw Cupid bending
His tight-strung little bow. "O silly youngster,"
He said, "What are you doing with such weapons?
Those are for grown-ups! The bow is for my shoulders;
I never fail in wounding beast or mortal,
And not so long ago I slew the Python
With countless darts; his bloated body covered
Acre on endless acre, and I slew him!
The torch, my boy, is enough for you to play with,
To get the love-fires burning. Do not meddle
With honors that are mine!" And Cupid answered:
"Your bow shoots everything, Apollo—maybe—
But mine will fix you! You are far above
All creatures living, and by just that distance
Your glory less than mine." He shook his wings,
Soared high, came down to the shadows of Parnassus,
Drew from his quiver different kinds of arrows,
One causing love, golden and sharp and gleaming,
The other blunt, and tipped with lead, and serving
To drive all love away, and this blunt arrow
He used on Daphne, but he fired the other,
The sharp and golden shaft, piercing Apollo
Through bones, through marrow, and at once he loved
And she at once fled from the name of lover,
Rejoicing in the woodland hiding places
And spoils of beasts which she had taken captive,
A rival of Diana, virgin goddess.
She had many suitors, but she scorned them all;
Wanting no part of any man, she travelled
The pathless groves, and had no care whatever
For husband, love, or marriage. Her father often
Said, "Daughter, give me a son-in-law!" and "Daughter,
Give me some grandsons!" But the marriage torches
Were something hateful, criminal, to Daphne,

So she would blush, and put her arms around him,
And coax him: "Let me be a virgin always;
Diana's father said she might. Dear father!
Dear father—please!" He yielded, but her beauty
Kept arguing against her prayer. Apollo
Loves at first sight; he wants to marry Daphne,
He hopes for what he wants—all wishful thinking!—
Is fooled by his own oracles. As stubble
Burns when the grain is harvested, as hedges
Catch fire from torches that a passer-by
Has brought too near, or left behind in the morning,
So the god burned, with all his heart, and burning
Nourished that futile love of his by hoping.
He sees the long hair hanging down her neck
Uncared for, says, "But what if it were combed?"
He gazes at her eyes—they shine like stars!
He gazes at her lips, and knows that gazing
Is not enough. He marvels at her fingers,
Her hands, her wrists, her arms, bare to the shoulder,
And what he does not see he thinks is better.
But still she flees him, swifter than the wind,
And when he calls she does not even listen:
"Don't run away, dear nymph! Daughter of Peneus,
Don't run away! I am no enemy,
Only your follower: don't run away!
The lamb flees from the wolf, the deer the lion,
The dove, on trembling wing, flees from the eagle.
All creatures flee their foes. But I, who follow,
Am not a foe at all. Love makes me follow,
Unhappy fellow that I am, and fearful
You may fall down, perhaps, or have the briars
Make scratches on those lovely legs, unworthy
To be hurt so, and I would be the reason.
The ground is rough here. Run a little slower,
And I will run, I promise, a little slower.
Or wait a minute: be a little curious
Just who it is you charm. I am no shepherd,
No mountain-dweller, I am not a ploughboy,
Uncouth and stinking of cattle. You foolish girl,
You don't know who it is you run away from,
That must be why you run. I am lord of Delphi
And Tenedos and Claros and Patara.

Jove is my father. I am the revealer
Of present, past and future; through my power
The lyre and song make harmony; my arrow
Is sure in aim—there is only one arrow surer,
The one that wounds my heart. The power of healing
Is my discovery; I am called the Healer
Through all the world: all herbs are subject to me.
Alas for me, love is incurable
With any herb; the arts which cure the others
Do me, their lord, no good!"
                          He would have said
Much more than this, but Daphne, frightened, left him
With many words unsaid, and she was lovely
Even in flight, her limbs are in the wind,
Her garments fluttering, and her soft hair streaming,
More beautiful than ever. But Apollo,
Too young a god to waste his time in coaxing,
Came following fast. When a hound starts a rabbit
In an open field, one runs for game, one safety,
He has her, or thinks he has, and she is doubtful
Whether she's caught or not, so close the margin,
So ran the god and girl, one swift in hope,
The other in terror, but he ran more swiftly,
Borne on the wings of love, gave her no rest,
Shadowed her shoulder, breathed on her streaming hair.
Her strength was gone, worn out by the long effort
Of the long flight; she was deathly pale, and seeing
The river of her father, cried "O help me,
If there is any power in the rivers,
Change and destroy the body which has given
Too much delight!" And hardly had she finished,
When her limbs grew numb and heavy, her soft breasts
Were closed with delicate bark, her hair was leaves,
Her arms were branches, and her speedy feet
Rooted and held, and her head became a tree top,
Everything gone except her grace, her shining.
Apollo loved her still. He placed his hand
Where he had hoped and felt the heart still beating
Under the bark; and he embraced the branches
As if they still were limbs, and kissed the wood,
And the wood shrank from his kisses, and the god
Exclaimed: "Since you can never be my bride,

My tree at least you shall be! Let the laurel
Adorn, henceforth, my hair, my lyre, my quiver:
Let Roman victors, in the long procession,
Wear laurel wreaths for triumph and ovation.
Beside Augustus' portals let the laurel
Guard and watch over the oak, and as my head
Is always youthful, let the laurel always
Be green and shining!" He said no more. The laurel,
Stirring, seemed to consent, to be saying *Yes*.

Translated by Rolphe Humphries

From BOOK IV

PYRAMUS AND THISBE

"Next door to each other, in the brick-walled city
Built by Semiramis, lived a boy and girl,
Pyramus, a most handsome fellow, Thisbe,
Loveliest of all those Eastern girls. Their nearness
Made them acquainted, and love grew, in time,
So that they would have married, but their parents
Forbade it. But their parents could not keep them
From being in love: their nods and gestures showed it—
You know how fire suppressed burns all the fiercer.
There was a chink in the wall between the houses,
A flaw the careless builder had never noticed,
Nor anyone else, for many years, detected,
But the lovers found it—love is a finder, always—
Used it to talk through, and the loving whispers
Went back and forth in safety. They would stand
One on each side, listening for each other,
Happy if each could hear the other's breathing,
And then they would scold the wall: 'You envious barrier,
Why get in our way? Would it be too much to ask you
To open wide for an embrace, or even
Permit us room to kiss in? Still, we are grateful,
We owe you something, we admit; at least
You let us talk together.' But their talking
Was futile, rather; and when evening came
They would say *Good-night!* and give the good-night kisses
That never reached the other.

                    "The next morning
Came, and the fires of night burnt out, and sunshine
Dried the night frost, and Pyramus and Thisbe
Met at the usual place, and first, in whispers,
Complained, and came—high time! —to a decision.
That night, when all was quiet, they would fool
Their guardians, or try to, come outdoors,
Run away from home, and even leave the city.
And, not to miss each other, as they wandered
In the wide fields, where should they meet? At Ninus'
Tomb, they supposed, was best; there was a tree there,
A mulberry-tree, loaded with snow-white berries,
Near a cool spring. The plan was good, the daylight
Was very slow in going, but at last
The sun went down into the waves, as always,
And the night rose, as always, from those waters.

And Thisbe opened her door, so sly, so cunning,
There was no creaking of the hinge, and no one
Saw her go through the darkness, and she came,
Veiled, to the tomb of Ninus, sat there waiting
Under the shadow of the mulberry-tree.
Love made her bold. But suddenly, here came something!—
A lioness, her jaws a crimson froth
With the blood of cows, fresh-slain, came there for water,
And far off through the moonlight Thisbe saw her
And ran, all scared, to hide herself in a cave,
And dropped her veil as she ran. The lioness,
Having quenched her thirst, came back to the woods, and saw
The girl's light veil, and mangled it and mouthed it
With bloody jaws. Pyramus, coming there
Too late, saw tracks in the dust, turned pale, and paler
Seeing the bloody veil. 'One night,' he cried,
'Will kill two lovers, and one of them, most surely,
Deserved a longer life. It is all my fault,
I am the murderer, poor girl; I told you
To come here in the night, to all this terror,
And was not here before you, to protect you.
Come, tear my flesh, devour my guilty body,
Come, lions, all of you, whose lairs lie hidden
Under this rock! I am acting like a coward,
Praying for death.' He lifts the veil and takes it

Into the shadow of their tree; he kisses
The veil he knows so well, his tears run down
Into its folds: 'Drink my blood too!' he cries,
And draws his sword, and plunges it into his body,
And, dying, draws it out, warm from the wound.
As he lay there on the ground, the spouting blood
Leaped high, just as a pipe sends water spurting
Through a small hissing opening, when broken
With a flaw in the lead, and all the air is sprinkled.
The fruit of the tree, from that red spray, turned crimson,
And the roots, soaked with the blood, dyed all the berries
The same dark hue.
                    "Thisbe came out of hiding,
Still frightened, but a little fearful, also,
To disappoint her lover. She kept looking
Not only with her eyes, but all her heart,
Eager to tell him of those terrible dangers,
About her own escape. She recognized
The place, the shape of the tree, but there was something
Strange or peculiar in the berries' color.
Could this be right? And then she saw a quiver
Of limbs on bloody ground, and started backward,
Paler than boxwood, shivering, as water
Stirs when a little breeze ruffles the surface.
It was not long before she knew her lover,
And tore her hair, and beat her innocent bosom
With her little fists, embraced the well-loved body,
Filling the wounds with tears, and kissed the lips
Cold in his dying. 'O my Pyramus,'
She wept, 'What evil fortune takes you from me?
Pyramus, answer me! Your dearest Thisbe
Is calling you. Pyramus, listen! Lift your head!'
He heard the name of Thisbe, and he lifted
His eyes, with the weight of death heavy upon them,
And saw her face, and closed his eyes.
                                        "And Thisbe
Saw her own veil, and saw the ivory scabbard
With no sword in it, and understood. 'Poor boy,'
She said, 'So, it was your own hand,
Your love, that took your life away. I too
Have a brave hand for this one thing, I too
Have love enough, and this will give me strength

For the last wound. I will follow you in death,
Be called the cause and comrade of your dying.
Death was the only one could keep you from me,
Death shall not keep you from me. Wretched parents
Of Pyramus and Thisbe, listen to us,
Listen to both our prayers, do not begrudge us,
Whom death has joined, lying at last together
In the same tomb. And you, O tree, now shading
The body of one, and very soon to shadow
The bodies of two, keep in remembrance always
The sign of our death, the dark and mournful color.'
She spoke, and fitting the sword-point at her breast,
Fell forward on the blade, still warm and reeking
With her lover's blood. Her prayers touched the gods,
And touched her parents, for the mulberry fruit
Still reddens at its ripeness, and the ashes
Rest in a common urn."

Translated by Rolphe Humphries

TEREUS, PROCNE, AND PHILOMELA

*Tereus, king of Thrace, came to the aid of Pandion, king of Athens,
when his city was besieged; in return Pandion gave Tereus the hand of
his daughter Procne in marriage. The story of the ghastly events that
followed was treated by many ancient poets (a lost play of Sophocles was
called* Tereus*), but Ovid's version has become the classic text, and has
many echoes in our own literature.*

*Ovid does not specify which sister "flew to the woods" and became
the nightingale and which one flew "to the roof-top" and became the
swallow. In the Greek tradition, it was Procne who turned into the
nightingale, her song a lamentation for her son Itys; in the Latin poets,
Philomela became the nightingale, probably because her name was, mis-
takenly, thought to mean "lover of song" (Greek* melos*). This identifi-
cation has been generally followed by English poets, as, for example,
Eliot in* The Waste Land: *"The change of Philomel, by the barbarous
king / So rudely forced; yet there the nightingale / Filled all the desert
with inviolable voice . . ."*

The omens, though, were baleful: neither Juno,
Nor Hymen, nor the Graces, blessed the marriage;
The Furies swung, or, maybe, brandished torches

Snatched from a funeral; the Furies lighted
The bridal bed; and above the bridal chamber
Brooded the evil hoot-owl. With such omens
Tereus and Procne married, with such omens
The bride and bridegroom soon were father and mother,
And Thrace rejoiced, and they rejoiced, and offered
Thanks to the gods, making the day of marriage,
The day of Itys' birth, both festal days.
People never know, it seems.
                                    Five years went by,
And Procne asked a favor of her husband:
"My lord, if any ways of mine have been
A source of satisfaction to my husband,
Let me go see my sister, or let her come
To visit us, with a promise to her father
Of quick return. The sight of my dear sister
Would be the finest present you could give me."
So Tereus promptly had the ship made ready,
Sailed off to Athens, landed at Piraeus,
Found Pandion, and they joined hands in greeting
And wished each other well, and Tereus started
To explain the reasons of his coming there,
His wife's request, and the expected promise
Of a stay not over-long, and, as they chatted,
Here Philomela came, in rich apparel,
In richer grace, as lovely as the naiads,
As lovely as the dryads of the woodlands,
As lovely, rather, as they would be, if only
They had such clothes as hers, and such a bearing.
And Tereus looked at her, and in that moment
Took fire, as ripe grain burns, or dry leaves burn,
Or hay stored in the hay-mow; and this tribute
She well deserved, but there were other reasons.
He was a passionate man, and all the Thracians
Are all too quick at loving; a double fire
Burnt in him, his own passion and his nation's.
So his first impulse was to bribe her guardians,
Corrupt her faithful nurse, or by rich presents,
Even if it cost him all his kingdom, win her,
Or take her, and defend what he had taken
By violent war. In that unbridled passion
There was nothing he would not dare, with the flame bursting

Out of his breast. Delay, delay! He suffered,
Was all too eager, and when he spoke for Procne
Spoke for himself. Love made him eloquent,
If he went too far, he would lay the blame on Procne,
Saying she wished it so, and he added tears,
As if the tears were shed at her instructions!
The hearts of men have such blind darkness in them.
Tereus seems a most devoted husband,
So eager to please Procne, and wins praises,
The secret crime-contriver. Philomela
Is eager to go, wants the same thing, or seems to,
Wheedles her father, and fondles him, and coaxes,
And argues how much good it will do them both,
Her sister and her self (little she knows!)
If she can make the visit. And Tereus, watching,
Sees beyond what he sees: she is in his arms,
That is not her father whom her arms go around,
Not her father she is kissing. Everything
Is fuel to his fire. He would like to be
Her father, at that moment; and if he were
He would be as wicked a father as he is husband.
So Pandion says Yes, and Philomela,
Poor girl, is happy, and thanks him; both his daughters,
She thinks, have won; they are losers, both his daughters,
But how was she to know?
              And the Sun's horses
Swung low to the West, and there was a great banquet,
Feasting, and wine in golden cups, then slumber;
And Tereus went to bed, and did not slumber,
In heat for Philomela, thinking of her,
The way she looked, the way she moved, her gestures,
Her visible charms, and what he has not seen,
Or not yet seen, at least he can imagine,
And does, and feeds his fires, and cannot slumber.
And morning came, and the old king and the younger
Shook hands before the leaving, and the older
Spoke through his tears: "Dear son, in all devotion,
Since both the sisters wish it, and since you
Appear to share their wish, I trust her to you.
I beg you, by your honor and our kinship,
Protect her with a father's love, and send her
Safe home, as soon as may be, the sweet comfort

Of my declining years. However brief
Her visit, it will seem to me a long one.
And you, my Philomela, if you love me,
Come home to me soon!" And, saying so, he kissed her
With his last plea, and wept, and hands were joined
To bind the agreement, and one thing more, he told them,
Give all my love to Procne and to Itys,
And his voice broke, and underneath his sorrow
Foreboding lay.
            And the painted ship went sailing
Over the sea, and Tereus, the savage,
Knew he had won, having, as passenger,
His heart's desire, exults, can wait no more,
Or almost cannot wait, and looks her over
The way an eagle does, who has brought home
To his high nest, hooked by the cruel talons,
The prey, still warm, still living, the poor captive
Hopeless before the captor's gloating gaze.

And now the voyage ended, and the vessel
Was worn from travel, and they came stepping down
To their own shores, and Tereus dragged her with him
To the deep woods, to some ramshackle building
Dark in that darkness, and he shut her in there,
Pale, trembling, fearing everything, and asking
Where was her sister? And he told her then
What he was going to do, and straightway did it,
Raped her, a virgin, all alone, and calling
For her father, for her sister, but most often
For the great gods. In vain. She shook and trembled
As a frightened lamb which a gray wolf has mangled
And cast aside, poor creature, to a safety
It cannot quite believe. She is like a dove
With her own blood all over her feathers, fearing
The talons that have pierced and left her. Soon
As sense comes back, she tears her loosened hair,
She beats her breast, wild as a woman in mourning,
Crying: "O wicked deed! O cruel monster,
Barbarian, savage! Were my father's orders
Nothing to you, his tears, my sister's love,
My own virginity, the bonds of marriage?
Now it is all confused, mixed up; I am

My sister's rival, a second-class wife, and you,
For better and worse, the husband of two women,
Procne my enemy now, at least she should be.
Why not have been my murderer? That crime
Would have been cleaner, have no treachery in it,
And I an innocent ghost. If those on high
Behold these things, if there are any gods,
If anything is left, not lost as I am,
What punishment you will pay me, late or soon!
Now that I have no shame, I will proclaim it.
Given the chance, I will go where people are,
Tell everybody; if you shut me here,
I will move the very woods and rocks to pity.
The air of Heaven will hear, and any god,
If there is any god in Heaven, will hear me."
The words had their effect. The cruel king
Was moved to a fierce anger, to equal fear;
The double drive of fear and anger drove him
To draw the sword, to catch her by the hair,
To pull the head back, tie the arms behind her,
And Philomela, at the sight of the blade,
Was happy, filled with hope, the thought of death
Most welcome: her throat was ready for the stroke.
But Tereus did not kill her; he seized her tongue
With pincers, though it cried against the outrage,
Babbled and made a sound something like *Father*,
Till the sword cut it off. The mangled root
Quivered, the severed tongue along the ground
Lay quivering, making a little murmur,
Jerking and twitching, the way a serpent does
Run over by a wheel, and with its dying movement
Came to its mistress' feet. And even then—
It seems too much to believe—even then, Tereus
Took her, and took her again, the injured body
Still giving satisfaction to his lust.

And after that, Tereus went on to Procne,
And Procne asked, of course, about her sister
Asked where she was. And Tereus, with a groan,
Lamented, wept, and told some kind of story,
Saying that she was dead, oh, most convincing
With all his show of sorrow. Therefore Procne

Tore from her shoulders the robe with golden border,
Put on plain black, and built a tomb to honor
The spirit of her sister, and brought gifts
As funeral offerings to the fictive ghost,
Mourning a fate that should have been resented
Rather than mourned for.
                                    And a year went by,
And what of Philomela? Guarded against flight,
Stone blocks around her cottage, no power of speech
To help her tell her wrongs, her grief has taught her
Sharpness of wit, and cunning comes in trouble.
She had a loom to work with, and with purple
On a white background, wove her story in,
Her story in and out, and when it was finished,
Gave it to one old woman, with signs and gestures
To take it to the queen, so it was taken,
Unrolled and understood. Procne said nothing—
What could she say?—grief choked her utterance,
Passion her sense of outrage. There was no room
For tears, but for confusion only, and vengeance,
But something must be done, and in a hurry.
It was the time when all the Thracian mothers
Held festival for Bacchus, and the night
Shared in their secrets; Rhodope by night
Resounded as the brazen cymbals clashed,
And so by night the queen went from her palace,
Armed for the rites of Bacchus, in all the dress
Of frenzy, trailing vines for head-dress, deer-skin
Down the left side, and a spear over the shoulder.
So, swiftly through the forest with attendants,
Comrades and worshippers in throngs, and driven
By madness, terrible in rage and anger,
Went Procne, went the Bacchanal, and came
At last to the hidden cottage, came there shrieking,
"Hail, Bacchus!" broke the doors in, found her sister,
Dressed her like all the others, hid her face
With ivy-leaves, and dragged her on, and brought her
Home to the palace.
                                    And when Philomela
Saw where she was, she trembled and grew pale,
As pale as death, and Procne found her a place,
Took off the Bacchic trappings, and uncovered

Her sister's features, white with shame, and took her
Into her arms, but Philomela could not
So much as lift her eyes to face her sister,
Her sister, whom she knew she had wronged. She kept
Her gaze on the ground, longing with all her heart
To have the power to call the gods to witness
It was not her fault, but something forced upon her.
She tried to say so with her hand. And Procne,
Burning, could not restrain her wrath; she scolded
Her sister's weeping. "This is no time," she told her,
"For tears, but for the sword, for something stronger
Than sword, if you have any such weapon on you.
I am prepared for any crime, my sister,
To burn the palace, and into the flaming ruin
Hurl Tereus, the author of our evils.
I would cut out his tongue, his eyes, cut off
The parts which brought you shame, inflict a thousand
Wounds on his guilty soul. I am prepared
For some great act of boldness, but what it is
I do not know, I wish I did."
                              The answer
Came to her as her son came in, young Itys.
She looked at him with pitiless eyes; she thought
How like his father he is! That was enough,
She knew, now, what she had to do, all burning
With rage inside her, but when the little fellow
Came close and put both arms around his mother,
And kissed her in appealing boyish fashion,
She was moved to tenderness; against her will,
Her eyes filled up with tears, her purpose wavered.
She knew it, and she looked at Philomela,
No more at Itys, then from one to the other,
Saying: "And why should one make pretty speeches,
The other be dumb, and ravished tongue unable
To tell of ravish? Since he calls me mother,
Why does she not say Sister? Whose wife are you,
Daughter of Pandion? Will you disgrace him,
Your husband, Tereus? But devotion to him
Is a worse crime." Without more words, a tigress
With a young fawn, she dragged the youngster with her
To a dark corner somewhere in the palace,
And Itys, who seemed to see his doom approaching,

Screamed, and held out his hands, with *Mother, Mother!*
And tried to put his little arms around her
But she, with never a change in her expression,
Drove the knife home through breast, through side, one wound,
Enough to kill him, but she made another,
Cutting the throat, and they cut up the body
Still living, still keeping something of the spirit,
And part of the flesh leaped in the boiling kettles,
Part hissed on turning skewers, and the room
Dripped blood.
         And this was the feast they served to Tereus,
Who did not know, for the queen made up some story
About a ritual meal, for husbands only,
Which even servants might not watch. High in the chair
Sat Tereus, proud, and feasting, almost greedy
On the flesh of his own flesh, and in his darkness
Of mind, he calls: "Bring Itys here!" and Procne
Cannot conceal her cruel joy; she is eager
To be the herald of her bloody murder.
"He has come in," she answers, and he looks
Around, asks where the boy is, asks again,
Keeps calling, and Philomela, with hair all bloody,
Springs at him, and hurls the bloody head of Itys
Full in his father's face. There was no time, ever,
When she would rather have had the use of her tongue,
The power to speak, to express her full rejoicing.
With a great cry he turns the table over,
Summons the snaky Furies from their valley
Deep in the pit of Styx. Now, if he could,
If he only could, he would open up his belly,
Eject the terrible feast: all he can do
Is weep, call himself the pitiful resting-place
Of his dear son. He draws the sword, pursues them,
Both Pandion's daughters. They went flying from him
As if they were on wings. They were on wings!
One flew to the woods, the other to the roof-top,
And even so the red marks of the murder
Stayed on their breasts; the feathers were blood-colored.
Tereus, swift in grief and lust for vengeance,
Himself becomes a bird: a stiff crest rises
Upon his head, and a huge beak juts forward,

Not too unlike a sword. He is the hoopoe,
The bird who looks like war.

Translated by Rolphe Humphries

MIDAS: THE GOLDEN TOUCH

Virgil (see p. 643) has the Thracian women, in a Bacchic frenzy, tear Orpheus apart because after the death of Eurydice he lost all interest in women. Ovid gives them a stronger motive: Orpheus' "love was given / To young boys only, and he told the Thracians / That was the better way . . ." Bacchus (Dionysus) was appalled by the murder of the singer who had celebrated his worship and taught his rites; he changed the women into trees. He also left Thrace for Lydia in Asia Minor, where near Mount Tmolus, the Pactolus River comes down to the sea. All his customary train of nymphs and satyrs was with him, but in the course of his travels, Silenus, the old father of the satyrs, got lost.

And even this was not enough for Bacchus.
He left those fields, and with a worthier band
He sought the vineyards of his own Timolus
And Pactolus, a river not yet gold
Nor envied for its precious sands. The throng
He always had surrounded him, the satyrs,
The Bacchanals; Silenus, though, was missing.
The Phrygian rustics found him, staggering
Under the weight of years, and maybe also
From more than too much wine, bound him with wreaths
And led him to King Midas. Now this king
Together with the Athenian Eumolpus
Had learned the rites of Bacchic lore from Orpheus.
And therefore, since he recognized a comrade,
A brother in the lodge, he gave a party
For ten long days and nights, and then, rejoicing,
Came to the Lydian fields and gave Silenus
Back to his precious foster son. And Bacchus,
Happy and grateful, and meaning well, told Midas
To make his choice of anything he wanted.
And Midas, never too judicious, answered:
"Grant that whatever I touch may turn to gold!"
Bacchus agreed, gave him the ruinous gift,

Sorry the monarch had not chosen better.
So Midas went his cheerful way, rejoicing
In his own bad luck, and tried to test the promise
By touching this and that. It all was true,
He hardly dared believe it! From an oak-tree
He broke a green twig loose: the twig was golden.
He picked a stone up from the ground; the stone
Paled with light golden color; he touched a clod,
The clod became a nugget. Awns of grain
Were a golden harvest; if he picked an apple
It seemed a gift from the Hesperides.
He placed his fingers on the lofty pillars
And saw them gleam and shine. He bathed his hands
In water, and the stream was golden rain
Like that which came to Danae. His mind
Could scarcely grasp his hopes—all things were golden,
Or would be, at his will! A happy man,
He watched his servants set a table before him
With bread and meat. He touched the gift of Ceres
And found it stiff and hard; he tried to bite
The meat with hungry teeth, and where the teeth
Touched food they seemed to touch on golden ingots.
He mingled water with the wine of Bacchus;
It was molten gold that trickled through his jaws.
Midas, astonished at his new misfortune,
Rich man and poor man, tries to flee his riches
Hating the favor he had lately prayed for.
No food relieves his hunger; his throat is dry
With burning thirst; he is tortured, as he should be,
By the hateful gold. Lifting his hands to Heaven,
He cries: "Forgive me, father! I have sinned.
Have mercy upon me, save me from this loss
That looks so much like gain!" The gods are kind,
And Bacchus, since he owned his fault, forgave him,
Took back the gift. "You need not be forever
Smeared with that foolish color: go to the stream
That flows by Sardis, take your way upstream
Into the Lydian hills, until you find
The tumbling river's source. There duck your head
And body under the foaming white of the fountain,
And wash your sin away." The king obeyed him,
And the power of the golden touch imbued the water,

So that even now the fields grow hard and yellow
If that vein washes over them to flood
Their fields with the water of the touch of gold.

Translated by Rolphe Humphries

From TRISTIA

*Ovid's last poems, written in exile in Tomi, are all in the elegiac meter he
had used for his erotic poems, but his theme now is sadness;* Tristia
(Sorrows) *is the title of the collection of poems, in five books, that he
sent back to friends in Rome during the four years from A.D. 8 to 12. His
earlier books had been removed from the public libraries in Rome, and
the usual avenues for circulation of his poems—public readings and
copies made for sale by the booksellers—were not available to him, but
there is no doubt that private copies were made and widely circulated.
Ovid was Rome's most famous and popular poet, and though his laments
and appeals to Augustus for repeal or mitigation of his sentence sometimes verge on the lachrymose, he had lost none of his literary skill.
Indeed, the* Tristia *are in some ways the most virtuoso performance of
his career.*

OVID'S LAST NIGHT IN ROME

*The account of Ovid's last night in Rome is justly famous. His wife
wished to go with him to Tomi, but at his insistence she agreed to stay in
Rome, to look after his property and to work for his pardon.*
*Theseus is referred to as an example of faithful friendship because of
his love for Pirithous, his comrade in his exploits. Mettus (usually Met-
tius) was commander of the Alban troops allied to the Romans against
the Etruscans; his dubious conduct in battle raised suspicion that he had
perhaps intended to change sides at a critical moment. After the Roman
victory, he was tied to two teams of horses that were driven in different
directions, tearing his body apart.*

Nagging reminders: the black ghost-melancholy vision
    of my final night in Rome,
the night I abandoned so much I dearly treasured—
    to think of it, even now, starts tears.

That day was near dawning on which, by Caesar's fiat,
    I must leave the frontiers of Italy behind.
I'd lacked time—and inclination—to get things ready,
    long procrastination had numbed my will:
Too listless to bother with choosing slaves, attendants,
    the wardrobe, the outfit an exile needs,
I was dazed, like someone struck by Jove's own lightning
    (had I not been?), who survives, yet remains unsure
whether he's dead or alive. Sheer force of grief unclouded
    my mind in the end. When my poor wits revived
I had one last word with my friends before departure—
    those few friends, out of many, who'd stood firm.
My wife, my lover, embraced me, outwept my weeping,
    her undeserving cheeks
rivered with tears. Far away in North Africa, my daughter
    could know nothing of my fate. From every side,
wherever you looked, came the sounds of grief and lamentation,
    just like a noisy funeral. The whole house
mourned at my obsequies—men, women, even children,
    every nook and corner had its tears.
If I may gloss the trite with a lofty comparison,
    such was Troy's state when it fell.
By now all was still, no voices, no barking watchdogs,
    just the Moon on her course aloft in the night sky.
Gazing at her, and the Capitol—clear now by moonlight,
    close (but what use?) to my home,
I cried: "All you powers who dwell in that neighbour citadel,
    you temples, never more to be viewed
by me, you high gods of Rome, whom I must now abandon,
    accept my salutation for all time!
And although I assume my shield so late, after being wounded,
    yet free this my exile from the burden of hate,
and tell that *heavenly man* what error beguiled me, let him
    not think my remissness a crime—so that what *you* know
may likewise be discerned by the author of my expulsion:
    with godhead appeased, I cannot be downcast."
Such my prayer to the powers above; my wife's were countless,
    sobs choked each half-spoken word;
she flung herself down, hair loose, before our familial
    shrine, touched the dead-cold hearth with trembling lips,
poured out torrential appeals on behalf of the husband
    she mourned in vain. Our little household gods

turned a deaf ear, the Bear wheeled round the pole-star,
  and ebbing dark left no room
for further delay. What to do? Seductive love of country
  held me back—but this night was decreed my last,
tomorrow came exile. The times friends said "Hurry!" "Why?"
    I'd ask them,
  "Think to what place you're rushing me—and from where!"
The times I lied, swearing I'd set up an appropriate
  departure-time for my journey! Thrice I tripped
on the threshold, thrice turned back, dragging lethargic
  feet, their pace matched to my mood.
Often I'd make my farewells—and then go on talking,
  kiss everyone goodbye all over again,
unconsciously repeat identical instructions, eyes yearning
  back to my loved ones. In the end—
"Why make haste?" I exclaimed, "it's Scythia I'm being sent to,
  it's Rome I must leave: each one a prime excuse
for postponement: my living wife is denied her living
  husband for evermore: dear family, home,
loyal and much-loved companions, bonded in brotherhood
  that Theseus might have envied—all
now lost to me. This may well be my final chance to embrace them—
  let me make the most of one last extra hour."
With that I broke off, leaving my speech unfinished,
  and hugged all my dear ones in turn—
but while I'd been speaking, and amid their tears, the morning
  star (so baneful to me) had risen high
and bright in the heavens. I felt myself ripped asunder
  as though I'd lost a limb; a part of me
seemed wrenched from my body. So Mettus must have suffered
  when the horses avenging his treachery tore him in two.
Now my family's clamorous weeping reached its climax,
  sad hands beat naked breasts,
and my wife clung to me at the moment of my departure,
  making one last agonised tearful plea:
"They can't tear you from me—together," she cried, "we'll voyage
  together, I'll follow you into exile, be
an exile's wife. Mine, too, the journey: that frontier station
  has room for me as well; I'll make little weight
on the vessel of banishment! While your expulsion's caused by
  the wrath of Caesar, mine springs from loyal love:
this love will be Caesar for me." Her argument was familiar,

she'd tried it before, and she only gave it up—
still reluctant—on practical grounds. So I made my exit,
    dirty, unshaven, hair anyhow—like a corpse
minus the funeral. Grief-stricken, mind whirling-black, she fainted
    (they tell me), fell down half-dead,
and when she came round, hair foul with dust, and staggered
    back to her feet from the cold floor,
wept now for herself, and now for hearth and household
    bereft of their lord, cried her lost husband's name
again and again, groaning as though she'd witnessed
    her daughter's corpse, or mine,
on the high-stacked pyre; longed to die, to expunge by dying
    all awareness—yet through her regard for me
could not perish. Let her live, then, ever to succour
Ovid's exile, since this is what fate has willed.

Translated by Peter Green

OVID'S AUTOBIOGRAPHY

Sulmo mihi patria est. . . . *It is called Sulmona now, and there is a statue
of Ovid in the main piazza. The year "both consuls perished" (their
names were Hirtius and Pansa) was 43 B.C.; they fell fighting against
Mark Antony near Mutina, now called Modena. Ovid was a "knight";
the Latin term,* eques, *for which this is a rather misleading equivalent,
denoted a social rank just below that of the senatorial aristocracy. His
birthday came in March, on the second of the days sacred to Minerva
(Athena), the day on which the gladiatorial combats began. The birthday cake was offered to the* genius, *the tutelary spirit or guardian angel of
the celebrant. Ovid "dressed for a freer life" when he and his brother put
on the toga with the "broad stripe and the purple draped from our
shoulders" worn by senators and those embarked on the official career
that would lead to senatorial rank after the highest office, the consulate.
But Ovid decided against embarking on the* cursus honorum, *the ladder
of elective offices that led to the consulate; he "chose to narrow" his
"purple stripe."*

*Aemilius Macer was, like Catullus, a native of Verona; his works on
birds,* Ornithogonia, *and snakes,* Theriaca, *have not survived. Ponticus
and Bassus are little more than names to us. Gallus—who is credited
with the invention of the Latin love elegy, but whose works are lost—
was a prominent partisan and close associate of Octavian, but fell into
disfavor with the* princeps *and committed suicide. The work that Ovid*

claims to have burned "on the brink of exile" was the Metamorphoses, *but evidently, and fortunately, there were other copies in circulation. When the sentence of exile came, he was fifty years old: "ten times since my birth . . . the victorious Olympic / charioteer had carried off the prize."*

Who was this I you read, this trifler in tender passions?
   You want to know, posterity? Then attend:—
Sulmo is my homeland, where ice-cold mountain torrents
   make lush our pastures, and Rome is ninety miles off.
Here I was born, in the year both consuls perished
   at Antony's hands; heir (for what that's worth)
to an ancient family, no brand-new knight promoted
   just yesterday for his wealth.
I was not the eldest child: I came after a brother
   born a twelvemonth before me, to the day,
so that we shared a birthday, celebrated one occasion
   with two cakes, in March, at the time
of that festival sacred to armed Minerva—the first day in it
   stained by the blood of combat. We began
our education young: our father sent us to study
   with Rome's best teachers in the liberal arts.
My brother from his green years had the gift of eloquence,
   was born for the clash of words in a public court:
but I, even in boyhood, held out for higher matters,
   and the Muse was seducing me subtly to her work.
My father kept saying: "Why study such useless subjects?
   Even Homer left no inheritance." Convinced
by his argument, I abandoned Helicon completely,
   struggled to write without poetic form:
but a poem, spontaneously, would shape itself to metre—
   whatever I tried to write turned into verse.
The years sped silently by: we arrived at manhood,
   my brother and I, dressed for a freer life,
with the broad stripe and the purple draped from our shoulders,
   each still obsessed by his own early pursuits.
But when he was barely twenty years old, my brother
   died—and from then I lost a part of myself.
I did take the first step up the governmental ladder,
   became a member of the Board of Three;
the Senate awaited me; but I chose to narrow my purple

stripe: there lay a burden beyond my strength.
For such a career I lacked both endurance and inclination;
   the stress of ambition left me cold,
while the Muse, the creative spirit, was for ever urging on me
   that haven of leisure to which I'd always leaned.
The poets of those days I cultivated and cherished:
   for me, bards were so many gods.
Often the ageing Macer would read me what he'd written
   on birds or poisonous snakes or healing herbs;
often Propertius, by virtue of that close-binding
   comradeship between us, would recite
his burning verses. Ponticus, noted for epic, and Bassus,
   preeminent in iambics, both belonged
to my circle: Horace, that metrical wizard, held us
   spellbound with songs to the lyre.
Virgil I only saw, while greedy fate left Tibullus
   scant time for our friendship. He
came after Gallus, then Propertius followed:
   I was next, the fourth in line.
And as I looked up to my elders, so a younger generation
   looked up to me: my reputation soon spread.
When first I recited my earliest poems in public
   my beard had only been shaved once or twice:
she fired my genius, who now is a Roman byword
   because of those verses, the girl to whom I gave
the pseudonym of "Corinna." My writing was prolific,
   but what I thought defective, I myself
let the flames claim for revision. On the brink of exile,
   raging against my vocation, my poems, I burnt work
that could have found favour. My heart was soft, no stronghold
   against Cupid's assaults, prey to the lightest pang.
Yet, despite my nature, though the smallest spark would
   ignite me, no scandal ever smeared my name.
When I was scarce past boyhood I was briefly married
   to a wife both worthless and useless; next
came a bride you could not find fault with, yet not destined
   to warm my bed for long; third and last
there's the partner who's grown old with me, who's learnt to shoulder
   the burden of living as an exile's wife.
My daughter, twice pregnant (but by different husbands), made me
   a grandfather early on, while she was still
just a slip of a girl. By then *my* father had completed

his lifespan of ninety years. For him I wept
just as he would have done had I been the one taken.
Then, next, I saw my mother to her grave.
Ah, lucky the pair of them, so timely dead and buried,
before the black day of my disgrace!
And lucky for me, that they are not still living
to witness my misery, that they felt no grief
on my account. Yet if there survives from a life's extinction
something more than a name, if an insubstantial wraith
does escape the pyre, if some word, my parental spirits,
has reached you about me, if charges stand to my name
in the Stygian court, then understand, I implore you
—and you I may not deceive—that my exile's cause
was not a crime, but an error. So much for the dead. I return now
to you, my devoted readers, who would know
the events of my life. Already my best years were behind me—
age had brindled my hair, and ten times since my birth,
head wreathed with Pisan olive, the victorious Olympic
charioteer had carried off the prize
when the wrath of an injured prince compelled me to make my way to
Tomis, on the left shore of the Black Sea.
The cause (though too familiar to everyone) of my ruin
must not be revealed through testimony of mine.
Why rake up associates' meannesses, harm done me by house-slaves,
and much further suffering, not a whit less harsh
than the exile itself? Yet my mind disdained to yield to trouble,
showed itself invincible, drew on its strength,
till I, forgetting myself and my old leisured existence,
took arms on occasion with unpractised hand:
by sea and land I suffered as many misfortunes
as the stars between the unseen and the visible poles.
Through long wanderings driven I at length made landfall
on this coast, where native bowmen roam; and here,
though the din of neighbouring arms surrounds me, I still lighten
my sad fate as best I can
with the composition of verse: though there are none to listen
this is how I spend, and beguile, my days.
So that I live still, to grapple with such grim hardships,
unwearied, yet, of the light and all it brings
I owe, my Muse, to you: it's you who afford me solace,
who come as rest, as medicine to my cares;
you my guide and comrade, who spirit me from the Danube

to an honoured seat on Helicon; who have
offered me that rare benefit, fame while still living,
    a title rarely granted till after death.
Nor has Envy, belittler of all that's present, sunk her
    malignant fangs into any work of mine:
for although our age has produced some classic poets
    Fame has not grudged my gifts renown.
There are many I'd rank above me: yet I am no less quoted
    than they are, and most read throughout the world.
So if there's any truth in poetic predictions, even
    should I die tomorrow, I'll not be wholly earth's.
Which I was it triumphed? True poet or fashion's pander?
    Either way, generous reader, it is you I must thank.

Translated by Peter Green

TACITUS

A.D. 56/7–After 117

*Cornelius Tacitus had a distinguished career in the imperial service
under the emperors Vespasian, Titus, Domitian, and Trajan. His major
works were the* Histories, *covering the years* A.D. *69 to 96, and, published
later, the* Annals, *dealing with the years from the death of Augustus in*
A.D. *14 to the suicide of Nero in 68.*

From THE ANNALS

*Typical of Tacitus' dramatic presentation of conflict at the level of su-
preme power is his account, in the* Annals, *of the fall of Agrippina, the
mother of Nero, a formidable woman of whose ascent to imperial power
when she married, the aging emperor Claudius Tacitus remarked:
"From this moment the country was transformed. Complete obedience
was accorded to a woman. . . . This was a rigorous, almost masculine*

despotism. In public Agrippina was austere and often arrogant. Her private life was chaste—unless power was to be gained. Her passion to acquire money was unbounded. She wanted it as a stepping-stone to supremacy."

Her father, Germanicus, had been a successful general on the Rhine frontier, a favorite of the troops; adopted by Tiberius, he was in the line of succession to the principate when he died in A.D. 19. Agrippina's son by her first marriage was to become the emperor Nero. During the reign of her brother Gaius Caligula, she was sent into exile, but recalled by his successor, her uncle Claudius, who married her after the disgrace and death of his first wife, Messalina. Agrippina persuaded Claudius to adopt Nero as his son and as guardian to his own, younger son, Britannicus, and to marry his daughter Octavia to Nero. When Claudius died in A.D. 54 (with the help, many believed, of poison administered by Agrippina), her prompt action ensured that with the support of Burrus, commander of the praetorian guard, Nero was proclaimed emperor.

THE DEATH OF AGRIPPINA

Nero, who was sixteen years old when he came to power, relied on Burrus and the philosopher and tragic poet Seneca as advisers in his resistance to his mother's attempts to rule through him. When she tried to build up support for Britannicus against Nero, Britannicus died, almost certainly by poison, in A.D. 55. Nero was estranged from Octavia (who was finally put to death in 62) and consoled himself with a former slave called Acte. But soon another woman came into his life.

Lusitania was the Roman province of western Spain. Baiae and Antium (Anzio) were seaside resorts south of Rome.

There was at Rome a woman called Poppaea. Friendship with Sejanus had ruined her father, Titus Ollius, before he held office, and she had assumed the name of her brilliant maternal grandfather, Gaius Poppaeus Sabinus, of illustrious memory for his consulship and honorary Triumph. Poppaea had every asset except goodness. From her mother, the loveliest woman of her day, she inherited distinction and beauty. Her wealth, too, was equal to her birth. She was clever and pleasant to talk to. She seemed respectable. But her life was depraved. Her public appearances were few; she would half-veil her face at them, to stimulate curiosity (or because it suited her). To her, married or bachelor bedfellows were alike. She was indifferent to her reputation—yet insensible to men's love, and herself unloving. Advantage dictated the bestowal of her favours.

While married to a knight called Rufrius Crispinus—to whom she had borne a son—she was seduced by Marcus Salvius Otho, an extravagant youth who was regarded as peculiarly close to Nero. Their liaison was quickly converted into marriage. Otho praised her charms and graces to the emperor. This was either a lover's indiscretion or a deliberate stimulus prompted by the idea that joint possession of Poppaea would be a bond reinforcing Otho's own power. As he left the emperor's table he was often heard saying he was going to his wife, who had brought him what all men want and only the fortunate enjoy—nobility and beauty.

Under such provocations, delay was brief. Poppaea obtained access to Nero, and established her ascendancy. First she used flirtatious wiles, pretending to be unable to resist her passion for Nero's looks. Then, as the emperor fell in love with her, she became haughty, and if he kept her for more than two nights she insisted that she was married and could not give up her marriage. "I am devoted to Otho. My relations with him are unique. His character and way of living are both fine. *There* is a man for whom nothing is too good. Whereas you, Nero, are kept down because the mistress you live with is a servant, Acte. What a sordid, dreary, menial association!"

Ortho lost his intimacy with the emperor. Soon he was excluded from Nero's receptions and company. Finally, to eliminate his rivalry from the Roman scene, he was made governor of Lusitania. There, until the civil war, he lived moderately and respectably—enjoying himself in his spare time, officially blameless.

* * *

He loved Poppaea more every day. While Agrippina lived, Poppaea saw no hope of his divorcing Octavia and marrying her. So she nagged and mocked him incessantly. He was under his guardian's thumb, she said—master neither of the empire nor of himself. "Otherwise," she said, "why these postponements of our marriage? I suppose my looks and victorious ancestors are not good enough. Or do you distrust my capacity to bear children? Or the sincerity of my love?

"No! I think you are afraid that, if we were married, I might tell you frankly how the senate is downtrodden and the public enraged by your mother's arrogance and greed. If Agrippina can only tolerate daughters-in-law who hate her son, let me be Otho's wife again! I will go anywhere in the world where I only need hear of the emperor's humiliations rather than see them—and see you in danger, like myself!" This appeal was reinforced by tears and all a lover's tricks. Nero was won. Nor was there any opposition. Everyone longed for the mother's domination to end. But no one believed that her son's hatred would go as far as murder.

According to one author, Cluvius Rufus, Agrippina's passion to retain power carried her so far that at midday, the time when food and drink were beginning to raise Nero's temperature, she several times appeared before her inebriated son all decked out and ready for incest. Their companions observed sensual kisses and evilly suggestive caresses. Seneca, supposing that the answer to a woman's enticements was a woman, called in the ex-slave Acte. She feared for Nero's reputation— and for her own safety. Now she was instructed to warn Nero that Agrippina was boasting of her intimacy with her son, that her boasts had received wide publicity, and that the army would never tolerate a sacrilegious emperor.

Another writer, Fabius Rusticus, agrees in attributing successful intervention to Acte's wiles, but states that the desires were not Agrippina's but Nero's. But the other authorities support the contrary version. So does the tradition. That may be because Agrippina really did intend this monstrosity. Or perhaps it is because no sexual novelty seemed incredible in such a woman. In her earliest years she had employed an illicit relationship with Marcus Aemilius Lepidus as a means to power. Through the same ambition she had sunk to be Pallas' mistress. Then, married to her uncle, her training in abomination was complete. So Nero avoided being alone with her. When she left for her gardens or country mansions at Tusculum and Antium, he praised her intention of taking a holiday.

Finally, however, he concluded that wherever Agrippina was she was intolerable. He decided to kill her. His only doubt was whether to employ poison, or the dagger, or violence of some other kind. Poison was the first choice. But a death at the emperor's table would not look fortuitous after Britannicus had died there. Yet her criminal conscience kept her so alert for plots that it seemed impracticable to corrupt her household. Moreover, she had strengthened her physical resistance by a preventive course of antidotes. No one could think of a way of stabbing her without detection. And there was another danger: that the selected assassin might shrink from carrying out his dreadful orders.

However, a scheme was put forward by Anicetus, an ex-slave who commanded the fleet at Misenum. In Nero's boyhood Anicetus had been his tutor; he and Agrippina hated each other. A ship could be made, he now said, with a section which would come loose at sea and hurl Agrippina into the water without warning. Nothing is so productive of surprises as the sea, remarked Anicetus; if a shipwreck did away with her, who could be so unreasonable as to blame a human agency instead of wind and water? Besides, when she was dead the emperor could allot her a temple and altars and the other public tokens of filial duty.

This ingenious plan found favour. The time of year, too, was suitable, since Nero habitually attended the festival of Minerva at Baiae. Now he enticed his mother there. "Parents' tempers must be borne!" he kept announcing. "One must humour their feelings." This was to create the general impression that they were friends again, and to produce the same effect on Agrippina. For women are naturally inclined to believe welcome news.

As she arrived from Antium, Nero met her at the shore. After welcoming her with outstretched hands and embraces, he conducted her to Bauli, a mansion on the bay between Cape Misenum and the waters of Baiae. Some ships were standing there. One, more sumptuous than the rest, was evidently another compliment to his mother, who had formerly been accustomed to travel in warships manned by the imperial navy. Then she was invited out to dinner. The crime was to take place on the ship under cover of darkness. But an informer, it was said, gave the plot away; Agrippina could not decide whether to believe the story, and preferred a sedan-chair as her conveyance to Baiae.

There her alarm was relieved by Nero's attentions. He received her kindly, and gave her the place of honour next himself. The party went on for a long time. They talked about various things; Nero was boyish and intimate—or confidentially serious. When she left, he saw her off, gazing into her eyes and clinging to her. This may have been a final piece of shamming—or perhaps even Nero's brutal heart was affected by his last sight of his mother, going to her death.

But heaven seemed determined to reveal the crime. For it was a quiet, star-lit night and the sea was calm. The ship began to go on its way. Agrippina was attended by two of her friends. One of them, Crepereius Gallus, stood near the tiller. The other, Acerronia, leant over the feet of her resting mistress, happily talking about Nero's remorseful behaviour and his mother's re-established influence. Then came the signal. Under the pressure of heavy lead weights, the roof fell in. Crepereius was crushed, and died instantly. Agrippina and Acerronia were saved by the raised sides of their couch, which happened to be strong enough to resist the pressure. Moreover, the ship held together.

In the general confusion, those in the conspiracy were hampered by the many who were not. But then some of the oarsmen had the idea of throwing their weight on one side, to capsize the ship. However, they took too long to concert this improvised plan, and meanwhile others brought weight to bear in the opposite direction. This provided the opportunity to make a gentler descent into the water. Acerronia ill-advisedly started crying out, "I am Agrippina! Help, help the emperor's mother!" She was struck dead by blows from poles and oars and whatever ship's gear happened to be available. Agrippina herself kept quiet and avoided recognition. Though she was hurt—she had a wound in the shoulder—she swam until she came to some sailing-boats. They brought her to the Lucrine lake, from which she was taken home.

There she realized that the invitation and special compliment had been treacherous, and the collapse of her ship planned. The collapse had started at the top, like a stage-contrivance. The shore was close by, there had been no wind, no rock to collide with. Acerronia's death and her own wound also invited reflection. Agrippina decided that the only escape from the plot was to profess ignorance of it. She sent an ex-slave Agerinus to tell her son that by divine mercy and his lucky star she had survived a serious accident. The messenger was to add, however, that despite anxiety about his mother's dangerous experience Nero must not yet trouble to visit her—at present rest was what she needed. Meanwhile, pretending unconcern, she cared for her wound and physical condition generally. She also ordered Acerronia's will to be found and her property sealed. Here alone no pretence was needed.

To Nero, awaiting news that the crime was done, came word that she had escaped with a slight wound—after hazards which left no doubt of their instigator's identity. Half-dead with fear, he insisted she might arrive at any moment. "She may arm her slaves! She may whip up the army, or gain access to the senate or Assembly, and incriminate me for wrecking and wounding her and killing her friends! What can I do to save myself?" Could Burrus and Seneca help? Whether they were in the plot is uncertain. But they were immediately awakened and summoned.

For a long time neither spoke. They did not want to dissuade and be rejected. They may have felt matters had gone so far that Nero had to strike before Agrippina, or die. Finally Seneca ventured so far as to turn to Burrus and ask if the troops should be ordered to kill her. He replied that the Guard were devoted to the whole imperial house and to Germanicus' memory; they would commit no violence against his offspring. Anicetus, he said, must make good his promise. Anicetus unhesitatingly claimed the direction of the crime. Hearing him, Nero cried that this was the first day of his reign—and the magnificent gift came from a former slave! "Go quickly!" he said. "And take men who obey orders scrupulously!"

Agrippina's messenger arrived. When Nero was told, he took the initiative, and staged a fictitious incrimination. While Agerinus delivered his message, Nero dropped a sword at the man's feet and had him arrested as if caught red-handed. Then he could pretend that his mother had plotted against the emperor's life, been detected, and—in shame—committed suicide.

Meanwhile Agrippina's perilous adventure had become known. It was believed to be accidental. As soon as people heard of it they ran to the beach, and climbed on to the embankment, or fishing-boats nearby. Others waded out as far as they could, or waved their arms. The whole shore echoed with wails and prayers and the din of all manner of inquiries and ignorant answers. Huge crowds gathered with lights. When she was known to be safe, they prepared to make a show of rejoicing.

But a menacing armed column arrived and dispersed them. Anicetus surrounded her house and broke in. Arresting every slave in his path, he came to her bedroom door. Here stood a few servants—the rest had been frightened away by the invasion. In her dimly lit room a single maid waited with her. Agrippina's alarm had increased as nobody, not even Agerinus, came from her son. If things had been well there would not be this terribly ominous isolation, then this sudden uproar. Her maid vanished. "Are you leaving me, too?" called Agrippina. Then she saw Anicetus. Behind him were a naval captain and lieutenant named Herculeius and Obaritus respectively. "If you have come to visit me," she said, "you can report that I am better. But if you are assassins, I know my son is not responsible. He did not order his mother's death." The murderers closed round her bed. First the captain hit her on the head with a truncheon. Then as the lieutenant was drawing his sword to finish her off, she cried out: "Strike here!"—pointing to her womb. Blow after blow fell, and she died.

So far accounts agree. Some add that Nero inspected his mother's corpse and praised her figure; but that is contested. She was cremated that night, on a dining couch, with meagre ceremony. While Nero reigned, her grave was not covered with earth or enclosed, though later her household gave her a modest tomb beside the road to Misenum, on the heights where Julius Caesar's mansion overlooks the bay beneath. During the cremation one of her former slaves, Mnester, stabbed himself to death. Either he loved his patroness, or he feared assassination.

This was the end which Agrippina had anticipated for years. The prospect had not daunted her. When she asked astrologers about Nero, they had answered that he would become emperor but kill his mother. Her reply was, "Let him kill me—provided he becomes emperor!" But Nero only understood the horror of his crime when it was done. For the rest of the night, witless and speechless, he alternately lay paralysed and leapt to his feet in terror—waiting for the dawn which he thought would be his last. Hope began to return to him when at Burrus' suggestion the colonels and captains of the Guard came and cringed to him, with congratulatory handclasps for his escape from the unexpected menace of his mother's evil activities. Nero's friends crowded to the temples. Campanian towns nearby followed their lead and displayed joy by sacrifices and deputations.

Translated by Michael Grant

PETRONIUS ARBITER
?–A.D. 65

Petronius deserves a brief obituary. He spent his days sleeping, his nights working and enjoying himself. Others achieve fame by energy, Petronius by laziness. Yet he was not, like others who waste their resources, regarded as dissipated or extravagant, but as a refined voluptuary. People liked the apparent freshness of his unconventional and unself-conscious sayings and doings. Nevertheless, as governor of Bithynia and later as consul, he had displayed a capacity for business.

Then, reverting to a vicious or ostensibly vicious way of life, he had been admitted into the small circle of Nero's intimates, as Arbiter of Taste: to the blasé emperor nothing was smart and elegant unless Petronius had given it his approval. So Tigellinus, loathing him as a rival and a more expert hedonist, denounced him on the grounds of his friendship with Flavius Scaevinus. This appealed to the emperor's outstanding passion—his cruelty. A slave was bribed to incriminate Petronius. No defence was heard. Indeed, most of his household were under arrest.

The emperor happened to be in Campania. Petronius too had reached Cumae; and there he was arrested. Delay, with its hopes and fears, he refused to endure. He severed his own veins. Then, having them bound up again when the fancy took him, he talked with his friends—but not seriously, or so as to gain a name for fortitude. And he listened to them reciting, not discourses about the immortality of the soul or philosophy, but light lyrics and frivolous poems. Some slaves received presents—others beatings. He appeared at dinner, and dozed, so that his death, even if compulsory, might look natural.

Even his will deviated from the routine death-bed flatteries of Nero, Tigellinus, and other leaders. Petronius wrote out a list of Nero's sen-

sualities—*giving names of each male and female bed-fellow and details of every lubricious novelty—and sent it under seal to Nero. Then Petronius broke his signet-ring, to prevent its subsequent employment to incriminate others.*

Tacitus, The Annals

Translated by Michael Grant

From THE SATYRICON

Tacitus does not mention it, but Petronius was the author of one of the most remarkable productions of Latin literature, a picaresque novel entitled Satyricon. *We have only fragments of what must have been a very long narrative; our fragments are from Books XIV to XVI. As might be expected from the title, which means something like "Satyr Stories," sexual adventures bulk large in the lives of the three principal characters.*

TRIMALCHIO'S DINNER PARTY

Encolpius, the narrator, is on the road in southern Italy with his boy love Giton and his friend Ascyltus, who is his rival for Giton's love. Together with Agamemnon, a professor of rhetoric, they are invited to a dinner at the palatial establishment of Trimalchio. The banquet, complete with full orchestra, singing and dancing slave waiters, rich, pretentious food, and expensive wines, not to mention performances of various kinds designed to allow the host to show off his ponderous wit or his capacity for literary allusions (all of them grotesquely confused), drags on through one tasteless exhibition after another until Trimalchio has to answer the call of nature and the guests get a chance to talk.

When Seleucus says, "Your bath's a fuller," he means that it is very hard on your skin; a fuller was a cleaner of woolen garments who used strong solvents, one of the most common being human urine. Most of those present at Chrysanthus' funeral were "slaves he set free" because it was a frequent gesture to set one's slaves free in one's will. The "spread" Mammaea is going to offer, according to Echion, is a move to gain votes in an election; the incumbent, Norbanus, is vulnerable—the gladiatorial show he put on was a cheap affair. Trimalchio's phrase, "Bacchante mincemeat," is a literary reference (correct for once); he is thinking of the dismemberment of Pentheus in Euripides' play The Bacchae. *He goes on, however, to offer a wildly distorted version of the Cyclops episode in the* Odyssey. *The Sybil of Cumae (the one Aeneas went to see) was immortal but not ageless; she has now shrunk to such small stature that she lives in a bottle. In the text, the boys' question and the Sybil's reply are in Greek. The passage was made famous in the twentieth century by its appearance as the epigraph to T. S. Eliot's* The Waste Land.

Corinthian bronze was a famous alloy, the secret of which has been lost. There was a story, certainly false, that it was accidentally produced when Mummius sacked and burned Corinth in 146 B.C., but Trimalchio seems to think that this happened at the sack of Troy and that the Carthaginian general Hannibal was responsible. He goes on to confuse Cassandra with Medea, and of course the stories of Daedalus, Niobe, and the Wooden Horse have no possible interconnection.

At this point Trimalchio heaved himself up from his couch and waddled off to the toilet. Once rid of our table tyrant, the talk began to flow more freely. Damas called for larger glasses and led off himself. "What's one day? Bah, nothing at all. You turn round and it's dark. Nothing for it, I say, but jump right from bed to table. Brrrr. Nasty spell of cold weather we've been having. A bath hardly warmed me up. But a hot drink's the best overcoat of all; that's what I always say. Whoosh, I must have guzzled gallons. I'm tight and no mistake. Wine's gone right to my head . . ."

"As for me," Seleucus broke in, "I don't take a bath every day. Your bath's a fuller; the water's got teeth like a comb. Saps your vital juices. But once I've had a slug of mead, then bugger the cold. Couldn't have had a bath today anyway. Had to go to poor old Chrysanthus' funeral. Yup, he's gone for good, folded his tent forever. And a grand little guy he was; they don't make 'em any better these days. I might almost be talking to him now. Just goes to show you. What are men anyway but balloons on legs, a lot of blown-up bladders? Flies, that's what we are. No, not even flies. Flies have something inside. But a man's a bubble, all air, nothing else. And, you know, Chrysanthus might still be with us if he hadn't tried that starvation diet. Five days and not a crumb of bread, not a drop of water, passed his lips. Tch, tch. And now he's gone, joined the great majority. Doctors killed him. Maybe not doctors, call it fate. What good's a doctor but for peace of mind? But the funeral was fine, they did it up brown: nice bier, fancy drapes, and a good bunch of mourners turned out too. Mostly slaves he'd set free, of course. But his old lady was sure stingy with the tears. Not that he didn't lead her a hard life, mind. But women, they're a race of kites. Don't deserve love. You might as well drop it down a well. And old love's a real cancer . . ."

He was beginning to be tiresome and Phileros shouted him down.

"Whoa there," he cut in, "let's talk about the living. He got what was
coming to him. He lived well, he died well. What the hell more did he
want? And got rich from nothing too. And no wonder, I say. That boy
would have grubbed in the gutter for a coin and picked it out with his
teeth too. God knows what he had salted away. Just got fatter and fatter,
bloated with the stuff. Why, that man oozed money the way a honeycomb oozes honey. But I'll give you the lowdown on him, and no frills
either. He talked tough, sure, but he was a born gabber. And a real
scrapper too, regular pair of fists on legs. But you take his brother: now
that's a real man for you, friendly and generous as they come, and what's
more, he knows how to put on a spread. Anyway, as I was saying, what
does our boy do but flop on his first big deal and end up eating crow? But
come the vintage and he got right back on his feet and sold his wine at
his own figure. What really gave him a boost was some legacy he got.
And I don't mind telling you, he milked that legacy for all it was worth
and then some. So what does the sap do next but pick a fight with his
own brother and leave everything to a total stranger? I mean, it just
shows you. Run from your kin and you run a damn long ways, as the
saying goes. Well, you know, he had some slaves and he listened to them
as though they were a lot of oracles, so naturally they took him in the
end. It's like I always say, a sucker gets screwed. And that goes double
when a man's in business. But there's a saying, it isn't what you're given,
but what you can get that counts. Well, he got the meat out of that one
all his life. He was Lady Luck's fair-haired boy and no mistake. Lead
turned to gold in his hand. Of course, it's easy when the stuff comes
rolling in on its own. And you know how old he was when he died?
Seventy and then some. But carried it beautifully, hard as nails and his
hair as black as a crow. I knew him for ages, and he was horny, right to
the end. By god, I'll bet he even pestered the dog. Boys were what he
really liked, but he wasn't choosy: he'd jump anything with legs. I don't
blame him a bit, you understand. He won't have any fun where he's gone
now."

But Ganymedes struck in, "Stuff like that doesn't matter a bit to man
or beast. But nobody mentions the real thing, the way the price of bread
is pinching. God knows, I couldn't buy a mouthful of bread today. And
this damn drought goes on and on. Nobody's had a bellyful for years
now. It's those rotten officials, you take my word for it. They're in
cahoots with the bakers: you scratch me and I'll scratch you. So the little
people get it in the neck, but in the rich man's jaws it's jubilee all year.
By god, if we only had the kind of men we used to have, the sort I found
here when I arrived from Asia. Then life was something like living. Man,
milk and honey day in and day out, and the way they'd wallop those

blood-sucking officials, you'd have thought old Jupiter was having himself a tantrum. I remember old Safinius now. He used to live down by the
old arch when I was a boy. More peppercorn than man. Singed the
ground wherever he went. But honest and square and a real friend! Why,
you could have matched coins with him in the dark. And in the townhall
he'd lay it right on the line, no frills at all, just square on the target. And
when he made a speech in the main square, he'd let loose like a bugle
blowing. But neat as a pin all the time, never ruffled, never spat: there
was something Asiatic about him. And you know, he always spoke to
you, even remembered your name, just as though he were one of us. And
bread was dirt-cheap in his day. For a penny you got a loaf that two men
couldn't finish. Nowadays bulls' eyes come bigger than bread. But that's
what I mean, things are just getting worse and worse. Why, this place is
running downhill like a heifer's ass. You tell me, by god, the good of this
three-fig official of ours who thinks more of his graft than what's happening to us. Why, that boy's just living it up at home and making more in a
day than most men ever inherit. If we had any balls, let me tell you, he'd
be laughing out of the other side of his face. But not us. Oh no, we're big
lions at home and scared foxes in public. Why, I've practically had to
pawn my clothes and if bread prices don't drop soon, I'll have to put my
houses on the market. Mark my words, we're in for bad times if some
man or god doesn't have a heart and take pity on this place. I'll stake my
luck on it, the gods have got a finger in what's been happening here. And
you know why? Because no one believes in the gods, that's why. Who
observes the fast days any more, who cares a rap for Jupiter? One and all,
bold as brass, they sit there pretending to pray, but cocking their eyes on
the chances and counting up their cash. Once upon a time, let me tell
you, things were different. The women would dress up in their best and
climb barefoot up to the temple on the hill. Their hair was unbound and
their hearts were pure and they went to beg Jupiter for rain. And you
know what happened? Then or never, the rain would come sloshing
down by the bucket, and they'd all stand there like a pack of drowned
rats, just grinning away. Well, that's why the gods have stuffed their ears,
because we've gotten unreligious. The fields are lying barren and . . ."

"For god's sake," the ragseller Echion broke in, "cut out the damned
gloom, will you? 'Sometimes it's good, sometimes it's bad,' as the old
peasant said when he sold the spotted pig. Luck changes. If things are
lousy today, there's always tomorrow. That's life, man. Sure, the times
are bad, but they're no better anywhere else. We're all in the same boat,
so what's the fuss? If you lived anywhere else, you'd be swearing the pigs
here went waddling around already roasted. And don't forget, there's a
big gladiator show coming up the day after tomorrow. Not the same old

fighters either; they've got a fresh shipment in and there's not a slave in the batch. You know how old Titus works. Nothing's too good for him when he lets himself go. Whatever it is, it'll be something special. I know the old boy well, and he'll go whole hog. Just wait. There'll be cold steel for the crowd, no quarter, and the amphitheater will end up looking like a slaughterhouse. He's got what it takes too. When the old man died—and a nasty way to die, I'm telling you—he left Titus a cool million. Even if he spent ten thousand, he'd never feel it, and people won't forget him in a hurry either. He's already raked together a troupe of whirling dervishes, and there's a girl who fights from a chariot. And don't forget that steward that Glyco caught in bed with his wife. You just wait, there'll be a regular free-for-all between the lovers and the jealous husbands. But that Glyco's a cheap bastard. Sent the steward down to be pulled to pieces by the wild beasts, you know. So that just gave his little secret away, of course. And what's the crime, I'd like to know, when the poor slave is told to do it? It's that piss-pot-bitch of his that ought to be thrown to the bulls, by god! Still, those who can't beat the horse must whop the saddle. But what stumps me is why Glyco ever thought old Hermogenes' brat would turn out well anyway. The old man would have pared a hawk's claws in mid-air, and like father, like daughter, as I always say. But Glyco's thrown away his own flesh and blood; he'll carry the marks of this mess as long as he lives and only hell will burn it away. Yes sir, that boy has dug his own grave and no mistake.

"Well, they say Mammaea's going to put on a spread. Mmmm, I can sniff it already. There'll be a nice little handout all around. And if he does, he'll knock old Norbanus out of the running for good. Beat him hands down. And what's Norbanus ever done anyway, I'd like to know. A lot of two-bit gladiators and half-dead at that: puff at them and they'd fall down dead. Why, I've seen better men tossed to the wild animals. A lot of little clay statues, barnyard strutters, that's what they were. One was an old jade, another was a clubfoot, and the replacement they sent in for him was half-dead and hamstrung to boot. There was one Thracian with some guts but he fought by the book. And after the fight they had to flog the whole lot of them the way the mob was screaming, 'Let 'em have it!' Just a pack of runaway slaves. Well, says Norbanus, at least I gave you a show. So you did, says I, and you got my cheers for it. But tot it up and you'll see you got as much as you gave. So there too, and tit for tat, says I.

"Well, Agamemnon, I can see you're thinking, 'What's that bore blabbing about now?' You're the professor here, but I don't catch you opening your mouth. No, you think you're a cut above us, don't you, so you just sit there and smirk at the way we poor men talk. Your learning's

made you a snob. Still, let it go. I tell you what. Someday you come down
to my villa and look it over. We'll find something to nibble on, a chicken,
a few eggs maybe. This crazy weather's knocked everything topsy-turvy,
but we'll come up with something you like. Don't worry your head about
it, there'll be loads to eat.

"You remember that little shaver of mine? Well, he'll be your pupil
one of these days. He's already doing division up to four, and if he comes
through all right, he'll sit at your feet someday. Every spare minute he
has, he buries himself in his books. He's smart all right, and there's good
stuff in him. His real trouble is his passion for birds. I killed three of his
pet goldfinches the other day and told him the cat had got them. He
found some other hobby soon enough. And, you know, he's mad about
painting. And he's already started wading into Greek and he's keen on
his Latin. But the tutor's a little stuck on himself and won't keep him in
line. The older boy now, he's a bit slow. But he's a hard worker and
teaches the others more than he knows. Every holiday he spends at
home, and whatever you give him, he's content. So I bought him some
of those big red lawbooks. A smattering of law, you know, is a useful
thing around the house. There's money in it too. He's had enough
literature, I think. But if he doesn't stick it out in school, I'm going to
have him taught a trade. Barbering or auctioneering, or at least a little
law. The only thing that can take a man's trade away is death. But
everyday I keep pounding the same thing into his head: 'Son, get all the
learning you can. Anything you learn is money in the bank. Look at
Lawyer Phileros. If he hadn't learned his law, he'd be going hungry and
chewing on air. Not so long ago he was peddling his wares on his back;
now he's running neck and neck with old Norbanus. Take my word for
it, son, there's a mint of money in books, and learning a trade never
killed a man yet.' "

Conversation was running along these lines when Trimalchio returned, wiping the sweat from his brow. He splashed his hands in perfume and stood there for a minute in silence. "You'll excuse me,
friends," he began, "but I've been constipated for days and the doctors
are stumped. I got a little relief from a prescription of pomegranate rind
and resin in a vinegar base. Still, I hope my tummy will get back its
manners soon. Right now my bowels are bumbling around like a bull.
But if any of you has any business that needs attending to, go right
ahead; no reason to feel embarrassed. There's not a man been born yet
with solid insides. And I don't know any anguish on earth like trying to
hold it in. Jupiter himself couldn't stop it from coming.—What are you
giggling about, Fortunata? You're the one who keeps me awake all night
with your trips to the potty. Well, anyone at table who wants to go has

my permission, and the doctors tell us not to hold it in. Everything's ready outside—water and pots and the rest of the stuff. Take my word for it, friends, the vapors go straight to your brain. Poison your whole system. I know of some who've died from being too polite and holding it in." We thanked him for his kindness and understanding, but we tried to hide our snickers in repeated swallows of wine.

As yet we were unaware that we had slogged only halfway through this "forest of refinements," as the poets put it. But when the tables had been wiped—to the inevitable music, of course—servants led in three hogs rigged out with muzzles and bells. According to the headwaiter, the first hog was two years old, the second three, but the third was all of six. I supposed that we would now get tumblers and rope dancers and that the pigs would be put through the kind of clever tricks they perform for the crowds in the street. But Trimalchio dispelled such ideas by asking, "Which one of these hogs would you like cooked for your dinner? Now your ordinary country cook can whip you up a chicken or make a Bacchante mincemeat or easy dishes of that sort. But my cooks frequently broil calves whole." With this he had the cook called in at once, and without waiting for us to choose our pig, ordered the oldest slaughtered. Then he roared at the cook, "What's the number of your corps, fellow?"

"The fortieth, sir," the cook replied.

"Were you born on the estate or bought?"

"Neither, sir. Pansa left me to you in his will."

"Well," barked Trimalchio, "see that you do a good job or I'll have you demoted to the messenger corps."

The cook, freshly reminded of his master's power, meekly led the hog off toward the kitchen, while Trimalchio gave us all an indulgent smile. "If you don't like the wine," he said, "we'll have it changed for you. I'll know by the amount you drink what you think of it. Luckily too I don't have to pay a thing for it. It comes with a lot of other good things from a new estate of mine near town. I haven't seen it yet, but I'm told it adjoins my lands at Terracina and Tarentum. Right now what I'd really like to do is buy up Sicily. Then I could go to Africa without ever stepping off my own property."

"But tell me," he said, turning to Agamemnon, "what was the subject of your debate today? Of course, I'm no orator myself, but I've learnt a thing or two about law for use around the place. And don't think I'm one of those people who look down on learning. No sir, I've got two libraries, one Greek and the other Latin. So tell us, if you will, what your debate was about."

"Well," said Agamemnon, "it seems that a rich man and a poor man had gone to court . . ."

"A *poor* man?" Trimalchio broke in, "what's that?"

"Very pretty, very pretty," chuckled Agamemnon and then launched out into an exposition of god knows which of his debating topics. But Trimalchio immediately interrupted him: "If that's the case, there's no argument; if it isn't the case, then what does it matter?" Needless to say, we pointedly applauded all of Trimalchio's sallies.

"But tell me, my dear Agamemnon," continued our host, "do you remember the twelve labors of Hercules or the story about Ulysses and how the Cyclops broke his thumb trying to get the log out of his eye? When I was a kid, I used to read all those stories in Homer. And, you know, I once saw the Sybil of Cumae in prison. She was hanging in a bottle, and when the boys asked her, 'Sybil, what do you want?' she said, 'I want to die.' "

He was still chattering away when the servants came in with an immense hog on a tray almost the size of the table. We were, of course, astounded at the chef's speed and swore it would have taken longer to roast an ordinary chicken, all the more since the pig looked even bigger than the one served to us earlier. Meanwhile Trimalchio had been scrutinizing the pig very closely and suddenly roared, "What! What's this? By god, this hog hasn't even been gutted! Get that cook in here on the double!"

Looking very miserable, the poor cook came shuffling up to the table and admitted that he had forgotten to gut the pig.

"You *forgot?*" bellowed Trimalchio. "*You forgot to gut a pig?* And I suppose you think that's the same thing as merely forgetting to add salt and pepper. Strip that man!"

The cook was promptly stripped and stood there stark naked between two bodyguards, utterly forlorn. The guests to a man, however, interceded for the chef. "Accidents happen," they said, "please don't whip him. If he ever does it again, we promise we won't say a word for him." My own reaction was anger, savage and unrelenting. I could barely restrain myself and leaning over, I whispered to Agamemnon, "Did you ever hear of anything worse? Who could forget to gut a pig? By god, you wouldn't catch me letting him off, not if it was just a fish he'd forgotten to clean."

Not so Trimalchio, however. He sat there, a great grin widening across his face, and said: "Well, since your memory's so bad, you can gut the pig here in front of us all." The cook was handed back his clothes, drew out his knife with a shaking hand and then slashed at the pig's belly with crisscross cuts. The slits widened out under the pressure from inside, and suddenly out poured, not the pig's bowels and guts, but link upon link of tumbling sausages and blood puddings.

The slaves saluted the success of the hoax with a rousing, "LONG LIVE GAIUS!" The vindicated chef was presented with a silver crown and honored by the offer of a drink served on a platter of fabulous Corinthian bronze. Noticing that Agamemnon was admiring the platter, Trimalchio said, "I'm the only man in the world who owns genuine Corinthian bronze." I expected him to brag in his usual way that he'd had the stuff imported directly from Corinth, but he was way ahead of me. "Perhaps," he said, "you'd like to know why I'm the only man who owns genuine Corinthian. Well, I'll tell you. It's because I have it made by a craftsman of mine called Corinthus, and what's Corinthian, I'd like to know, if not something Corinthus makes? And don't think I'm just a stupid half-wit. I know very well how Corinthian bronze got invented. You see, when Troy was taken, there was this fellow called Hannibal, a real swindler, and he ordered all the bronze and gold and silver statues to be melted down in a pile. Well, the stuff melted and made a kind of mixture. So the smiths came and started carting it off and turning out platters and side dishes and little statues. And that's how real Corinthian began, a kind of mishmash metal, and nothing on its own. If you don't mind my saying so though, I like glass better. It doesn't stink like bronze, and if it weren't so breakable, I'd prefer it to gold. Besides, it's cheap as cheap.

"But, you know, there was once a workman who invented a little glass bottle that wouldn't break. Well, he got in to see the emperor with this bottle as a present. Then he asked the emperor to hand it back to him and managed to drop it on the floor on purpose. Well, the emperor just about died. But the workman picked the bottle back up from the floor and, believe it or not, it was dented just a little, as though it were made out of bronze. So he pulled a little hammer out of his pocket and tapped it back into shape. Well, by this time he thought he had Jupiter by the balls, especially when the emperor asked him if anyone else was in on the secret. But you know what happened? When the workman told him that nobody else knew, the emperor ordered his head chopped off. Said that if the secret ever got out, gold would be as cheap as dirt.

"But silver's my real passion. I've got a hundred bowls that hold three or four gallons apiece, all of them with the story of Cassandra engraved on them: how she killed her sons, you know, and the kids are lying there dead so naturally that you'd think they were still alive. And there's a thousand goblets too which Mummius left my old master. There's pictures on them too, things like Daedalus locking up Niobe in the Trojan Horse. And on my cups, the heavy ones, I've got the fights of Hermeros and Petraites. No sir, I wouldn't take cash down for my taste in silver."

In the midst of this harangue, a slave dropped a goblet on the floor. Once he had finished talking, Trimalchio wheeled on him and said, "Why don't you go hang yourself? You're no damn good to me." The slave began to whimper and beg for mercy. But Trimalchio was stern: "Why come whining to me for pity? As if I got you into your mess. Next time tell yourself not to be so damn dumb." However, we interceded once more and managed to get the slave off. The instant he was pardoned, he began to scamper around the table . . .

Then Trimalchio shouted, "Out with the water, in with the wine!" We dutifully applauded the joke, and particularly Agamemnon who was an old hand at wangling return invitations.

By now Trimalchio was drinking heavily and was, in fact, close to being drunk. "Hey, everybody!" he shouted, "nobody's asked Fortunata to dance. Believe me, you never saw anyone do grinds the way she can." With this he raised his hands over his forehead and did an impersonation of the actor Syrus singing one of his numbers, while the whole troupe of slaves joined in on the chorus. He was just about to get up on the table when Fortunata went and whispered something in his ear, probably a warning that these drunken capers were undignified. Never was a man so changeable: sometimes he would bow down to Fortunata in anything she asked; at other times, as now, he went his own way.

But it was the secretary, not Fortunata, who effectively dampened his desire to dance, for quite without warning he began to read from the estate records as though he were reading some government bulletin.

"Born," he began, "on July 26th, on Trimalchio's estate at Cumae, thirty male and forty female slaves.

"Item, five hundred thousand bushels of wheat transferred from the threshing rooms into storage.

"On the same date, the slave Mithridates crucified alive for blaspheming the guardian spirit of our master Gaius.

"On the same date, the sum of three hundred thousand returned to the safe because it could not be invested.

"On the same date, in the gardens at Pompeii, fire broke out in the house of the bailiff Nasta . . ."

"What?" roared Trimalchio. "When did I buy any gardens at Pompeii?"

"Last year," the steward replied. "That's why they haven't yet appeared on the books."

"I don't care what you buy," stormed Trimalchio, "but if it's not reported to me within six months, I damn well won't have it appearing on the books at all!"

[*After a great many more courses and some garbled lectures on literature, astronomy, and philosophy from Trimalchio, the proceedings get so ridiculous that Ascyltus bursts out laughing, provoking the wrath of Hermeros, one of Trimalchio's friends. He recognizes the gold ring on Ascyltus' finger as a sign that he was born (like Ovid) into the equestrian class, and in his tirade against Ascyltus we can recognize the contempt of a man who has worked his way up from the lower depths for one who, born to higher station, has drifted into vagrancy. Hermeros' claim that he would "rather be a Roman slave than a tax-paying savage" refers to the fact that under the empire Roman citizens paid no taxes, so a Roman slave, once he attained freedom and citizenship, would be better off than the freeborn provincials. Hermeros has come a long way from slavery; he is, like Trimalchio, a member of the prestigious local board supervising the worship of the emperor. His final taunt to Ascyltus, that he is "gaping . . . like a goat in vetch" (such a goat would be awestruck by the richness of the food facing him), sets Giton off into helpless laughter, and Hermeros now attacks him in his turn. December is the time of the Saturnalia, the festival at which slaves, for one day in the year, could act like free men. Giton is unable to answer Hermeros' riddle, and so are we.*

Rhapsodes were professional reciters of epic, and especially Homeric, poetry, but only in Trimalchio's banquet do they bang shields on spears. The host's explanation of the Homeric scenes they have just recited in Greek reaches new heights of absurdity. The point of naming the slave who comes in to cut up the calf "Ajax" is that Ajax, in the mad fit inflicted on him by Athena, slaughtered cattle under the impression he was killing Agamemnon and Menelaus.]

Ascyltus, however, was no longer able to swallow his snickers and he finally tossed back his head and roared and guffawed until he was almost in tears. At this one of Trimalchio's freedmen friends, the man just above me at the table, took offense and flared out in wild rage. "You cheap muttonhead," he snarled, "what are you cackling about? Entertainment isn't good enough for the likes of you, I suppose? You're richer, huh? And eat better too? I'll bet! So help me, if you were down here by me, I'd stop your damn bleating!

"Some nerve he's got, laughing at us. Stinking runaway, that's what he is. A burglar. A bum. Bah, he's not worth a good boot in the ass. By god, if I tangle with him, he won't know where he's headed! So help me, I don't often fly off the handle like this. Still, if the flesh is soft, I say, the worms will breed.

"Still cackling, are you? Who the hell are you to snicker? Where'd your daddy buy you? Think you're made out of gold, eh? So that's it, you're a Roman knight? That makes me a king's son. Then why was I a slave? Because I wanted to be. Because I'd rather be a Roman slave than a tax-paying savage. And as I live and breathe, I hope no man thinks I'm funny. I walk like a free man. I don't owe any man a thing. I've never been hauled into court. That's right: no man ever had to tell me to pay up. I've bought a few little plots of land and a nice bit of silver plate. I feed twenty stomachs, not counting the dog. I bought my wife's freedom so no man could put his dirty paws on her. I paid a good two hundred for my own freedom. Right now, I'm on the board for the emperor's worship, and I hope when I die, I won't have to blush for anything. But you're so damn busy sneering at us, you don't look at your own behind. You see the lice on us but not the ticks on yourself. Nobody but you thinks we're funny. Look at your old professor there: he appreciates us. Bah, you're still sucking tit; you're limp leather, limper, no damn better. Oh, you're rich, are you? Then cram down two lunches; bolt two suppers, sonny. As for me, I'd rather have my credit than all your cash. Who ever had to dun me twice? Forty years, boy and man, I spent as a slave, but no one could tell now whether I was slave or free. I was just a curly-headed kid when I came to this place. The town hall wasn't even built then. But I did everything I could to please my master. He was a good man, a real gentleman, whose fingernail was worth more than your whole carcass. And there were some in that house who would have liked to see me stumble. But thanks to my master I gave them the slip. Those are real trials, those are real triumphs. But when you're born free everything's as easy as saying, 'Hurry on down.' Well, what are you gaping at now, like a goat in vetch?"

At these last words, Giton, who was sitting at our feet, went rudely off into a great gale of whooping laughter which he had been trying to stifle for some time. Ascyltus' tormentor promptly trained his fire on the boy. "So you're snorting too, are you, you frizzle-headed scallion? You think it's time for capers, do you, carnival days and cold December? When did you pay your freedom tax, eh? Well, what are you smirking at, you little gallowsbird? Look, birdbait, I'll give it to you proper and the same for that master who won't keep you in line. May I never eat bread again, if I let you off for anyone except our host here; if it weren't for him, I'd fix you right now. We were all feeling good, nice happy party, and then those half-baked masters of yours let you cut out of line. Like master, like slave, I always say.

"Damnation, I'm so hopping mad, I can't stop. I'm no sorehead either, but when I let go, I don't give a damn for my own mother. Just you wait, I'll catch you out in the street someday. You mouse, you little potato! And when I do, if I don't knock your master into the cabbage patch, my name's not Hermeros. You can holler for Jupiter on Olympus as loud as you like, and it won't help you one little bit. By god, I'll fix those frizzle-curls of yours, and I'll fix your two-bit master too! You'll feel my teeth, sonny boy. And you won't snicker then, or I don't know who I am. No, not if your beard were made out of gold! By god, I'll give you Athena's own anger, and that goes for the blockhead who set you free! I never learned geometry or criticism or hogwash of that kind, but I know how to read words carved in stone and divide up to a hundred, money, measure, or weights. Come on, I'll lay you a little bet. I'll stake a piece of my silver set. You may have learned some rhetoric in school, but let me prove your daddy wasted his money educating you. Ready? Then answer me this: 'I come long and I come broad. What am I?' I'll give you a clue. One of us runs, the other stays put. One grows bigger; the other stays small. Well, that's you, skittering around, bustling and your elders and betters who don't know you exist. Or do you think I'm impressed by those phony gold rings of yours? Swipe them from your girl? Sweet Mercury, come down to the main square in town and try to take out a loan. Then you'll see this plain iron ring of mine makes plenty of credit. Hah, that finished you. You look like a fox in the rain. By god, if I don't pull up my toga and hound you all over town, may I fail in my business and die broke! So help me! And isn't he something, that professor who taught you your manners? Him a professor? A bum, that's what he is. In my time, a teacher was a teacher. Why, my old teacher used to say, 'Now, boys, is everything in order? Then go straight home. No dawdling, no gawking on the way. And don't be sassy to your elders.' But nowadays teachers are trash. Not worth a damn. As for me, I'm grateful to my old teacher for what he taught me . . ."

Ascyltus was on the point of replying, but Trimalchio, charmed by his friend's eloquence, broke in first: "Come on now. That's enough. No more hard feelings. I want everyone feeling good. As for you, Hermeros, don't be too hard on the boy. He's a little hotheaded, so show him you're made of better stuff. It's the man who gives in in arguments like this who wins every time. Besides, when you were just a little bantam strutting around the yard, you were all cockadoodledoo and no damn sense. So let bygones be bygones. Come on, everybody, smile! The rhapsodes are going to perform for us now."

Immediately a troupe of rhapsodes burst into the room, all banging away on their shields with spears. Trimalchio hoisted himself up on his pillows and while the rhapsodes were gushing out their Greek poetry with the usual bombast, he sat there reading aloud in Latin. At the end there was a brief silence; then Trimalchio asked us if we knew the scene from Homer the rhapsodes had just recited. "Well," he said, "I'll tell you. You see, there were these two brothers, Ganymede and Diomedes. Now they had this sister called Helen, see. Well, Agamemnon eloped with her and Diana left a deer as a fill-in for Helen. Now this poet called Homer describes the battle between the Trojans and the people of a place called Paros, which is where Paris came from. Well, as you'd expect, Agamemnon won and gave his daughter Iphigeneia to Achilles in marriage. And that's why Ajax went mad, but here he comes in person to explain the plot himself."

At this the rhapsodes burst into cheers, the slaves went scurrying about and promptly appeared with a barbecued calf on a huge platter— it must have weighed two hundred pounds at the very least. Behind it came Trimalchio's so-called Ajax. He pulled out his sword and began slashing away at the calf, sawing up and down, first with the edge and then with the flat of his blade. Then with the point of the sword he neatly skewered the slices of veal he had cut and handed them around to the astounded guests.

[*After more courses and more entertainment (including stories told about werewolves and witches), a late guest arrives. It is Habinnas, whose business is making tombstones and funeral monuments. He is quite drunk already, coming as he does from a funeral feast. He happens to be fond of Trimalchio's wife Fortunata and calls for her presence; when she comes in, she sits next to Habinnas' wife Scintilla, and the two ladies proceed to get tipsy. So does everyone else, and the slaves, invited by Trimalchio, crowd into the room and even, to the disgust of Encolpius the narrator, take up position on the couches. One of them, the cook, makes a bet with his master that the green team will win the chariot race in the Circus.*]

But Trimalchio was charmed by the challenge. "My friends," he brayed, "slaves are human too. They drink the same mother's milk that we do, though an evil fate grinds them down. But I swear that it won't be long—if nothing happens to me—before they all taste the good water of freedom. For I plan to free them all in my will. To Philargyrus here I leave a farm and his woman. Cario inherits a block of flats and the tax on his freedom and his bed and bedding. To my dear Fortunata I leave everything I have, and I commend her to the kindness of my friends. But I'm telling you the contents of my will so my whole household will love me as much when I'm still alive as after I'm dead."

Once the slaves heard this, of course, they burst out with cheers and effusive thanks. But Trimalchio suddenly began to take the whole farce quite seriously and ordered his will brought out and read aloud from beginning to end while the slaves sat there groaning and moaning. At the close of the reading, he turned to Habinnas. "Well, old friend, will you make me my tomb exactly as I order it? First, of course, I want a statue of myself. But carve my dog at my feet, and give me garlands of flowers, jars of perfume and every fight in Petraites' career. Then, thanks to your good offices, I'll live on long after I'm gone. . . . Around it I want an orchard with every known variety of fruit tree. You'd better throw in a vineyard too. For it's wrong, I think, that a man should concern himself with the house where he lives his life but give no thought to the home he'll have forever. But above all I want you to carve this notice:

THIS MONUMENT DOES NOT PASS INTO
THE POSSESSION OF MY HEIRS.

In any case I'll see to it in my will that my grave is protected from damage after my death. I'll appoint one of my ex-slaves to act as custodian to chase off the people who might come and crap on my tomb. Also, I want you to carve me several ships with all sail crowded and a picture of myself sitting on the judge's bench in official dress with five gold rings on my fingers and handing out a sack of coins to the people. For it's a fact, and you're my witness, that I gave a free meal to the whole town and a cash handout to everyone. Also make me a dining room, a frieze maybe, but however you like, and show the whole town celebrating at my expense. On my right I want a statue of Fortunata with a dove in her hand. And oh yes, be sure to have her pet dog tied to her girdle. And don't forget my pet slave. Also I'd like huge jars of wine, well stoppered so the wine won't slosh out. Then sculpt me a broken vase with a little boy sobbing out his heart over it. And in the middle stick a sundial so that anyone who wants the time of day will have to read my name. And how will this do for the epitaph?

HERE LIES GAIUS POMPEIUS TRIMALCHIO
MAECENATIANUS,
VOTED IN ABSENTIA AN OFFICIAL OF THE
IMPERIAL CULT.
HE COULD HAVE BEEN REGISTERED
IN ANY CATEGORY OF THE CIVIL SERVICE AT ROME
BUT CHOSE OTHERWISE.
PIOUS AND COURAGEOUS,

A LOYAL FRIEND,
HE DIED A MILLIONAIRE,
THOUGH HE STARTED LIFE WITH NOTHING.
LET IT BE SAID TO HIS ETERNAL CREDIT
THAT HE NEVER LISTENED TO PHILOSOPHERS.
PEACE TO HIM.
FAREWELL.

At the end he burst into tears. Then Fortunata started wailing, Habinnas began to cry, and every slave in the room burst out sobbing as though Trimalchio were dying then and there. The whole room throbbed and pulsed to the sound of mourning. I was almost in tears myself, when Trimalchio suddenly cried, "We all have to die, so let's live while we're waiting! Come on, everybody, smile, be happy. We'll all go down to the baths for a dip. The water's hot as an oven."

[*They all go off to the baths and are then ushered into a different dining room. Trimalchio sends the slaves off to eat and a new crew comes in to wait on table.*]

At this moment an incident occurred on which our little party almost foundered. Among the incoming slaves there was a remarkably pretty boy. Trimalchio literally launched himself upon him and, to Fortunata's extreme annoyance, began to cover him with rather prolonged kisses. Finally, Fortunata asserted her rights and began to abuse him. "You turd!" she shrieked, "you hunk of filth." At last she used the supreme insult: "Dog!" At this Trimalchio exploded with rage, reached for a wine cup and slammed it into her face. Fortunata let out a piercing scream and covered her face with trembling hands as though she'd just lost an eye. Scintilla, stunned and shocked, tried to comfort her sobbing friend in her arms, while a slave solicitously applied a glass of cold water to her livid cheek. Fortunata herself hunched over the glass heaving and sobbing.

But Trimalchio was still shaking with fury. "Doesn't that slut remember what she used to be? By god, I took her off the sale platform and made her an honest woman. But she blows herself up like a bullfrog. She's forgotten how lucky she is. She won't remember the whore she used to be. People in shacks shouldn't dream of palaces, I say. By god, if I don't tame that strutting Cassandra, my name isn't Trimalchio! And to think, sap that I was, that I could have married an heiress worth half a million. And that's no lie. Old Agatho, who sells perfume to the lady next door, slipped me the word: 'Don't let your line die out old boy,' he said. But not me. Oh no, I was a good little boy, nothing fickle about me. And now I've gone and slammed the axe into my shins good and proper.—But someday, slut, you'll come scratching at my grave to get me back! And just so you undertsand what you've done, I'll remove your statue from my tomb. That's an order, Habinnas. No sir, I don't want anymore domestic squabbles in my grave. And what's more, just to show her I can dish it out too, I won't have her kissing me or my deathbed."

After this last thunderbolt, Habinnas begged him to calm himself and forgive her. "None of us is perfect," he said, "we're men, not gods." Scintilla burst into tears, called him her dear dear Gaius and implored him by everything holy to forgive Fortunata. Finally, even Trimalchio began to blubber. "Habinnas," he whined, "as you hope to make a fortune, tell me the truth; if I've done anything wrong, spit right in my face. So I admit I kissed the boy, not because of his looks, but because he's a good boy, a thrifty boy, a boy of real character. He can divide up to ten, he reads at sight, he's saved his freedom price from his daily allowance and bought himself an armchair and two ladles out of his own pocket. Now doesn't a boy like that deserve his master's affection? But Fortunata says no.—Is that your idea, you high-stepping bitch? Take my advice, vulture, and keep your own nose clean. Don't make me show my teeth, sweetheart, or you'll feel my anger. You know me. Once I make up my mind, I'm as stubborn as a spike in wood.

"But the hell with her. Friends, make yourselves comfortable. Once I used to be like you, but I rose to the top by my ability. Guts are what make the man; the rest is garbage. I buy well, I sell well. Others have different notions. But I'm like to bust with good luck.—You slut, are you still blubbering? By god, I'll give you something to blubber about.

"But like I was saying, friends, it's through my business sense that I shot up. Why, when I came here from Asia, I stood no taller than that candlestick there. In fact, I used to measure myself by it every day; what's more, I used to rub my mouth with lamp oil to make my beard sprout faster. Didn't do a bit of good, though. For fourteen years I was my master's pet. But what's the shame in doing what you're told to do? But all the same, if you know what I mean, I managed to do my mistress a favor or two. But mum's the word: I'm none of your ordinary blowhards.

"Well, then heaven gave me a push and I became master in the house. I was my master's brains. So he made me joint heir with the emperor to everything he had, and I came out of it with a senator's fortune. But we never have enough, and I wanted to try my hand at business. To cut it short, I had five ships built. Then I stocked them with wine—worth its weight in gold at the time—and shipped them off to Rome. I might as well have told them to go sink themselves since that's what they did. Yup, all five of them wrecked. No kidding. In one day old Neptune swallowed down a cool million. Was I licked? Hell, no. That loss just whetted my appetite as though nothing had happened at all. So I built some more ships, bigger and better and a damn sight luckier. No one could say I didn't have guts. But big ships make a man feel big himself. I shipped a cargo of wine, bacon, beans, perfume and slaves. And then Fortunata came through nicely in the nick of time: sold her gold and the clothes off her back and put a hundred gold coins in the palm of my hand. That was the yeast of my wealth. Besides, when the gods want something done, it gets done in a jiffy. On that one voyage alone, I cleared about five hundred thousand. Right away I bought up all my old master's property. I built a house, I went into slave-trading and cattle-buying. Everything I touched just grew and grew like a honeycomb. Once I was worth more than all the people in my home town put together, I picked up my winnings and pulled out. I retired from trade and started lending money to ex-slaves. To tell the truth, I was tempted to quit for keeps, but on the advice of an astrologer who'd just come to town, I decided to keep my hand in. He was a Greek, fellow by the name of Serapa, and clever enough to set up as consultant to the gods. Well, he told me things I'd clean forgotten and laid it right on the line from A to Z. Why, that man could have peeked into my tummy and told me everything except what I'd eaten the day before. You'd have thought he'd lived with me all his life.

"Remember what he said, Habinnas? You were there, I think, when he told my fortune. 'You have bought yourself a mistress and a tyrant,' he said, 'out of your own profits. You are unlucky in your friends. No one is as grateful to you as he should be. You own vast estates. You nourish a viper in your bosom.' There's no reason why I shouldn't tell you, but according to him, I have thirty years, four months, and two days left to live. And soon, he said, I am going to receive an inheritance. Now if I could just add Apulia to the lands I own, I could die content.

"Meanwhile, with Mercury's help, I built this house. As you know, it used to be a shack; now it's a shrine. It has four dining rooms, twenty bedrooms, two marble porticoes, an upstairs dining room, the master bedroom where I sleep, the nest of that viper there, a fine porter's lodge, and guestrooms enough for all my guests. In fact, when Scaurus came down here from Rome, he wouldn't put up anywhere else, though his father has lots of friends down on the shore who would have been glad to have him. And there are lots of other things I'll show you in a bit. But take my word for it: money makes the man. No money and you're nobody. But big money, big man. That's how it was with yours truly: from mouse to millionaire.

"In the meantime, Stichus," he called to a slave, "go and fetch out the clothes I'm going to be buried in. And while you're at it, bring along some perfume and a sample of that wine I'm having poured on my bones."

Stichus hurried off and promptly returned with a white grave-garment and a very splendid robe with a broad purple stripe. Trimalchio told us to inspect them and see if we approved of the material. Then he added with a smile, "See to it, Stichus, that no mice or moths get into them, or I'll have you burned alive. Yes sir, I'm going to be buried in such splendor that everybody in town will go out and pray for me." He then unstoppered a jar of fabulously expensive spikenard and had us all anointed with it. "I hope," he chuckled, "I like this perfume as much after I'm dead as I do now." Finally he ordered the slaves to pour the wine into the bowl and said, "Imagine that you're all present at my funeral feast."

The whole business had by now become absolutely revolting. Trimalchio was obviously completely drunk, but suddenly he had a hankering for funeral music too and ordered a brass band sent into the dining room. Then he propped himself on piles of cushions and stretched out full length along the couch. "Pretend I'm dead," he said, "say something nice about me." The band blared a dead march, but one of the slaves belonging to Habinnas—who was, incidentally, one of the most respectable people present—blew so loudly that he woke up the entire neighborhood. Immediately the firemen assigned to that quarter of town, thinking that Trimalchio's house was on fire, smashed down the door and rushed in with buckets and axes to do their job. Utter confusion followed, of course, and we took advantage of the heaven-sent opportunity, gave Agamemnon the slip, and rushed out of there as though the place were really in flames.

Translated by William Arrowsmith

"DOING, A FILTHY PLEASURE IS, AND SHORT"

The expert parodies of contemporary poets which appear in the Satyricon *vouch for Petronius' skill as a poet, and the manuscripts have preserved for us a number of his own poems, among them this remarkable short lyric, here presented in a famous translation by Ben Jonson.*

Doing, a filthy pleasure is, and short;
And done, we straight repent us of the sport:
Let us not then rush blindly on unto it,
Like lustful beasts, that only know to do it:
For lust will languish, and that heat decay.
But thus, thus, keeping endless holiday,
Let us together closely lie and kiss,
There is no labour, nor no shame in this;
This hath pleas'd, doth please, and long will please; never
Can this decay, but is beginning ever.

Translated by Ben Jonson

JUVENAL
55?–138?

From SATIRE I

WHY SATIRE?

About the life of Decimus Junius Juvenalis we know very little. To judge from allusions in the poems, his sixteen Satires were published between about A.D. 110 and some time after 127, in the benevolent administrations of Trajan and Hadrian that followed the tyrannical regime of Domitian, who was assassinated in A.D. 96. In the First Satire, Juvenal announces his program: he intends to get his own back on all the poets who have bored him with their interminable epics and trite mythological allusions by writing poetry himself. After all, he has been to school, like them, and like them, has done his rhetorical exercises, such as recommending that the dictator Sulla (who had been dead for a very long time) should relinquish power and retire (which he did). But Juvenal is not going to write epics; he will follow the path of Lucilius, the first Roman satirist, and Horace, his successor. He goes on to explain his choice:

Rome being what it is, it is difficult not to write satire—difficile est
saturam non scribere.
   *At Caligula's "competitions" in public speaking, held at Lyon, those
who came in last, according to the report of Suetonius, had to erase their
entries with a sponge, or by licking it off the page with their tongues.
Locusta was a famous expert on poisons, who got rid of Claudius for
Agrippina and of Britannicus for Nero.*

Must I *always* be stuck in the audience at these poetry-readings, never
Up on the platform myself, taking it out on Cordus
For the times he's bored me to death with ranting speeches
From that *Theseid* of his? Is X to get off scot-free
After inflicting his farces on me, or Y his elegies? Is there
No recompense for whole days wasted on prolix
Versions of *Telephus?* And what about that *Orestes*—
Each margin of the roll crammed solid, top and bottom,
More on the back, and *still* it wasn't finished!
I know all the mythical landscapes like my own back-room:
The grove of Mars, that cave near Aeolus' island
Belonging to Vulcan. The stale themes are bellowed daily
In rich patrons' colonnades, till their marble pillars
Crack with a surfeit of rhetoric. The plane-trees echo
Every old trope—what the winds are up to, whose ghost
Aeacus has on his hellish rack, from what far country
The other fellow is sneaking off with that golden sheepskin,
The monstrous size of those ash-trees the Centaurs used for spears:
You get the same stuff from them all, established poet
And raw beginner alike. I too have winced under the cane
And concocted "Advice to Sulla": *Let the despot retire
Into private life, take a good long sleep,* and so on. When you find
Hordes of poets on each street-corner, it's misplaced kindness
To refrain from writing. The paper will still be wasted.
Why then have I chosen to drive my team down the track
Which great Lucilius blazed? If you have the leisure to listen
Calmly and reasonably, I will enlighten you.
When a flabby eunuch marries, when well-born girls go crazy
For pig-sticking up-country, bare-breasted, spear in fist;
When the barber who rasped away at my youthful beard has risen
To challenge good society with his millions; when Crispinus—
That Delta-bred house-slave, silt washed down by the Nile—
Now hitches his shoulders under Tyrian purple, airs

A thin gold ring in summer on his sweaty finger
("My dear, I couldn't *bear* to wear my *heavier* jewels")—
Why then, it is harder *not* to be writing satires; for who
Could endure this monstrous city, however callous at heart,
And swallow his wrath? Look: here comes a brand-new litter,
Crammed with its corpulent owner, some chiselling advocate.
Who's next? An informer. He turned in his noble patron,
And soon he'll have gnawed away that favourite bone of his,
The aristocracy. Lesser informers dread him, grease
His palm with ample bribes, while the wives of trembling actors
Grease him the other way. Today we are elbowed aside
By men who earn legacies in bed, who rise to the top
Via that quickest, most popular route—the satisfied desires
Of some rich old matron. Each lover will get his cut,
A twelfth share in the estate, or eleven-twelfths, depending
On the size of his—services rendered. I suppose he deserves
Some recompense for all that sweat and exertion: he looks
As pale as the man who steps barefoot on a snake—or is waiting
His turn to declaim, at Lyons, in Caligula's competitions.
    Need I tell you how anger burns in my heart when I see
The bystanders jostled back by a mob of bravos
Whose master has first debauched his ward, and later
Defrauded the boy as well? The courts condemned him,
But the verdict was a farce. Who cares for reputation
If he keeps his cash? A provincial governor, exiled
For extortion, boozes and feasts all day, basks cheerfully
In the wrathful eye of the Gods; it's still his province,
After winning the case against him, that feels the pinch.
    Are not such themes well worthy of Horace's pen? Should I
Not attack them too? Must I stick to the usual round
Of Hercules' labours, what Diomede did, the bellowing
Of that thingummy in the Labyrinth, or the tale of the flying
Carpenter, and how his son went splash in the sea?
Will *these* suffice in an age when each pimp of a husband
Takes gifts from his own wife's lover—if she is barred in law
From inheriting legacies—and, while they paw each other,
Tactfully stares at the ceiling, or snores, wide awake, in his wine?
Will *these* suffice, when the young blade who has squandered
His family fortune on racing-stables still reckons to get
Command of a cohort? Just watch him lash his horses
Down the Flaminian Way like Achilles' charioteer,
Reins bunched in one hand, showing off to his mistress

Who stands beside him, wrapped in his riding-cloak!
Don't you want to cram whole notebooks with scribbled invective
When you stand at the corner and see some forger carried past
On the necks of six porters, lounging back like Maecenas
In his open litter? A counterfeit seal, a will, a mere scrap
Of paper—these were enough to convert him to wealth and honour.
Do you see that distinguished lady? She has the perfect dose
For a thirsty husband—old wine with a dash of toad's blood.
Locusta's a child to her; she trains her untutored neighbours
To ignore all unkind rumours, to stalk through angry crowds
With their black and bloated husbands before them on the hearse.
If you want to be someone today you must nerve yourself
For deeds that could earn you an island exile, or years in gaol.
Honesty's praised, but honest men freeze. Wealth springs from crime:
Landscape-gardens, palaces, furniture, antique silver—
Those cups embossed with prancing goats—all, all are tainted.
Who can sleep easy today? If your greedy daughter-in-law
Is not being seduced for cash, it'll be your bride: mere schoolboys
Are adulterers now. Though talent be wanting, yet
Indignation will drive me to verse, such as I—or any scribbler—
May still command. All human endeavours, men's prayers,
Fears, angers, pleasures, joys and pursuits, these make
The mixed mash of my verse.

Translated by Peter Green

From SATIRE III

LIFE IN THE BIG CITY

*Juvenal's old friend Umbricius has finally decided to clear out of Rome
and settle at Cumae, where Aeneas went to consult the Sybil and where
Daedalus, the "inventor of wings," landed after his flight from Crete. It
is now an almost deserted site along the coast from the fashionable resort
of Baiae. The Capuan Gate of Rome, starting point for the journey
south, was under an aqueduct; it was on the site of the grove where
Numa, the second (mythical) king of Rome, was instructed in the law
(and according to Juvenal in other matters, too) by the nymph Egeria. It
now housed a settlement of Jewish refugees; after the suppression of the
Jewish revolt and the sack of Jerusalem in A.D. 70, Jews had migrated to*

many different parts of the Roman Empire. The "Sabbath haybox" kept food warm on a day cooking was forbidden; the Latin is ambiguous and has also been taken to mean "hay and a box"—the box to store food and the hay to sleep on. "Frog's guts" were used in magical charms and spells designed to harm enemies or business rivals. Verres was the infamous republican governor of Sicily whose large-scale extortion and theft was denounced by Cicero in a series of famous speeches.

The pissing contest mentioned at the end of the catalogue of Greek feats of flattery is our translator's reading of a puzzling couple of lines in the Latin original. Other solutions to the puzzle have been proposed. Though we cannot be certain about what Juvenal meant, Peter Green's suggestion has an unmistakably Juvenalian sound.

Tarsus, a city in Asia Minor (the birthplace, incidentally, of Saint Paul) was supposed to be named after a feather or a hoof (Greek tarsos) of Pegasus, the flying horse, born from the Gorgon, on which Bellerophon rode to kill the Chimaera. The Reserved Seat Act was the work of the tribune L. Roscius Otho, who in 67 B.C. had the first fourteen rows of seats in the theater reserved for members of the equestrian class, people whose assets were above a fixed high level. The rich man whose losses by fire were quickly made up by sympathetic friends was a bachelor; he had no wife or children to leave his wealth to—hence his popularity. Heavy daytime traffic in Rome was forbidden; it all had to roll at night, when the noise was enough to wake up even as sound a sleeper as the emperor Claudius, who often dozed off in the middle of the trial over which he was presiding.

Despite the wrench of parting, I applaud my old friend's
Decision to make his home in lonely Cumae—the poor
Sibyl will get at least one fellow-citizen now!
It's a charming coastal retreat, and just across the point
From our smartest watering-spot. Myself, I would value
A barren offshore island more than Rome's urban heart:
Squalor and isolation are minor evils compared
To this endless nightmare of fires and collapsing houses,
The cruel city's myriad perils—and poets reciting
Their work in *August!*
                    While his goods were being loaded
On one small waggon, my old friend lingered a while
By the ancient dripping arches of the Capuan Gate, where once
King Numa had nightly meetings with his mistress. (But today
Egeria's grove and shrine and sacred spring are rented

To Jewish squatters, their sole possession a Sabbath haybox.
Each tree must show a profit, the Muses have been evicted,
The wood's aswarm with beggars.)
                                 From here we strolled down
To the nymph's new, modernized grotto. (What a gain in sanctity
And atmosphere there would be if grassy banks
Surrounded the pool, if no flash marble affronted
Our native limestone!) Here Umbricius stood, and
Opened his heart to me.
                        "There's no room in this city,"
He said, "for the decent professions: they don't show any profit.
My resources have shrunk since yesterday, and tomorrow
Will eat away more of what's left. So I am going
Where Daedalus put off his weary wings, while as yet
I'm in vigorous middle age, while active years are left me,
While my white hairs are still few, and I need no stick
To guide my tottering feet. So farewell Rome, I leave you
To sanitary engineers and municipal architects, men
Who by swearing black is white land all the juicy contracts
Just like that—a new temple, swamp-drainage, harbour-works,
River-clearance, undertaking, the lot—then pocket the cash
And fraudulently file their petition in bankruptcy.
Once these fellows were horn-players, stumping the provinces
In road-shows, their puffed-out cheeks a familiar sight
To every country village. But now they stage shows themselves,
Of the gladiatorial sort, and at the mob's thumbs-down
Will butcher a loser for popularity's sake, and
Pass on from that to erecting public privies. Why not?
These are such men as Fortune, by way of a joke,
Will sometimes raise from the gutter and make Top People.
What can I do in Rome? I never learnt how
To lie. If a book is bad, I cannot puff it, or bother
To ask around for a copy; astrological clap-trap
Is not in my stars. I cannot and will not promise
To encompass any man's death by way of obliging his son.
I have never meddled with frogs' guts; the task of carrying
Letters and presents between adulterous lovers
I resign to those who know it. I refuse to become
An accomplice in theft—which means that no governor
Will accept me on his staff. It's like being a cripple
With a paralysed right hand. Yet who today is favoured
Above the conspirator, his head externally seething

With confidential matters, never to be revealed?
Harmless secrets carry no obligations, and he
Who shares them with you feels no great call thereafter
To keep you sweet. But if Verres promotes a man
You can safely assume that man has the screws on Verres
And could turn him in tomorrow. Not all the gold
Washed seaward with the silt of tree-lined Tagus
Is worth the price you pay, racked by insomnia, seeing
Your high-placed friends all cringe at your approach—and
For what? Too-transient prizes, unwillingly resigned.
   "Now let me turn to that race which goes down so well
With our millionaires, but remains *my* special pet aversion,
And not mince my words. I cannot, citizens, stomach
A Greek-struck Rome. Yet what fraction of these sweepings
Derives, in fact, from Greece? For years now Syrian
Orontes has poured its sewerage into our native Tiber—
Its lingo and manners, its flutes, its outlandish harps
With their transverse strings, its native tambourines,
And the whores who hang out round the race-course. (That's where
      to go
If you fancy a foreign piece in one of those saucy toques.)
Our beloved Founder should see how his homespun rustics
Behave today, with their dinner-pumps—*trechedipna*
They call them—not to mention their *niceteria*
(Decorations to you) hung round their *ceromatic* (that's
Well-greased) wrestlers' necks. Here's one from Sicyon,
Another from Macedonia, two from Aegean islands—
Andros, say, or Samos—two more from Caria,
All of them lighting out for the City's classiest districts
And burrowing into great houses, with a long-term plan
For taking them over. Quick wit, unlimited nerve, a gift
Of the gab that outsmarts a professional public speaker—
These are their characteristics. What do you take
That fellow's profession to be? He has brought a whole bundle
Of personalities with him—schoolmaster, rhetorician,
Surveyor, artist, masseur, diviner, tightrope-walker,
Magician or quack, your versatile hungry Greekling
Is all by turns. Tell him to fly—he's airborne.
The inventor of wings was no Moor or Slav, remember,
Or Thracian, but born in the very heart of Athens.
   "When such men as these wear the purple, when some creature
Blown into Rome along with the figs and damsons

Precedes me at dinner-parties, or for the witnessing
Of manumissions and wills—*me,* who drew my first breath
On these Roman hills, and was nourished on Sabine olives!—
Things have reached a pretty pass. What's more, their talent
For flattery is unmatched. They praise the conversation
Of their dimmest friends; the ugly they call handsome,
So that your scrag-necked weakling finds himself compared
To Hercules holding the giant Antaeus aloft
Way off the earth. They go into ecstasies over
Some shrill and scrannel voice that sounds like a hen
When the cock gets at her. We can make the same compliments, but
It's they who convince. On the stage they remain supreme
In female parts, courtesan, matron or slave-girl,
With no concealing cloak: you'd swear it was a genuine
Woman you saw, and not a masked performer.
Look there, beneath that belly: no bulge, all smooth, a neat
Nothingness—even a hint of the Great Divide. Yet back home
These queens and dames pass unnoticed. Greece is a nation
Of actors. Laugh, and they split their sides. At the sight
Of a friend's tears, they weep too—though quite unmoved.
If you ask for a fire in winter, the Greek puts on his cloak;
If you say 'I'm hot,' *he* starts sweating. So you see
We are not on an equal footing: he has the great advantage
Of being able on all occasions, night and day,
To take his cue, his mask, from others. He's always ready
To throw up his hands and applaud when a friend delivers
A really resounding belch, or pisses right on the mark,
With a splendid drumming sound from the upturned golden basin.
    "Besides, he holds nothing sacred, not a soul is safe
From his randy urges, the lady of the house, her
Virgin daughter, her daughter's still unbearded
Husband-to-be, her hitherto virtuous son—
And if none of these are to hand, he'll cheerfully lay
His best friend's grandmother. (Anything to ferret
Domestic secrets out, and get a hold over people.)
    "And while we are on the subject of Greeks, let us consider
Academics and their vices—not the gymnasium crowd
But big philosophical wheels, like that Stoic greybeard
Who narked on his friend and pupil, and got him liquidated.
He was brought up in Tarsus, by the banks of that river
Where Bellerophon fell to earth from the Gorgon's flying nag.
No room for honest Romans when Rome's ruled by a junta

Of Greek-born secret agents, who—like all their race—
Never share friends or patrons. One small dose of venom
(Half Greek, half personal) dropped in that ready ear
And I'm out, shown the back-door, my years of obsequious
Service all gone for nothing. Where can a hanger-on
Be ditched with less fuss than in Rome? Besides (not to flatter
    ourselves)
What use are our poor efforts, where does it all get us,
Dressing up while it's dark still, hurrying along
To pay our morning respects to a couple of wealthy
Maiden aunts? But the practor's really worked up, his
Colleague may get there before him, the ladies have been awake
For hours already, the minions catch it—'Get
A *move* on there, can't you?' Here a citizen, free-born,
Must stand aside on the pavement for some wealthy tycoon's slave:
He can afford to squander a senior officer's income
On classy amateur harlots, just for the privilege
Of laying them once or twice. But when *you* fancy
A common-or-garden tart, you dither and hesitate:
Can I afford to accost her? With witnesses in court
The same applies. Their morals may be beyond cavil, and yet
If Scipio took the stand (and he was selected
To escort the Mother Goddess on her journey to Rome) or Metellus
Who rescued Minerva's image from her blazing shrine, or even
King Numa himself, still the first and foremost question
Would be: 'What's he worth?' His character would command
Little if any respect. 'How many slaves does he keep?
What's his acreage? What sort of dinner-service
Appears on his table—how many pieces, how big?'
Each man's word is as good as his bond—or rather,
The number of bonds in his strong-box. A pauper can swear by every
Altar, and every god between Rome and Samothrace, still
(Though the gods themselves forgive him) he'll pass for a perjuror
Defying the wrath of heaven. The poor man's an eternal
Butt for bad jokes, with his torn and dirt-caked top-coat,
His grubby toga, one shoe agape where the leather's
Split—those clumsy patches, that coarse and tell-tale stitching
Only a day or two old. The hardest thing to bear
In poverty is the fact that it makes us ridiculous.
'Out of those front-row seats,' we're told. 'You ought to be
Ashamed of yourselves—your incomes are far too small, and
The law's the law. Make way for some pander's son,

Spawned in an unknown brothel, let your place be occupied
By that natty auctioneer's offspring, with his high-class companions
The trainer's brat and the son of the gladiator
Applauding beside him.' Such were the fruits of that pinhead
Otho's Reserved Seat Act. What prospective son-in-law
Ever passed muster here if he was short on cash
To match the girl's dowry? What poor man ever inherits
A legacy, or is granted that meanest of sinecures—
A job with the Office of Works? All lower-income citizens
Should have marched out of town, in a body, years ago.
Nobody finds it easy to get to the top if meagre
Resources cripple his talent. But in Rome the problem's worse
Than anywhere else. Inflation hits the rental
Of your miserable apartment, inflation distends
The ravenous maws of your slaves; your humble dinner
Suffers inflation too. You feel ashamed to eat
Off earthenware dishes—yet if you were transported
To some rural village, you'd be content enough
And happily wear a cloak of coarse blue broadcloth
Complete with hood. Throughout most of Italy—we
Might as well admit it—no one is seen in a toga
Till the day he dies. Even on public holidays,
When the same old shows as last year are cheerfully staged
In the grassgrown theatre, when peasant children, sitting
On their mothers' laps, shrink back in terror at the sight
Of those gaping, whitened masks, you will still find the whole
Audience—top row or bottom—dressed exactly alike;
Even the magistrates need no better badge of status
Than a plain white tunic. But here in Rome we must toe
The line of fashion, living beyond our means, and
Often on borrowed credit: every man jack of us
Is keeping up with his neighbours. To cut a long story short,
Nothing's for free in Rome. How much does it cost you
To salute our noble Cossus (rare privilege!) or extract
One casual, tight-lipped nod from Veiento the honours-broker?
X will be having his beard trimmed, Y just offering up
His boy-friend's kiss-curls: the whole house swarms with barbers,
Each of them on the make. You might as well swallow
Your bile, and face the fact that we hangers-on
Have to bribe our way, swell some sleek menial's savings.
    "What countryman ever bargained, besides, for his house collapsing

About his cars? Such things are unheard-of in cool
Praeneste, or rural Gabii, or Tivoli perched on its hillside,
Or Volsinii, nestling amid its woodland ridges. But here
We live in a city shored up, for the most part, with gimcrack
Stays and props: that's how our landlords arrest
The collapse of their property, papering over great cracks
In the ramshackle fabric, reassuring the tenants
They can sleep secure, when all the time the building
Is poised like a house of cards. I prefer to live where
Fires and midnight panics are not quite such common events.
By the time the smoke's got up to your third-floor apartment
(And you still asleep) your downstairs neighbour is roaring
For water, and shifting his bits and pieces to safety.
If the alarm goes at ground-level, the last to fry
Will be the attic tenant, way up among the nesting
Pigeons, with nothing but tiles between himself and the weather.
What did friend Cordus own? One truckle bed, too short
For even a midget nympho; one marble-topped sideboard
On which stood six little mugs; beneath it, a pitcher
And an up-ended bust of Chiron; one ancient settle
Crammed with Greek books (though by now analphabetic mice
Had gnawed their way well into his texts of the great poets).
Cordus could hardly be called a property-owner, and yet
What little the poor man had, he lost. Today the final
Straw on his load of woe (clothes worn to tatters, reduced
To begging for crusts) is that no one will offer him lodging
Or shelter, not even stand him a decent meal. But if
Some millionaire's mansion is gutted, women rend their garments,
Top people put on mourning, the courts go into recess:
Then you hear endless complaints about the hazards
Of city life, these deplorable outbreaks of fire;
Then contributions pour in while the shell is still ash-hot—
Construction materials, marble, fresh-gleaming sculptured nudes.
Up comes A with bronzes (genuine antique works
By a real Old Master) acquired, as part of his booty,
From their hallowed niche in some Asiatic temple;
B provides bookshelves, books, and a study bust of Minerva;
C a sackful of silver. So it goes on, until
This dandified bachelor's losses are all recouped—
And more than recouped—with even rarer possessions,
And a rumour (well-founded) begins to circulate

That he fired the place himself, a deliberate piece of arson.
"If you can face the prospect of no more public games
Purchase a freehold house in the country. What it will cost you
Is no more than you pay in annual rent for some shabby
And ill-lit garret here. A garden plot's thrown in
With the house itself, and a well with a shallow basin—
No rope-and-bucket work when your seedlings need some water!
Learn to enjoy hoeing, work and plant your allotment
Till a hundred vegetarians could feast off its produce.
It's quite an achievement, even out in the backwoods,
To have made yourself master of—well, say one lizard, even.
    "Insomnia causes more deaths amongst Roman invalids
Than any other factor (the most common *complaints*, of course,
Are heartburn and ulcers, brought on by over-eating.)
How much sleep, I ask you, can one get in lodgings here?
Unbroken nights—and this is the root of the trouble—
Are a rich man's privilege. The waggons thundering past
Through those narrow twisting streets, the oaths of draymen
Caught in a traffic-jam—these alone would suffice
To jolt the doziest sea-cow of an Emperor into
Permanent wakefulness. If a business appointment
Summons the tycoon, *he* gets there fast, by litter,
Tacking above the crowd. There's plenty of room inside:
He can read, or take notes, or snooze as he jogs along—
Those drawn blinds are most soporific. Even so
He outstrips us: however fast we pedestrians hurry
We're blocked by the crowds ahead, while those behind us
Tread on our heels. Sharp elbows buffet my ribs,
Poles poke into me; one lout swings a crossbeam
Down on my skull, another scores with a barrel.
My legs are mud-encrusted, big feet kick me, a hobnailed
Soldier's boot lands squarely on my toes. Do you see
All that steam and bustle? The great man's hangers-on
Are getting their free dinner, each with his own
Kitchen-boy in attendance. Those outsize dixies,
And all the rest of the gear one poor little slave
Must balance on his head, while he trots along
To keep the charcoal glowing, would tax the strength
Of a musclebound general. Recently-patched tunics
Are ripped to shreds. Here's the great trunk of a fir-tree
Swaying along on its waggon, and look, another dray

Behind it, stacked high with pine-logs, a nodding threat
Over the heads of the crowd. If that axle snapped, and a
Cartload of marble avalanched down on them, what
Would be left of their bodies? Who could identify bits
Of ownerless flesh and bone? The poor man's flattened corpse
Would vanish along with his soul. And meanwhile, all unwitting,
The folk at home are busily scouring dishes,
Blowing the fire to a glow, clattering over greasy
Flesh-scrapers, filling up oil-flasks, laying out clean towels.
But all the time, as his houseboys hasten about their chores,
Himself is already sitting—the latest arrival—
By the bank of the Styx, and gawping in holy terror
At its filthy old ferryman. No chance of a passage over
That mud-thick channel for him, poor devil, without so much
As a copper stuck in his mouth to pay for the ride.
    "There are other nocturnal perils, of various sorts,
Which you should consider. It's a long way up to the rooftops,
And a falling tile can brain you—not to mention all
Those cracked or leaky pots that people toss out through windows.
Look at the way they smash, the weight of them, the damage
They do to the pavement! You'll be thought most improvident,
A catastrophe-happy fool, if you don't make your will before
Venturing out to dinner. Each open upper casement
Along your route at night may prove a death-trap:
So pray and hope (poor you!) that the local housewives
Drop nothing worse on your head than a pailful of slops.
    "Then there's the drunken bully, in an agonized state
For lack of a victim, who lies there tossing and turning
The whole night through, like Achilles after the death
Of his boy-friend Patroclus. [This lout is doomed to insomnia
Unless he gets a fight.] Yet however flown with wine
Our young hothead may be, he carefully keeps his distance
From the man in a scarlet cloak, the man surrounded
By torches and big brass lamps and a numerous bodyguard.
But for me, a lonely pedestrian, trudging home by moonlight
Or with hand cupped round the wick of one poor guttering candle,
He has no respect whatever. This is the way the wretched
Brawl comes about (if you can term it a brawl
When you do the fighting and I'm just cast as punchbag).
He blocks my way. 'Stop,' he says. I have no option
But to obey—what else can one do when attacked

By a huge tough, twice one's size and fighting-mad as well?
    " 'Where have *you* sprung from?' he shouts. 'Ugh, what a stench
Of beans and sour wine! I know your sort, you've been round
With some cobbler-crony, scoffing a boiled sheep's head
And a dish of spring leeks. What? Nothing to say for yourself?
Speak up, or I'll kick your teeth in! Tell me, where's your pitch?
What synagogue do you doss in?' It makes not a jot of difference
Whether you try to answer, or back away from him
Without saying a word, you get beaten up just the same—
And then your irate 'victim' takes *you* to court on a charge
Of assault and battery. Such is the poor man's 'freedom':
After being slugged to a pulp, he may beg, as a special
Favour, to be left with his last few remaining teeth.
    "Nor is this the sum of your terrors: when every house
Is shut up for the night, when shops stand silent, when bolts
Are shot, and doors on the chain, there are still burglars
Lurking around, or maybe some street-apache will settle
Your hash with a knife, the quick way. (Whenever armed detachments
Are patrolling the swamps and forests, Rome becomes
A warren for this sort of scum.) Our furnaces glow, our anvils
Groan everywhere under their output of chains and fetters:
That's where most of our iron goes nowadays: one wonders
Whether ploughshares, hoes and mattocks may not soon be obsolete.
How fortunate they were (you well may think) those early
Forbears of ours, how happy the good old days
Of Kings and Tribunes, when Rome made do with one prison only!
'There are many other arguments I could adduce: but the sun
Slants down, my cattle are lowing, I must be on my way—
The muleteer has been signalling me with his whip
For some while now. So goodbye, and don't forget me—
Whenever you go back home for a break from the City, invite
Me over too, to share your fields and coverts,
Your country festivals: I'll put on my thickest boots
And make the trip to those chilly uplands—and listen
To your *Satires*, if I am reckoned worthy of that honour."

Translated by Peter Green

MARCUS AURELIUS
121–180
Emperor, 161–180

MEDITATIONS

Although Marcus Aurelius Antoninus was a Roman, and Latin was his native language, he was fluent in Greek (his tutor had been the famous Athenian littérateur Herodes Atticus), and when he came to write down his occasional philosophic meditations it was to the language of Plato, Aristotle, and his Stoic teachers that he turned. Meditations *is the English title of his book, but the Greek title in the manuscripts,* Pros Heauton, *means* To Himself, *which is an accurate description. This is a book of self-exhortation; when Marcus writes "you" he means himself. It is a remarkable document. The ruler of a world empire who had to deal not only with hard-fought campaigns on the threatened Balkan frontier but also with the ravages of a devastating plague here jots down his inmost thoughts as he steels himself for the daily struggle with the problems of a world in crisis.*

The opening extract in this selection is a tribute to his adoptive father, the emperor Antoninus Pius, who reigned from 138 to 161. It is a portrait of an ideal ruler, the model Marcus hoped to live up to.

From BOOK I

The qualities I admired in my father were his lenience, his firm refusal to be diverted from any decision he had deliberately reached, his complete indifference to meretricious honours; his industry, perseverance, and willingness to listen to any project for the common good; the unvarying insistence that rewards must depend on merit; the expert's sense of when to tighten the reins and when to relax them; and the efforts he made to suppress pederasty.

He was aware that social life must have its claims: his friends were under no obligation to join him at his table or attend his progresses, and when they were detained by other engagements it made no difference to him. Every question that came before him in council was painstakingly and patiently examined; he was never content to dismiss it on a cursory first impression. His friendships were enduring; they were not capricious, and they were not extravagant. He was always equal to an occasion; cheerful, yet long-sighted enough to have all his dispositions unobtrusively perfected down to the last detail. He had an ever-watchful eye to the needs of the Empire, prudently conserving its resources and putting up with the criticisms that resulted. Before his gods he was not superstitious; before his fellow-men he never stooped to bid for popularity or woo the masses, but pursued his own calm and steady way, disdaining anything that savoured of the flashy or new-fangled. He accepted without either complacency or compunction such material comforts as fortune had put at his disposal; when they were to hand he would avail himself of them frankly, but when they were not he had no regrets.

Not a vestige of the casuist's quibbling, the lackey's pertness, the pedant's over-scrupulosity could be charged against him; all men recognized in him a mature and finished personality, that was impervious to flattery and entirely capable of ruling both himself and others. Moreover, he had a high respect for all genuine philosophers; and though refraining from criticism of the rest, he preferred to dispense with their guidance. In society he was affable and gracious without being fulsome. The care he took of his body was reasonable; there was no solicitous anxiety to prolong its existence, or to embellish its appearance, yet he was far from unmindful of it, and indeed looked after himself so successfully that he was seldom in need of medical attention or physic or liniments. No hint of jealousy showed in his prompt recognition of outstanding abilities, whether in public speaking, law, ethics, or any other department, and he took pains to give each man the chance of earning a reputation in his own field. Though all his actions were guided by a respect for constitutional precedent, he would never go out of his way to court public recognition of this.

From BOOK II

1

Begin each day by telling yourself: Today I shall be meeting with interference, ingratitude, insolence, disloyalty, ill-will, and selfishness—all of them due to the offenders' ignorance of what is good or evil. But for my part I have long perceived the nature of good and its nobility, the nature of evil and its meanness, and also the nature of the culprit himself, who is my brother (not in the physical sense, but as a fellow-creature similarly endowed with reason and a share of the divine); therefore none of those things can injure me, for nobody can implicate me in what is degrading. Neither can I be angry with my brother or fall foul of him; for he and I were born to work together, like a man's two hands, feet, or eyelids, or like the upper and lower rows of his teeth. To obstruct each other is against Nature's law—and what is irritation or aversion but a form of obstruction?

2

In the life of a man, his time is but a moment, his being an incessant flux, his senses a dim rushlight, his body a prey of worms, his soul an unquiet eddy, his fortune dark, and his fame doubtful. In short, all that is of the body is as coursing waters, all that is of the soul as dreams and vapours; life a warfare, a brief sojourning in an alien land; and after repute, oblivion. Where, then, can man find the power to guide and guard his steps? In one thing and one alone: Philosophy. To be a philosopher is to keep unsullied and unscathed the divine spirit within him, so that it may transcend all pleasure and all pain, take nothing in hand without purpose and nothing falsely or with dissimulation, depend not on another's actions or inactions, accept each and every dispensation as coming from the same Source as itself—and last and chief, wait with a good grace for death, as no more than a simple dissolving of the elements whereof each living thing is composed. If those elements themselves take no harm from their ceaseless forming and re-forming, why look with mistrust upon the change and dissolution of the whole? It is but Nature's way; and in the ways of Nature there is no evil to be found.

From BOOK III

1

In your actions let there be a willing promptitude, yet a regard for the common interest; due deliberation, yet no irresolution; and in your sentiments no pretentious over-refinement. Avoid talkativeness, avoid officiousness. The god within you should preside over a being who is virile and mature, a statesman, a Roman, and a ruler; one who has held his ground, like a soldier waiting for the signal to retire from life's battlefield and ready to welcome his relief; a man whose credit need neither be sworn to by himself nor avouched by others. Therein is the secret of cheerfulness, of depending on no help from without and needing to crave from no man the boon of tranquillity. We have to stand upright ourselves, not be set up.

2

Mislead yourself no longer; you will never read these notebooks again now, nor the annals of bygone Romans and Greeks, nor that choice selection of writings you have put by for your old age. Press on, then, to the finish; cast away vain hopes; and if you have any regard at all for self, see to your own security while still you may.

From BOOK IV

Remind yourself constantly of all the physicians, now dead, who used to knit their brows over their ailing patients; of all the astrologers who so solemnly predicted their clients' doom; the philosophers who expatiated so endlessly on death or immortality; the great commanders who slew their thousands; the despots who wielded powers of life and death with such terrible arrogance, as if themselves were gods who could never die; the whole cities which have perished completely, Helice, Pompeii, Herculaneum, and others without number. After that, recall one by one each of your own acquaintances; how one buried another, only to be laid low himself and buried in turn by a third, and all in so brief a space of time. Observe, in short, how transient and trivial is all mortal life; yesterday a drop of semen, tomorrow a handful of spice or ashes. Spend, therefore, these fleeting moments on earth as Nature would have you spend them, and then go to your rest with a good grace, as an olive falls in its season, with a blessing for the earth that bore it and a thanksgiving to the tree that gave it life.

From BOOK V

1

You will never be remarkable for quick-wittedness. Be it so, then; yet there are still a host of other qualities whereof you cannot say, "I have no bent for them." Cultivate these, then, for they are wholly within your power: sincerity, for example, and dignity; industriousness, and sobriety. Avoid grumbling; be frugal, considerate, and frank; be temperate in manner and in speech; carry yourself with authority. See how many qualities there are which could be yours at this moment. You can allege no native incapacity or inaptitude for them; and yet you choose to linger still on a less lofty plane. Furthermore, is it any lack of natural endowments that necessitates those fits of querulousness and parsimony and fulsome flattery, of railing at your ill-health, of cringing and bragging and continually veering from one mood to another? Most assuredly not; you could have rid yourself of all these long ago, and remained chargeable with nothing worse than a certain slowness and dulness of comprehension—and even this you can correct with practice, so long as you do not make light of it or take pleasure in your own obtuseness.

2

The Athenians pray, "Rain, rain, dear Zeus, upon the fields and plains of Athens." Prayers should either not be offered at all, or else be as simple and ingenuous as this.

From BOOK VI

1

Either the world is a mere hotch-potch of random cohesions and dispersions, or else it is a unity of order and providence. If the former, why wish to survive in such a purposeless and chaotic confusion; why care about anything, save the manner of the ultimate return to dust; why trouble my head at all; since, do what I will, dispersion must overtake me sooner or later? But if the contrary be true, then I do reverence, I stand firmly, and I put my trust in the directing Power.

2

If you had a stepmother at the same time as a mother, you would do your duty by the former, but would still turn continually to your mother. Here, you have both: the court and philosophy. Time and again turn back to philosophy for refreshment; then even the court life, and yourself in it, will seem bearable.

From BOOK VII

An empty pageant; a stage play; flocks of sheep, herds of cattle; a tussle of spearmen; a bone flung among a pack of curs; a crumb tossed into a pond of fish; ants, loaded and labouring; mice, scared and scampering; puppets, jerking on their strings—that is life. In the midst of it all you must take your stand, good-temperedly and without disdain, yet always aware that a man's worth is no greater than the worth of his ambitions.

From BOOK X

1

Now your remaining years are few. Live them, then, as though on a mountain-top. Whether a man's lot be cast in this place or in that matters nothing, provided that in all places he views the world as a city and himself its citizen. Give men the chance to see and know a true man, living by Nature's law. If they cannot brook the sight, let them do away with him. Better so, than to live as they live.

2

Reflect often how all the life of today is a repetition of the past; and observe that it also presages what is to come. Review the many complete dramas and their settings, all so similar, which you have known in your own experience, or from bygone history: the whole court-circle of Hadrian, for example, or the court of Antonius, or the courts of Philip, Alexander, and Croesus. The performance is always the same; it is only the actors who change.

3

No man is so fortunate but that some who stand beside his death-bed will be hailing the coming loss with delight. He was virtuous, let us say, and wise; even so, will there not be one at the end who murmurs under his breath, "At last we can breathe freely again, without our master! To be sure, he was never harsh with any of us; but I always felt that he had a silent contempt for us"? Such is the fate of the virtuous; as for the rest of us, what a host of other good reasons there are to make not a few of our friends glad to be rid of us! Think of this when you come to die; it will ease your passing to reflect, "I am leaving a world in which the very companions I have so toiled for, prayed for and thought for, themselves wish me gone, and hope to win some relief thereby; then how can any man cling to a lengthening of his days therein?" Yet do not on that account leave with any diminished kindness for them; maintain your own accustomed friendliness, good-will, and charity; and do not feel the departure to be a wrench, but let your leave-taking be like those painless deaths in which the soul glides easily forth from the body. Before, Nature had joined you to these men and made you one with them; now she looses the tie. I am loosed, then, as from my own kinsfolk; yet all unresisting, and all unforced; it is simply one more of Nature's ways.

From BOOK XII

O man, citizenship of this great world-city has been yours. Whether for five years or fivescore, what is that to you? Whatever the law of that city decrees is fair to one and all alike. Wherein, then, is your grievance? You are not ejected from the city by any unjust judge or tyrant, but by the selfsame Nature which brought you into it; just as when an actor is dismissed by the manager who engaged him. "But I have played no more than three of the five acts." Just so; in your drama of life, three acts are all the play. Its point of completeness is determined by him who formerly sanctioned your creation, and today sanctions your dissolution. Neither of those decisions lay within yourself. Pass on your way, then, with a smiling face, under the smile of him who bids you go.

Translated by Maxwell Staniforth

AURELIUS AUGUSTINUS
(SAINT AUGUSTINE)
354–530

From CONFESSIONS

Unlike Marcus Aurelius, Augustine did not know Greek well (though he was much influenced by Greek Neoplatonic philosophy), but he is one of the masters of Latin prose. He was a prolific writer, an ecclesiastical controversialist on the grand scale (with ninety-three titles to his credit), and an eloquent upholder and mainstay of the authority of the hierarchy of the Church. His zeal was probably in part a form of compensation for the lateness of his conversion—he was thirty-three years old at the time.

In his Confessions *he tells the story of his long, wandering way to final acceptance of the Christian religion and the sacrifice priesthood in its Church would entail.*

CHILDHOOD

Augustine begins with a fascinating account of his childhood, a subject almost entirely ignored in other ancient writers. In the fifty biographies of great men, Greek and Roman, written by Plutarch, for example, there is hardly a mention of childhood; it is as if the ancient world thought of it as a sort of pre-human stage. For Augustine, however, the infant's exhibition of greed and jealousy is one more proof of the doctrine of Original Sin, a doctrine which he was to develop to the full and hand on to the Church of later ages.

. . . I do not know where I came from. But the consolations of your mercies (cf. Ps. 50: 3; 93: 19) upheld me, as I have heard from the parents of my flesh, him from whom and her in whom you formed me in time. For I do not remember. So I was welcomed by the consolations of human milk; but it was not my mother or my nurses who made any decision to fill their breasts, but you who through them gave me infant food, in accordance with your ordinance and the riches which are distributed deep in the natural order. You also granted me not to wish for more than you were giving, and to my nurses the desire to give me what you gave them. For by an impulse which you control their instinctive wish was to give me the milk which they had in abundance from you. For the good which came to me from them was a good for them; yet it was not from them but through them. Indeed all good things come from you, O God, and "from my God is all my salvation" (2 Sam. 23: 5). I became aware of this only later when you cried aloud to me through the gifts which you bestow both inwardly in mind and outwardly in body. For at that time I knew nothing more than how to suck and to be quietened by bodily delights, and to weep when I was physically uncomfortable.

Afterwards I began to smile, first in my sleep, then when awake. That at least is what I was told, and I believed it since that is what we see other infants doing. I do not actually remember what I then did.

Little by little I began to be aware where I was and wanted to manifest my wishes to those who could fulfil them as I could not. For my desires were internal; adults were external to me and had no means of entering into my soul. So I threw my limbs about and uttered sounds, signs resembling my wishes, the small number of signs of which I was capable but such signs as lay in my power to use: for there was no real resemblance. When I did not get my way, either because I was not understood or lest it be harmful to me, I used to be indignant with my seniors for their disobedience, and with free people who were not slaves to my interests; and I would revenge myself upon them by weeping. That this is the way of infants I have learnt from those I have been able to watch. That is what I was like myself and, although they have not been aware of it, they have taught me more than my nurses with all their knowledge of how I behaved.

Translated by Henry Chadwick

EDUCATION

Augustine also gives a lively account of his schooldays. Virgil's Aeneid *had become the classic text on which the young were reared; it was the base for rhetorical exercises, such as the prose paraphrase of a speech of Juno from Book I that Augustine was assigned as his task. Underlying Augustine's harsh criticism of the educational texts and methods is a disgust with its products, the professors of rhetoric and the lawyers and bureaucrats they had trained—a privileged class to which Augustine had aspired and in which he had risen high, only to abandon it and become first a priest and then a bishop of the Church. The "veils" or curtains that "hang at the entrances to the schools of literature" were, in the eyes of the world, a sign of professional prestige; but to Augustine they now seemed "the cover up of error."*

In his youth, however, he had despised useful accomplishments such as arithmetic and delighted in the sorrows of Dido, the Wooden Horse, and ipsius umbra Creusae—*the vision of Aeneas' wife Creusa. She had followed him as he carried his old father on his back, leading his little son by the hand, but was missing when he reached safety. As he rushed back to find her, she appeared to him as a shade, a ghost, to tell him that she must stay in Troy, detained by the goddess Cybele. Outside school Augustine seems to have been as capable of mischief as most schoolboys, but it is typical of the depths of his conviction of human sinfulness that he now sees the theft of some pears (and not very good pears at that) as "foul," as "wickedness," "self-destruction," the work of a "depraved soul."*

O God, my God, "what miseries I experienced" at this stage of my life, and what delusions when in my boyhood it was set before me as my moral duty in life to obey those who admonished me with the purpose that I should succeed in this world, and should excel in the arts of using my tongue to gain access to human honours and to acquire deceitful riches. I was next sent to school to learn to read and write. Poor wretch, I did not understand for what such knowledge is useful. Yet if ever I was indolent in learning, I was beaten. This method was approved by adults, and many people living long before me had constructed the laborious courses which we were compelled to follow by an increase of the toil and sorrow (Gen. 3: 16) of Adam's children. We found however, Lord, people who prayed to you and from them we learnt to think of you, in our limited way, as some large being with the power, even when not present to our senses, of hearing us and helping us. As a boy I began to pray to you, "my help and my refuge" (Ps. 93: 22), and for my prayer to you I broke the bonds of my tongue. Though I was only a small child, there was great feeling when I pleaded with you that I might not be caned at school. And when you did not hear me, which was so as "not to give me to foolishness", (Ps. 21: 3), adult people, including even my parents, who wished no evil to come upon me, used to laugh at my stripes, which were at that time a great and painful evil to me.

Lord, is there anyone, any mind so great, united to you by a strong love—is there, I say, anyone (as with the character produced by a certain stolidity)—is there a man who is so devotedly united to you with mighty affection that he holds of small account racks and hooks and various torments of this brutal nature, which in all countries people with great terror pray you they may escape, and yet loves those who are utterly terrified of them? Is this comparable to the way our parents laughed at the torments which our teachers inflicted on us as boys? We at least were no less scared and prayed no less passionately to escape them. Yet we were at fault in paying less attention than was required of us to writing or reading or using our minds about our books. Not, Lord, that there was a deficiency in memory or intelligence. It was your will to endow us sufficiently with the level appropriate to our age. But we loved to play, and punishments were imposed on us by those who were engaged in adult games. For "the amusement of adults is called business." But when boys play such games they are punished by adults, and no one feels sorry either for the children or for the adults or indeed for both of them. Perhaps some refined arbiter of things might approve of my being beaten. As a boy I played ball-games, and that play slowed down the speed at which I learnt letters with which, as an adult, I might play a less creditable game. The schoolmaster who caned me was behaving no bet-

ter than I when, after being refuted by a fellow-teacher in some pedantic
question, he was more tormented by jealousy and envy than I when my
opponent overcame me in a ball-game.

* * *

Even during boyhood when there was less reason to fear than during
adolescence, I had no love for reading books and hated being forced to
study them. Yet pressure was put on me and was good for me. It was not
of my own inclination that I did well, for I learnt nothing unless compelled. No one is doing right if he is acting against his will, even when
what he is doing is good. Those who put compulsion on me were not
doing right either; the good was done to me by you, my God. They gave
no consideration to the use that I might make of the things they forced
me to learn. The objective they had in view was merely to satisfy the
appetite for wealth and for glory, though the appetite is insatiable, the
wealth is in reality destitution of spirit, and the glory something to be
ashamed of. But you, by whom "the hairs of our head are numbered"
(Matt. 10: 30), used the error of all who pressed me to learn to turn out
to my advantage. And my reluctance to learn you used for a punishment
which I well deserved: so tiny a child, so great a sinner. So by making use
of those who were failing to do anything morally right you did good to
me, and from me in my sin you exacted a just retribution. For you have
imposed order, and so it is that the punishment of every disordered mind
is its own disorder.

Even now I have not yet discovered the reasons why I hated Greek
literature when I was being taught it as a small boy. Latin I deeply loved,
not at the stage of my primary teachers but at the secondary level taught
by the teachers of literature called "grammarians" *(grammatici)*. The
initial elements, where one learns the three Rs of reading, writing, and
arithmetic, I felt to be no less a burden and an infliction than the entire
series of Greek classes. The root of this aversion must simply have been
sin and the vanity of life, by which I was "mere flesh and wind going on
its way and not returning" (Ps. 77: 39). Of course, those first elements of
the language were better, because more fundamental. On that foundation I came to acquire the faculty which I had and still possess of being
able to read whatever I find written, and to write myself whatever I wish.
This was better than the poetry I was later forced to learn about the
wanderings of some legendary fellow named Aeneas (forgetful of my
own wanderings) and to weep over the death of a Dido who took her
own life from love. In reading this, O God my life, I myself was meanwhile dying by my alienation from you, and my miserable condition in
that respect brought no tear to my eyes.

What is more pitiable than a wretch without pity for himself who weeps over the death of Dido dying for love of Aeneas, but not weeping over himself dying for his lack of love for you, my God, light of my heart, bread of the inner mouth of my soul, the power which begets life in my mind and in the innermost recesses of my thinking. I had no love for you and "committed fornication against you" (Ps. 72: 27); and in my fornications I heard all round me the cries "Well done, well done" (Ps. 34: 21; 39: 16). "For the friendship of this world is fornication aagainst you" (Jas. 4: 4), and "Well done" is what they say to shame a man who does not go along with them. Over this I wept not a tear. I wept over Dido who "died in pursuing her ultimate end with a sword." I abandoned you to pursue the lowest things of your creation. I was dust going to dust. Had I been forbidden to read this story, I would have been sad that I could not read what made me sad. Such madness is considered a higher and more fruitful literary education than being taught to read and write.

"But now may my God cry out in my soul and may your truth tell me: "It is not so, it is not so. The best education you received was the primary." Obviously I much prefer to forget the wanderings of Aeneas and all that stuff than to write and read. It is true, veils hang at the entrances to the schools of literature; but they do not signify the prestige of élite teaching so much as the covering up of error.

Let no critics shout against me (I am not afraid of them now) while I confess to you the longing of my soul, my God, and when I accept rebuke for my evil ways and wish to love your good ways (Ps. 118: 101). Let there be no abuse of me from people who sell or buy a literary education. If I put the question to them whether the poet's story is true that Aeneas once came to Carthage, the uneducated will reply that they do not know, while the educated will say it is false. But if I ask with what letters Aeneas' name is spelled, all who have learnt to read will reply correctly in accordance with the agreement and convention by which human beings have determined the value of these signs. Similarly, if I ask which would cause the greater inconvenience to someone's life, to forget how to read and write or to forget these fabulous poems, who does not see what answer he would give, unless he has totally lost his senses? So it was a sin in me as a boy when I gave pride of place in my affection to those empty fables rather than to more useful studies, or rather when I hated the one and loved the other. But to me it was a hateful chant to recite "one and one is two," and "two and two are four"; delightful was the vain spectacle of the wooden horse full of armed soldiers and the burning of Troy and the very ghost of Creusa.

Why then did I hate Greek which has similar songs to sing? Homer was skilled at weaving such stories, and with sheer delight mixed vanity. Yet to me as a boy he was repellent. I can well believe that Greek boys feel the same about Virgil when they are forced to learn him in the way that I learnt Homer. The difficulty lies there: the difficulty of learning a foreign language at all. It sprinkles gall, as it were, over all the charm of the stories the Greeks tell. I did not know any of the words, and violent pressure on me to learn them was imposed by means of fearful and cruel punishments. At one time in my infancy I also knew no Latin, and yet by listening I learnt it with no fear or pain at all, from my nurses caressing me, from people laughing over jokes, and from those who played games and were enjoying them. I learnt Latin without the threat of punishment from anyone forcing me to learn it. My own heart constrained me to bring its concepts to birth, which I could not have done unless I had learnt some words, not from formal teaching but by listening to people talking; and they in turn were the audience for my thoughts. This experience sufficiently illuminates the truth that free curiosity has greater power to stimulate learning than rigorous coercion. Nevertheless, the free-ranging flux of curiosity is channelled by discipline under your laws, God. By your laws we are disciplined, from the canes of schoolmasters to the ordeals of martyrs. Your laws have the power to temper bitter experiences in a constructive way, recalling us to yourself from the pestilential life of easy comforts which have taken us away from you.

* * *

Let me, my God, say something also about the intelligence which was your gift to me, and the ways in which I wasted it on follies. A task was set me which caused me deep psychological anxiety. The reward was praise but I feared shame and blows if I did badly. I was to recite the speech of Juno in her anger and grief that she "could not keep the Trojan king out of Italy." I had understood that Juno never said this. But we were compelled to follow in our wanderings the paths set by poetic fictions, and to express in plain prose the sense which the poet had put in verse. The speaker who received highest praise was the one who had regard to the dignity of the imaginary characters, who most effectively expressed feelings of anger and sorrow, and who clothed these thoughts in appropriate language.

What could all this matter to me, true life, my God? What importance could it have for me that my recitation was acclaimed beyond many other readers of my age group? Was not the whole exercise mere smoke and wind? Was there no other subject on which my talent and tongue might be exercised? Your praises, Lord, your praises expressed through your scriptures would have upheld the tender vine of my heart, and it would not have been snatched away by empty trifles to become "a shameful prey for the birds." There is more than one way of offering sacrifice to the fallen angels.

SIN

I intend to remind myself of my past foulnesses and carnal corruptions, not because I love them but so that I may love you, my God. It is from love of your love that I make the act of recollection. The recalling of my wicked ways is bitter in my memory, but I do it so that you may be sweet to me, a sweetness touched by no deception, a sweetness serene and content. You gathered me together from the state of disintegration in which I had been fruitlessly divided. I turned from unity in you to be lost in multiplicity.

At one time in adolescence I was burning to find satisfaction in hellish pleasures. I ran wild in the shadowy jungle of erotic adventures. "My beauty wasted away and in your sight I became putrid" (Dan. 10: 8), by pleasing myself and by being ambitious to win human approval.

"The single desire that dominated my search for delight was simply to love and to be loved. But no restraint was imposed by the exchange of mind with mind, which marks the brightly lit pathway of friendship. Clouds of muddy carnal concupiscence filled the air. The bubbling impulses of puberty befogged and obscured my heart so that it could not see the difference between love's serenity and lust's darkness. Confusion of the two things boiled within me. It seized hold of my youthful weakness sweeping me through the precipitous rocks of desire to submerge me in a whirlpool of vice. Your wrath was heavy upon me and I was unaware of it. I had become deafened by the clanking chain of my mortal condition, the penalty of my pride. I travelled very far from you, and you did not stop me. I was tossed about and spilt, scattered and boiled dry in my fornications. And you were silent. How slow I was to find my joy! At that time you said nothing, and I travelled much further away from you into more and more sterile things productive of unhappiness, proud in my self-pity, incapable of rest in my exhaustion.

Where was I in the sixteenth year of the age of my flesh? "Far away in exile from the pleasures of your house" (Mic. 2: 9). Sensual folly assumed domination over me, and I gave myself totally to it in acts allowed by shameful humanity but under your laws illicit. My family did not try to extricate me from my headlong course by means of marriage. The only concern was that I should learn to speak as effectively as possible and carry conviction by my oratory.

* * *

Theft receives certain punishment by your law (Exod. 20: 15), Lord, and by the law written in the hearts of men (Rom. 2: 14) which not even iniquity itself destroys. For what thief can with equanimity endure being robbed by another thief? He cannot tolerate it even if he is rich and the other is destitute. I wanted to carry out an act of theft and did so, driven by no kind of need other than my inner lack of any sense of, or feeling for, justice. Wickedness filled me. I stole something which I had in plenty and of much better quality. My desire was to enjoy not what I sought by stealing but merely the excitement of thieving and the doing of what was wrong. There was a pear tree near our vineyard laden with fruit, though attractive in neither colour nor taste. To shake the fruit off the tree and carry off the pears, I and a gang of naughty adolescents set off late at night after (in our usual pestilential way) we had continued our game in the streets. We carried off a huge load of pears. But they were not for our feasts but merely to throw to the pigs. Even if we ate a few, nevertheless our pleasure lay in doing what was not allowed.

Such was my heart, O God, such was my heart. You had pity on it when it was at the bottom of the abyss. Now let my heart tell you what it was seeking there in that I became evil for no reason. I had no motive for my wickedness except wickedness itself. It was foul, and I loved it. I loved the self-destruction, I loved my fall, not the object for which I had fallen but my fall itself. My depraved soul leaped down from your firmament to ruin. I was seeking not to gain anything by shameful means, but shame for its own sake.

Translated by Henry Chadwick

CARTHAGE

Augustine left his home town Thagaste for Carthage, the capital of the province, to continue his studies on a higher level and eventually to teach. He remained there from his nineteenth to his twentieth year, winning a reputation as a teacher, enjoying the life of the capital, especially the theater, and settling into a regular liaison with a woman.

The Hortensius, *the Ciceronian work that set him on the philosophical quest for understanding that led him to Neoplatonist philosophy and, eventually, to acceptance of Christianity, has not survived. His road to that end was long and erratic. While at Carthage he became a member of a sect of ascetic mystics, the Manichees, who recognized the divinity of Christ but also accepted the claim of Mani, a third-century Babylonian prophet, that he was the Paraclete, the Comforter whom Christ promised his Disciples he would send them (John 14:16). Their congregation consisted of the Elect, who were denied occupation or possessions, but who were destined to escape transmigration of their souls, and the lower order of Hearers, to which Augustine belonged for nine years.*

I came to Carthage and all around me hissed a cauldron of illicit loves. As yet I had never been in love and I longed to love; and from a subconscious poverty of mind I hated the thought of being less inwardly destitute. I sought an object for my love; I was in love with love, and I hated safety and a path free of snares (Wisd. 14: 11; Ps. 90: 3). My hunger was internal, deprived of inward food, that is of you yourself, my God. But that was not the kind of hunger I felt. I was without any desire for incorruptible nourishment, not because I was replete with it, but the emptier I was, the more unappetizing such food became. So my soul was in rotten health. In an ulcerous condition it thrust itself to outward things, miserably avid to be scratched by contact with the world of the senses. Yet physical things had no soul. Love lay outside their range. To me it was sweet to love and to be loved, the more so if I could also enjoy the body of the beloved. I therefore polluted the spring water of friendship with the filth of concupiscence. I muddied its clear stream by the hell of lust, and yet, though foul and immoral, in my excessive vanity, I used to carry on in the manner of an elegant man about town. I rushed headlong into love, by which I was longing to be captured. "My God, my mercy" (Ps. 58: 18) in your goodness you mixed in much vinegar with that sweetness. My love was returned and in secret I attained the joy that enchains. I was glad to be in bondage, tied with troublesome chains, with the result that I was flogged with the red-hot iron rods of jealousy, suspicion, fear, anger, and contention.

I was captivated by theatrical shows. They were full of representations of my own miseries and fuelled my fire. Why is it that a person should wish to experience suffering by watching grievous and tragic events which he himself would not wish to endure? Nevertheless he wants to suffer the pain given by being a spectator of these sufferings, and the pain itself is his pleasure. What is this but amazing folly? For the more anyone is moved by these scenes, the less free he is from similar passions. Only, when he himself suffers, it is called misery; when he feels compassion for others, it is called mercy. But what quality of mercy is it in fictitious and theatrical inventions? A member of the audience is not excited to offer help, but invited only to grieve. The greater his pain, the greater his approval of the actor in these representations. If the human calamities, whether in ancient histories or fictitious myths, are so presented that the theatregoer is not caused pain, he walks out of the theatre disgusted and highly critical. But if he feels pain, he stays riveted in his seat enjoying himself.

* * *

My studies which were deemed respectable had the objective of leading me to distinction as an advocate in the lawcourts, where one's reputation is high in proportion to one's success in deceiving people. The blindness of humanity is so great that people are actually proud of their blindness. I was already top of the class in the rhetor's school, and was pleased with myself for my success and was inflated with conceit. Yet I was far quieter than the other students (as you know, Lord), and had nothing whatever to do with the vandalism which used to be carried out by the Wreckers. This sinister and diabolical self-designation was a kind of mark of their urbane sophistication. I lived among them shamelessly ashamed of not being one of the gang. I kept company with them and sometimes delighted in their friendship, though I always held their actions in abhorrence. The Wreckers used wantonly to persecute shy and unknown freshmen. Their aim was to persecute them by mockery and so to feed their own malevolent amusement. Nothing more resembles the behaviour of devils than their manner of carrying on. So no truer name could be given them than the Wreckers. Clearly they are themselves wrecked first of all and perverted by evil spirits, who are mocking them and seducing them in the very acts by which they love to mock and deceive others.

This was the society in which at a vulnerable age I was to study the textbooks on eloquence. I wanted to distinguish myself as an orator for a damnable and conceited purpose, namely delight in human vanity. Following the usual curriculum I had already come across a book by a certain Cicero, whose language (but not his heart) almost everyone admires. That book of his contains an exhortation to study philosophy and is entitled *Hortensius*. The book changed my feelings. It altered my prayers, Lord, to be towards you yourself. It gave me different values and priorities. Suddenly every vain hope became empty to me, and I longed for the immortality of wisdom with an incredible ardour in my heart. I began to rise up to return to you. For I did not read the book for a sharpening of my style, which was what I was buying with my mother's financial support now that I was 18 years old and my father had been dead for two years. I was impressed not by the book's refining effect on my style and literary expression but by the content.

During this same period of nine years, from my nineteenth to my twenty-eighth year, our life was one of being seduced and seducing, being deceived and deceiving (2 Tim. 3: 13), in a variety of desires. Publicly I was a teacher of the arts which they call liberal; privately I professed a false religion—in the former role arrogant, in the latter superstitious, in everything vain. On the one side we pursued the empty glory of popularity, ambitious for the applause of the audience at the theatre when entering for verse competitions to win a garland of mere grass, concerned with the follies of public entertainments and unrestrained lusts. On the other side, we sought to purge ourselves of that filth by supplying food to those whose title was the Elect and Holy, so that in the workshop of their stomach they could manufacture for us angels and gods to bring us liberation. This was how my life was spent, and these were the activities of myself and my friends who had been deceived through me and with me.

* * *

In those years I had a woman. She was not my partner in what is called lawful marriage. I had found her in my state of wandering desire and lack of prudence. Nevertheless, she was the only girl for me, and I was faithful to her. With her I learnt by direct experience how wide a difference there is between the partnership of marriage entered into for the sake of having a family and the mutual consent of those whose love is a matter of physical sex, and for whom the birth of a child is contrary to their intention—even though, if offspring arrive, they compel their parents to love them.

Translated by Henry Chadwick

ROME

From Carthage, Augustine went to Rome, hoping to find a less rowdy student body than he had to deal with in Carthage. His mother Monica, who was a devout Christian and hoped always to see her son regain his childhood faith, was opposed to the move, and Augustine had to deceive her in order to get away. But the students in Rome proved as bad as, if not worse than, those in Carthage. Augustine accepted a call to Milan, which by this time, because it was closer to the frontiers and the lateral lines of communication of the empire, was the seat of the imperial administration in the West.

You were at work in persuading me to go to Rome and to do my teaching there rather than at Carthage. The consideration which persuaded me I will not omit to confess to you because in this also your profoundly mysterious providence and your mercy very present to us are proper matters for reflection and proclamation. My motive in going to Rome was not that the friends who urged it on me promised higher fees and a greater position of dignity, though at that time these considerations had an influence on my mind. The principal and almost sole reason was that I had heard how at Rome the young men went quietly about their studies and were kept in order by a stricter imposition of discipline.

They did not rush all at once and in a mob into the class of a teacher with whom they were not enrolled, nor were pupils admitted at all unless the teacher gave them leave. By contrast at Carthage the licence of the students is foul and uncontrolled. They impudently break in and with almost mad behaviour disrupt the order which each teacher has established for his pupils' benefit. They commit many acts of vandalism with an astonishing mindlessness, which would be punished under the law were it not that custom protects them. Thereby their wretched self-delusion is shown up. They act as if they were allowed to do what would never be permitted by your eternal law. They think they are free to act with impunity when by the very blindness of their behaviour they are being punished, and inflict on themselves incomparably worse damage than on others. When I was a student, I refused to have anything to do with these customs; as a professor I was forced to tolerate them in outsiders who were not my own pupils. So I decided to go where all informed people declared that such troubles did not occur. But it was you, "my hope and my portion in the land of the living" (Ps. 141: 6) who wished me to change my earthly home for "the salvation of my soul" (Ps. 34: 3). You applied the pricks which made me tear myself away from Carthage, and you put before me the attractions of Rome to draw me there, using people who love a life of death, committing insane actions in this world, promising vain rewards in the next. To correct my "steps" (Ps. 36: 23; Prov. 20: 20) you secretly made use of their and my perversity. For those who disturbed my serenity were blinded with a disgraceful frenzy. Those who invited me to go elsewhere had a taste only for this earth. I myself, while I hated a true misery here, pursued a false felicity there.

But you knew, God, why I left Carthage and went to Rome, and of that you gave no hint either to me or to my mother, who was fearfully upset at my going and followed me down to the sea. But as she vehemently held on to me calling me back or saying she would come with me, I deceived her. I pretended I had a friend I did not want to leave until the wind was right for him to sail. I lied to my mother—to such a mother—and I gave her the slip. Even this you forgave me, mercifully saving me from the waters of the sea, when I was full of abominable filth, so as to bring me to the water of your grace [in baptism]. This water was to wash me clean, and to dry the rivers flowing from my mother's eyes which daily before you irrigated the soil beneath her face.

Nevertheless since she refused to return home without me, with difficulty I persuaded her to stay that night in a place close to our ship, the memorial shrine to blessed Cyprian. But that night I secretly set out; she did not come, but remained praying and weeping. By her floods of tears what was she begging of you, my God, but that you would not allow me to sail? Yet in your deep counsel you heard the central point of her longing, though not granting her what she then asked, namely that you would make me what she continually prayed for. The wind blew and filled our sails and the shore was lost to our sight. There, when morning came, she was crazed with grief, and with recriminations and groans she filled your ears. But you paid no heed to her cries. You were using my ambitious desires as a means towards putting an end to those desires, and the longing she felt for her own flesh and blood was justly chastised by the whip of sorrows. As mothers do, she loved to have me with her, but much more than most mothers; and she did not undertsand that you were to use my absence as a means of bringing her joy. She did not know that. So she wept and lamented, and these agonies proved that there survived in her the remnants of Eve, seeking with groaning for the child she had brought forth in sorrow (Gen. 3: 16). And yet after accusing me of deception and cruelty, she turned again to pray for me and to go back to her usual home. Meanwhile I came to Rome.

You had not yet "put a guard on my mouth and a gate of continence about my lips" (Ps. 140: 2) to prevent my heart slipping into evil words to find excuses for sinning with "people who do iniquity" (Ps. 140: 3). That is why I was still in close association "with their Elect" (Ps. 140: 4), even though I had already lost hope of being able to advance higher in that false doctrine. I had decided to be content to remain with them if I should find nothing better; but my attitude was increasingly remiss and negligent.

The thought had come into my mind that the philosophers whom they call Academics were shrewder than others. They taught that everything is a matter of doubt, and that an understanding of the truth lies beyond human capacity. For to me that seemed clearly to be their view, and so they are popularly held to think. I did not yet understand their intention.

I did not neglect to tell my host that he should not put the excessive trust, which I perceived him to have, in the fabulous matters of which Manichee books are full. But I was in more intimate friendship with them than with others who were not in that heresy. I did not defend it with the zest that at one time I had. Nevertheless my close association with them (the number of them secretly living in Rome was large) made me reluctant to look elsewhere. In particular I had no hope that truth could be found in your Church, Lord of heaven and earth (Gen. 24: 3), maker of all things visible and invisible (Col. 1: 16).

* * *

I began to be busy about the task of teaching the art of rhetoric for which I had come to Rome. I first gathered some pupils at my lodging, and with them and through them I began to be known. I quickly discovered that at Rome students behaved in a way which I would never have had to endure in Africa. Acts of vandalism, it was true, by young hooligans did not occur at Rome; that was made clear to me. But, people told me, to avoid paying the teacher his fee, numbers of young men would suddenly club together and transfer themselves to another tutor, breaking their word and out of love of money treating fairness as something to be flouted.

Translated by Henry Chadwick

MILAN

In Milan, Augustine came under the influence of Ambrose, the bishop of Milan, and by the time his mother came to join him had finally broken completely with the Manichees, although he was not yet ready to accept baptism and join the Church. His mother arranged a marriage for him, hoping that the break with his longtime mistress (who was the mother of his son) might bring about his conversion; he complied, and sent his mistress away.

So after a notification came from Milan to Rome to the city prefect saying that at Milan a teacher of rhetoric was to be appointed with his travel provided by the government service, I myself applied through the mediation of those intoxicated with Manichee follies. My move there was to end my association with them, but neither of us knew that. An oration I gave on a prescribed topic was approved by the then prefect Symmachus, who sent me to Milan.

And so I came to Milan to Ambrose the bishop, known throughout the world as among the best of men, devout in your worship. At that time his eloquence valiantly ministered to your people "the abundance of your sustenance" and "the gladness of oil" (Ps. 44: 8; 80: 17; 147: 14), and the sober intoxication of your wine. I was led to him by you, unaware that through him, in full awareness, I might be led to you. That "man of God" (2 Kgs. 1: 9) received me like a father and expressed pleasure at my coming with a kindness most fitting in a bishop. I began to like him, at first indeed not as a teacher of the truth, for I had absolutely no confidence in your Church, but as a human being who was kind to me. I used enthusiastically to listen to him preaching to the people, not with the intention which I ought to have had, but as if testing out his oratorical skill to see whether it merited the reputation it enjoyed or whether his fluency was better or inferior than it was reported to be. I hung on his diction in rapt attention, but remained bored and contemptuous of the subject-matter. My pleasure was in the charm of his language. It was more learned than that of Faustus, but less witty and entertaining, as far as the manner of his speaking went. But in content there could be no comparison. Through Manichee deceits Faustus wandered astray. Ambrose taught the sound doctrine of salvation. From sinners such as I was at that time, salvation is far distant. Nevertheless, gradually, though I did not realize it, I was drawing closer.

My mother, strong in her devotion, had already come to join me, following me by land and sea, and in all dangers serenely confident in you. During a hazardous voyage she encouraged the crew themselves who are accustomed to offering consolation to frightened travellers with no experience of the deep sea. She promised them a safe arrival, for in a vision you had promised this to her. She found me in a dangerous state of depression. I had lost all hope of discovering the truth. Yet when I informed her that I was not now a Manichee, though neither was I a Catholic Christian, she did not leap for joy as if she had heard some unexpected news; she was already free from anxiety about that part of my wretched condition, for which she wept over me as a person dead but to be revived by you.

* * *

I aspired to honours, money, marriage, and you laughed at me. In those ambitions I suffered the bitterest difficulties; that was by your mercy—so much the greater in that you gave me the less occasion to find sweet pleasure in what was not you. Look into my heart, Lord. In obedience to your will I recall this and confess to you. May my soul now adhere to you. You detached it from the birdlime which held me fast in death. How unhappy it was! Your scalpel cut to the quick of the wound, so that I should leave all these ambitions and be converted to you, who are "above all things" (Rom. 9: 5) and without whom all things are nothing, and that by conversion I should be healed. How unhappy I was, and how conscious you made me of my misery, on that day when I was preparing to deliver a panegyric on the emperor! In the course of it I would tell numerous lies and for my mendacity would win the good opinion of people who knew it to be untrue. The anxiety of the occasion was making my heart palpitate and perspire with the destructive fever of worry, when I passed through a Milan street and noticed a destitute beggar. Already drunk, I think, he was joking and laughing. I groaned and spoke with the friends accompanying me about the many sufferings that result from our follies. In all our strivings such as those efforts that were then worrying me, the goads of ambition impelled me to drag the burden of my unhappiness with me, and in dragging it to make it even worse; yet we had no goal other than to reach a carefree cheerfulness. That beggar was already there before us, and perhaps we would never achieve it. For what he had gained with a few coins, obtained by begging, that is the cheerfulness of temporal felicity, I was going about to reach by painfully twisted and roundabout ways. True joy he had not. But my quest to fulfil my ambitions was much falser. There was no question that he was happy and I racked with anxiety. He had no worries; I was frenetic, and if anyone had asked me if I would prefer to be merry or to be racked with fear, I would have answered "to be merry." Yet if he asked whether I would prefer to be a beggar like that man or the kind of person I then was, I would have chosen to be myself, a bundle of anxieties and fears. What an absurd choice! Surely it could not be the right one. For I ought not to have put myself above him on the ground of being better educated, a matter from which I was deriving no pleasure. My education enabled me to seek to please men, not to impart to them any instruction, but merely to purvey pleasure. For that reason you "broke my bones" (Ps. 41: 11; 50: 10) with the rod of your discipline (Ps. 22: 4).

* * *

Meanwhile my sins multiplied. The woman with whom I habitually slept was torn away from my side because she was a hindrance to my marriage. My heart which was deeply attached was cut and wounded, and left a trail of blood. She had returned to Africa vowing that she would never go with another man. She left with me the natural son I had by her. But I was unhappy, incapable of following a woman's example, and impatient of delay. I was to get the girl I had proposed to only at the end of two years. As I was not a lover of marriage but a slave of lust, I procured another woman, not of course as wife. By this liason the disease of my soul would be sustained and kept active, either in full vigour or even increased, so that the habit would be guarded and fostered until I came to the kingdom of marriage. But my wound, inflicted by the earlier parting, was not healed. After inflammation and sharp pain, it festered. The pain made me as it were frigid but desperate.

HESITATION

Such was my sickness and my torture, as I accused myself even more bitterly than usual. I was twisting and turning in my chain until it would break completely: I was now only a little bit held by it, but I was still held. You, Lord, put pressure on me in my hidden depths with a severe mercy wielding the double whip of fear and shame, lest I should again succumb, and lest that tiny and tenuous bond which still remained should not be broken, but once more regain strength and bind me even more firmly. Inwardly I said to myself: Let it be now, let it be now. And by this phrase I was already moving towards a decision; I had almost taken it, and then I did not do so. Yet I did not relapse into my original condition, but stood my ground very close to the point of deciding and recovered my breath. Once more I made the attempt and came only a little short of my goal; only a little short of it—yet I did not touch it or hold on to it. I was hesitating whether to die to death and to live to life. Ingrained evil had more hold over me than unaccustomed good. The nearer approached the moment of time when I would become different, the greater the horror of it struck me. But it did not thrust me back nor turn me away, but left me in a state of suspense.

Vain trifles and the triviality of the empty-headed, my old loves, held me back. They tugged at the garment of my flesh and whispered: "Are you getting rid of us?" And "from this moment we shall never be with you again, not for ever and ever." And "from this moment this and that are forbidden to you for ever and ever." What they were suggesting in what I have called "this and that"—what they were suggesting, my God, may your mercy avert from the soul of your servant! What filth, what disgraceful things they were suggesting! I was listening to them with much less than half my attention. They were not frankly confronting me face to face on the road, but as it were whispering behind my back, as if they were furtively tugging at me as I was going away, trying to persuade me to look back. Nevertheless they held me back. I hesitated to detach myself, to be rid of them, to make the leap to where I was being called. Meanwhile the overwhelming force of habit was saying to me: "Do you think you can live without them?"

Translated by Henry Chadwick

CONVERSION

The end of Augustine's long spiritual odyssey came in the garden of a house outside Milan. With him was Alypius, a young man from Augustine's home town, Thagaste, who had been one of his students at Carthage.

I blushed with embarrassment because I was still listening to the mutterings of those vanities, and racked by hesitations I remained undecided. But once more it was as if she said: "Stop your ears to your impure members on earth and mortify them' (Col. 3: 5). They declare delights to you, but "not in accord with the law of the Lord your God" (Ps. 118: 85). This debate in my heart was a struggle of myself against myself. Alypius stood quite still at my side, and waited in silence for the outcome of my unprecedented state of agitation.

From a hidden depth a profound self-examination had dredged up a heap of all my misery and set it "in the sight of my heart" (Ps. 18: 15). That precipitated a vast storm bearing a massive downpour of tears. To pour it all out with the accompanying groans, I got up from beside Alypius (solitude seemed to me more appropriate for the business of weeping), and I moved further away to ensure that even his presence put no inhibition upon me. He sensed that this was my condition at that moment. I think I may have said something which made it clear that the sound of my voice was already choking with tears. So I stood up while in profound astonishment he remained where we were sitting. I threw myself down somehow under a certain figtree, and let my tears flow freely. Rivers streamed from my eyes, a sacrifice acceptable to you (Ps. 50: 19), and (though not in these words, yet in this sense) I repeatedly said to you: "How long, O Lord? How long, Lord, will you be angry to the uttermost? Do not be mindful of our old iniquities" (Ps. 6: 4). For I felt my past to have a grip on me. It uttered wretched cries: "How long, how long is it to be?" "Tomorrow, tomorrow." "Why not now? Why not an end to my impure life in this very hour?"

As I was saying this and weeping in the bitter agony of my heart, suddenly I heard a voice from the nearby house chanting as if it might be a boy or a girl (I do not know which), saying and repeating over and over again "Pick up and read, pick up and read." At once my countenance changed, and I began to think intently whether there might be some sort of children's game in which such a chant is used. But I could not remember having heard of one. I checked the flood of tears and stood up. I interpreted it solely as a divine command to me to open the book and read the first chapter I might find. For I had heard how Antony happened to be present at the gospel reading, and took it as an admonition addressed to himself when the words were read: "Go, sell all you have, give to the poor, and you shall have treasure in heaven; and come, follow me" (Matt. 19: 21). By such an inspired utterance he was immediately converted to you" (Ps. 50: 15). So I hurried back to the place where Alypius was sitting. There I had put down the book of the apostle when I got up. I seized it, opened it and in silence read the first passage on which my eyes lit: "Not in riots and drunken parties, not in eroticism and indecencies, not in strife and rivalry, but put on the Lord Jesus Christ and make no provision for the flesh in its lusts" (Rom. 13: 13–14).

I neither wished nor needed to read further. At once, with the last words of this sentence, it was as if a light of relief from all anxiety flooded into my heart. All the shadows of doubt were dispelled.

Then I inserted my finger or some other mark in the book and closed it. With a face now at peace I told everything to Alypius. What had been going on in his mind, which I did not know, he disclosed in this way. He asked to see the text I had been reading. I showed him, and he noticed a passage following that which I had read. I did not know how the text went on; but the continuation was "Receive the person who is weak in faith" (Rom. 14: 1). Alypius applied this to himself, and he made that known to me. He was given confidence by this admonition. Without any agony of hesitation he joined me in making a good resolution and affirmation of intention, entirely congruent with his moral principles in which he had long been greatly superior to me. From there we went in to my mother, and told her. She was filled with joy. We told her how it had happened. She exulted, feeling it to be a triumph, and blessed you who "are powerful to do more than we ask or think" (Eph. 3: 20). She saw that you had granted her far more than she had long been praying for in her unhappy and tearful groans.

The effect of your converting me to yourself was that I did not now seek a wife and had no ambition for success in this world. I stood firm upon that rule of faith on which many years before you had revealed me to her. You "changed her grief into joy" (Ps. 29: 12) far more abundantly than she desired, far dearer and more chaste than she expected when she looked for grandchildren begotten of my body.

Translated by Henry Chadwick

FOR FURTHER READING

In the list of permissions acknowledgments following, the reader will find publishing data for all the translations from which our texts have been selected. For an eminently readable (and profusely illustrated) history of the ancient world that pays special attention to literature, see *The Oxford History of the Classical World*, edited by John Boardman, Jasper Griffin, and Oswyn Murray (Oxford University Press, 1986). For a detailed survey of the classical literatures (with full bibliographical and biographical data), see *The Cambridge History of Classical Literature. Volume I: Greek Literature*, edited by P. E. Easterling and B. M. W. Knox (Cambridge University Press, 1985); *Volume II: Latin Literature*, edited by E. J. Kenney and W. V. Clausen (Cambridge University Press, 1982).

PERMISSIONS

INDEX